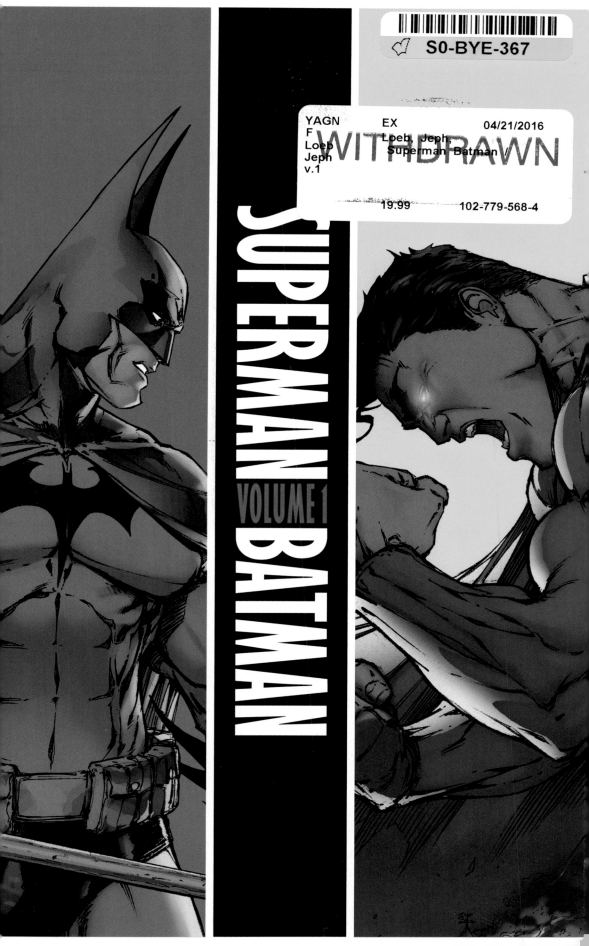

SUPERMAN BATMAN

VOLUME 1

JEPH LOEB
WRITER

ED McGUINNESS
MICHAEL TURNER
PAT LEE
PENCILLERS

DEXTER VINES
MICHAEL TURNER
DREAMWAVE PRODUCTIONS
INKERS

DAVE STEWART
PETER STEIGERWALD
DREAMWAVE PRODUCTIONS
COLORISTS

RICHARD STARKINGS
LETTERER

ED McGUINNESS & DEXTER VINES
WITH DAVE STEWART
COLLECTION COVER ART

BATMAN CREATED BY BOB KANE WITH BILL FINGER
SUPERMAN CREATED BY JERRY SIEGEL AND JOE SHUSTER
SUPERGIRL BASED ON CHARACTERS CREATED BY JERRY SIEGEL AND JOE SHUSTER
BY SPECIAL ARRANGEMENT WITH THE JERRY SIEGEL FAMILY

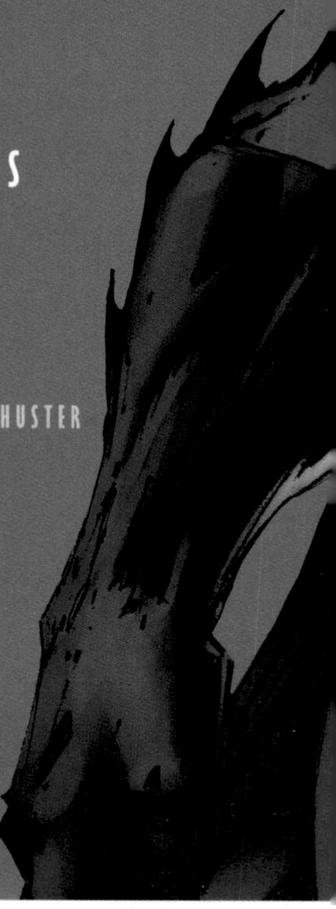

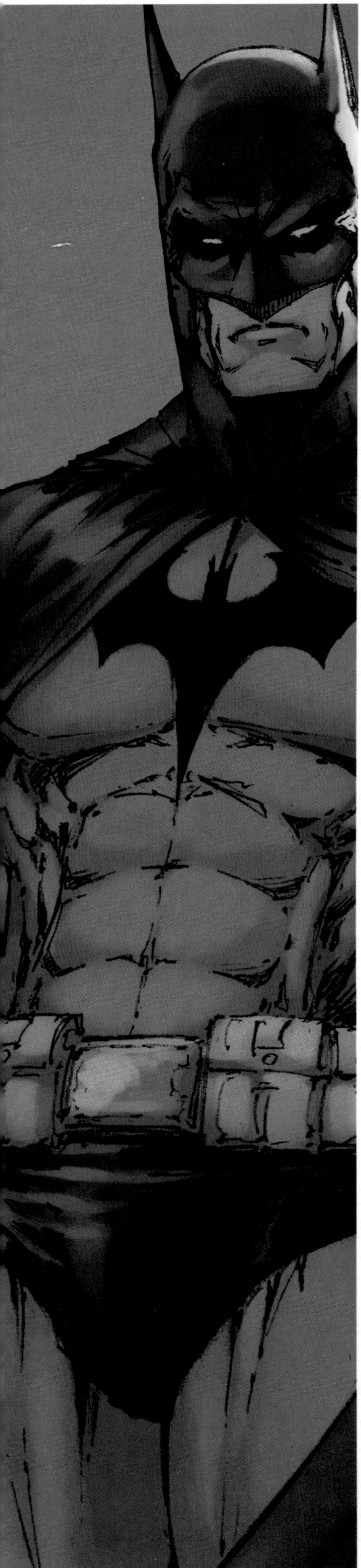

SUPERMAN BATMAN

VOLUME 1

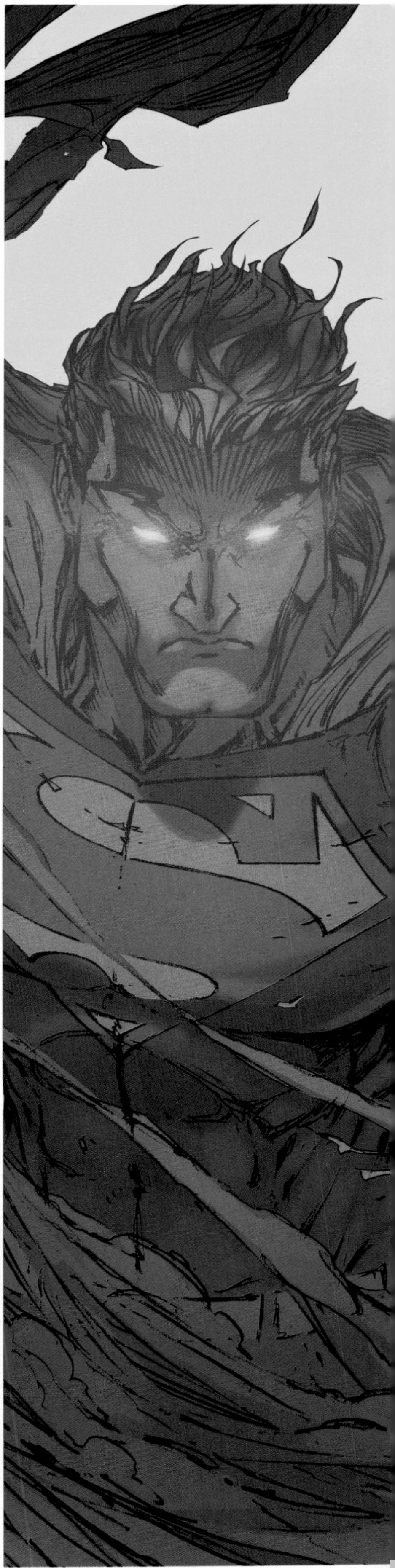

Eddie Berganza, Matt Idelson Editors—Original Series   Tom Palmer, Jr. Associate Editor—Original Series
Jeb Woodard Group Editor—Collected Editions   Peter Hamboussi Editor—Collected Edition   Rachel Pinnelas Assistant Editor—Collected Edition   Steve Cook Design Director—Books   Damian Ryland Publication Design

Bob Harras Senior VP—Editor-in-Chief, DC Comics

Diane Nelson President   Dan DiDio and Jim Lee Co-Publishers   Geoff Johns Chief Creative Officer   Amit Desai Senior VP—Marketing & Global Franchise Management   Nairi Gardiner Senior VP—Finance
Sam Ades VP—Digital Marketing   Bobbie Chase VP—Talent Development   Mark Chiarello Senior VP—Art, Design & Collected Editions   John Cunningham VP—Content Strategy   Anne DePies VP—Strategy Planning & Reporting
Don Falletti VP—Manufacturing Operations   Lawrence Ganem VP—Editorial Administration & Talent Relations   Alison Gill Senior VP—Manufacturing & Operations   Hank Kanalz Senior VP—Editorial Strategy & Administration
Jay Kogan VP—Legal Affairs   Derek Maddalena Senior VP—Sales & Business Development   Jack Mahan VP—Business Affairs   Dan Miron VP—Sales Planning & Trade Development   Nick Napolitano VP—Manufacturing Administration
Carol Roeder VP—Marketing   Eddie Scannell VP—Mass Account & Digital Sales   Courtney Simmons Senior VP—Publicity & Communications   Jim (Ski) Sokolowski VP—Comic Book Specialty & Newsstand Sales
Sandy Yi Senior VP—Global Franchise Management

SUPERMAN/BATMAN VOLUME 1

Published by DC Comics. Copyright © 2014 DC Comics. All Rights Reserved.

Originally published in single magazine form in SUPERMAN/BATMAN 1-13 and SUPERMAN/BATMAN SECRET FILES 2003 Copyright © 2003, 2004 DC Comics. All Rights Reserved.
All characters, their distinctive likenesses and related elements featured in this publication are trademarks of DC Comics. The stories, characters and incidents featured in this publication are entirely fictional.
DC Comics does not read or accept unsolicited ideas, stories or artwork.

DC Comics, 2900 W. Alameda Avenue, Burbank, CA 91505. Printed by RR Donnelley, Owensville, MO, USA. 5/6/16. Second Printing. ISBN: 978-1-4012-4818-5

PEFC Certified

Printed on paper from
sustainably managed
forests and controlled
sources
PEFC/29-31-75   www.pefc.org

Library of Congress Cataloging-in-Publication Data

Loeb, Jeph, author.
    Absolute Superman/Batman vol. 1 / Jeph Loeb, Ed McGuinness.
        pages cm
    "Originally published in single magazine form in Superman/Batman 1-13."
    ISBN 978-1-4012-4096-7
    1. Graphic novels.   I. McGuinness, Ed, illustrator. II. Title.
    PN6728.S9L59 2013
    741.5'973 — dc23
                                        2013011672

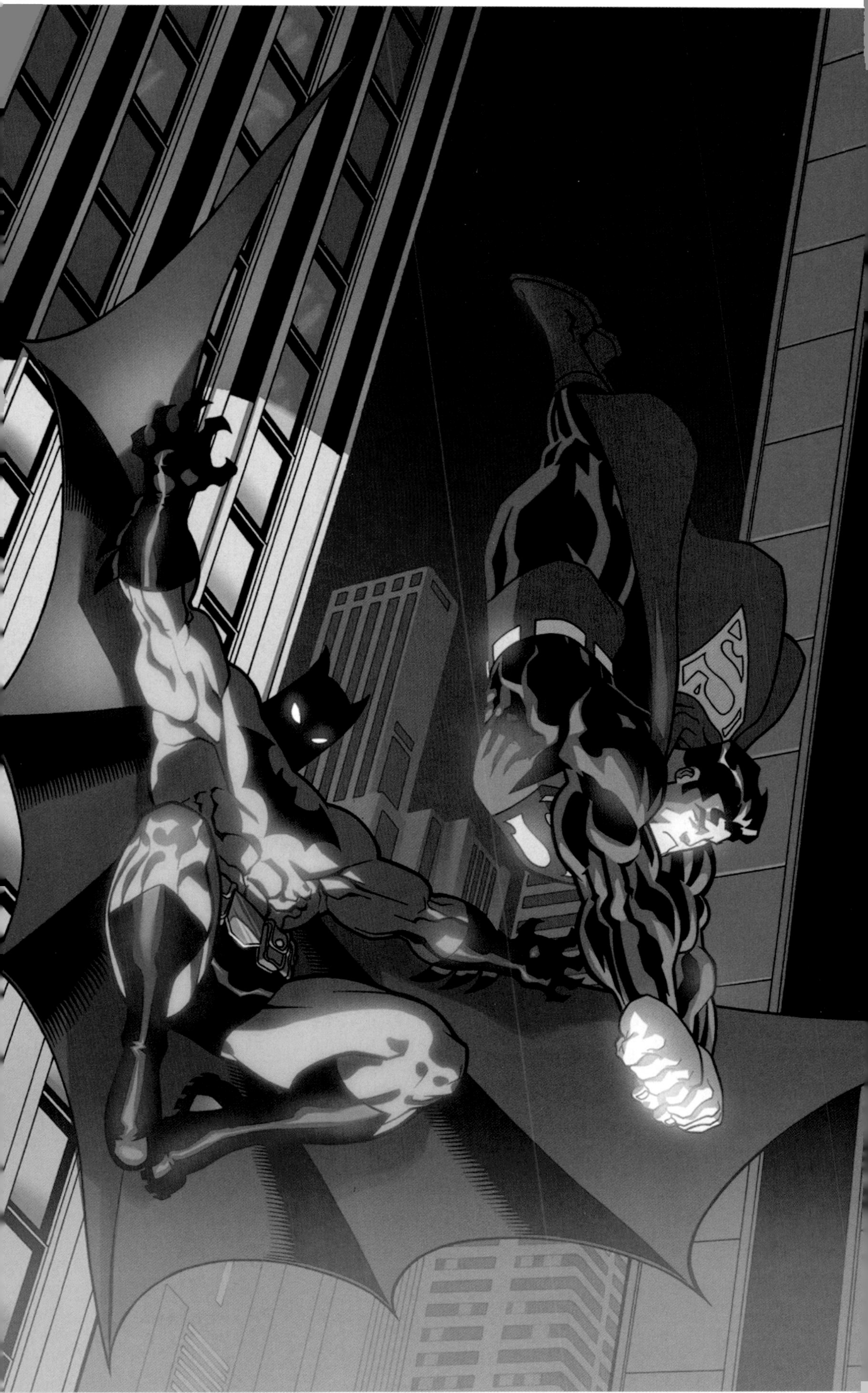

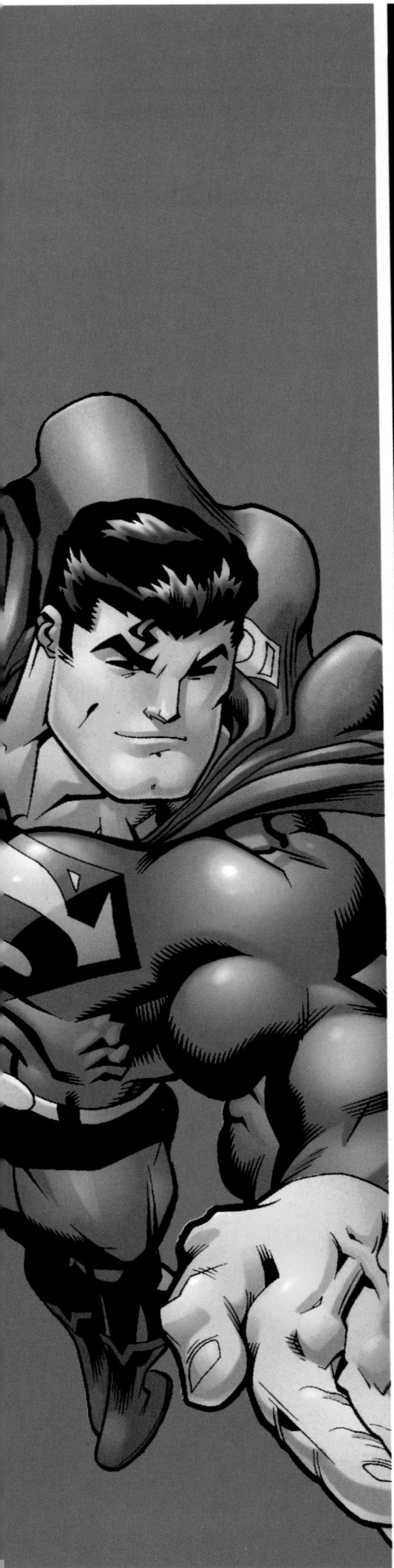

SUPERMAN PART ONE BATMAN

WORLD'S FINEST

JEPH LOEB
WRITER
ED McGUINNESS
PENCILLER
DEXTER VINES
INKER
DAVE STEWART
COLORIST
RICHARD STARKINGS
LETTERER
ED McGUINNESS
DEXTER VINES
WITH
DAVE STEWART
COVER

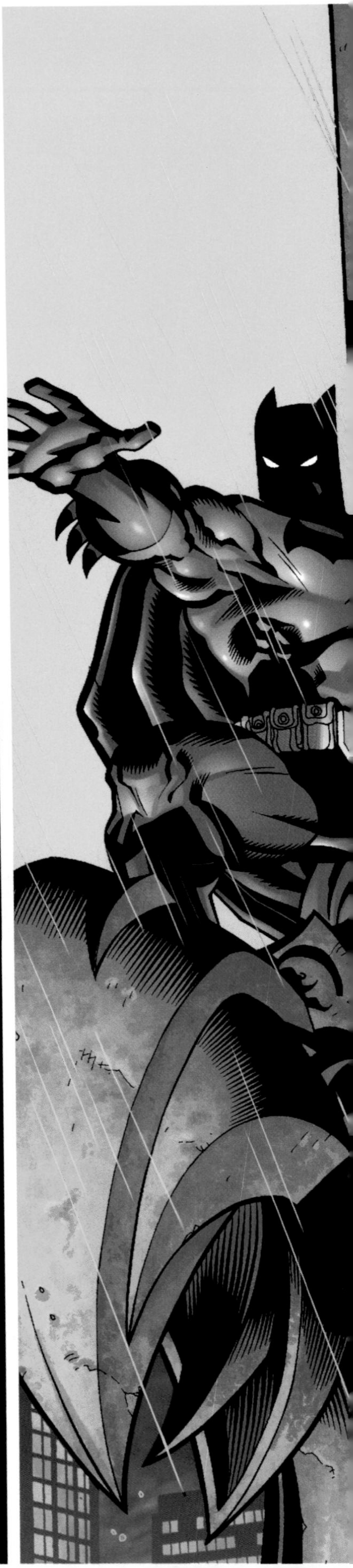

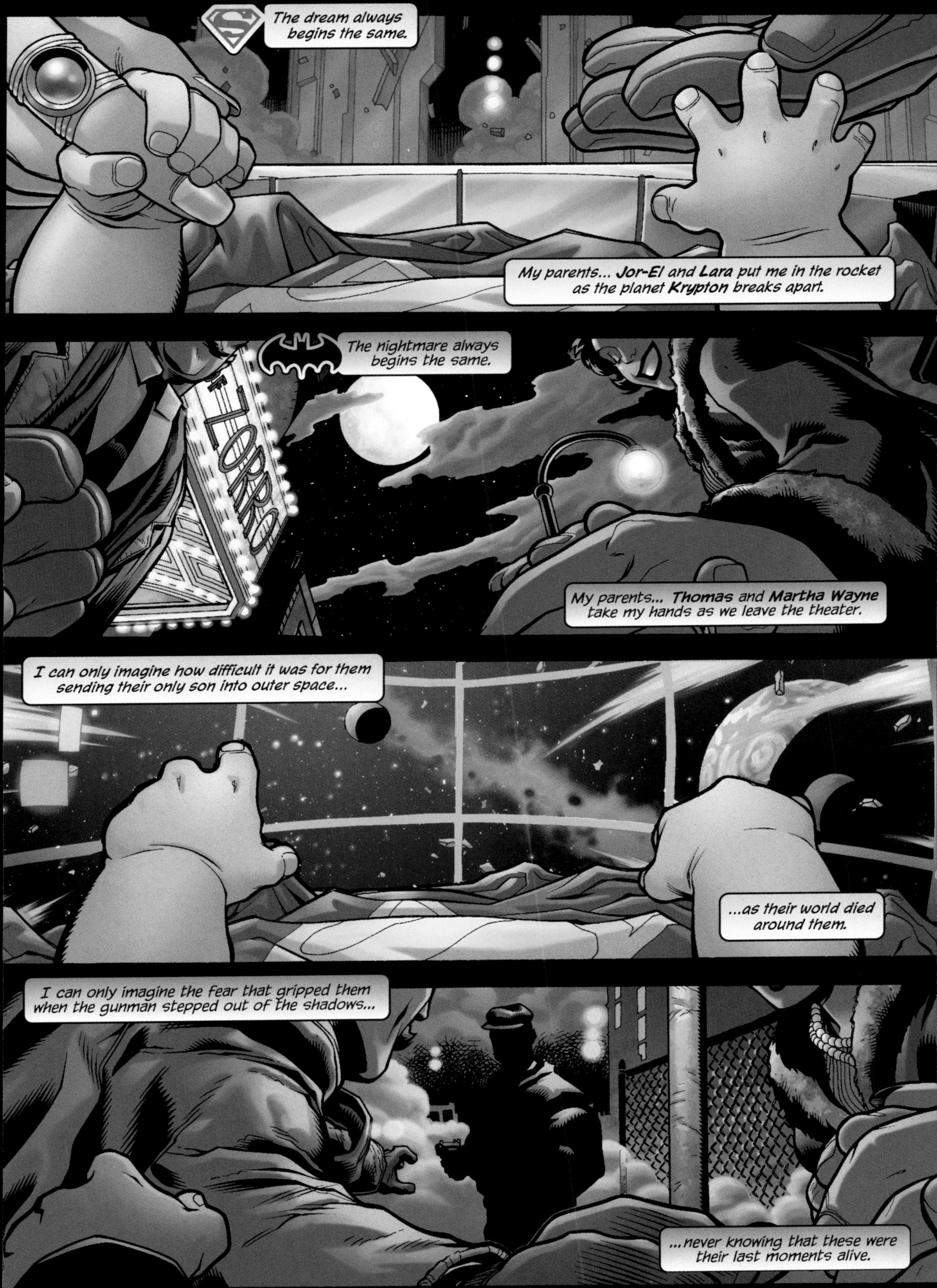
The dream always begins the same.
My parents... Jor-El and Lara put me in the rocket as the planet Krypton breaks apart.
The nightmare always begins the same.
ZORRO
My parents... Thomas and Martha Wayne take my hands as we leave the theater.
I can only imagine how difficult it was for them sending their only son into outer space...
...as their world died around them.
I can only imagine the fear that gripped them when the gunman stepped out of the shadows...
...never knowing that these were their last moments alive.

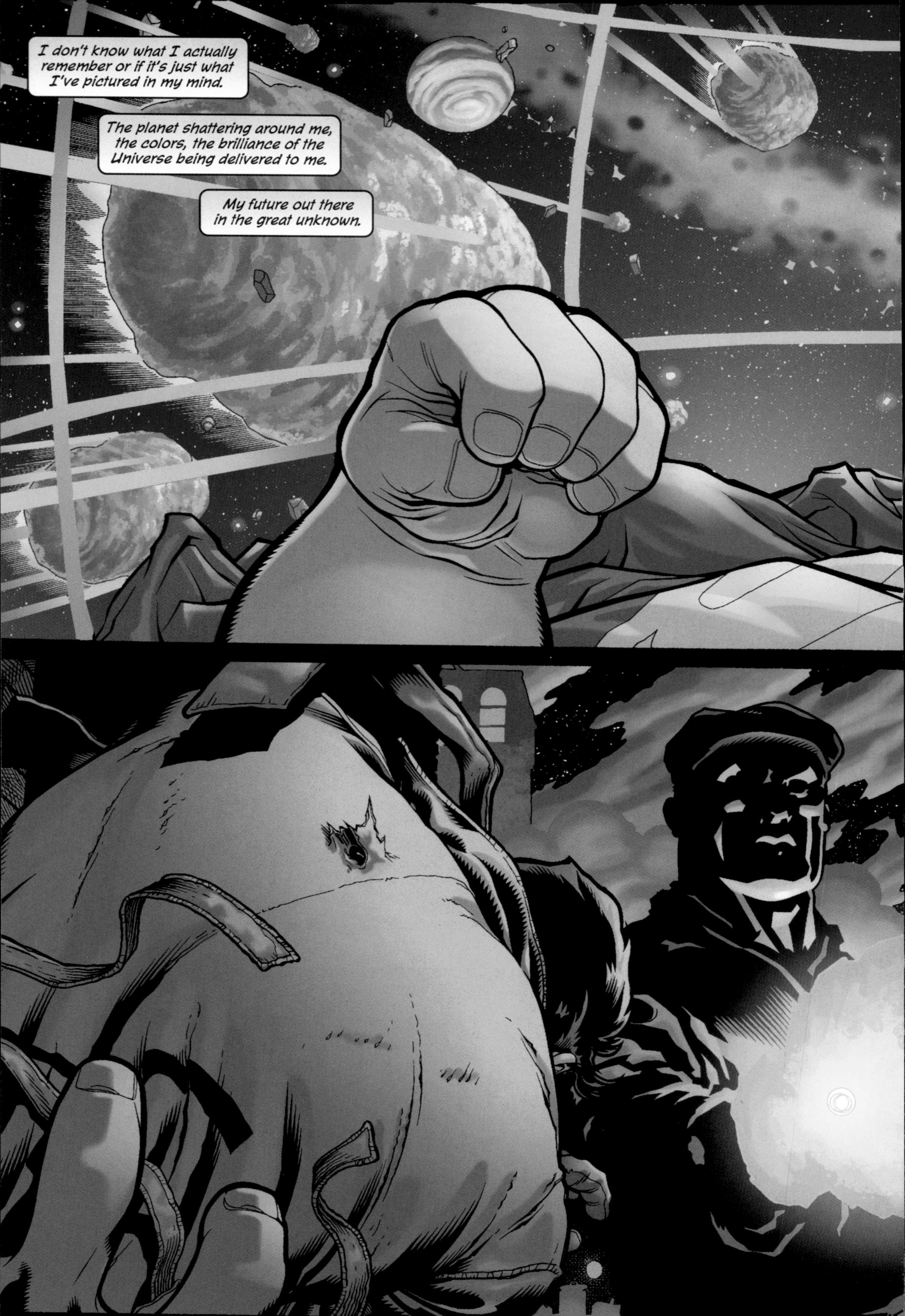
I don't know what I actually remember or if it's just what I've pictured in my mind.
The planet shattering around me, the colors, the brilliance of the Universe being delivered to me.
My future out there in the great unknown.

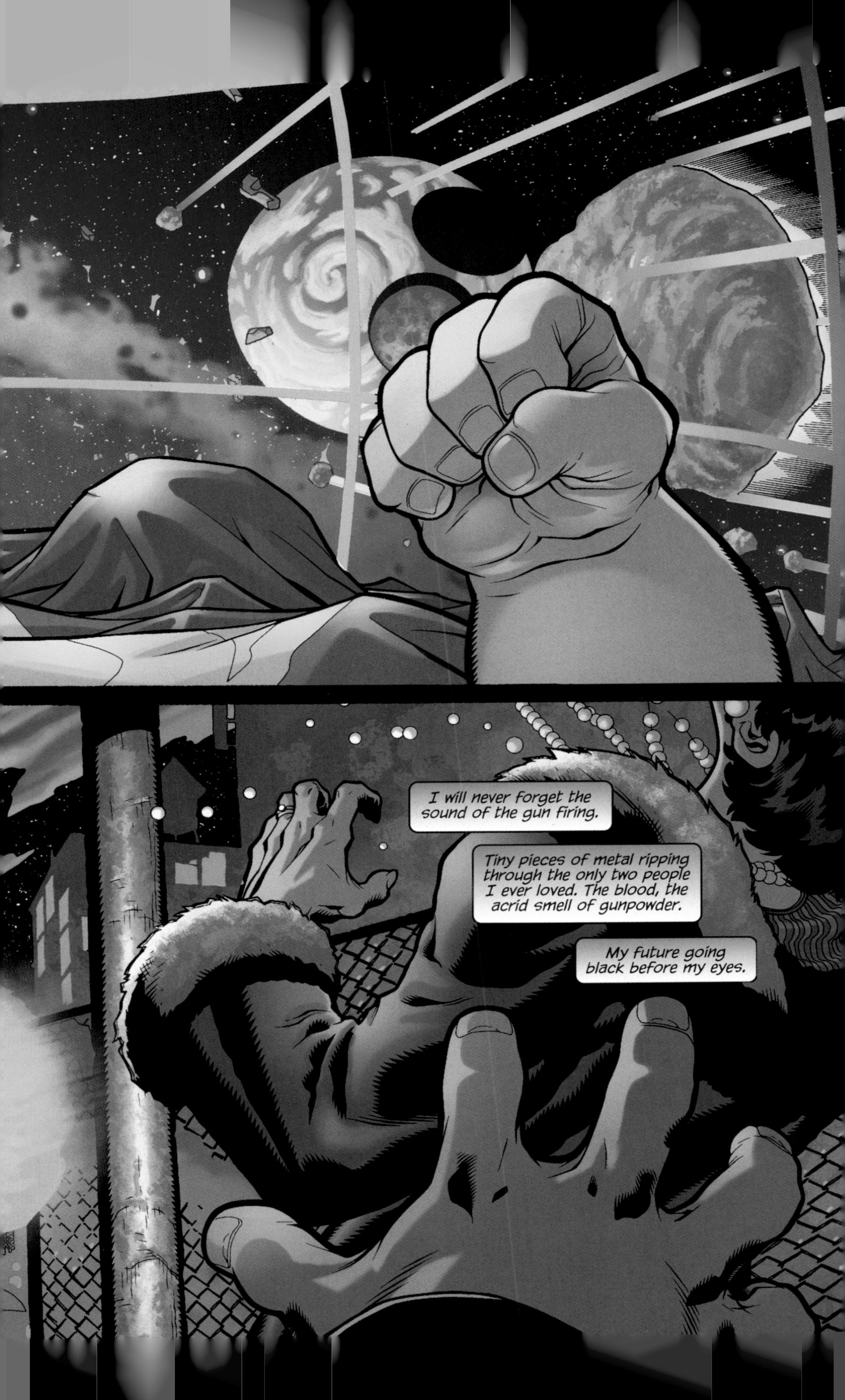
I will never forget the sound of the gun firing.
Tiny pieces of metal ripping through the only two people I ever loved. The blood, the acrid smell of gunpowder.
My future going black before my eyes.

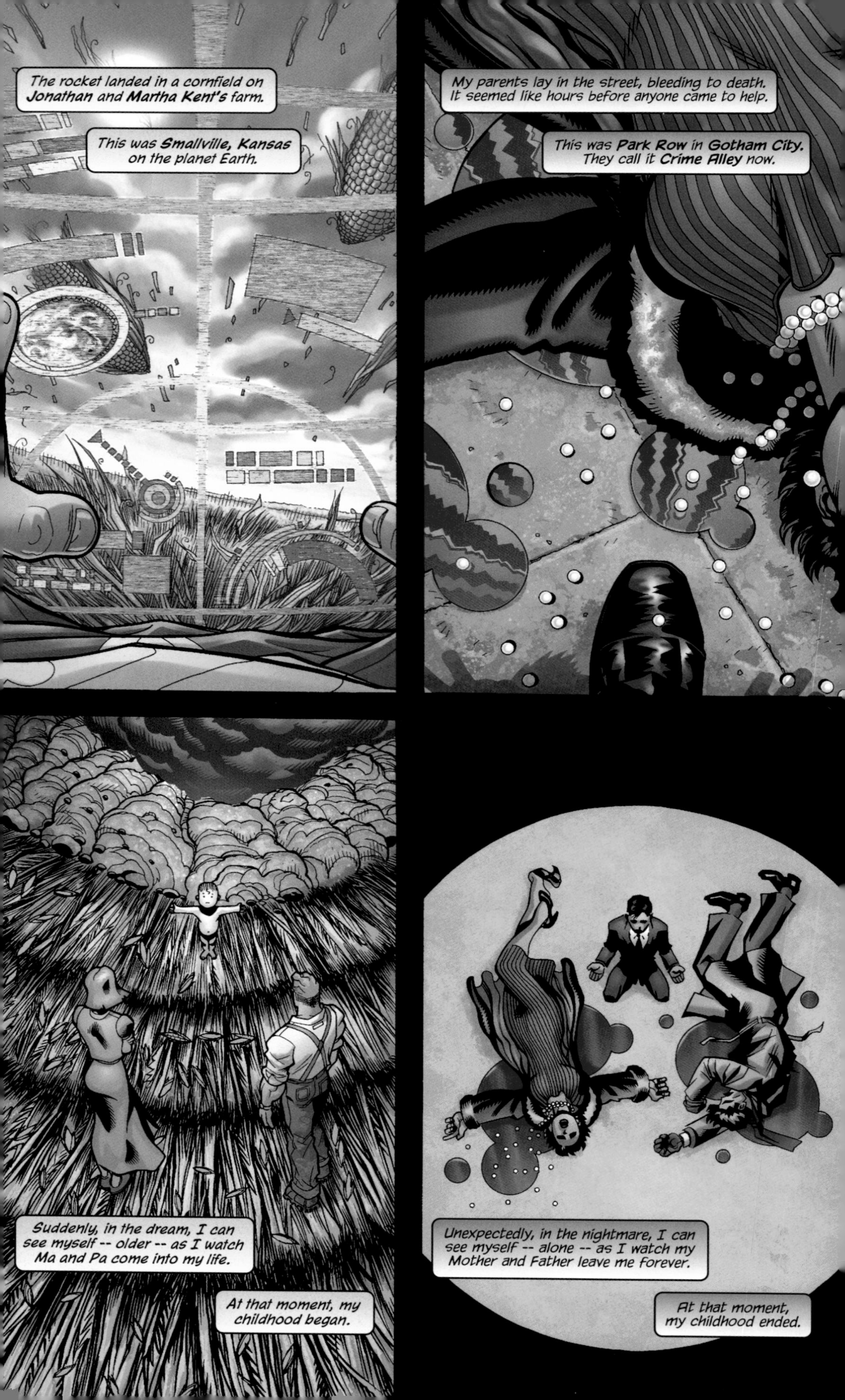
The rocket landed in a cornfield on Jonathan and Martha Kent's farm.
This was Smallville, Kansas on the planet Earth.
My parents lay in the street, bleeding to death. It seemed like hours before anyone came to help.
This was Park Row in Gotham City. They call it Crime Alley now.
Suddenly, in the dream, I can see myself -- older -- as I watch Ma and Pa come into my life.
At that moment, my childhood began.
Unexpectedly, in the nightmare, I can see myself -- alone -- as I watch my Mother and Father leave me forever.
At that moment, my childhood ended.

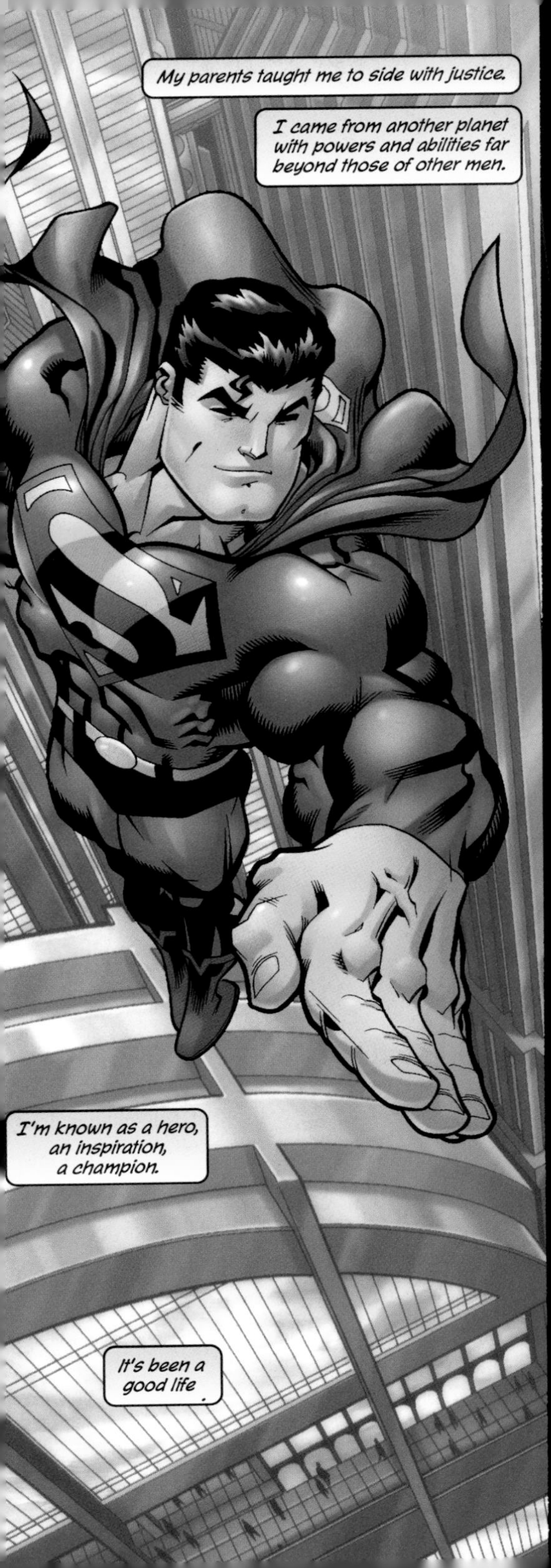
My parents taught me to side with justice.
I came from another planet with powers and abilities far beyond those of other men.
I'm known as a hero, an inspiration, a champion.
It's been a good life.

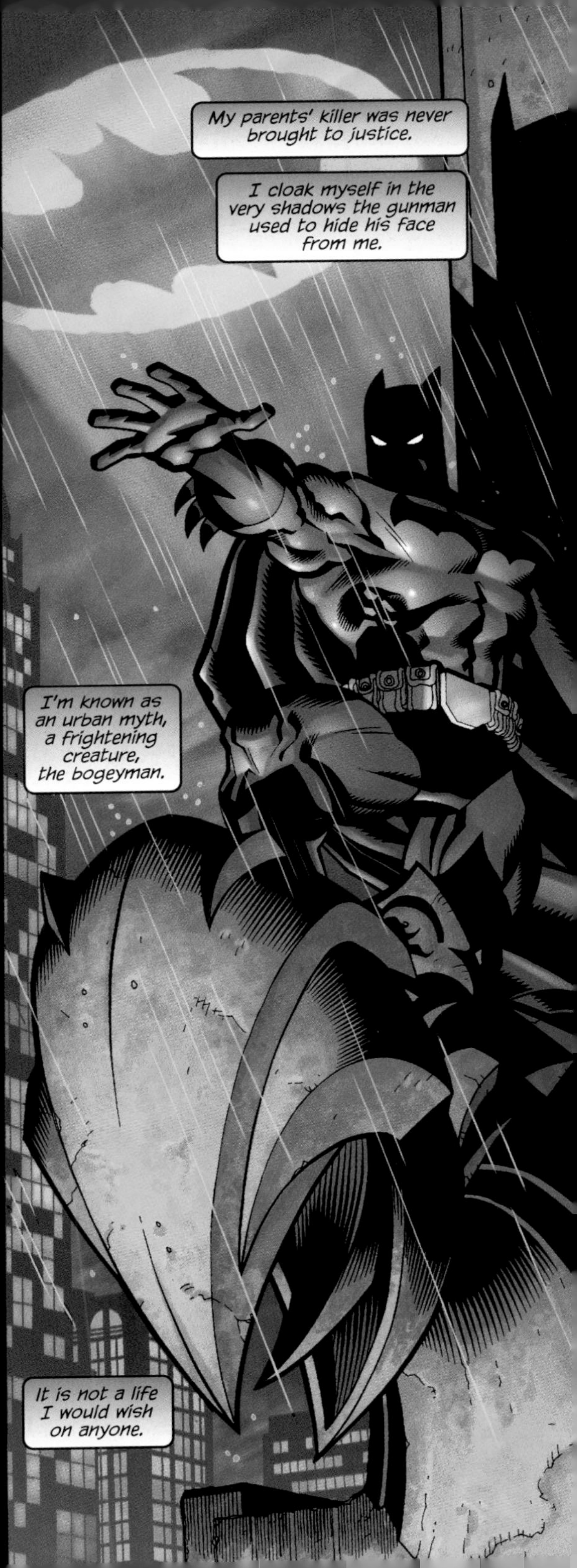
My parents' killer was never brought to justice.
I cloak myself in the very shadows the gunman used to hide his face from me.
I'm known as an urban myth, a frightening creature, the bogeyman.
It is not a life I would wish on anyone.

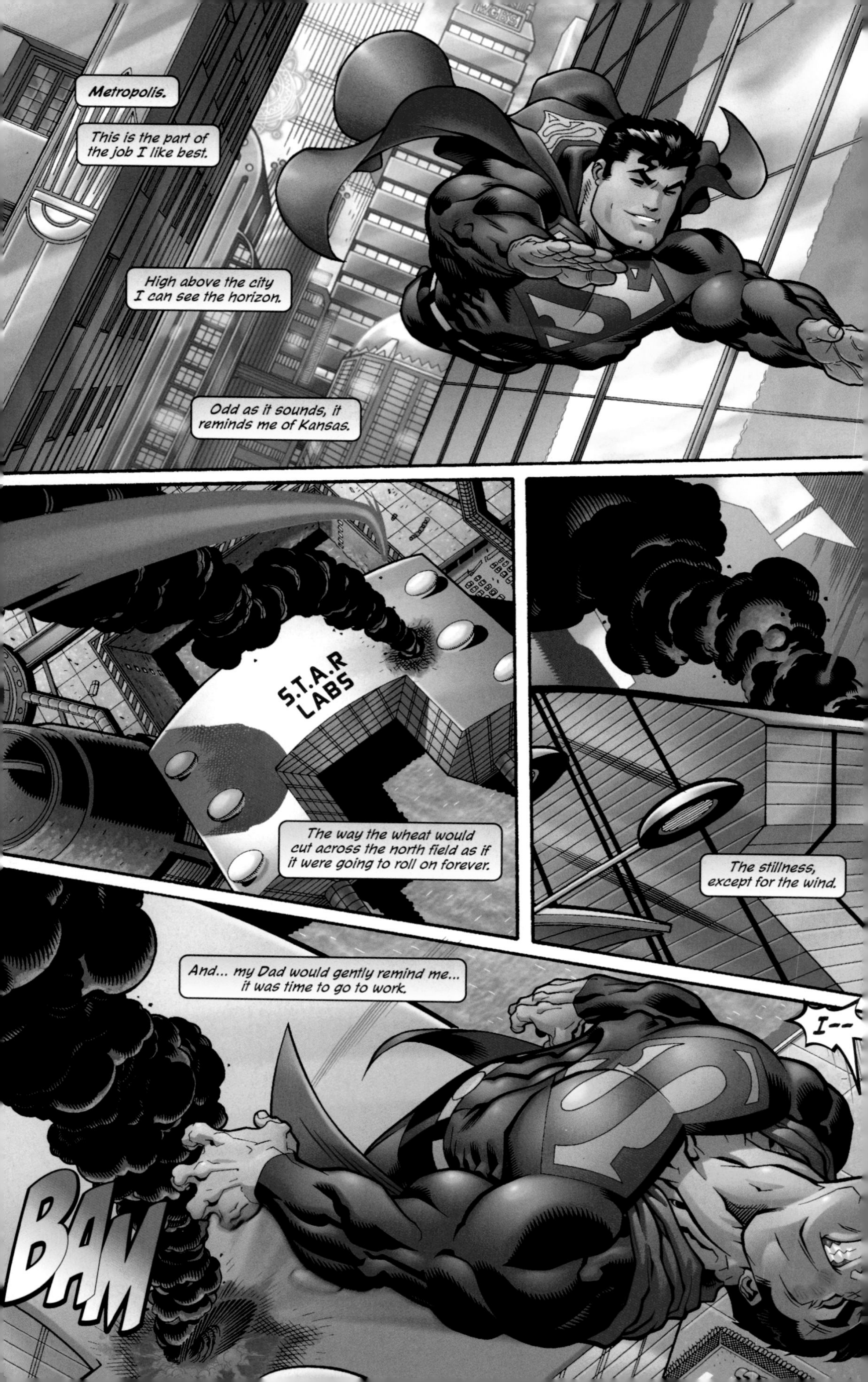

Metropolis.
This is the part of the job I like best.
High above the city I can see the horizon.
Odd as it sounds, it reminds me of Kansas.
S.T.A.R LABS
The way the wheat would cut across the north field as if it were going to roll on forever.
The stillness, except for the wind.
And... my Dad would gently remind me... it was time to go to work.
I--
BAM

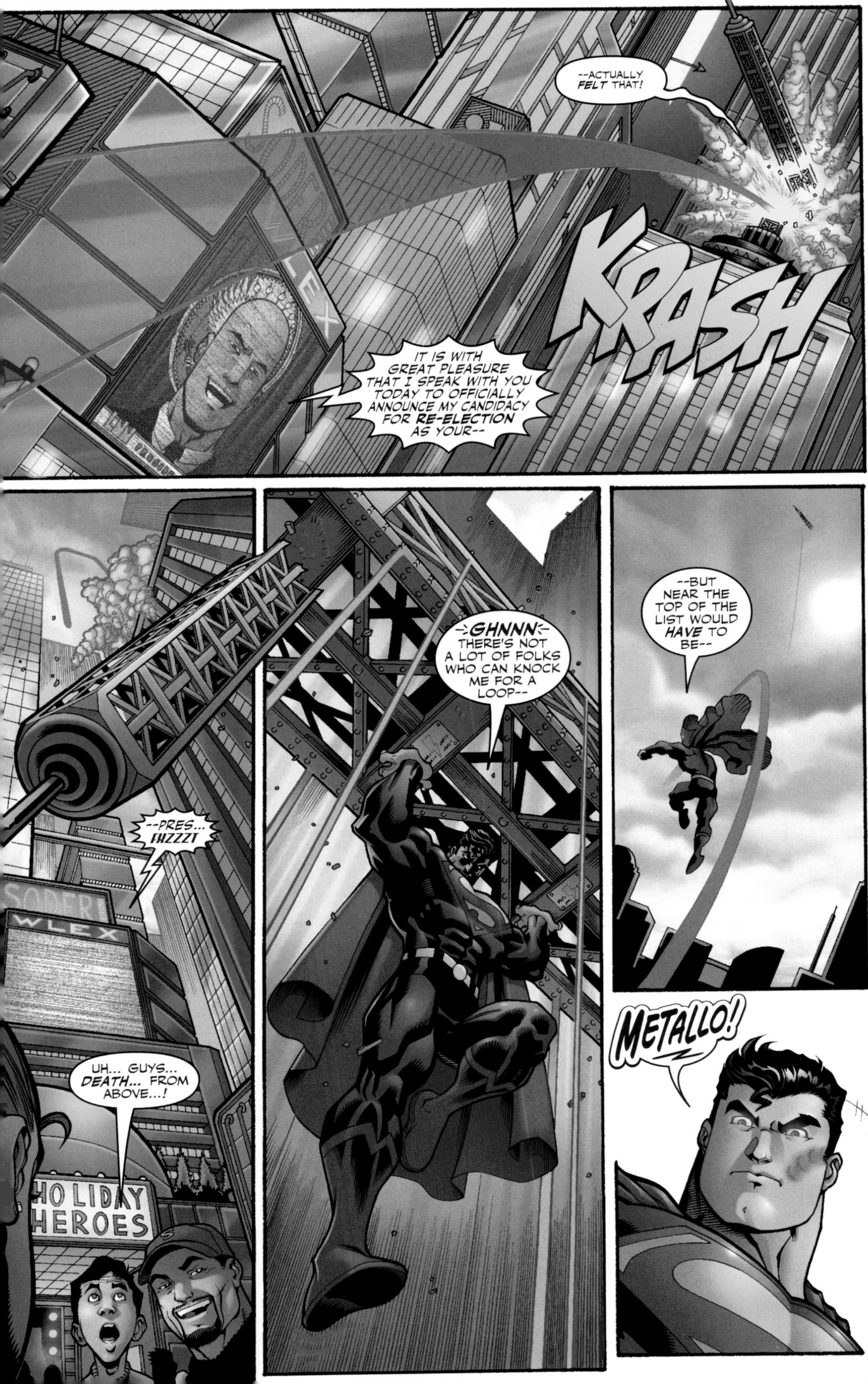
--ACTUALLY FELT THAT!
KRASH
IT IS WITH GREAT PLEASURE THAT I SPEAK WITH YOU TODAY TO OFFICIALLY ANNOUNCE MY CANDIDACY FOR RE-ELECTION AS YOUR--
WLEX
--PRES... FHZZZT
WLEX
UH... GUYS... DEATH... FROM ABOVE...!
HOLIDAY HEROES
-GHNNN- THERE'S NOT A LOT OF FOLKS WHO CAN KNOCK ME FOR A LOOP--
--BUT NEAR THE TOP OF THE LIST WOULD HAVE TO BE--
METALLO!

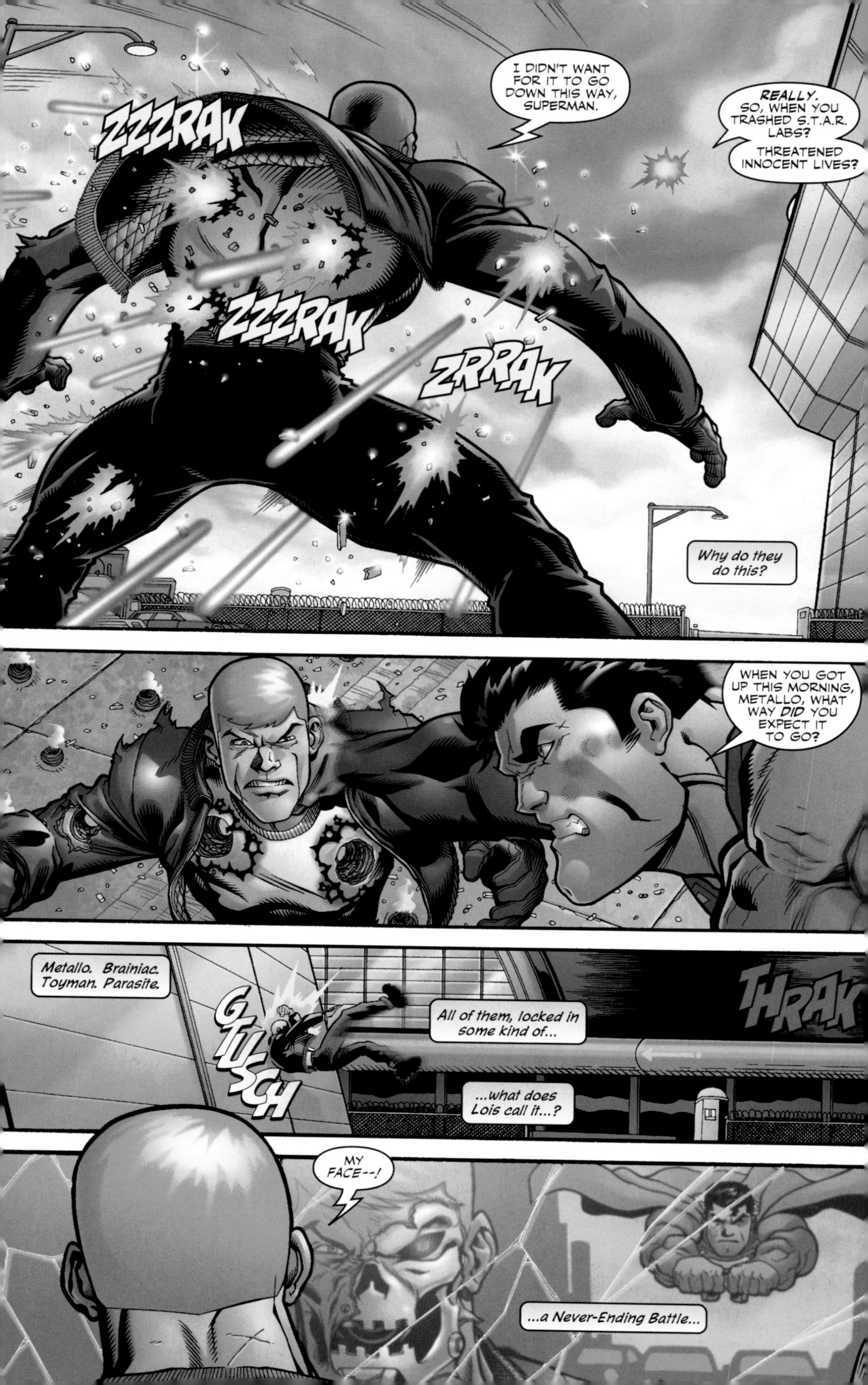
ZZZRAK
I DIDN'T WANT FOR IT TO GO DOWN THIS WAY, SUPERMAN.
REALLY. SO, WHEN YOU TRASHED S.T.A.R. LABS?
THREATENED INNOCENT LIVES?
ZZZRAK
ZRRAK
Why do they do this?
WHEN YOU GOT UP THIS MORNING, METALLO, WHAT WAY DID YOU EXPECT IT TO GO?
Metallo. Brainiac. Toyman. Parasite.
GTUSCH
All of them, locked in some kind of...
THRAK
...what does Lois call it...?
MY FACE--!
...a Never-Ending Battle...

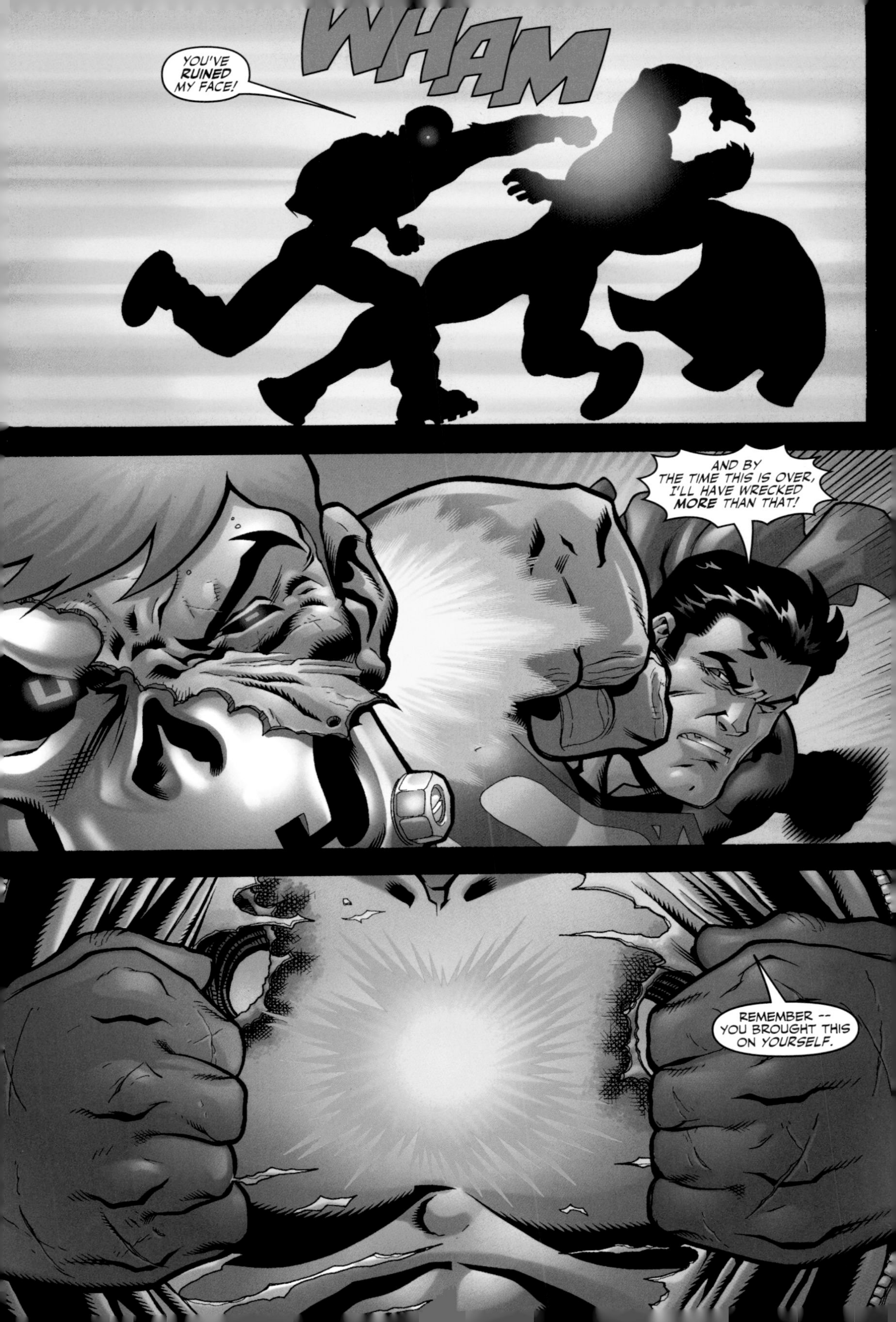
WHAM
YOU'VE RUINED MY FACE!
AND BY THE TIME THIS IS OVER, I'LL HAVE WRECKED MORE THAN THAT!
REMEMBER -- YOU BROUGHT THIS ON YOURSELF.

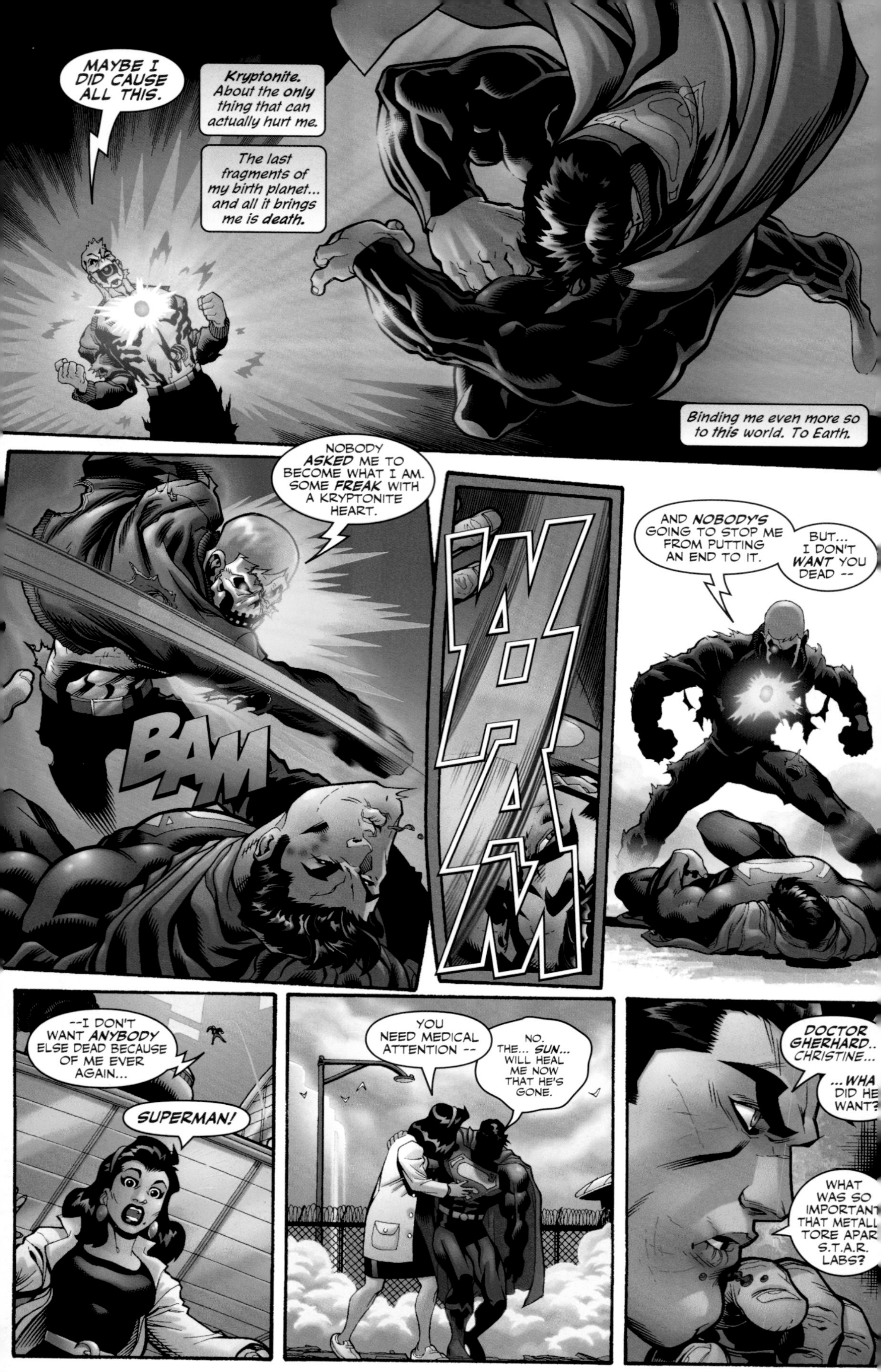
MAYBE I DID CAUSE ALL THIS.
Kryptonite. About the only thing that can actually hurt me.
The last fragments of my birth planet... and all it brings me is death.
Binding me even more so to this world. To Earth.
NOBODY ASKED ME TO BECOME WHAT I AM. SOME FREAK WITH A KRYPTONITE HEART.
BAM
WHAM
AND NOBODY'S GOING TO STOP ME FROM PUTTING AN END TO IT.
BUT... I DON'T WANT YOU DEAD --
--I DON'T WANT ANYBODY ELSE DEAD BECAUSE OF ME EVER AGAIN...
SUPERMAN!
YOU NEED MEDICAL ATTENTION --
NO. THE... SUN... WILL HEAL ME NOW THAT HE'S GONE.
DOCTOR GHERHARD... CHRISTINE...
...WHA DID HE WANT?
WHAT WAS SO IMPORTANT THAT METALL TORE APAR S.T.A.R. LABS?

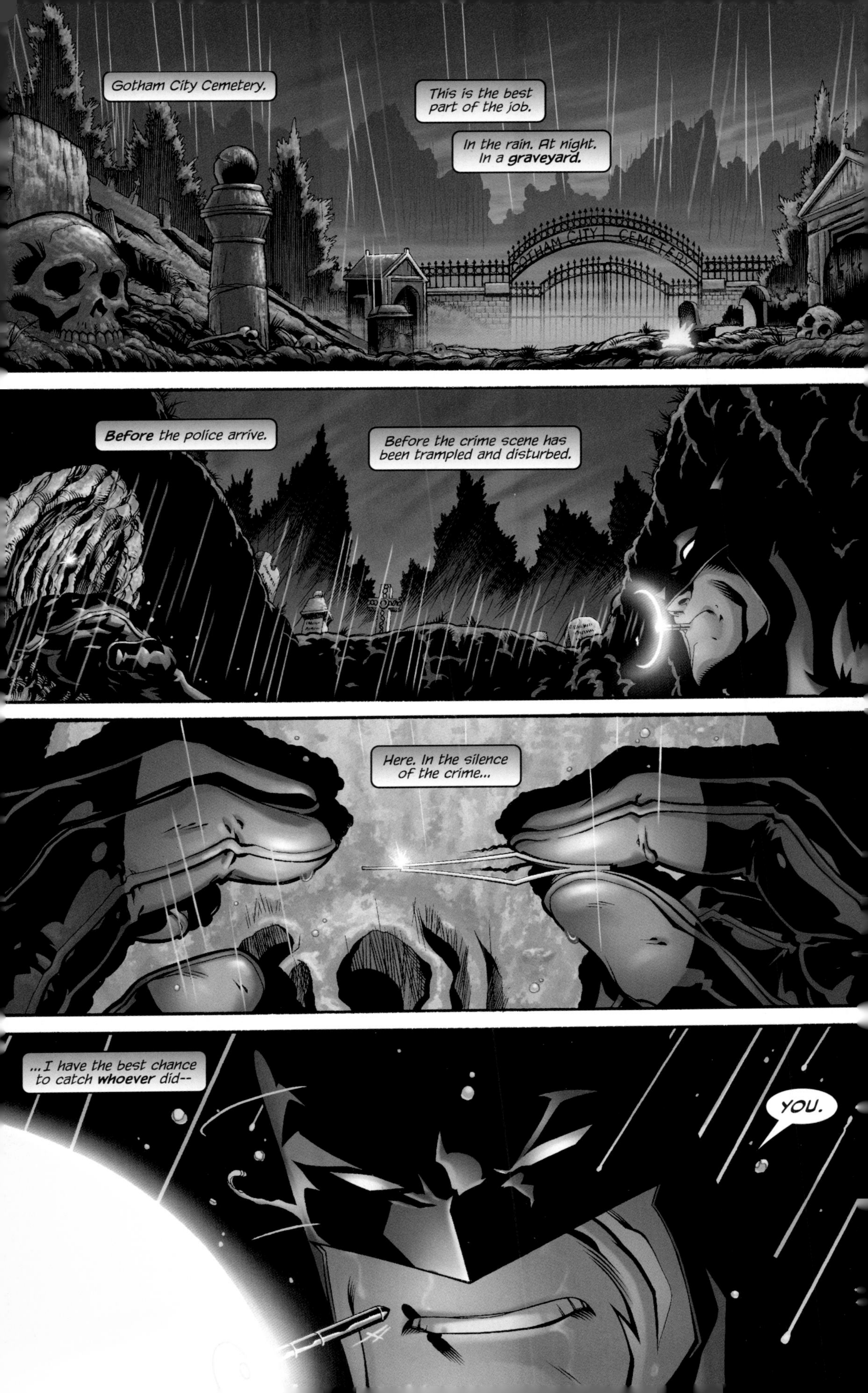
Gotham City Cemetery.
This is the best part of the job.
In the rain. At night. In a **graveyard.**
GOTHAM CITY CEMETERY
Before the police arrive.
Before the crime scene has been trampled and disturbed.
Here. In the silence of the crime...
...I have the best chance to catch **whoever** did--
YOU.

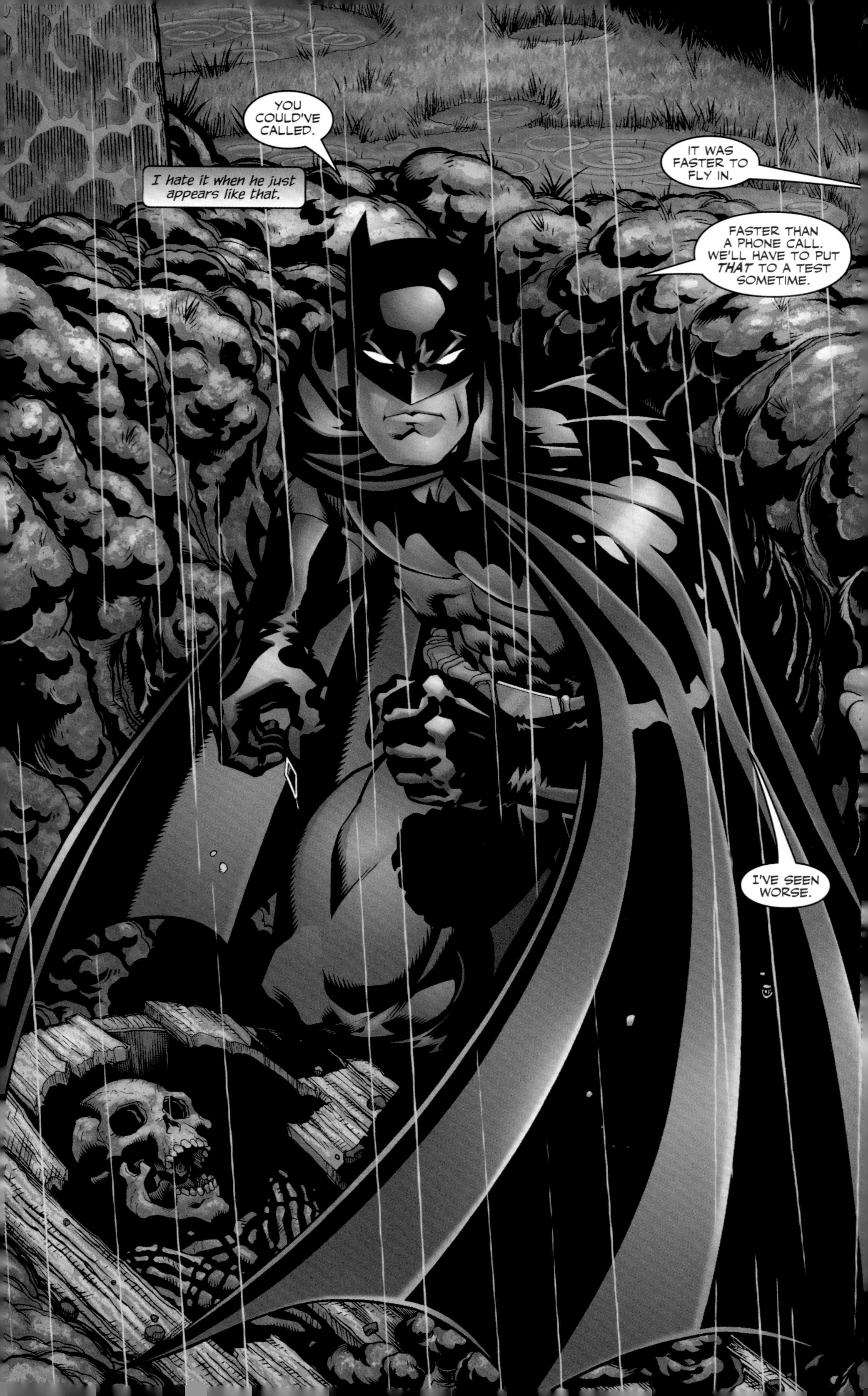
I hate it when he just appears like that.
YOU COULD'VE CALLED.
IT WAS FASTER TO FLY IN.
FASTER THAN A PHONE CALL. WE'LL HAVE TO PUT *THAT* TO A TEST SOMETIME.
I'VE SEEN WORSE.

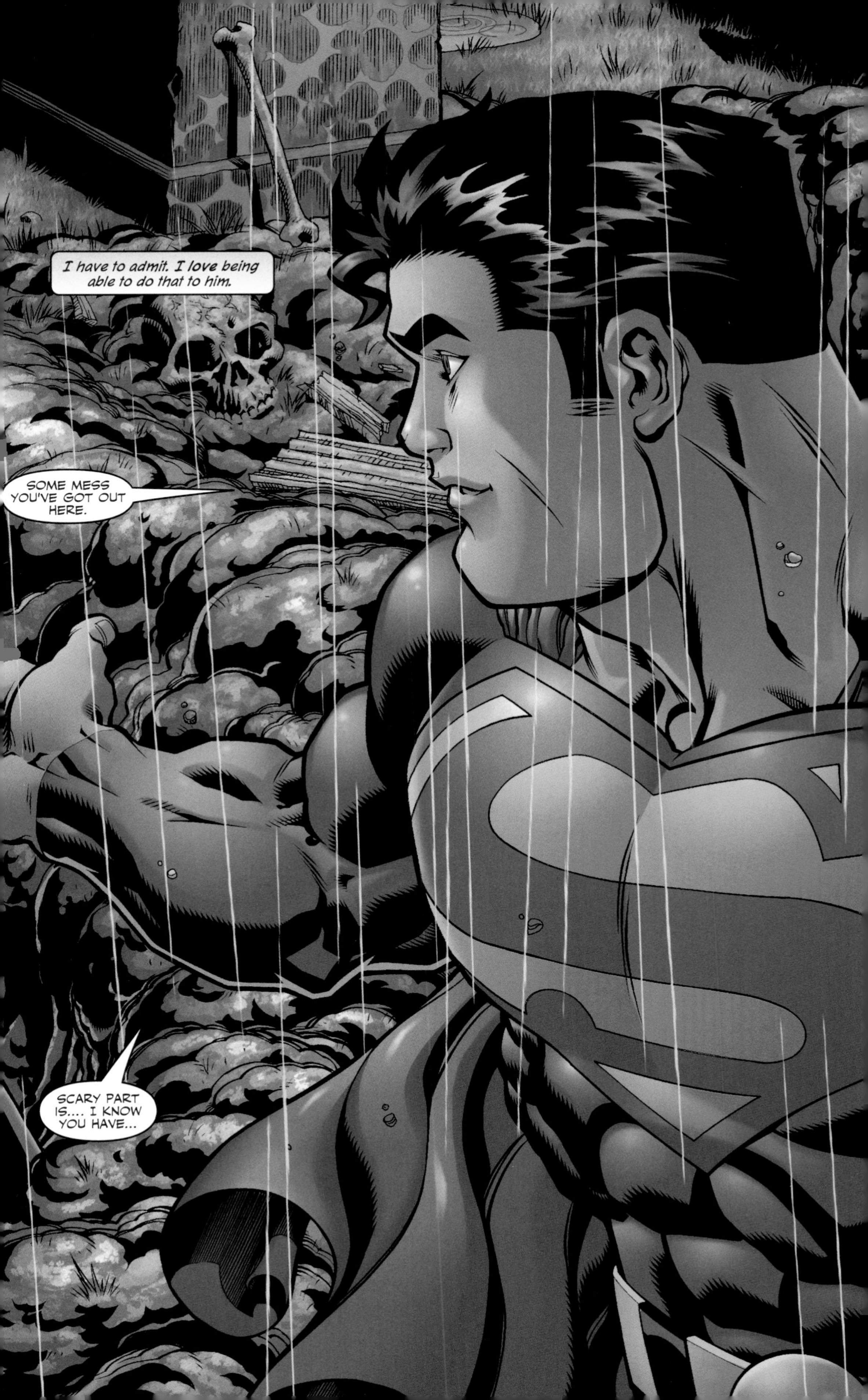
I have to admit. I love being able to do that to him.
SOME MESS YOU'VE GOT OUT HERE.
SCARY PART IS.... I KNOW YOU HAVE...

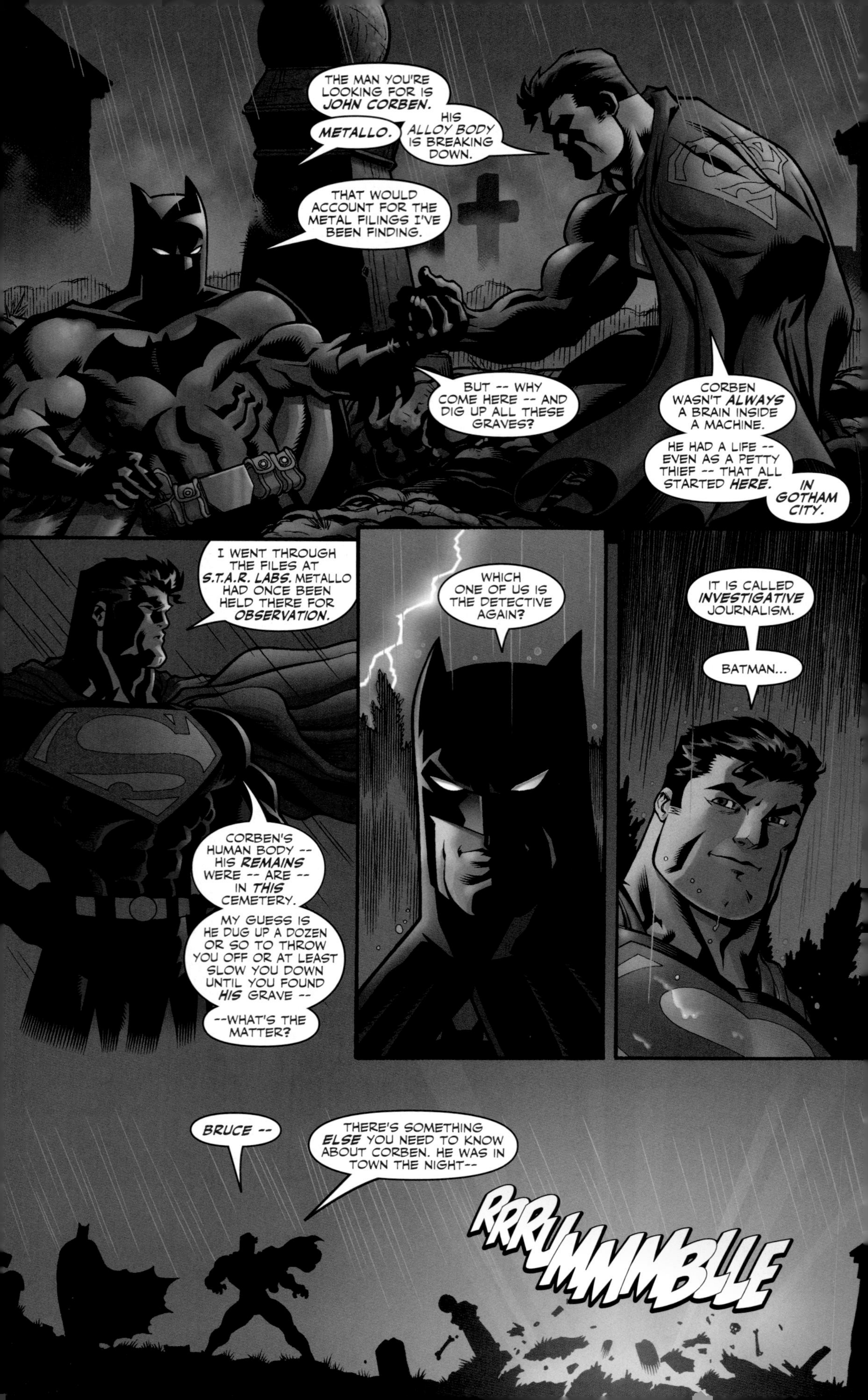

THE MAN YOU'RE LOOKING FOR IS JOHN CORBEN.
METALLO.
HIS ALLOY BODY IS BREAKING DOWN.
THAT WOULD ACCOUNT FOR THE METAL FILINGS I'VE BEEN FINDING.
BUT -- WHY COME HERE -- AND DIG UP ALL THESE GRAVES?
CORBEN WASN'T ALWAYS A BRAIN INSIDE A MACHINE.
HE HAD A LIFE -- EVEN AS A PETTY THIEF -- THAT ALL STARTED HERE.
IN GOTHAM CITY.
I WENT THROUGH THE FILES AT S.T.A.R. LABS. METALLO HAD ONCE BEEN HELD THERE FOR OBSERVATION.
CORBEN'S HUMAN BODY -- HIS REMAINS WERE -- ARE -- IN THIS CEMETERY.
MY GUESS IS HE DUG UP A DOZEN OR SO TO THROW YOU OFF OR AT LEAST SLOW YOU DOWN UNTIL YOU FOUND HIS GRAVE --
--WHAT'S THE MATTER?
WHICH ONE OF US IS THE DETECTIVE AGAIN?
IT IS CALLED INVESTIGATIVE JOURNALISM.
BATMAN...
BRUCE --
THERE'S SOMETHING ELSE YOU NEED TO KNOW ABOUT CORBEN. HE WAS IN TOWN THE NIGHT--
RRRUMMMMBLLE

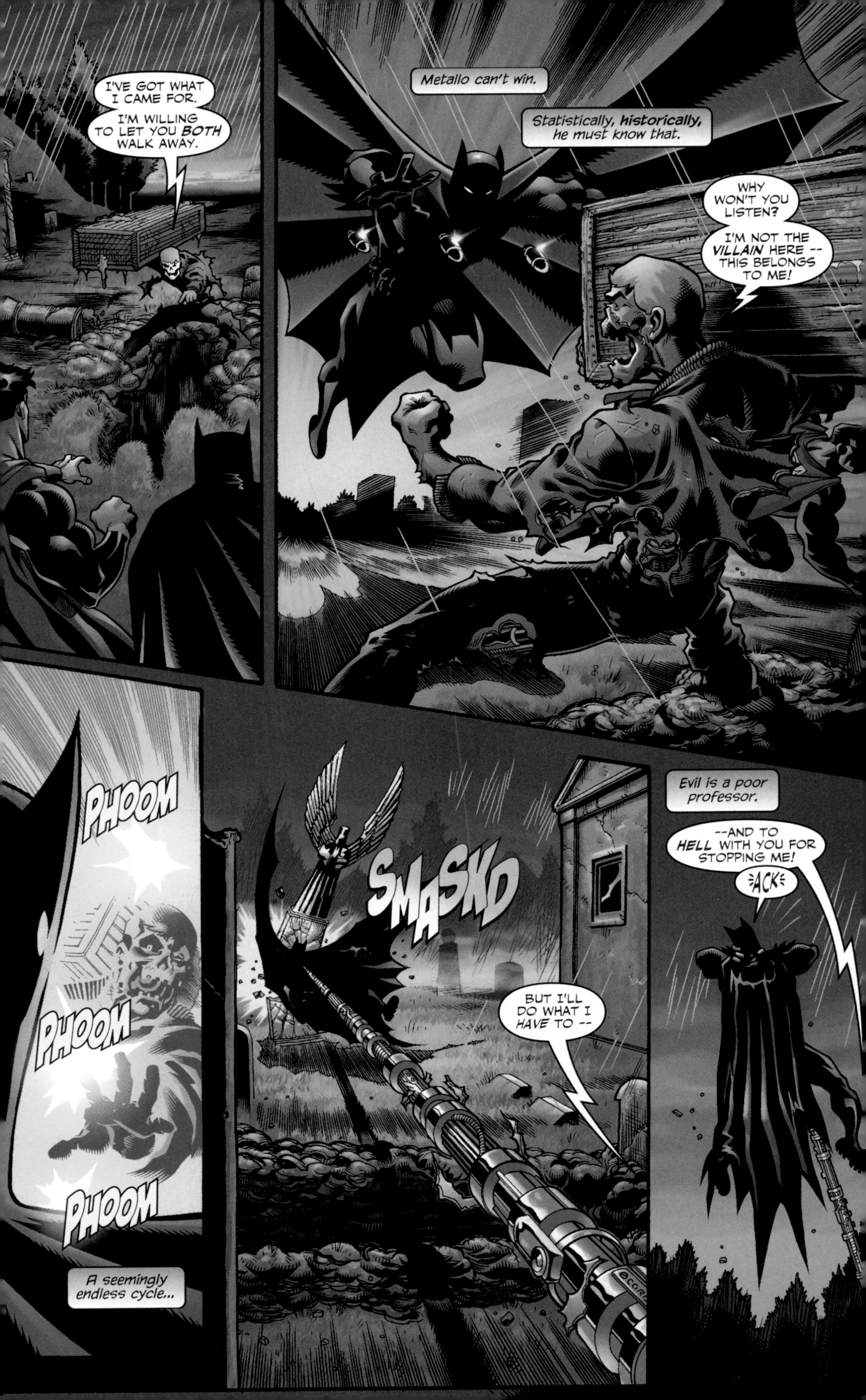
I'VE GOT WHAT I CAME FOR.
I'M WILLING TO LET YOU BOTH WALK AWAY.
Metallo can't win.
Statistically, historically, he must know that.
WHY WON'T YOU LISTEN?
I'M NOT THE VILLAIN HERE -- THIS BELONGS TO ME!
PHOOM
PHOOM
PHOOM
A seemingly endless cycle...
SMASKD
BUT I'LL DO WHAT I HAVE TO --
Evil is a poor professor.
--AND TO HELL WITH YOU FOR STOPPING ME!
ACK

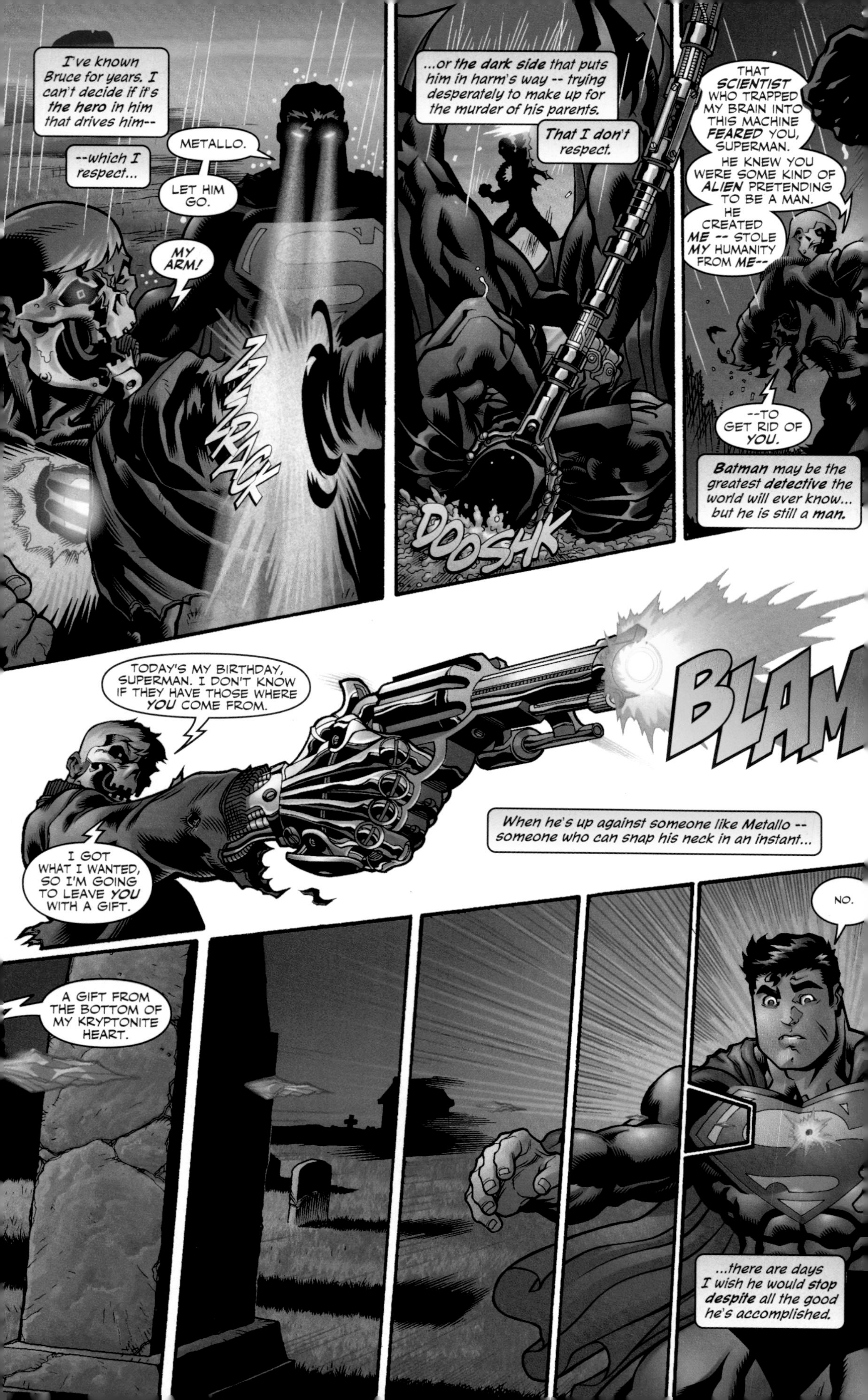
I've known Bruce for years. I can't decide if it's the hero in him that drives him--
--which I respect...
METALLO.
LET HIM GO.
MY ARM!
ZZZZRACK
...or the dark side that puts him in harm's way -- trying desperately to make up for the murder of his parents.
That I don't respect.
DOOSHK
THAT SCIENTIST WHO TRAPPED MY BRAIN INTO THIS MACHINE FEARED YOU, SUPERMAN.
HE KNEW YOU WERE SOME KIND OF ALIEN PRETENDING TO BE A MAN.
HE CREATED ME -- STOLE MY HUMANITY FROM ME--
--TO GET RID OF YOU.
Batman may be the greatest detective the world will ever know... but he is still a man.
TODAY'S MY BIRTHDAY, SUPERMAN. I DON'T KNOW IF THEY HAVE THOSE WHERE YOU COME FROM.
BLAM
I GOT WHAT I WANTED, SO I'M GOING TO LEAVE YOU WITH A GIFT.
When he's up against someone like Metallo -- someone who can snap his neck in an instant...
A GIFT FROM THE BOTTOM OF MY KRYPTONITE HEART.
NO.
...there are days I wish he would stop despite all the good he's accomplished.

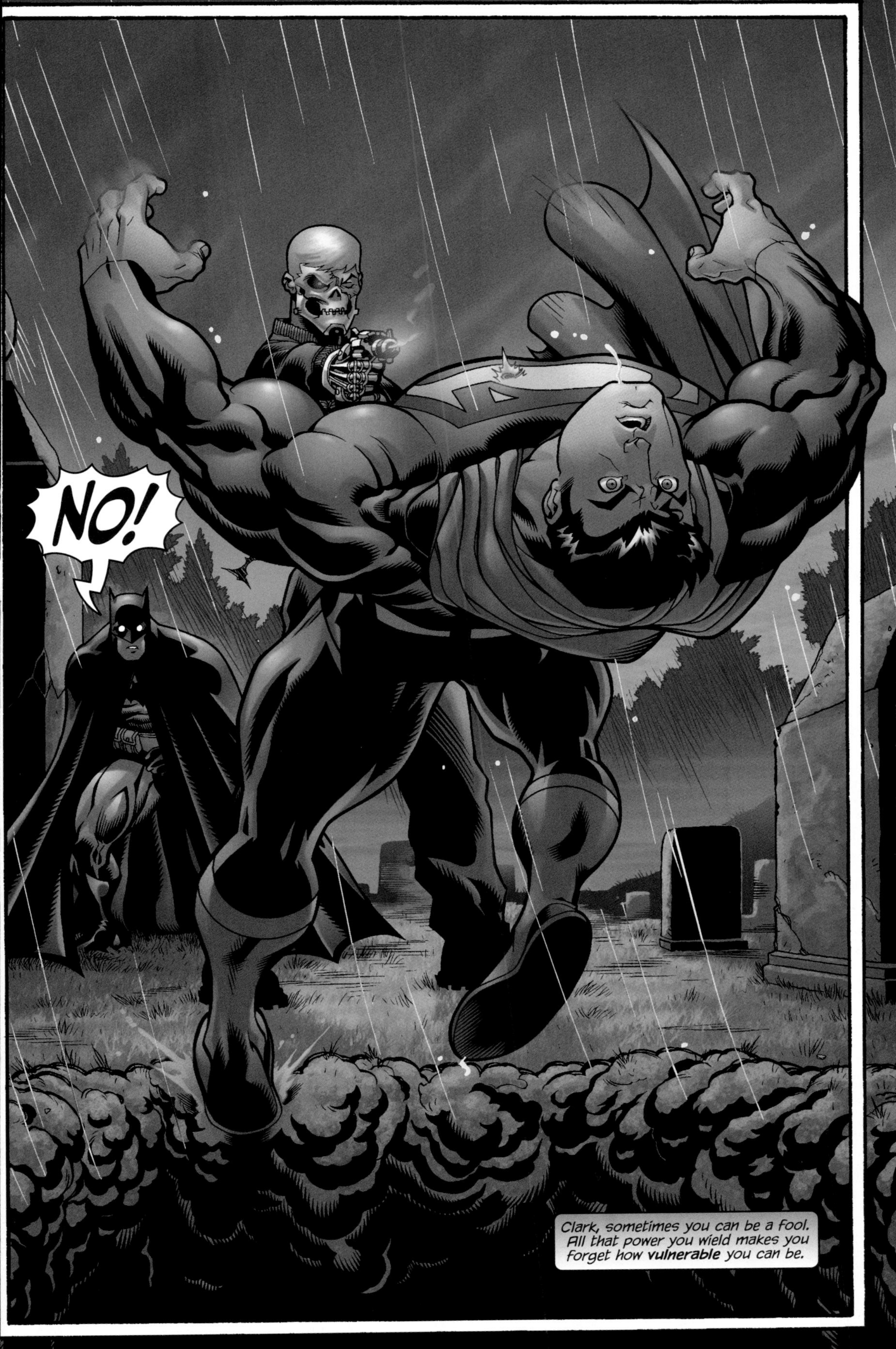
NO!
Clark, sometimes you can be a fool. All that power you wield makes you forget how **vulnerable** you can be.

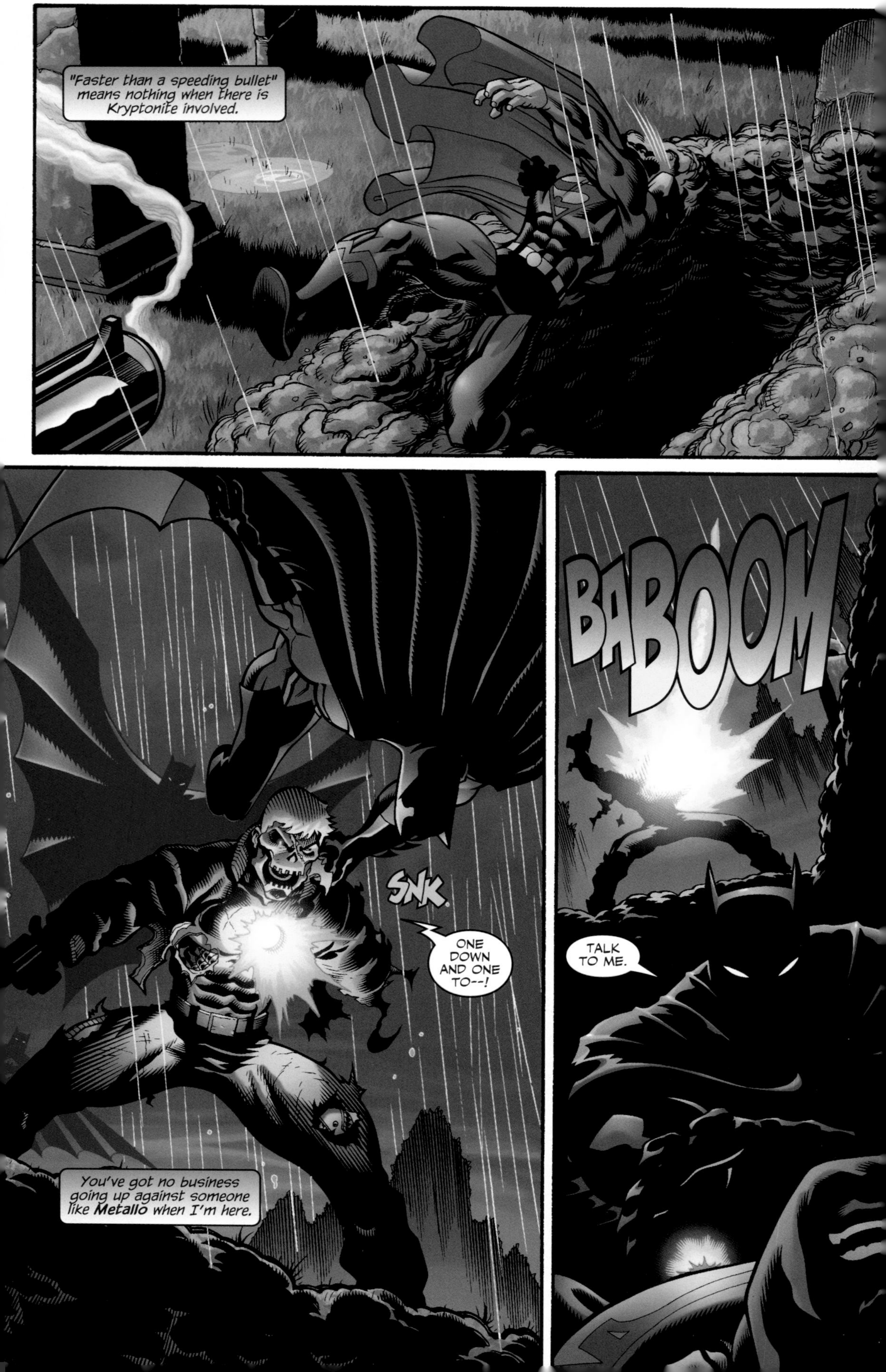
"Faster than a speeding bullet" means nothing when there is Kryptonite involved.
SNK
ONE DOWN AND ONE TO--!
You've got no business going up against someone like **Metallo** when I'm here.
BABOOM
TALK TO ME.

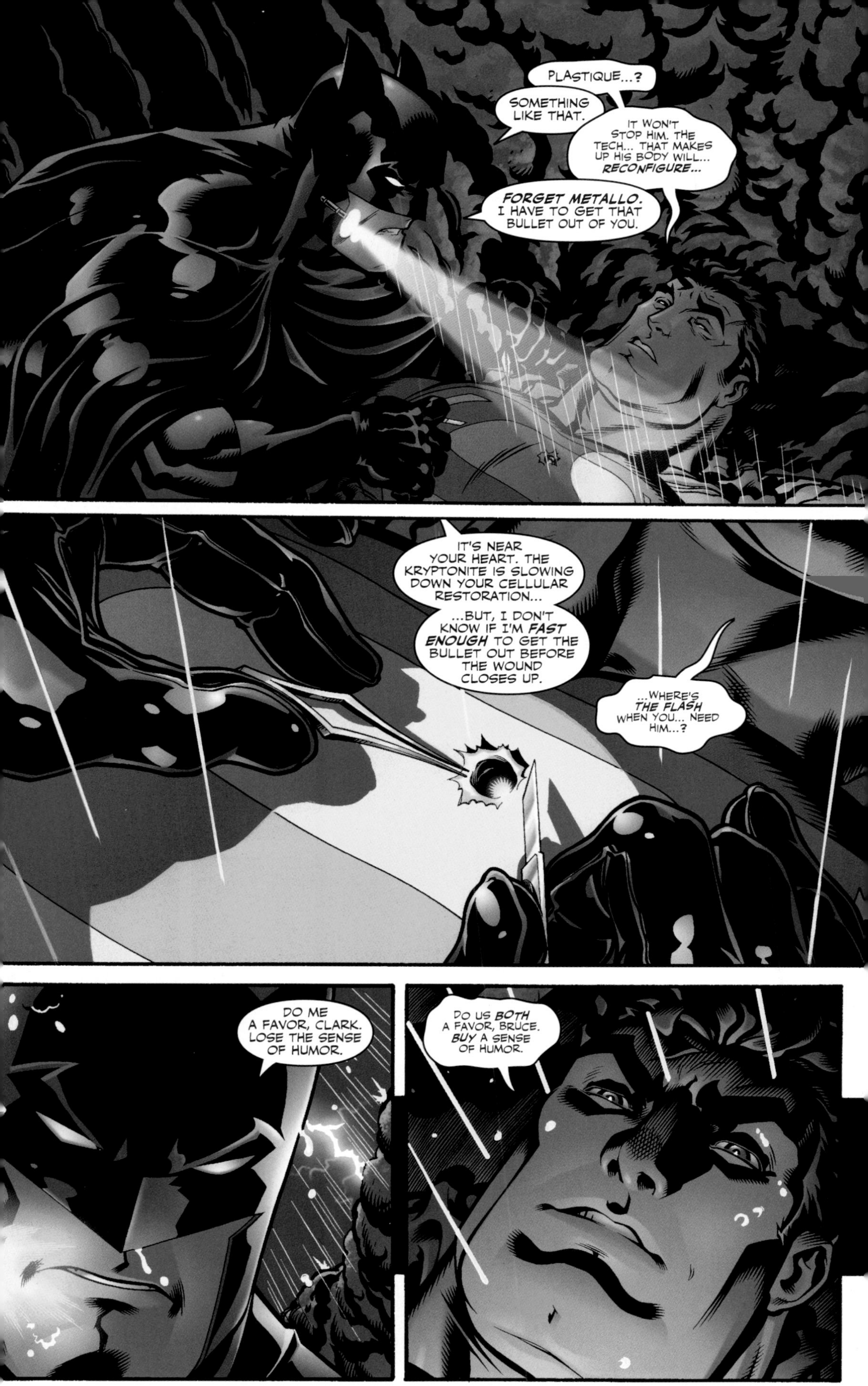
PLASTIQUE...?
SOMETHING LIKE THAT.
IT WON'T STOP HIM. THE TECH... THAT MAKES UP HIS BODY WILL... *RECONFIGURE...*
FORGET METALLO. I HAVE TO GET THAT BULLET OUT OF YOU.
IT'S NEAR YOUR HEART. THE KRYPTONITE IS SLOWING DOWN YOUR CELLULAR RESTORATION...
...BUT, I DON'T KNOW IF I'M *FAST ENOUGH* TO GET THE BULLET OUT BEFORE THE WOUND CLOSES UP.
...WHERE'S *THE FLASH* WHEN YOU... NEED HIM...?
DO ME A FAVOR, CLARK. LOSE THE SENSE OF HUMOR.
DO US *BOTH* A FAVOR, BRUCE. *BUY* A SENSE OF HUMOR.

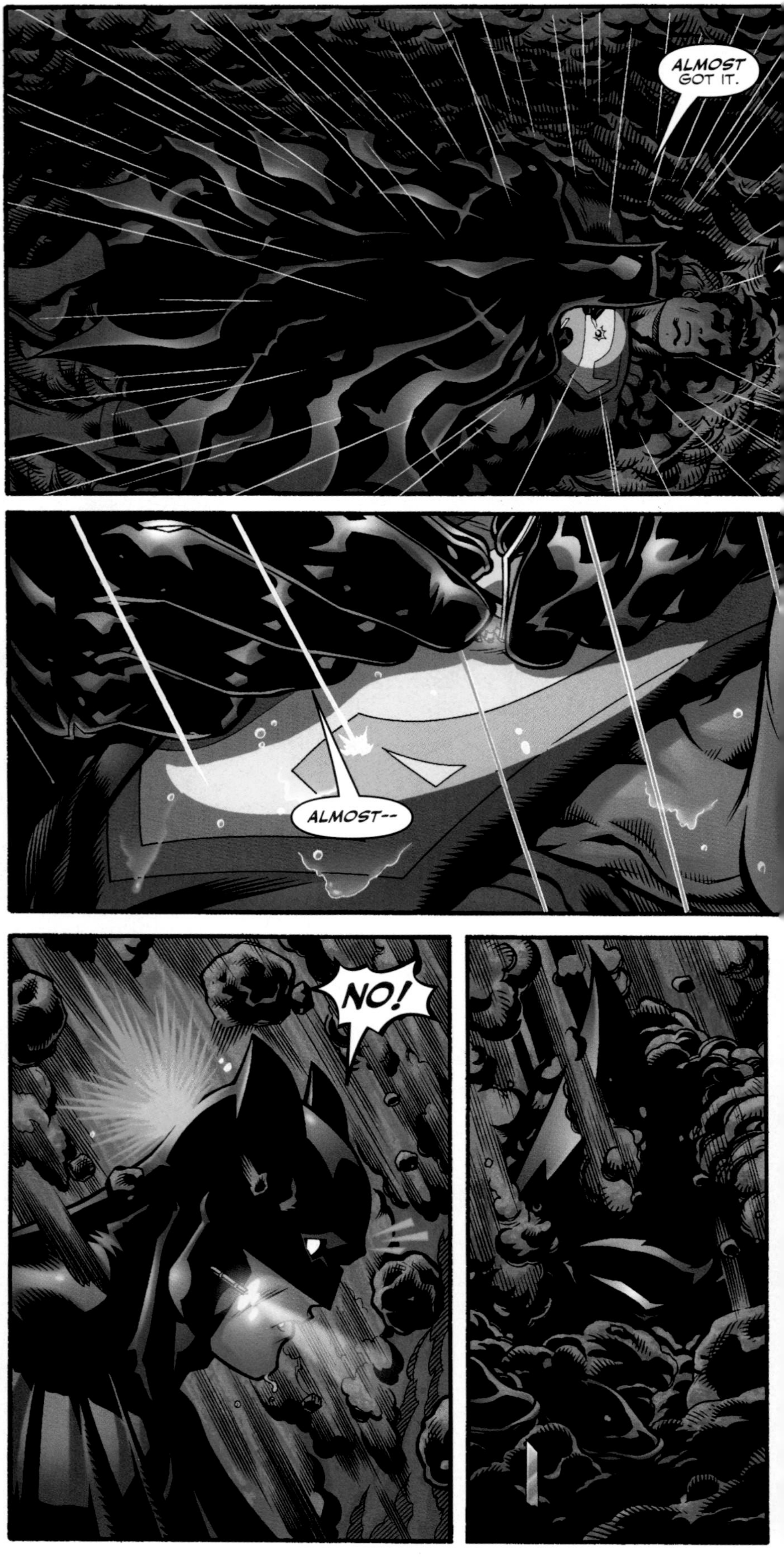
ALMOST GOT IT.
ALMOST--
NO!

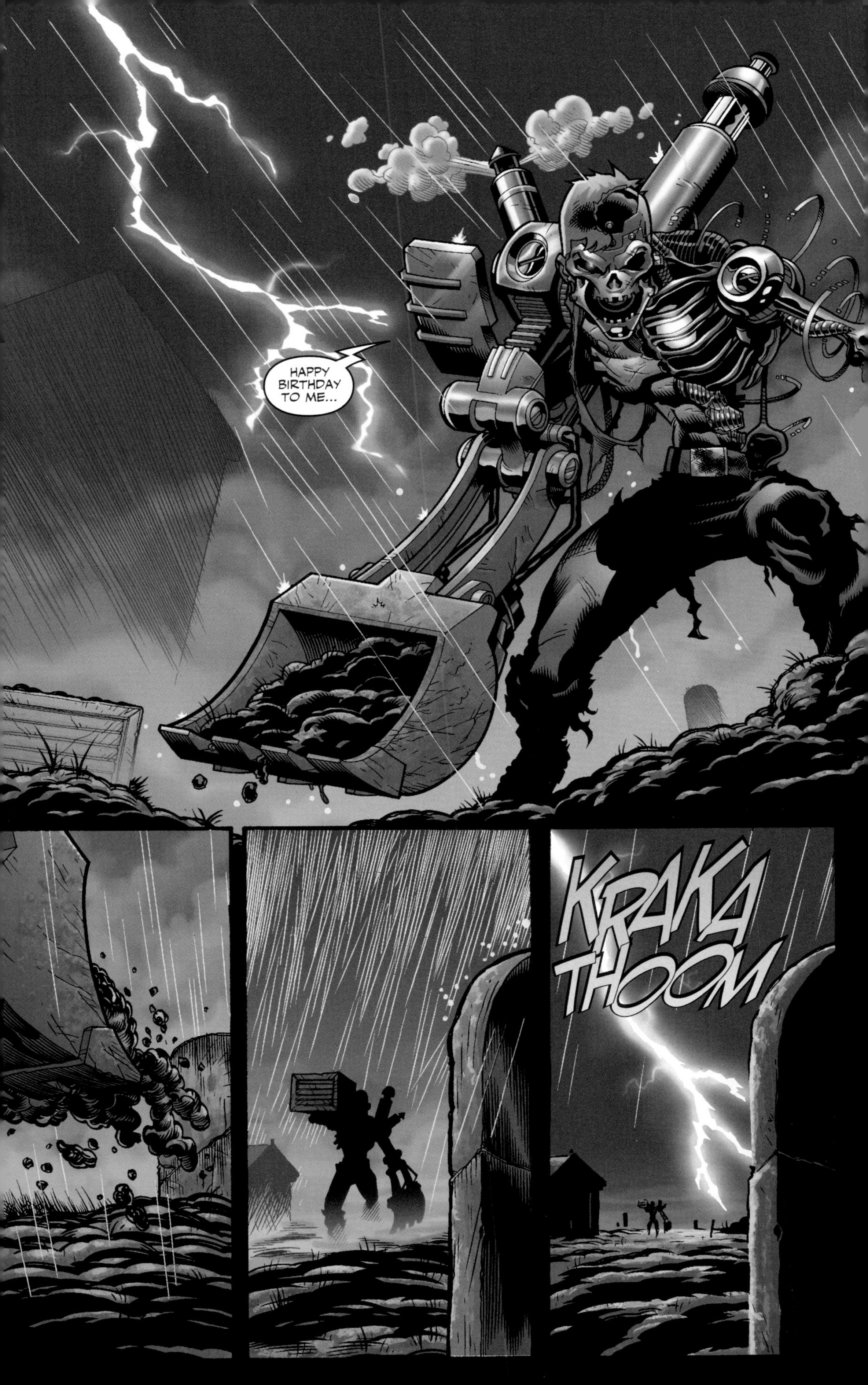
HAPPY BIRTHDAY TO ME...
KRAKA THOOM

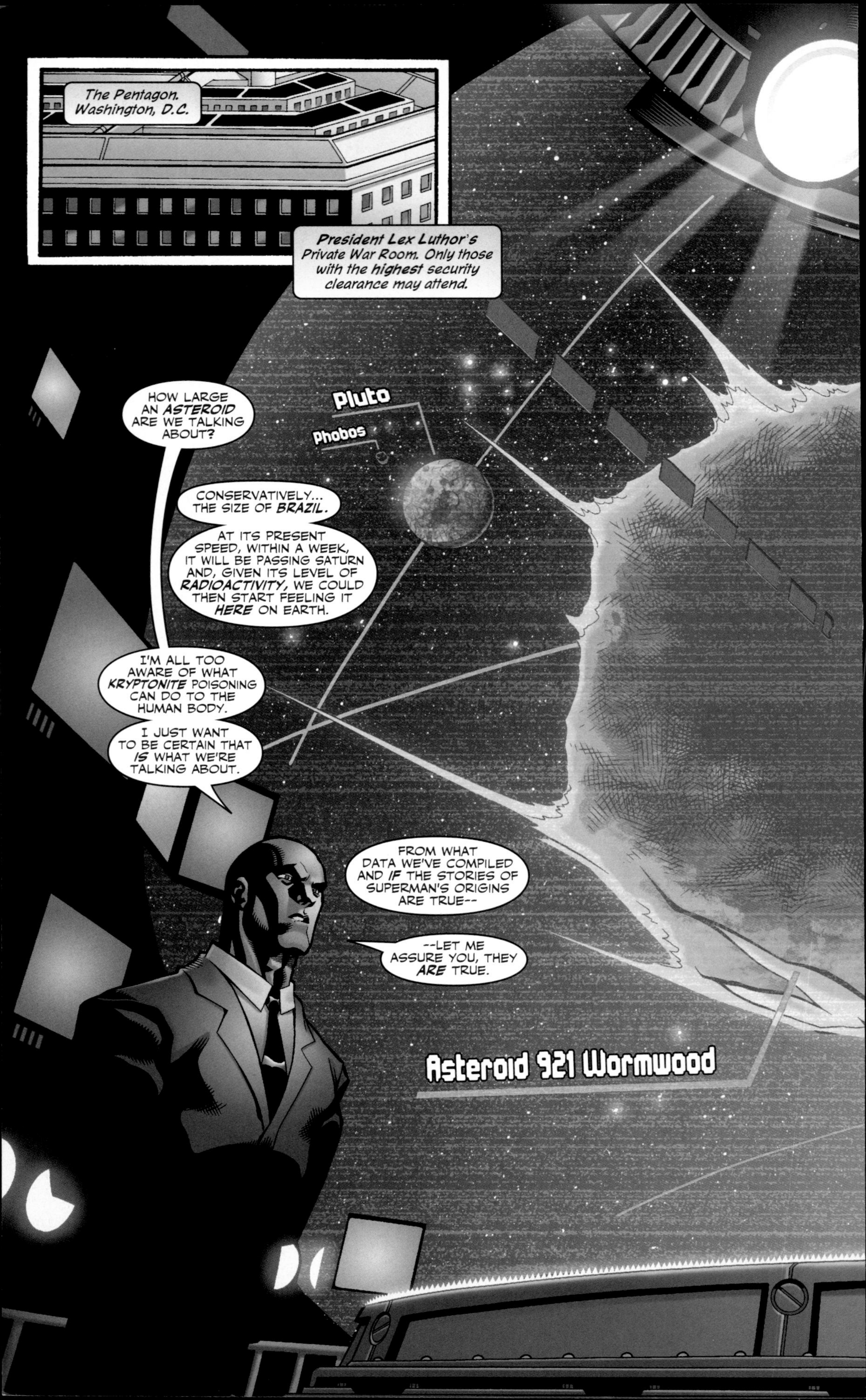
The Pentagon. Washington, D.C.
President Lex Luthor's Private War Room. Only those with the highest security clearance may attend.
HOW LARGE AN ASTEROID ARE WE TALKING ABOUT?
Pluto
Phobos
CONSERVATIVELY... THE SIZE OF BRAZIL.
AT ITS PRESENT SPEED, WITHIN A WEEK, IT WILL BE PASSING SATURN AND, GIVEN ITS LEVEL OF RADIOACTIVITY, WE COULD THEN START FEELING IT HERE ON EARTH.
I'M ALL TOO AWARE OF WHAT KRYPTONITE POISONING CAN DO TO THE HUMAN BODY.
I JUST WANT TO BE CERTAIN THAT IS WHAT WE'RE TALKING ABOUT.
FROM WHAT DATA WE'VE COMPILED AND IF THE STORIES OF SUPERMAN'S ORIGINS ARE TRUE--
--LET ME ASSURE YOU, THEY ARE TRUE.
Asteroid 921 Wormwood

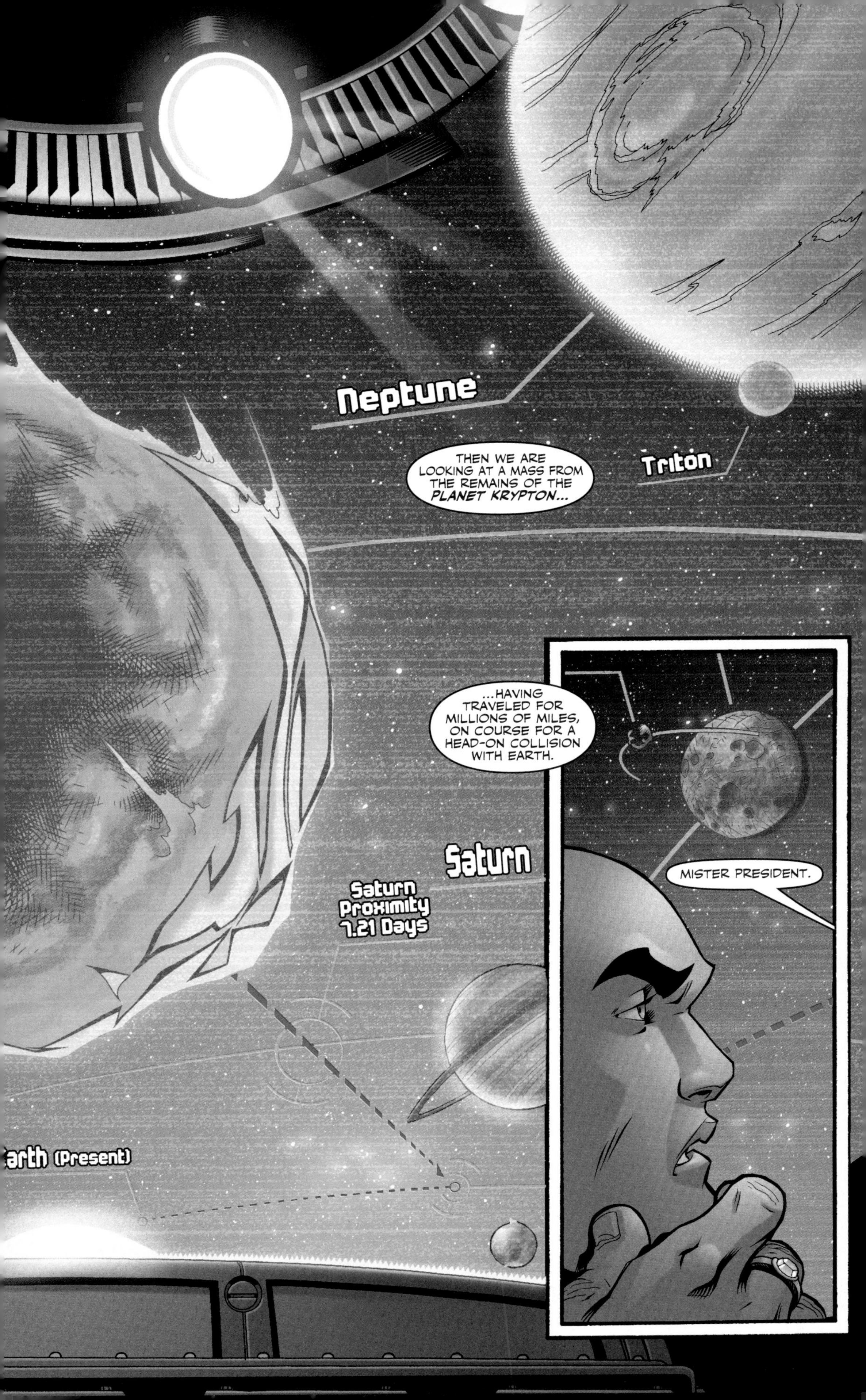
Neptune
Triton
THEN WE ARE LOOKING AT A MASS FROM THE REMAINS OF THE PLANET KRYPTON...
...HAVING TRAVELED FOR MILLIONS OF MILES, ON COURSE FOR A HEAD-ON COLLISION WITH EARTH.
Saturn
Saturn Proximity 7.21 Days
MISTER PRESIDENT.
Earth (Present)

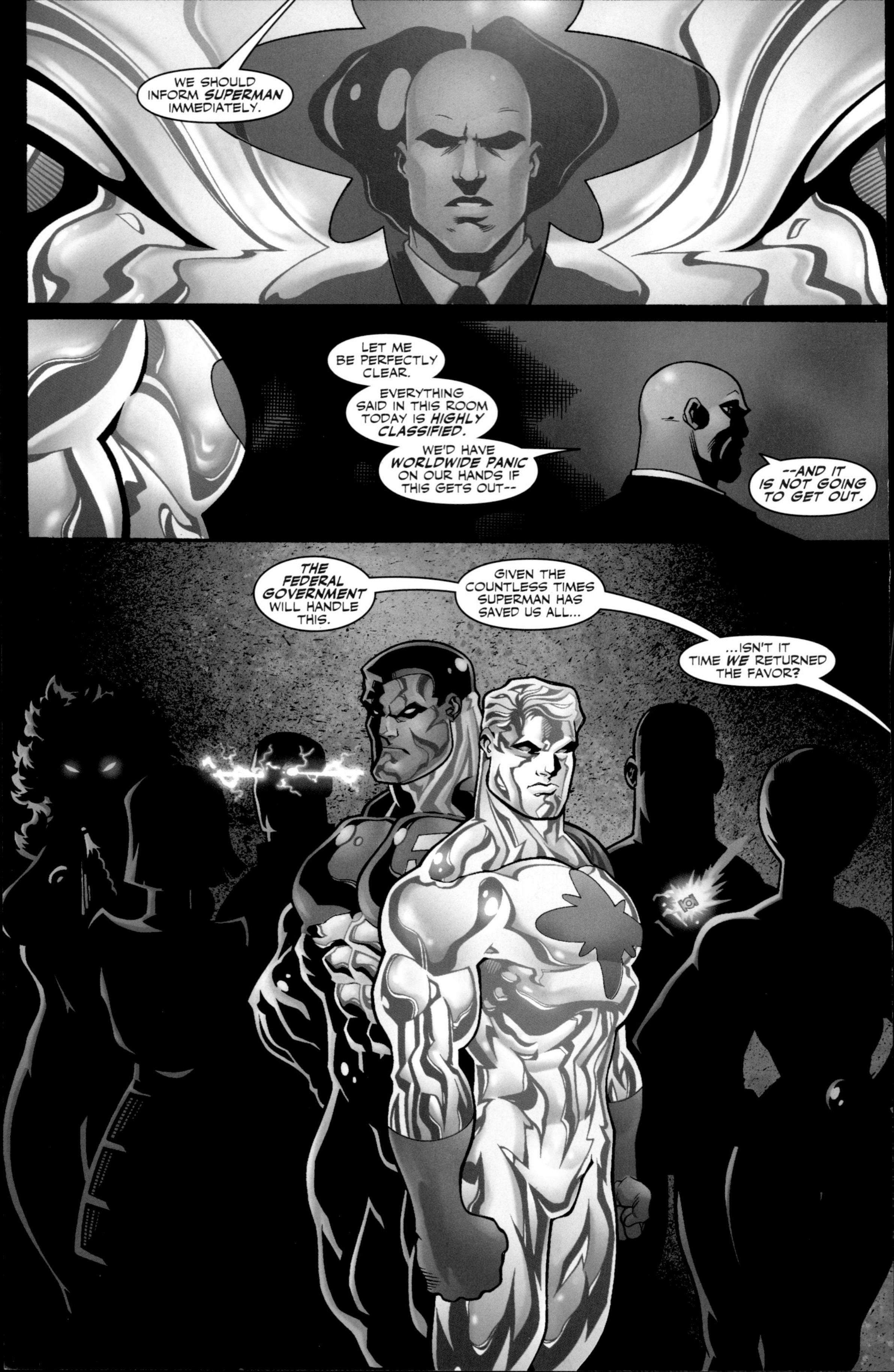
WE SHOULD INFORM SUPERMAN IMMEDIATELY.
LET ME BE PERFECTLY CLEAR.
EVERYTHING SAID IN THIS ROOM TODAY IS HIGHLY CLASSIFIED.
WE'D HAVE WORLDWIDE PANIC ON OUR HANDS IF THIS GETS OUT--
--AND IT IS NOT GOING TO GET OUT.
THE FEDERAL GOVERNMENT WILL HANDLE THIS.
GIVEN THE COUNTLESS TIMES SUPERMAN HAS SAVED US ALL...
...ISN'T IT TIME WE RETURNED THE FAVOR?

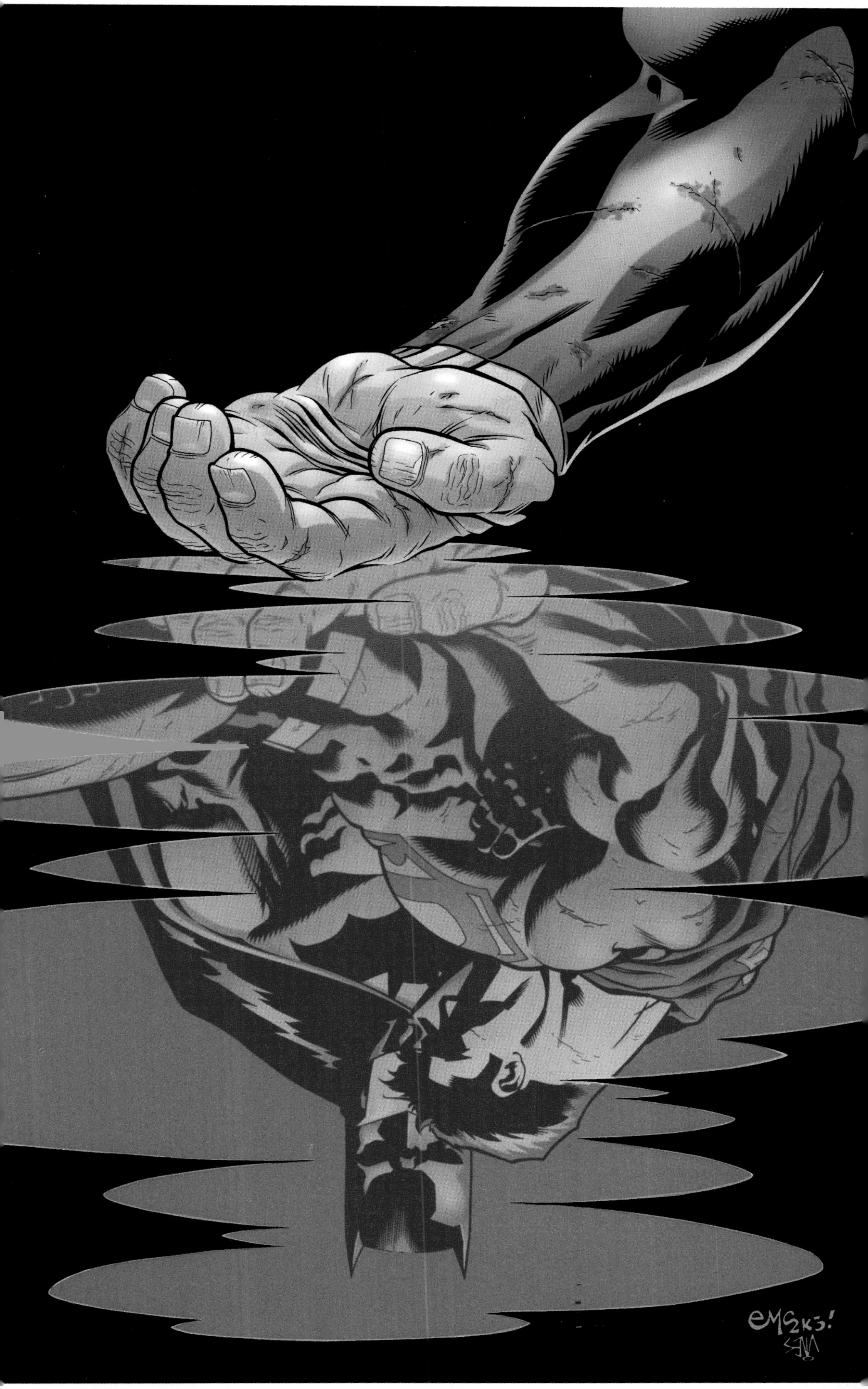

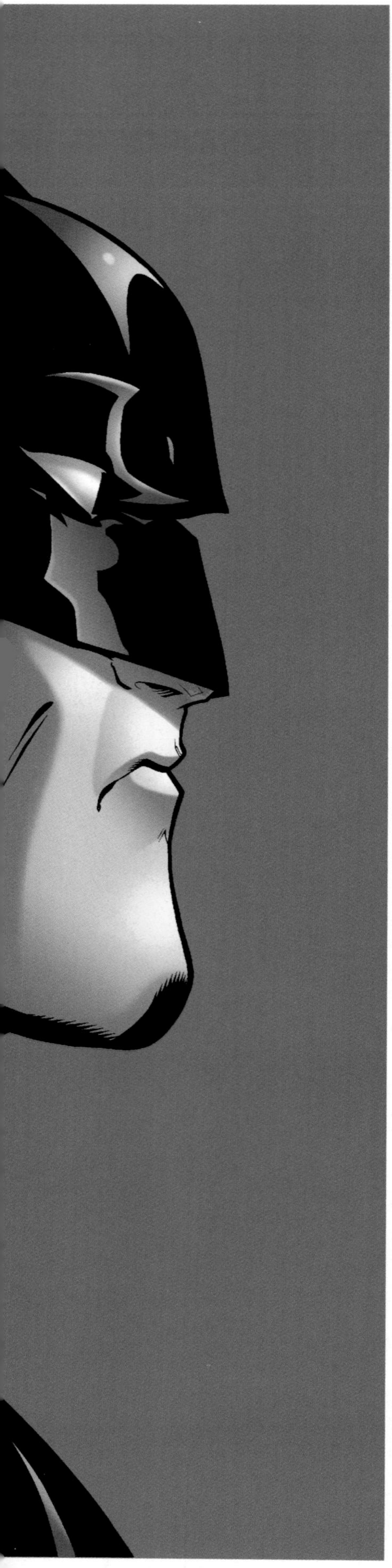

SUPERMAN
PART TWO
BATMAN

EARLY WARNING

JEPH LOEB
WRITER
ED McGUINNESS
PENCILLER
DEXTER VINES
INKER
DAVE STEWART
COLORIST
RICHARD STARKINGS
LETTERER
ED McGUINNESS
DEXTER VINES
WITH
DAVE STEWART
COVER

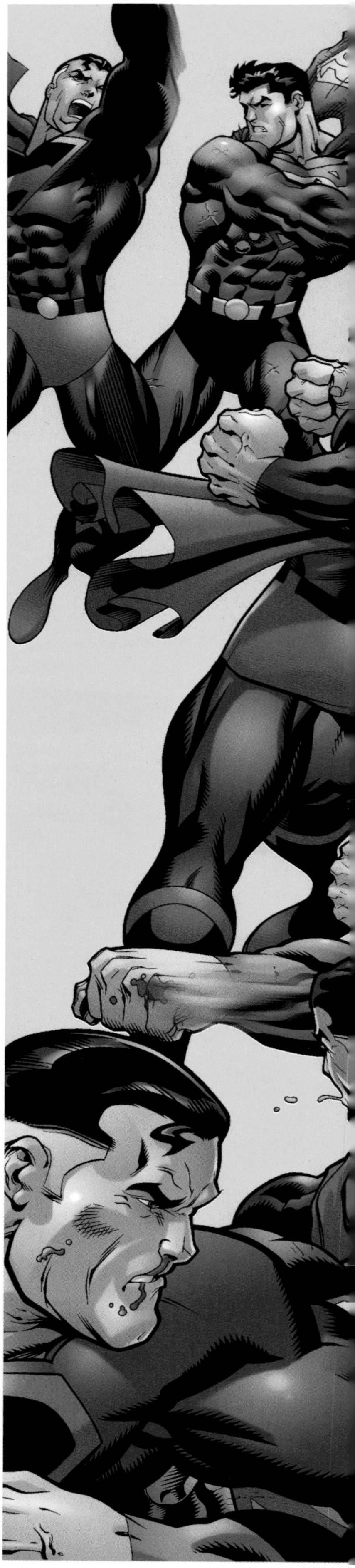

It's... odd what goes through your head when... it seems like the worst of times.

No more air.

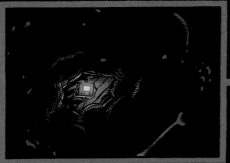

We were kids, **Pete Ross** and I. We had gone camping in this horrible storm back in Smallville.

The Kryptonite bullet lodged in Clark's chest has immobilized him.

003

The ground had softened and I fell into an old well. It was maybe a hundred feet down. And all around me were these green rocks. **Meteor rocks.**

002

We can't go up. **Metallo** may still be there, and neither of us is in any shape to take him on.

I'd never felt anything like it before. My head was spinning. My stomach going upside-down. I didn't know then it was **Kryptonite.** I only knew I was hurt.

I need you to be **The Man of Steel,** Clark. Be the shield --

001

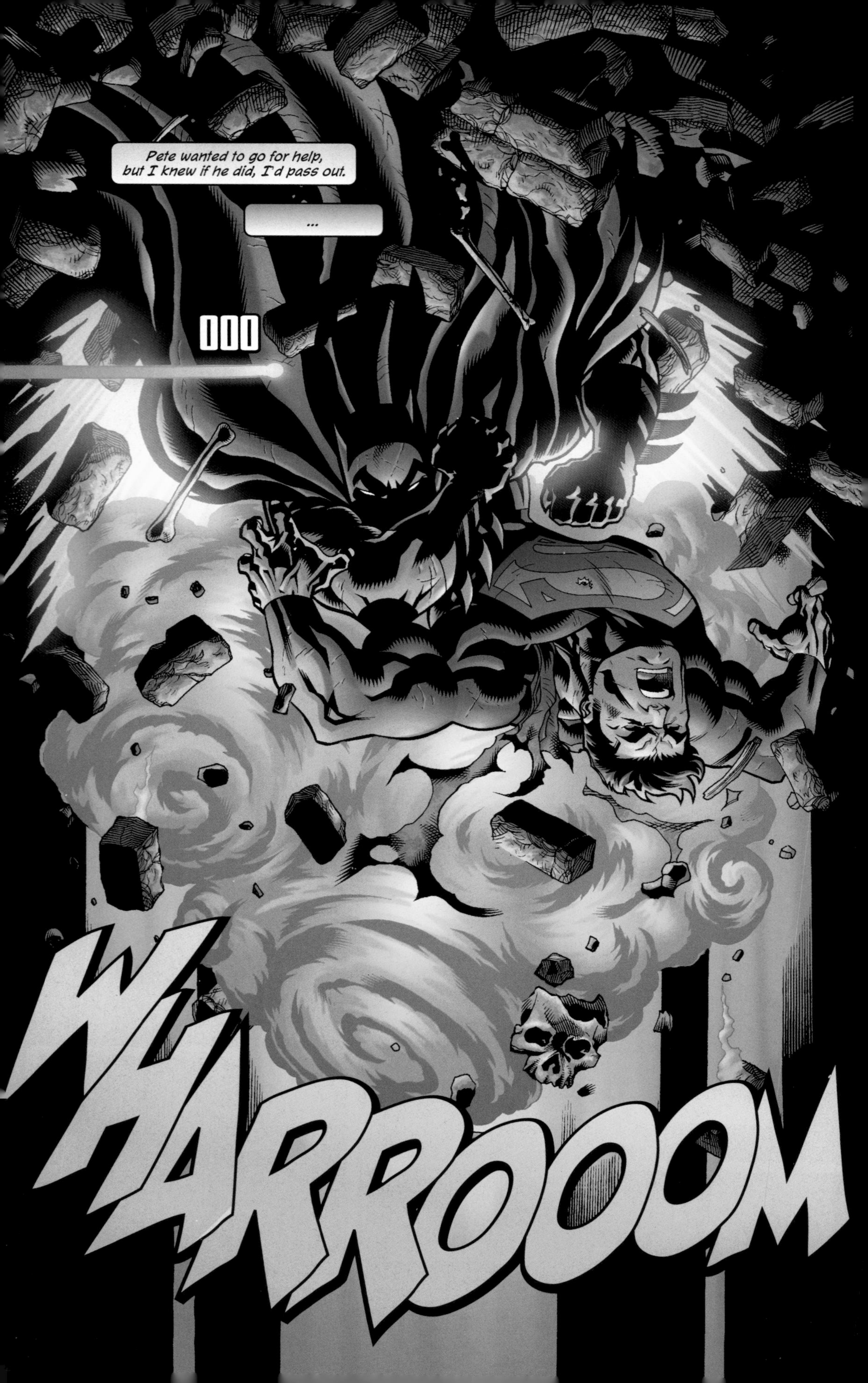
Pete wanted to go for help, but I knew if he did, I'd pass out.
...
OOO
WHARROOOM

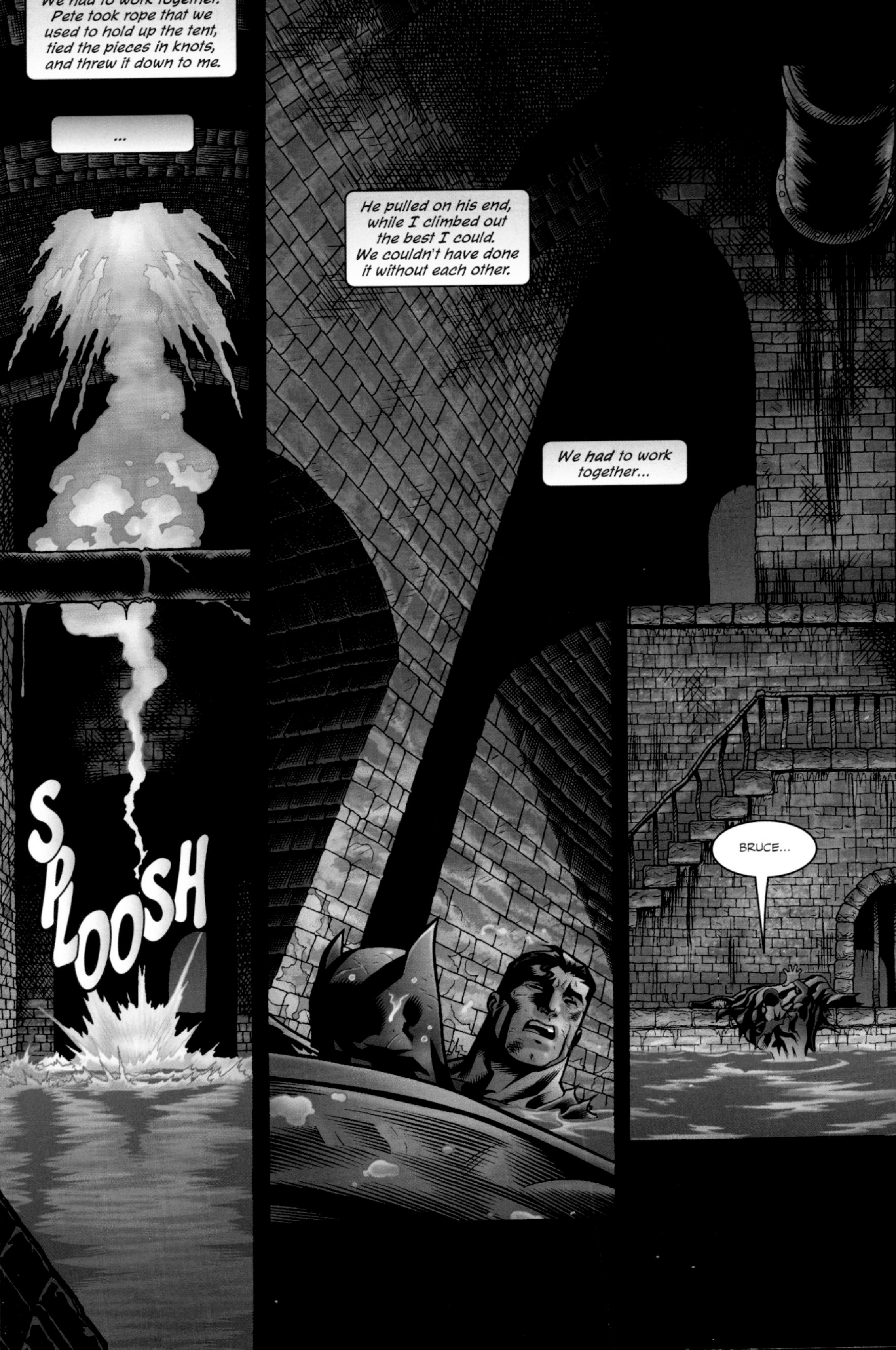

Pete took rope that we used to hold up the tent, tied the pieces in knots, and threw it down to me.
...
SPLOOSH
He pulled on his end, while I climbed out the best I could. We couldn't have done it without each other.
We had to work together...
BRUCE...

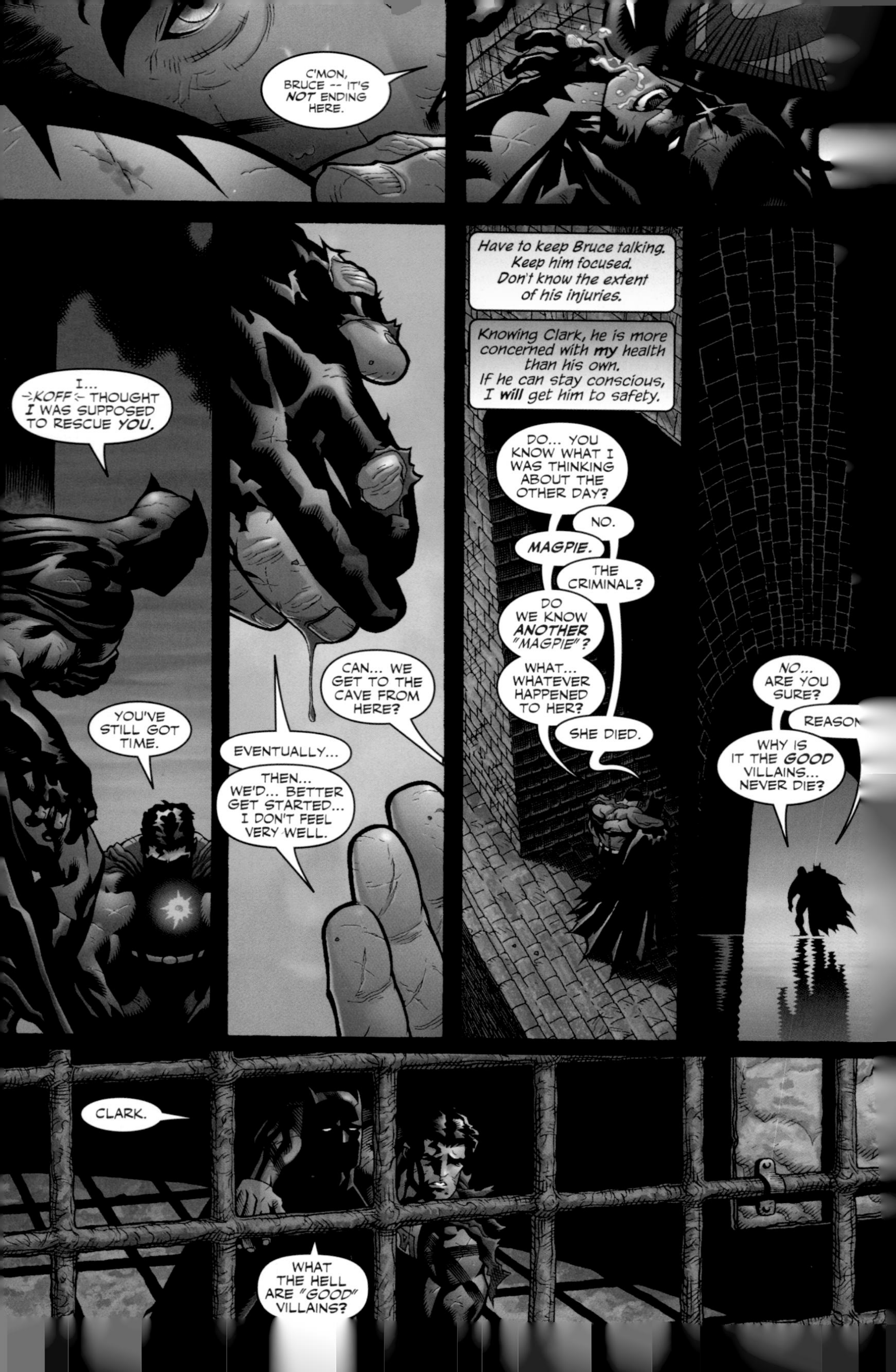
C'MON, BRUCE -- IT'S NOT ENDING HERE.
I... ⇢KOFF⇠ THOUGHT I WAS SUPPOSED TO RESCUE YOU.
YOU'VE STILL GOT TIME.
CAN... WE GET TO THE CAVE FROM HERE?
EVENTUALLY...
THEN... WE'D... BETTER GET STARTED... I DON'T FEEL VERY WELL.
Have to keep Bruce talking. Keep him focused. Don't know the extent of his injuries.
Knowing Clark, he is more concerned with my health than his own. If he can stay conscious, I will get him to safety.
DO... YOU KNOW WHAT I WAS THINKING ABOUT THE OTHER DAY?
NO.
MAGPIE.
THE CRIMINAL?
DO WE KNOW ANOTHER "MAGPIE"?
WHAT... WHATEVER HAPPENED TO HER?
SHE DIED.
NO... ARE YOU SURE?
REASON
WHY IS IT THE GOOD VILLAINS... NEVER DIE?
CLARK.
WHAT THE HELL ARE "GOOD" VILLAINS?

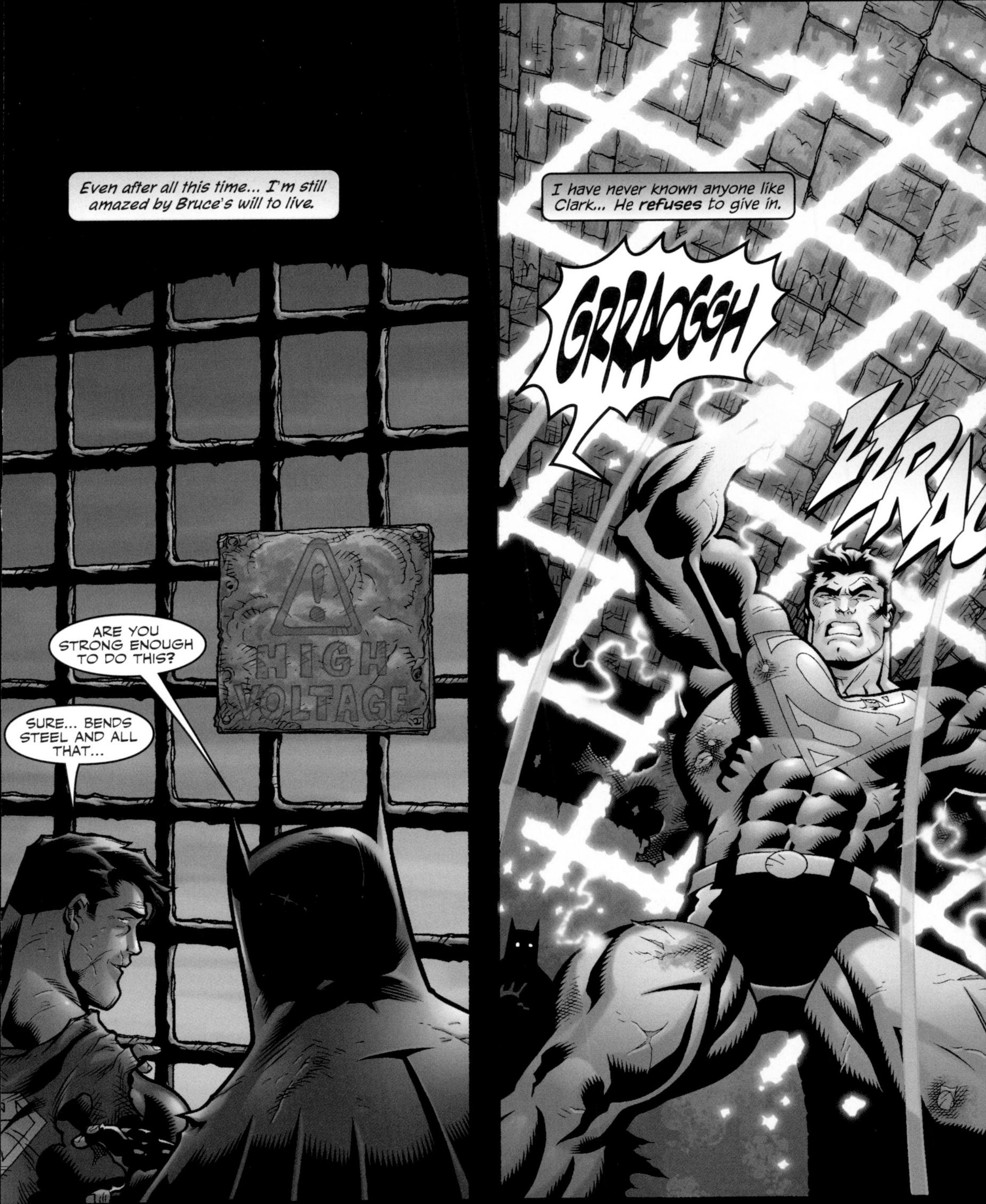
Even after all this time... I'm still amazed by Bruce's will to live.
HIGH VOLTAGE
ARE YOU STRONG ENOUGH TO DO THIS?
SURE... BENDS STEEL AND ALL THAT...
I have never known anyone like Clark... He refuses to give in.
GRRAOGGH

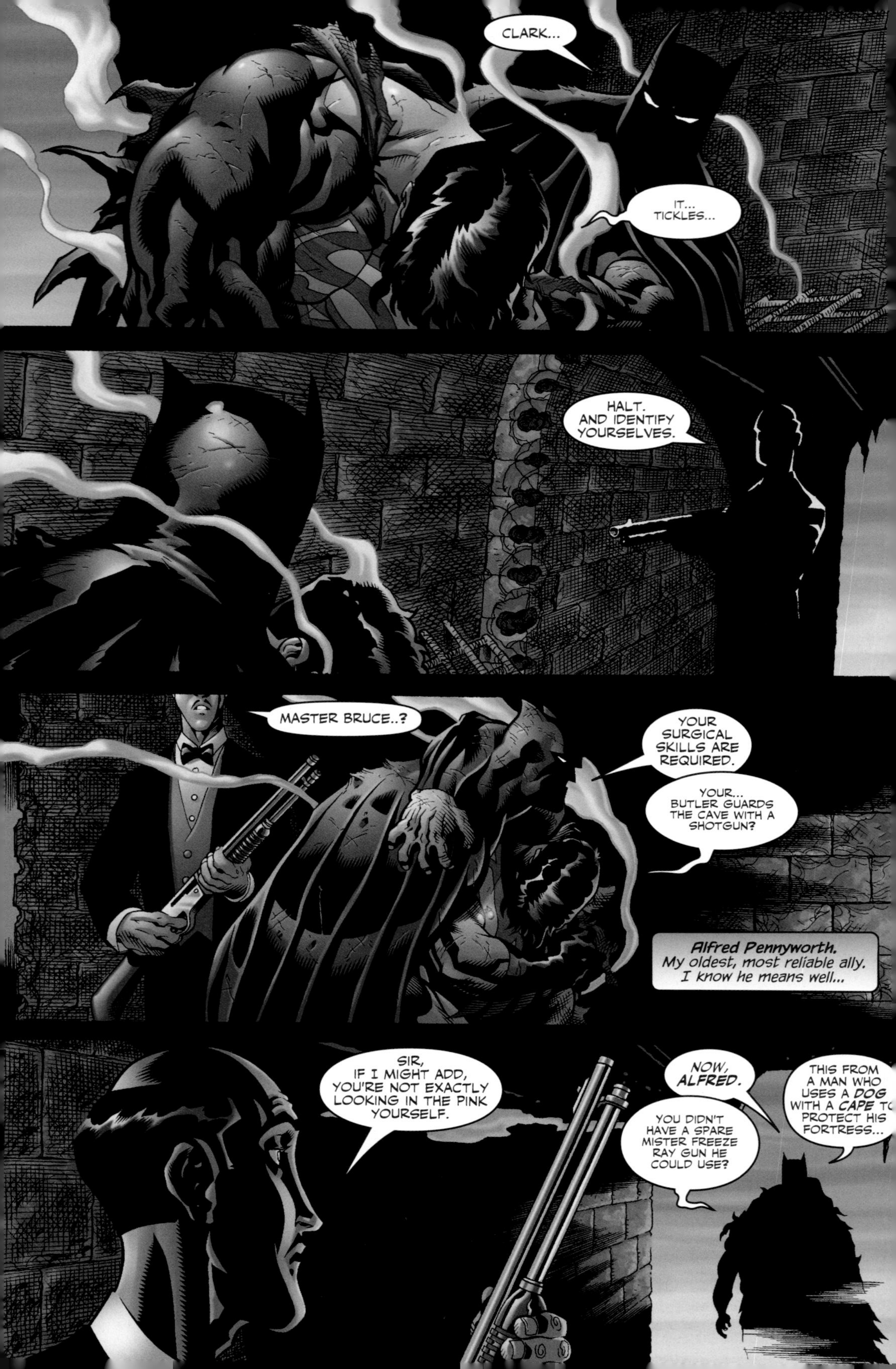
CLARK...
IT... TICKLES...
HALT. AND IDENTIFY YOURSELVES.
MASTER BRUCE..?
YOUR SURGICAL SKILLS ARE REQUIRED.
YOUR... BUTLER GUARDS THE CAVE WITH A SHOTGUN?
Alfred Pennyworth. My oldest, most reliable ally. I know he means well...
SIR, IF I MIGHT ADD, YOU'RE NOT EXACTLY LOOKING IN THE PINK YOURSELF.
NOW, ALFRED.
YOU DIDN'T HAVE A SPARE MISTER FREEZE RAY GUN HE COULD USE?
THIS FROM A MAN WHO USES A DOG WITH A CAPE TO PROTECT HIS FORTRESS...

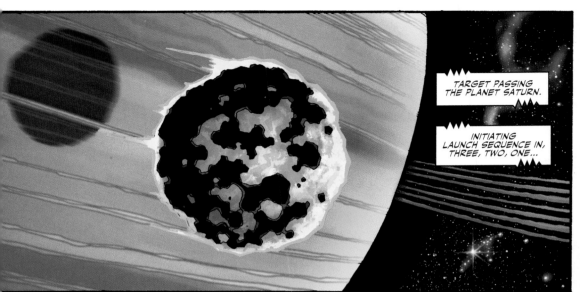

TARGET PASSING THE PLANET SATURN.

INITIATING LAUNCH SEQUENCE IN, THREE, TWO, ONE...

MISTER PRESIDENT. PERMISSION TO SPEAK FREELY, SIR.

CAPTAIN ATOM. A PORTION OF THE PLANET KRYPTON IS ON A COLLISION COURSE WITH EARTH.

DO YOU THINK THAT WHATEVER IT IS YOU HAVE TO SAY COULD WAIT UNTIL THOSE NUCLEAR MISSILES HAVE ELIMINATED THAT THREAT?

WITH ALL DUE RESPECT, SIR... NO.

THAT WAS A BOOM TUBE.

TECHNOLOGY WHICH IS NOT ONLY ILLEGAL, IT REPRESENTS TRADE WITH AN EMBARGOED--

--DON'T TAKE THAT SANCTIMONIOUS TONE WITH ME, CAPTAIN.

HOW ELSE WERE WE GOING TO GET THAT MUCH FIREPOWER ACROSS THE SOLAR SYSTEM IN TIME TO SAVE OUR WORLD?

YOU BETTER THAN ANYONE KNOW THAT WHEN THE AMERICAN PEOPLE LEARN THAT THEIR LIVES ARE THREATENED--

--THAT INNOCENT WOMEN AND CHILDREN ARE GOING TO LIE DEAD IN THE STREETS--

--THEY AREN'T GOING TO WONDER HOW WE STOPPED IT.

JUST THAT WE DID.

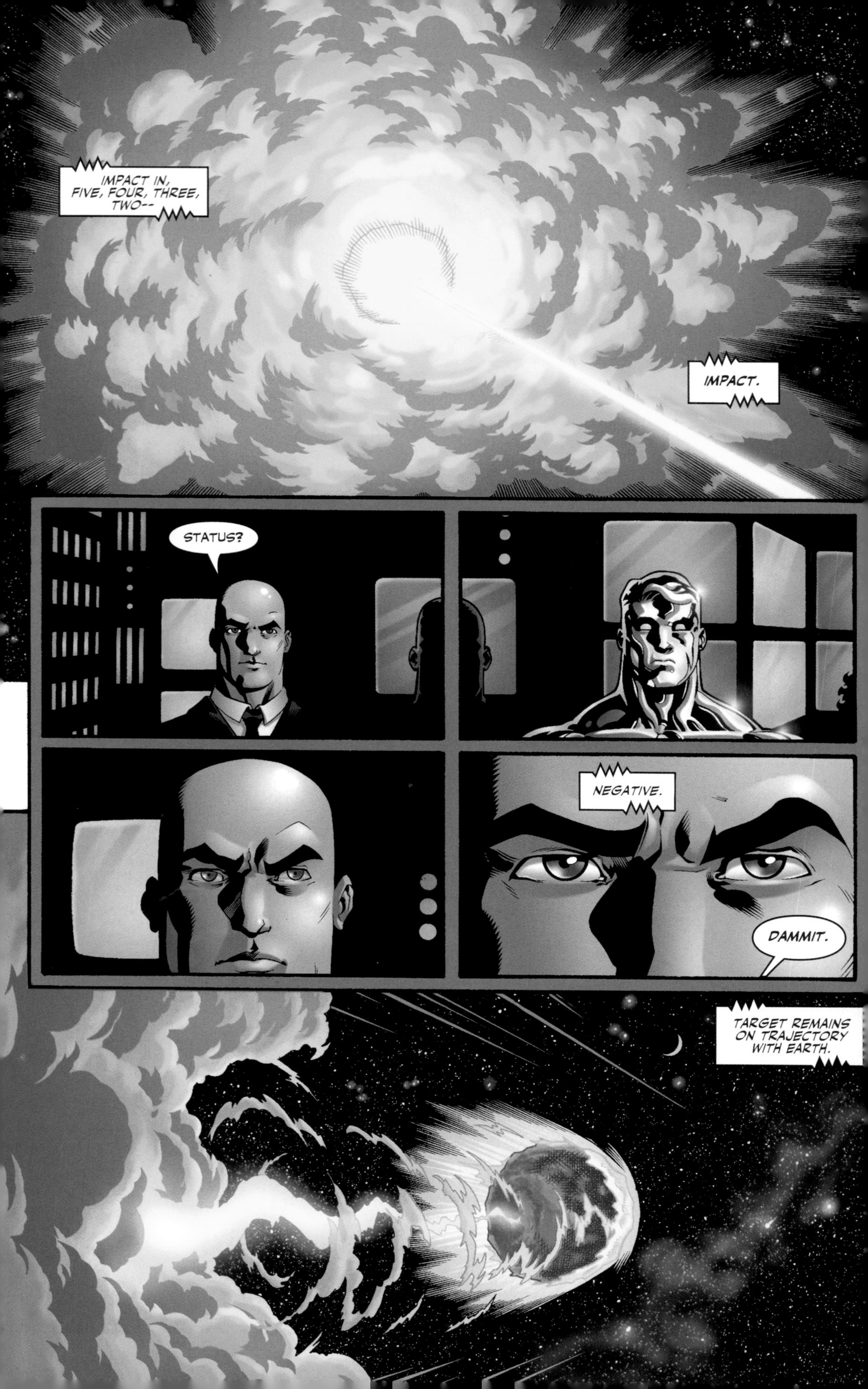

IMPACT IN, FIVE, FOUR, THREE, TWO--
IMPACT.
STATUS?
NEGATIVE.
DAMMIT.
TARGET REMAINS ON TRAJECTORY WITH EARTH.

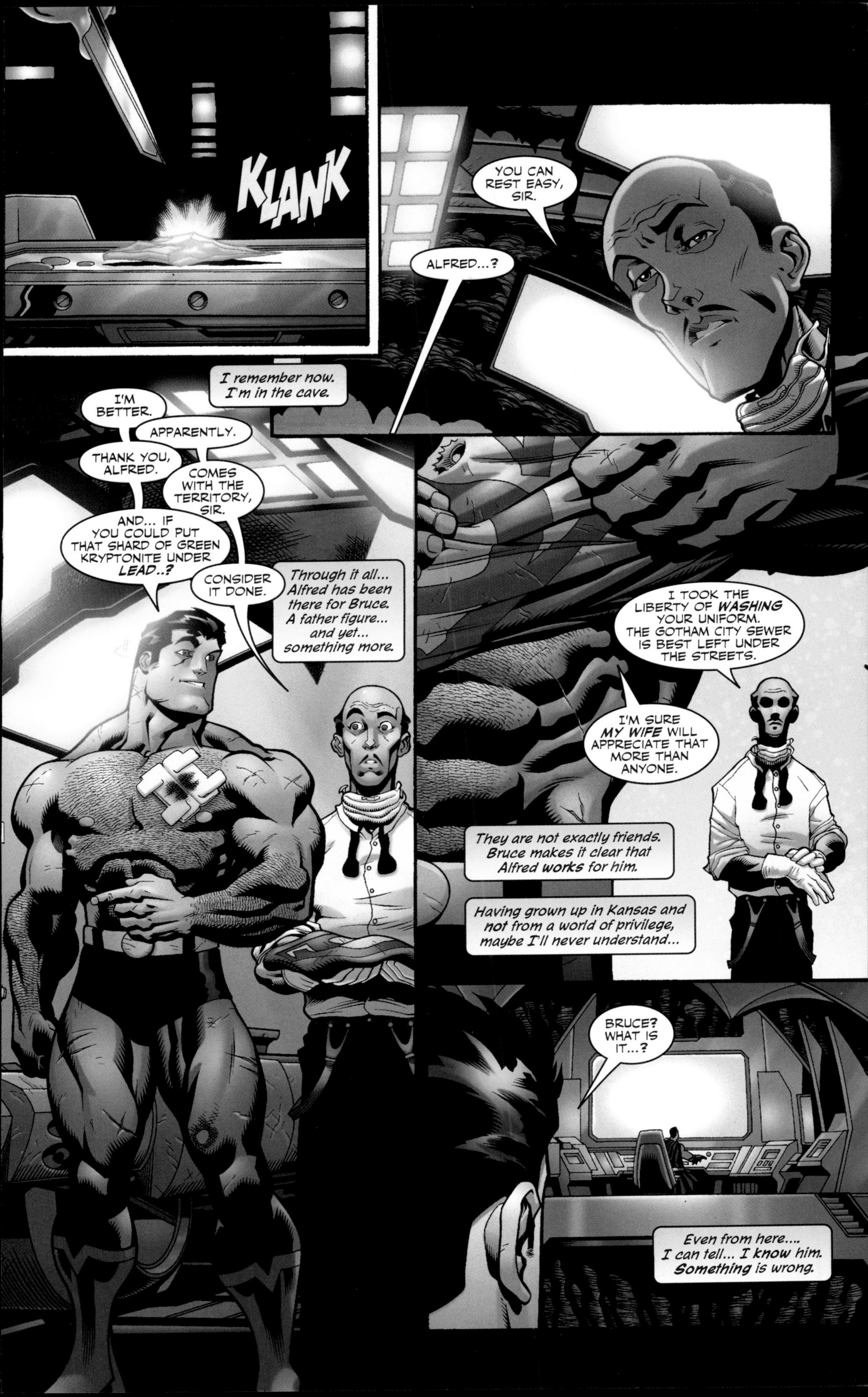
KLANK
YOU CAN REST EASY, SIR.
ALFRED...?
I remember now. I'm in the cave.
I'M BETTER.
APPARENTLY.
THANK YOU, ALFRED.
COMES WITH THE TERRITORY, SIR.
AND... IF YOU COULD PUT THAT SHARD OF GREEN KRYPTONITE UNDER LEAD..?
CONSIDER IT DONE.
Through it all... Alfred has been there for Bruce. A father figure... and yet... something more.
I TOOK THE LIBERTY OF WASHING YOUR UNIFORM. THE GOTHAM CITY SEWER IS BEST LEFT UNDER THE STREETS.
I'M SURE MY WIFE WILL APPRECIATE THAT MORE THAN ANYONE.
They are not exactly friends. Bruce makes it clear that Alfred works for him.
Having grown up in Kansas and not from a world of privilege, maybe I'll never understand...
BRUCE? WHAT IS IT...?
Even from here.... I can tell... I know him. Something is wrong.

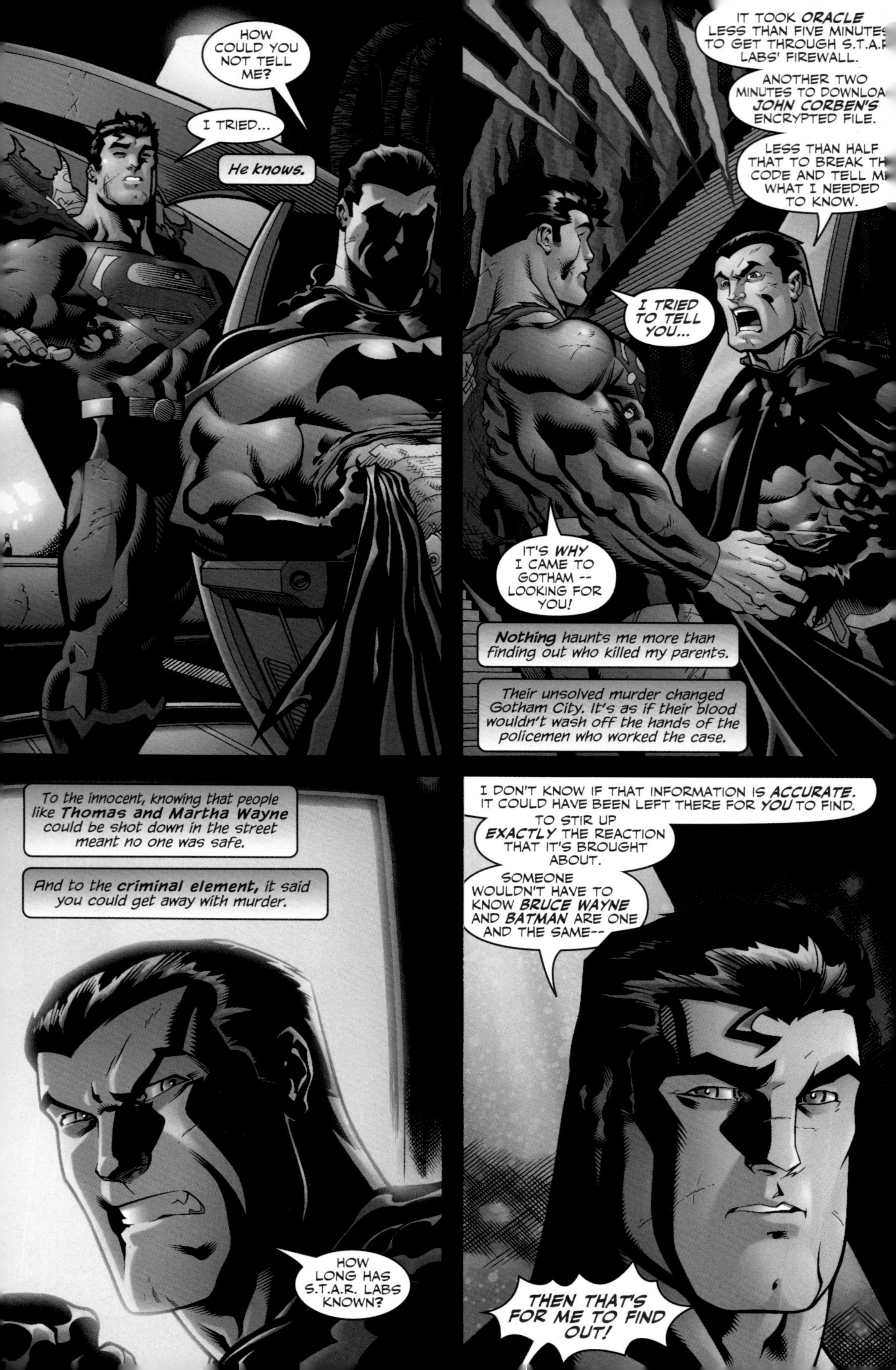
HOW COULD YOU NOT TELL ME?
I TRIED...
He knows.
IT TOOK ORACLE LESS THAN FIVE MINUTES TO GET THROUGH S.T.A.R. LABS' FIREWALL.
ANOTHER TWO MINUTES TO DOWNLOAD JOHN CORBEN'S ENCRYPTED FILE.
LESS THAN HALF THAT TO BREAK THE CODE AND TELL ME WHAT I NEEDED TO KNOW.
I TRIED TO TELL YOU...
IT'S WHY I CAME TO GOTHAM -- LOOKING FOR YOU!
Nothing haunts me more than finding out who killed my parents.
Their unsolved murder changed Gotham City. It's as if their blood wouldn't wash off the hands of the policemen who worked the case.
To the innocent, knowing that people like Thomas and Martha Wayne could be shot down in the street meant no one was safe.
And to the criminal element, it said you could get away with murder.
HOW LONG HAS S.T.A.R. LABS KNOWN?
I DON'T KNOW IF THAT INFORMATION IS ACCURATE. IT COULD HAVE BEEN LEFT THERE FOR YOU TO FIND.
TO STIR UP EXACTLY THE REACTION THAT IT'S BROUGHT ABOUT.
SOMEONE WOULDN'T HAVE TO KNOW BRUCE WAYNE AND BATMAN ARE ONE AND THE SAME--
THEN THAT'S FOR ME TO FIND OUT!

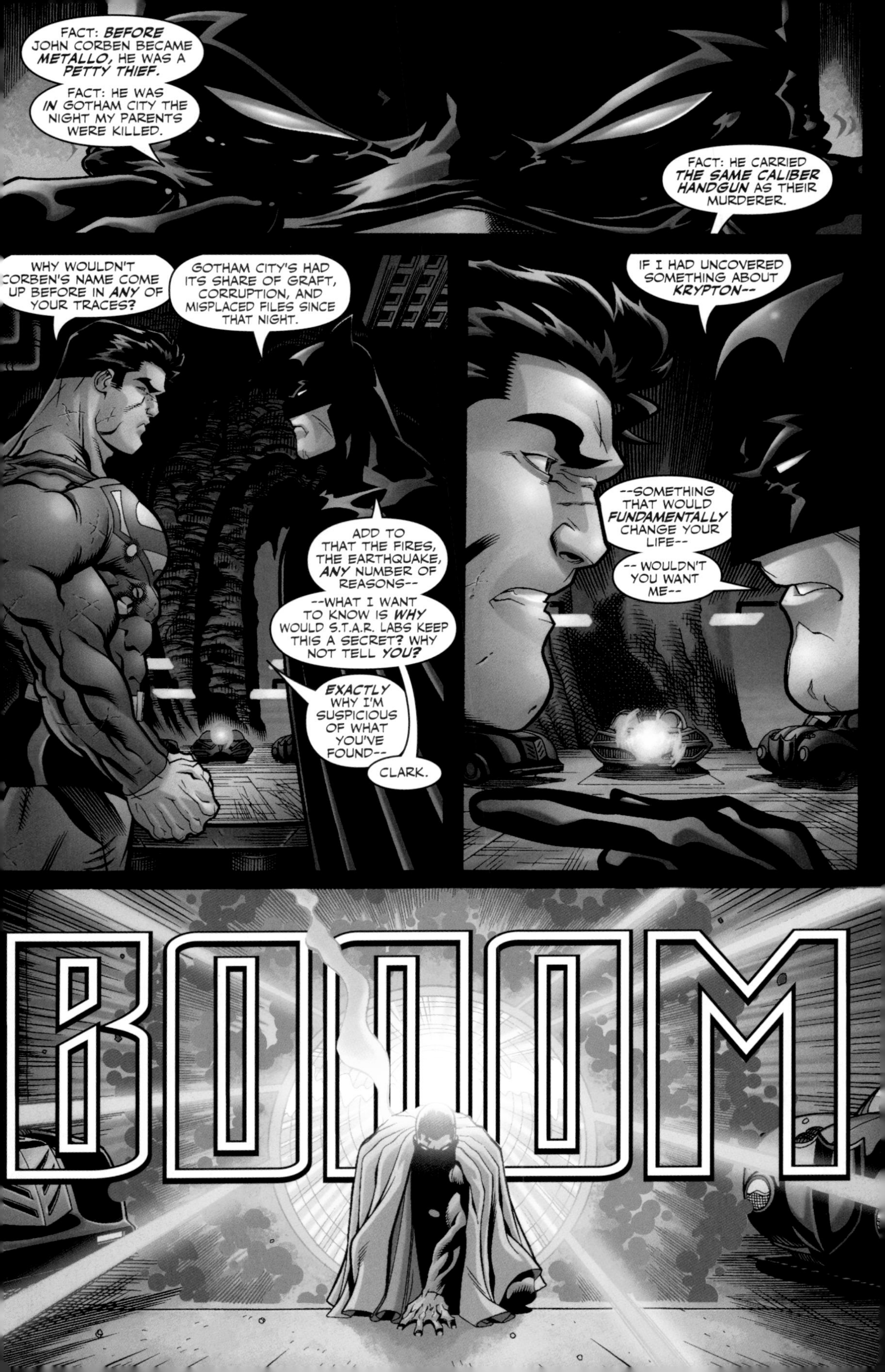
FACT: BEFORE JOHN CORBEN BECAME METALLO, HE WAS A PETTY THIEF.
FACT: HE WAS IN GOTHAM CITY THE NIGHT MY PARENTS WERE KILLED.
FACT: HE CARRIED THE SAME CALIBER HANDGUN AS THEIR MURDERER.
WHY WOULDN'T CORBEN'S NAME COME UP BEFORE IN ANY OF YOUR TRACES?
GOTHAM CITY'S HAD ITS SHARE OF GRAFT, CORRUPTION, AND MISPLACED FILES SINCE THAT NIGHT.
ADD TO THAT THE FIRES, THE EARTHQUAKE, ANY NUMBER OF REASONS--
--WHAT I WANT TO KNOW IS WHY WOULD S.T.A.R. LABS KEEP THIS A SECRET? WHY NOT TELL YOU?
EXACTLY WHY I'M SUSPICIOUS OF WHAT YOU'VE FOUND--
CLARK.
IF I HAD UNCOVERED SOMETHING ABOUT KRYPTON--
--SOMETHING THAT WOULD FUNDAMENTALLY CHANGE YOUR LIFE--
-- WOULDN'T YOU WANT ME--
BOOOM

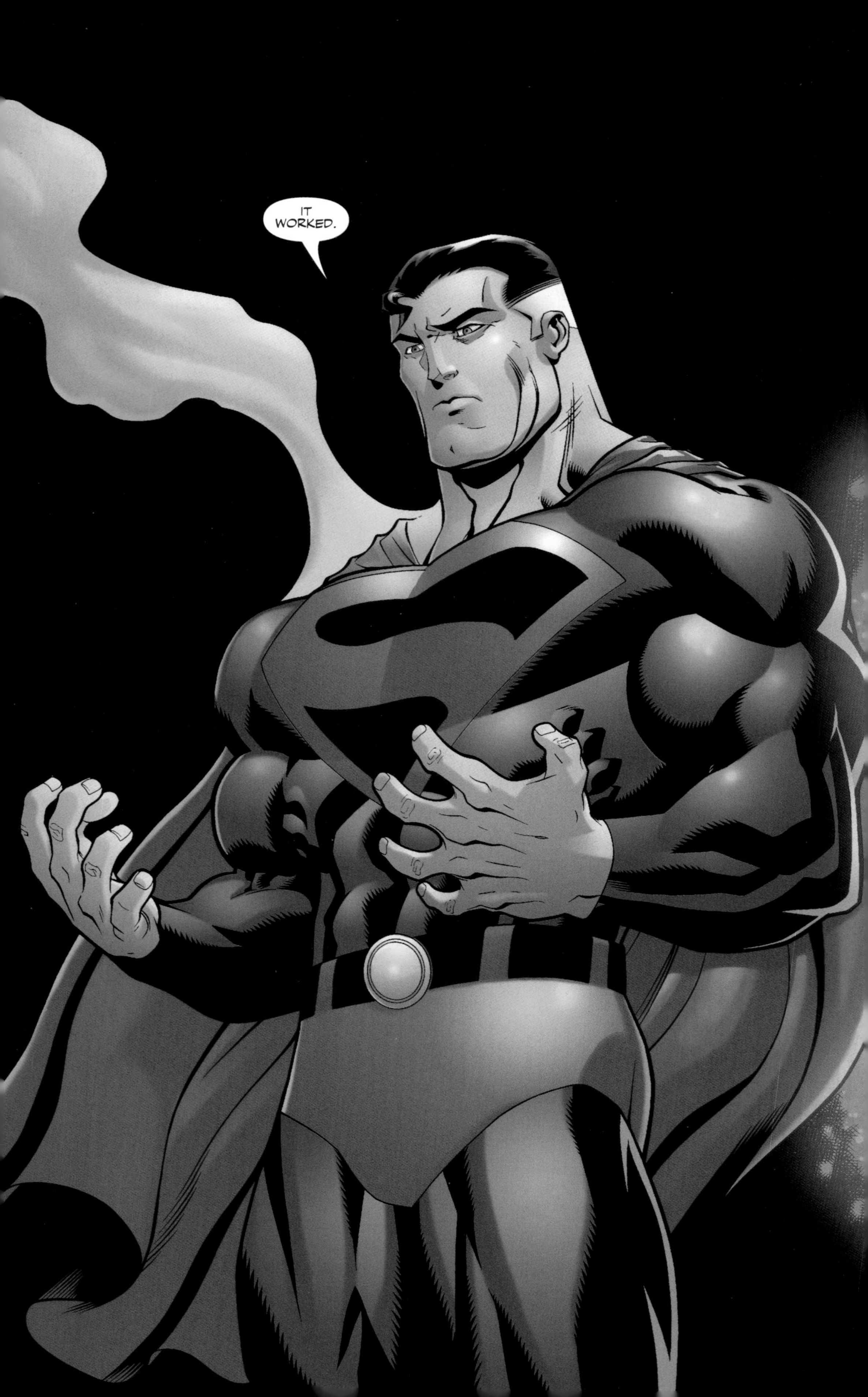
IT WORKED.

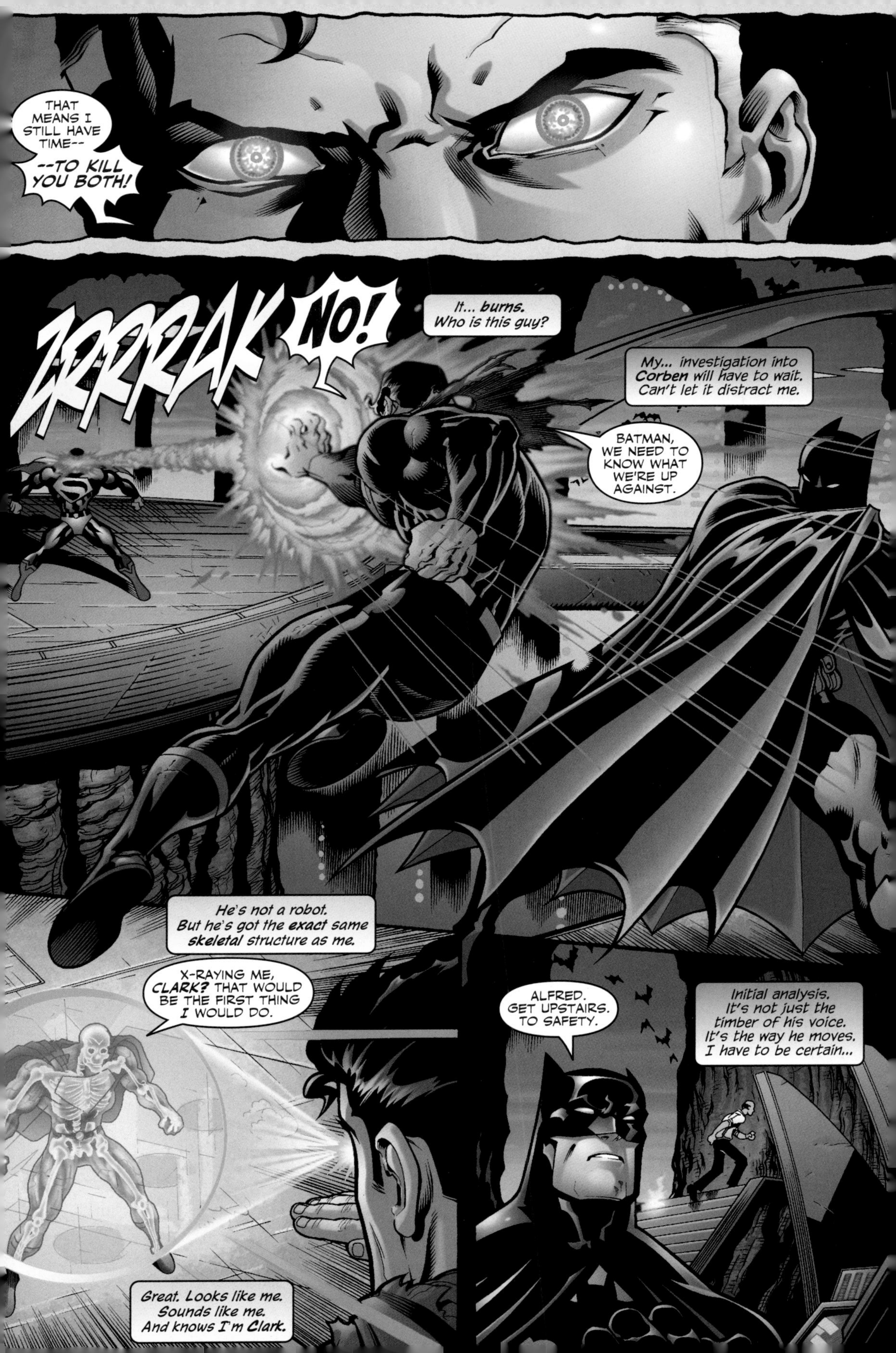
THAT MEANS I STILL HAVE TIME--
--TO KILL YOU BOTH!
ZRRRAK
NO!
It... burns. Who is this guy?
My... investigation into Corben will have to wait. Can't let it distract me.
BATMAN, WE NEED TO KNOW WHAT WE'RE UP AGAINST.
He's not a robot. But he's got the exact same skeletal structure as me.
X-RAYING ME, CLARK? THAT WOULD BE THE FIRST THING I WOULD DO.
Great. Looks like me. Sounds like me. And knows I'm Clark.
ALFRED. GET UPSTAIRS. TO SAFETY.
Initial analysis. It's not just the timber of his voice. It's the way he moves. I have to be certain...

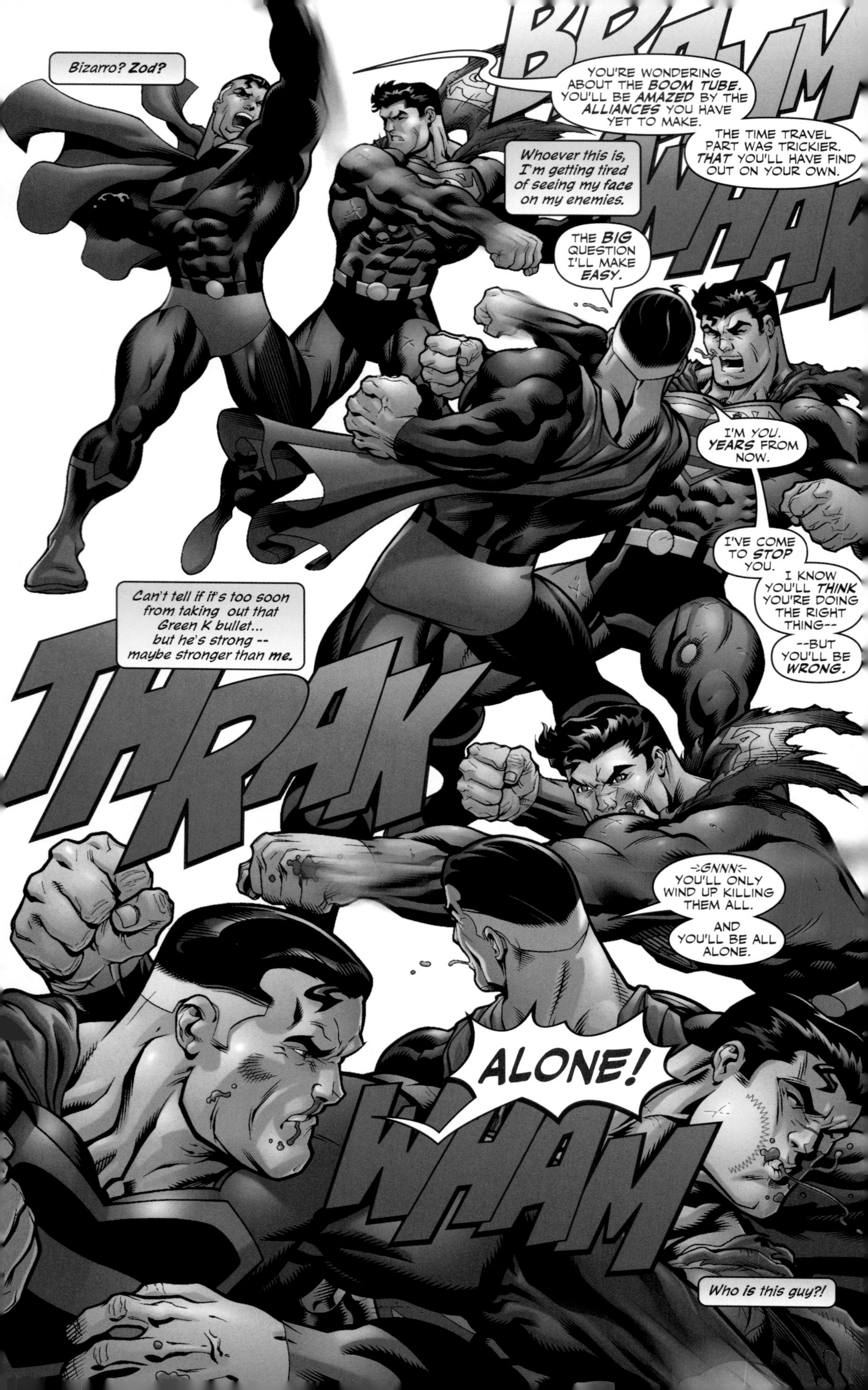
Bizarro? Zod?
BRAKM
YOU'RE WONDERING ABOUT THE BOOM TUBE. YOU'LL BE AMAZED BY THE ALLIANCES YOU HAVE YET TO MAKE.
THE TIME TRAVEL PART WAS TRICKIER. THAT YOU'LL HAVE FIND OUT ON YOUR OWN.
Whoever this is, I'm getting tired of seeing my face on my enemies.
THE BIG QUESTION I'LL MAKE EASY.
WHAK
I'M YOU. YEARS FROM NOW.
I'VE COME TO STOP YOU.
I KNOW YOU'LL THINK YOU'RE DOING THE RIGHT THING--
--BUT YOU'LL BE WRONG.
Can't tell if it's too soon from taking out that Green K bullet... but he's strong -- maybe stronger than me.
THRAK
-GNNN- YOU'LL ONLY WIND UP KILLING THEM ALL.
AND YOU'LL BE ALL ALONE.
ALONE!
WHAM
Who is this guy?!

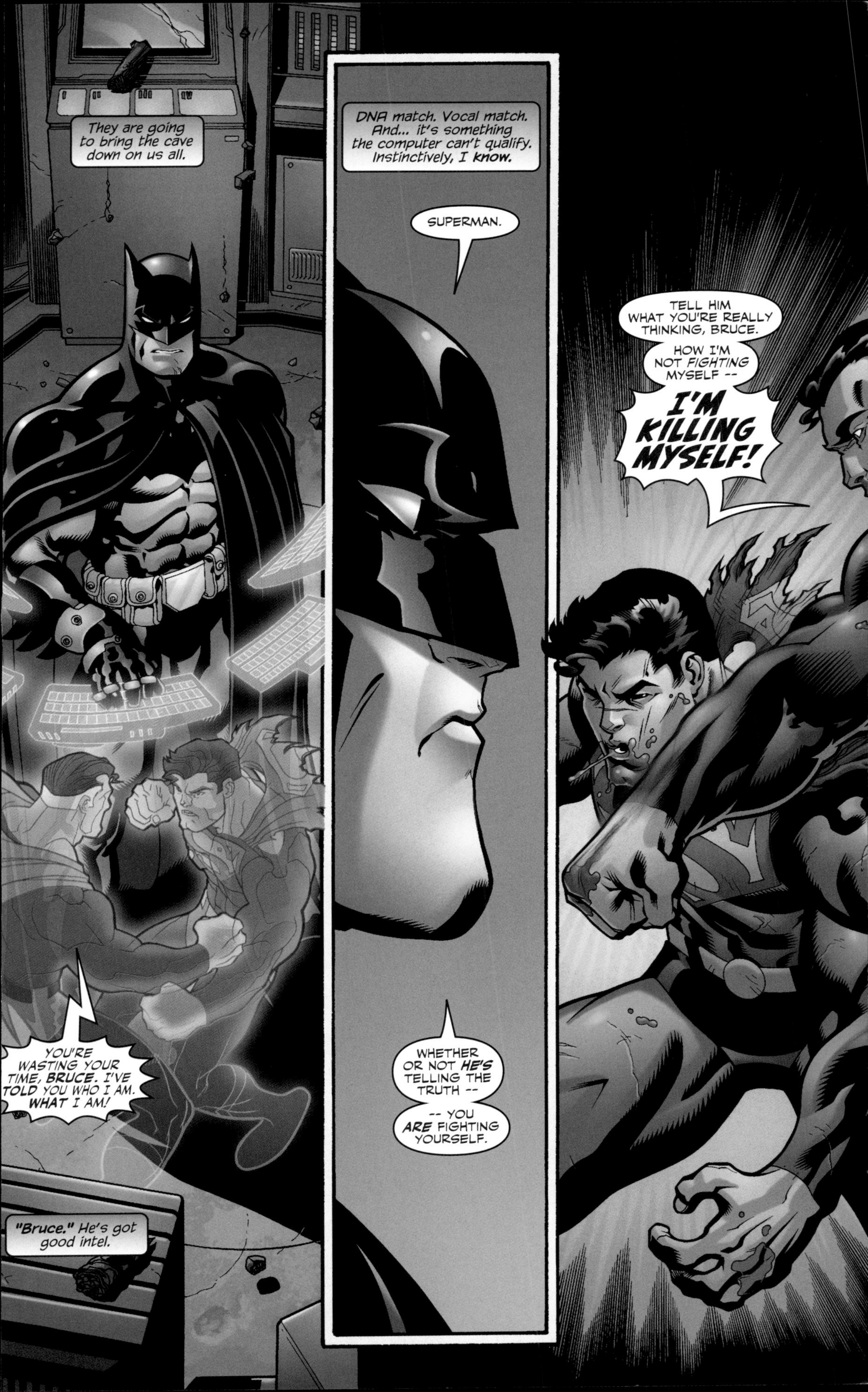

They are going to bring the cave down on us all.
YOU'RE WASTING YOUR TIME, BRUCE. I'VE TOLD YOU WHO I AM. WHAT I AM!
"Bruce." He's got good intel.
DNA match. Vocal match. And... it's something the computer can't qualify. Instinctively, I know.
SUPERMAN.
WHETHER OR NOT HE'S TELLING THE TRUTH --
-- YOU ARE FIGHTING YOURSELF.
TELL HIM WHAT YOU'RE REALLY THINKING, BRUCE.
HOW I'M NOT FIGHTING MYSELF --
I'M KILLING MYSELF!

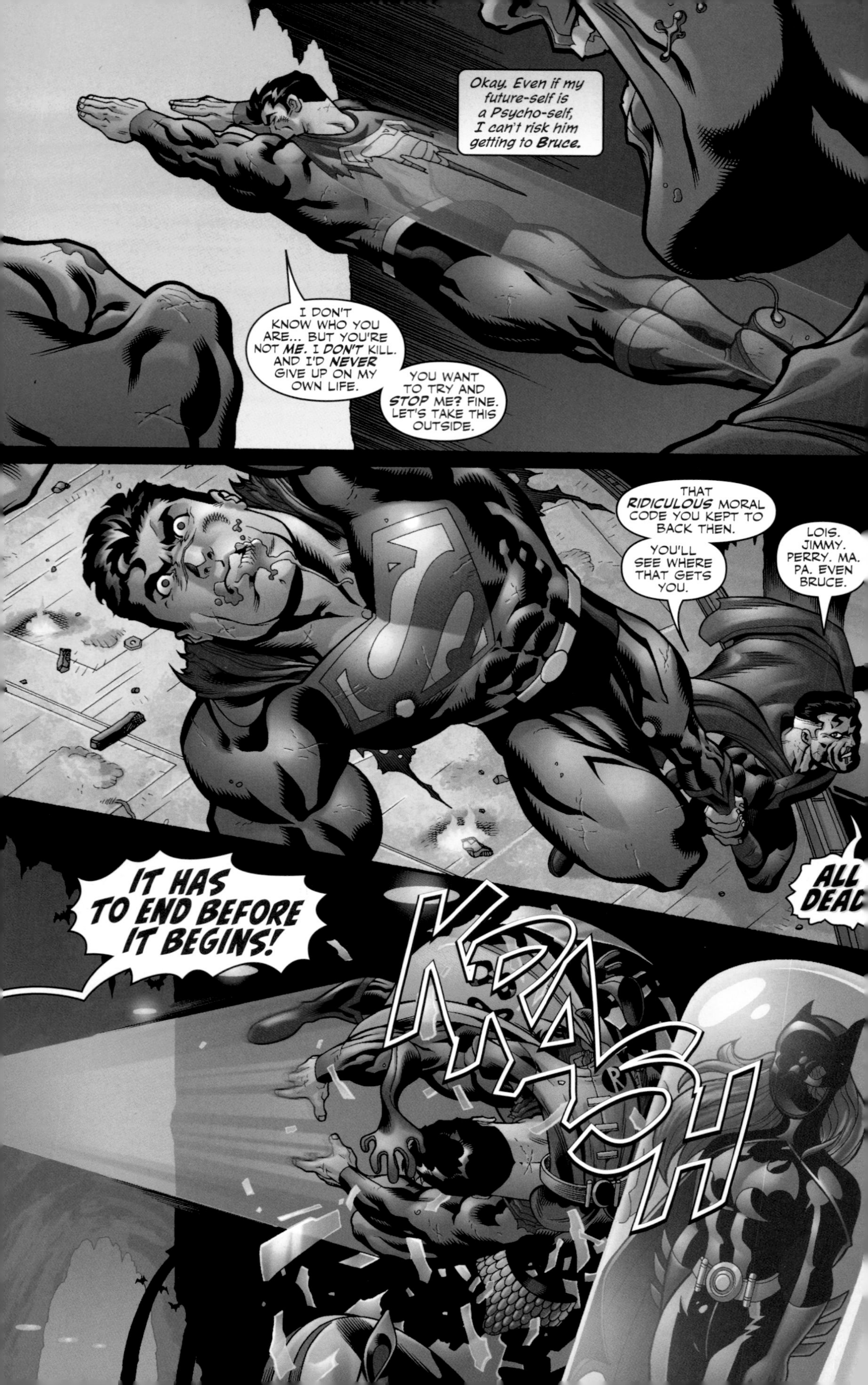
Okay. Even if my future-self is a Psycho-self, I can't risk him getting to Bruce.
I DON'T KNOW WHO YOU ARE... BUT YOU'RE NOT ME. I DON'T KILL. AND I'D NEVER GIVE UP ON MY OWN LIFE.
YOU WANT TO TRY AND STOP ME? FINE. LET'S TAKE THIS OUTSIDE.
THAT RIDICULOUS MORAL CODE YOU KEPT TO BACK THEN.
YOU'LL SEE WHERE THAT GETS YOU.
LOIS. JIMMY. PERRY. MA. PA. EVEN BRUCE.
ALL DEAD
IT HAS TO END BEFORE IT BEGINS!
KRASH

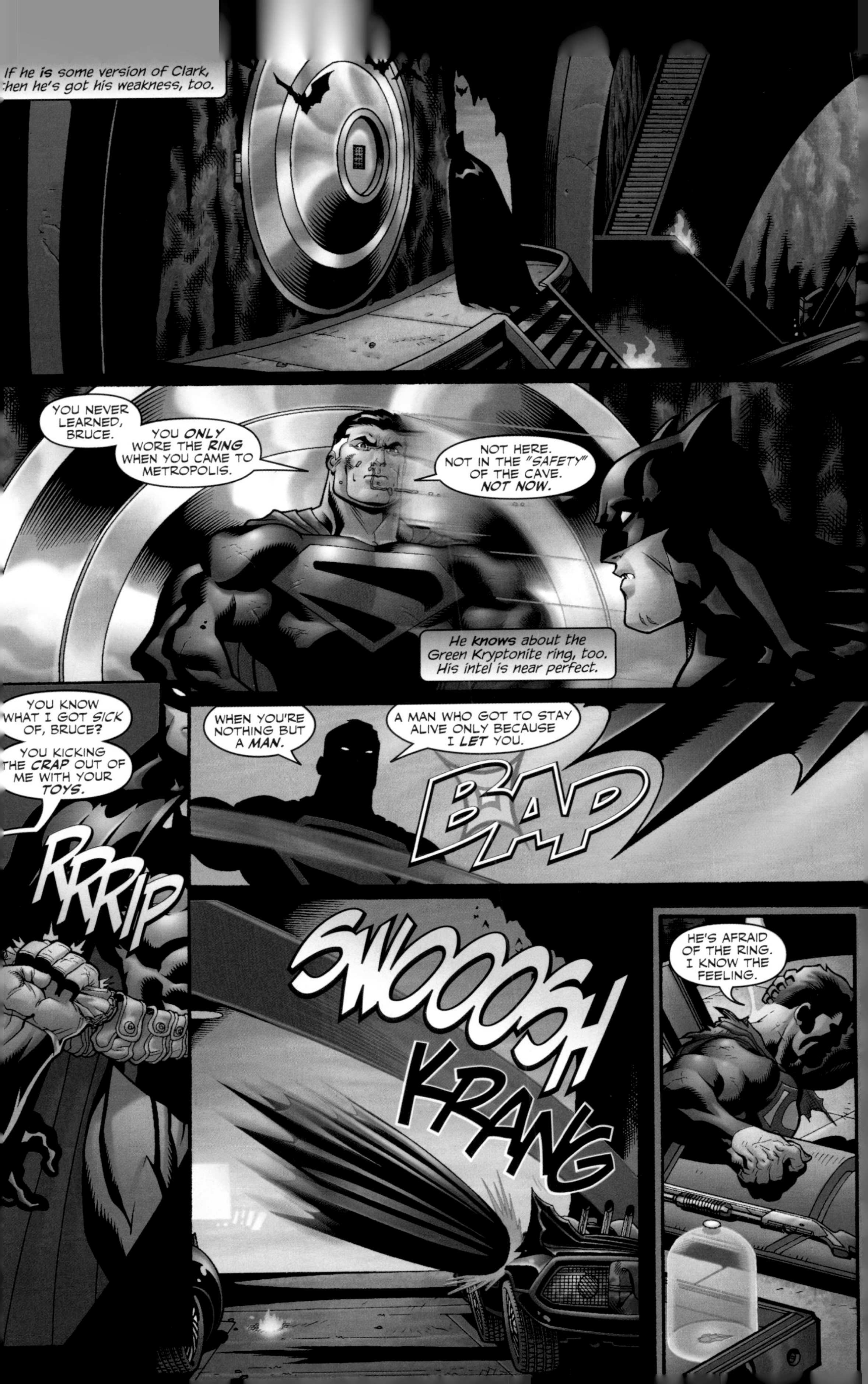

If he is some version of Clark, then he's got his weakness, too.
YOU NEVER LEARNED, BRUCE.
YOU ONLY WORE THE RING WHEN YOU CAME TO METROPOLIS.
NOT HERE. NOT IN THE "SAFETY" OF THE CAVE. NOT NOW.
He knows about the Green Kryptonite ring, too. His intel is near perfect.
YOU KNOW WHAT I GOT SICK OF, BRUCE?
YOU KICKING THE CRAP OUT OF ME WITH YOUR TOYS.
WHEN YOU'RE NOTHING BUT A MAN.
A MAN WHO GOT TO STAY ALIVE ONLY BECAUSE I LET YOU.
BAP
RRRIP
SWOOOSH
KRANG
HE'S AFRAID OF THE RING. I KNOW THE FEELING.

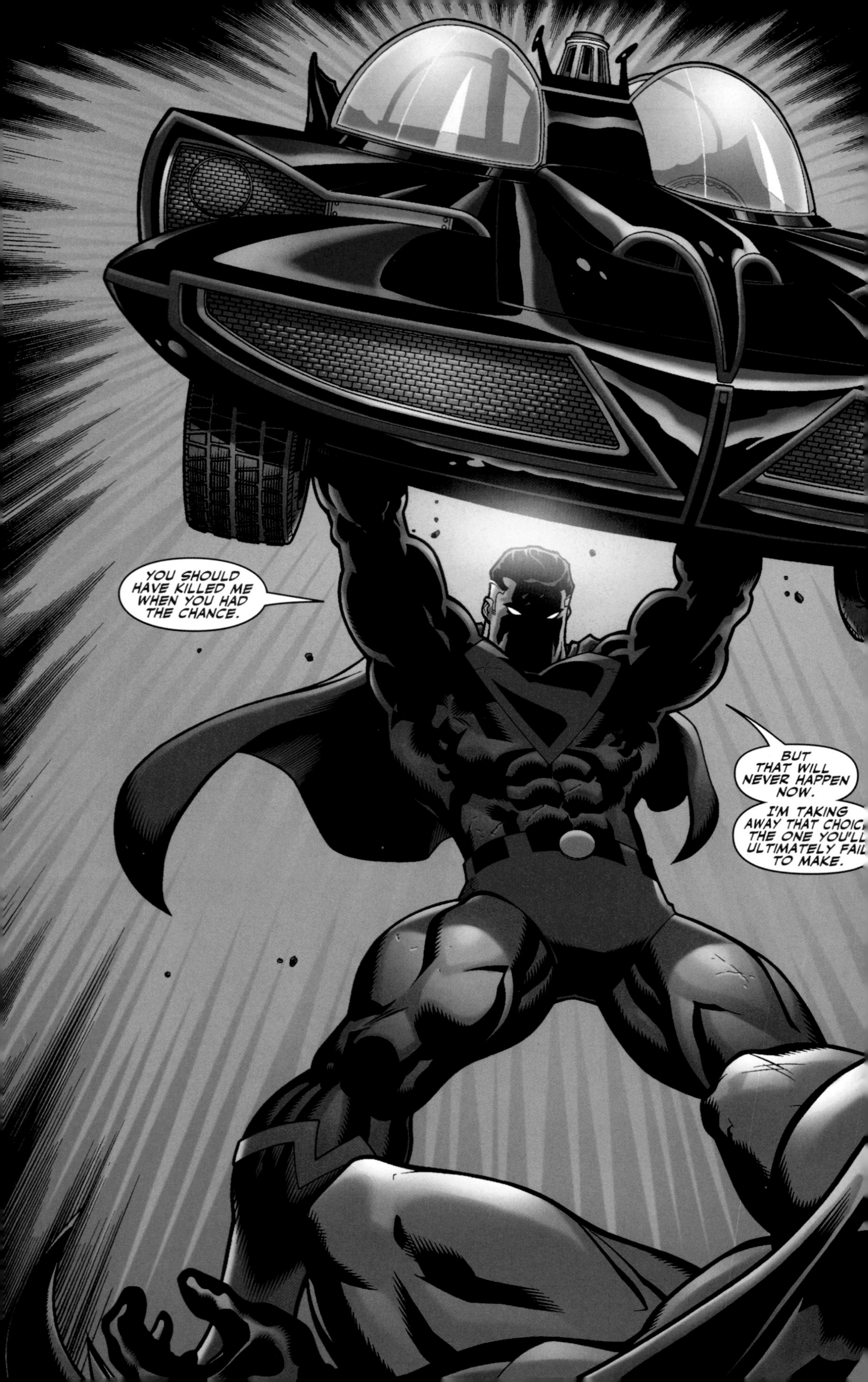
YOU SHOULD HAVE KILLED ME WHEN YOU HAD THE CHANCE.
BUT THAT WILL NEVER HAPPEN NOW.
I'M TAKING AWAY THAT CHOIC THE ONE YOU'LL ULTIMATELY FAIL TO MAKE.

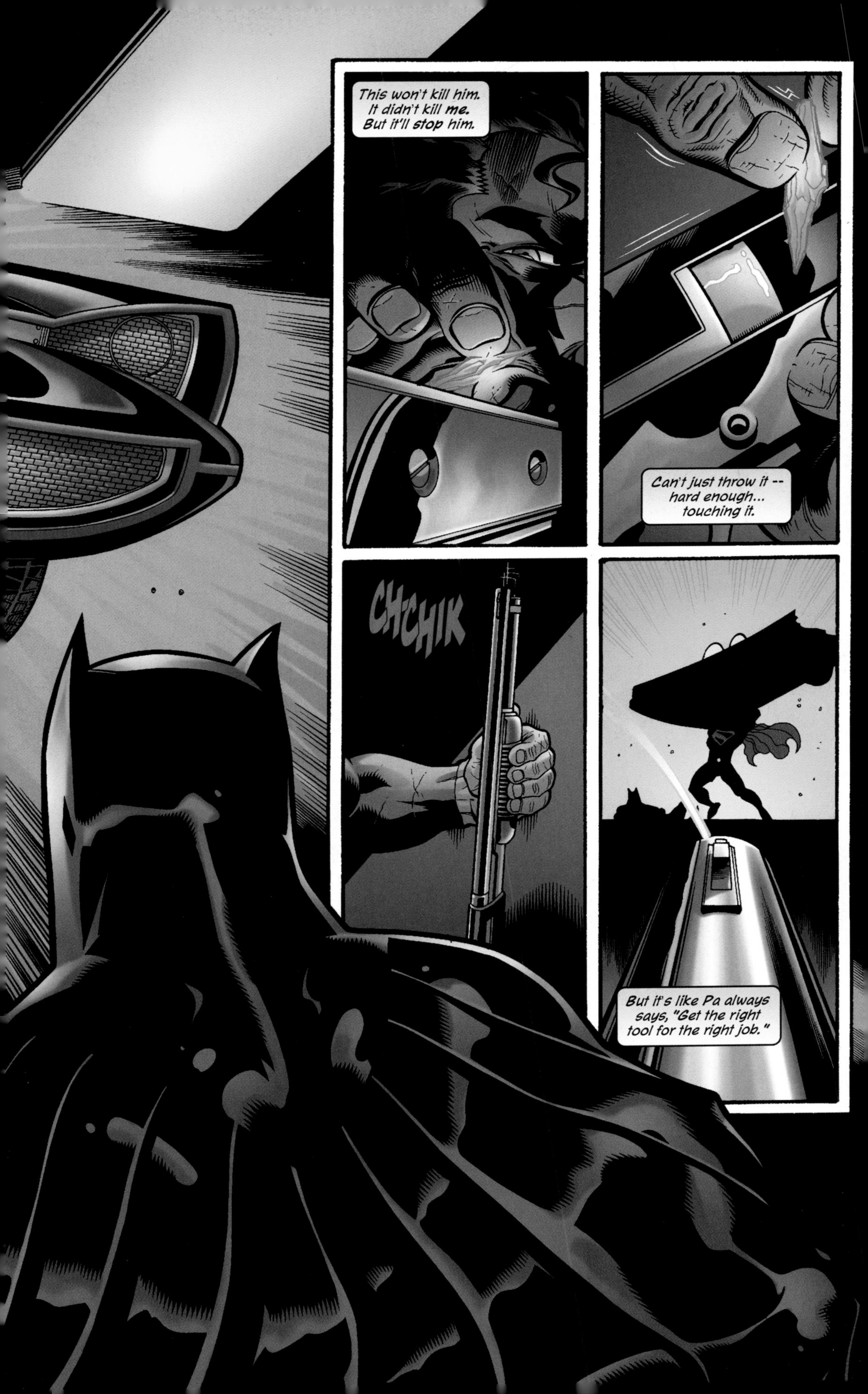
This won't kill him. It didn't kill me. But it'll stop him.
Can't just throw it -- hard enough... touching it.
CH-CHIK
But it's like Pa always says, "Get the right tool for the right job."

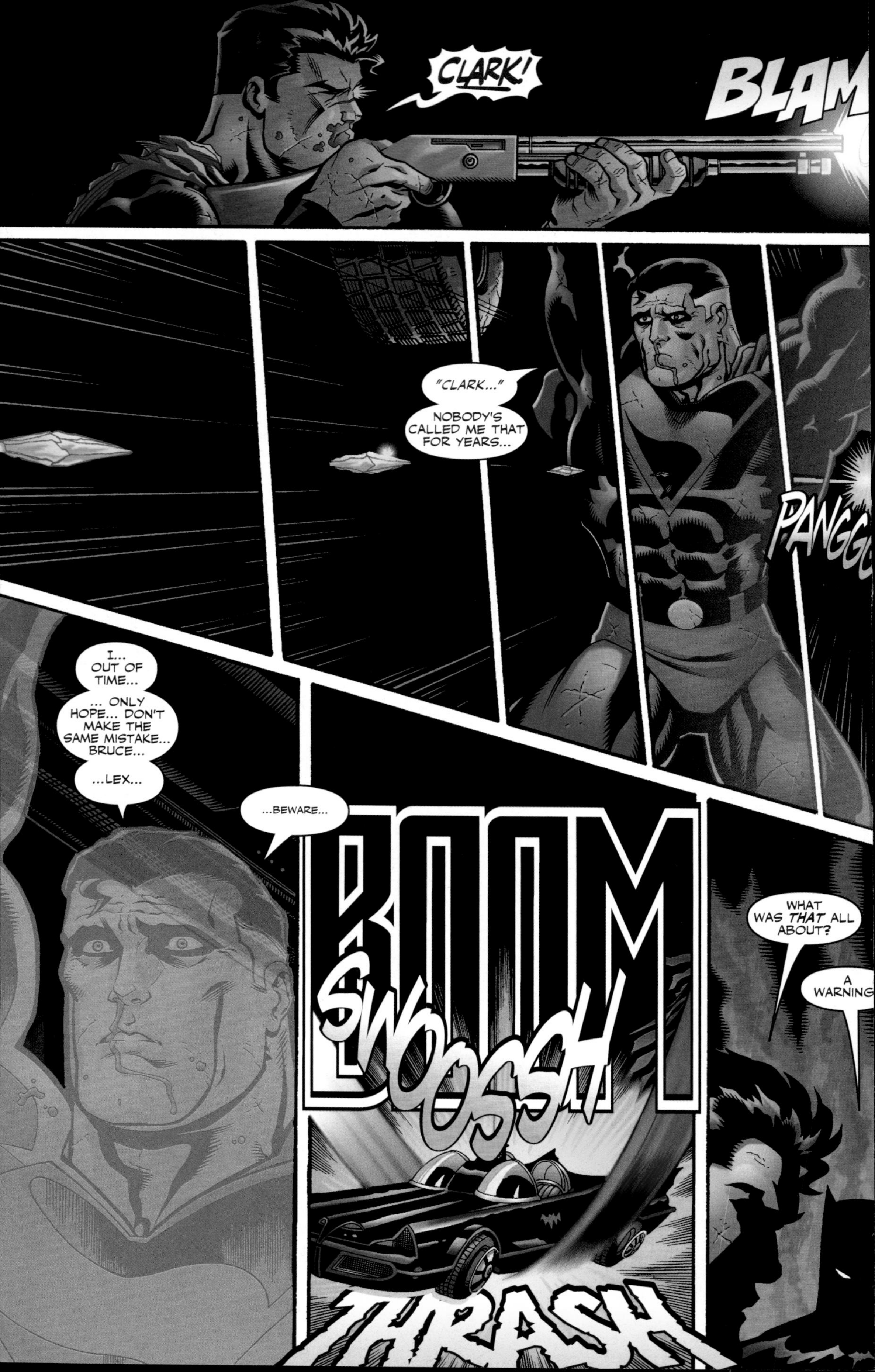
CLARK!
BLAM
"CLARK..."
NOBODY'S CALLED ME THAT FOR YEARS...
PANGG
I... OUT OF TIME...
... ONLY HOPE... DON'T MAKE THE SAME MISTAKE... BRUCE...
...LEX...
...BEWARE...
BOOM
SWOOSSH
WHAT WAS THAT ALL ABOUT?
A WARNING
THRASH

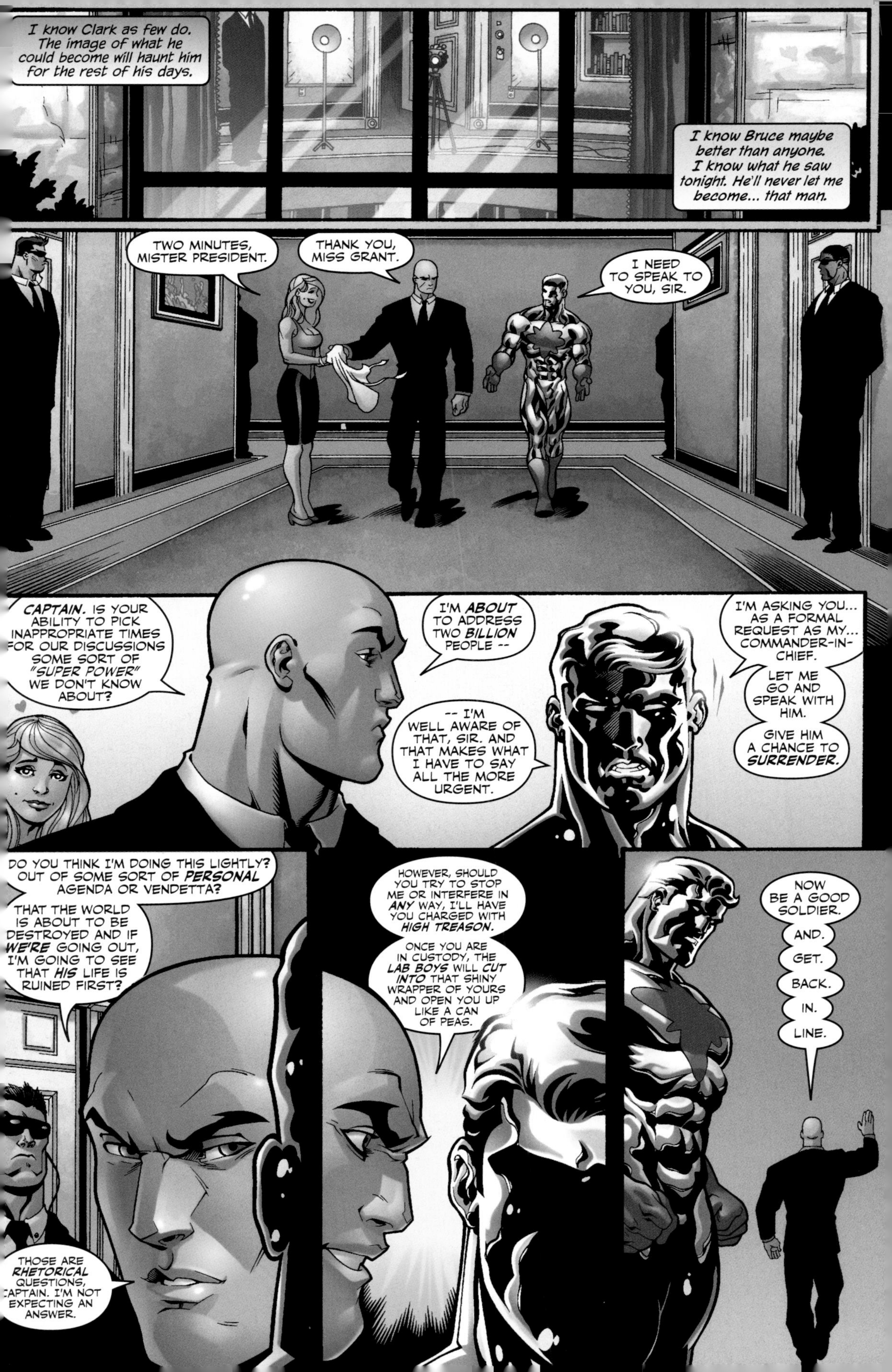
I know Clark as few do. The image of what he could become will haunt him for the rest of his days.
I know Bruce maybe better than anyone. I know what he saw tonight. He'll never let me become... that man.
TWO MINUTES, MISTER PRESIDENT.
THANK YOU, MISS GRANT.
I NEED TO SPEAK TO YOU, SIR.
CAPTAIN. IS YOUR ABILITY TO PICK INAPPROPRIATE TIMES FOR OUR DISCUSSIONS SOME SORT OF "SUPER POWER" WE DON'T KNOW ABOUT?
I'M ABOUT TO ADDRESS TWO BILLION PEOPLE --
-- I'M WELL AWARE OF THAT, SIR. AND THAT MAKES WHAT I HAVE TO SAY ALL THE MORE URGENT.
I'M ASKING YOU... AS A FORMAL REQUEST AS MY... COMMANDER-IN-CHIEF.
LET ME GO AND SPEAK WITH HIM.
GIVE HIM A CHANCE TO SURRENDER.
DO YOU THINK I'M DOING THIS LIGHTLY? OUT OF SOME SORT OF PERSONAL AGENDA OR VENDETTA?
THAT THE WORLD IS ABOUT TO BE DESTROYED AND IF WE'RE GOING OUT, I'M GOING TO SEE THAT HIS LIFE IS RUINED FIRST?
THOSE ARE RHETORICAL QUESTIONS, CAPTAIN. I'M NOT EXPECTING AN ANSWER.
HOWEVER, SHOULD YOU TRY TO STOP ME OR INTERFERE IN ANY WAY, I'LL HAVE YOU CHARGED WITH HIGH TREASON.
ONCE YOU ARE IN CUSTODY, THE LAB BOYS WILL CUT INTO THAT SHINY WRAPPER OF YOURS AND OPEN YOU UP LIKE A CAN OF PEAS.
NOW BE A GOOD SOLDIER.
AND.
GET.
BACK.
IN.
LINE.

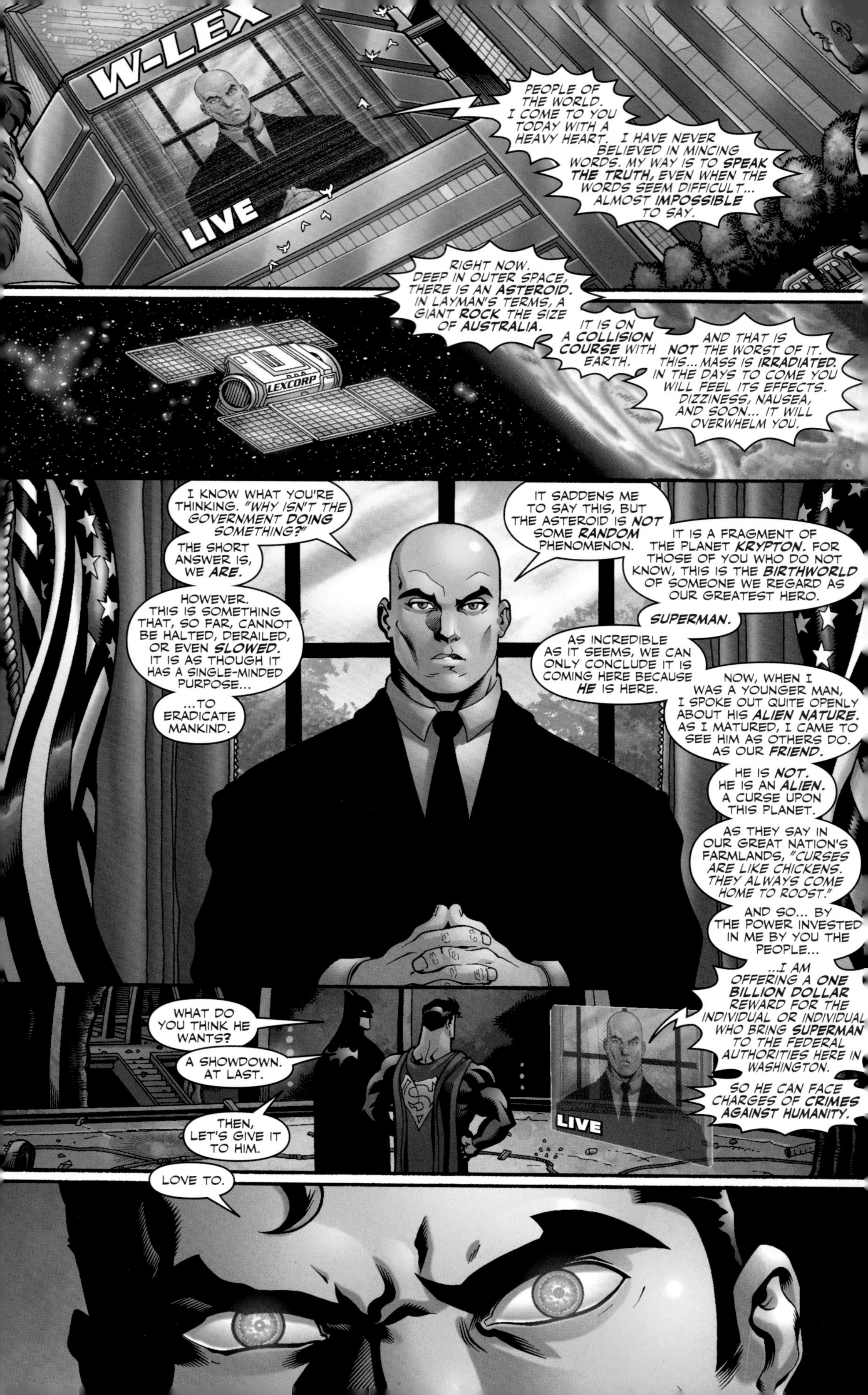
W-LEX
LIVE
PEOPLE OF THE WORLD. I COME TO YOU TODAY WITH A HEAVY HEART. I HAVE NEVER BELIEVED IN MINCING WORDS. MY WAY IS TO SPEAK THE TRUTH, EVEN WHEN THE WORDS SEEM DIFFICULT... ALMOST IMPOSSIBLE TO SAY.
RIGHT NOW. DEEP IN OUTER SPACE, THERE IS AN ASTEROID. IN LAYMAN'S TERMS, A GIANT ROCK THE SIZE OF AUSTRALIA.
LEXCORP
IT IS ON A COLLISION COURSE WITH EARTH.
AND THAT IS NOT THE WORST OF IT. THIS... MASS IS IRRADIATED. IN THE DAYS TO COME YOU WILL FEEL ITS EFFECTS. DIZZINESS, NAUSEA, AND SOON... IT WILL OVERWHELM YOU.
I KNOW WHAT YOU'RE THINKING. "WHY ISN'T THE GOVERNMENT DOING SOMETHING?"
THE SHORT ANSWER IS, WE ARE.
HOWEVER. THIS IS SOMETHING THAT, SO FAR, CANNOT BE HALTED, DERAILED, OR EVEN SLOWED. IT IS AS THOUGH IT HAS A SINGLE-MINDED PURPOSE...
...TO ERADICATE MANKIND.
IT SADDENS ME TO SAY THIS, BUT THE ASTEROID IS NOT SOME RANDOM PHENOMENON.
IT IS A FRAGMENT OF THE PLANET KRYPTON. FOR THOSE OF YOU WHO DO NOT KNOW, THIS IS THE BIRTHWORLD OF SOMEONE WE REGARD AS OUR GREATEST HERO.
SUPERMAN.
AS INCREDIBLE AS IT SEEMS, WE CAN ONLY CONCLUDE IT IS COMING HERE BECAUSE HE IS HERE.
NOW, WHEN I WAS A YOUNGER MAN, I SPOKE OUT QUITE OPENLY ABOUT HIS ALIEN NATURE. AS I MATURED, I CAME TO SEE HIM AS OTHERS DO. AS OUR FRIEND.
HE IS NOT. HE IS AN ALIEN. A CURSE UPON THIS PLANET.
AS THEY SAY IN OUR GREAT NATION'S FARMLANDS, "CURSES ARE LIKE CHICKENS. THEY ALWAYS COME HOME TO ROOST."
AND SO... BY THE POWER INVESTED IN ME BY YOU THE PEOPLE...
...I AM OFFERING A ONE BILLION DOLLAR REWARD FOR THE INDIVIDUAL OR INDIVIDUAL WHO BRING SUPERMAN TO THE FEDERAL AUTHORITIES HERE IN WASHINGTON.
SO HE CAN FACE CHARGES OF CRIMES AGAINST HUMANITY.
LIVE
WHAT DO YOU THINK HE WANTS?
A SHOWDOWN. AT LAST.
THEN, LET'S GIVE IT TO HIM.
LOVE TO.

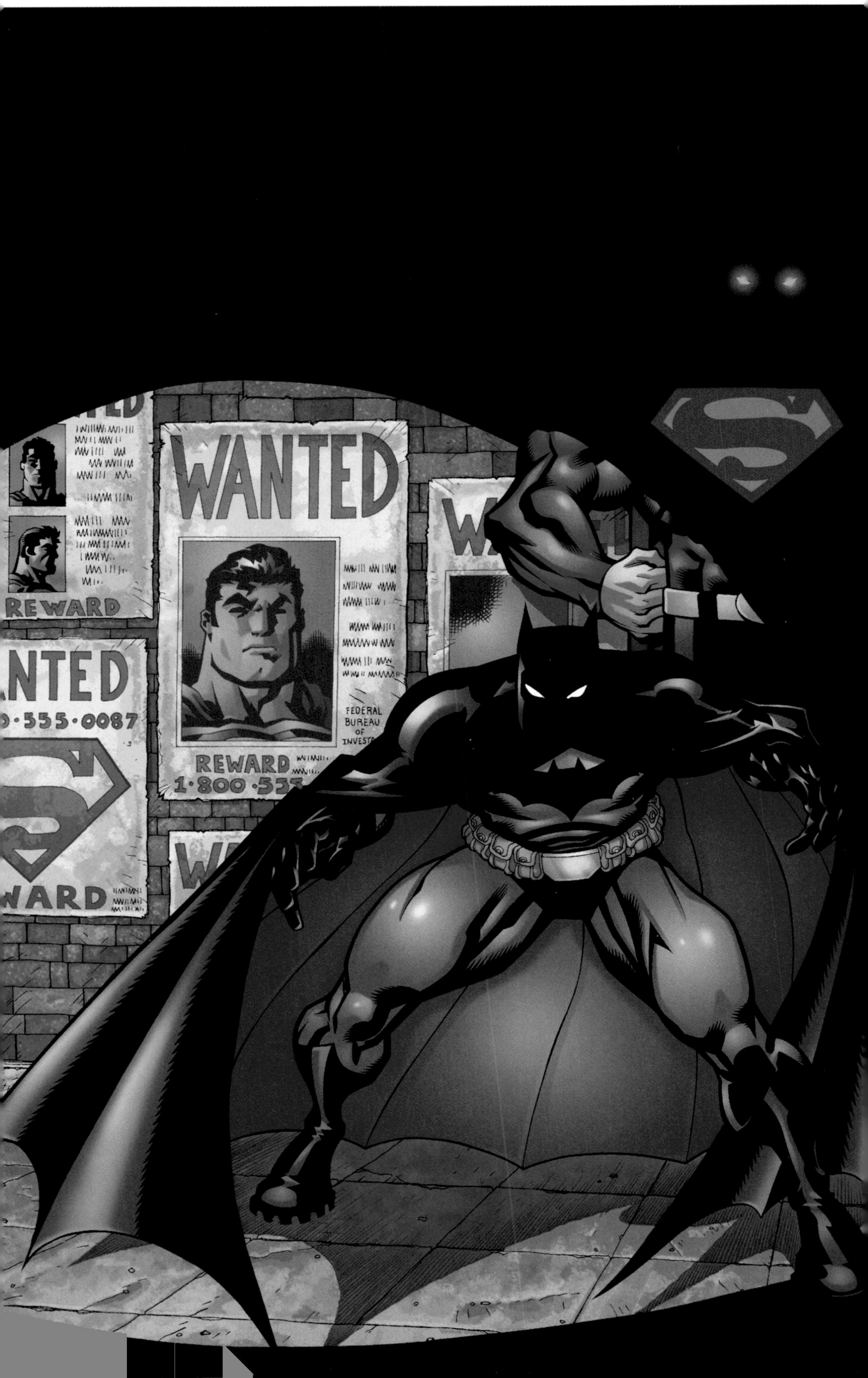

WANTED
REWARD
1·800·555
FEDERAL
BUREAU
OF
REWARD
ANTED
0·555·0087
WARD

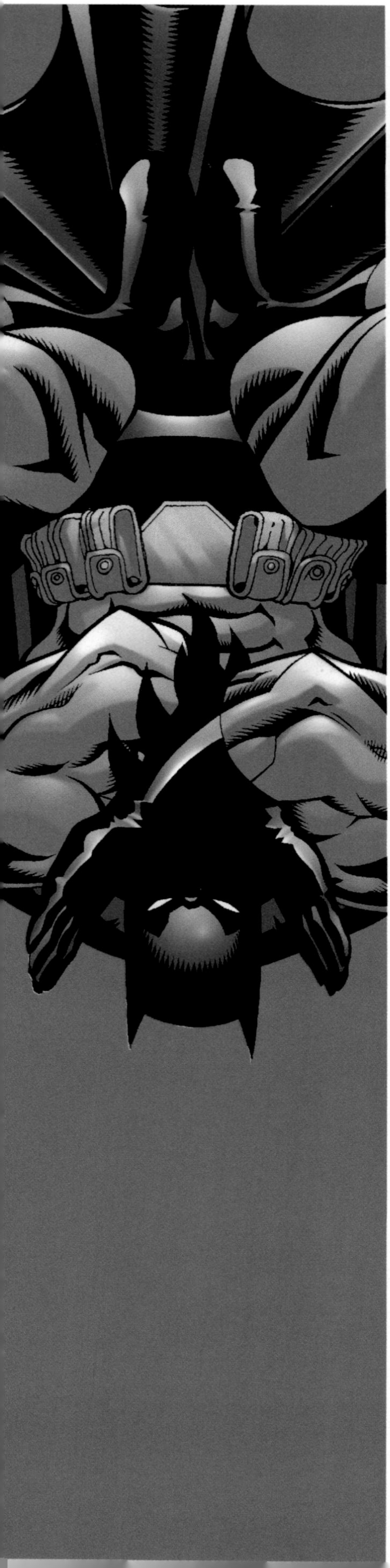

SUPERMAN BATMAN

PART THREE

RUNNING WILD

JEPH LOEB
WRITER

ED McGUINNESS
PENCILLER

DEXTER VINES
INKER

DAVE STEWART
COLORIST

RICHARD STARKINGS
LETTERER

ED McGUINNESS
DEXTER VINES
WITH
DAVE STEWART
COVER

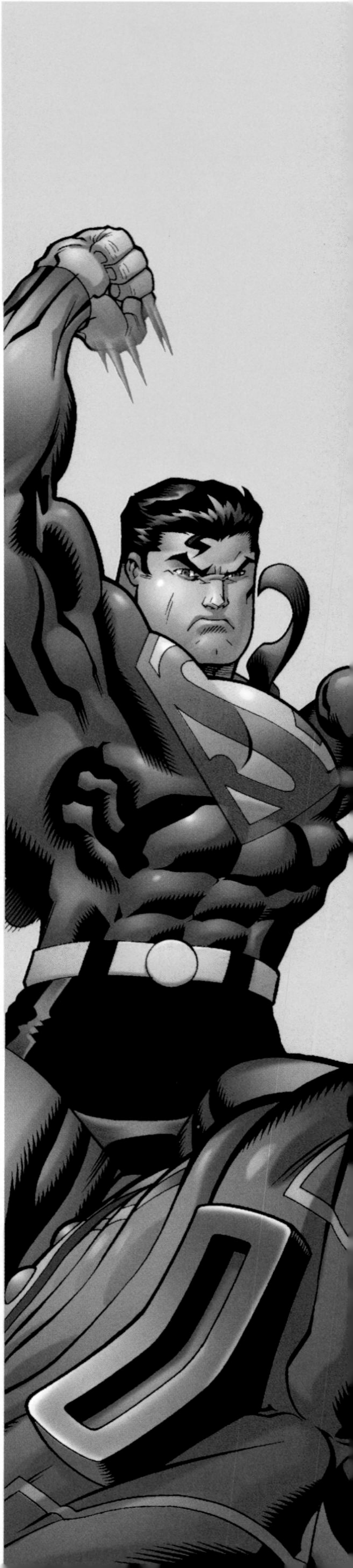

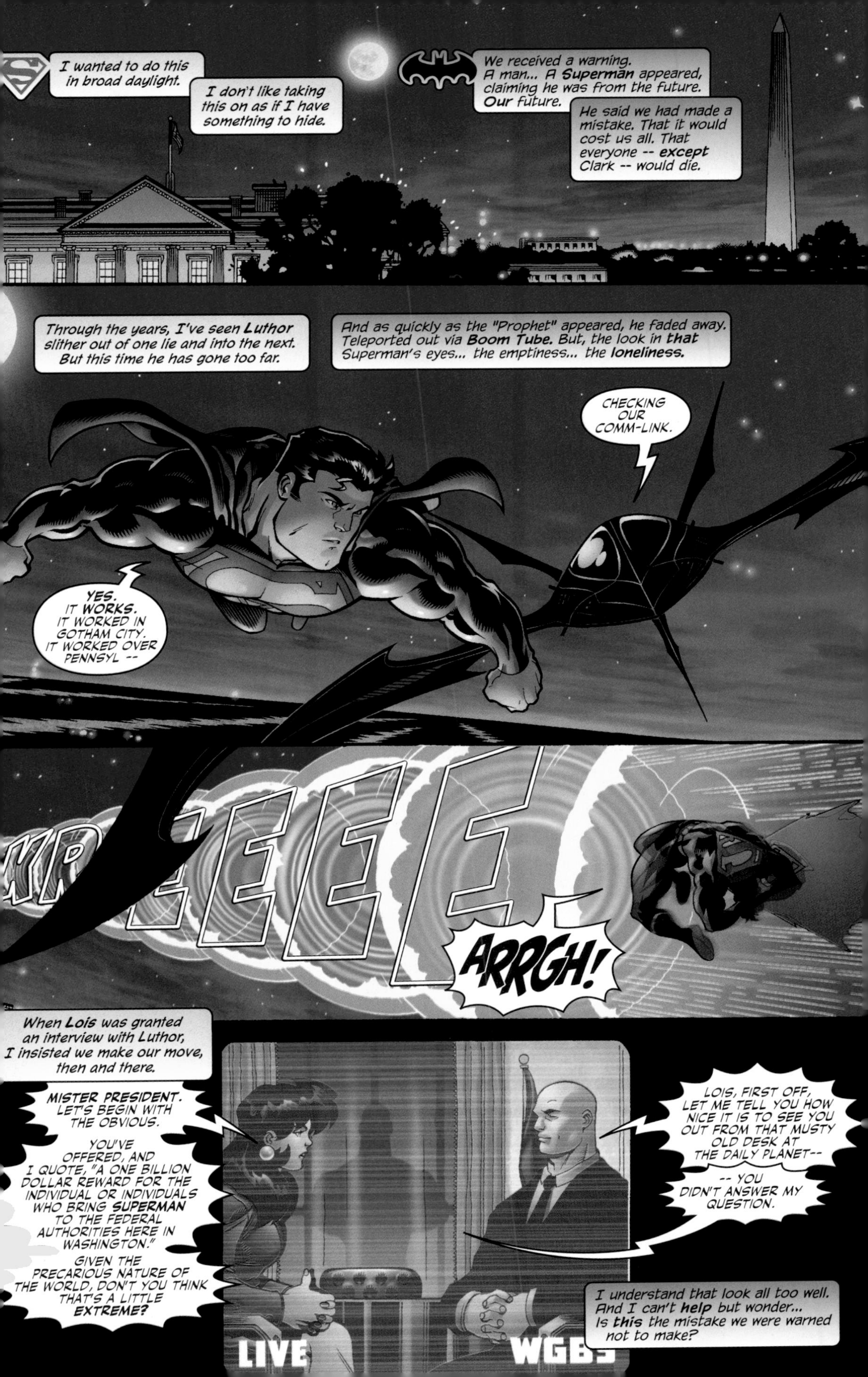

I wanted to do this in broad daylight.
I don't like taking this on as if I have something to hide.
We received a warning. A man... A Superman appeared, claiming he was from the future. Our future.
He said we had made a mistake. That it would cost us all. That everyone -- except Clark -- would die.
Through the years, I've seen Luthor slither out of one lie and into the next. But this time he has gone too far.
And as quickly as the "Prophet" appeared, he faded away. Teleported out via Boom Tube. But, the look in that Superman's eyes... the emptiness... the loneliness.
CHECKING OUR COMM-LINK.
YES. IT WORKS. IT WORKED IN GOTHAM CITY. IT WORKED OVER PENNSYL --
ARRGH!
When Lois was granted an interview with Luthor, I insisted we make our move, then and there.
MISTER PRESIDENT. LET'S BEGIN WITH THE OBVIOUS.
YOU'VE OFFERED, AND I QUOTE, "A ONE BILLION DOLLAR REWARD FOR THE INDIVIDUAL OR INDIVIDUALS WHO BRING SUPERMAN TO THE FEDERAL AUTHORITIES HERE IN WASHINGTON."
GIVEN THE PRECARIOUS NATURE OF THE WORLD, DON'T YOU THINK THAT'S A LITTLE EXTREME?
LOIS, FIRST OFF, LET ME TELL YOU HOW NICE IT IS TO SEE YOU OUT FROM THAT MUSTY OLD DESK AT THE DAILY PLANET--
-- YOU DIDN'T ANSWER MY QUESTION.
I understand that look all too well. And I can't help but wonder... Is this the mistake we were warned not to make?
LIVE
WGBS

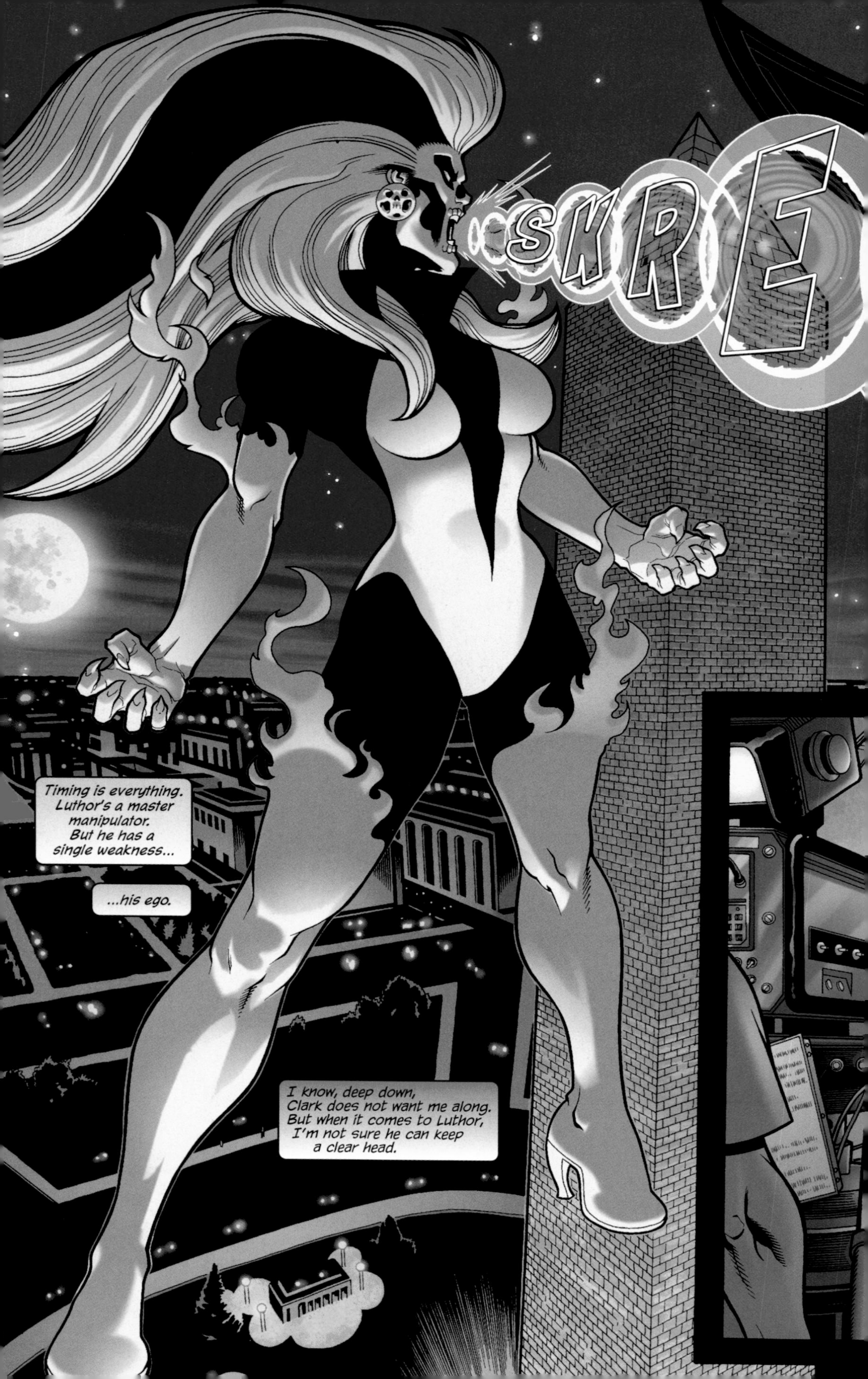
SKREE
Timing is everything. Luthor's a master manipulator. But he has a single weakness...
...his ego.
I know, deep down, Clark does not want me along. But when it comes to Luthor, I'm not sure he can keep a clear head.

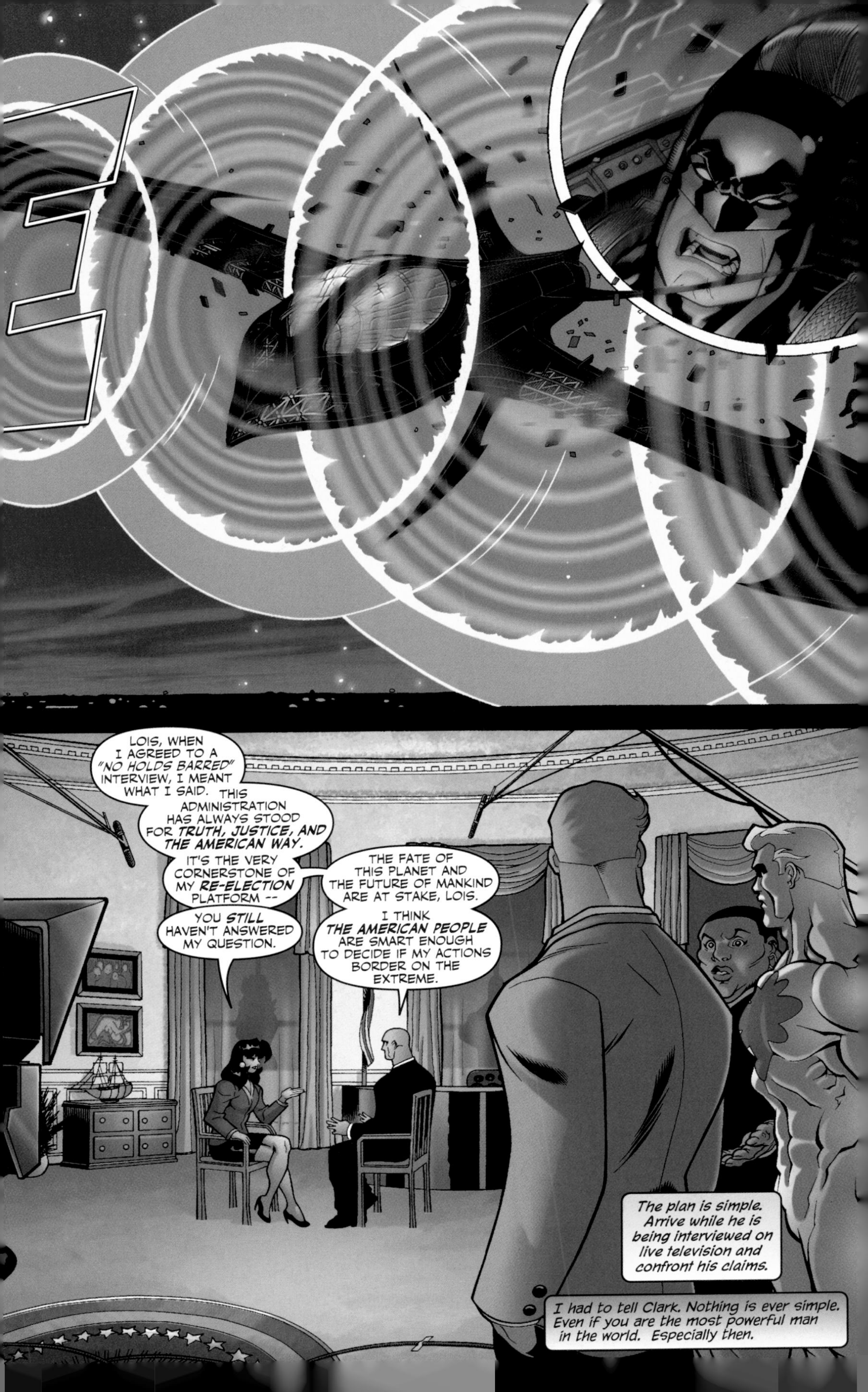
LOIS, WHEN I AGREED TO A "NO HOLDS BARRED" INTERVIEW, I MEANT WHAT I SAID.
THIS ADMINISTRATION HAS ALWAYS STOOD FOR TRUTH, JUSTICE, AND THE AMERICAN WAY.
IT'S THE VERY CORNERSTONE OF MY RE-ELECTION PLATFORM --
YOU STILL HAVEN'T ANSWERED MY QUESTION.
THE FATE OF THIS PLANET AND THE FUTURE OF MANKIND ARE AT STAKE, LOIS.
I THINK THE AMERICAN PEOPLE ARE SMART ENOUGH TO DECIDE IF MY ACTIONS BORDER ON THE EXTREME.
The plan is simple. Arrive while he is being interviewed on live television and confront his claims.
I had to tell Clark. Nothing is ever simple. Even if you are the most powerful man in the world. Especially then.

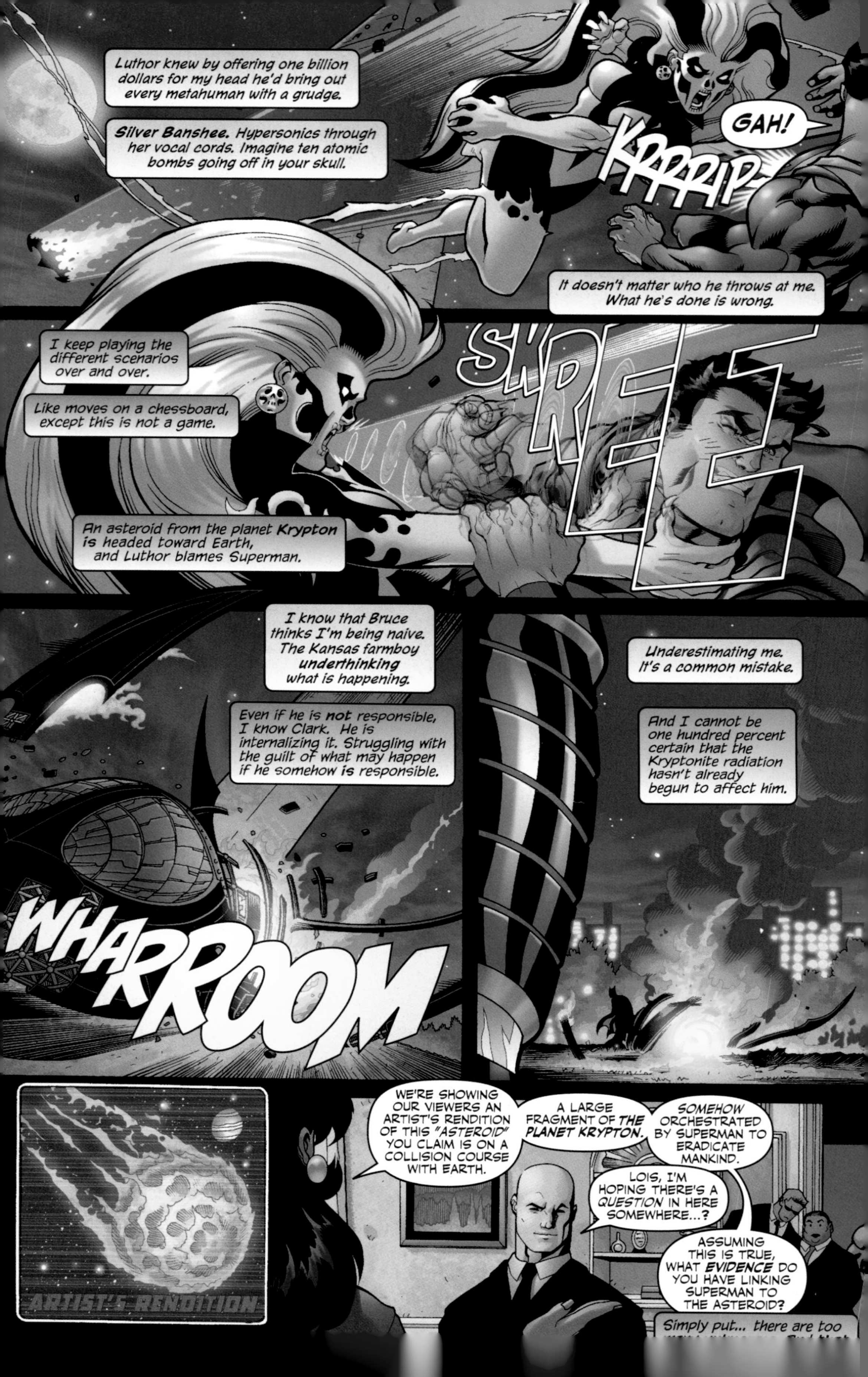

Luthor knew by offering one billion dollars for my head he'd bring out every metahuman with a grudge.
Silver Banshee. Hypersonics through her vocal cords. Imagine ten atomic bombs going off in your skull.
GAH!
KRRRRIP
It doesn't matter who he throws at me. What he's done is wrong.
I keep playing the different scenarios over and over.
Like moves on a chessboard, except this is not a game.
SKREEE
An asteroid from the planet Krypton is headed toward Earth, and Luthor blames Superman.
I know that Bruce thinks I'm being naive. The Kansas farmboy underthinking what is happening.
Even if he is not responsible, I know Clark. He is internalizing it. Struggling with the guilt of what may happen if he somehow is responsible.
WHARROOM
Underestimating me. It's a common mistake.
And I cannot be one hundred percent certain that the Kryptonite radiation hasn't already begun to affect him.
ARTIST'S RENDITION
WE'RE SHOWING OUR VIEWERS AN ARTIST'S RENDITION OF THIS "ASTEROID" YOU CLAIM IS ON A COLLISION COURSE WITH EARTH.
A LARGE FRAGMENT OF THE PLANET KRYPTON.
SOMEHOW ORCHESTRATED BY SUPERMAN TO ERADICATE MANKIND.
LOIS, I'M HOPING THERE'S A QUESTION IN HERE SOMEWHERE...?
ASSUMING THIS IS TRUE, WHAT EVIDENCE DO YOU HAVE LINKING SUPERMAN TO THE ASTEROID?
Simply put... there are too

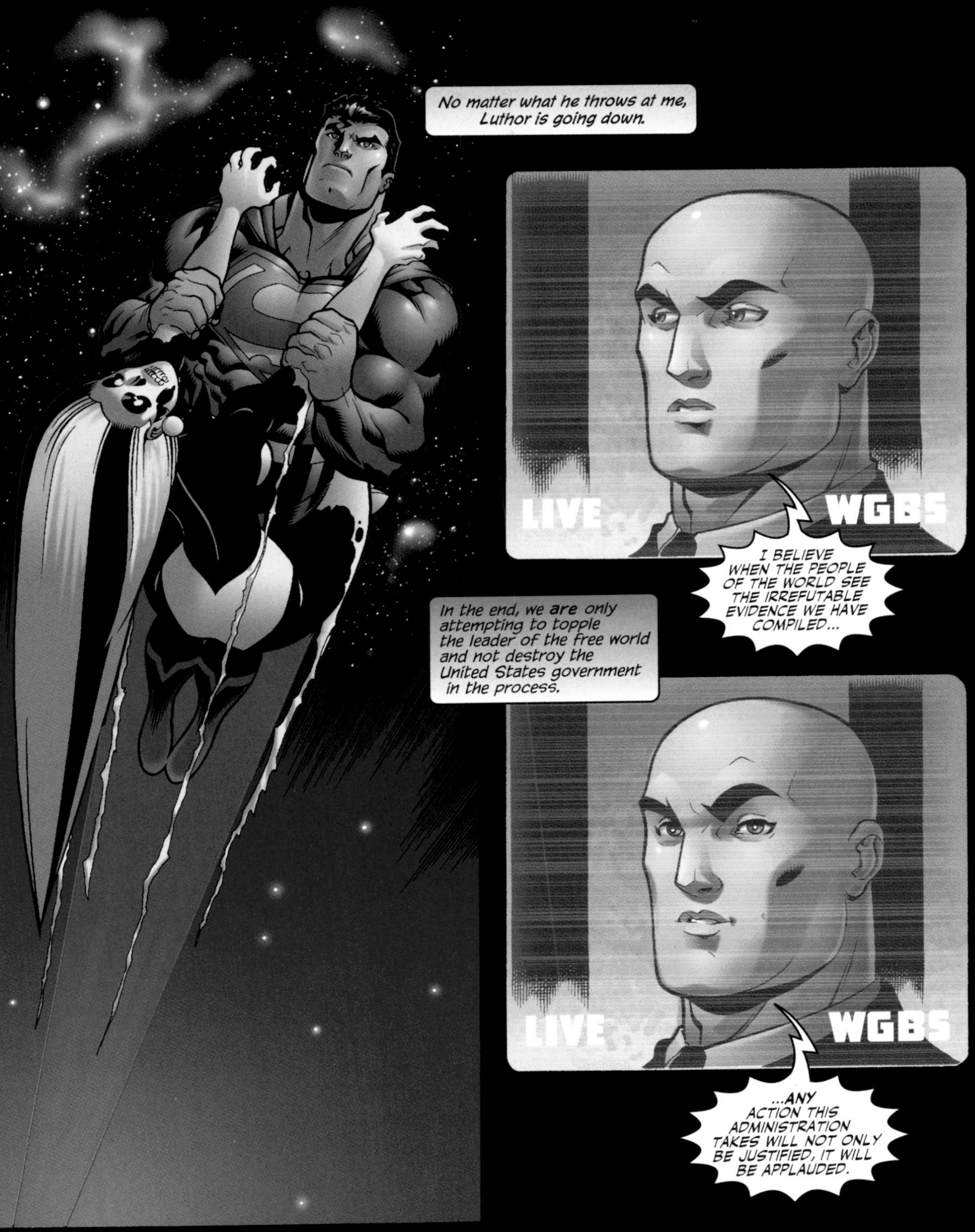
No matter what he throws at me, Luthor is going down.
LIVE
WGBS
I BELIEVE WHEN THE PEOPLE OF THE WORLD SEE THE IRREFUTABLE EVIDENCE WE HAVE COMPILED...
In the end, we are only attempting to topple the leader of the free world and not destroy the United States government in the process.
LIVE
WGBS
...ANY ACTION THIS ADMINISTRATION TAKES WILL NOT ONLY BE JUSTIFIED, IT WILL BE APPLAUDED.

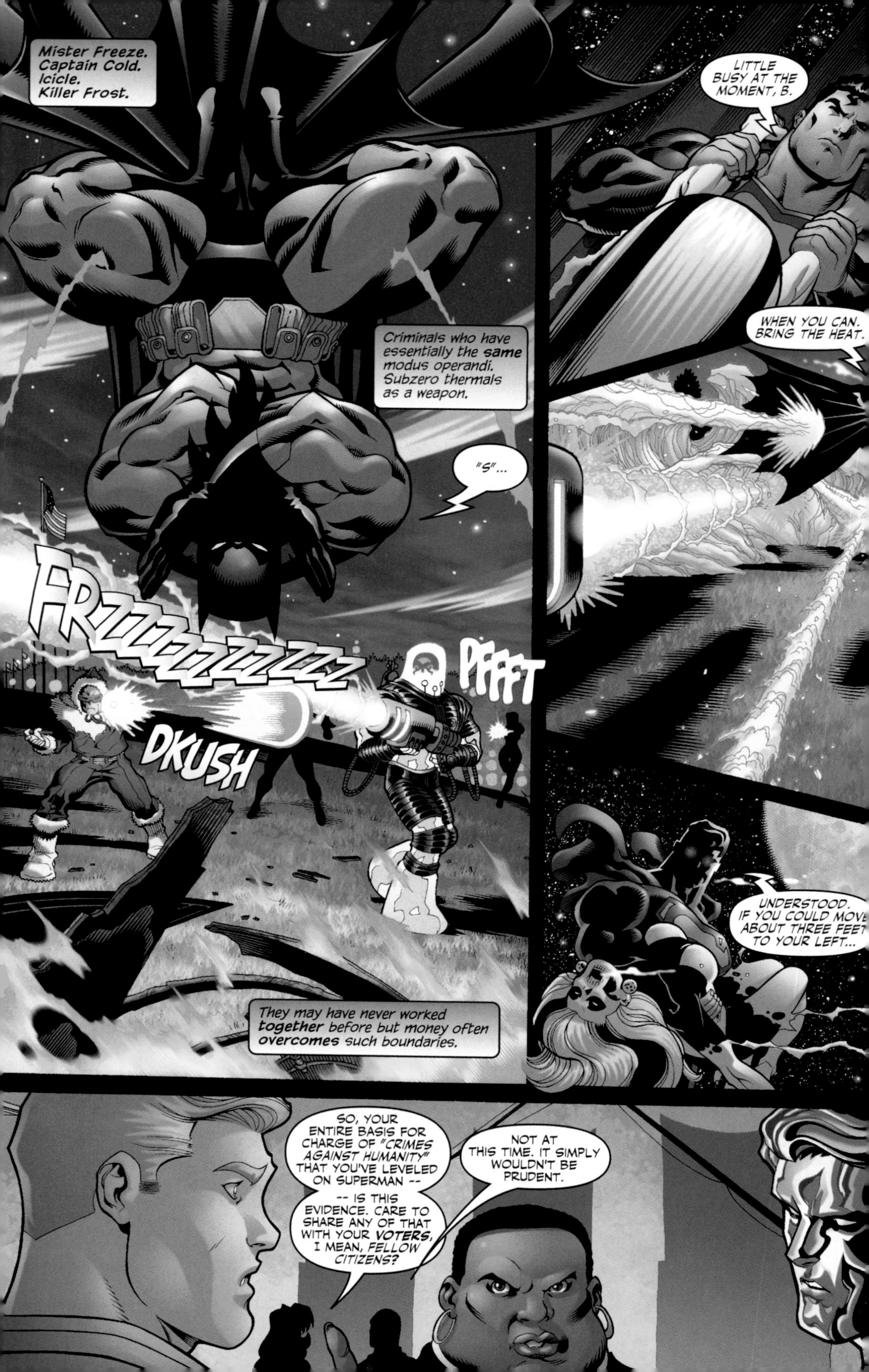
Mister Freeze. Captain Cold. Icicle. Killer Frost.
LITTLE BUSY AT THE MOMENT, B.
Criminals who have essentially the **same** modus operandi. Subzero thermals as a weapon.
WHEN YOU CAN. BRING THE HEAT.
"S"...
FRZZZZZZZZZZZZ
PFFFT
DKUSH
UNDERSTOOD. IF YOU COULD MOVE ABOUT THREE FEET TO YOUR LEFT...
They may have never worked **together** before but money often **overcomes** such boundaries.
SO, YOUR ENTIRE BASIS FOR CHARGE OF "CRIMES AGAINST HUMANITY" THAT YOU'VE LEVELED ON SUPERMAN --
-- IS THIS EVIDENCE. CARE TO SHARE ANY OF THAT WITH YOUR **VOTERS,** I MEAN, FELLOW CITIZENS?
NOT AT THIS TIME. IT SIMPLY WOULDN'T BE PRUDENT.

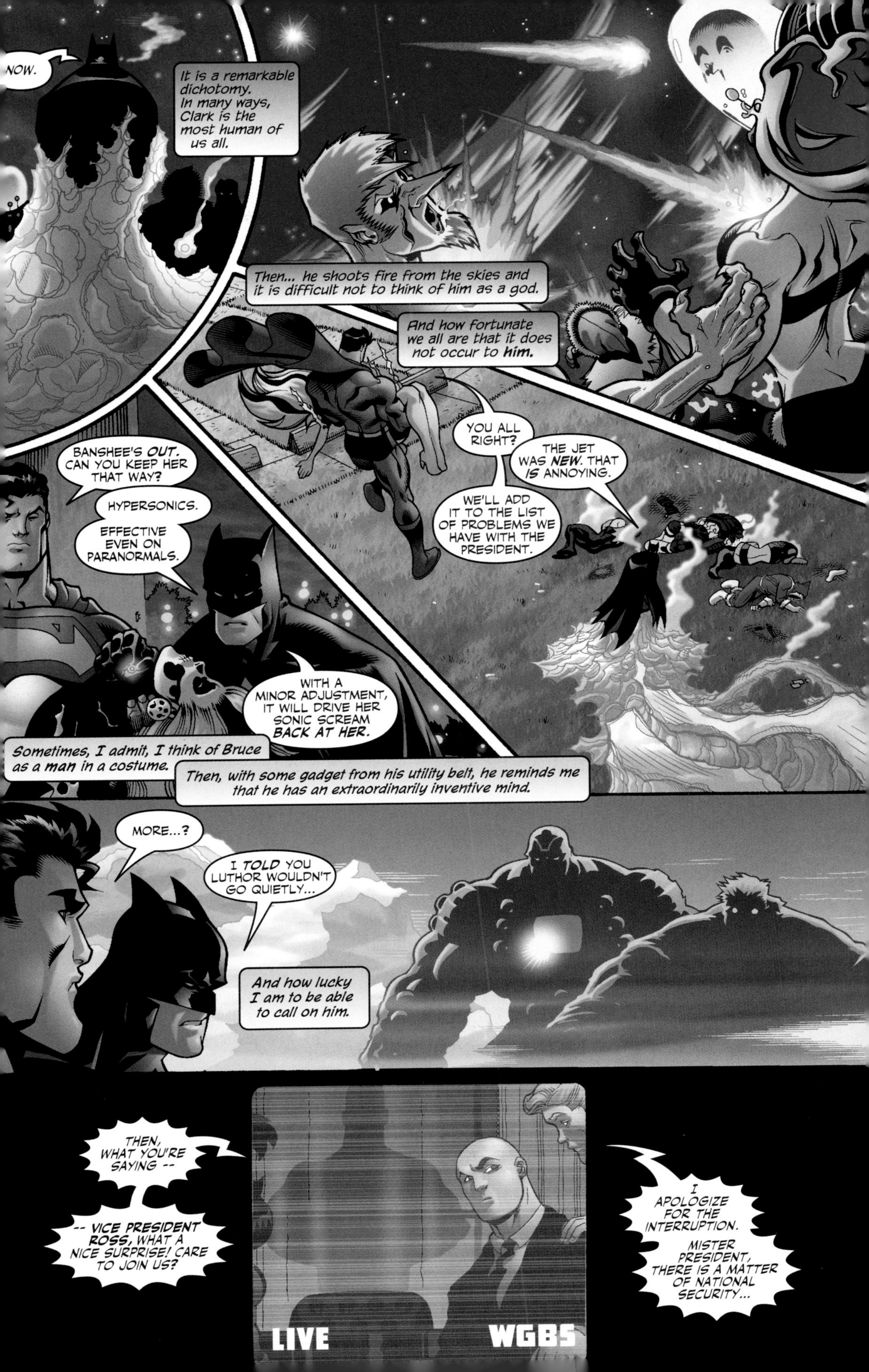
NOW.
It is a remarkable dichotomy. In many ways, Clark is the most human of us all.
Then... he shoots fire from the skies and it is difficult not to think of him as a god.
And how fortunate we all are that it does not occur to him.
YOU ALL RIGHT?
THE JET WAS NEW. THAT IS ANNOYING.
WE'LL ADD IT TO THE LIST OF PROBLEMS WE HAVE WITH THE PRESIDENT.
BANSHEE'S OUT. CAN YOU KEEP HER THAT WAY?
HYPERSONICS.
EFFECTIVE EVEN ON PARANORMALS.
WITH A MINOR ADJUSTMENT, IT WILL DRIVE HER SONIC SCREAM BACK AT HER.
Sometimes, I admit, I think of Bruce as a man in a costume.
Then, with some gadget from his utility belt, he reminds me that he has an extraordinarily inventive mind.
MORE...?
I TOLD YOU LUTHOR WOULDN'T GO QUIETLY...
And how lucky I am to be able to call on him.
THEN, WHAT YOU'RE SAYING --
-- VICE PRESIDENT ROSS, WHAT A NICE SURPRISE! CARE TO JOIN US?
I APOLOGIZE FOR THE INTERRUPTION.
MISTER PRESIDENT, THERE IS A MATTER OF NATIONAL SECURITY...
LIVE
WGBS

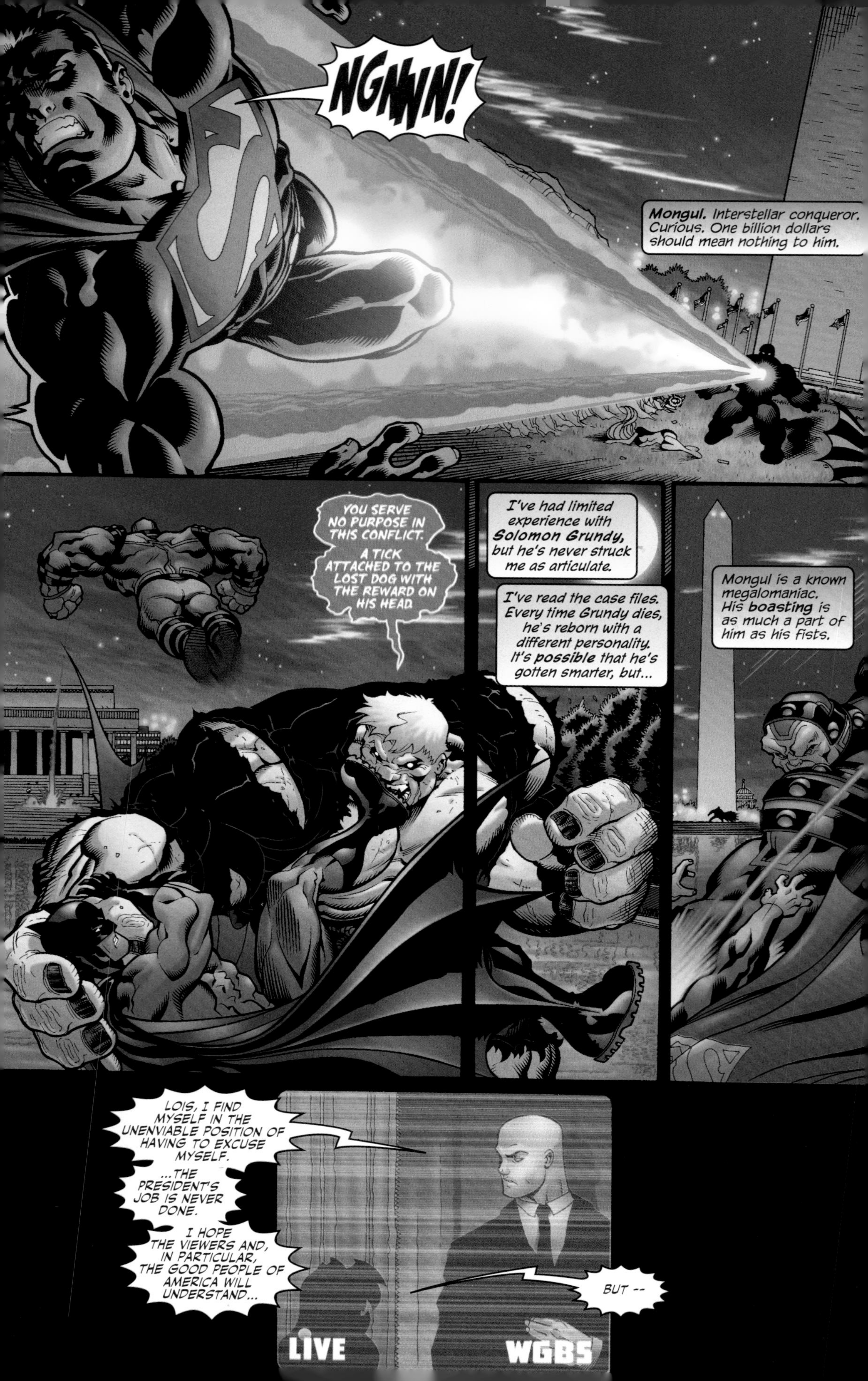
NGNNN!
Mongul. Interstellar conqueror. Curious. One billion dollars should mean nothing to him.
YOU SERVE NO PURPOSE IN THIS CONFLICT.
A TICK ATTACHED TO THE LOST DOG WITH THE REWARD ON HIS HEAD.
I've had limited experience with Solomon Grundy, but he's never struck me as articulate.
I've read the case files. Every time Grundy dies, he's reborn with a different personality. It's possible that he's gotten smarter, but...
Mongul is a known megalomaniac. His boasting is as much a part of him as his fists.
LOIS, I FIND MYSELF IN THE UNENVIABLE POSITION OF HAVING TO EXCUSE MYSELF.
...THE PRESIDENT'S JOB IS NEVER DONE.
I HOPE THE VIEWERS AND, IN PARTICULAR, THE GOOD PEOPLE OF AMERICA WILL UNDERSTAND...
BUT --
LIVE
WGBS

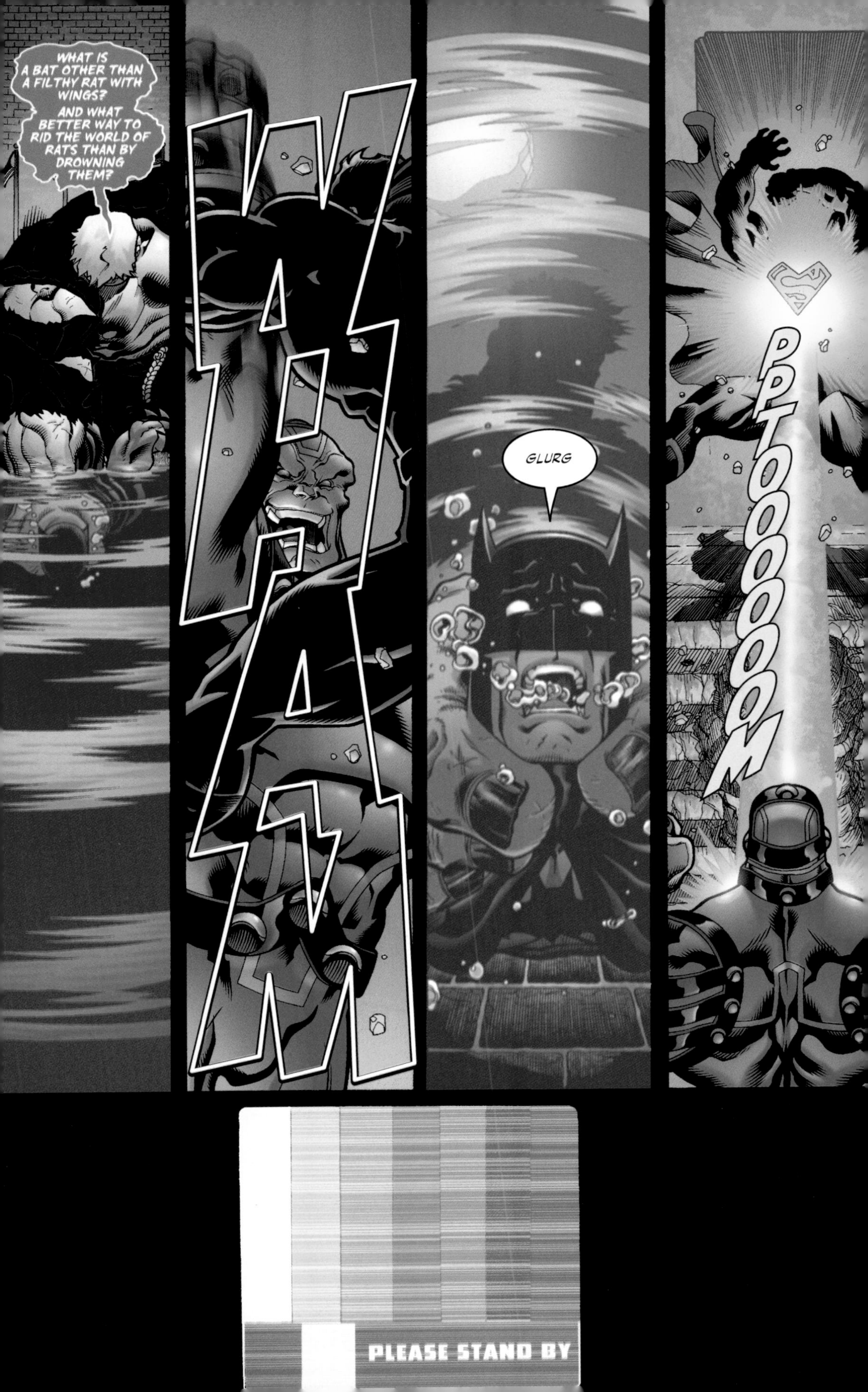
WHAT IS A BAT OTHER THAN A FILTHY RAT WITH WINGS?
AND WHAT BETTER WAY TO RID THE WORLD OF RATS THAN BY DROWNING THEM?
WHAM
GLURG
PPTOOOOOOOM
PLEASE STAND BY

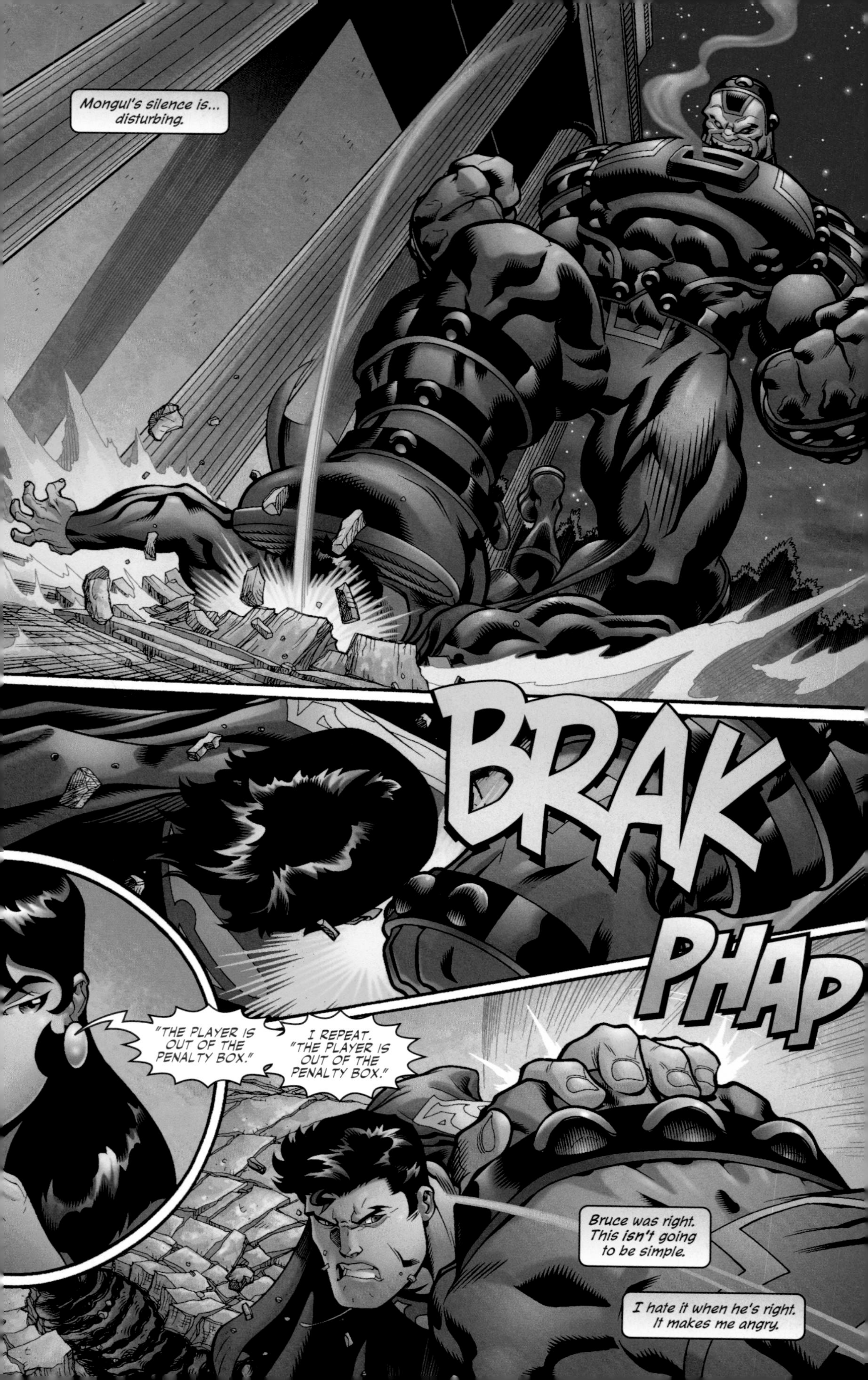

Mongul's silence is... disturbing.
BRAK
PHAP
"THE PLAYER IS OUT OF THE PENALTY BOX."
I REPEAT. "THE PLAYER IS OUT OF THE PENALTY BOX."
Bruce was right. This isn't going to be simple.
I hate it when he's right. It makes me angry.

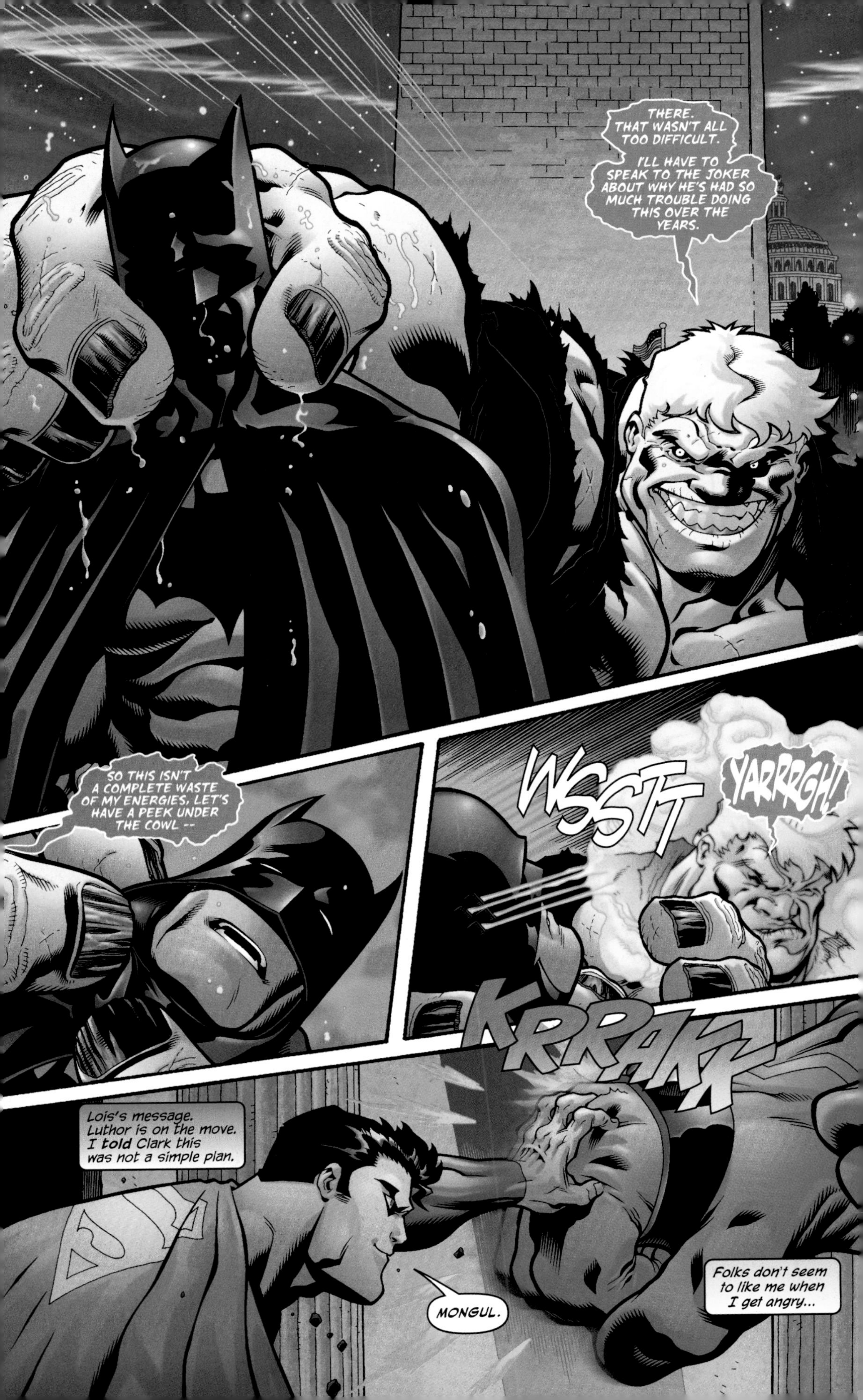
THERE. THAT WASN'T ALL TOO DIFFICULT.
I'LL HAVE TO SPEAK TO THE JOKER ABOUT WHY HE'S HAD SO MUCH TROUBLE DOING THIS OVER THE YEARS.
SO THIS ISN'T A COMPLETE WASTE OF MY ENERGIES, LET'S HAVE A PEEK UNDER THE COWL --
WSSTT
YARRRGH!
KRRAKK
Lois's message. Luthor is on the move. I told Clark this was not a simple plan.
MONGUL.
Folks don't seem to like me when I get angry...

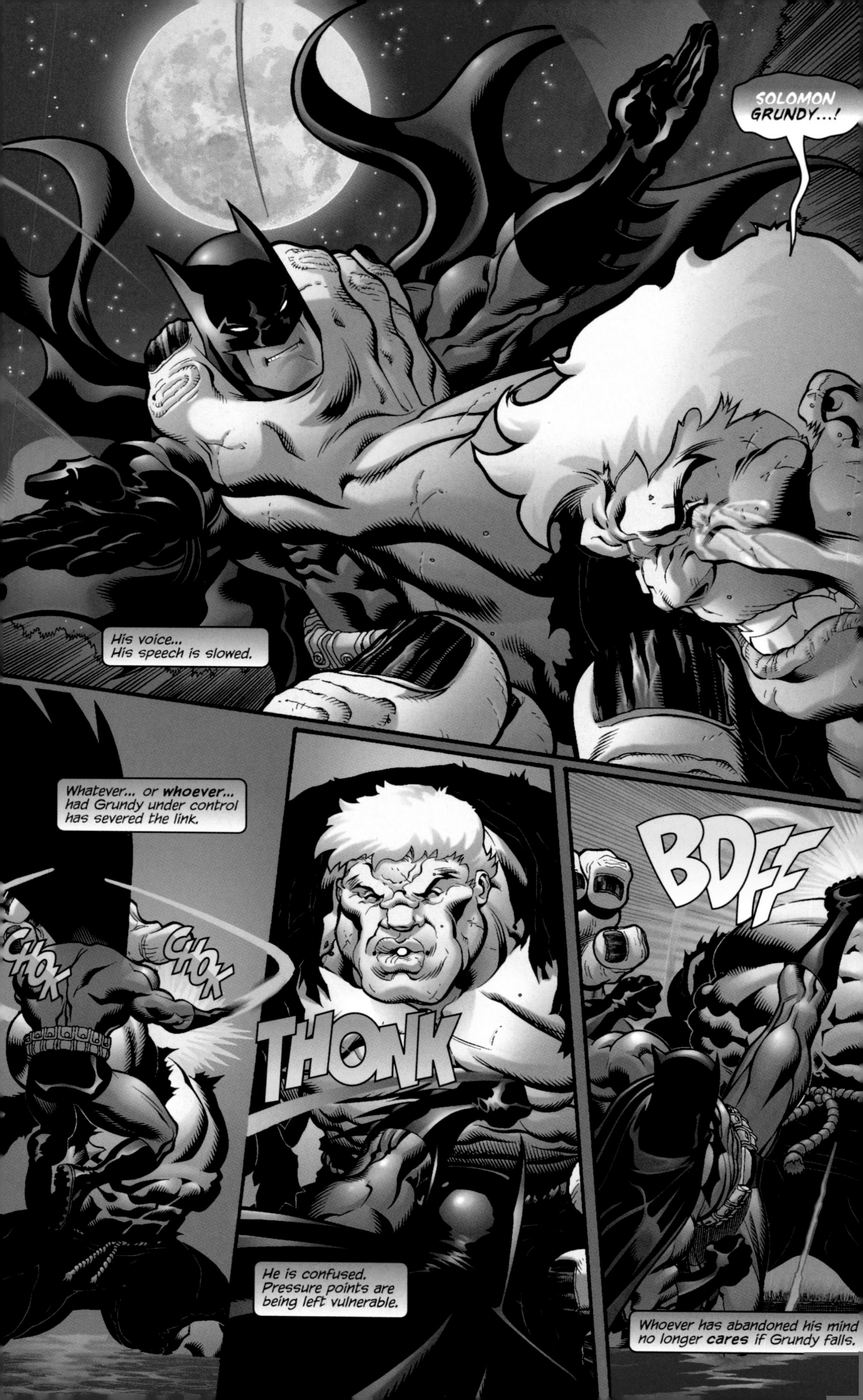
SOLOMON GRUNDY...!
His voice... His speech is slowed.
Whatever... or **whoever**... had Grundy under control has severed the link.
CHOK
CHOK
THONK
He is confused. Pressure points are being left vulnerable.
BDFF
Whoever has abandoned his mind no longer **cares** if Grundy falls.

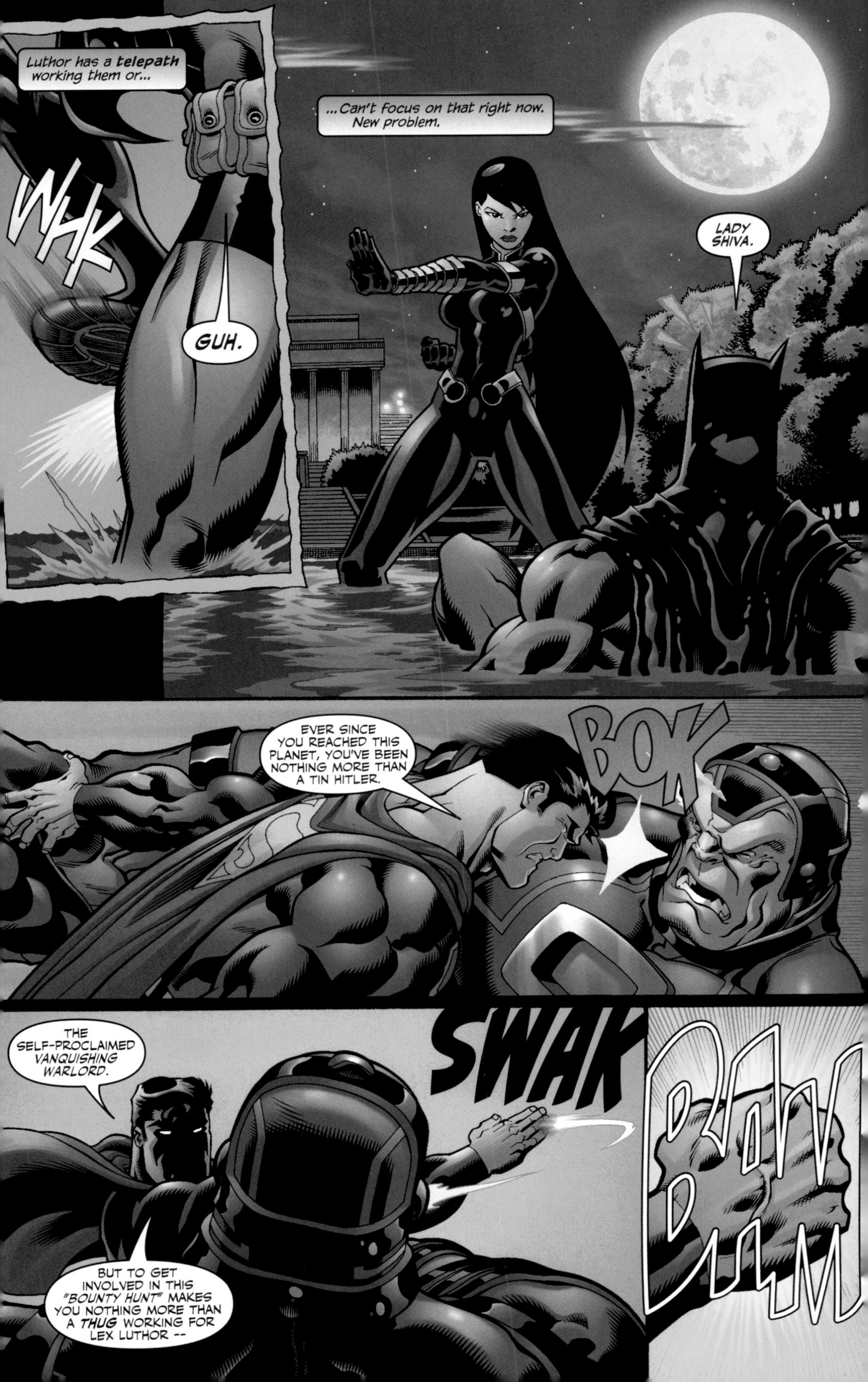
Luthor has a **telepath** working them or...
WHK
GUH.
...Can't focus on that right now. New problem.
LADY SHIVA.
EVER SINCE YOU REACHED THIS PLANET, YOU'VE BEEN NOTHING MORE THAN A TIN HITLER.
BOK
THE SELF-PROCLAIMED *VANQUISHING WARLORD.*
SWAK
BUT TO GET INVOLVED IN THIS *"BOUNTY HUNT"* MAKES YOU NOTHING MORE THAN A ***THUG*** WORKING FOR LEX LUTHOR --
BAM

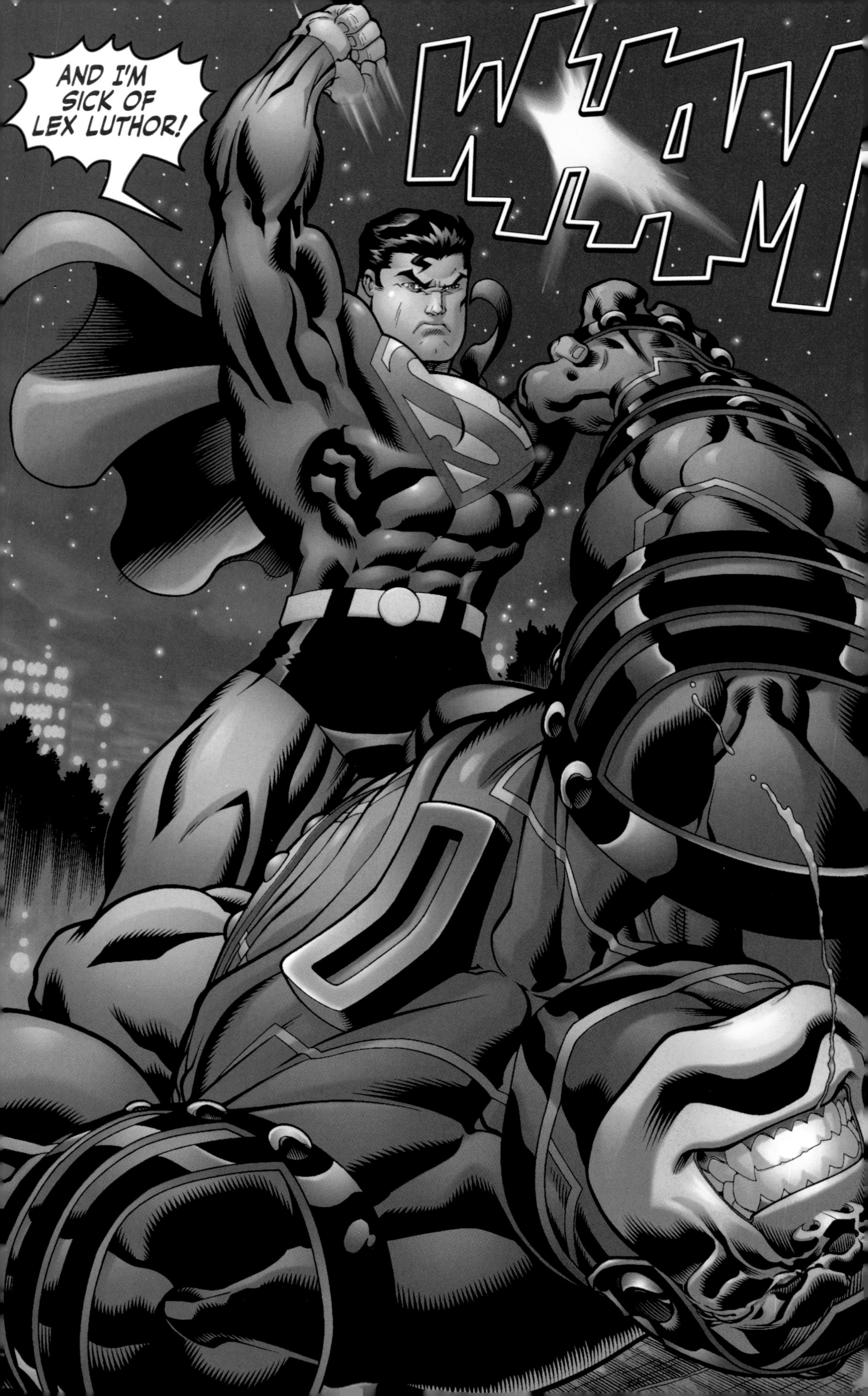
AND I'M SICK OF LEX LUTHOR!
WHAM

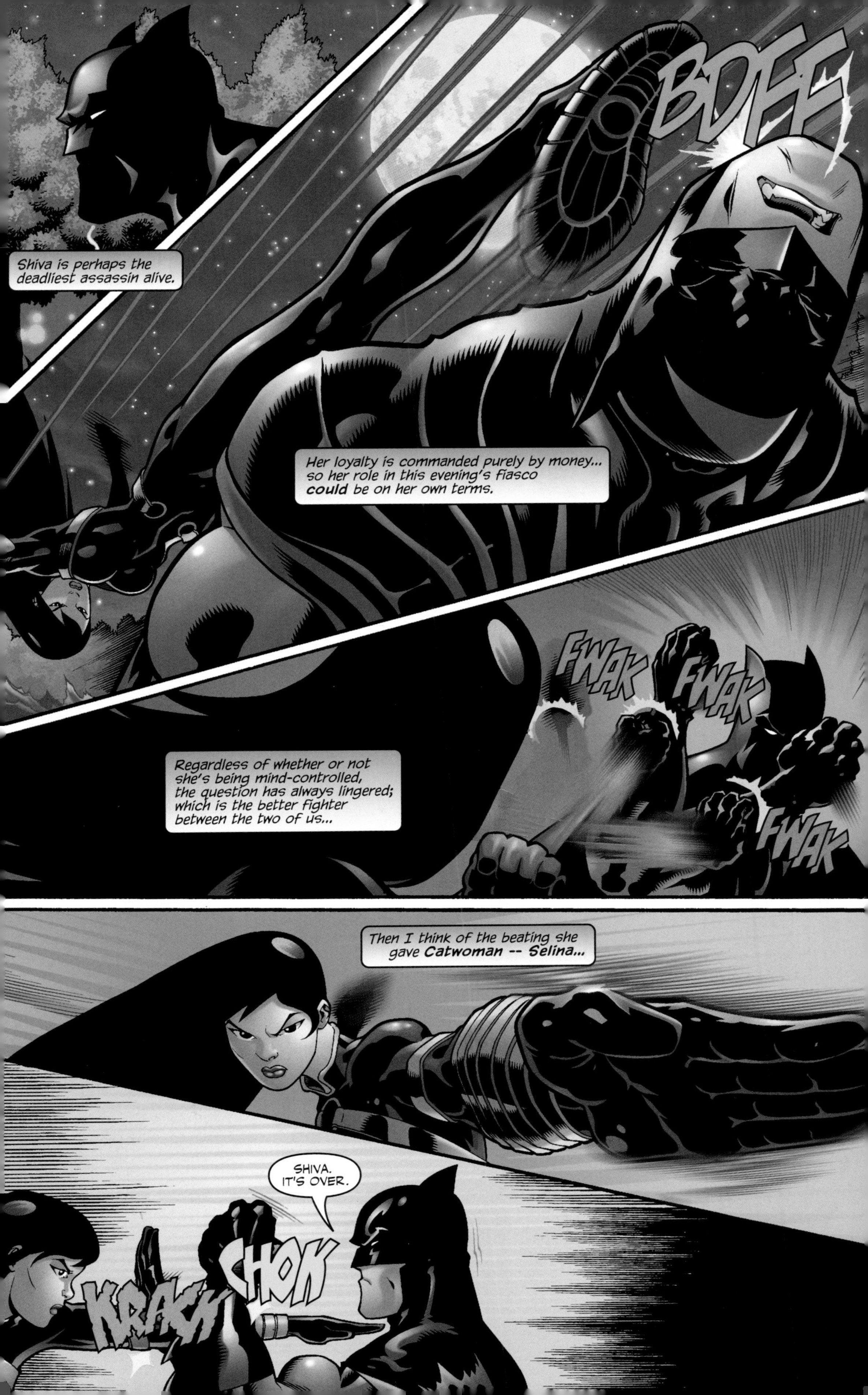

BDFF
Shiva is perhaps the deadliest assassin alive.
Her loyalty is commanded purely by money... so her role in this evening's fiasco **could** be on her own terms.
FWAK
FWAK
Regardless of whether or not she's being mind-controlled, the question has always lingered; which is the better fighter between the two of us...
FWAK
Then I think of the beating she gave **Catwoman -- Selina...**
SHIVA. IT'S OVER.
CHOK
KRACK

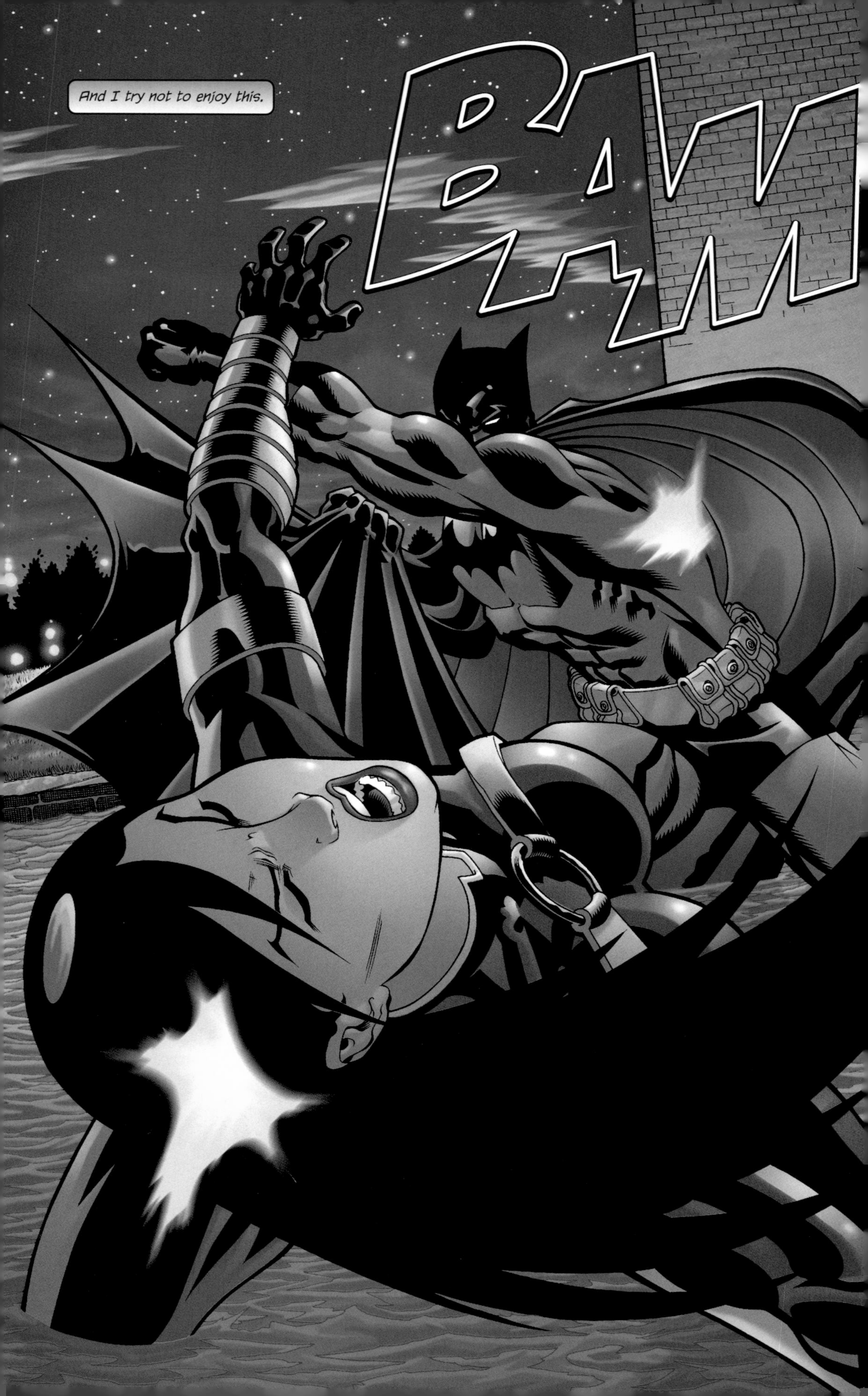
And I try not to enjoy this.
BAM

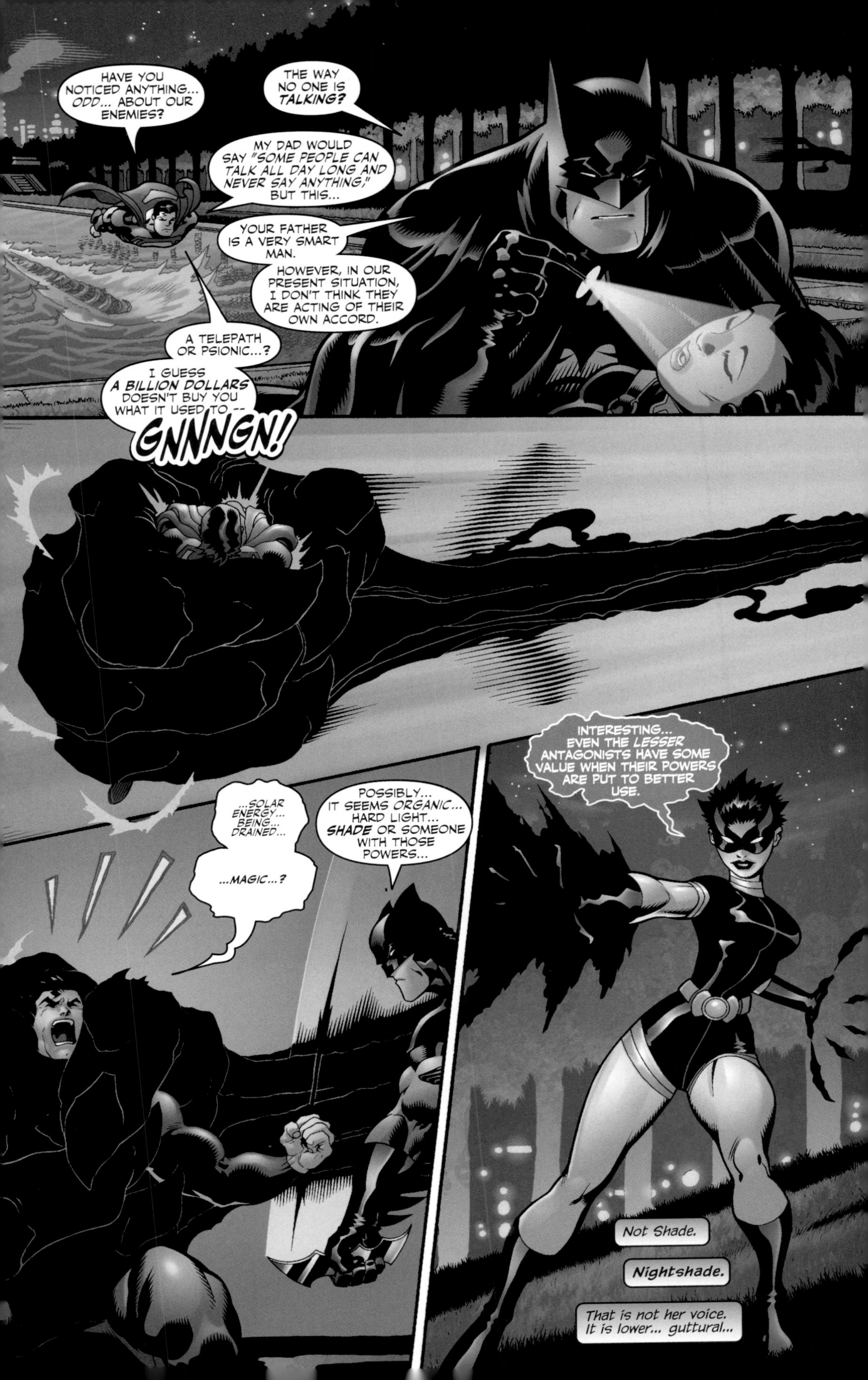
HAVE YOU NOTICED ANYTHING... ODD... ABOUT OUR ENEMIES?
THE WAY NO ONE IS TALKING?
MY DAD WOULD SAY "SOME PEOPLE CAN TALK ALL DAY LONG AND NEVER SAY ANYTHING," BUT THIS...
YOUR FATHER IS A VERY SMART MAN.
HOWEVER, IN OUR PRESENT SITUATION, I DON'T THINK THEY ARE ACTING OF THEIR OWN ACCORD.
A TELEPATH OR PSIONIC...?
I GUESS A BILLION DOLLARS DOESN'T BUY YOU WHAT IT USED TO --
GNNNGN!
...SOLAR ENERGY... BEING... DRAINED...
...MAGIC...?
POSSIBLY... IT SEEMS ORGANIC... HARD LIGHT... SHADE OR SOMEONE WITH THOSE POWERS...
INTERESTING... EVEN THE LESSER ANTAGONISTS HAVE SOME VALUE WHEN THEIR POWERS ARE PUT TO BETTER USE.
Not Shade.
Nightshade.
That is not her voice. It is lower... guttural...

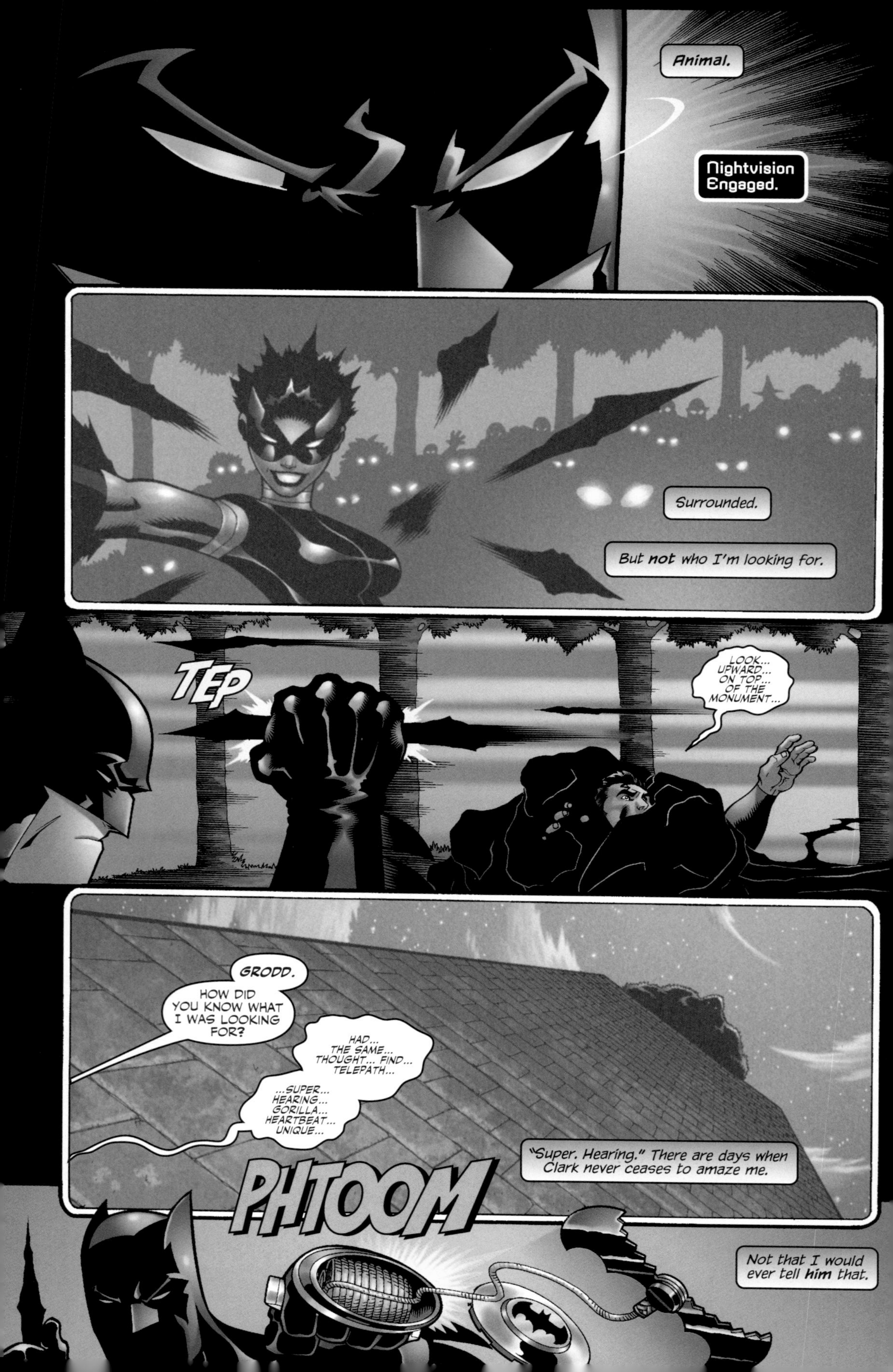
Animal.
Nightvision Engaged.
Surrounded.
But not who I'm looking for.
TEP
LOOK... UPWARD... ON TOP... OF THE MONUMENT...
GRODD.
HOW DID YOU KNOW WHAT I WAS LOOKING FOR?
HAD... THE SAME... THOUGHT... FIND... TELEPATH...
...SUPER... HEARING... GORILLA... HEARTBEAT... UNIQUE...
"Super. Hearing." There are days when Clark never ceases to amaze me.
PHTOOM
Not that I would ever tell him that.

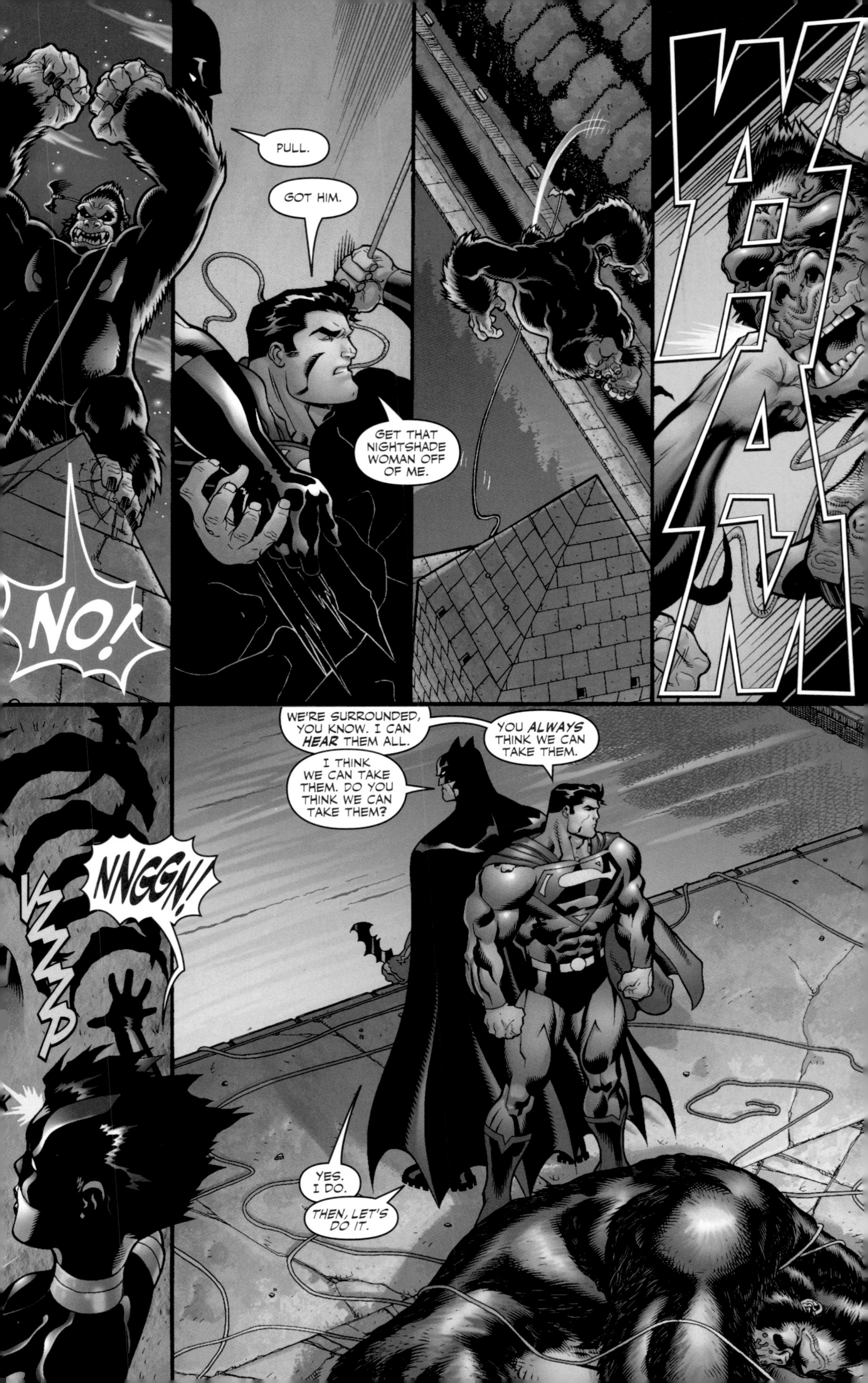
PULL.
GOT HIM.
GET THAT NIGHTSHADE WOMAN OFF OF ME.
NO!
WHAM
NNGGN!
VZZZAP
WE'RE SURROUNDED, YOU KNOW. I CAN *HEAR* THEM ALL.
I THINK WE CAN TAKE THEM. DO YOU THINK WE CAN TAKE THEM?
YOU *ALWAYS* THINK WE CAN TAKE THEM.
YES. I DO.
THEN, LET'S DO IT.

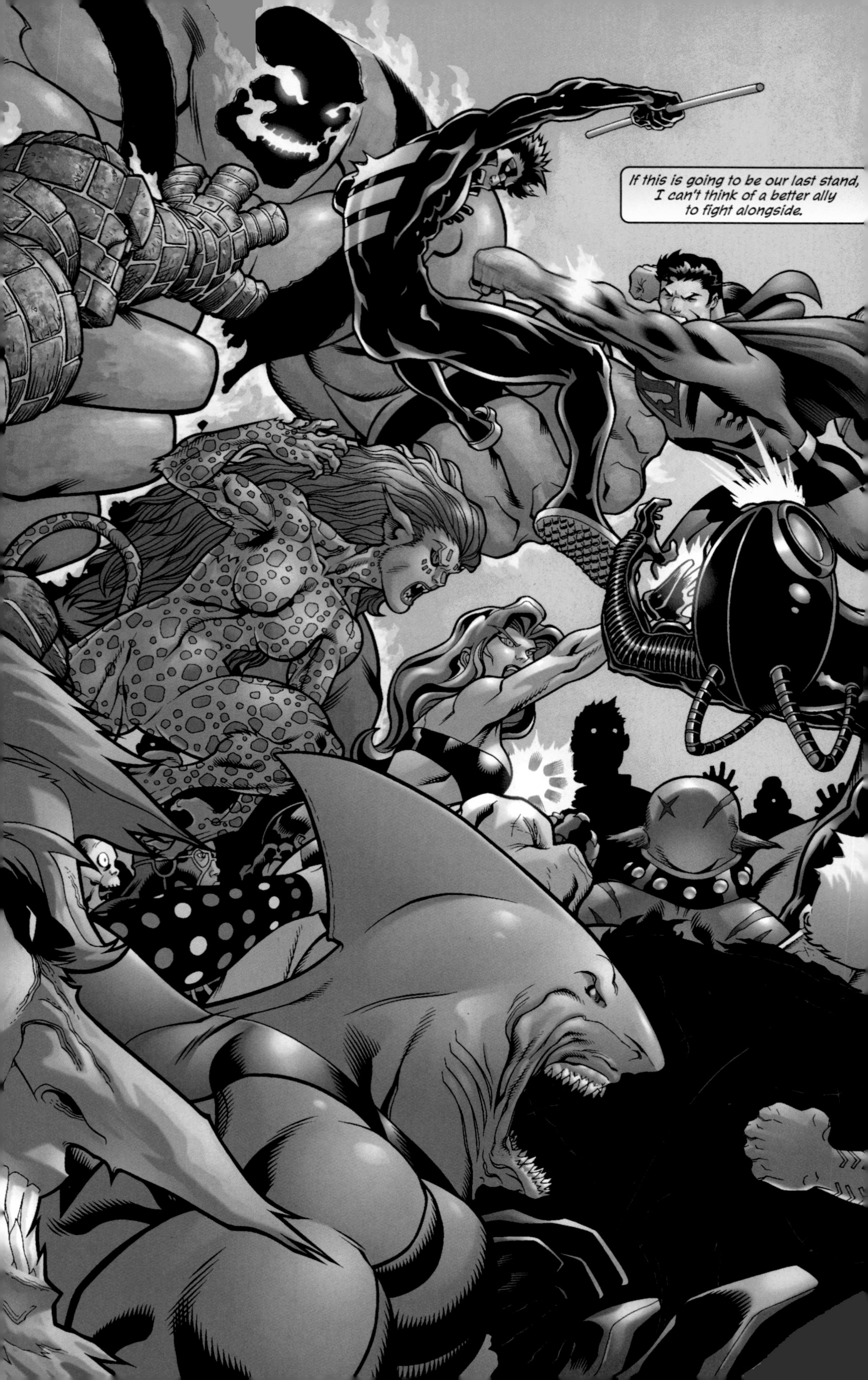
If this is going to be our last stand, I can't think of a better ally to fight alongside.

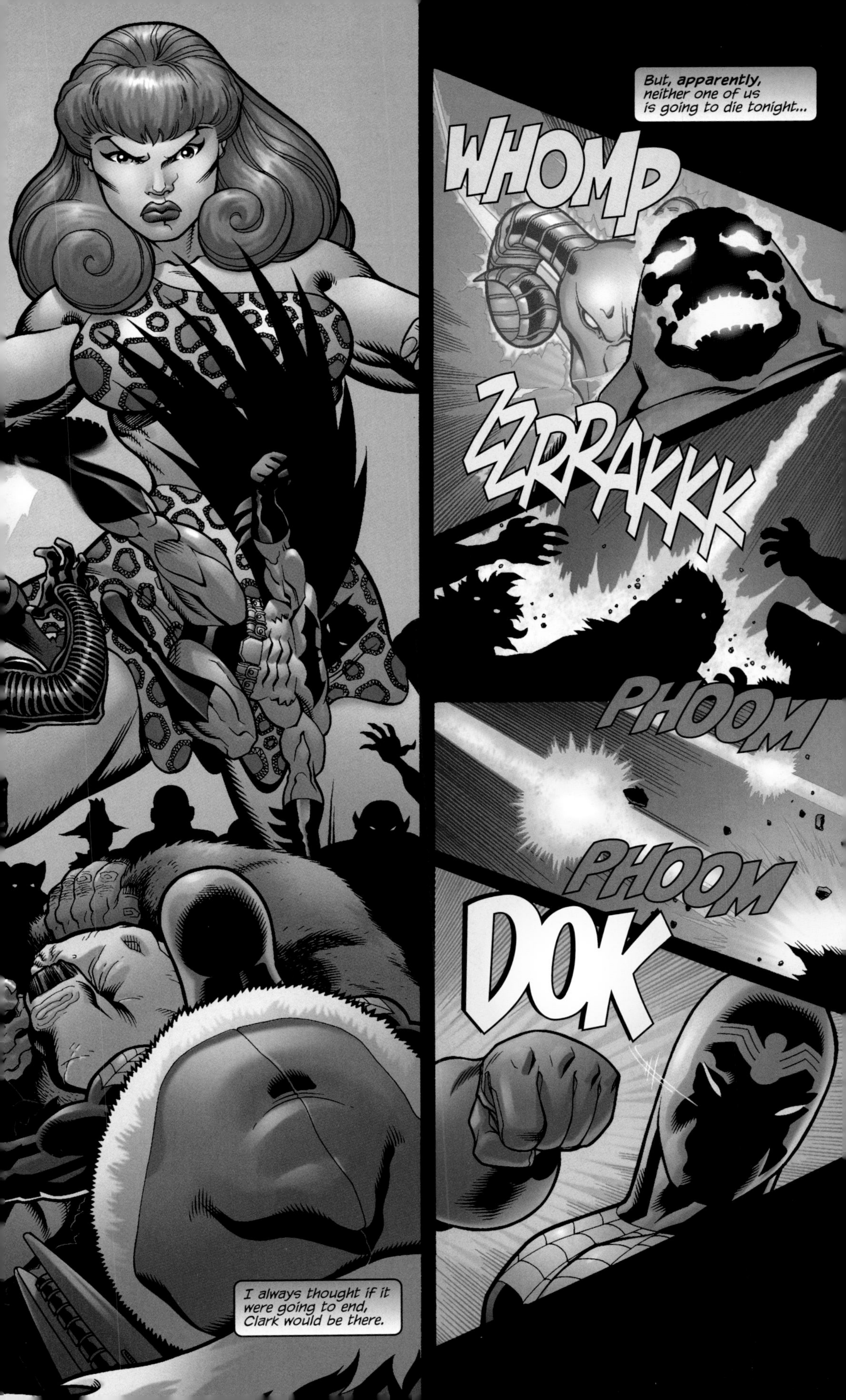
I always thought if it were going to end, Clark would be there.
But, apparently, neither one of us is going to die tonight...
WHOMP
ZZRAKKK
PHOOM
PHOOM
DOK

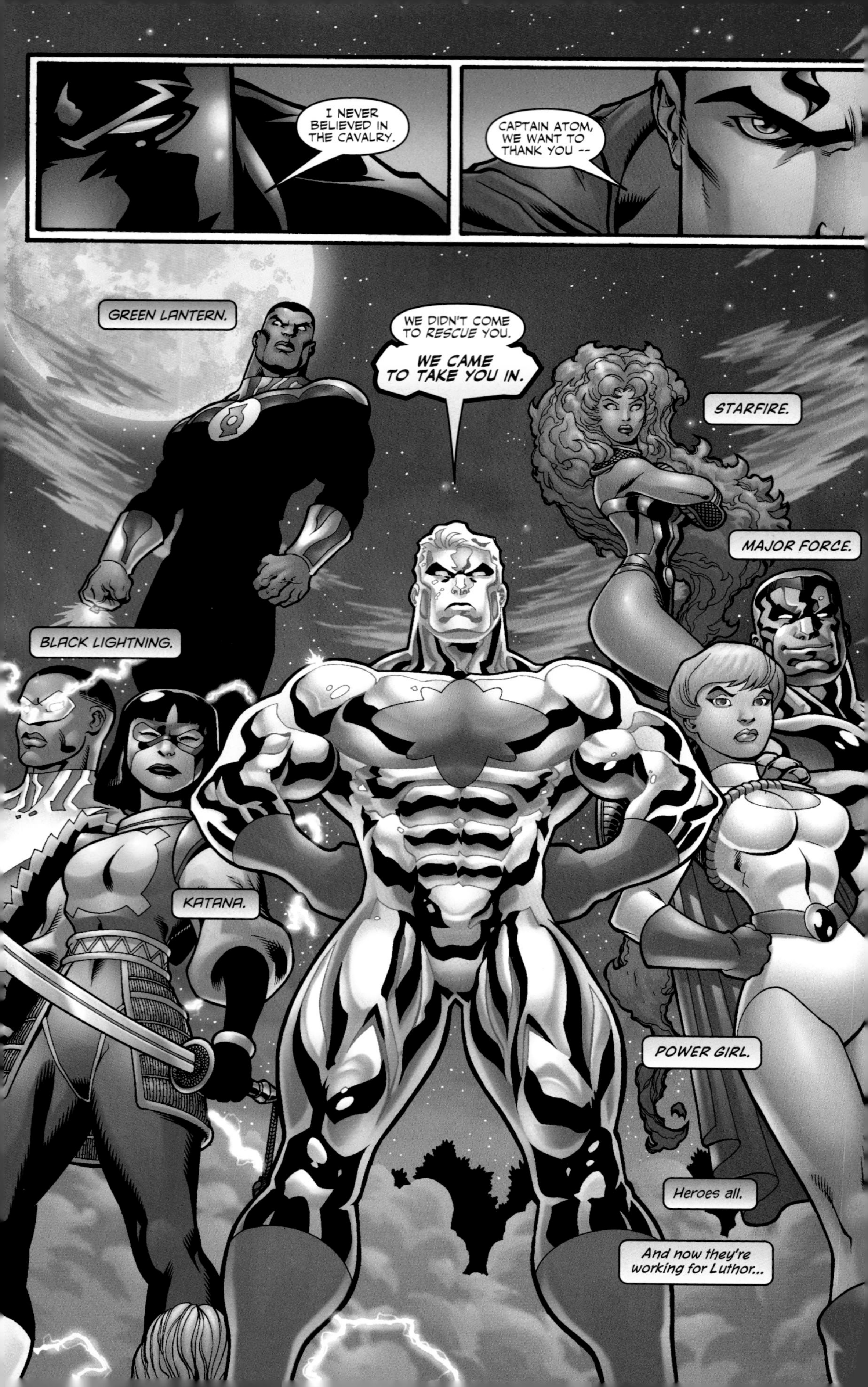
I NEVER BELIEVED IN THE CAVALRY.
CAPTAIN ATOM, WE WANT TO THANK YOU --
GREEN LANTERN.
WE DIDN'T COME TO RESCUE YOU.
WE CAME TO TAKE YOU IN.
STARFIRE.
MAJOR FORCE.
BLACK LIGHTNING.
KATANA.
POWER GIRL.
Heroes all.
And now they're working for Luthor...

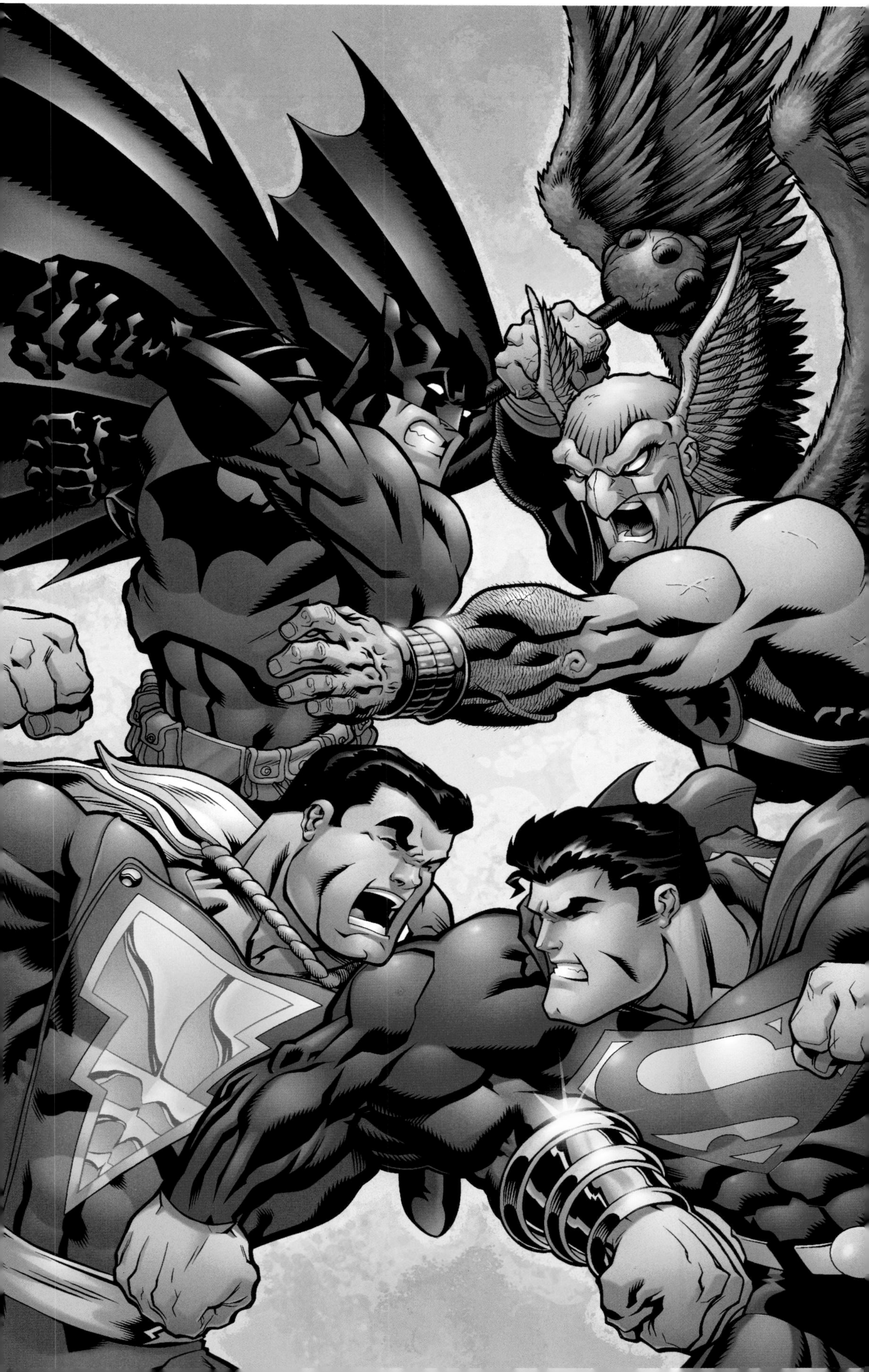

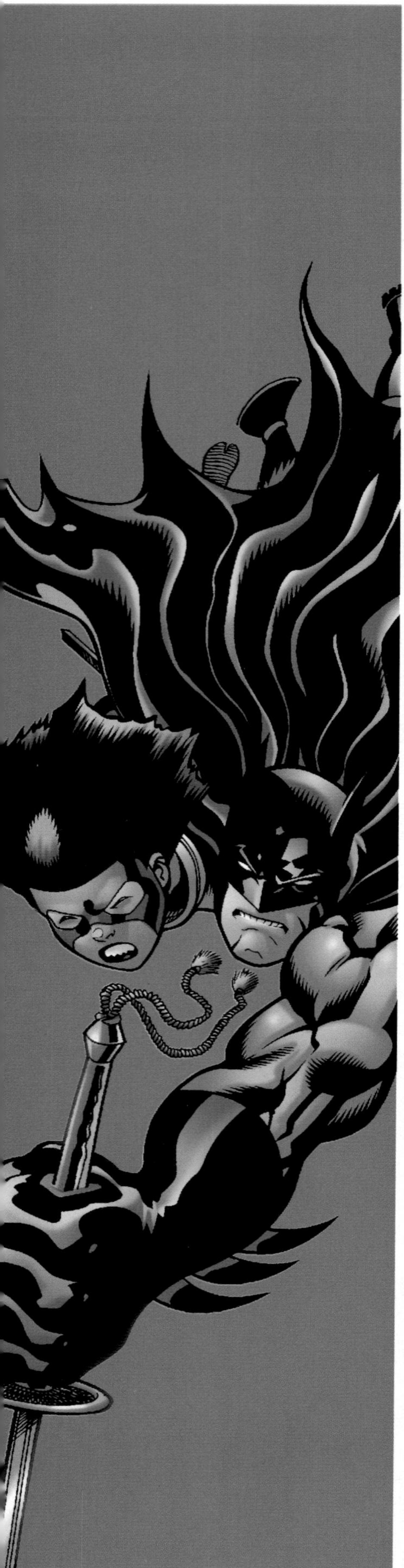

SUPERMAN
PART FOUR
BATMAN

BATTLE ON

JEPH LOEB
WRITER
ED McGUINNESS
PENCILLER
DEXTER VINES
INKER
DAVE STEWART
COLORIST
RICHARD STARKINGS
LETTERER
ED McGUINNESS
DEXTER VINES
WITH
DAVE STEWART
COVER

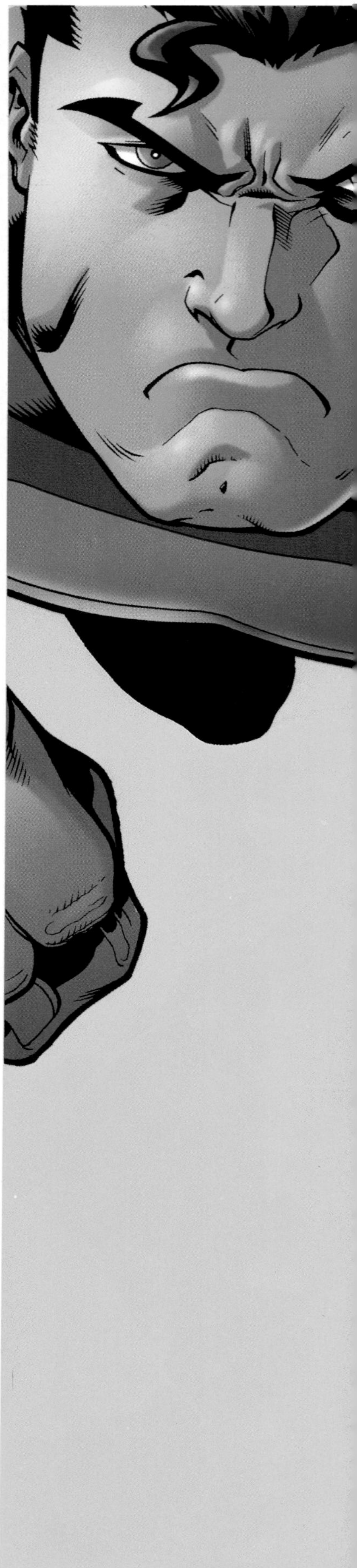

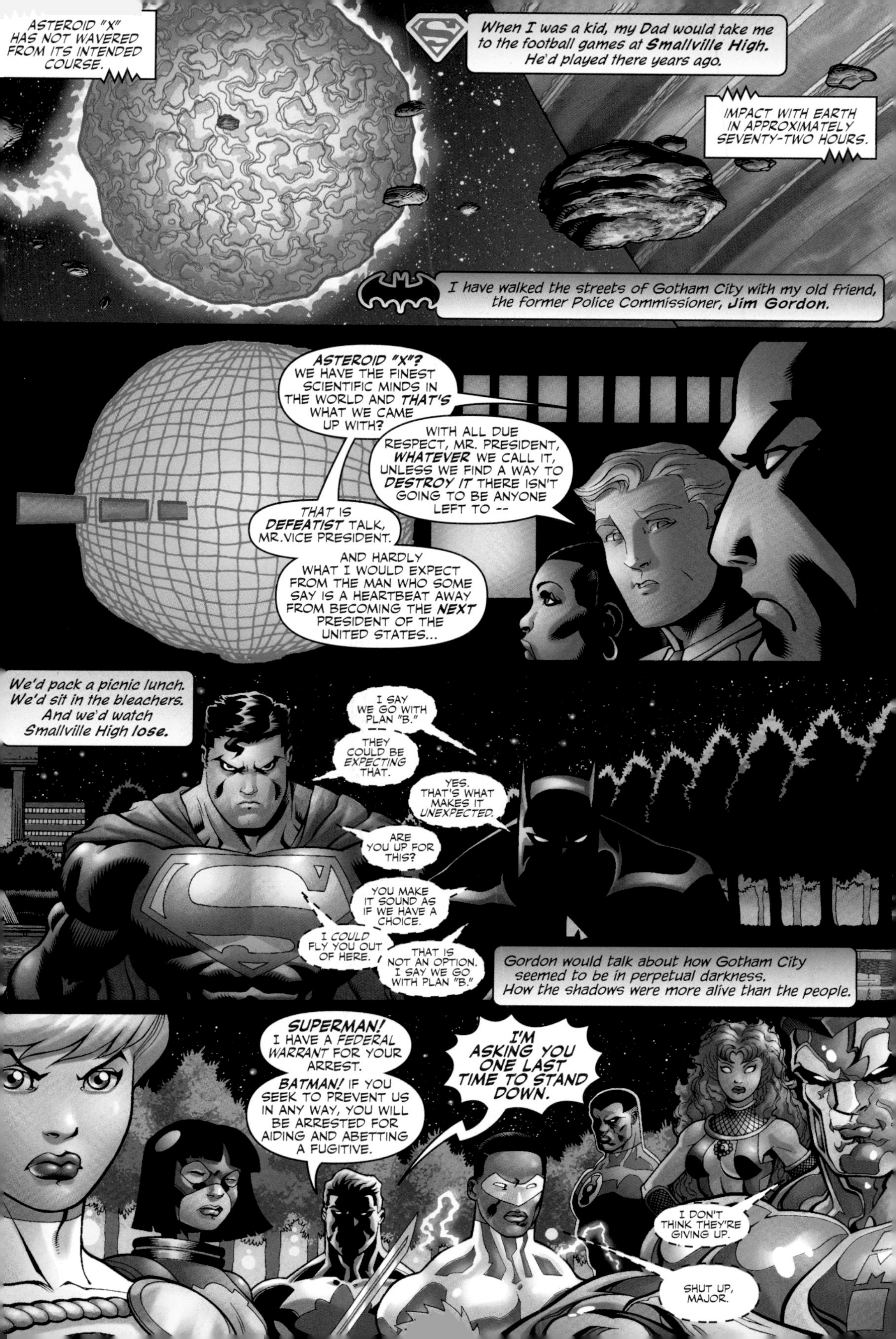
ASTEROID "X" HAS NOT WAVERED FROM ITS INTENDED COURSE.
When I was a kid, my Dad would take me to the football games at Smallville High. He'd played there years ago.
IMPACT WITH EARTH IN APPROXIMATELY SEVENTY-TWO HOURS.
I have walked the streets of Gotham City with my old friend, the former Police Commissioner, Jim Gordon.
ASTEROID "X"? WE HAVE THE FINEST SCIENTIFIC MINDS IN THE WORLD AND THAT'S WHAT WE CAME UP WITH?
WITH ALL DUE RESPECT, MR. PRESIDENT, WHATEVER WE CALL IT, UNLESS WE FIND A WAY TO DESTROY IT THERE ISN'T GOING TO BE ANYONE LEFT TO --
THAT IS DEFEATIST TALK, MR.VICE PRESIDENT.
AND HARDLY WHAT I WOULD EXPECT FROM THE MAN WHO SOME SAY IS A HEARTBEAT AWAY FROM BECOMING THE NEXT PRESIDENT OF THE UNITED STATES...
We'd pack a picnic lunch. We'd sit in the bleachers. And we'd watch Smallville High lose.
I SAY WE GO WITH PLAN "B."
THEY COULD BE EXPECTING THAT.
YES. THAT'S WHAT MAKES IT UNEXPECTED.
ARE YOU UP FOR THIS?
YOU MAKE IT SOUND AS IF WE HAVE A CHOICE.
I COULD FLY YOU OUT OF HERE.
THAT IS NOT AN OPTION. I SAY WE GO WITH PLAN "B."
Gordon would talk about how Gotham City seemed to be in perpetual darkness. How the shadows were more alive than the people.
SUPERMAN! I HAVE A FEDERAL WARRANT FOR YOUR ARREST.
BATMAN! IF YOU SEEK TO PREVENT US IN ANY WAY, YOU WILL BE ARRESTED FOR AIDING AND ABETTING A FUGITIVE.
I'M ASKING YOU ONE LAST TIME TO STAND DOWN.
I DON'T THINK THEY'RE GIVING UP.
SHUT UP, MAJOR.

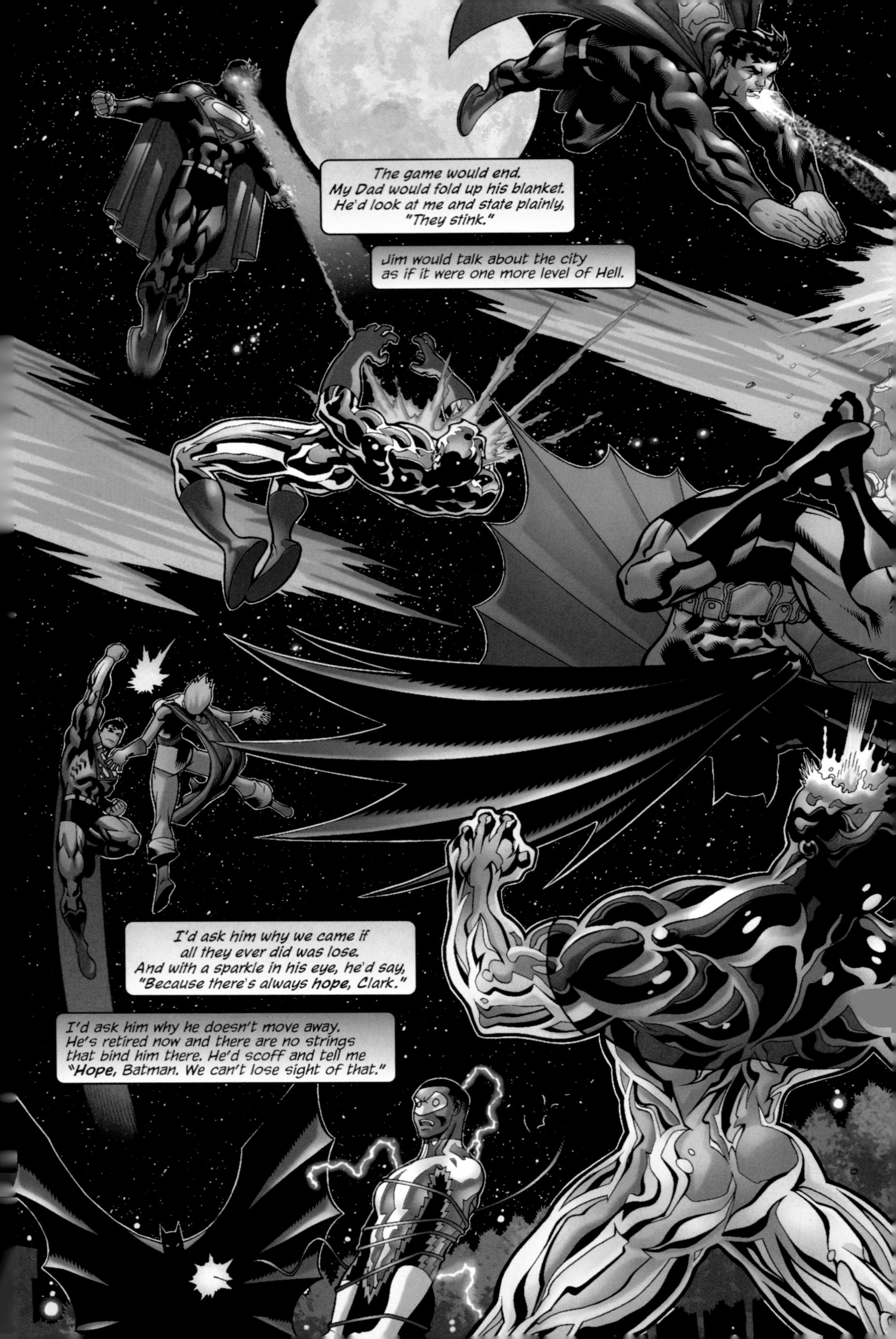
The game would end. My Dad would fold up his blanket. He'd look at me and state plainly, "They stink."
Jim would talk about the city as if it were one more level of Hell.
I'd ask him why we came if all they ever did was lose. And with a sparkle in his eye, he'd say, "Because there's always **hope**, Clark."
I'd ask him why he doesn't move away. He's retired now and there are no strings that bind him there. He'd scoff and tell me "**Hope**, Batman. We can't lose sight of that."

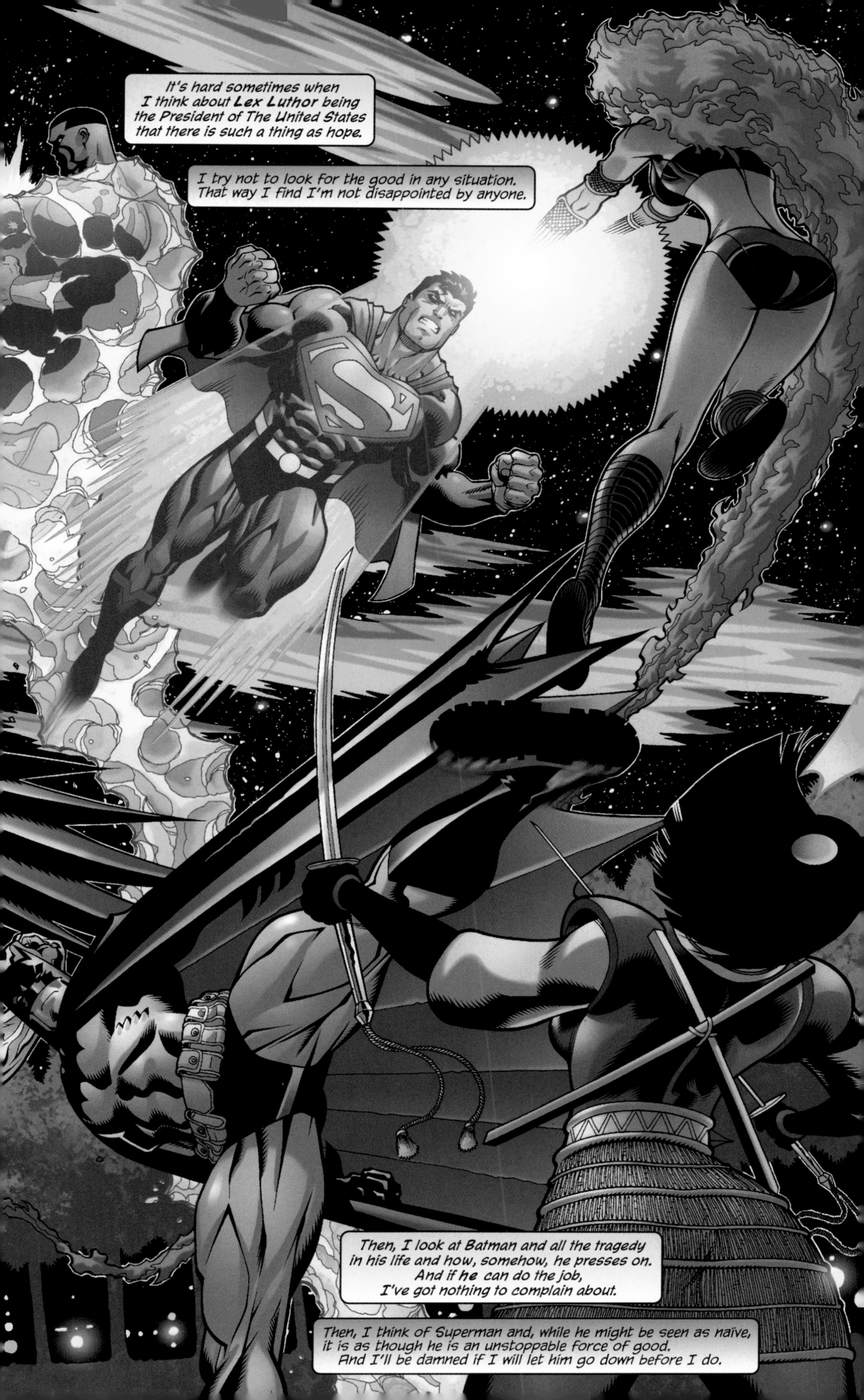
It's hard sometimes when I think about Lex Luthor being the President of The United States that there is such a thing as hope.
I try not to look for the good in any situation. That way I find I'm not disappointed by anyone.
Then, I look at Batman and all the tragedy in his life and how, somehow, he presses on. And if he can do the job, I've got nothing to complain about.
Then, I think of Superman and, while he might be seen as naïve, it is as though he is an unstoppable force of good. And I'll be damned if I will let him go down before I do.

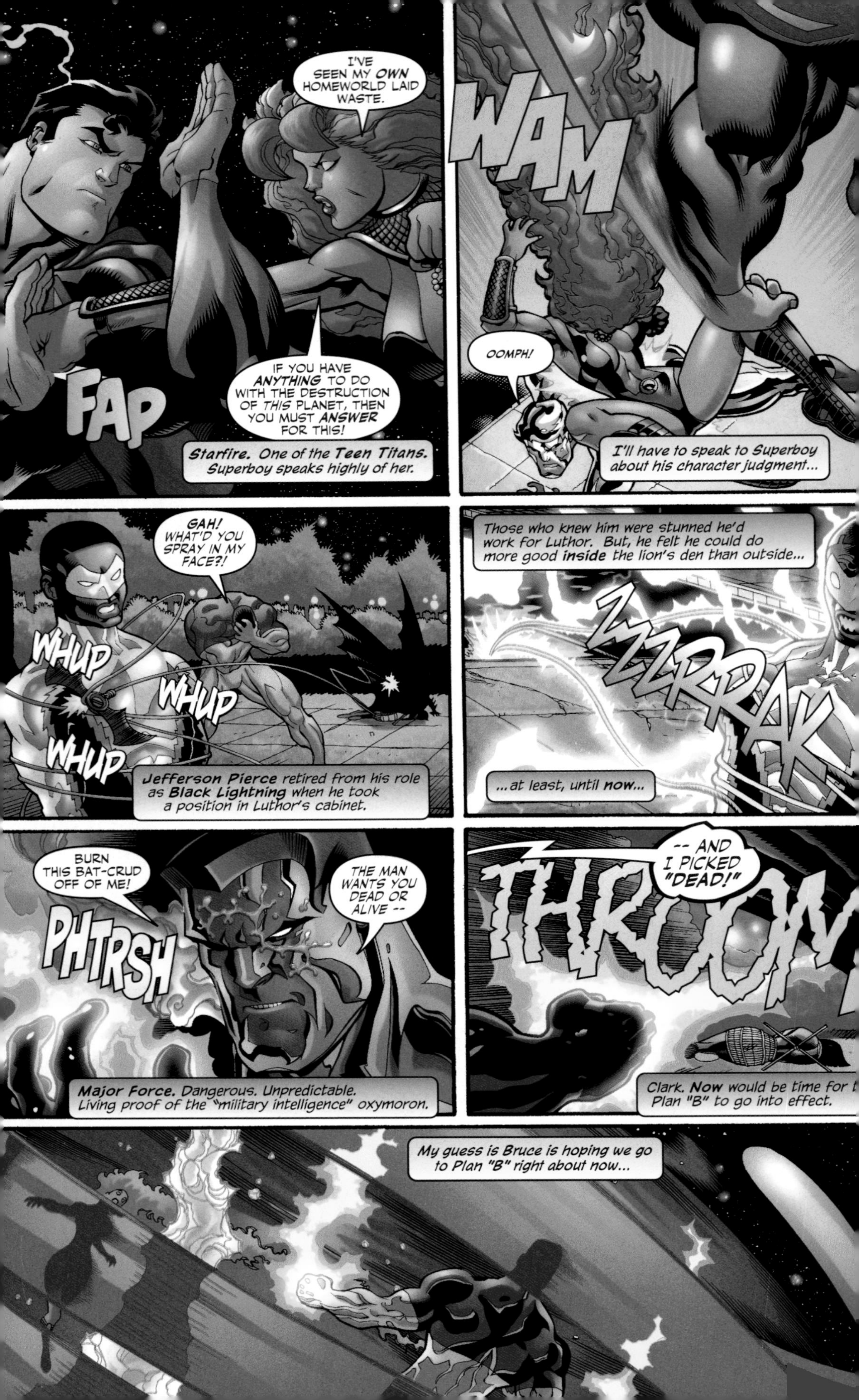
I'VE SEEN MY OWN HOMEWORLD LAID WASTE.
FAP
IF YOU HAVE ANYTHING TO DO WITH THE DESTRUCTION OF THIS PLANET, THEN YOU MUST ANSWER FOR THIS!
Starfire. One of the Teen Titans. Superboy speaks highly of her.
WAM
OOMPH!
I'll have to speak to Superboy about his character judgment...
GAH! WHAT'D YOU SPRAY IN MY FACE?!
WHUP
WHUP
WHUP
Jefferson Pierce retired from his role as Black Lightning when he took a position in Luthor's cabinet.
Those who knew him were stunned he'd work for Luthor. But, he felt he could do more good inside the lion's den than outside...
ZZZRRRAK
...at least, until now...
BURN THIS BAT-CRUD OFF OF ME!
PHTRSH
THE MAN WANTS YOU DEAD OR ALIVE --
Major Force. Dangerous. Unpredictable. Living proof of the "military intelligence" oxymoron.
-- AND I PICKED "DEAD!"
THROOM
Clark. Now would be time for t
Plan "B" to go into effect.
My guess is Bruce is hoping we go to Plan "B" right about now...

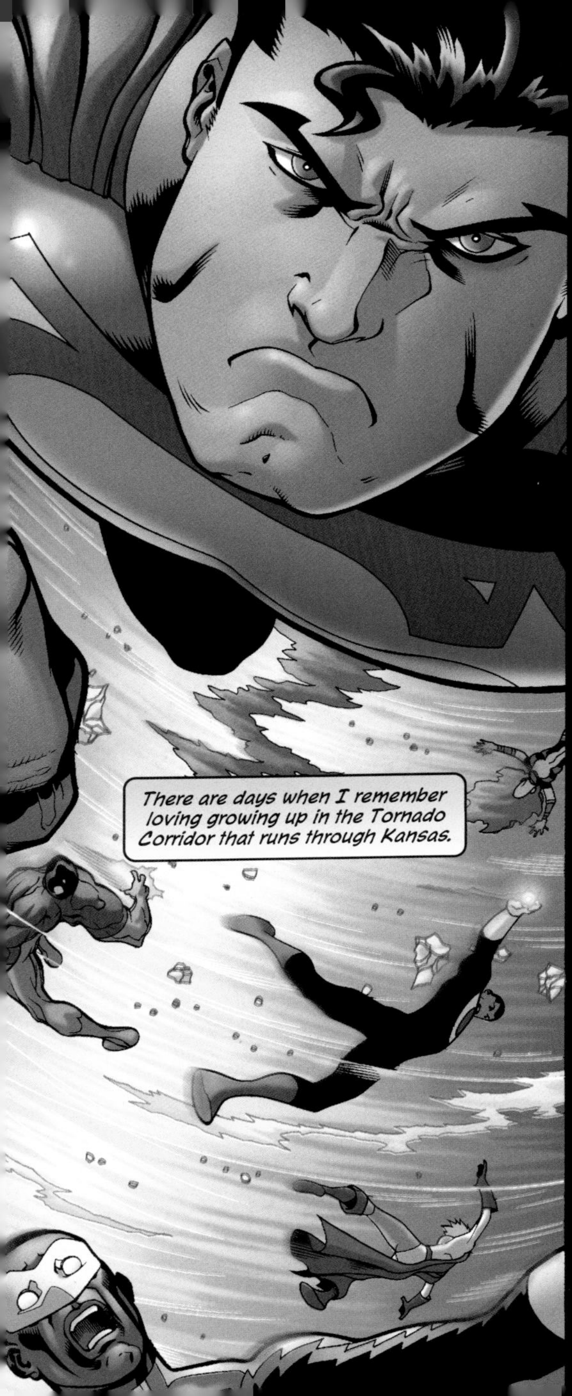
There are days when I remember loving growing up in the Tornado Corridor that runs through Kansas.

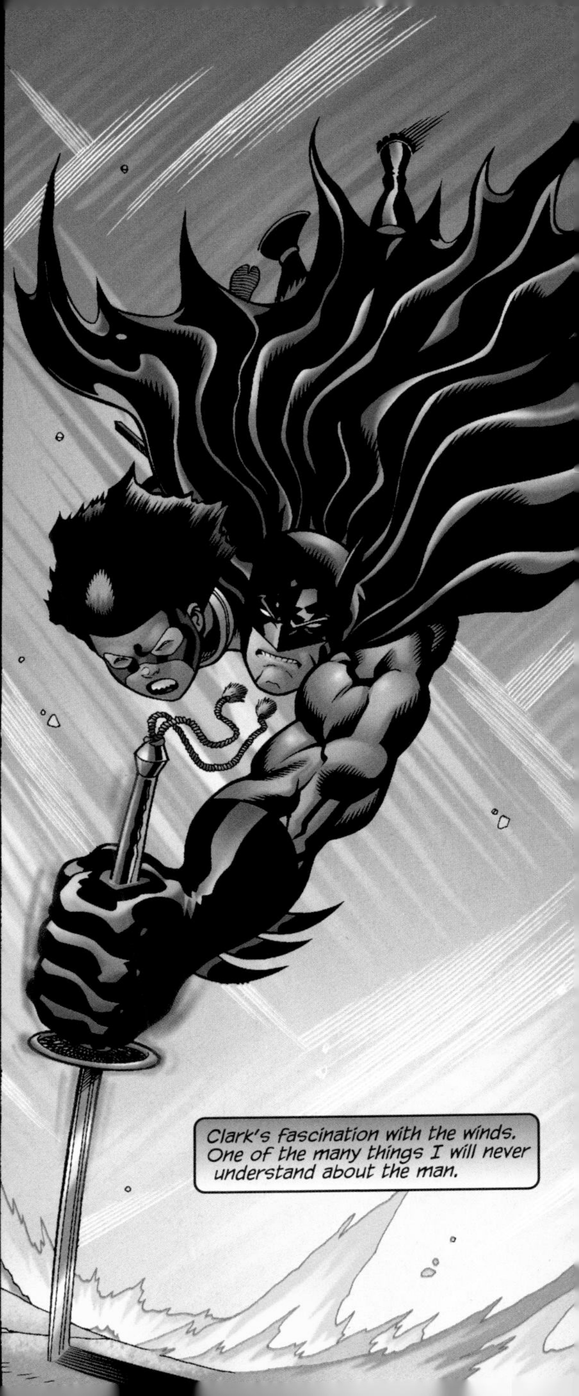
Clark's fascination with the winds. One of the many things I will never understand about the man.

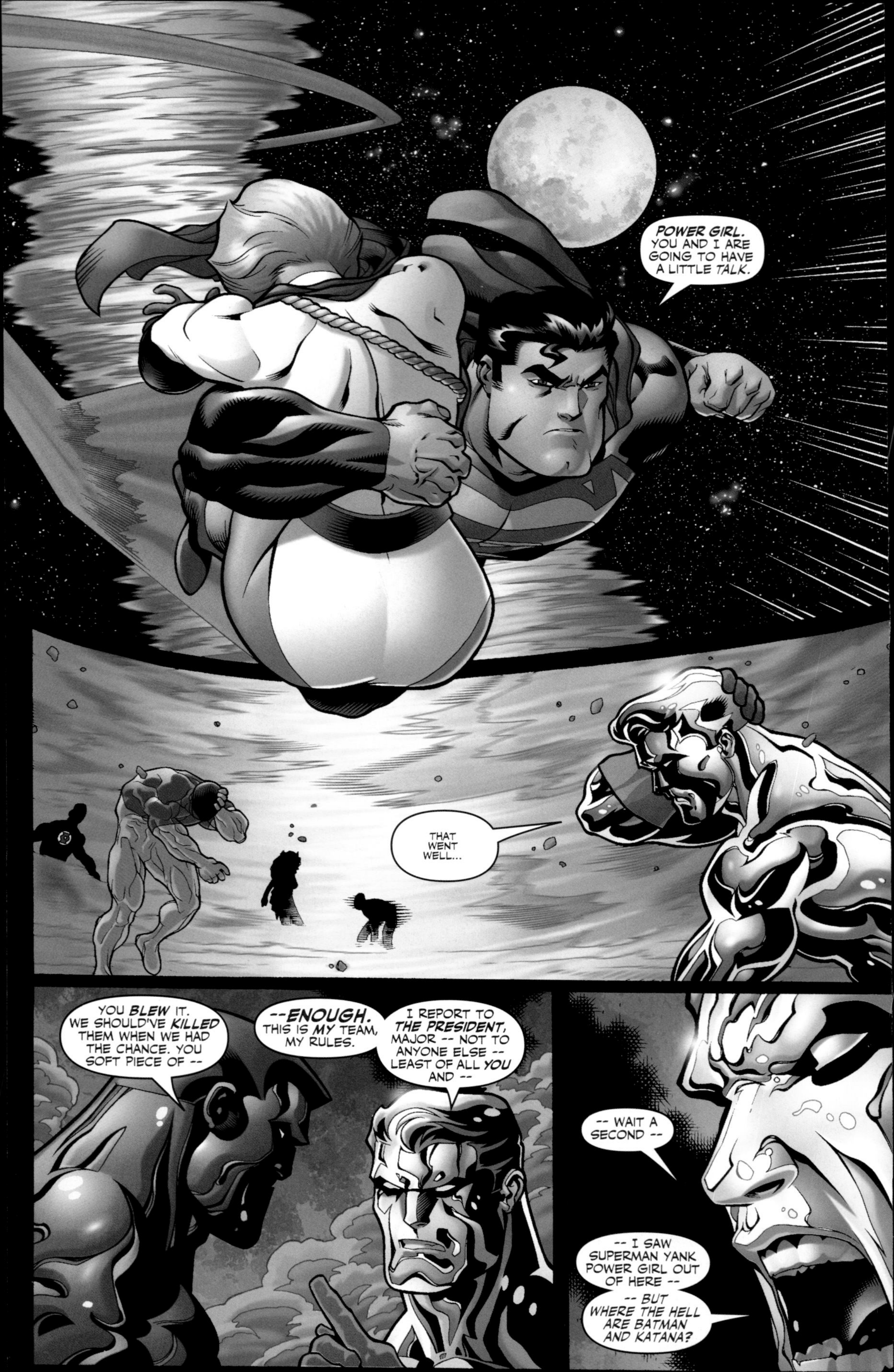
POWER GIRL. YOU AND I ARE GOING TO HAVE A LITTLE TALK.
THAT WENT WELL...
YOU BLEW IT. WE SHOULD'VE KILLED THEM WHEN WE HAD THE CHANCE. YOU SOFT PIECE OF --
--ENOUGH. THIS IS MY TEAM, MY RULES.
I REPORT TO THE PRESIDENT, MAJOR -- NOT TO ANYONE ELSE -- LEAST OF ALL YOU AND --
-- WAIT A SECOND --
-- I SAW SUPERMAN YANK POWER GIRL OUT OF HERE --
-- BUT WHERE THE HELL ARE BATMAN AND KATANA?

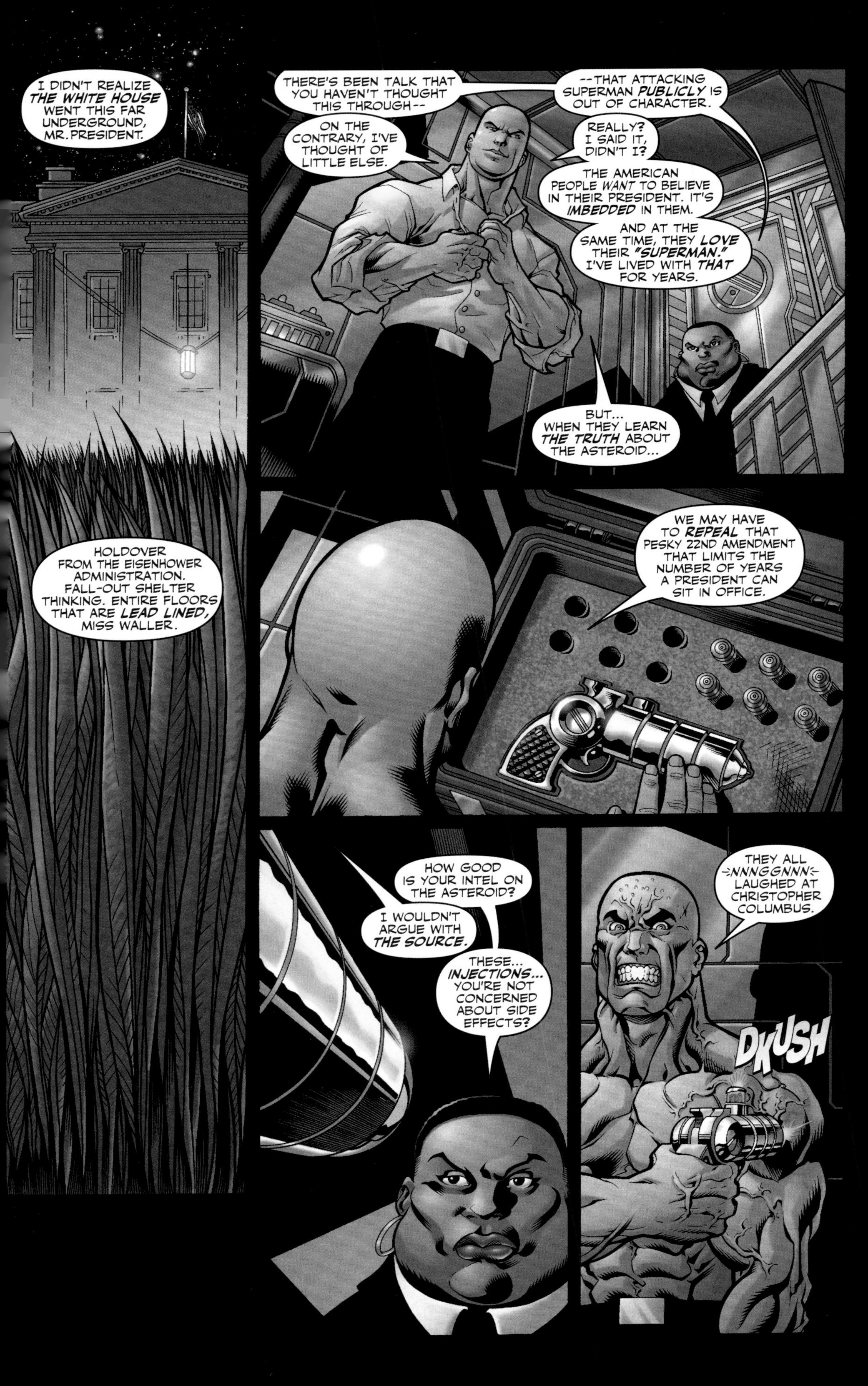
I DIDN'T REALIZE THE WHITE HOUSE WENT THIS FAR UNDERGROUND, MR. PRESIDENT.
HOLDOVER FROM THE EISENHOWER ADMINISTRATION. FALL-OUT SHELTER THINKING. ENTIRE FLOORS THAT ARE LEAD LINED, MISS WALLER.
THERE'S BEEN TALK THAT YOU HAVEN'T THOUGHT THIS THROUGH--
--THAT ATTACKING SUPERMAN PUBLICLY IS OUT OF CHARACTER.
ON THE CONTRARY, I'VE THOUGHT OF LITTLE ELSE.
REALLY? I SAID IT, DIDN'T I?
THE AMERICAN PEOPLE WANT TO BELIEVE IN THEIR PRESIDENT. IT'S IMBEDDED IN THEM.
AND AT THE SAME TIME, THEY LOVE THEIR "SUPERMAN." I'VE LIVED WITH THAT FOR YEARS.
BUT... WHEN THEY LEARN THE TRUTH ABOUT THE ASTEROID...
WE MAY HAVE TO REPEAL THAT PESKY 22ND AMENDMENT THAT LIMITS THE NUMBER OF YEARS A PRESIDENT CAN SIT IN OFFICE.
HOW GOOD IS YOUR INTEL ON THE ASTEROID?
I WOULDN'T ARGUE WITH THE SOURCE.
THESE... INJECTIONS... YOU'RE NOT CONCERNED ABOUT SIDE EFFECTS?
THEY ALL -NNNGGNNN- LAUGHED AT CHRISTOPHER COLUMBUS.
DKUSH

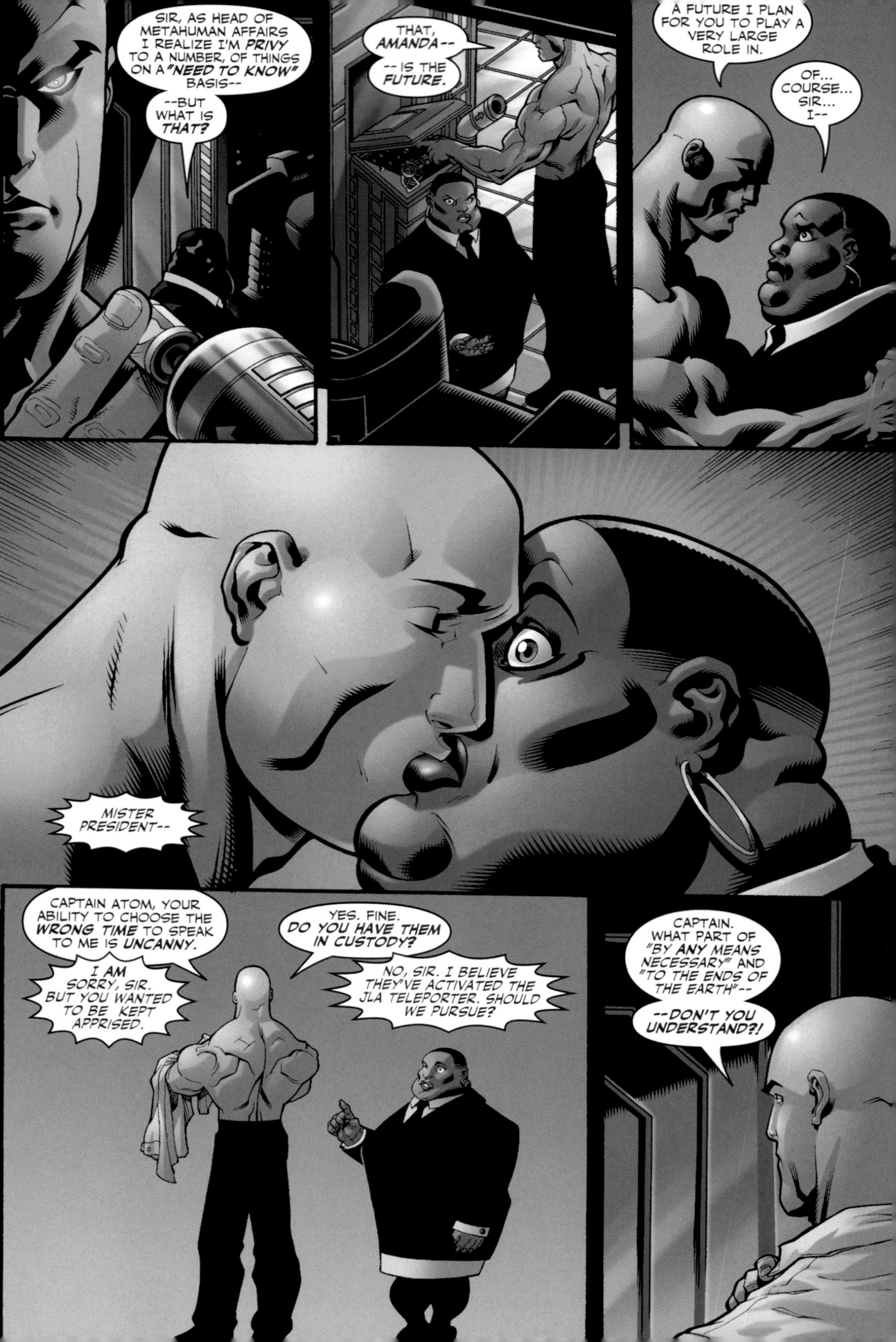
SIR, AS HEAD OF METAHUMAN AFFAIRS I REALIZE I'M PRIVY TO A NUMBER, OF THINGS ON A "NEED TO KNOW" BASIS--
--BUT WHAT IS THAT?
THAT, AMANDA--
-- IS THE FUTURE.
A FUTURE I PLAN FOR YOU TO PLAY A VERY LARGE ROLE IN.
OF... COURSE... SIR... I--
MISTER PRESIDENT--
CAPTAIN ATOM, YOUR ABILITY TO CHOOSE THE WRONG TIME TO SPEAK TO ME IS UNCANNY.
I AM SORRY, SIR. BUT YOU WANTED TO BE KEPT APPRISED.
YES. FINE. DO YOU HAVE THEM IN CUSTODY?
NO, SIR. I BELIEVE THEY'VE ACTIVATED THE JLA TELEPORTER. SHOULD WE PURSUE?
CAPTAIN. WHAT PART OF "BY ANY MEANS NECESSARY" AND "TO THE ENDS OF THE EARTH"--
--DON'T YOU UNDERSTAND?!

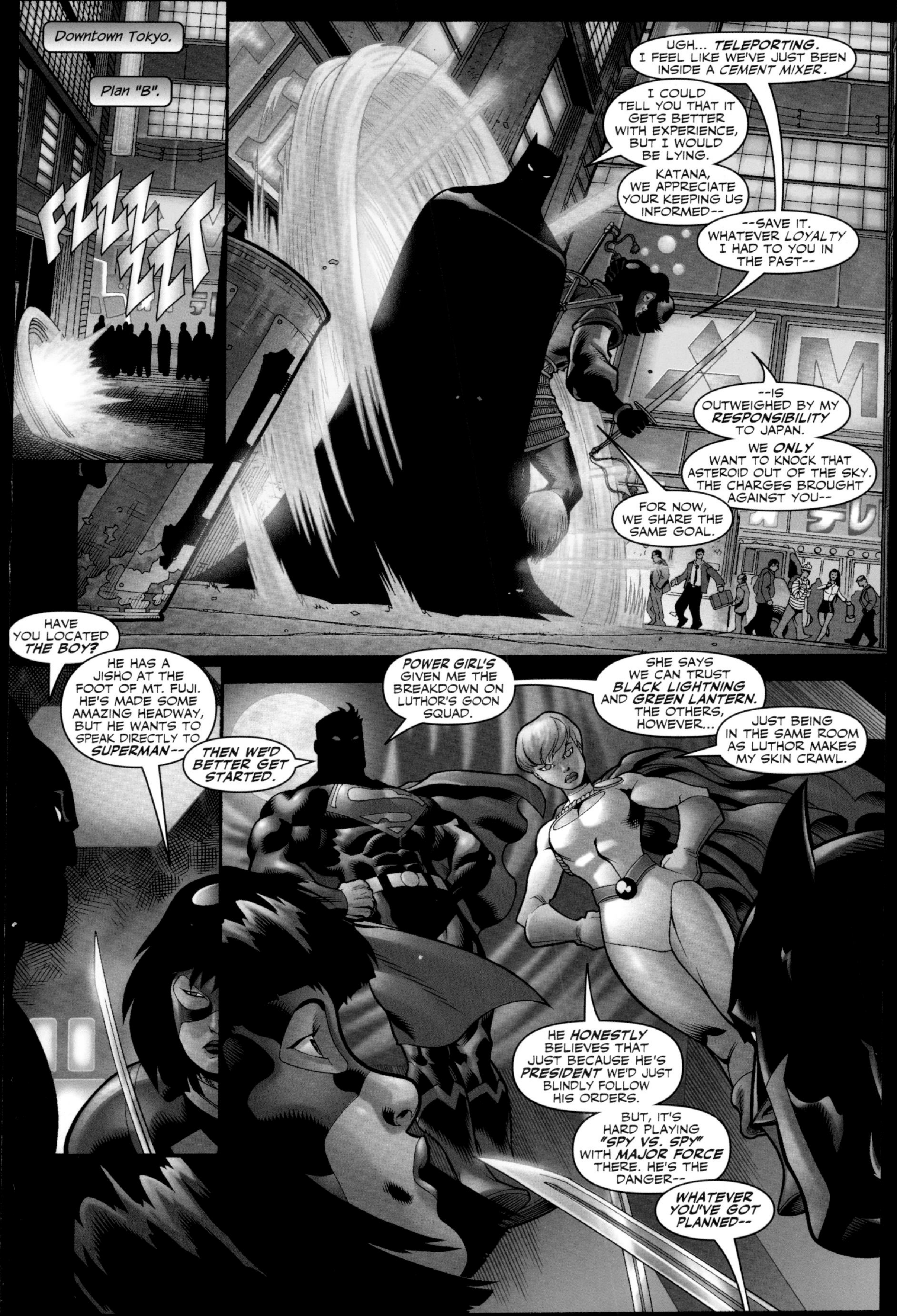

Downtown Tokyo.
Plan "B".
FZZZ
ZZZT
UGH... TELEPORTING. I FEEL LIKE WE'VE JUST BEEN INSIDE A CEMENT MIXER.
I COULD TELL YOU THAT IT GETS BETTER WITH EXPERIENCE, BUT I WOULD BE LYING.
KATANA, WE APPRECIATE YOUR KEEPING US INFORMED--
--SAVE IT. WHATEVER LOYALTY I HAD TO YOU IN THE PAST--
--IS OUTWEIGHED BY MY RESPONSIBILITY TO JAPAN.
WE ONLY WANT TO KNOCK THAT ASTEROID OUT OF THE SKY. THE CHARGES BROUGHT AGAINST YOU--
FOR NOW, WE SHARE THE SAME GOAL.
HAVE YOU LOCATED THE BOY?
HE HAS A JISHO AT THE FOOT OF MT. FUJI. HE'S MADE SOME AMAZING HEADWAY, BUT HE WANTS TO SPEAK DIRECTLY TO SUPERMAN--
THEN WE'D BETTER GET STARTED.
POWER GIRL'S GIVEN ME THE BREAKDOWN ON LUTHOR'S GOON SQUAD.
SHE SAYS WE CAN TRUST BLACK LIGHTNING AND GREEN LANTERN. THE OTHERS, HOWEVER...
JUST BEING IN THE SAME ROOM AS LUTHOR MAKES MY SKIN CRAWL.
HE HONESTLY BELIEVES THAT JUST BECAUSE HE'S PRESIDENT WE'D JUST BLINDLY FOLLOW HIS ORDERS.
BUT, IT'S HARD PLAYING "SPY VS. SPY" WITH MAJOR FORCE THERE. HE'S THE DANGER--
WHATEVER YOU'VE GOT PLANNED--

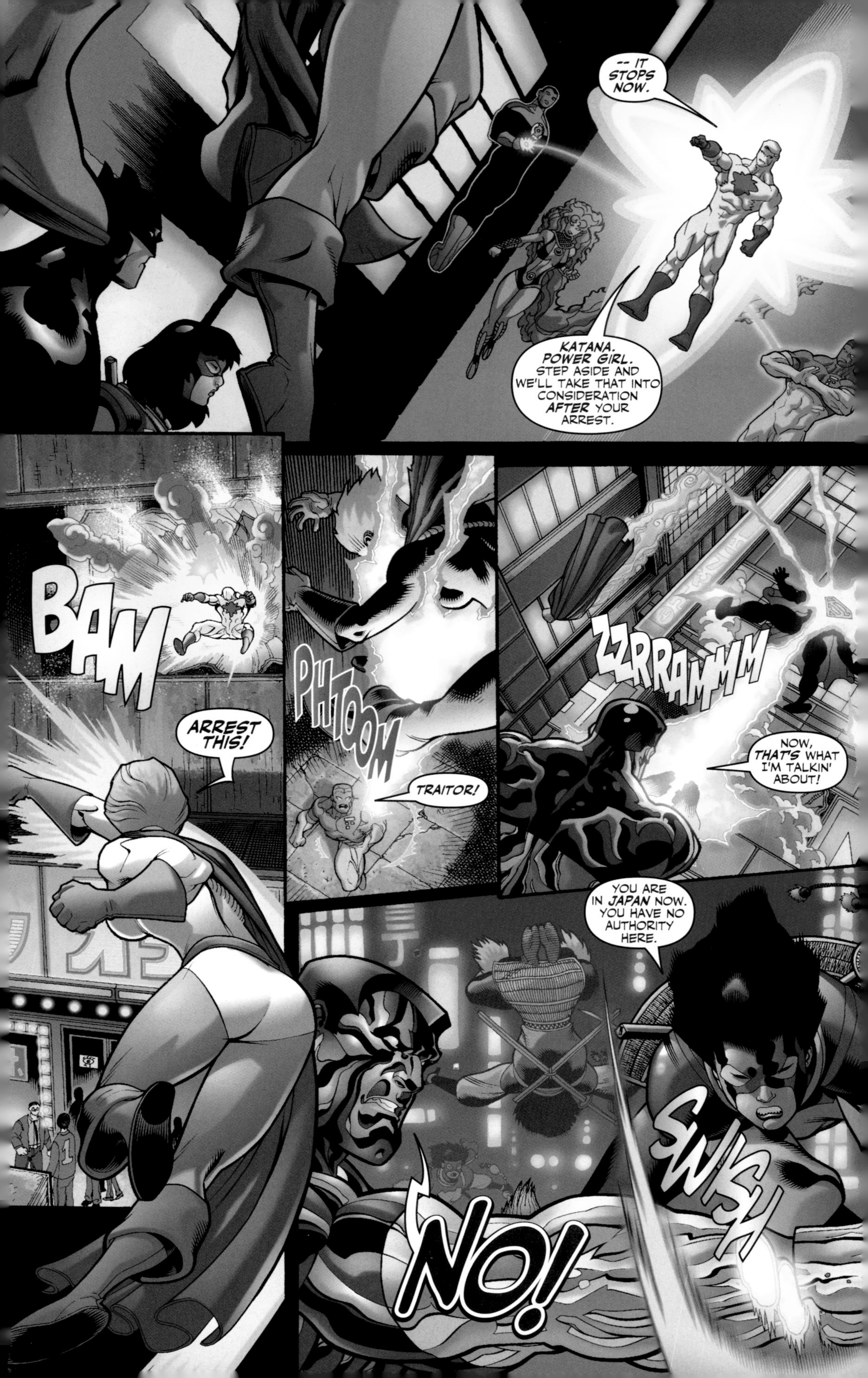
-- IT STOPS NOW.
KATANA. POWER GIRL. STEP ASIDE AND WE'LL TAKE THAT INTO CONSIDERATION AFTER YOUR ARREST.
BAM
ARREST THIS!
PHTOOM
TRAITOR!
ZZRRAMMMM
NOW, THAT'S WHAT I'M TALKIN' ABOUT!
YOU ARE IN JAPAN NOW. YOU HAVE NO AUTHORITY HERE.
SWISH
NO!

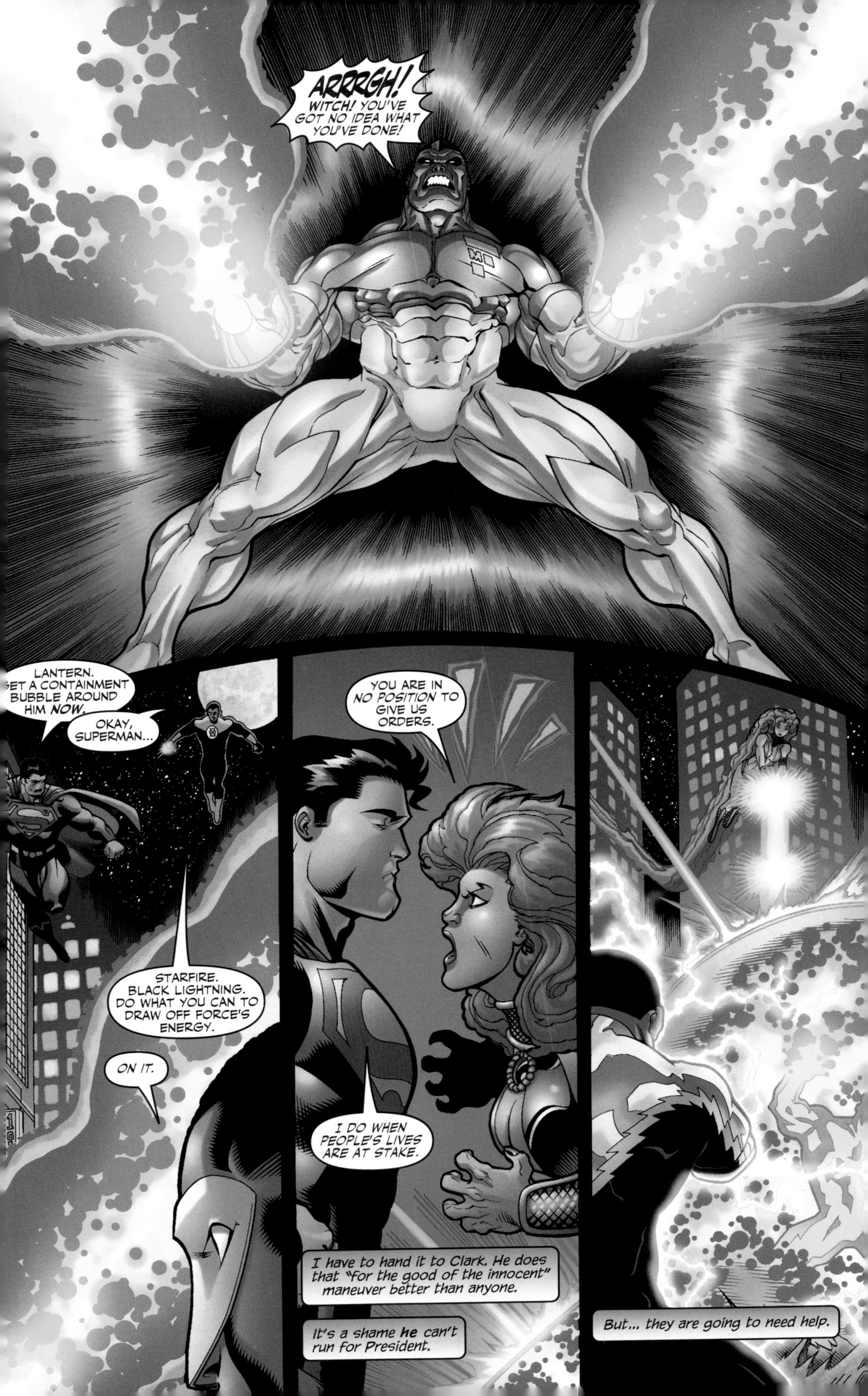
ARRRGH! WITCH! YOU'VE GOT NO IDEA WHAT YOU'VE DONE!
LANTERN. GET A CONTAINMENT BUBBLE AROUND HIM NOW.
OKAY, SUPERMAN...
STARFIRE. BLACK LIGHTNING. DO WHAT YOU CAN TO DRAW OFF FORCE'S ENERGY.
ON IT.
YOU ARE IN NO POSITION TO GIVE US ORDERS.
I DO WHEN PEOPLE'S LIVES ARE AT STAKE.
I have to hand it to Clark. He does that "for the good of the innocent" maneuver better than anyone.
It's a shame he can't run for President.
But... they are going to need help.

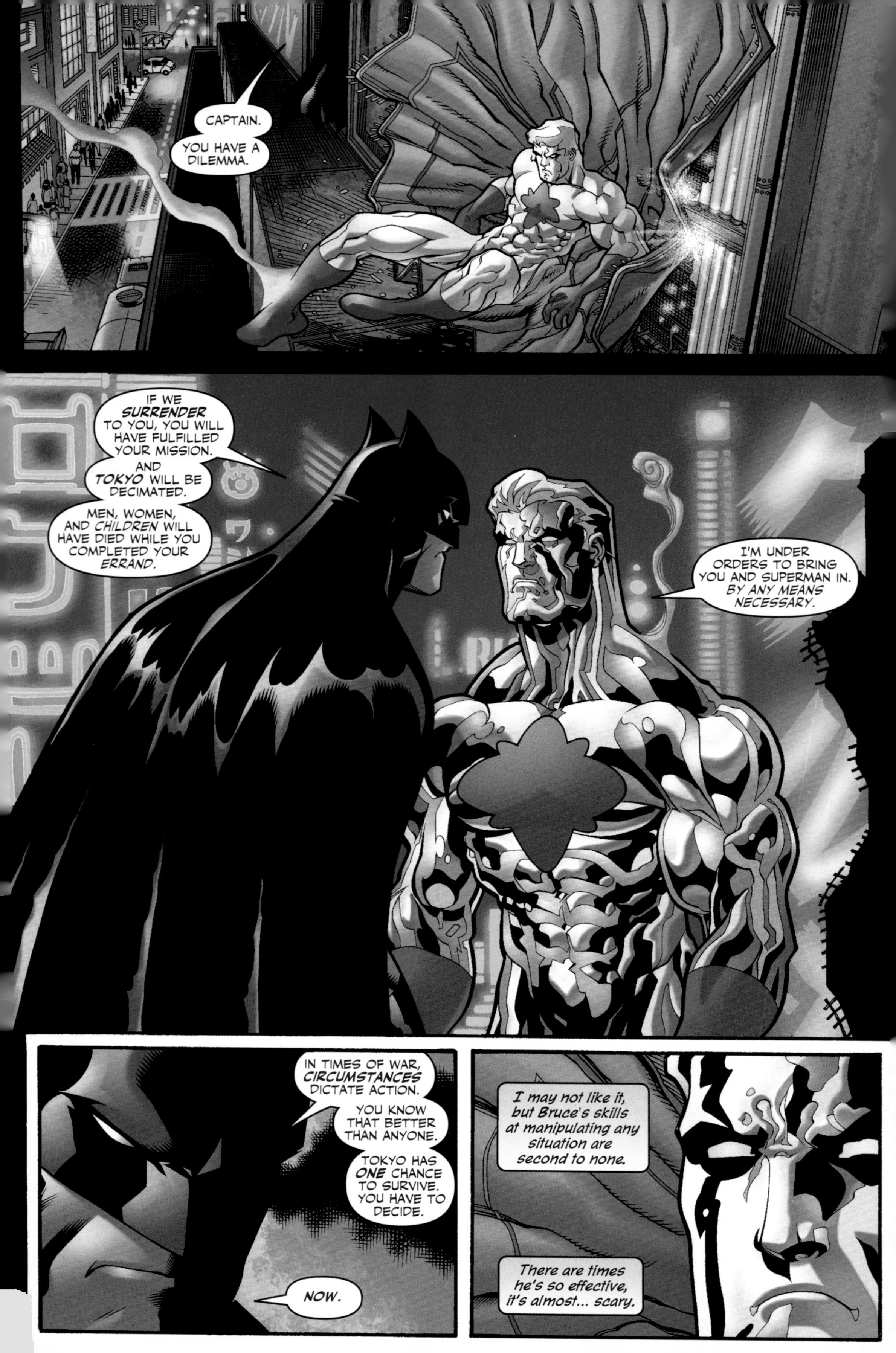
CAPTAIN.
YOU HAVE A DILEMMA.
IF WE SURRENDER TO YOU, YOU WILL HAVE FULFILLED YOUR MISSION.
AND TOKYO WILL BE DECIMATED.
MEN, WOMEN, AND CHILDREN WILL HAVE DIED WHILE YOU COMPLETED YOUR ERRAND.
I'M UNDER ORDERS TO BRING YOU AND SUPERMAN IN. BY ANY MEANS NECESSARY.
IN TIMES OF WAR, CIRCUMSTANCES DICTATE ACTION.
YOU KNOW THAT BETTER THAN ANYONE.
TOKYO HAS ONE CHANCE TO SURVIVE. YOU HAVE TO DECIDE.
NOW.
I may not like it, but Bruce's skills at manipulating any situation are second to none.
There are times he's so effective, it's almost... scary.

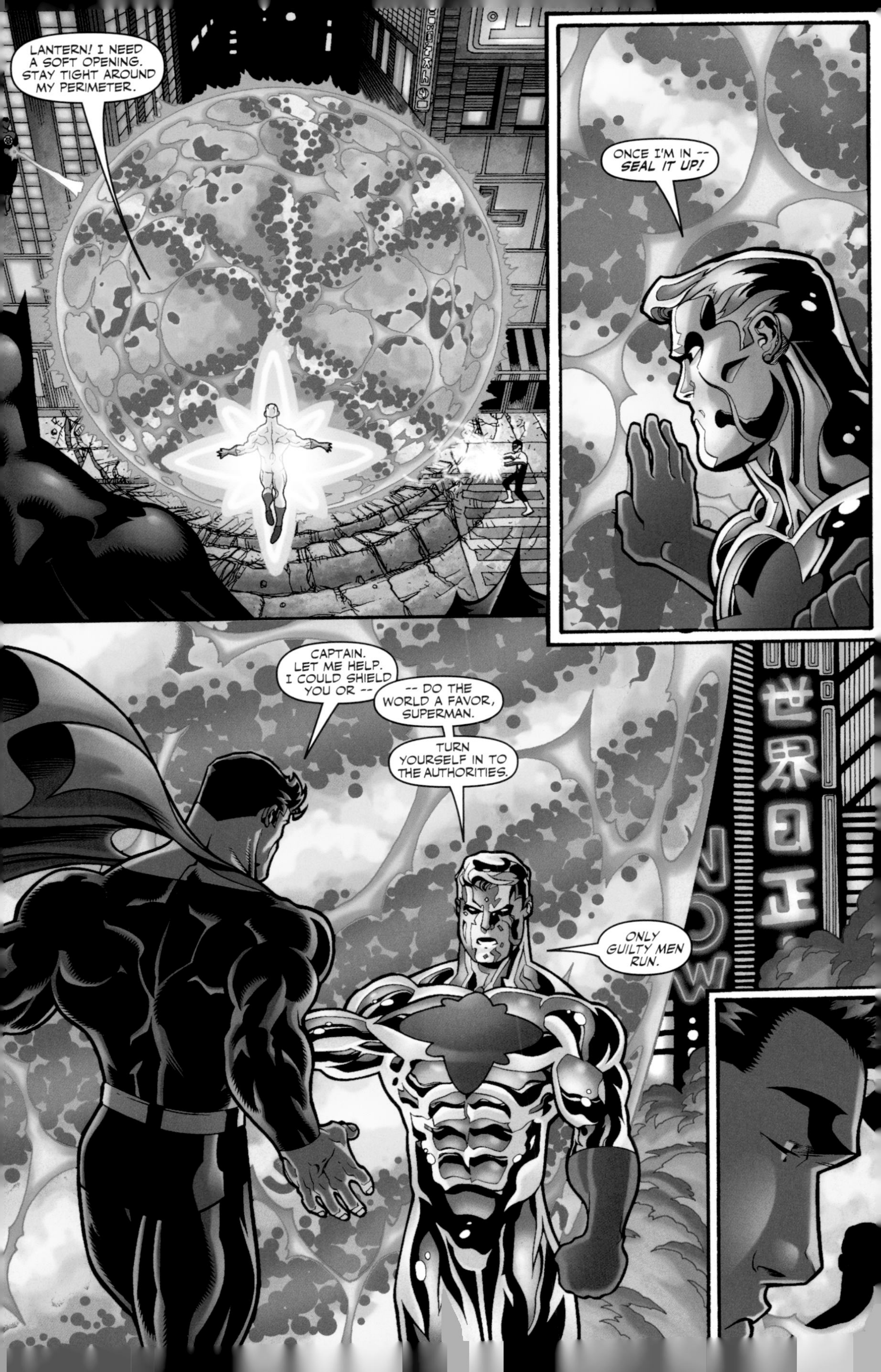
LANTERN! I NEED A SOFT OPENING. STAY TIGHT AROUND MY PERIMETER.
ONCE I'M IN -- SEAL IT UP!
CAPTAIN. LET ME HELP. I COULD SHIELD YOU OR --
-- DO THE WORLD A FAVOR, SUPERMAN.
TURN YOURSELF IN TO THE AUTHORITIES.
ONLY GUILTY MEN RUN.

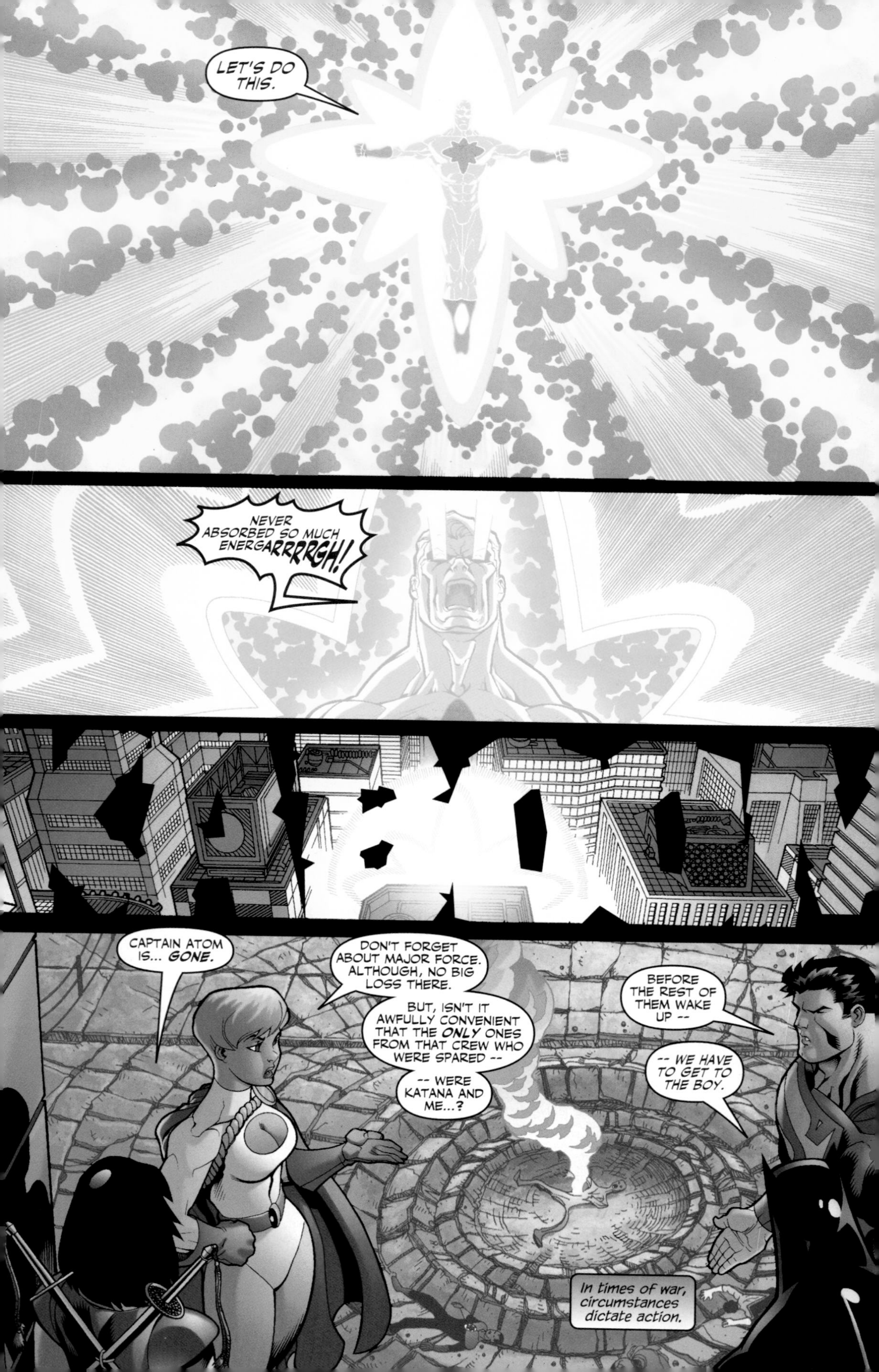
LET'S DO THIS.
NEVER ABSORBED SO MUCH ENERGARRRRGH!
CAPTAIN ATOM IS... GONE.
DON'T FORGET ABOUT MAJOR FORCE. ALTHOUGH, NO BIG LOSS THERE.
BUT, ISN'T IT AWFULLY CONVENIENT THAT THE ONLY ONES FROM THAT CREW WHO WERE SPARED --
-- WERE KATANA AND ME...?
BEFORE THE REST OF THEM WAKE UP --
-- WE HAVE TO GET TO THE BOY.
In times of war, circumstances dictate action.

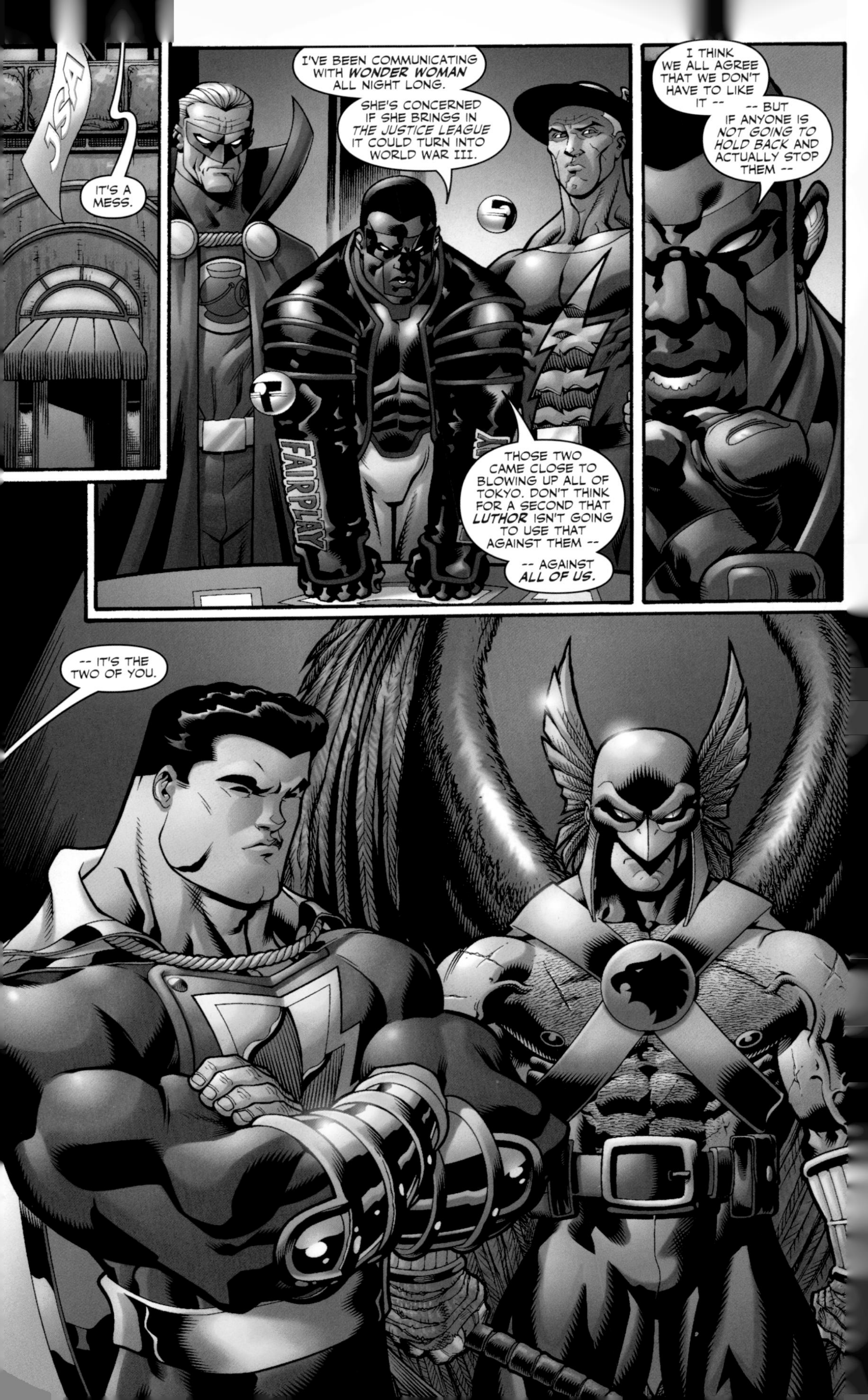
IT'S A MESS.
I'VE BEEN COMMUNICATING WITH WONDER WOMAN ALL NIGHT LONG.
SHE'S CONCERNED IF SHE BRINGS IN THE JUSTICE LEAGUE IT COULD TURN INTO WORLD WAR III.
THOSE TWO CAME CLOSE TO BLOWING UP ALL OF TOKYO. DON'T THINK FOR A SECOND THAT LUTHOR ISN'T GOING TO USE THAT AGAINST THEM --
-- AGAINST ALL OF US.
I THINK WE ALL AGREE THAT WE DON'T HAVE TO LIKE IT --
-- BUT IF ANYONE IS NOT GOING TO HOLD BACK AND ACTUALLY STOP THEM --
-- IT'S THE TWO OF YOU.

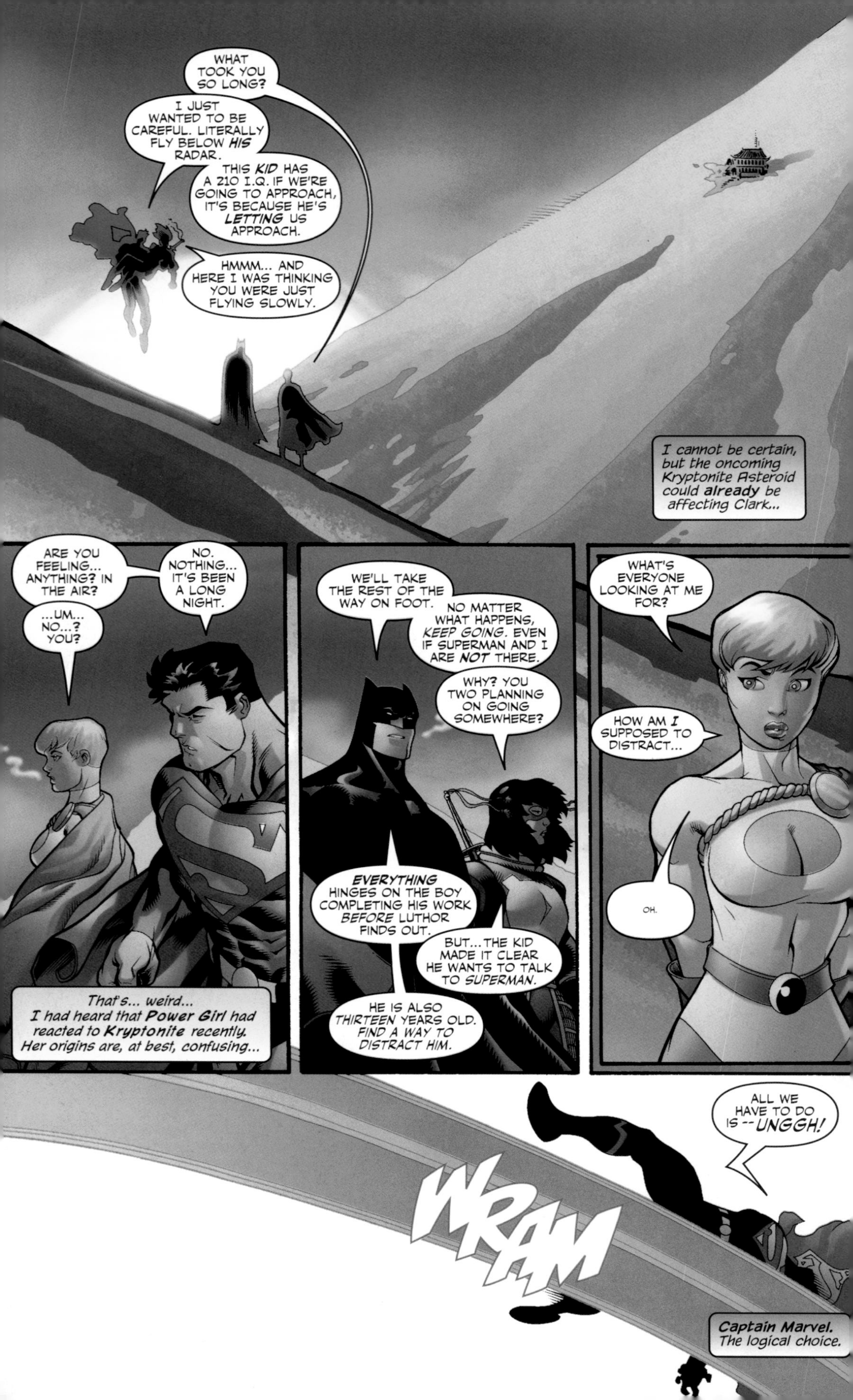
WHAT TOOK YOU SO LONG?
I JUST WANTED TO BE CAREFUL. LITERALLY FLY BELOW HIS RADAR.
THIS KID HAS A 210 I.Q. IF WE'RE GOING TO APPROACH, IT'S BECAUSE HE'S LETTING US APPROACH.
HMMM... AND HERE I WAS THINKING YOU WERE JUST FLYING SLOWLY.
I cannot be certain, but the oncoming Kryptonite Asteroid could already be affecting Clark...
ARE YOU FEELING... ANYTHING? IN THE AIR?
NO. NOTHING... IT'S BEEN A LONG NIGHT.
...UM... NO...? YOU?
That's... weird... I had heard that Power Girl had reacted to Kryptonite recently. Her origins are, at best, confusing...
WE'LL TAKE THE REST OF THE WAY ON FOOT.
NO MATTER WHAT HAPPENS, KEEP GOING. EVEN IF SUPERMAN AND I ARE NOT THERE.
WHY? YOU TWO PLANNING ON GOING SOMEWHERE?
EVERYTHING HINGES ON THE BOY COMPLETING HIS WORK BEFORE LUTHOR FINDS OUT.
BUT... THE KID MADE IT CLEAR HE WANTS TO TALK TO SUPERMAN.
HE IS ALSO THIRTEEN YEARS OLD. FIND A WAY TO DISTRACT HIM.
WHAT'S EVERYONE LOOKING AT ME FOR?
HOW AM I SUPPOSED TO DISTRACT...
OH.
ALL WE HAVE TO DO IS --UNGGH!
WRAM
Captain Marvel. The logical choice.

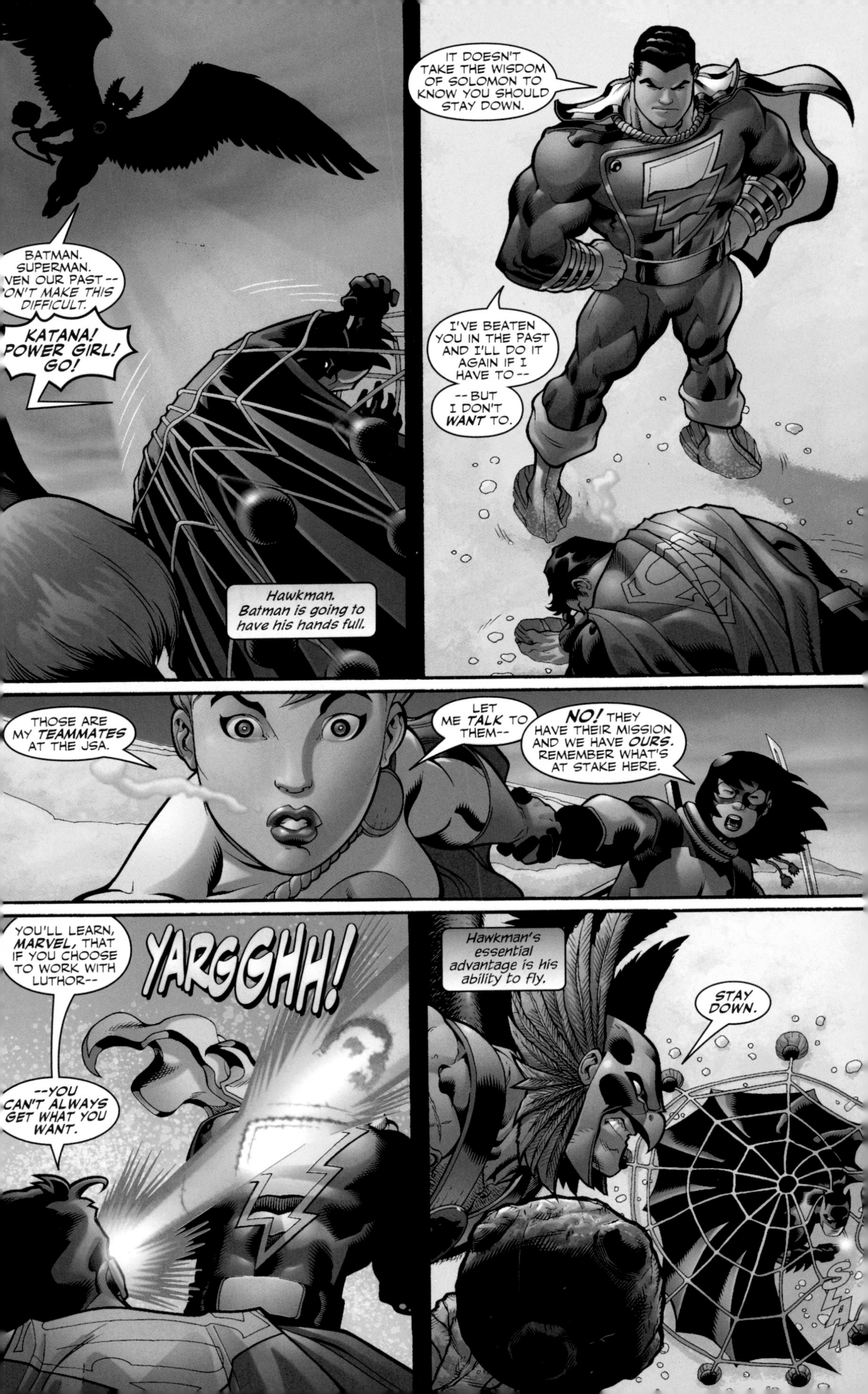
BATMAN. SUPERMAN. VEN OUR PAST-- ON'T MAKE THIS DIFFICULT.
KATANA! POWER GIRL! GO!
Hawkman. Batman is going to have his hands full.
IT DOESN'T TAKE THE WISDOM OF SOLOMON TO KNOW YOU SHOULD STAY DOWN.
I'VE BEATEN YOU IN THE PAST AND I'LL DO IT AGAIN IF I HAVE TO--
--BUT I DON'T WANT TO.
THOSE ARE MY TEAMMATES AT THE JSA.
LET ME TALK TO THEM--
NO! THEY HAVE THEIR MISSION AND WE HAVE OURS. REMEMBER WHAT'S AT STAKE HERE.
YOU'LL LEARN, MARVEL, THAT IF YOU CHOOSE TO WORK WITH LUTHOR--
YARGGHH!
--YOU CAN'T ALWAYS GET WHAT YOU WANT.
Hawkman's essential advantage is his ability to fly.
STAY DOWN.
SLAM

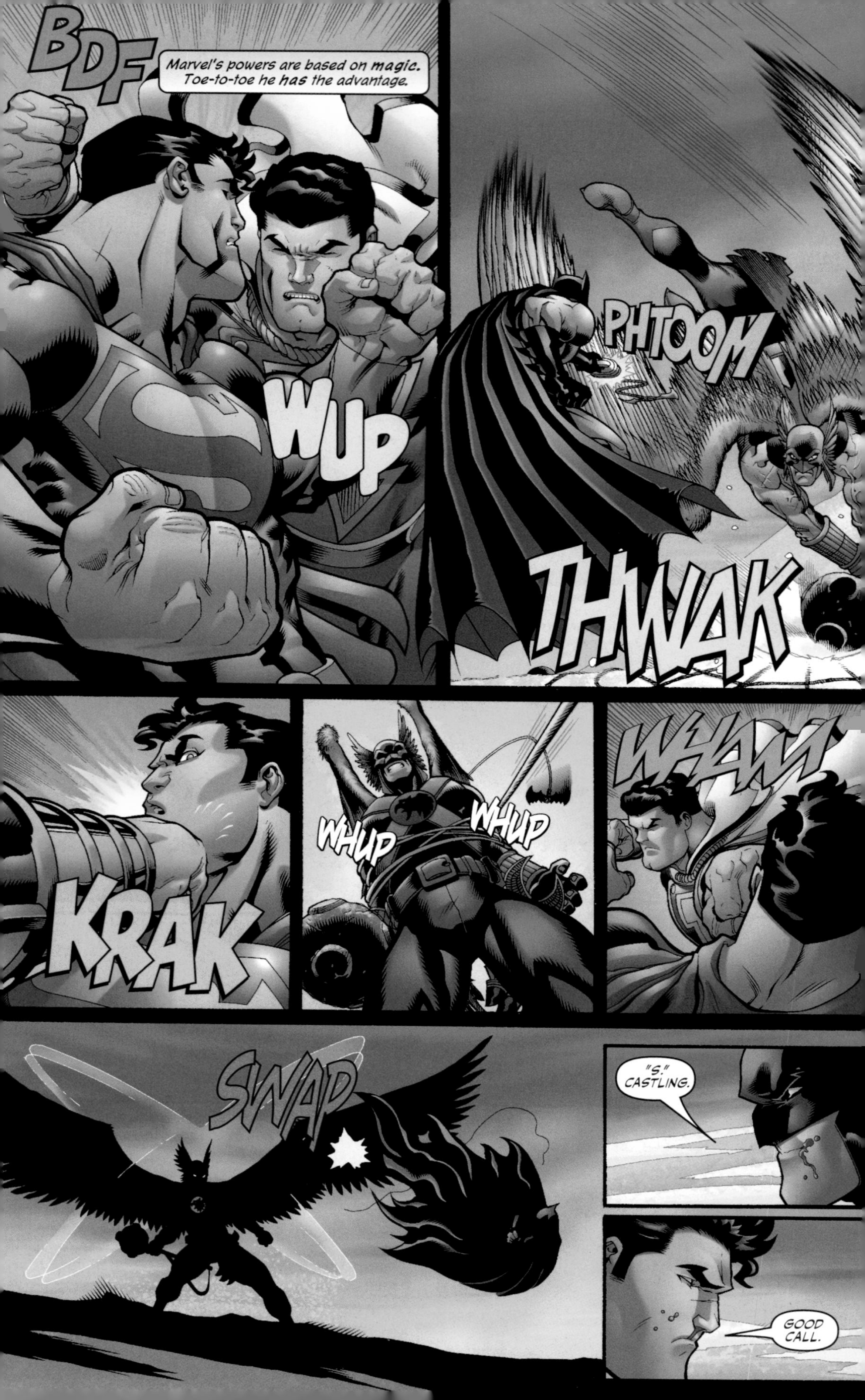
BDF
Marvel's powers are based on magic. Toe-to-toe he has the advantage.
WUP
PHTOOM
THWAK
KRAK
WHUP
WHUP
WHAM
SWAP
"S." CASTLING.
GOOD CALL.

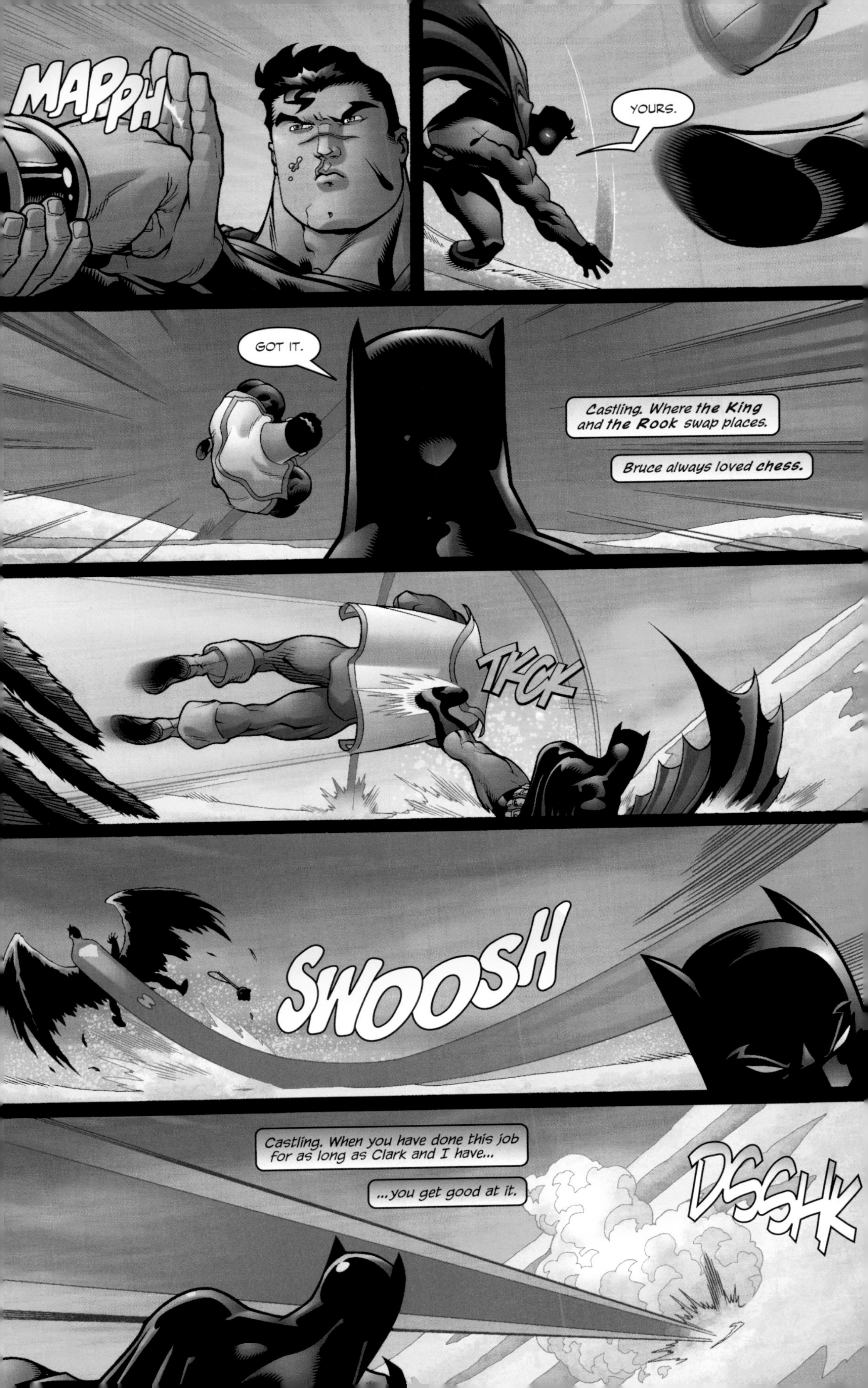
MAPPH
YOURS.
GOT IT.
Castling. Where the King and the Rook swap places.
Bruce always loved chess.
TKCK
SWOOSH
Castling. When you have done this job for as long as Clark and I have...
...you get good at it.
DSSHK

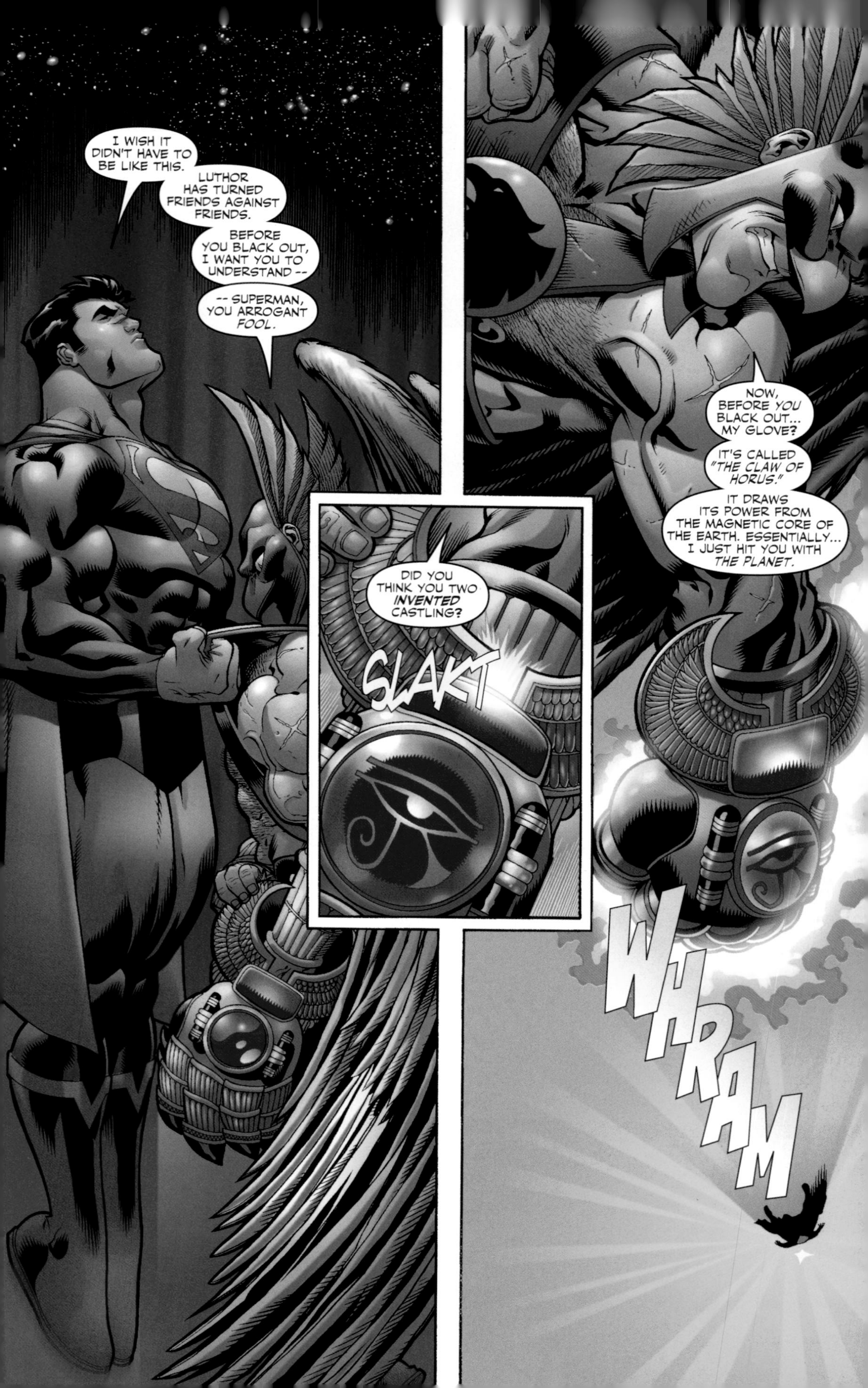
I WISH IT DIDN'T HAVE TO BE LIKE THIS.
LUTHOR HAS TURNED FRIENDS AGAINST FRIENDS.
BEFORE YOU BLACK OUT, I WANT YOU TO UNDERSTAND --
-- SUPERMAN, YOU ARROGANT *FOOL*.
DID YOU THINK YOU TWO ***INVENTED*** CASTLING?
SLAK!
NOW, BEFORE *YOU* BLACK OUT... MY GLOVE?
IT'S CALLED *"THE CLAW OF HORUS."*
IT DRAWS ITS POWER FROM THE MAGNETIC CORE OF THE EARTH. ESSENTIALLY... I JUST HIT YOU WITH *THE PLANET*.
WHRAM

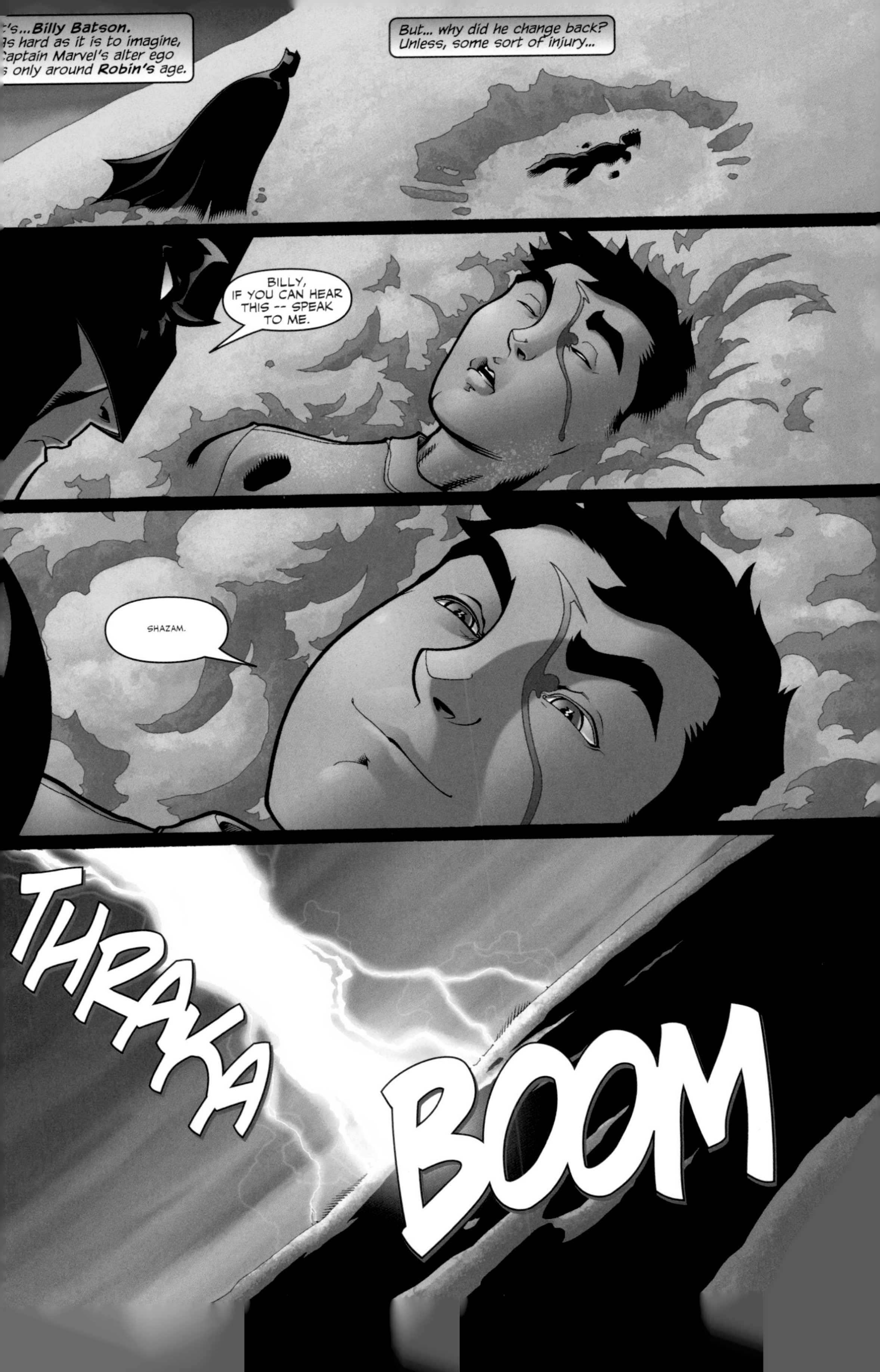
's...**Billy Batson.**
s hard as it is to imagine,
aptain Marvel's alter ego
s only around **Robin's** age.
But... why did he change back? Unless, some sort of injury...
BILLY, IF YOU CAN HEAR THIS -- SPEAK TO ME.
SHAZAM.
THRAKA
BOOM

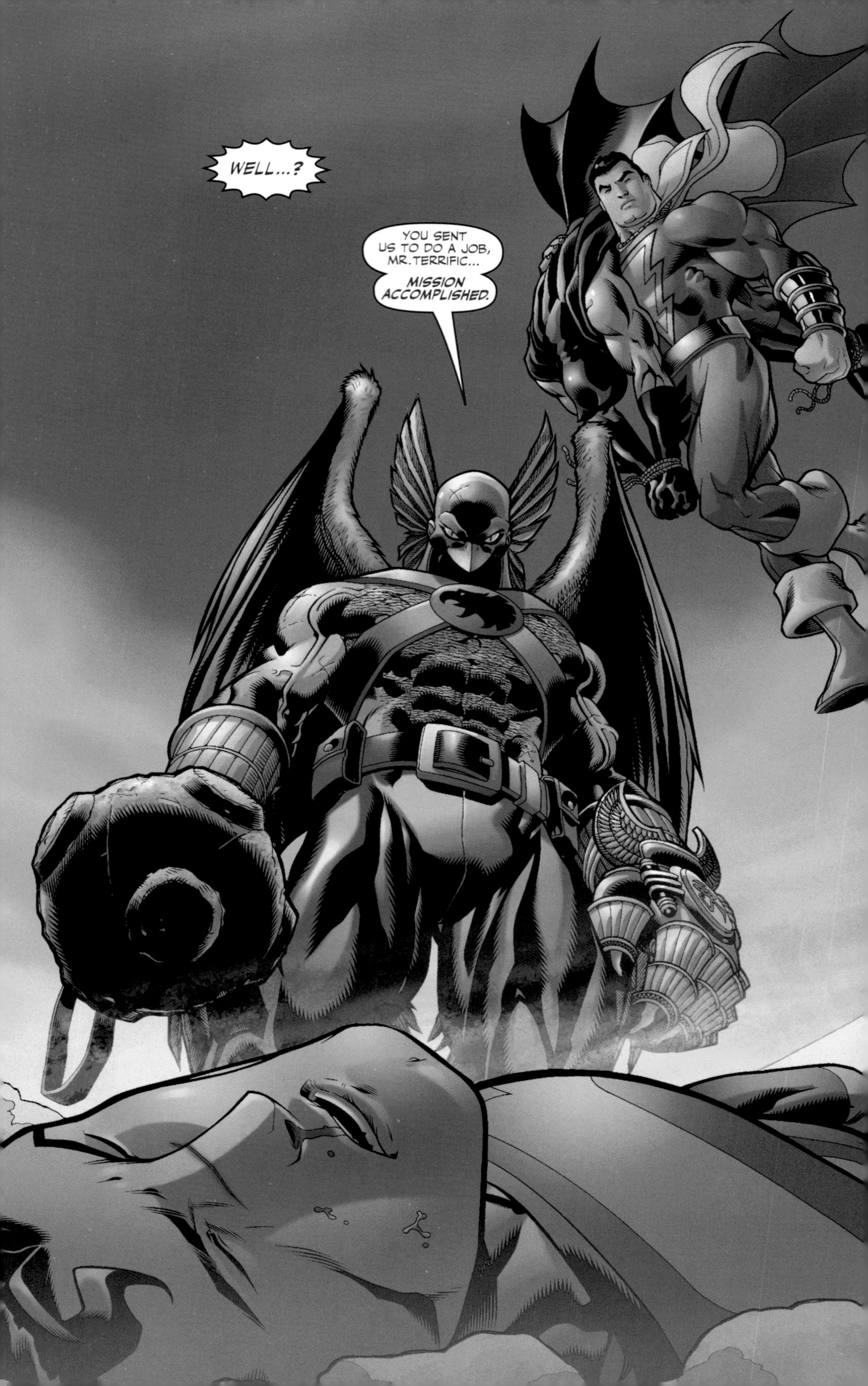
WELL...?
YOU SENT US TO DO A JOB, MR. TERRIFIC...
MISSION ACCOMPLISHED.

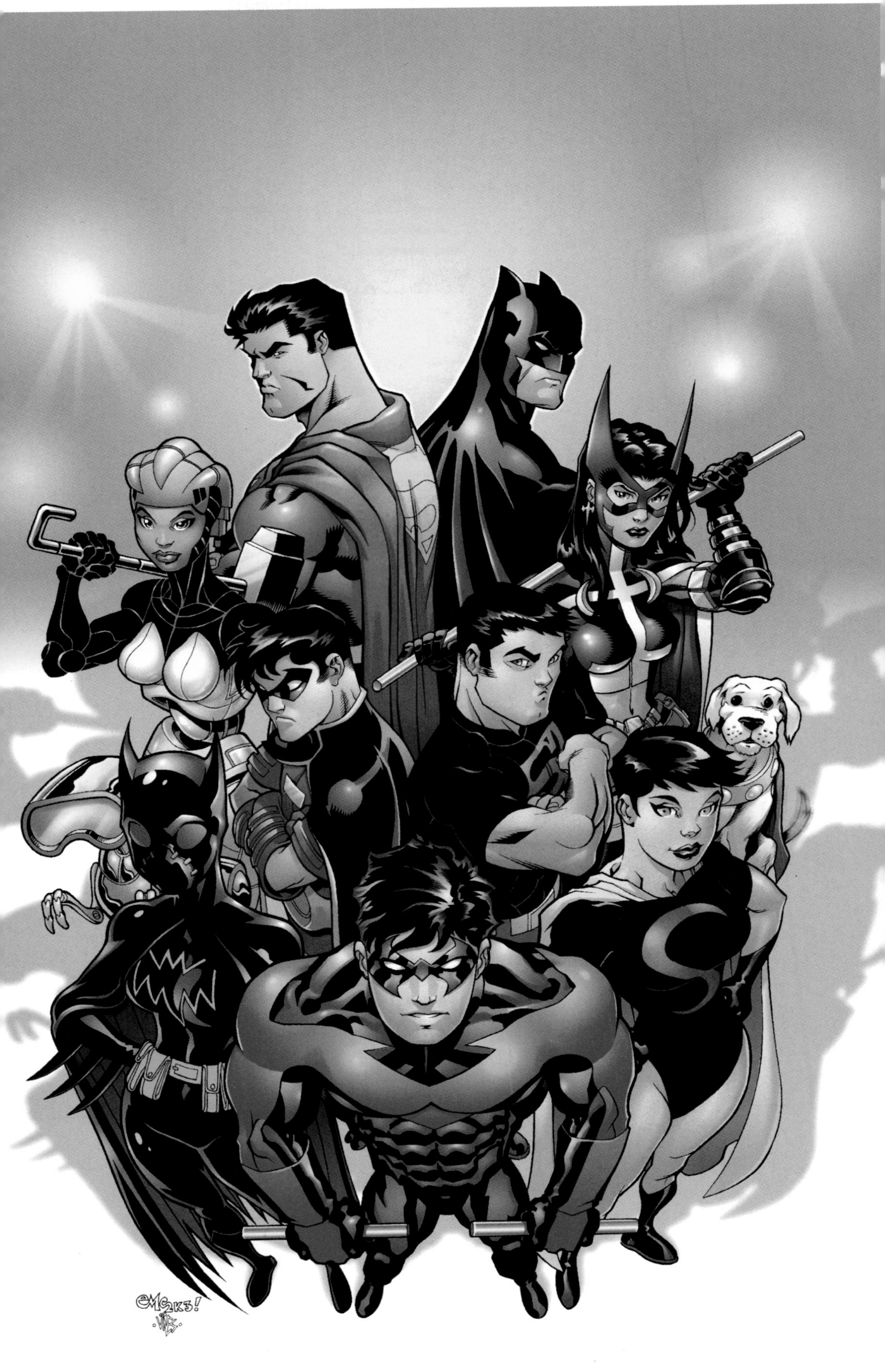

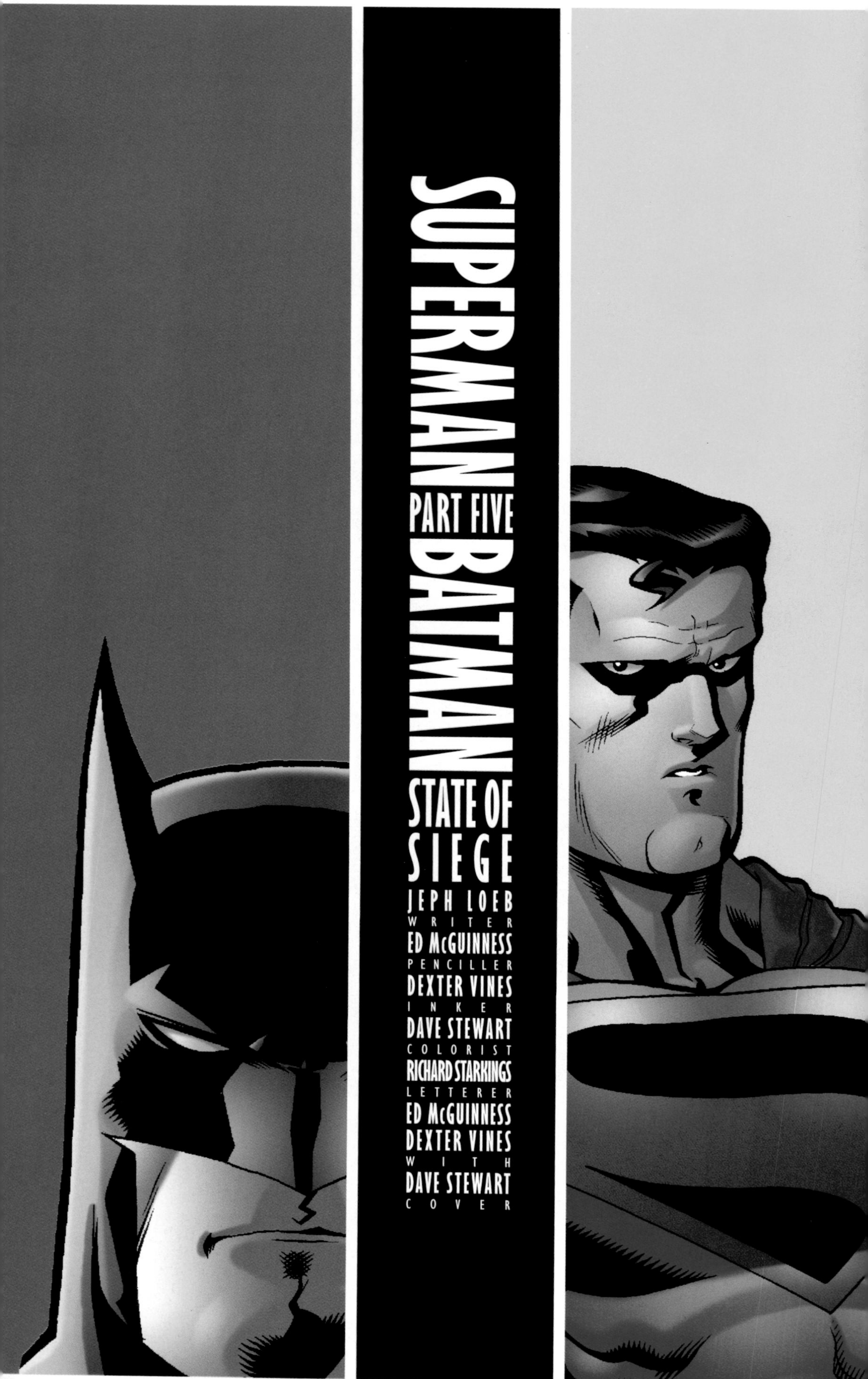
SUPERMAN
BATMAN
PART FIVE
STATE OF SIEGE
JEPH LOEB
WRITER
ED McGUINNESS
PENCILLER
DEXTER VINES
INKER
DAVE STEWART
COLORIST
RICHARD STARKINGS
LETTERER
ED McGUINNESS
DEXTER VINES
WITH
DAVE STEWART
COVER

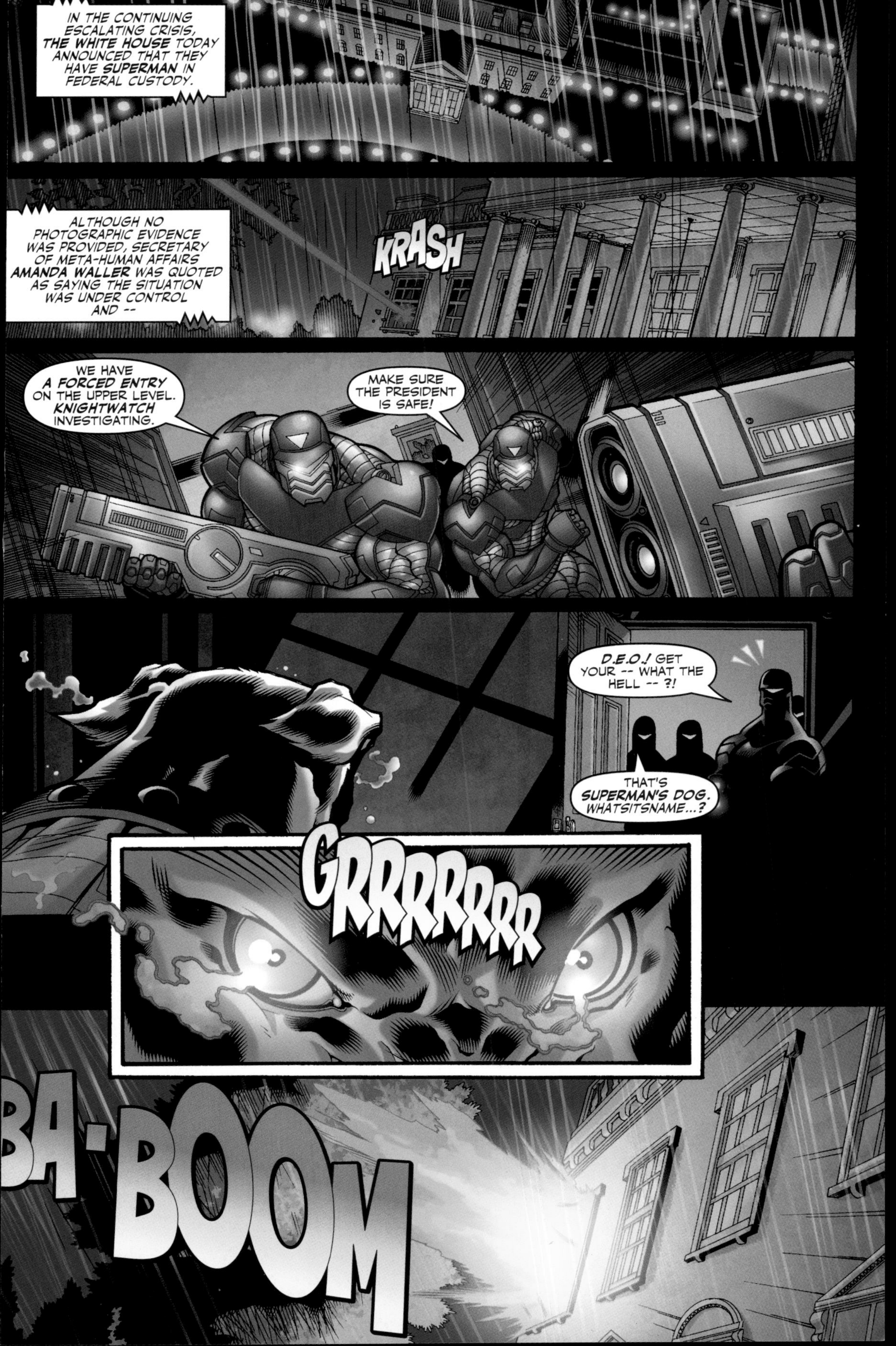
IN THE CONTINUING ESCALATING CRISIS, THE WHITE HOUSE TODAY ANNOUNCED THAT THEY HAVE SUPERMAN IN FEDERAL CUSTODY.
ALTHOUGH NO PHOTOGRAPHIC EVIDENCE WAS PROVIDED, SECRETARY OF META-HUMAN AFFAIRS AMANDA WALLER WAS QUOTED AS SAYING THE SITUATION WAS UNDER CONTROL AND --
KRASH
WE HAVE A FORCED ENTRY ON THE UPPER LEVEL. KNIGHTWATCH INVESTIGATING.
MAKE SURE THE PRESIDENT IS SAFE!
D.E.O.! GET YOUR -- WHAT THE HELL -- ?!
THAT'S SUPERMAN'S DOG. WHATSITSNAME...?
GRRRRRRR
BA-BOOM

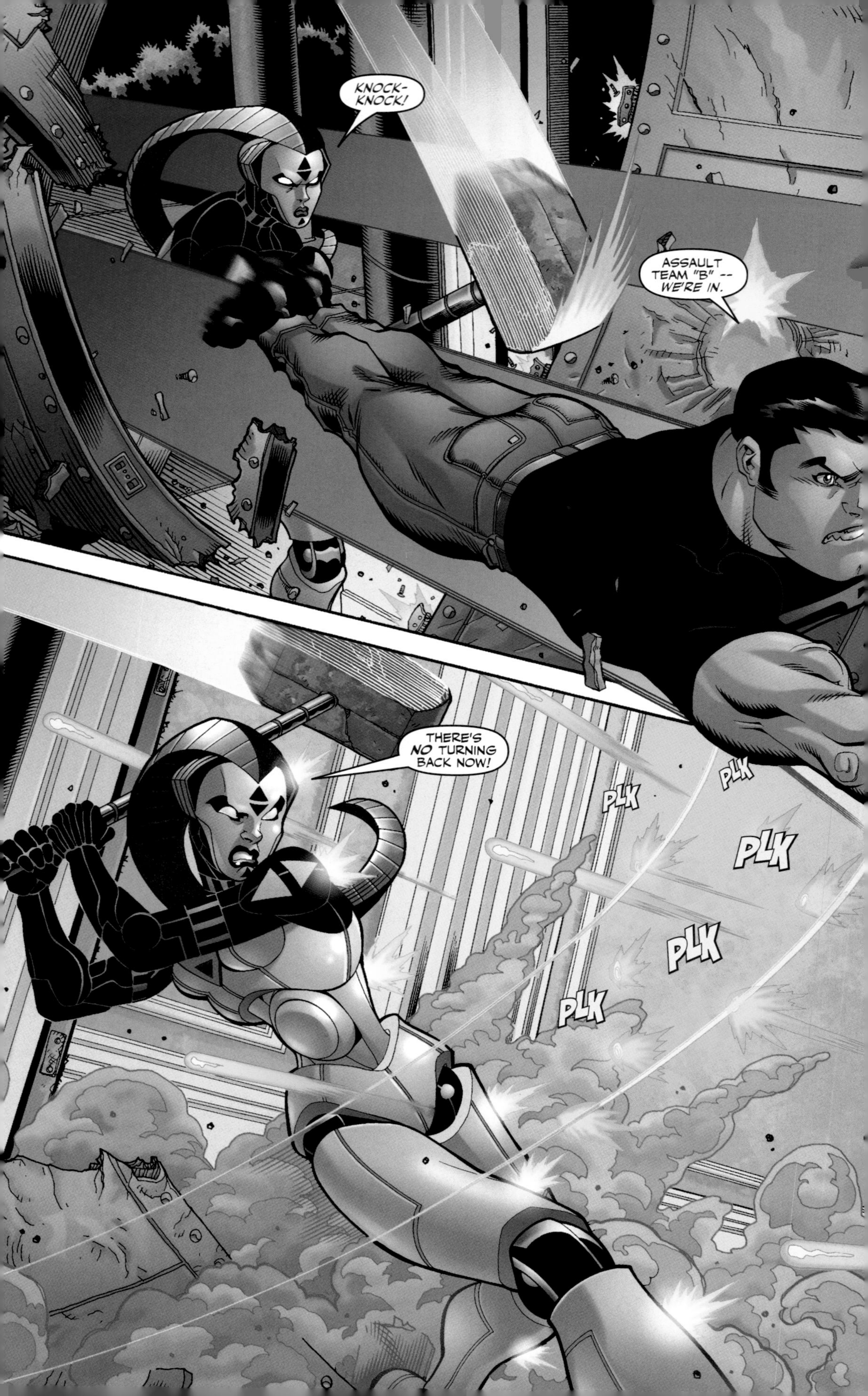
KNOCK-KNOCK!
ASSAULT TEAM "B" -- WE'RE IN.
THERE'S NO TURNING BACK NOW!
PLK
PLK
PLK
PLK
PLK

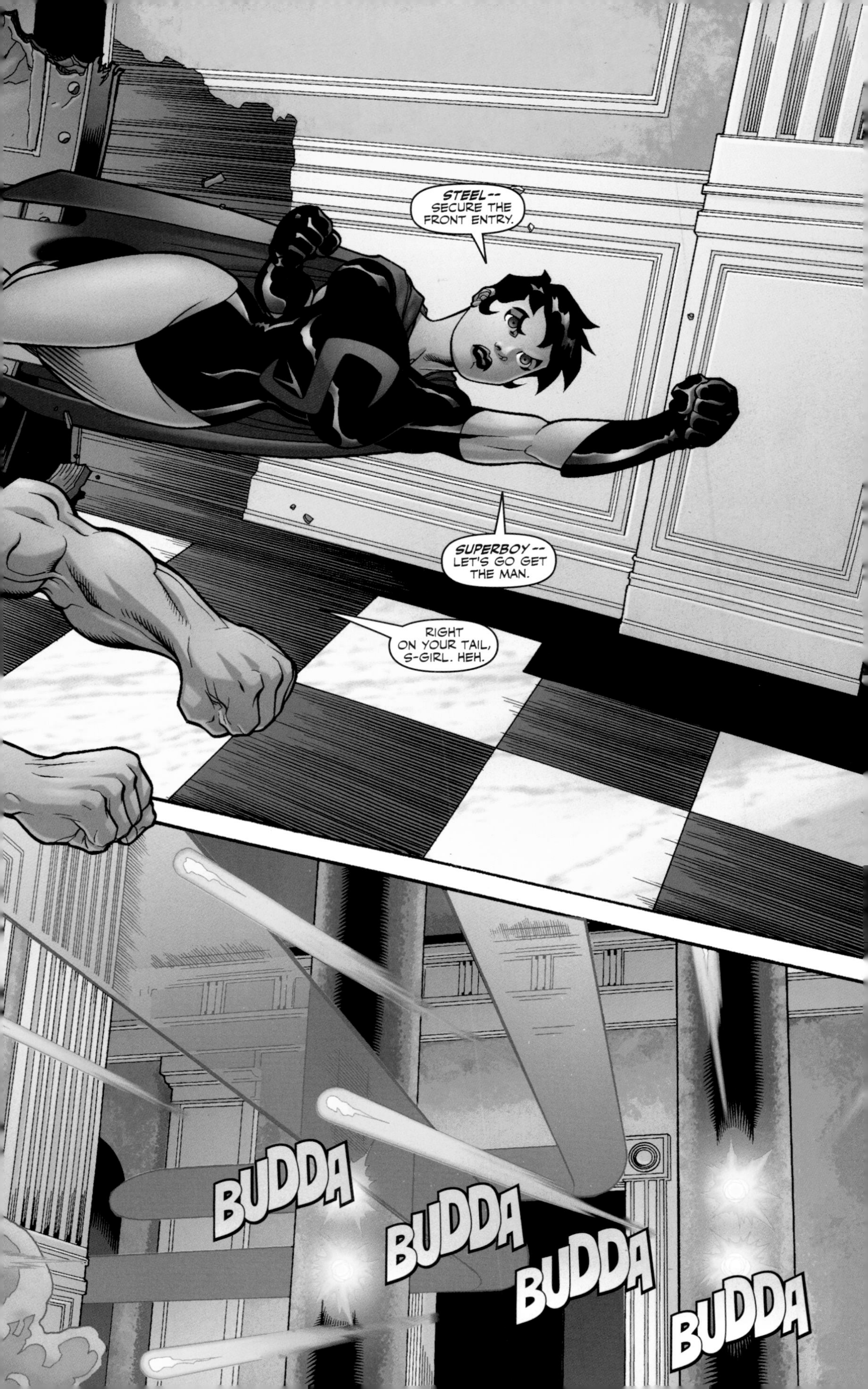
STEEL-- SECURE THE FRONT ENTRY.
SUPERBOY-- LET'S GO GET THE MAN.
RIGHT ON YOUR TAIL, S-GIRL. HEH.
BUDDA
BUDDA
BUDDA
BUDDA

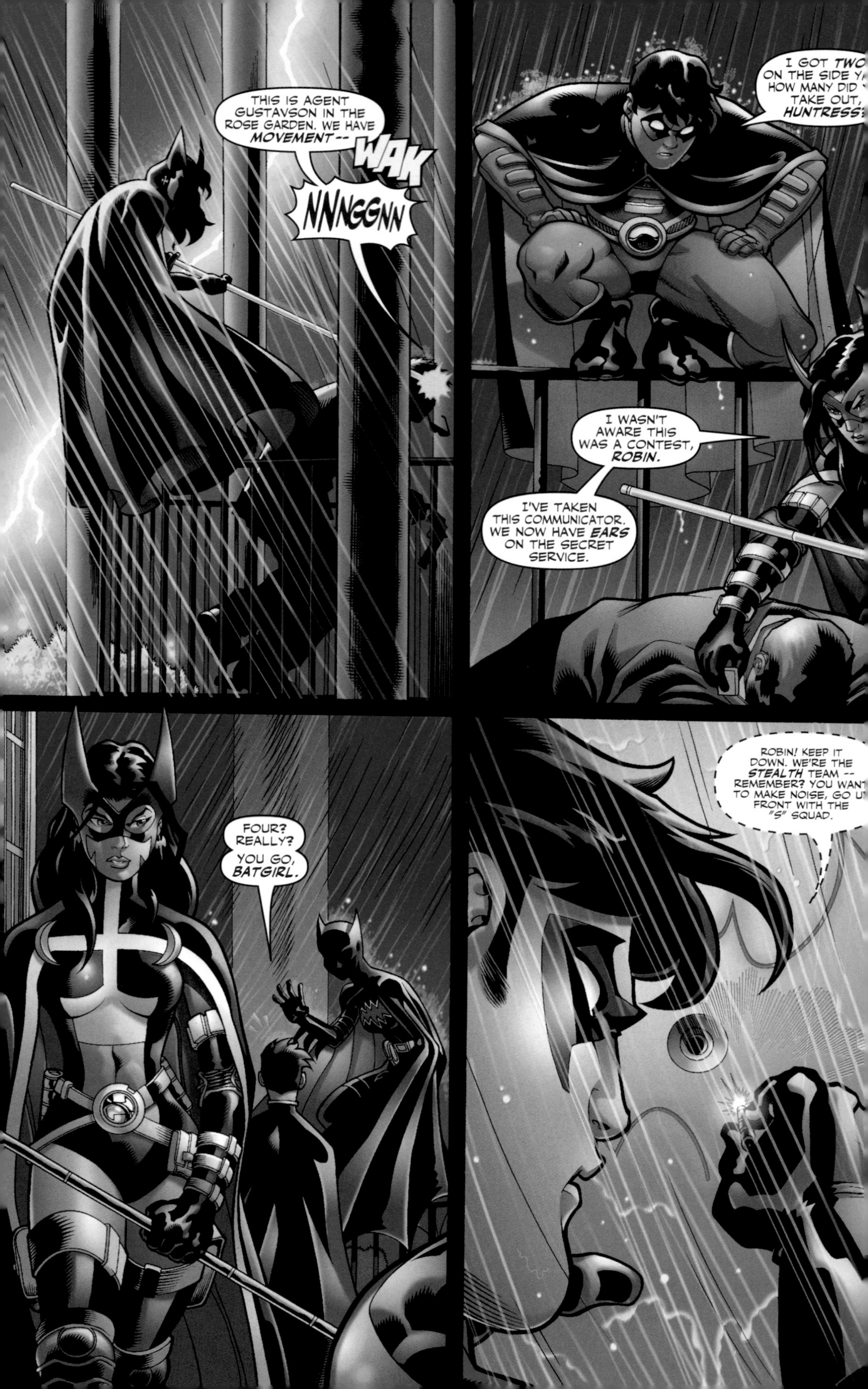

THIS IS AGENT GUSTAVSON IN THE ROSE GARDEN. WE HAVE MOVEMENT --
WAK
NNNGGNN
I GOT TWO ON THE SIDE Y HOW MANY DID TAKE OUT, HUNTRESS
I WASN'T AWARE THIS WAS A CONTEST, ROBIN.
I'VE TAKEN THIS COMMUNICATOR. WE NOW HAVE EARS ON THE SECRET SERVICE.
FOUR? REALLY?
YOU GO, BATGIRL.
ROBIN! KEEP IT DOWN. WE'RE THE STEALTH TEAM -- REMEMBER? YOU WANT TO MAKE NOISE, GO U FRONT WITH THE "S" SQUAD.

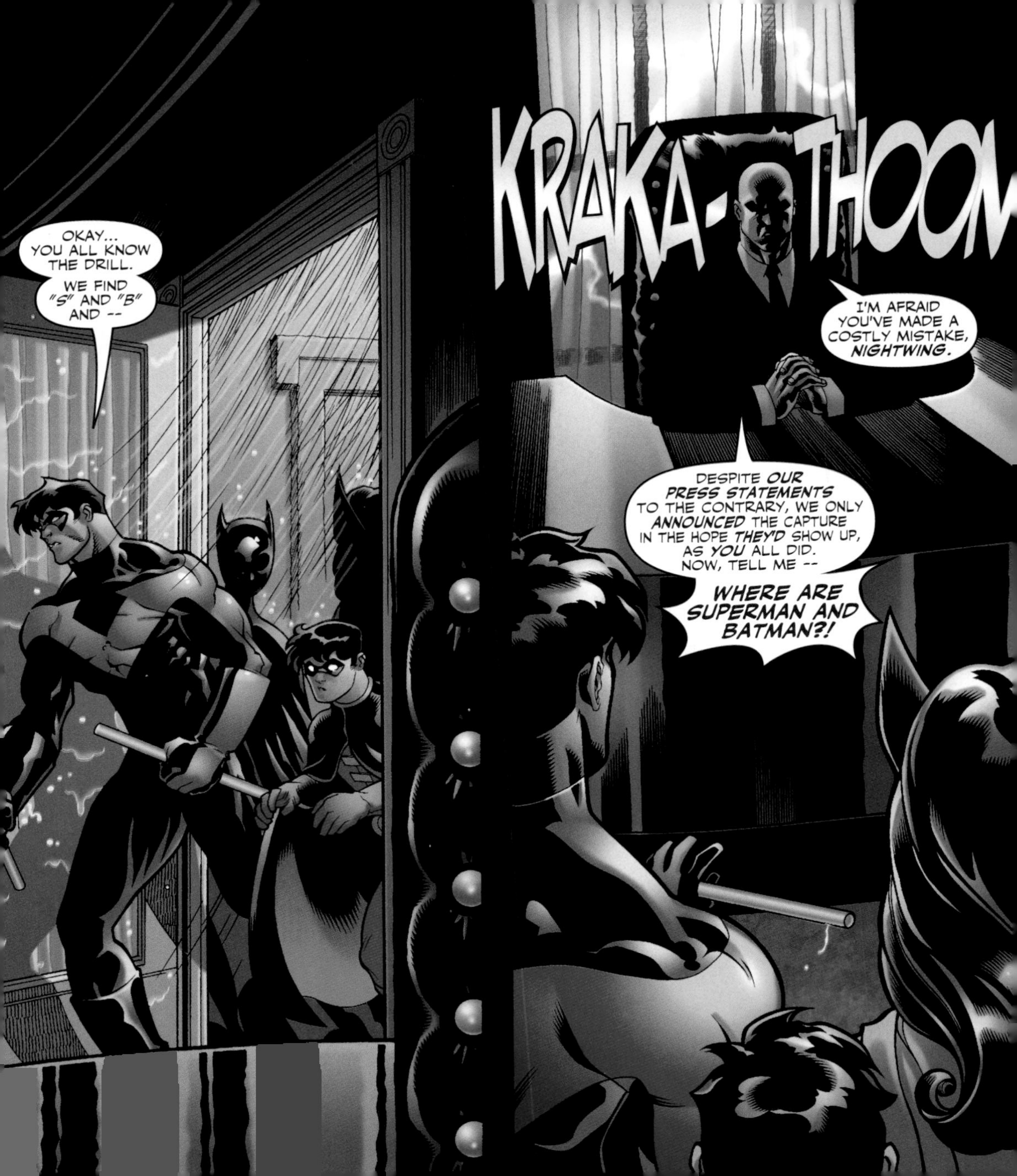
OKAY... YOU ALL KNOW THE DRILL.
WE FIND "S" AND "B" AND --
KRAKA-THOOM
I'M AFRAID YOU'VE MADE A COSTLY MISTAKE, NIGHTWING.
DESPITE OUR PRESS STATEMENTS TO THE CONTRARY, WE ONLY ANNOUNCED THE CAPTURE IN THE HOPE THEY'D SHOW UP, AS YOU ALL DID. NOW, TELL ME --
WHERE ARE SUPERMAN AND BATMAN?!

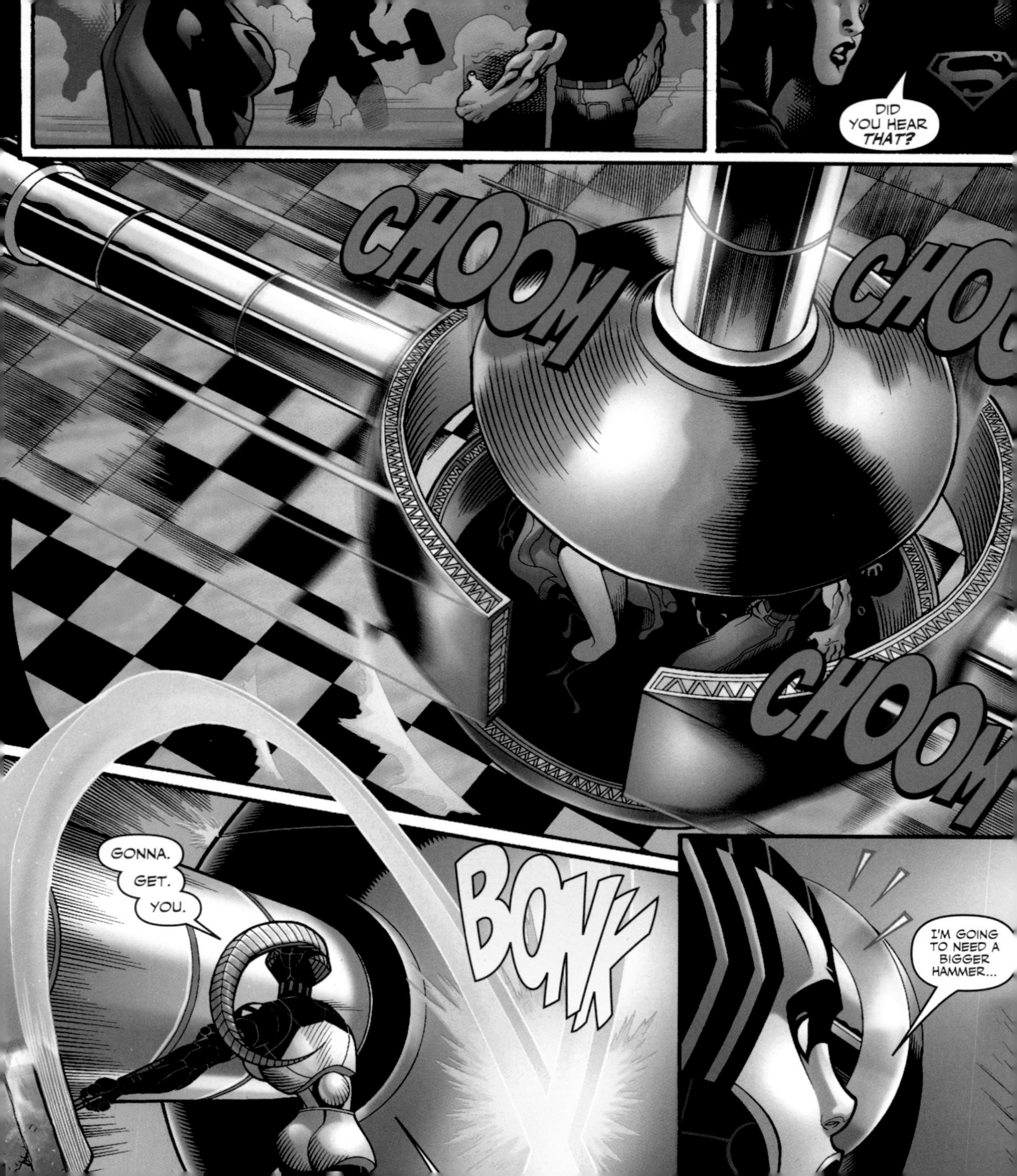
DID YOU HEAR THAT?
CHOOM
CHOOM
CHOOM
GONNA.
GET.
YOU.
BONK
I'M GOING TO NEED A BIGGER HAMMER...

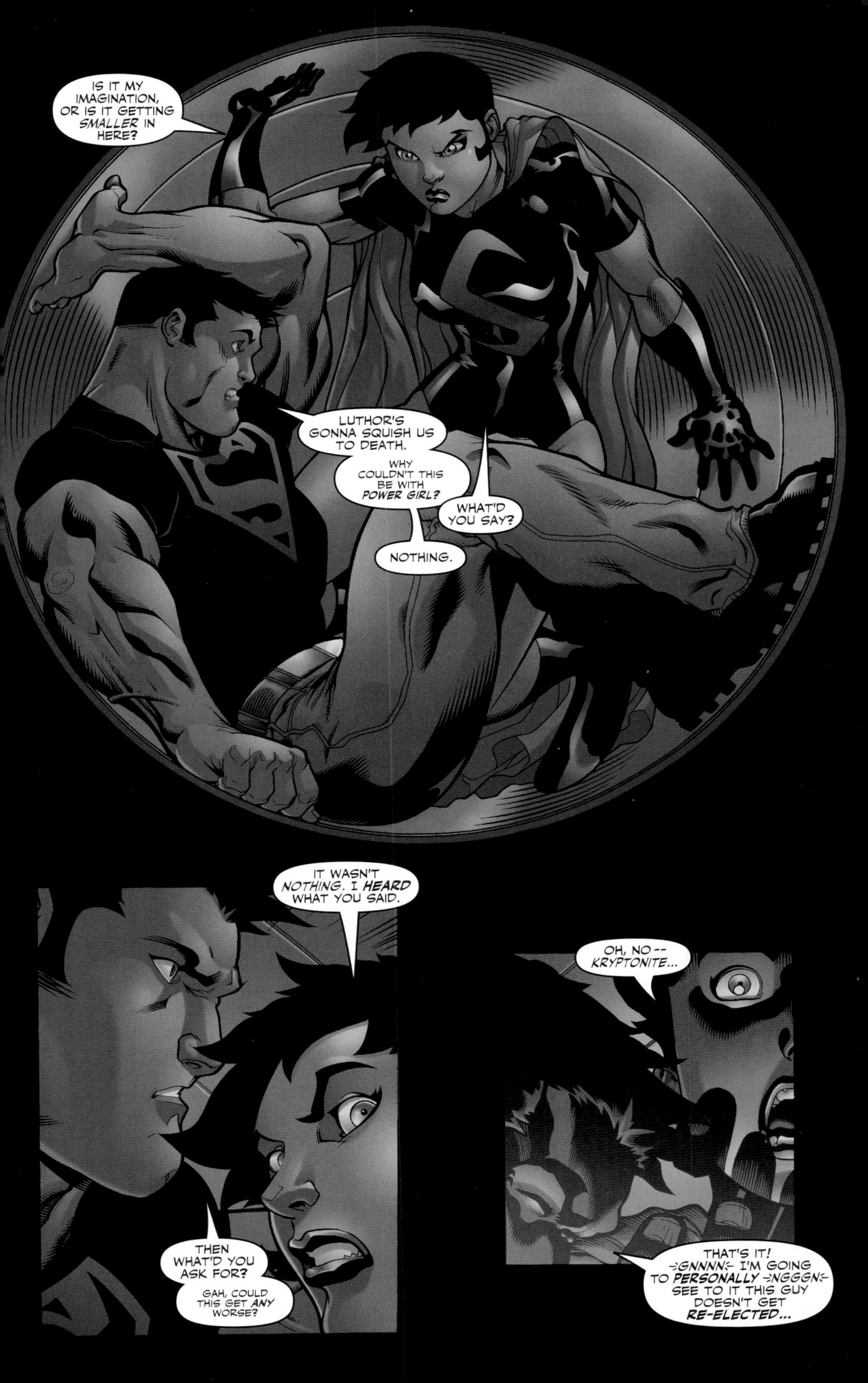
IS IT MY IMAGINATION, OR IS IT GETTING SMALLER IN HERE?
LUTHOR'S GONNA SQUISH US TO DEATH.
WHY COULDN'T THIS BE WITH POWER GIRL?
WHAT'D YOU SAY?
NOTHING.
IT WASN'T NOTHING. I HEARD WHAT YOU SAID.
THEN WHAT'D YOU ASK FOR?
GAH, COULD THIS GET ANY WORSE?
OH, NO-- KRYPTONITE...
THAT'S IT! GNNNN I'M GOING TO PERSONALLY NGGGN SEE TO IT THIS GUY DOESN'T GET RE-ELECTED...

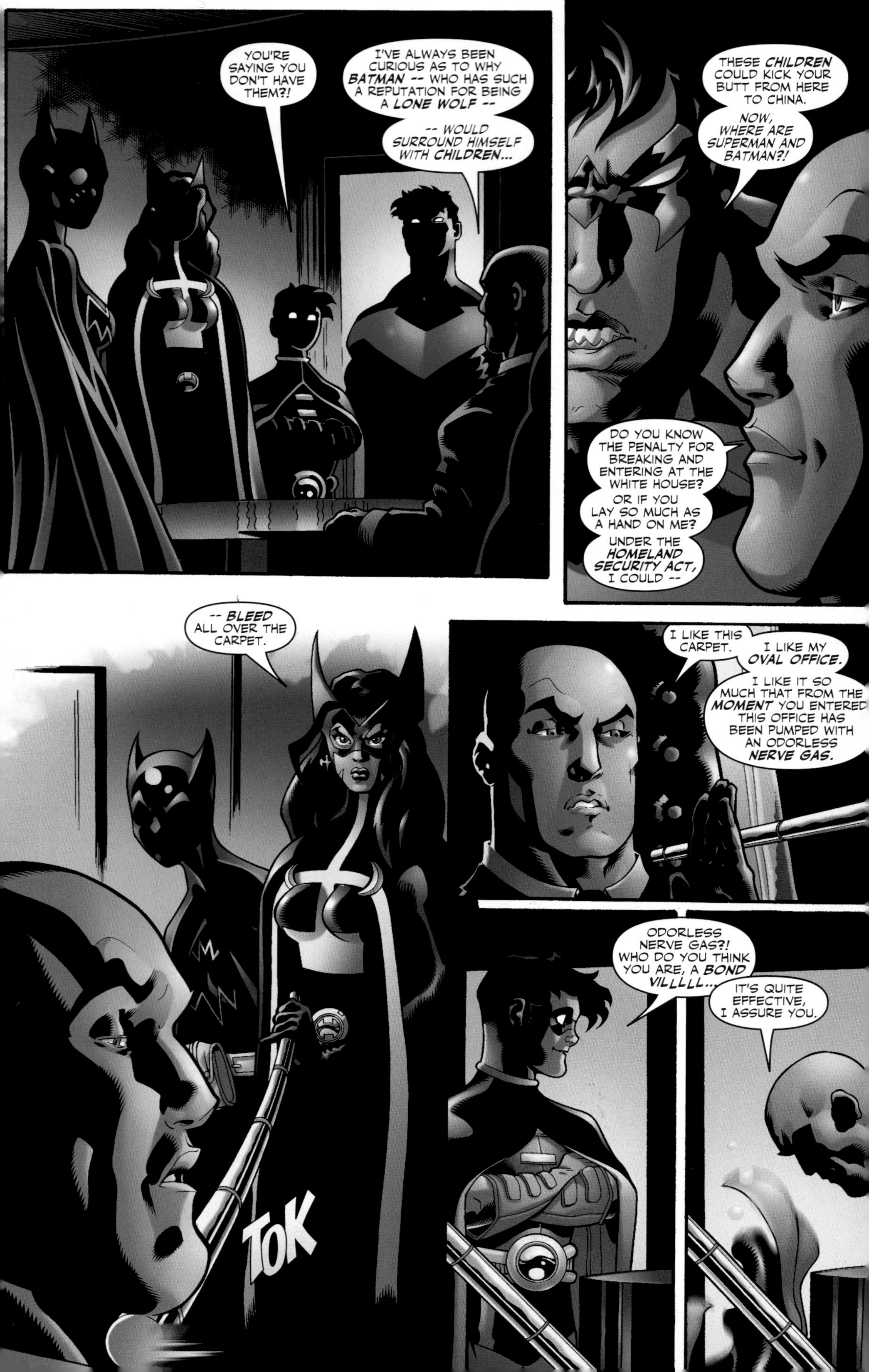
YOU'RE SAYING YOU DON'T HAVE THEM?!
I'VE ALWAYS BEEN CURIOUS AS TO WHY BATMAN -- WHO HAS SUCH A REPUTATION FOR BEING A LONE WOLF --
-- WOULD SURROUND HIMSELF WITH CHILDREN...
THESE CHILDREN COULD KICK YOUR BUTT FROM HERE TO CHINA.
NOW, WHERE ARE SUPERMAN AND BATMAN?!
DO YOU KNOW THE PENALTY FOR BREAKING AND ENTERING AT THE WHITE HOUSE?
OR IF YOU LAY SO MUCH AS A HAND ON ME?
UNDER THE HOMELAND SECURITY ACT, I COULD --
-- BLEED ALL OVER THE CARPET.
TOK
I LIKE THIS CARPET.
I LIKE MY OVAL OFFICE.
I LIKE IT SO MUCH THAT FROM THE MOMENT YOU ENTERED THIS OFFICE HAS BEEN PUMPED WITH AN ODORLESS NERVE GAS.
ODORLESS NERVE GAS?! WHO DO YOU THINK YOU ARE, A BOND VILLLLL...
IT'S QUITE EFFECTIVE, I ASSURE YOU.

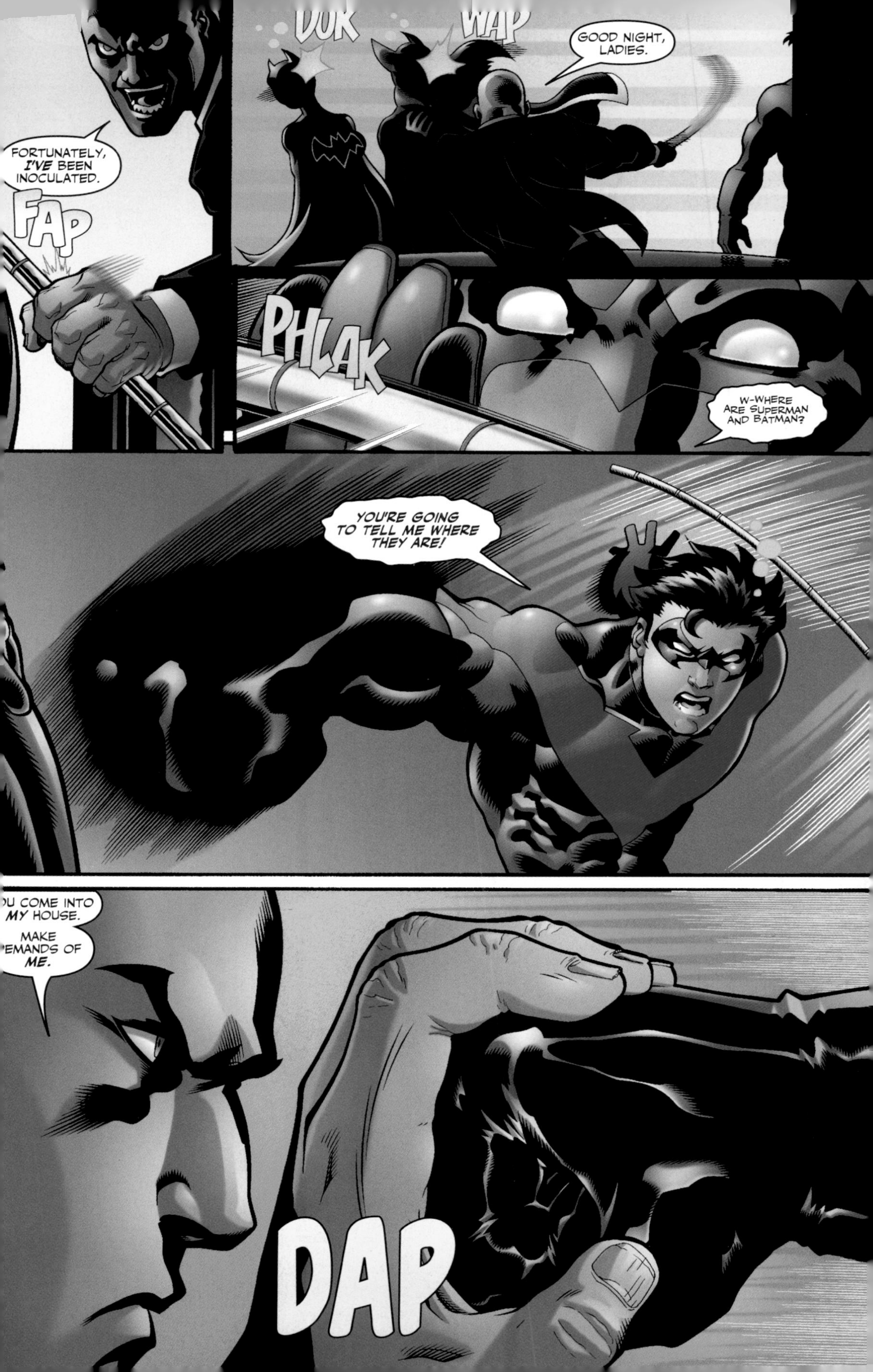

FORTUNATELY, I'VE BEEN INOCULATED.
FAP
DUK
WAP
GOOD NIGHT, LADIES.
PHLAK
W-WHERE ARE SUPERMAN AND BATMAN?
YOU'RE GOING TO TELL ME WHERE THEY ARE!
OU COME INTO MY HOUSE.
MAKE EMANDS OF ME.
DAP

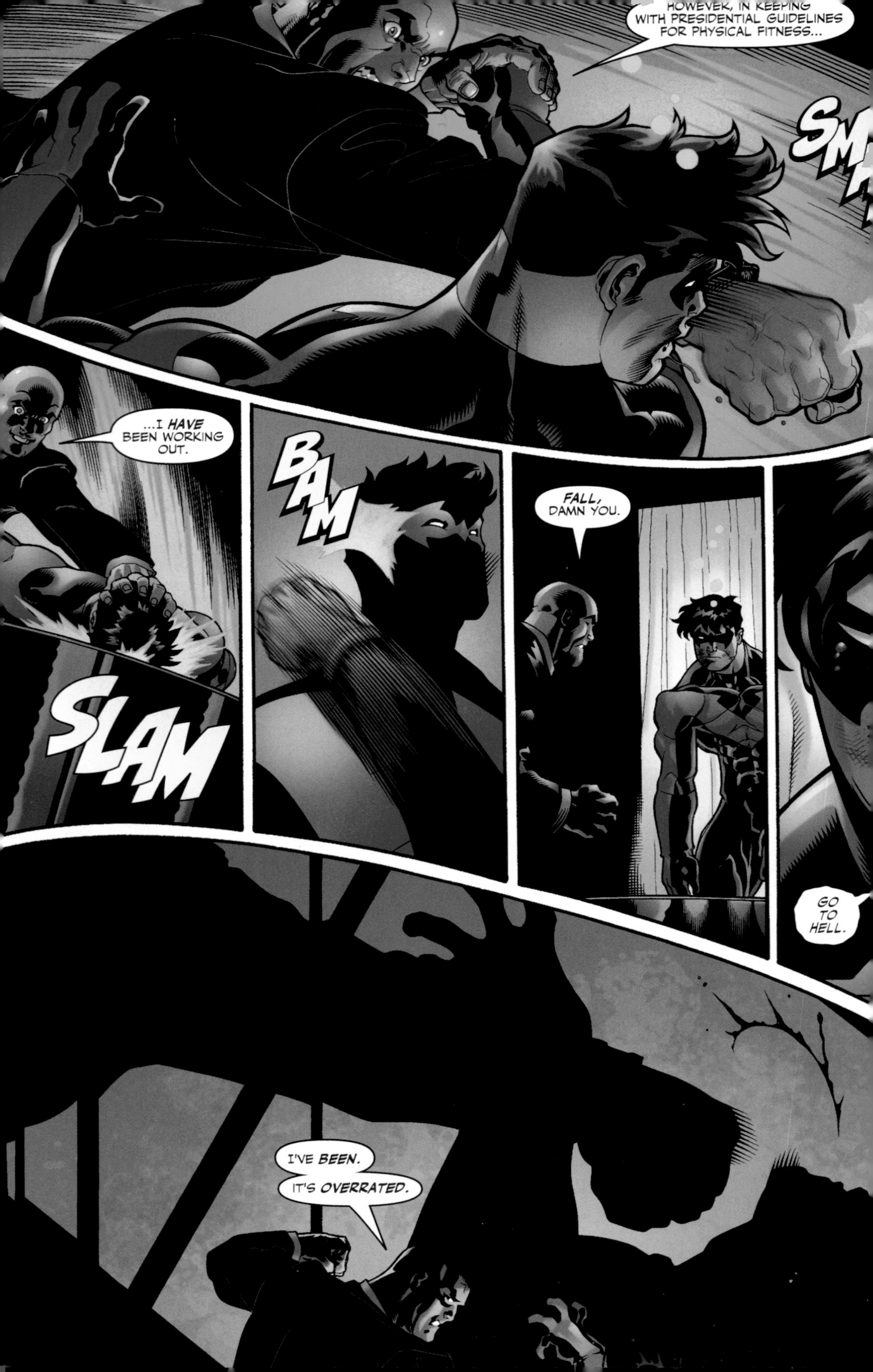
HOWEVER, IN KEEPING WITH PRESIDENTIAL GUIDELINES FOR PHYSICAL FITNESS...
...I HAVE BEEN WORKING OUT.
SLAM
BAM
FALL, DAMN YOU.
GO TO HELL.
I'VE BEEN.
IT'S OVERRATED.

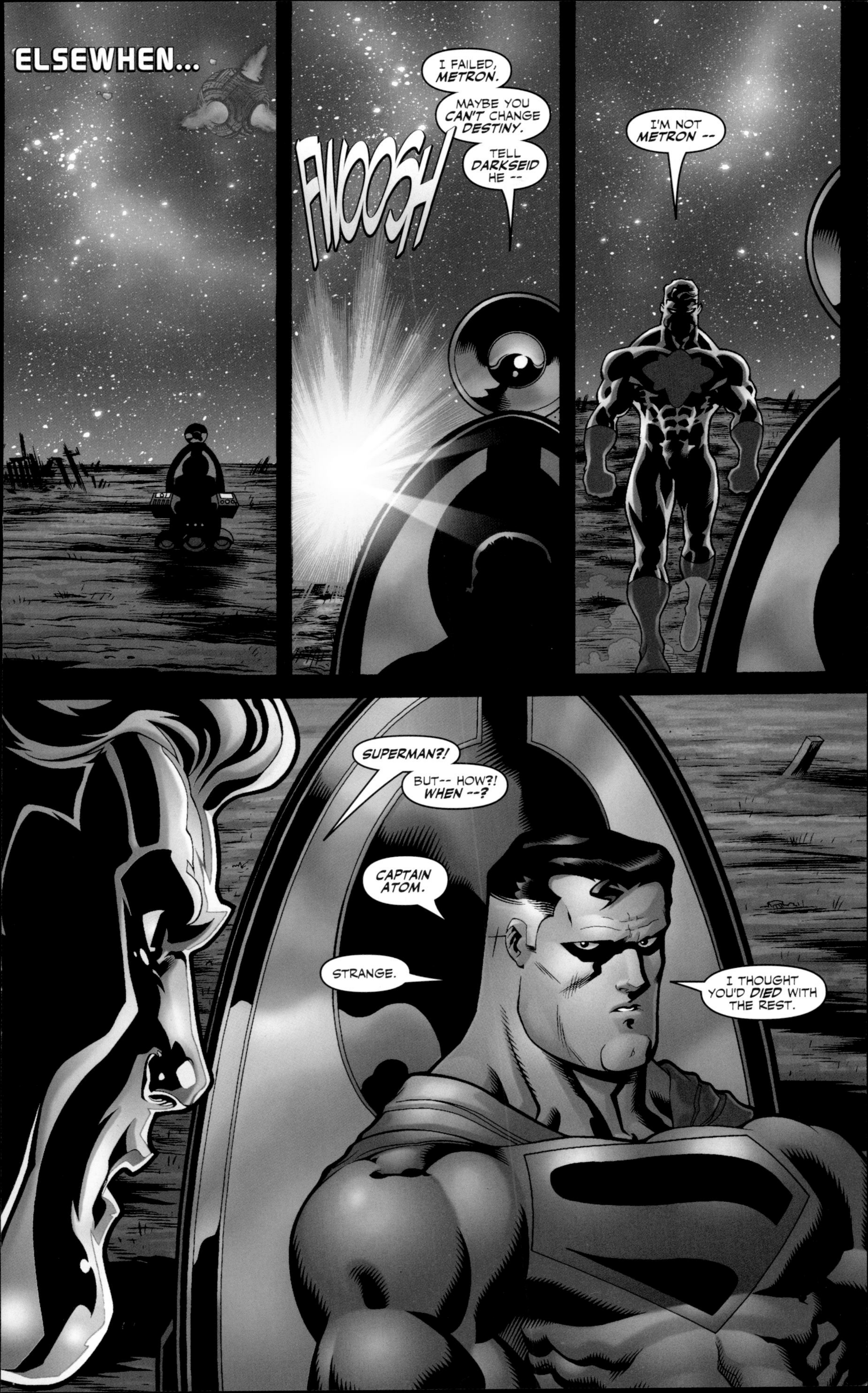
ELSEWHEN...
I FAILED, METRON.
MAYBE YOU CAN'T CHANGE DESTINY.
TELL DARKSEID HE --
FWOOSH
I'M NOT METRON --
SUPERMAN?!
BUT-- HOW?! WHEN --?
CAPTAIN ATOM.
STRANGE.
I THOUGHT YOU'D DIED WITH THE REST.

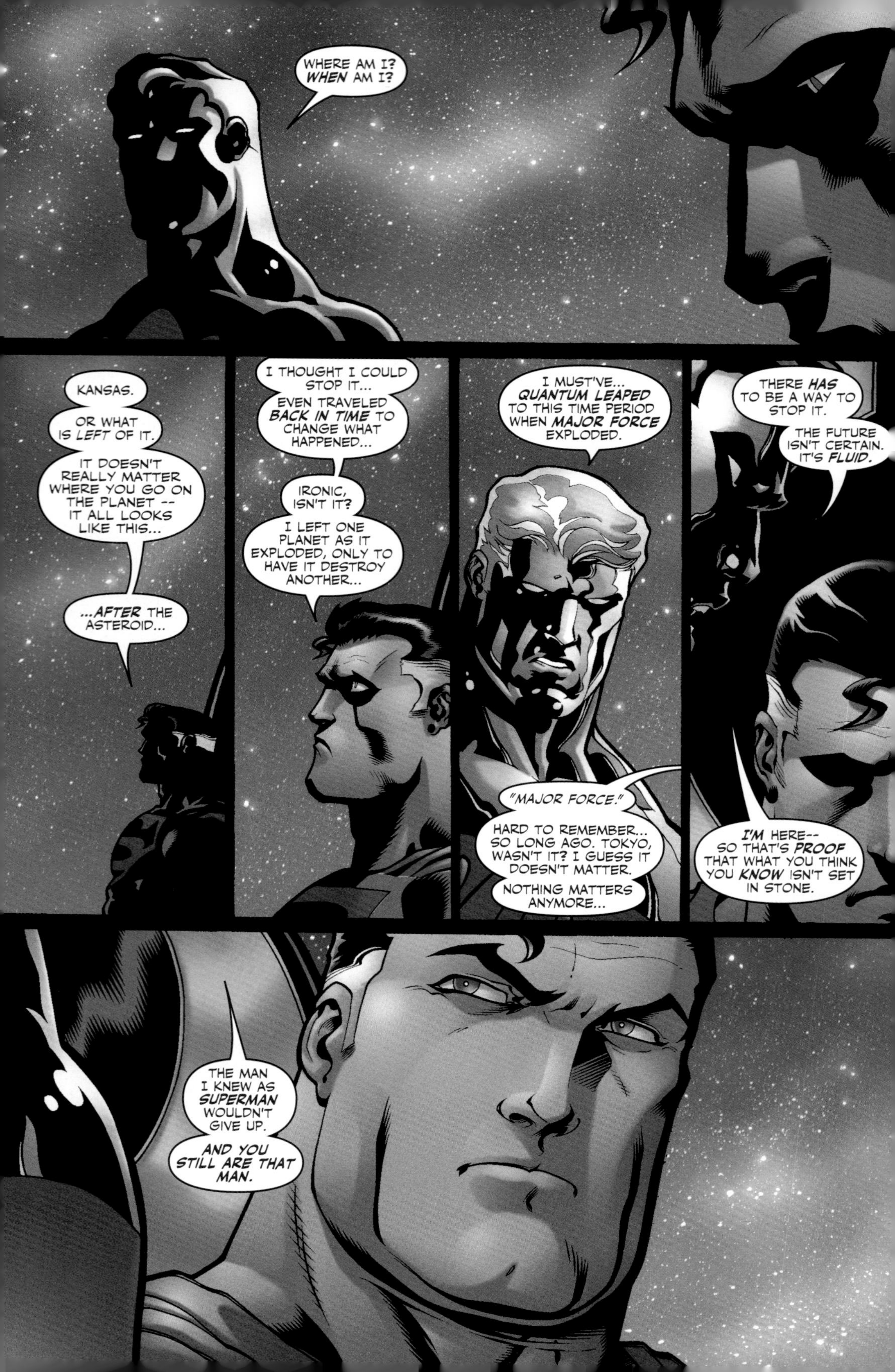
WHERE AM I? WHEN AM I?
KANSAS.
OR WHAT IS LEFT OF IT.
IT DOESN'T REALLY MATTER WHERE YOU GO ON THE PLANET -- IT ALL LOOKS LIKE THIS...
...AFTER THE ASTEROID...
I THOUGHT I COULD STOP IT...
EVEN TRAVELED BACK IN TIME TO CHANGE WHAT HAPPENED...
IRONIC, ISN'T IT?
I LEFT ONE PLANET AS IT EXPLODED, ONLY TO HAVE IT DESTROY ANOTHER...
I MUST'VE... QUANTUM LEAPED TO THIS TIME PERIOD WHEN MAJOR FORCE EXPLODED.
"MAJOR FORCE."
HARD TO REMEMBER... SO LONG AGO. TOKYO, WASN'T IT? I GUESS IT DOESN'T MATTER.
NOTHING MATTERS ANYMORE...
THERE HAS TO BE A WAY TO STOP IT.
THE FUTURE ISN'T CERTAIN. IT'S FLUID.
I'M HERE-- SO THAT'S PROOF THAT WHAT YOU THINK YOU KNOW ISN'T SET IN STONE.
THE MAN I KNEW AS SUPERMAN WOULDN'T GIVE UP.
AND YOU STILL ARE THAT MAN.

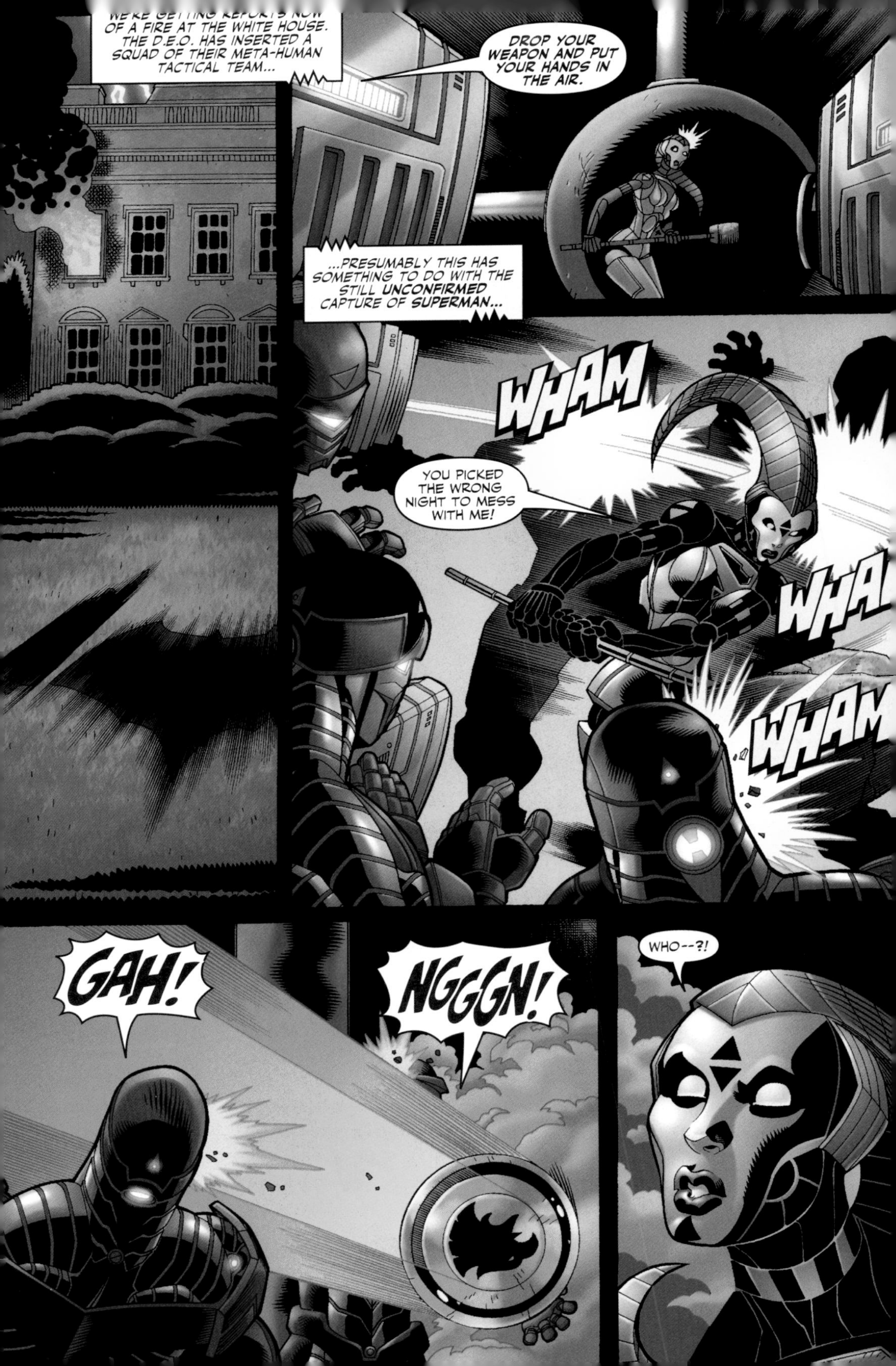
OF A FIRE AT THE WHITE HOUSE. THE D.E.O. HAS INSERTED A SQUAD OF THEIR META-HUMAN TACTICAL TEAM...
DROP YOUR WEAPON AND PUT YOUR HANDS IN THE AIR.
...PRESUMABLY THIS HAS SOMETHING TO DO WITH THE STILL UNCONFIRMED CAPTURE OF SUPERMAN...
WHAM
YOU PICKED THE WRONG NIGHT TO MESS WITH ME!
WHAM
GAH!
NGGGN!
WHO--?!

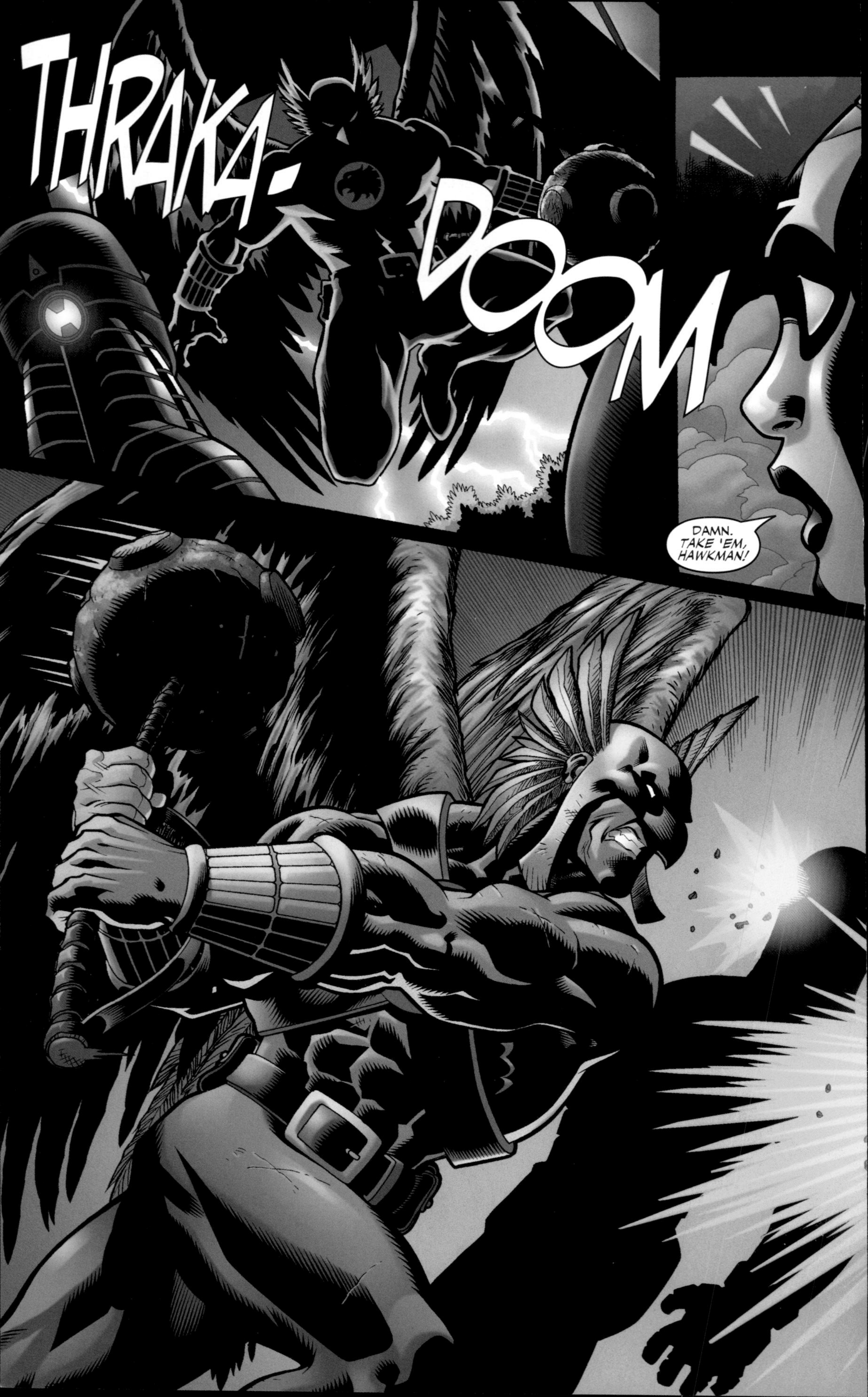
THRAKA-
DOOM
DAMN. TAKE 'EM, HAWKMAN!

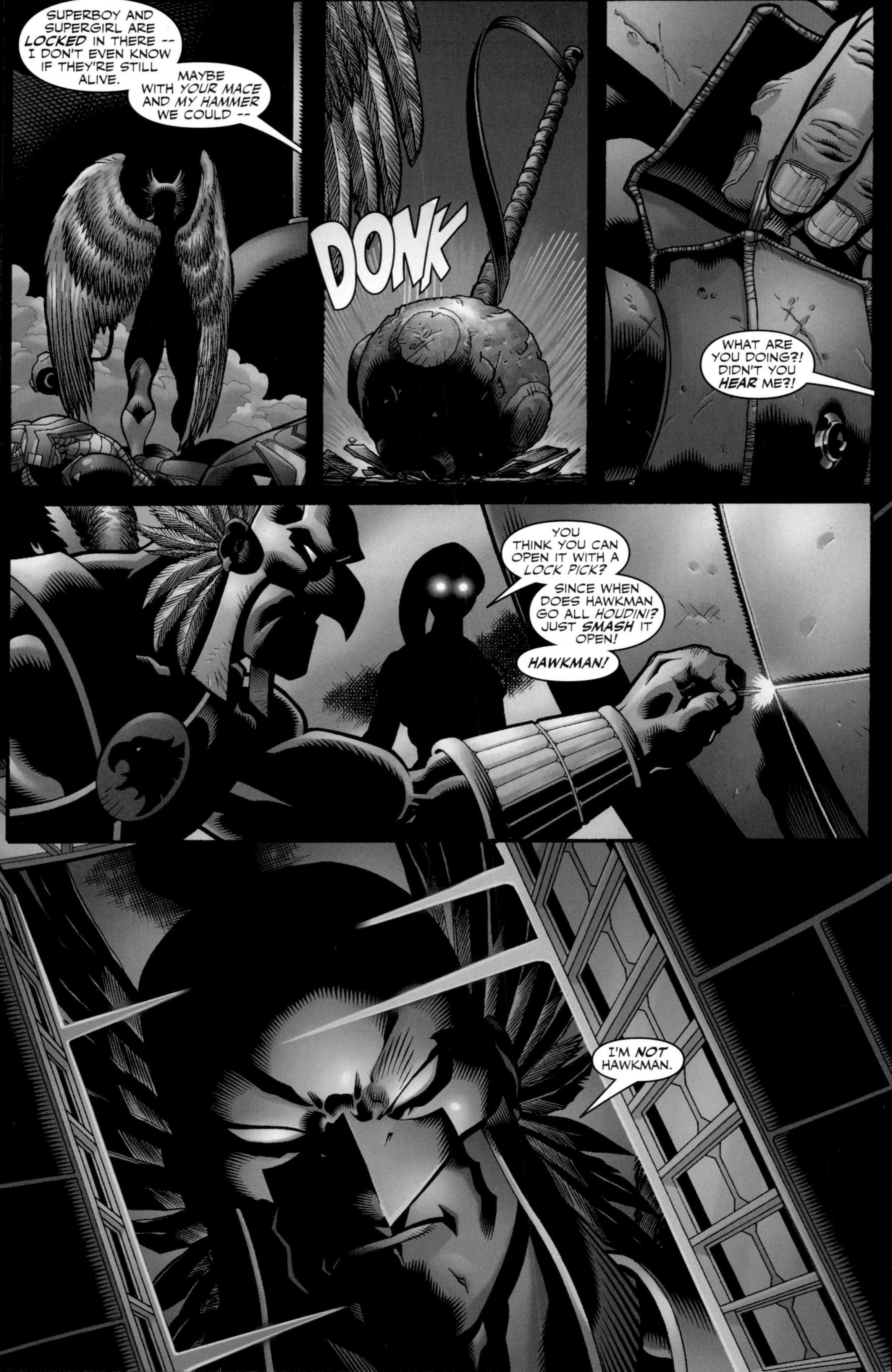
SUPERBOY AND SUPERGIRL ARE LOCKED IN THERE -- I DON'T EVEN KNOW IF THEY'RE STILL ALIVE.
MAYBE WITH YOUR MACE AND MY HAMMER WE COULD --
DONK
WHAT ARE YOU DOING?! DIDN'T YOU HEAR ME?!
YOU THINK YOU CAN OPEN IT WITH A LOCK PICK?
SINCE WHEN DOES HAWKMAN GO ALL HOUDINI? JUST SMASH IT OPEN!
HAWKMAN!
I'M NOT HAWKMAN.

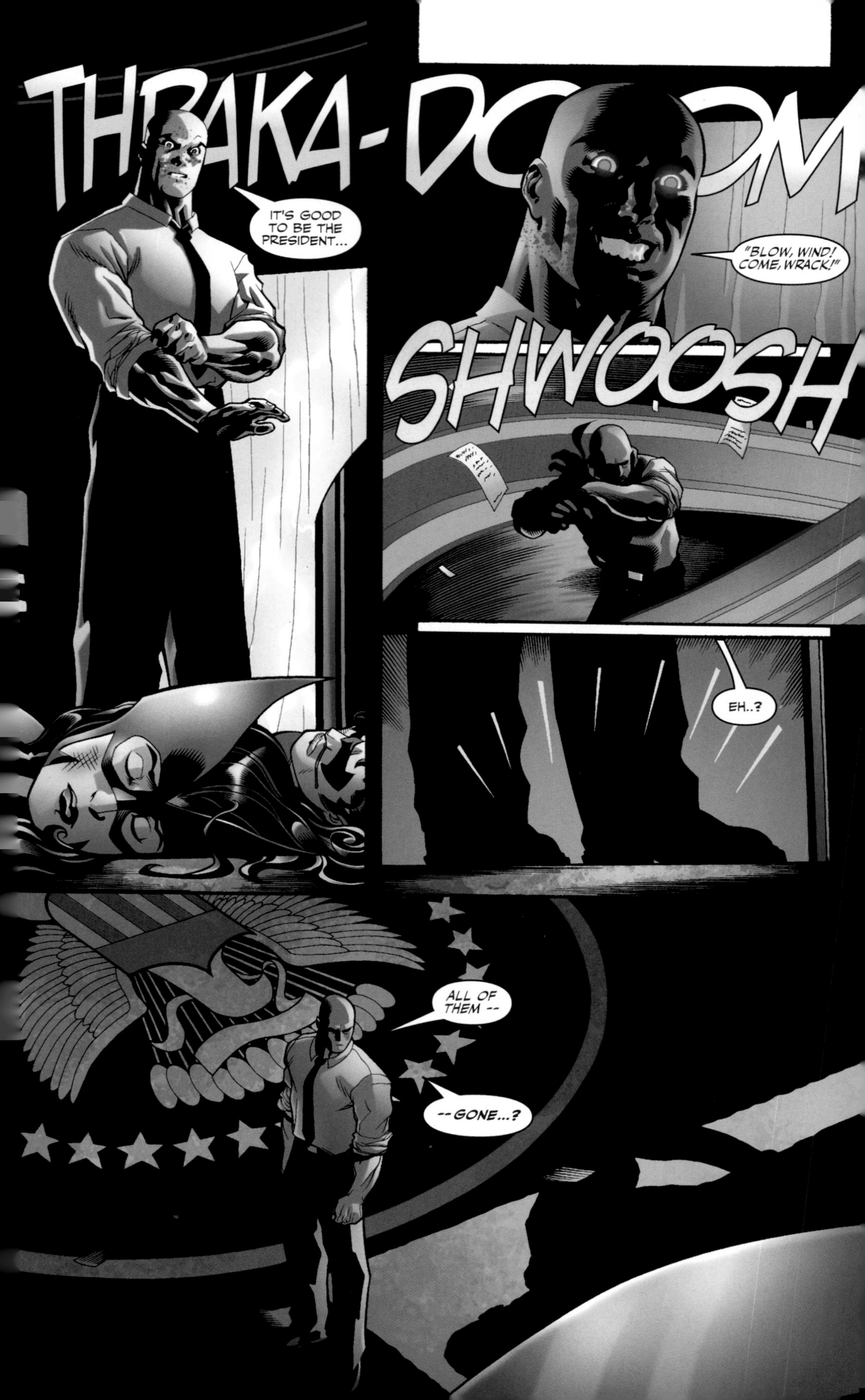
THRAKA-DOOOM
IT'S GOOD TO BE THE PRESIDENT...
"BLOW, WIND! COME, WRACK!"
SHWOOSH
EH..?
ALL OF THEM --
-- GONE...?

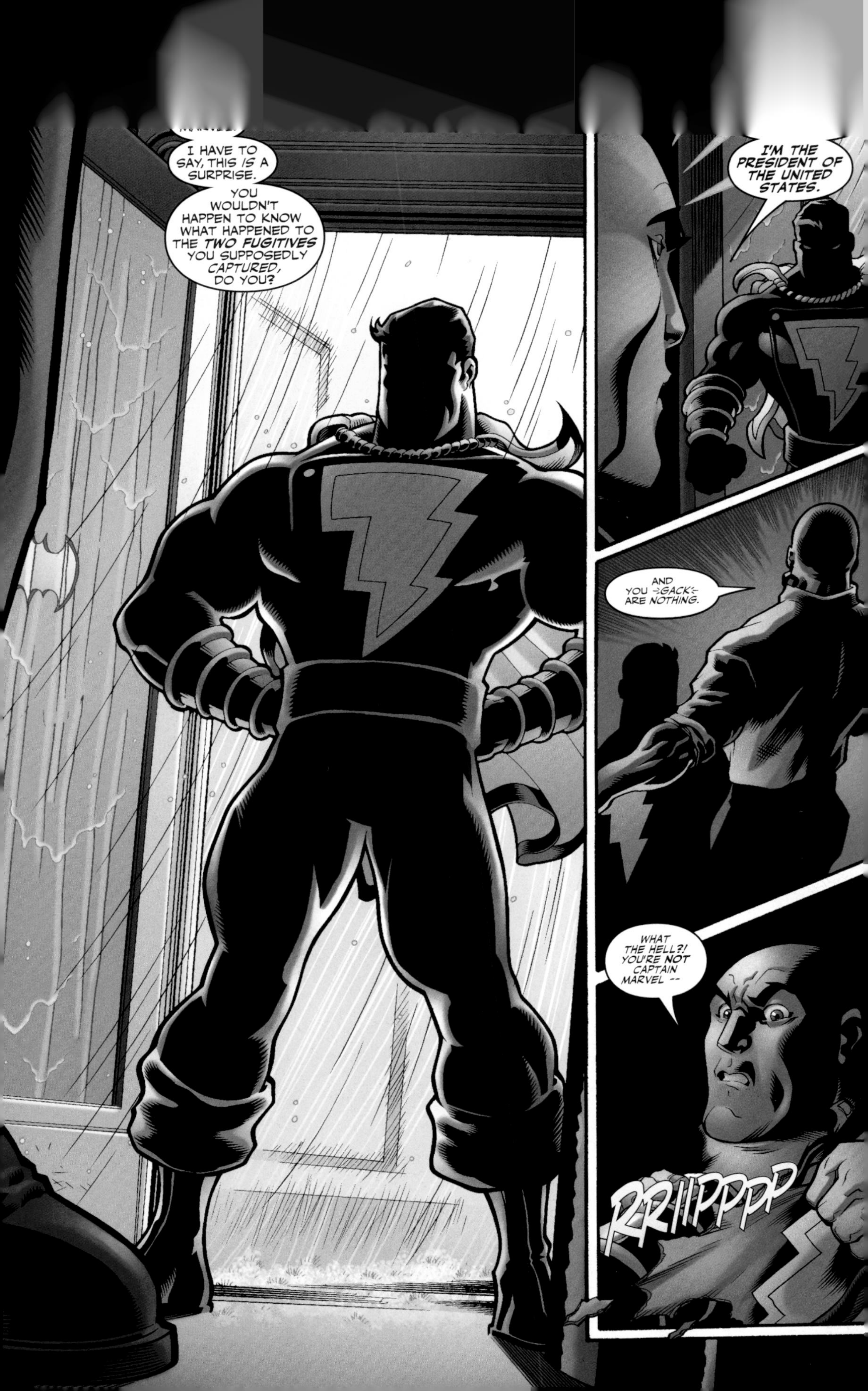
I HAVE TO SAY, THIS IS A SURPRISE.
YOU WOULDN'T HAPPEN TO KNOW WHAT HAPPENED TO THE TWO FUGITIVES YOU SUPPOSEDLY CAPTURED, DO YOU?
I'M THE PRESIDENT OF THE UNITED STATES.
AND YOU -GACK- ARE NOTHING.
WHAT THE HELL?! YOU'RE NOT CAPTAIN MARVEL --
RRIIPPPP

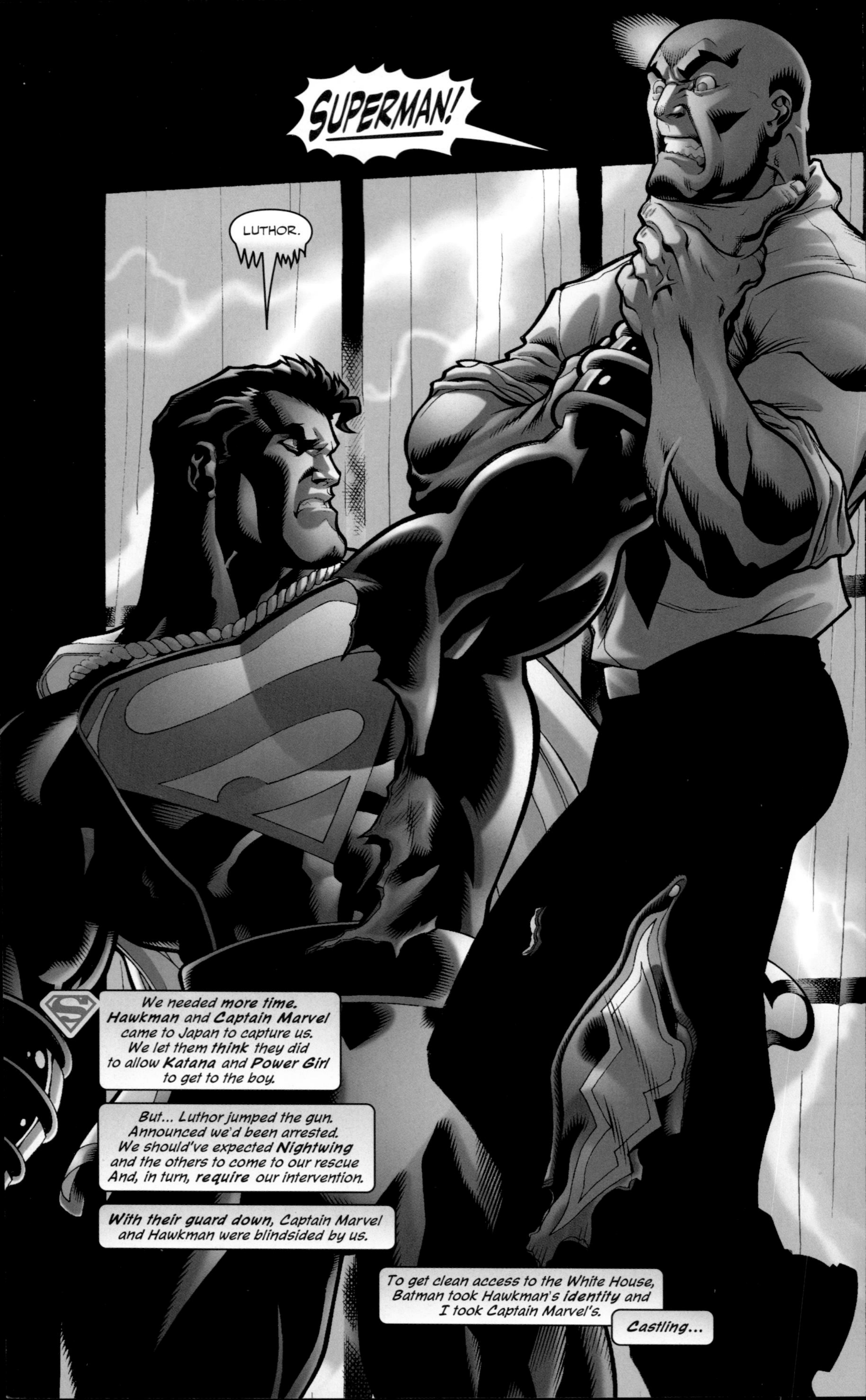
SUPERMAN!
LUTHOR.
We needed more time. Hawkman and Captain Marvel came to Japan to capture us. We let them think they did to allow Katana and Power Girl to get to the boy.
But... Luthor jumped the gun. Announced we'd been arrested. We should've expected Nightwing and the others to come to our rescue And, in turn, require our intervention.
With their guard down, Captain Marvel and Hawkman were blindsided by us.
To get clean access to the White House, Batman took Hawkman's identity and I took Captain Marvel's.
Castling...

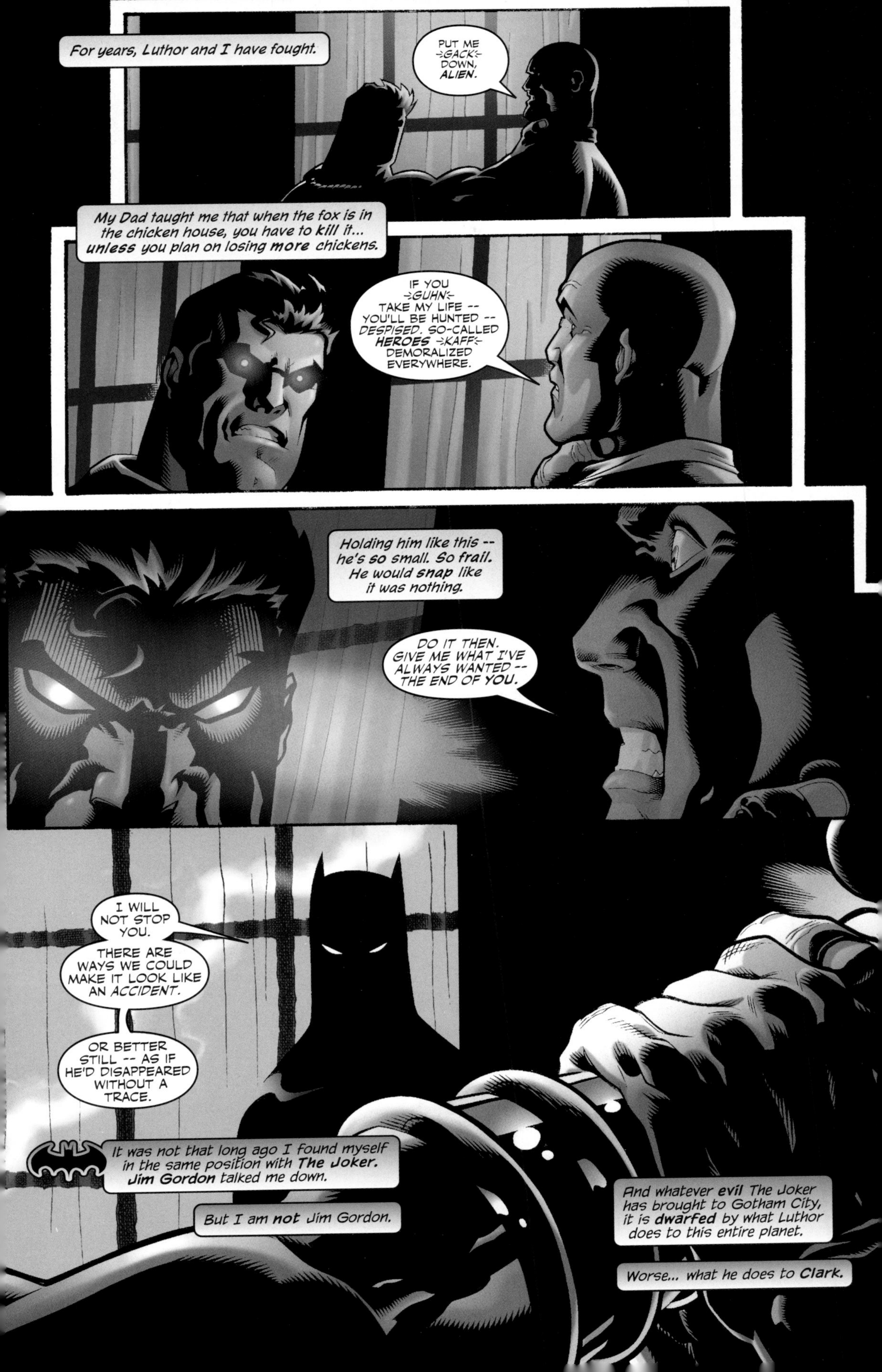
For years, Luthor and I have fought.
PUT ME -GACK- DOWN, ALIEN.
My Dad taught me that when the fox is in the chicken house, you have to kill it... unless you plan on losing more chickens.
IF YOU -GUHN- TAKE MY LIFE -- YOU'LL BE HUNTED -- DESPISED. SO-CALLED HEROES -KAFF- DEMORALIZED EVERYWHERE.
Holding him like this -- he's so small. So frail. He would snap like it was nothing.
DO IT THEN. GIVE ME WHAT I'VE ALWAYS WANTED -- THE END OF YOU.
I WILL NOT STOP YOU.
THERE ARE WAYS WE COULD MAKE IT LOOK LIKE AN ACCIDENT.
OR BETTER STILL -- AS IF HE'D DISAPPEARED WITHOUT A TRACE.
It was not that long ago I found myself in the same position with The Joker. Jim Gordon talked me down.
But I am not Jim Gordon.
And whatever evil The Joker has brought to Gotham City, it is dwarfed by what Luthor does to this entire planet.
Worse... what he does to Clark.

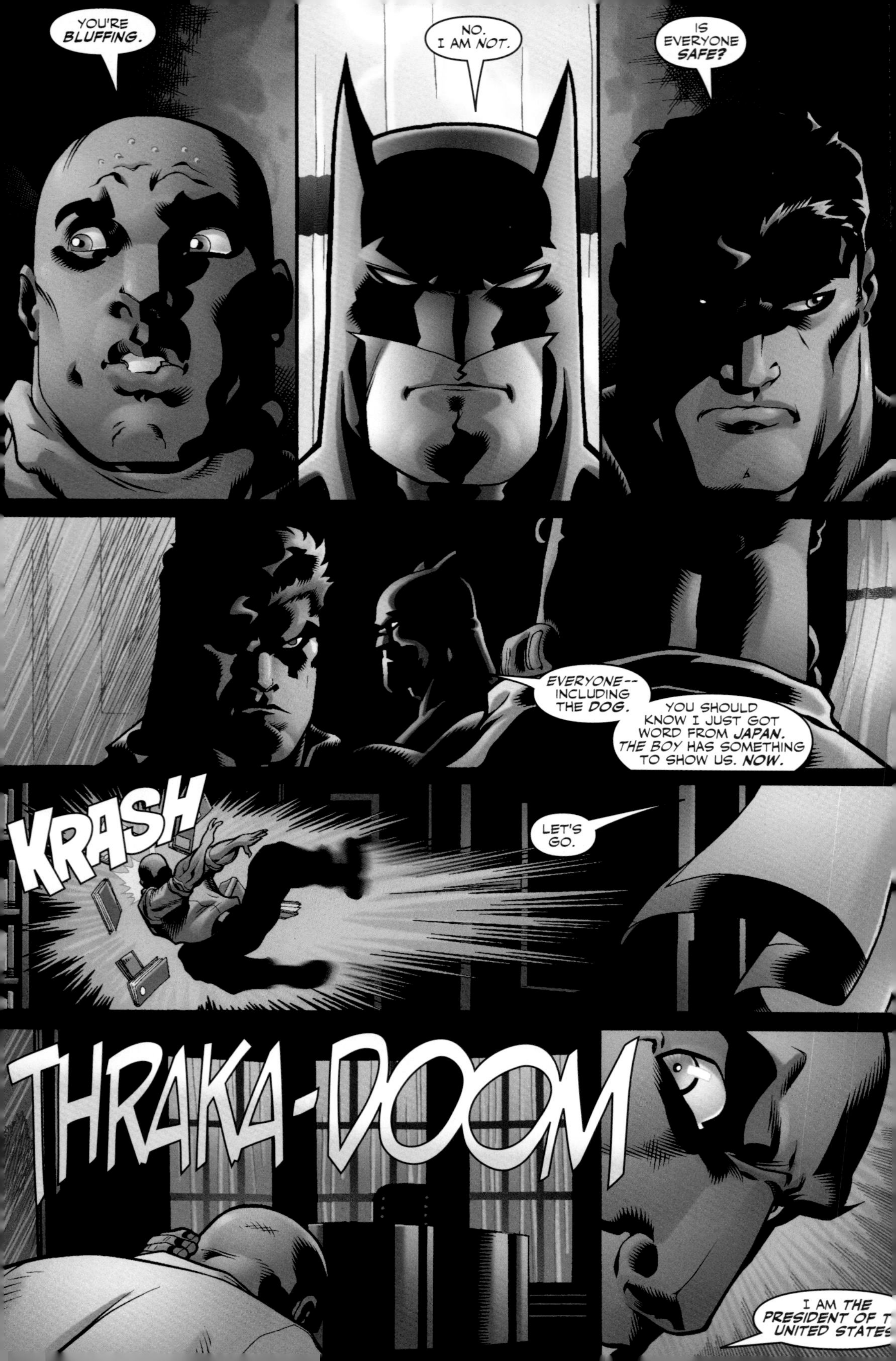
YOU'RE BLUFFING.
NO. I AM NOT.
IS EVERYONE SAFE?
EVERYONE-- INCLUDING THE DOG.
YOU SHOULD KNOW I JUST GOT WORD FROM JAPAN. THE BOY HAS SOMETHING TO SHOW US. NOW.
KRASH
LET'S GO.
THRAKA-DOOM
I AM THE PRESIDENT OF T UNITED STATES

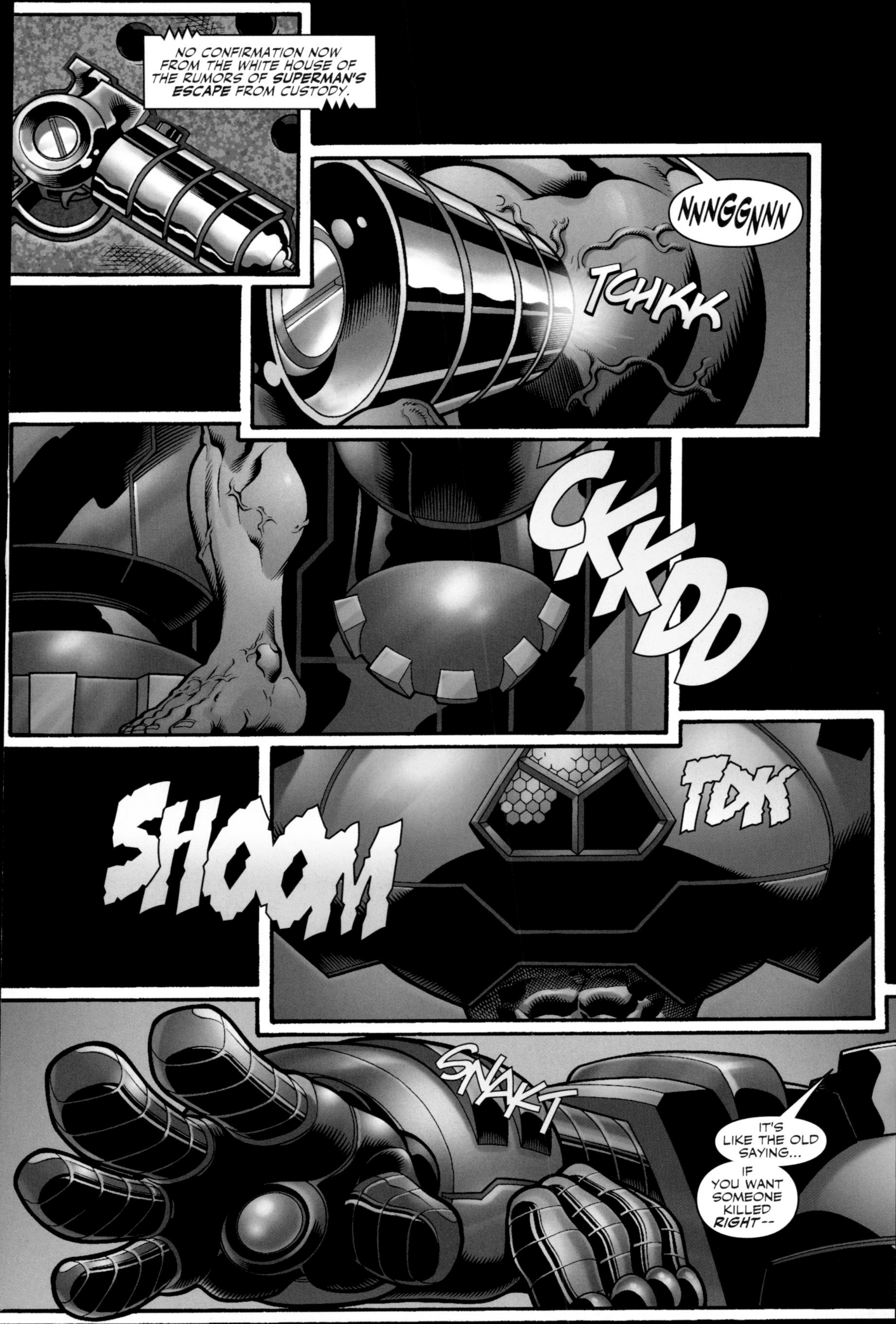
NO CONFIRMATION NOW FROM THE WHITE HOUSE OF THE RUMORS OF **SUPERMAN'S ESCAPE** FROM CUSTODY.
NNNGGNNN
TCHKK
CKKDD
SHOOM
TDK
SNAKT
IT'S LIKE THE OLD SAYING...
IF YOU WANT SOMEONE KILLED *RIGHT*--

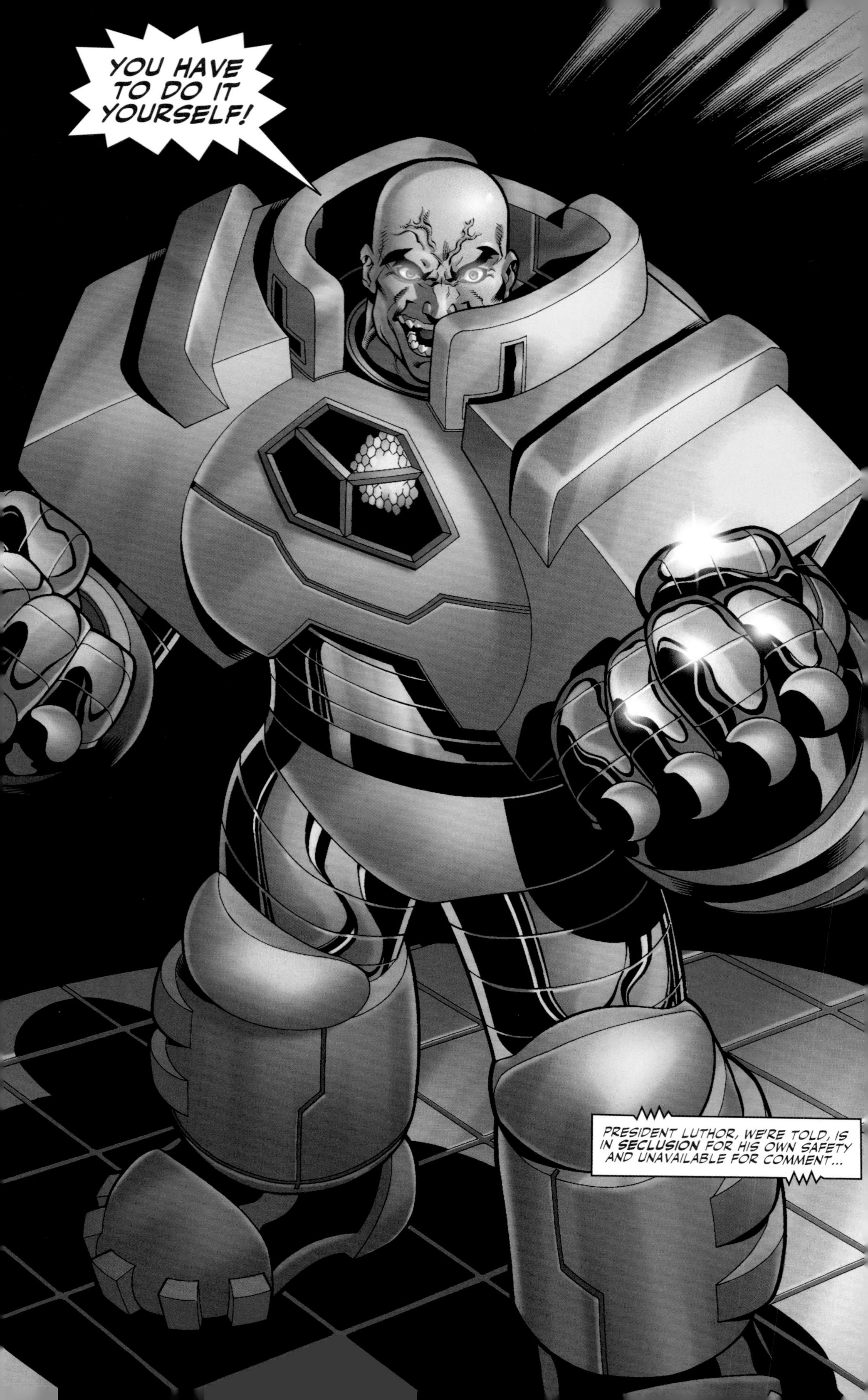
YOU HAVE TO DO IT YOURSELF!
PRESIDENT LUTHOR, WE'RE TOLD, IS IN SECLUSION FOR HIS OWN SAFETY AND UNAVAILABLE FOR COMMENT...

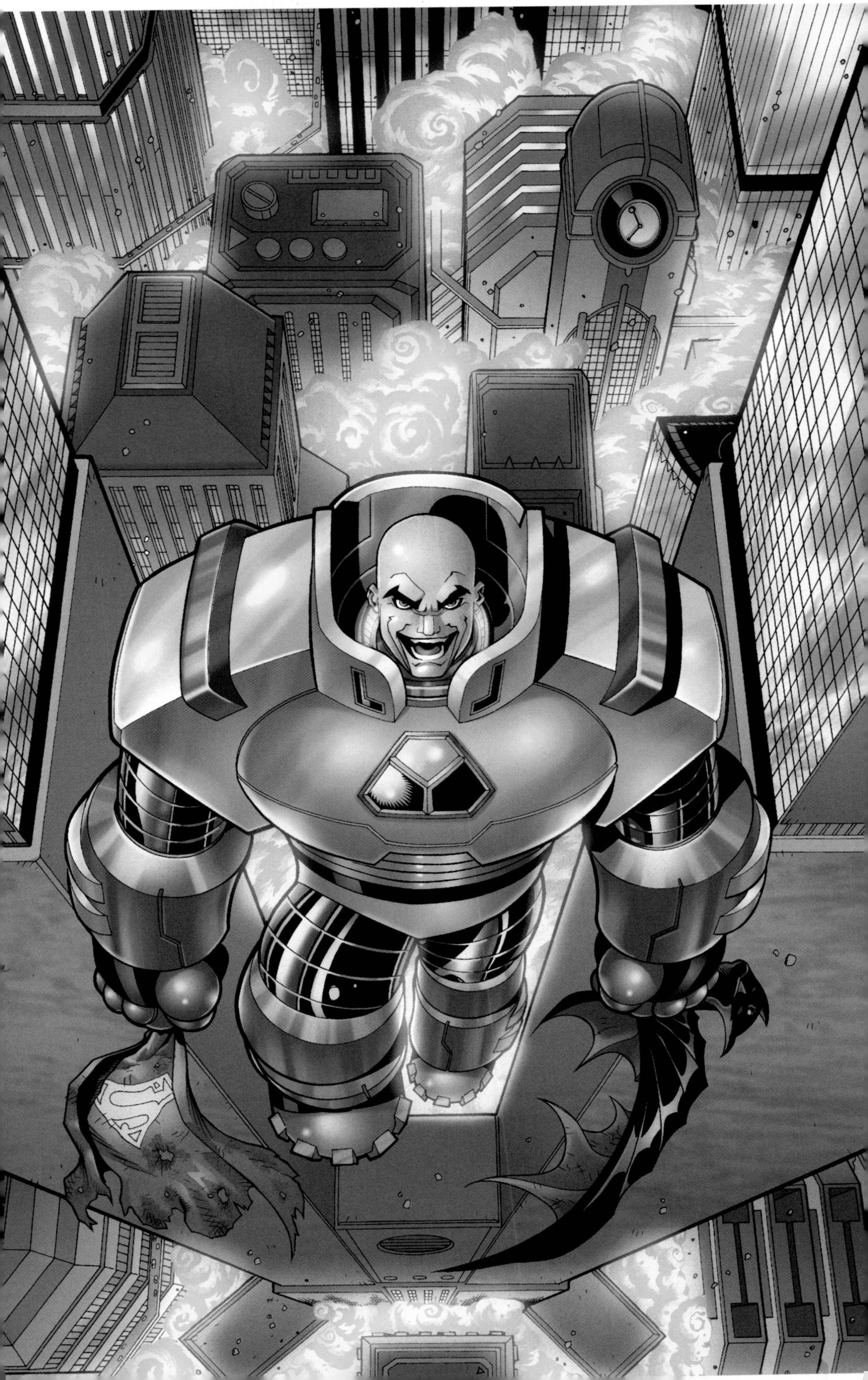

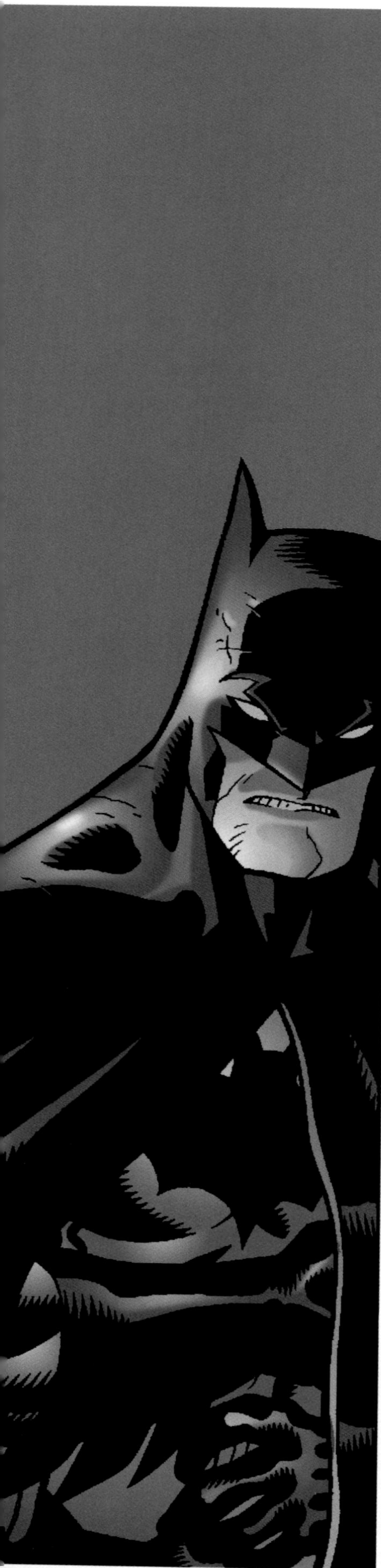

SUPERMAN

PART SIX

BATMAN

FINAL COUNTDOWN

JEPH LOEB
WRITER
ED McGUINNESS
PENCILLER
DEXTER VINES
INKER
DAVE STEWART
COLORIST
RICHARD STARKINGS
LETTERER
ED McGUINNESS
DEXTER VINES
WITH
DAVE STEWART
COVER

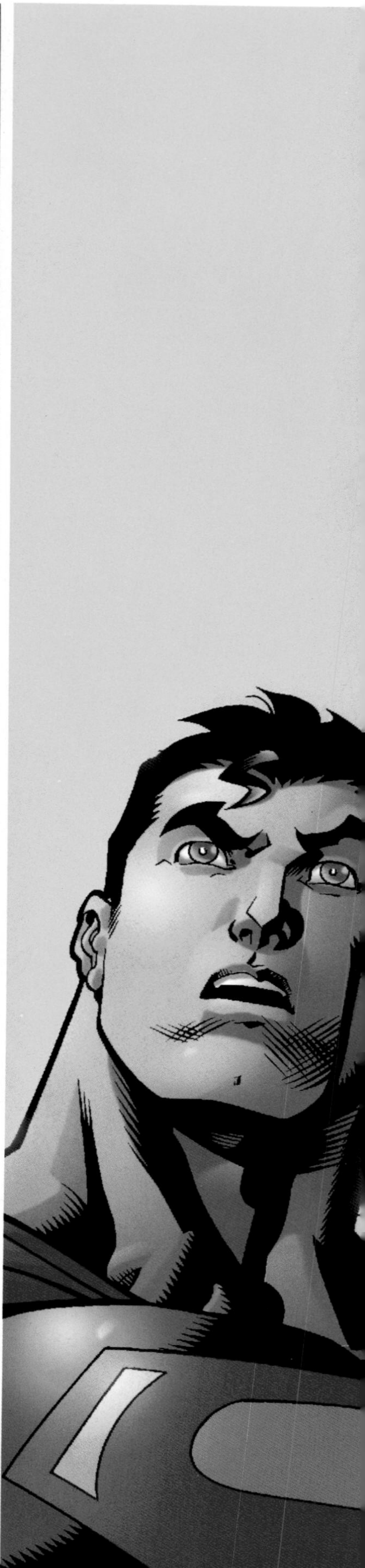

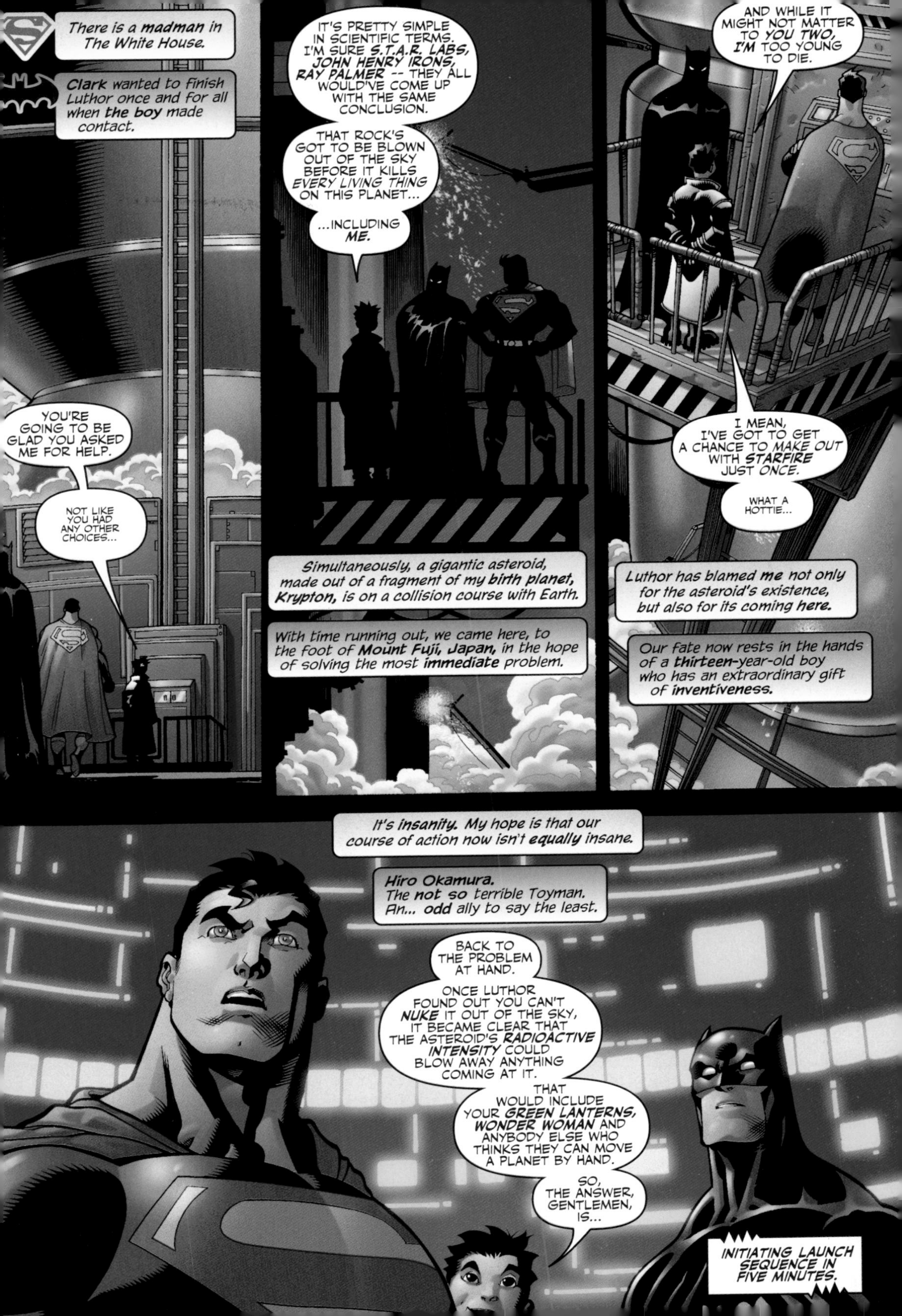

There is a madman in The White House.
Clark wanted to finish Luthor once and for all when the boy made contact.
YOU'RE GOING TO BE GLAD YOU ASKED ME FOR HELP.
NOT LIKE YOU HAD ANY OTHER CHOICES...
IT'S PRETTY SIMPLE IN SCIENTIFIC TERMS. I'M SURE S.T.A.R. LABS, JOHN HENRY IRONS, RAY PALMER -- THEY ALL WOULD'VE COME UP WITH THE SAME CONCLUSION.
THAT ROCK'S GOT TO BE BLOWN OUT OF THE SKY BEFORE IT KILLS EVERY LIVING THING ON THIS PLANET...
...INCLUDING ME.
Simultaneously, a gigantic asteroid, made out of a fragment of my birth planet, Krypton, is on a collision course with Earth.
With time running out, we came here, to the foot of Mount Fuji, Japan, in the hope of solving the most immediate problem.
AND WHILE IT MIGHT NOT MATTER TO YOU TWO, I'M TOO YOUNG TO DIE.
I MEAN, I'VE GOT TO GET A CHANCE TO MAKE OUT WITH STARFIRE JUST ONCE.
WHAT A HOTTIE...
Luthor has blamed me not only for the asteroid's existence, but also for its coming here.
Our fate now rests in the hands of a thirteen-year-old boy who has an extraordinary gift of inventiveness.
It's insanity. My hope is that our course of action now isn't equally insane.
Hiro Okamura. The not so terrible Toyman. An... odd ally to say the least.
BACK TO THE PROBLEM AT HAND.
ONCE LUTHOR FOUND OUT YOU CAN'T NUKE IT OUT OF THE SKY, IT BECAME CLEAR THAT THE ASTEROID'S RADIOACTIVE INTENSITY COULD BLOW AWAY ANYTHING COMING AT IT.
THAT WOULD INCLUDE YOUR GREEN LANTERNS, WONDER WOMAN AND ANYBODY ELSE WHO THINKS THEY CAN MOVE A PLANET BY HAND.
SO, THE ANSWER, GENTLEMEN, IS...
INITIATING LAUNCH SEQUENCE IN FIVE MINUTES.

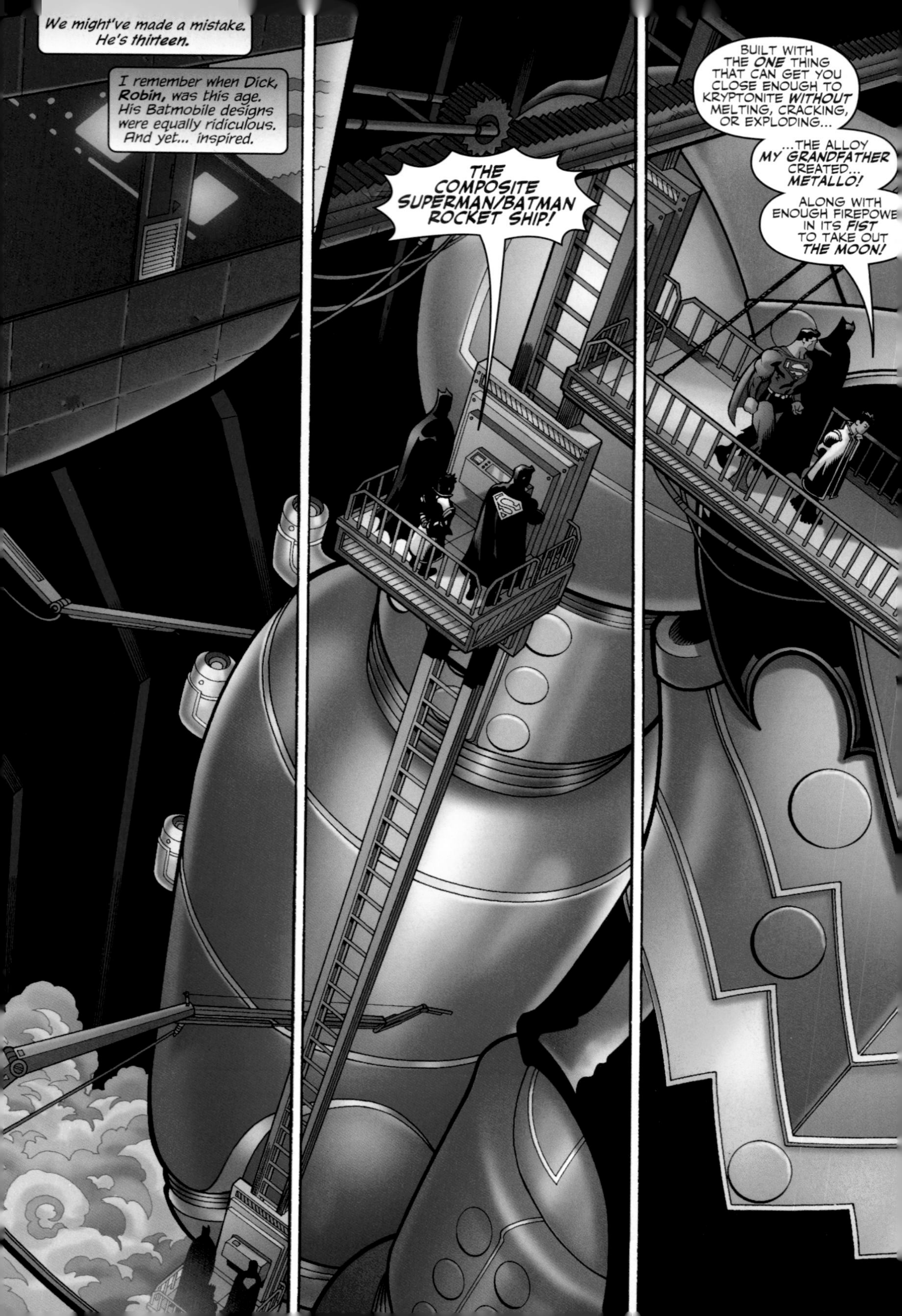

We might've made a mistake. He's thirteen.
I remember when Dick, Robin, was this age. His Batmobile designs were equally ridiculous. And yet... inspired.
THE COMPOSITE SUPERMAN/BATMAN ROCKET SHIP!
BUILT WITH THE ONE THING THAT CAN GET YOU CLOSE ENOUGH TO KRYPTONITE WITHOUT MELTING, CRACKING, OR EXPLODING...
...THE ALLOY MY GRANDFATHER CREATED... METALLO!
ALONG WITH ENOUGH FIREPOWE IN ITS FIST TO TAKE OUT THE MOON!

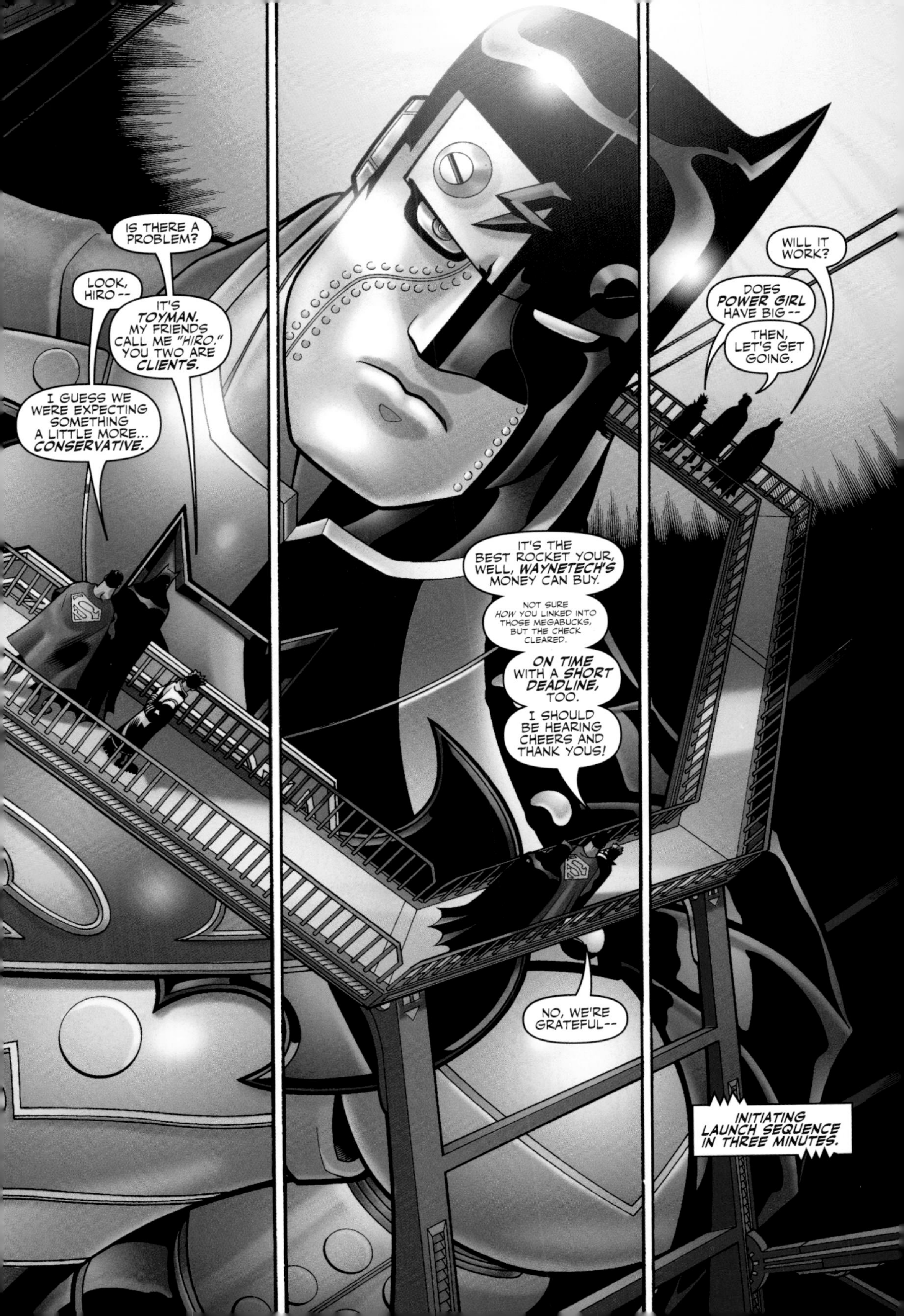
IS THERE A PROBLEM?
LOOK, HIRO--
IT'S TOYMAN. MY FRIENDS CALL ME "HIRO." YOU TWO ARE CLIENTS.
I GUESS WE WERE EXPECTING SOMETHING A LITTLE MORE... CONSERVATIVE.
IT'S THE BEST ROCKET YOUR, WELL, WAYNETECH'S MONEY CAN BUY.
NOT SURE HOW YOU LINKED INTO THOSE MEGABUCKS, BUT THE CHECK CLEARED.
ON TIME WITH A SHORT DEADLINE, TOO.
I SHOULD BE HEARING CHEERS AND THANK YOUS!
NO, WE'RE GRATEFUL--
WILL IT WORK?
DOES POWER GIRL HAVE BIG--
THEN, LET'S GET GOING.
INITIATING LAUNCH SEQUENCE IN THREE MINUTES.

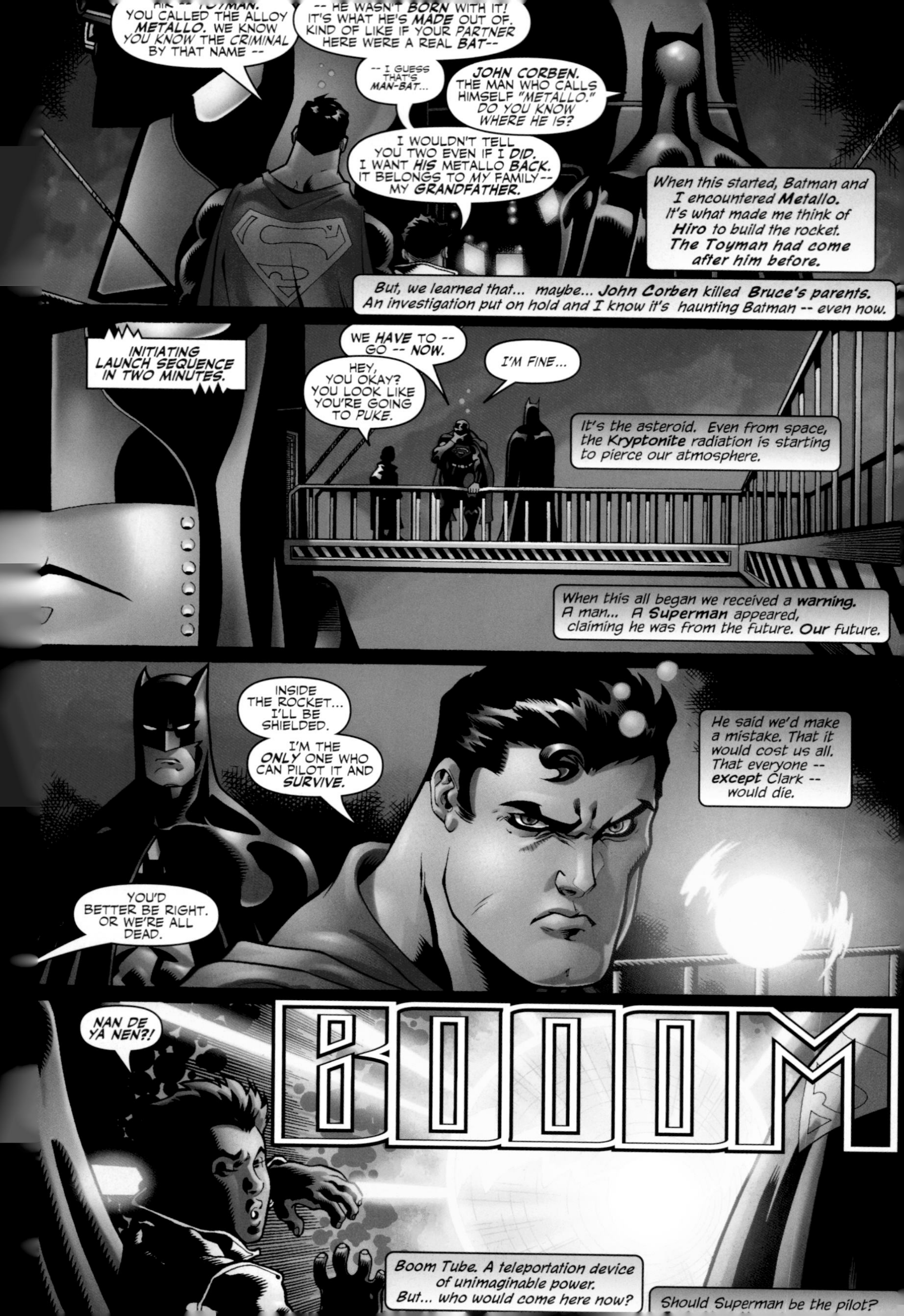
YOU CALLED THE ALLOY METALLO. WE KNOW YOU KNOW THE CRIMINAL BY THAT NAME --
-- HE WASN'T BORN WITH IT! IT'S WHAT HE'S MADE OUT OF. KIND OF LIKE IF YOUR PARTNER HERE WERE A REAL BAT--
-- I GUESS THAT'S MAN-BAT...
JOHN CORBEN. THE MAN WHO CALLS HIMSELF "METALLO." DO YOU KNOW WHERE HE IS?
I WOULDN'T TELL YOU TWO EVEN IF I DID. I WANT HIS METALLO BACK. IT BELONGS TO MY FAMILY-- MY GRANDFATHER.
When this started, Batman and I encountered Metallo. It's what made me think of Hiro to build the rocket. The Toyman had come after him before.
But, we learned that... maybe... John Corben killed Bruce's parents. An investigation put on hold and I know it's haunting Batman -- even now.
INITIATING LAUNCH SEQUENCE IN TWO MINUTES.
WE HAVE TO -- GO -- NOW.
HEY, YOU OKAY? YOU LOOK LIKE YOU'RE GOING TO PUKE.
I'M FINE...
It's the asteroid. Even from space, the Kryptonite radiation is starting to pierce our atmosphere.
When this all began we received a warning. A man... A Superman appeared, claiming he was from the future. Our future.
INSIDE THE ROCKET... I'LL BE SHIELDED.
I'M THE ONLY ONE WHO CAN PILOT IT AND SURVIVE.
He said we'd make a mistake. That it would cost us all. That everyone -- except Clark -- would die.
YOU'D BETTER BE RIGHT. OR WE'RE ALL DEAD.
NAN DE YA NEN?!
BOOOM
Boom Tube. A teleportation device of unimaginable power. But... who would come here now?
Should Superman be the pilot?

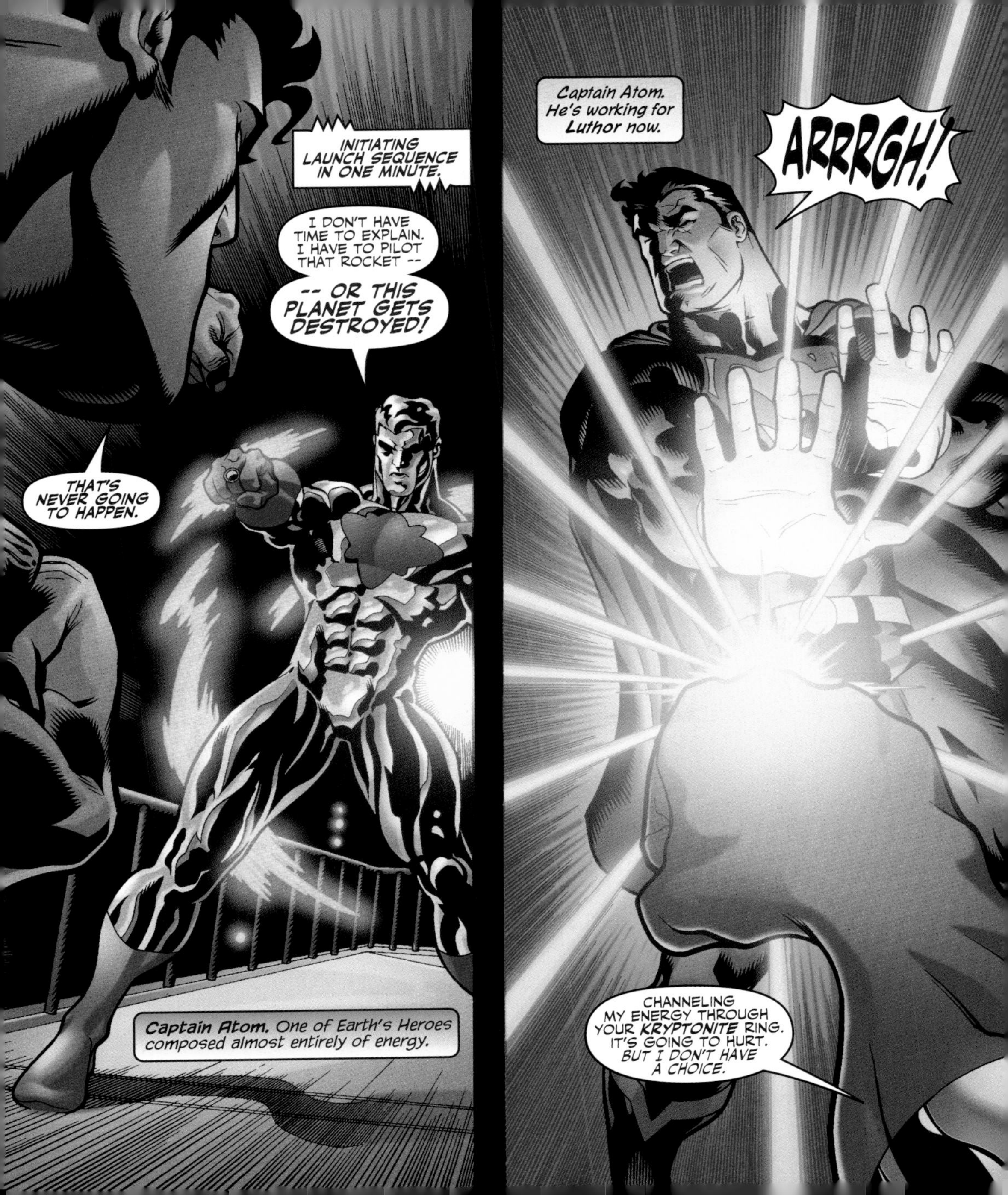

INITIATING LAUNCH SEQUENCE IN ONE MINUTE.
I DON'T HAVE TIME TO EXPLAIN. I HAVE TO PILOT THAT ROCKET --
-- OR THIS PLANET GETS DESTROYED!
THAT'S NEVER GOING TO HAPPEN.
Captain Atom. One of Earth's Heroes composed almost entirely of energy.
Captain Atom. He's working for Luthor now.
ARRRGH!
CHANNELING MY ENERGY THROUGH YOUR KRYPTONITE RING. IT'S GOING TO HURT. BUT I DON'T HAVE A CHOICE.

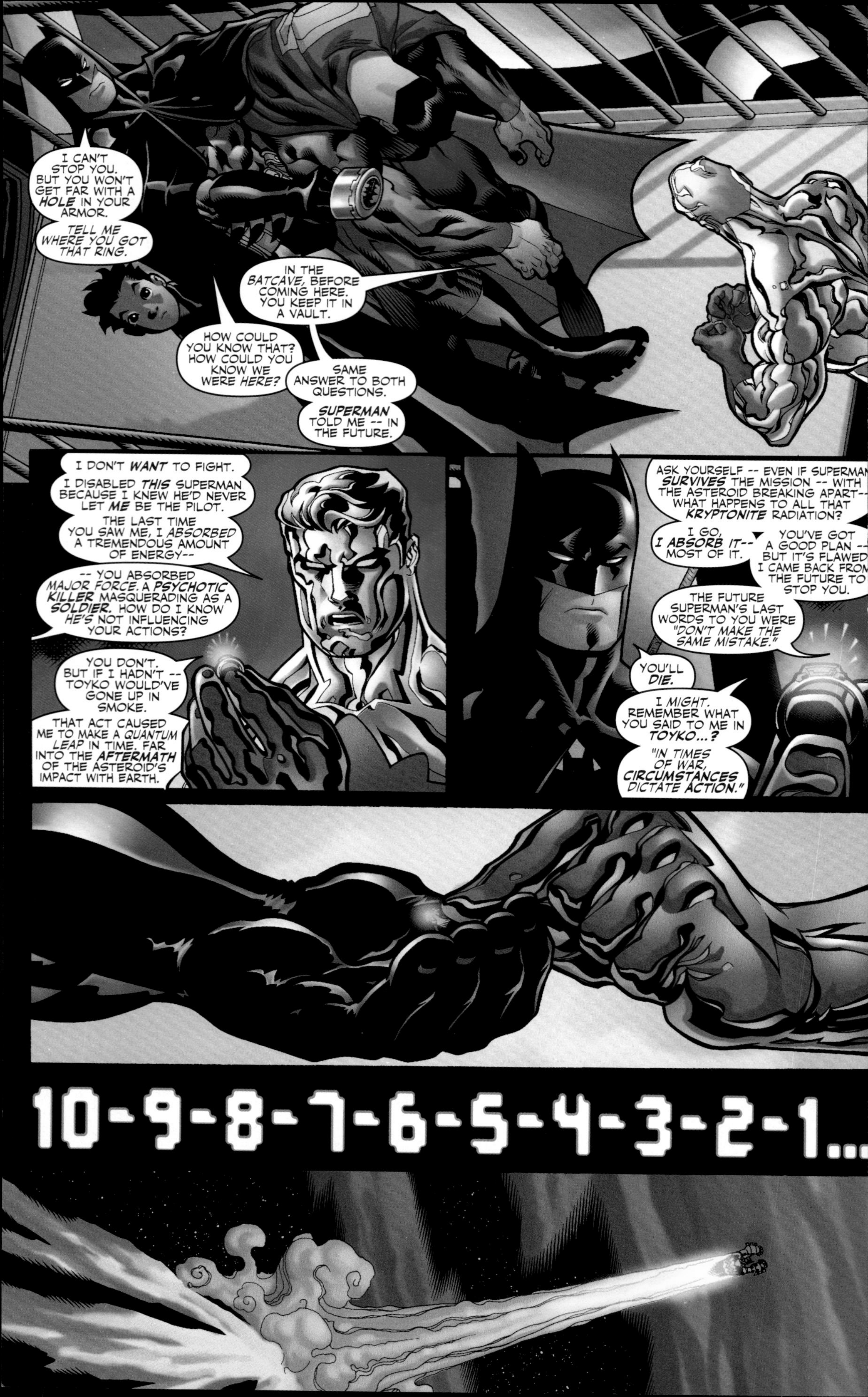
I CAN'T STOP YOU. BUT YOU WON'T GET FAR WITH A HOLE IN YOUR ARMOR.
TELL ME WHERE YOU GOT THAT RING.
IN THE BATCAVE, BEFORE COMING HERE. YOU KEEP IT IN A VAULT.
HOW COULD YOU KNOW THAT? HOW COULD YOU KNOW WE WERE HERE?
SAME ANSWER TO BOTH QUESTIONS.
SUPERMAN TOLD ME -- IN THE FUTURE.
I DON'T WANT TO FIGHT.
I DISABLED THIS SUPERMAN BECAUSE I KNEW HE'D NEVER LET ME BE THE PILOT.
THE LAST TIME YOU SAW ME, I ABSORBED A TREMENDOUS AMOUNT OF ENERGY--
-- YOU ABSORBED MAJOR FORCE. A PSYCHOTIC KILLER MASQUERADING AS A SOLDIER. HOW DO I KNOW HE'S NOT INFLUENCING YOUR ACTIONS?
YOU DON'T. BUT IF I HADN'T -- TOYKO WOULD'VE GONE UP IN SMOKE.
THAT ACT CAUSED ME TO MAKE A QUANTUM LEAP IN TIME. FAR INTO THE AFTERMATH OF THE ASTEROID'S IMPACT WITH EARTH.
ASK YOURSELF -- EVEN IF SUPERMAN SURVIVES THE MISSION -- WITH THE ASTEROID BREAKING APART-- WHAT HAPPENS TO ALL THAT KRYPTONITE RADIATION?
I GO, I ABSORB IT-- MOST OF IT.
YOU'VE GOT A GOOD PLAN -- BUT IT'S FLAWED. I CAME BACK FROM THE FUTURE TO STOP YOU.
THE FUTURE SUPERMAN'S LAST WORDS TO YOU WERE "DON'T MAKE THE SAME MISTAKE."
YOU'LL DIE.
I MIGHT. REMEMBER WHAT YOU SAID TO ME IN TOYKO...?
"IN TIMES OF WAR, CIRCUMSTANCES DICTATE ACTION."
10-9-8-7-6-5-4-3-2-1...

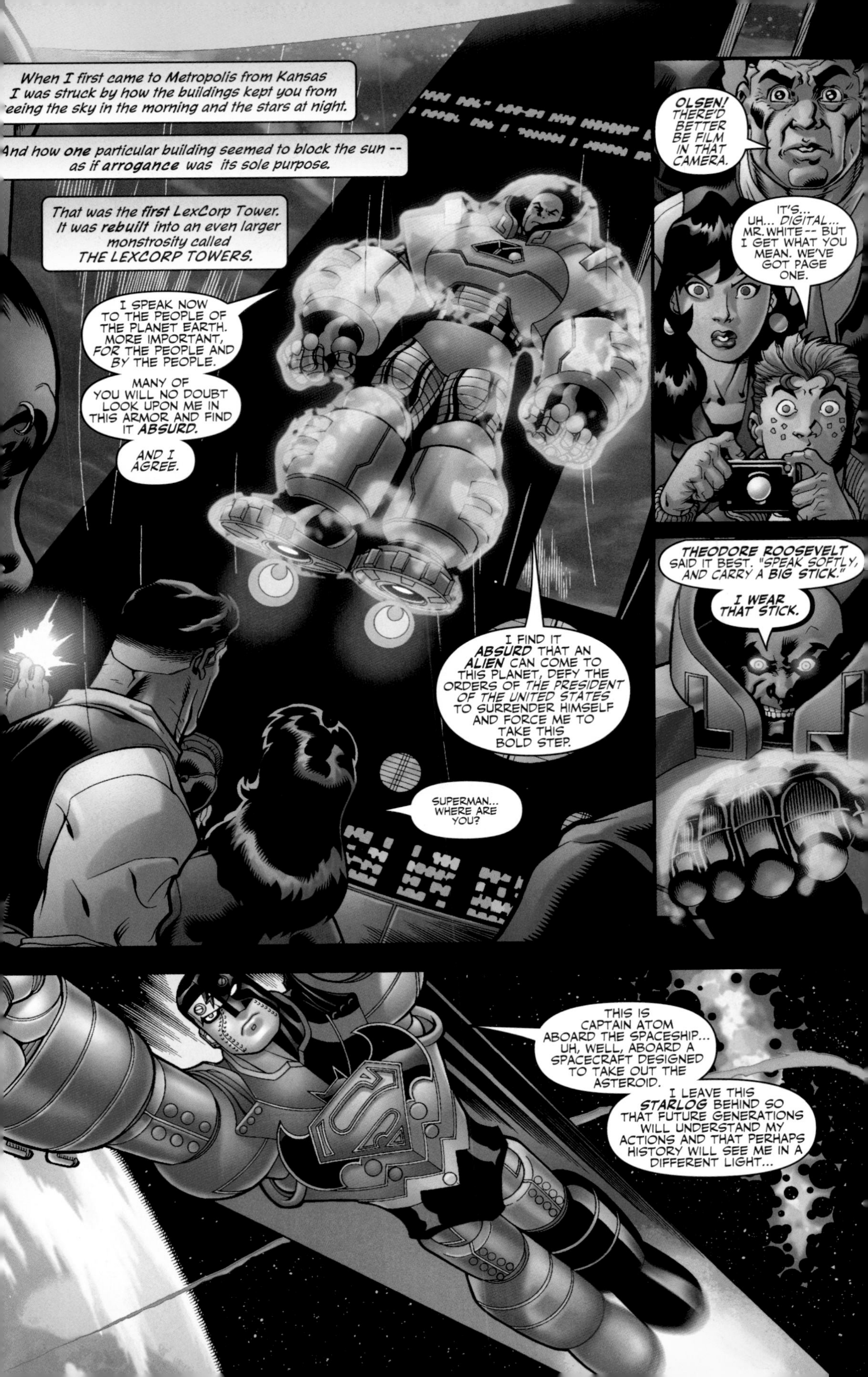
When I first came to Metropolis from Kansas I was struck by how the buildings kept you from seeing the sky in the morning and the stars at night.
And how one particular building seemed to block the sun -- as if arrogance was its sole purpose.
That was the first LexCorp Tower. It was rebuilt into an even larger monstrosity called THE LEXCORP TOWERS.
I SPEAK NOW TO THE PEOPLE OF THE PLANET EARTH. MORE IMPORTANT, FOR THE PEOPLE AND BY THE PEOPLE.
MANY OF YOU WILL NO DOUBT LOOK UPON ME IN THIS ARMOR AND FIND IT ABSURD.
AND I AGREE.
OLSEN! THERE'D BETTER BE FILM IN THAT CAMERA.
IT'S... UH... DIGITAL... MR. WHITE -- BUT I GET WHAT YOU MEAN. WE'VE GOT PAGE ONE.
I FIND IT ABSURD THAT AN ALIEN CAN COME TO THIS PLANET, DEFY THE ORDERS OF THE PRESIDENT OF THE UNITED STATES TO SURRENDER HIMSELF AND FORCE ME TO TAKE THIS BOLD STEP.
SUPERMAN... WHERE ARE YOU?
THEODORE ROOSEVELT SAID IT BEST. "SPEAK SOFTLY, AND CARRY A BIG STICK."
I WEAR THAT STICK.
THIS IS CAPTAIN ATOM ABOARD THE SPACESHIP... UH, WELL, ABOARD A SPACECRAFT DESIGNED TO TAKE OUT THE ASTEROID.
I LEAVE THIS STARLOG BEHIND SO THAT FUTURE GENERATIONS WILL UNDERSTAND MY ACTIONS AND THAT PERHAPS HISTORY WILL SEE ME IN A DIFFERENT LIGHT...

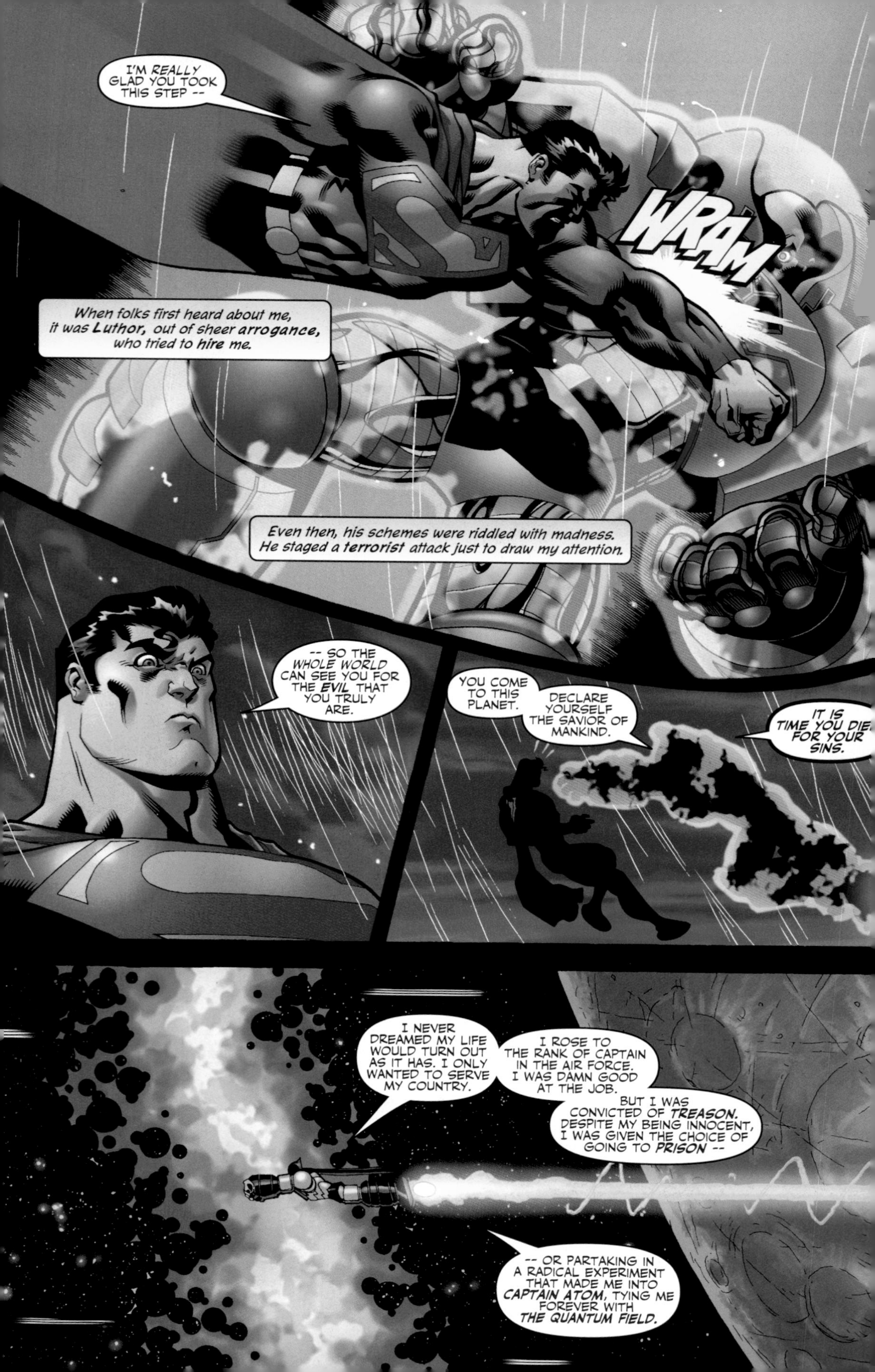
I'M REALLY GLAD YOU TOOK THIS STEP --
WRAM
When folks first heard about me, it was Luthor, out of sheer arrogance, who tried to hire me.
Even then, his schemes were riddled with madness. He staged a terrorist attack just to draw my attention.
-- SO THE WHOLE WORLD CAN SEE YOU FOR THE EVIL THAT YOU TRULY ARE.
YOU COME TO THIS PLANET.
DECLARE YOURSELF THE SAVIOR OF MANKIND.
IT IS TIME YOU DIE FOR YOUR SINS.
I NEVER DREAMED MY LIFE WOULD TURN OUT AS IT HAS. I ONLY WANTED TO SERVE MY COUNTRY.
I ROSE TO THE RANK OF CAPTAIN IN THE AIR FORCE. I WAS DAMN GOOD AT THE JOB.
BUT I WAS CONVICTED OF TREASON. DESPITE MY BEING INNOCENT, I WAS GIVEN THE CHOICE OF GOING TO PRISON --
-- OR PARTAKING IN A RADICAL EXPERIMENT THAT MADE ME INTO CAPTAIN ATOM, TYING ME FOREVER WITH THE QUANTUM FIELD.

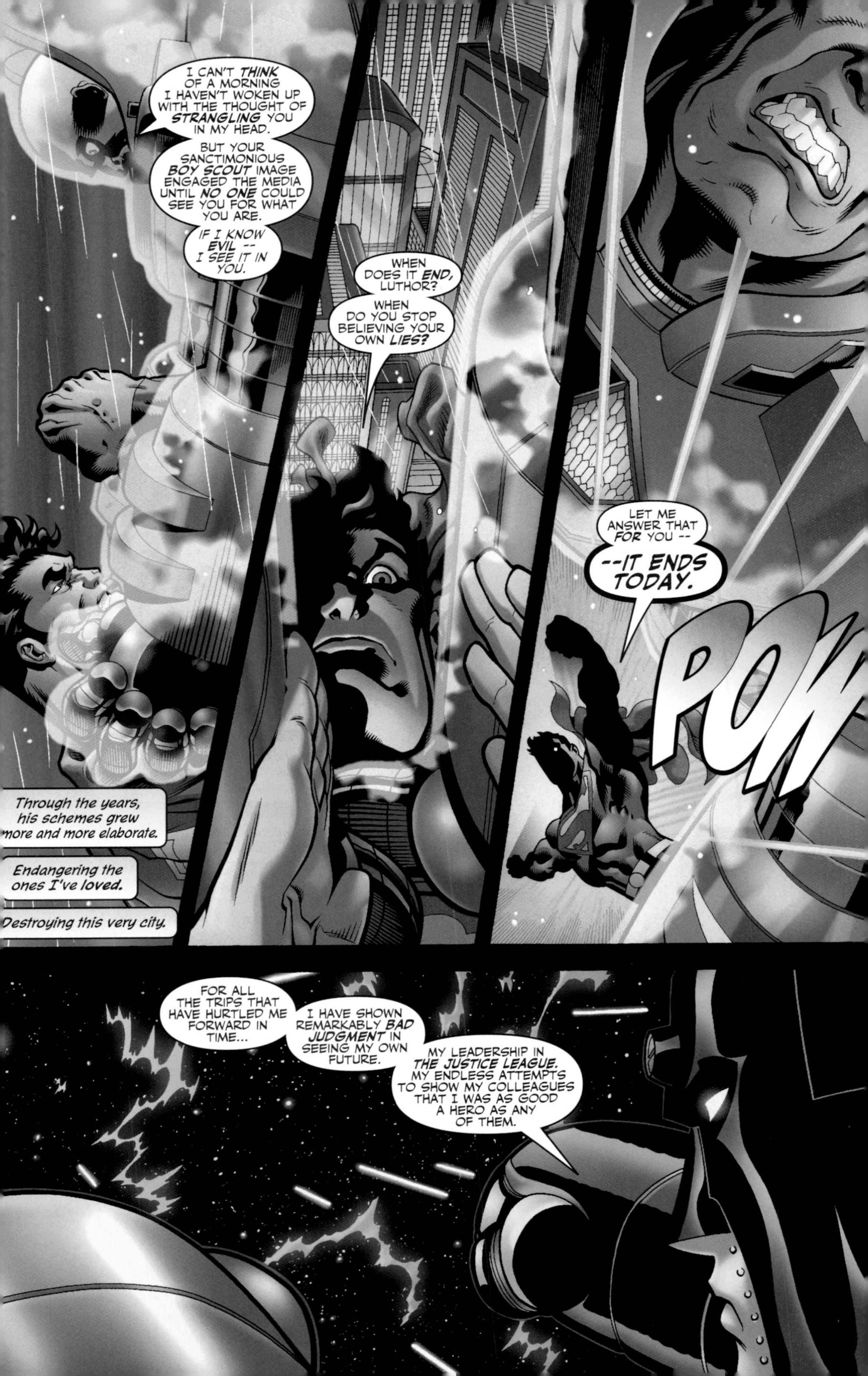
I CAN'T THINK OF A MORNING I HAVEN'T WOKEN UP WITH THE THOUGHT OF STRANGLING YOU IN MY HEAD.
BUT YOUR SANCTIMONIOUS BOY SCOUT IMAGE ENGAGED THE MEDIA UNTIL NO ONE COULD SEE YOU FOR WHAT YOU ARE.
IF I KNOW EVIL -- I SEE IT IN YOU.
Through the years, his schemes grew more and more elaborate.
Endangering the ones I've loved.
Destroying this very city.
WHEN DOES IT END, LUTHOR?
WHEN DO YOU STOP BELIEVING YOUR OWN LIES?
LET ME ANSWER THAT FOR YOU --
--IT ENDS TODAY.
POW
FOR ALL THE TRIPS THAT HAVE HURTLED ME FORWARD IN TIME...
I HAVE SHOWN REMARKABLY BAD JUDGMENT IN SEEING MY OWN FUTURE.
MY LEADERSHIP IN THE JUSTICE LEAGUE. MY ENDLESS ATTEMPTS TO SHOW MY COLLEAGUES THAT I WAS AS GOOD A HERO AS ANY OF THEM.

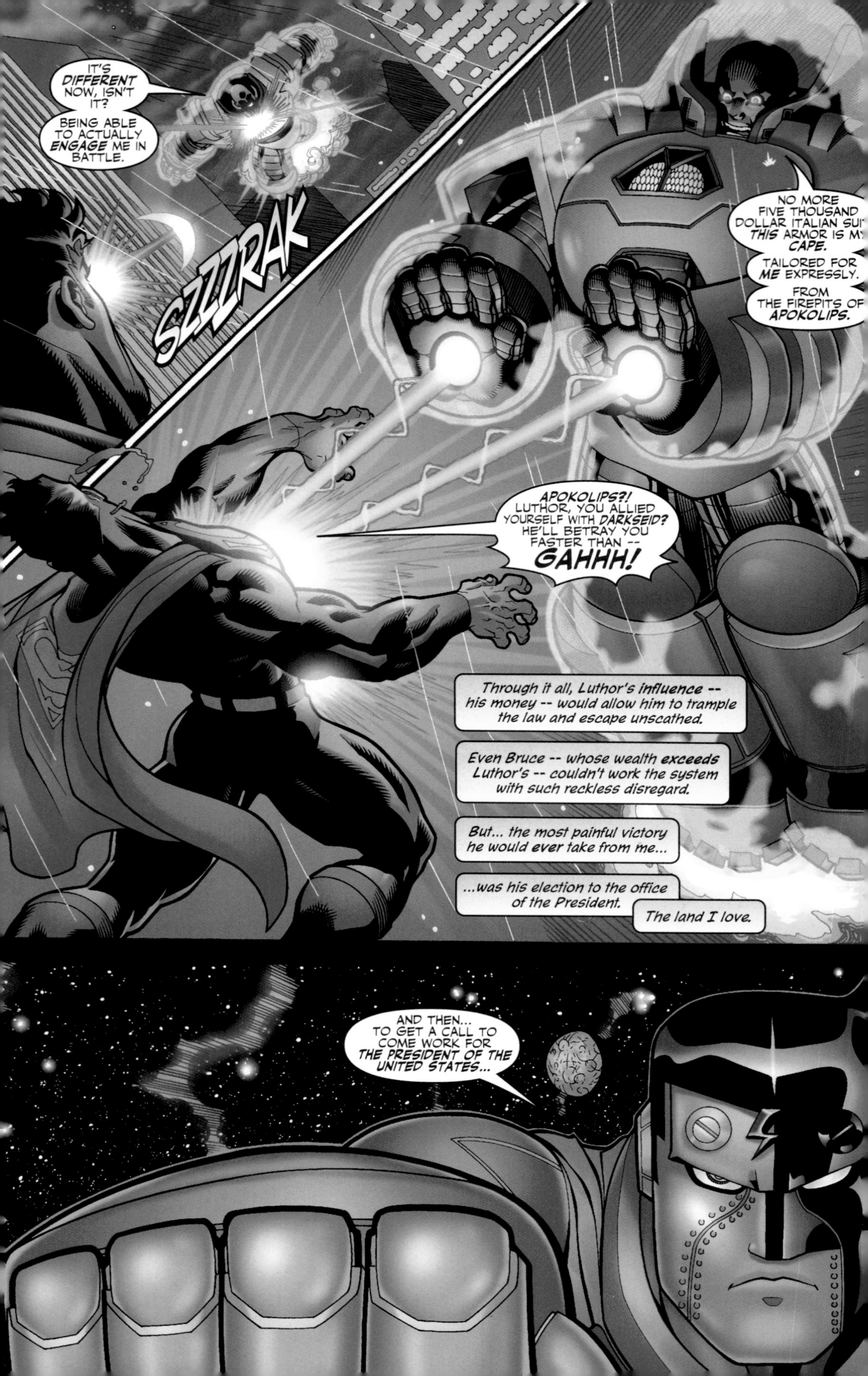
IT'S DIFFERENT NOW, ISN'T IT?
BEING ABLE TO ACTUALLY ENGAGE ME IN BATTLE.
SZZZRAK
NO MORE FIVE THOUSAND DOLLAR ITALIAN SUI THIS ARMOR IS M CAPE.
TAILORED FOR ME EXPRESSLY.
FROM THE FIREPITS OF APOKOLIPS.
APOKOLIPS?! LUTHOR, YOU ALLIED YOURSELF WITH DARKSEID? HE'LL BETRAY YOU FASTER THAN -- GAHHH!
Through it all, Luthor's influence -- his money -- would allow him to trample the law and escape unscathed.
Even Bruce -- whose wealth exceeds Luthor's -- couldn't work the system with such reckless disregard.
But... the most painful victory he would ever take from me...
...was his election to the office of the President.
The land I love.
AND THEN... TO GET A CALL TO COME WORK FOR THE PRESIDENT OF THE UNITED STATES...

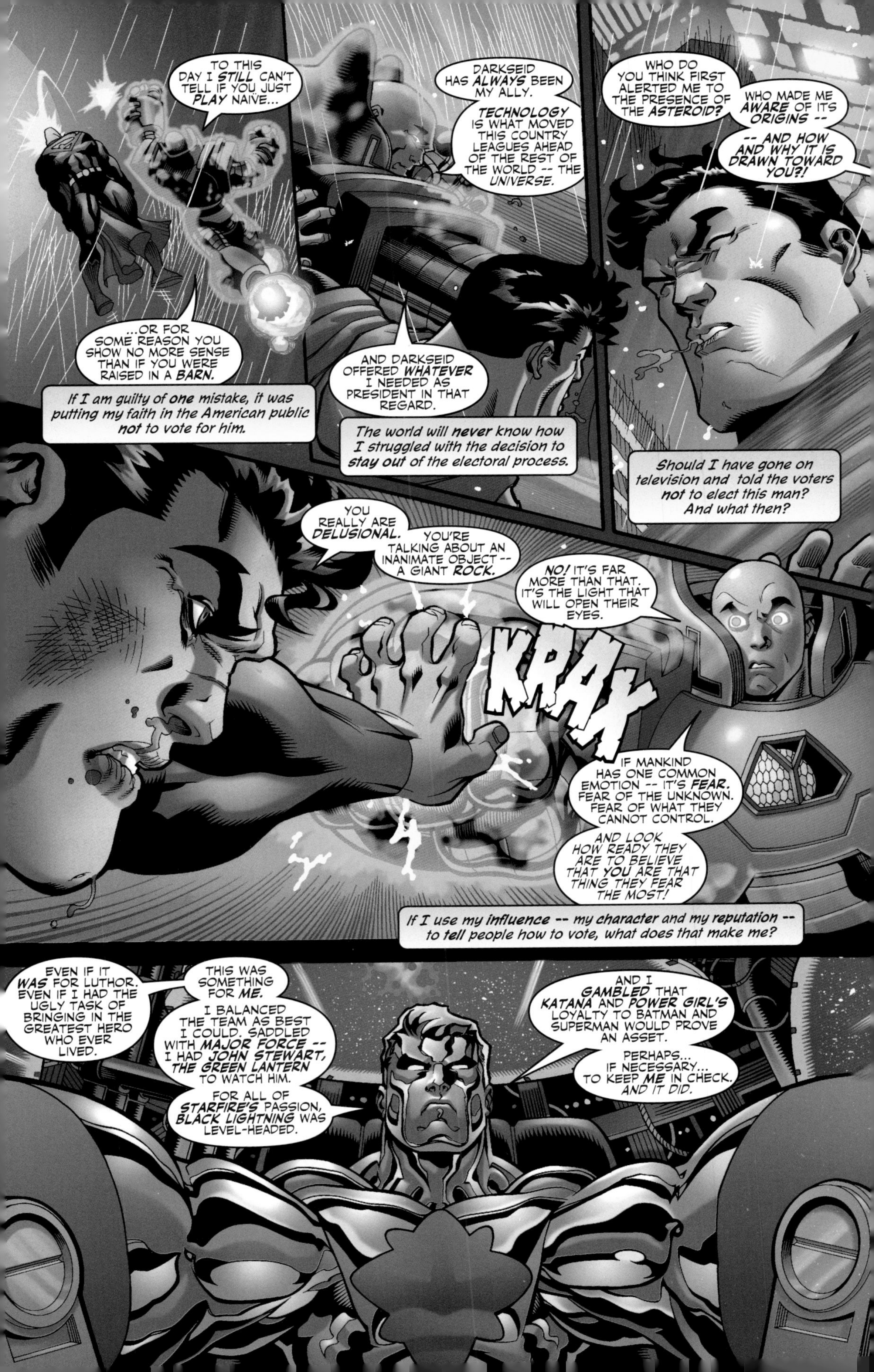

TO THIS DAY I STILL CAN'T TELL IF YOU JUST PLAY NAIVE...
...OR FOR SOME REASON YOU SHOW NO MORE SENSE THAN IF YOU WERE RAISED IN A BARN.
If I am guilty of one mistake, it was putting my faith in the American public not to vote for him.
DARKSEID HAS ALWAYS BEEN MY ALLY.
TECHNOLOGY IS WHAT MOVED THIS COUNTRY LEAGUES AHEAD OF THE REST OF THE WORLD -- THE UNIVERSE.
AND DARKSEID OFFERED WHATEVER I NEEDED AS PRESIDENT IN THAT REGARD.
The world will never know how I struggled with the decision to stay out of the electoral process.
WHO DO YOU THINK FIRST ALERTED ME TO THE PRESENCE OF THE ASTEROID?
WHO MADE ME AWARE OF ITS ORIGINS --
-- AND HOW AND WHY IT IS DRAWN TOWARD YOU?!
Should I have gone on television and told the voters not to elect this man? And what then?
YOU REALLY ARE DELUSIONAL.
YOU'RE TALKING ABOUT AN INANIMATE OBJECT -- A GIANT ROCK.
NO! IT'S FAR MORE THAN THAT. IT'S THE LIGHT THAT WILL OPEN THEIR EYES.
KRAK
IF MANKIND HAS ONE COMMON EMOTION -- IT'S FEAR. FEAR OF THE UNKNOWN. FEAR OF WHAT THEY CANNOT CONTROL.
AND LOOK HOW READY THEY ARE TO BELIEVE THAT YOU ARE THAT THING THEY FEAR THE MOST!
If I use my influence -- my character and my reputation -- to tell people how to vote, what does that make me?
EVEN IF IT WAS FOR LUTHOR. EVEN IF I HAD THE UGLY TASK OF BRINGING IN THE GREATEST HERO WHO EVER LIVED.
THIS WAS SOMETHING FOR ME.
I BALANCED THE TEAM AS BEST I COULD. SADDLED WITH MAJOR FORCE -- I HAD JOHN STEWART, THE GREEN LANTERN TO WATCH HIM.
FOR ALL OF STARFIRE'S PASSION, BLACK LIGHTNING WAS LEVEL-HEADED.
AND I GAMBLED THAT KATANA AND POWER GIRL'S LOYALTY TO BATMAN AND SUPERMAN WOULD PROVE AN ASSET.
PERHAPS... IF NECESSARY... TO KEEP ME IN CHECK. AND IT DID.

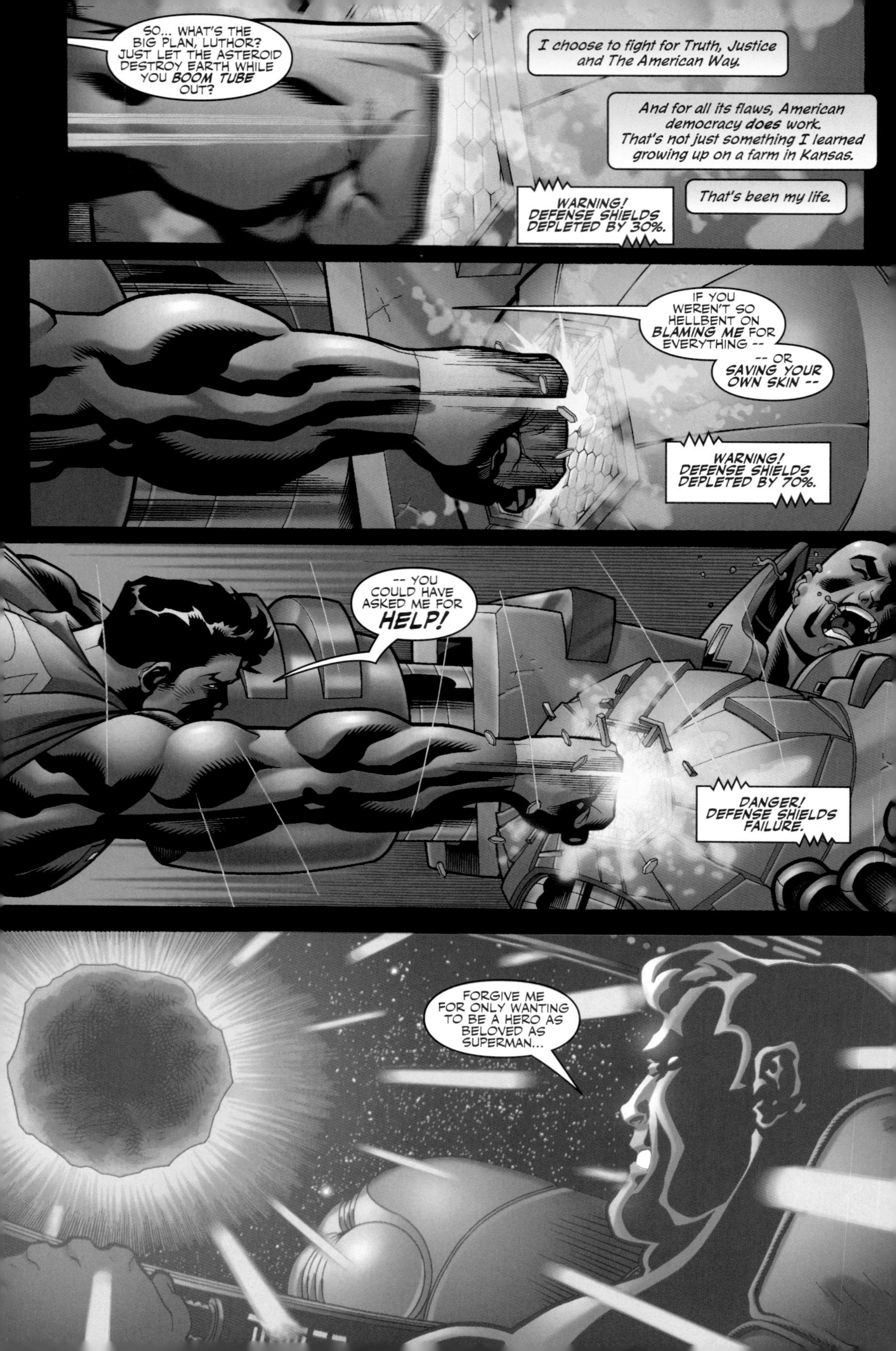
SO... WHAT'S THE BIG PLAN, LUTHOR? JUST LET THE ASTEROID DESTROY EARTH WHILE YOU BOOM TUBE OUT?
I choose to fight for Truth, Justice and The American Way.
And for all its flaws, American democracy does work. That's not just something I learned growing up on a farm in Kansas.
That's been my life.
WARNING! DEFENSE SHIELDS DEPLETED BY 30%.
IF YOU WEREN'T SO HELLBENT ON BLAMING ME FOR EVERYTHING --
-- OR SAVING YOUR OWN SKIN --
WARNING! DEFENSE SHIELDS DEPLETED BY 70%.
-- YOU COULD HAVE ASKED ME FOR HELP!
DANGER! DEFENSE SHIELDS FAILURE.
FORGIVE ME FOR ONLY WANTING TO BE A HERO AS BELOVED AS SUPERMAN...

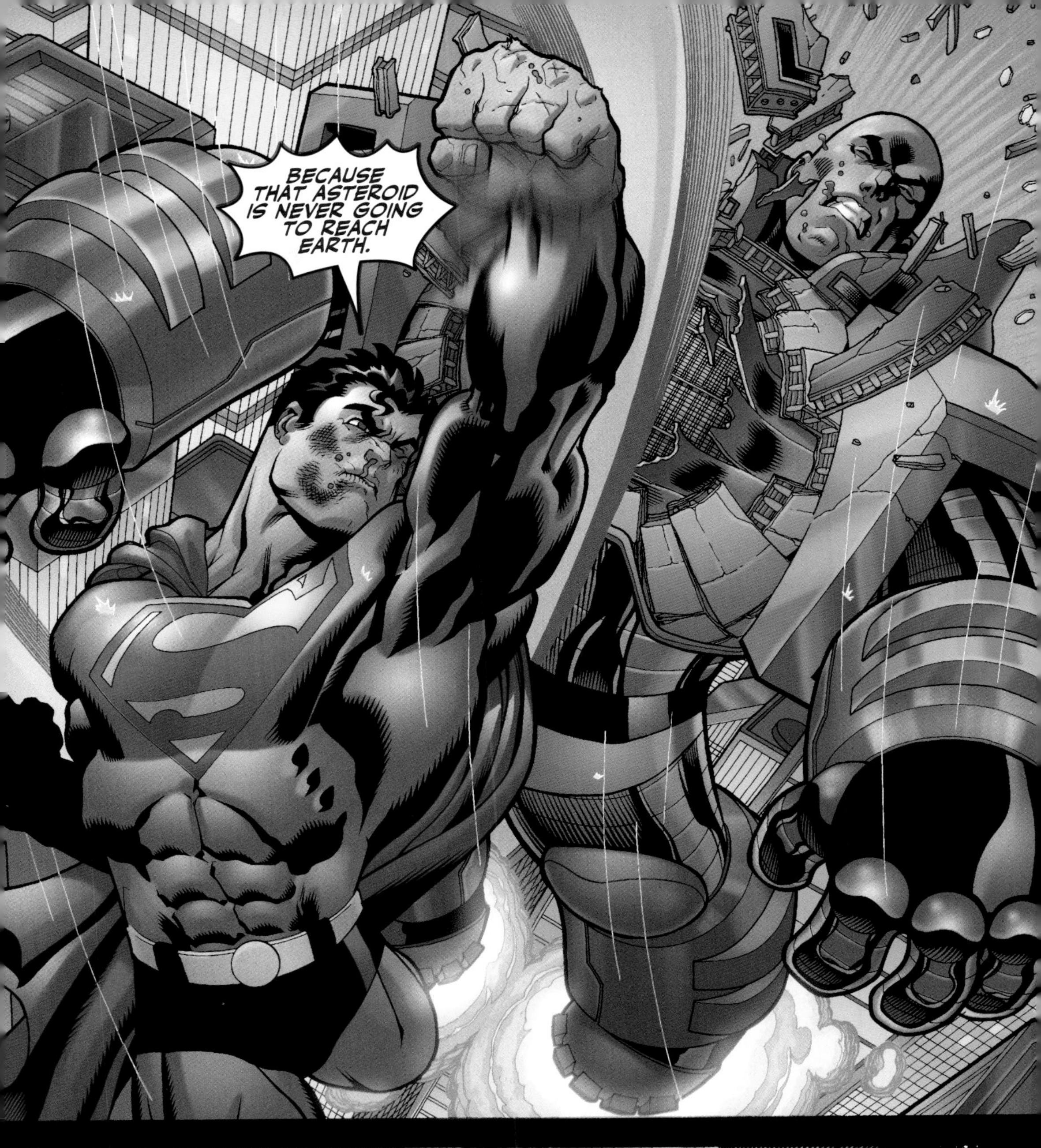
BECAUSE THAT ASTEROID IS NEVER GOING TO REACH EARTH.

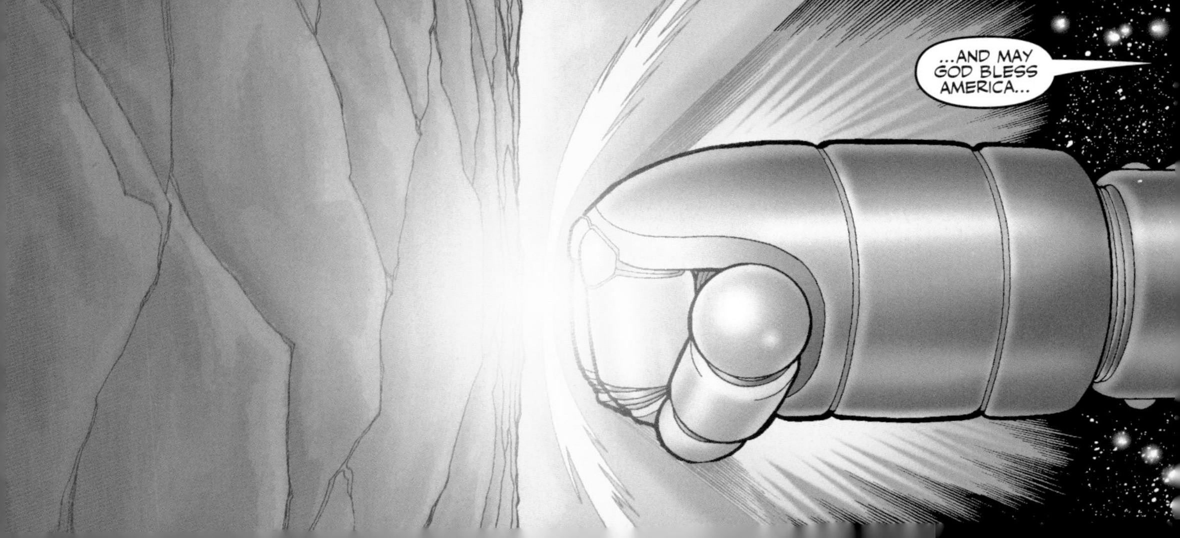
...AND MAY GOD BLESS AMERICA...

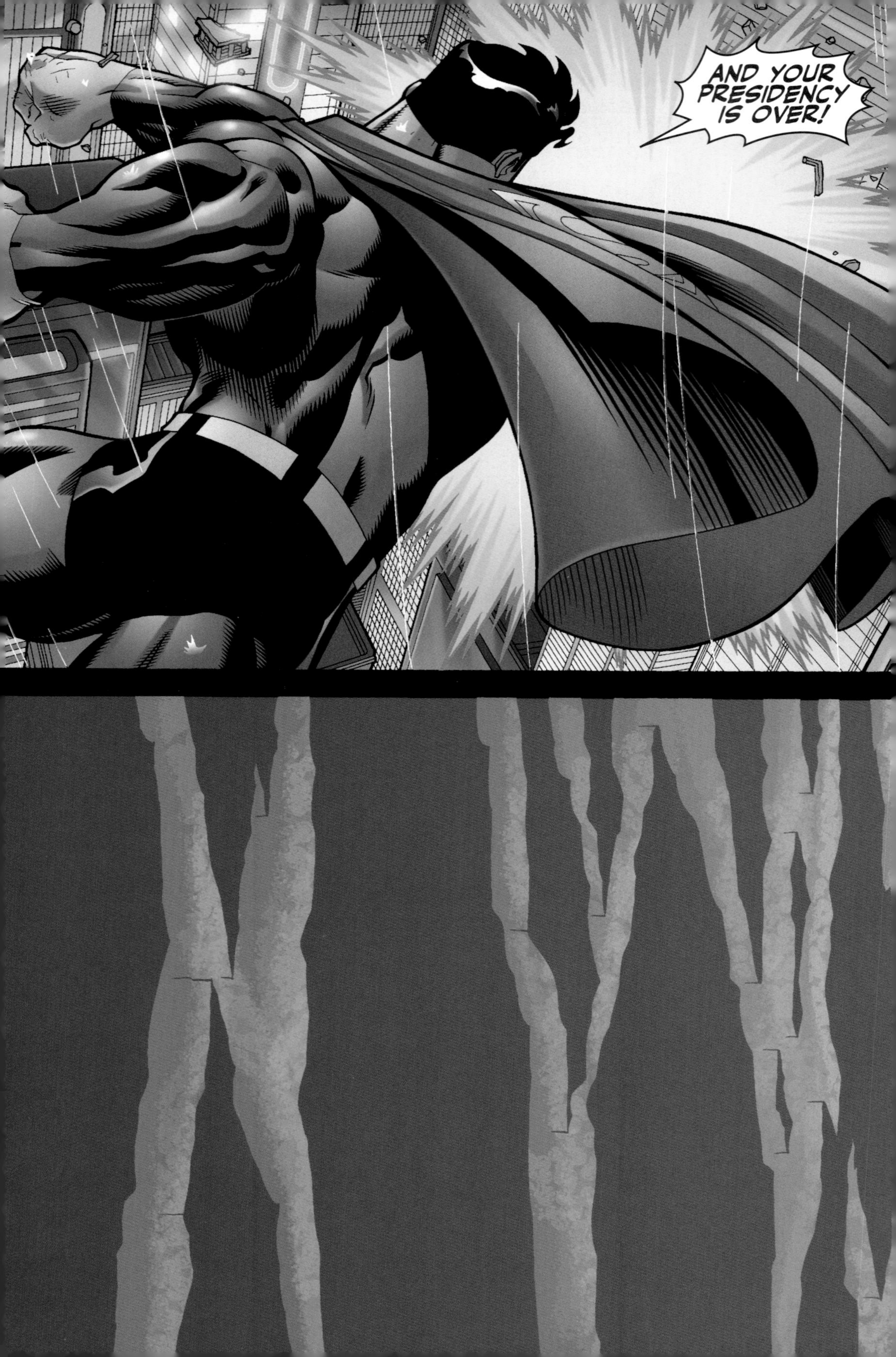
AND YOUR PRESIDENCY IS OVER!

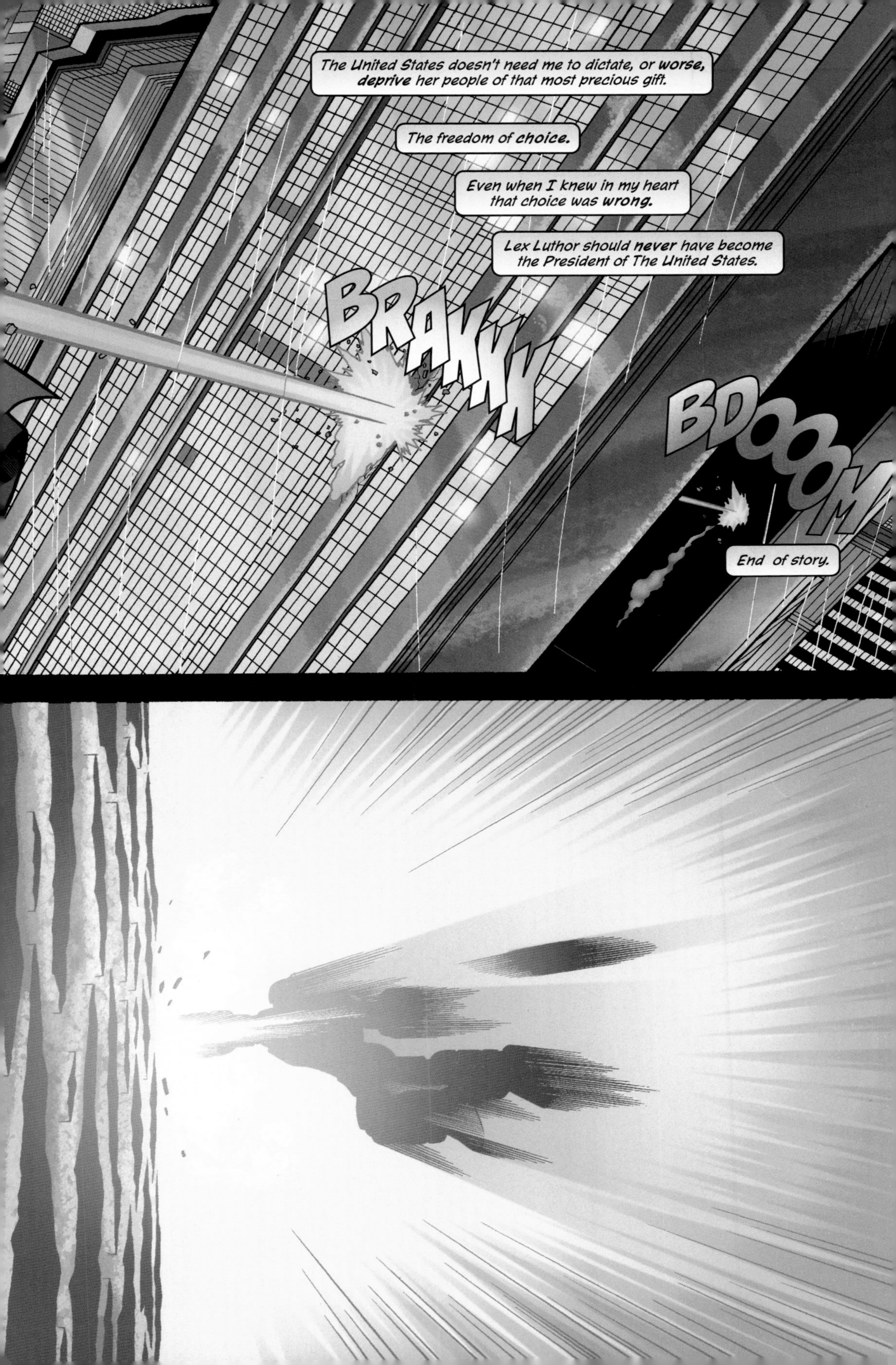
The United States doesn't need me to dictate, or worse, deprive her people of that most precious gift.
The freedom of choice.
Even when I knew in my heart that choice was wrong.
Lex Luthor should never have become the President of The United States.
BRAKKKK
BDOOOM
End of story.

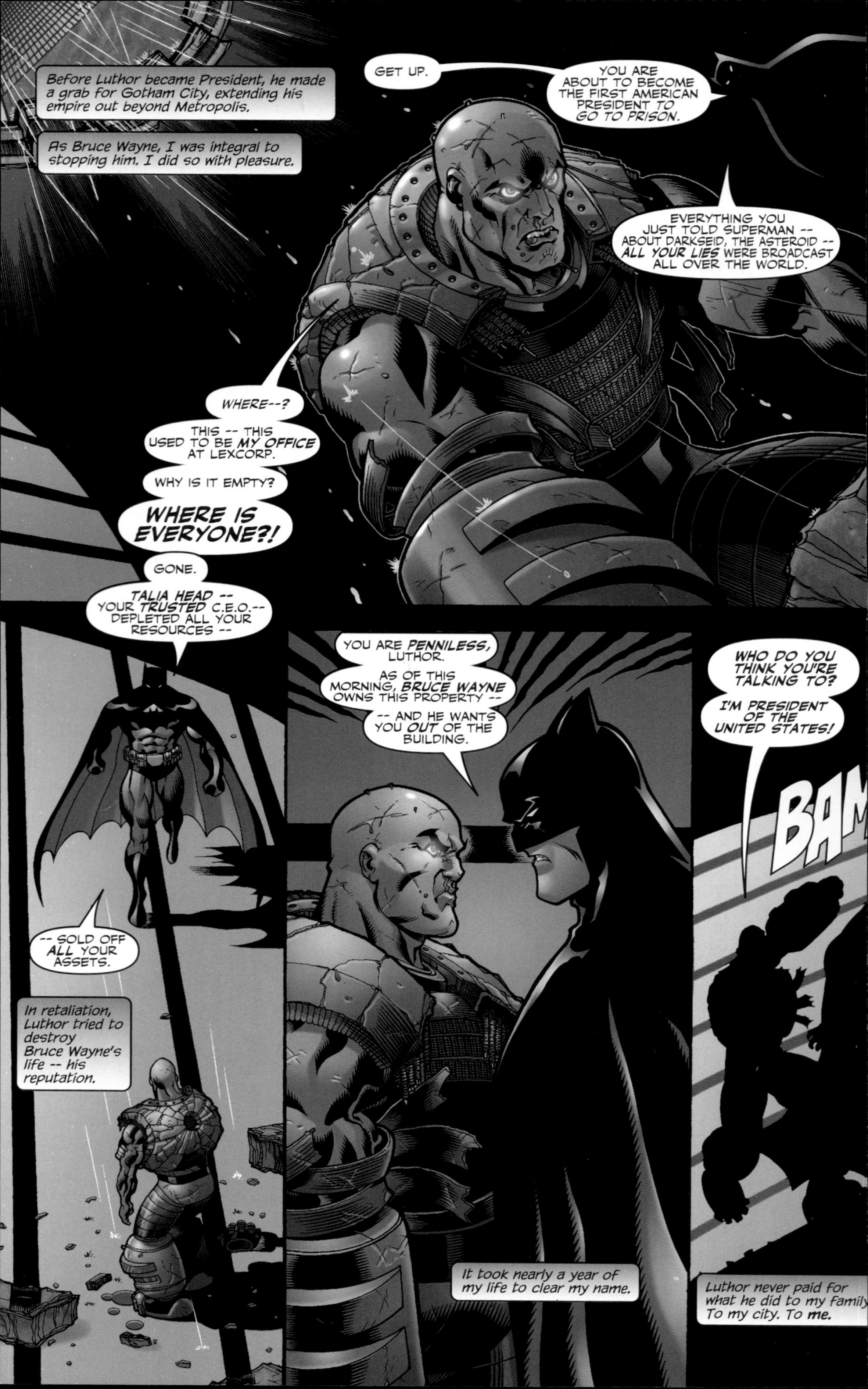

Before Luthor became President, he made a grab for Gotham City, extending his empire out beyond Metropolis.
As Bruce Wayne, I was integral to stopping him. I did so with pleasure.
GET UP.
YOU ARE ABOUT TO BECOME THE FIRST AMERICAN PRESIDENT TO GO TO PRISON.
EVERYTHING YOU JUST TOLD SUPERMAN -- ABOUT DARKSEID, THE ASTEROID -- ALL YOUR LIES WERE BROADCAST ALL OVER THE WORLD.
WHERE--?
THIS -- THIS USED TO BE MY OFFICE AT LEXCORP.
WHY IS IT EMPTY?
WHERE IS EVERYONE?!
GONE.
TALIA HEAD -- YOUR TRUSTED C.E.O.-- DEPLETED ALL YOUR RESOURCES --
-- SOLD OFF ALL YOUR ASSETS.
In retaliation, Luthor tried to destroy Bruce Wayne's life -- his reputation.
YOU ARE PENNILESS, LUTHOR.
AS OF THIS MORNING, BRUCE WAYNE OWNS THIS PROPERTY --
-- AND HE WANTS YOU OUT OF THE BUILDING.
It took nearly a year of my life to clear my name.
WHO DO YOU THINK YOU'RE TALKING TO?
I'M PRESIDENT OF THE UNITED STATES!
BAM
Luthor never paid for what he did to my family. To my city. To me.

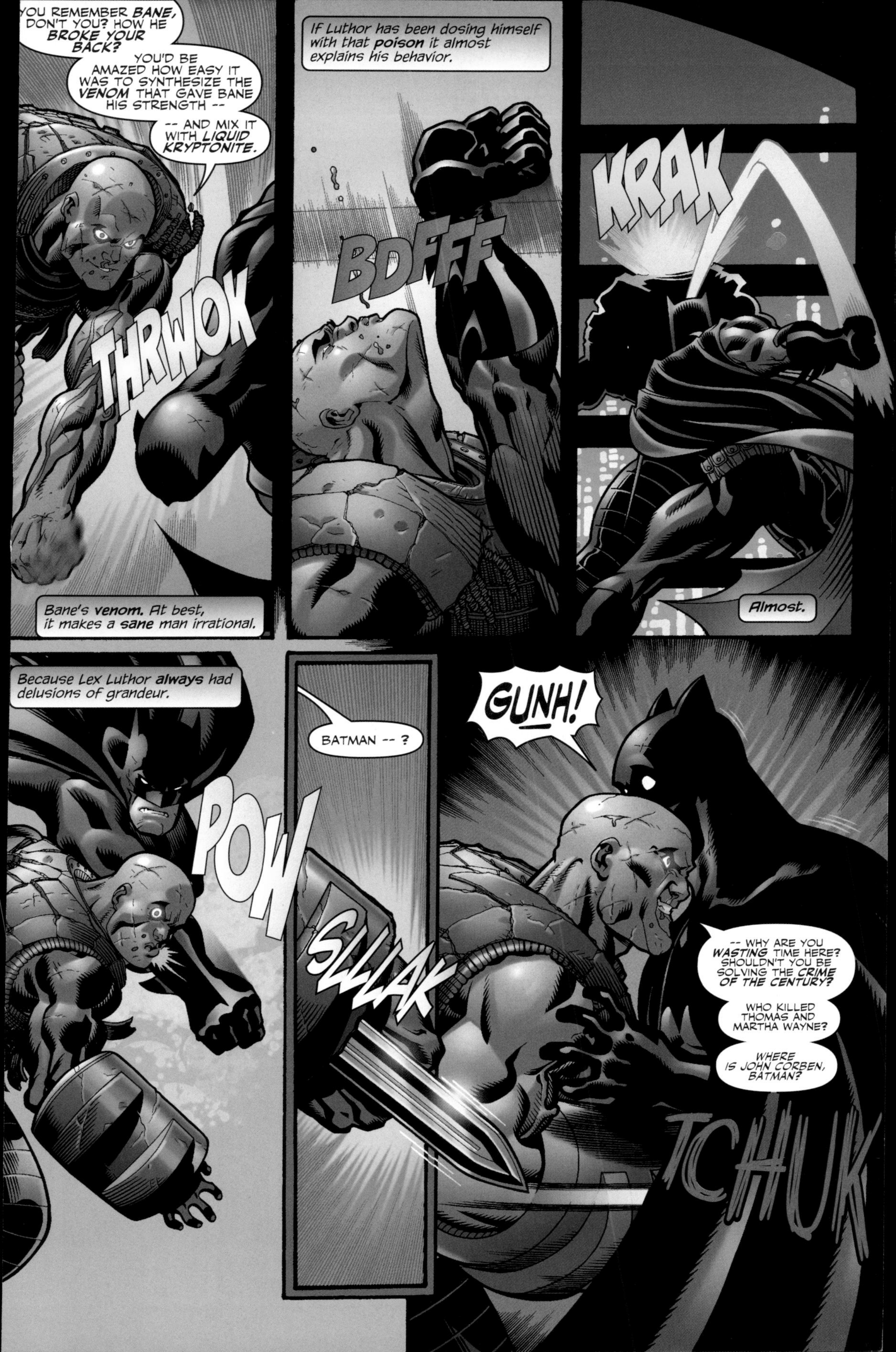

YOU REMEMBER BANE, DON'T YOU? HOW HE BROKE YOUR BACK?
YOU'D BE AMAZED HOW EASY IT WAS TO SYNTHESIZE THE VENOM THAT GAVE BANE HIS STRENGTH --
-- AND MIX IT WITH LIQUID KRYPTONITE.
THRWOK
Bane's venom. At best, it makes a sane man irrational.
If Luthor has been dosing himself with that poison it almost explains his behavior.
BDFFF
KRAK
Almost.
Because Lex Luthor always had delusions of grandeur.
POW
BATMAN -- ?
SLLAK
GUNH!
-- WHY ARE YOU WASTING TIME HERE? SHOULDN'T YOU BE SOLVING THE CRIME OF THE CENTURY?
WHO KILLED THOMAS AND MARTHA WAYNE?
WHERE IS JOHN CORBEN, BATMAN?
TCHUK

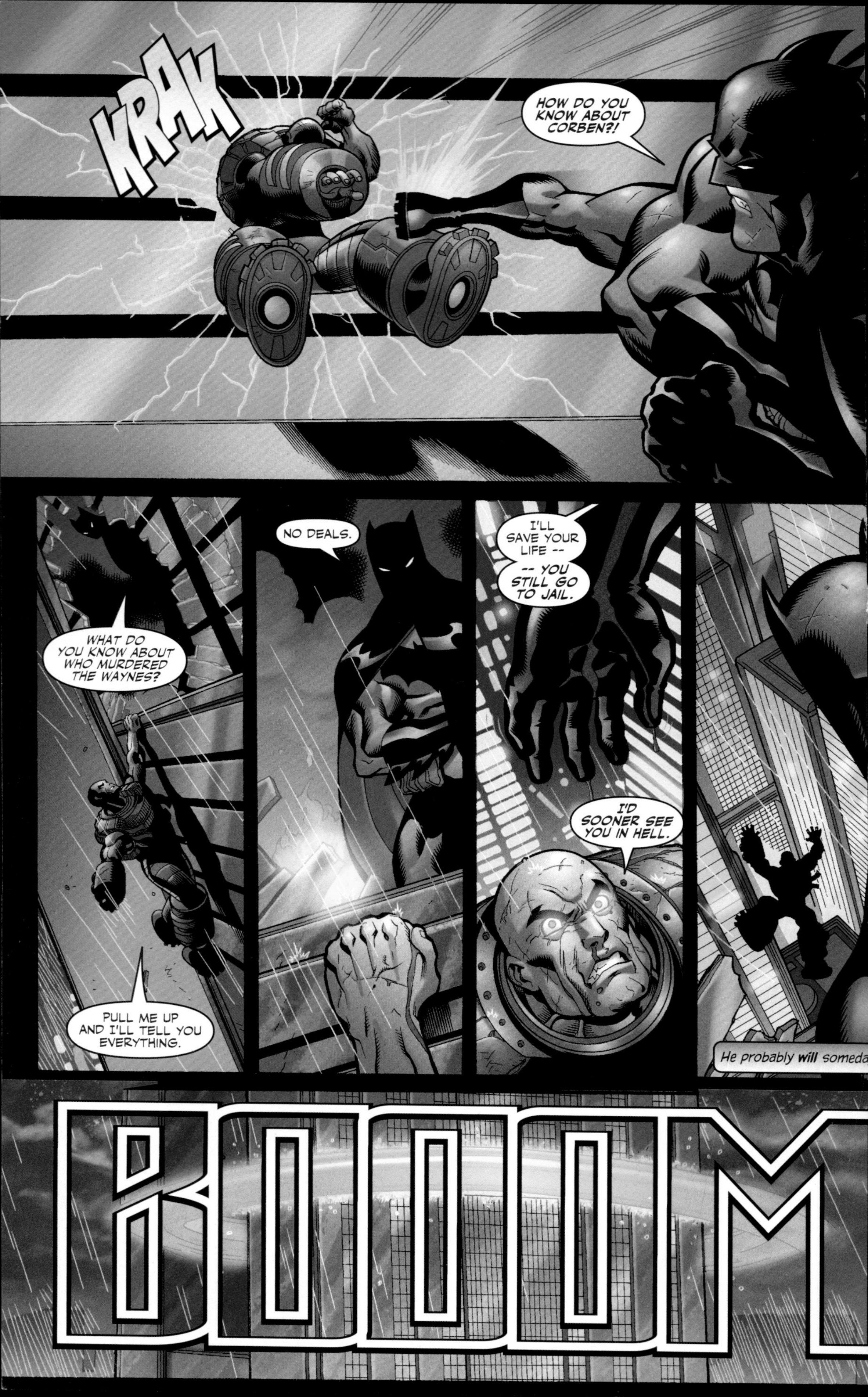
KRAK
HOW DO YOU KNOW ABOUT CORBEN?!
WHAT DO YOU KNOW ABOUT WHO MURDERED THE WAYNES?
PULL ME UP AND I'LL TELL YOU EVERYTHING.
NO DEALS.
I'LL SAVE YOUR LIFE --
-- YOU STILL GO TO JAIL.
I'D SOONER SEE YOU IN HELL.
He probably *will* someda
BOOOM

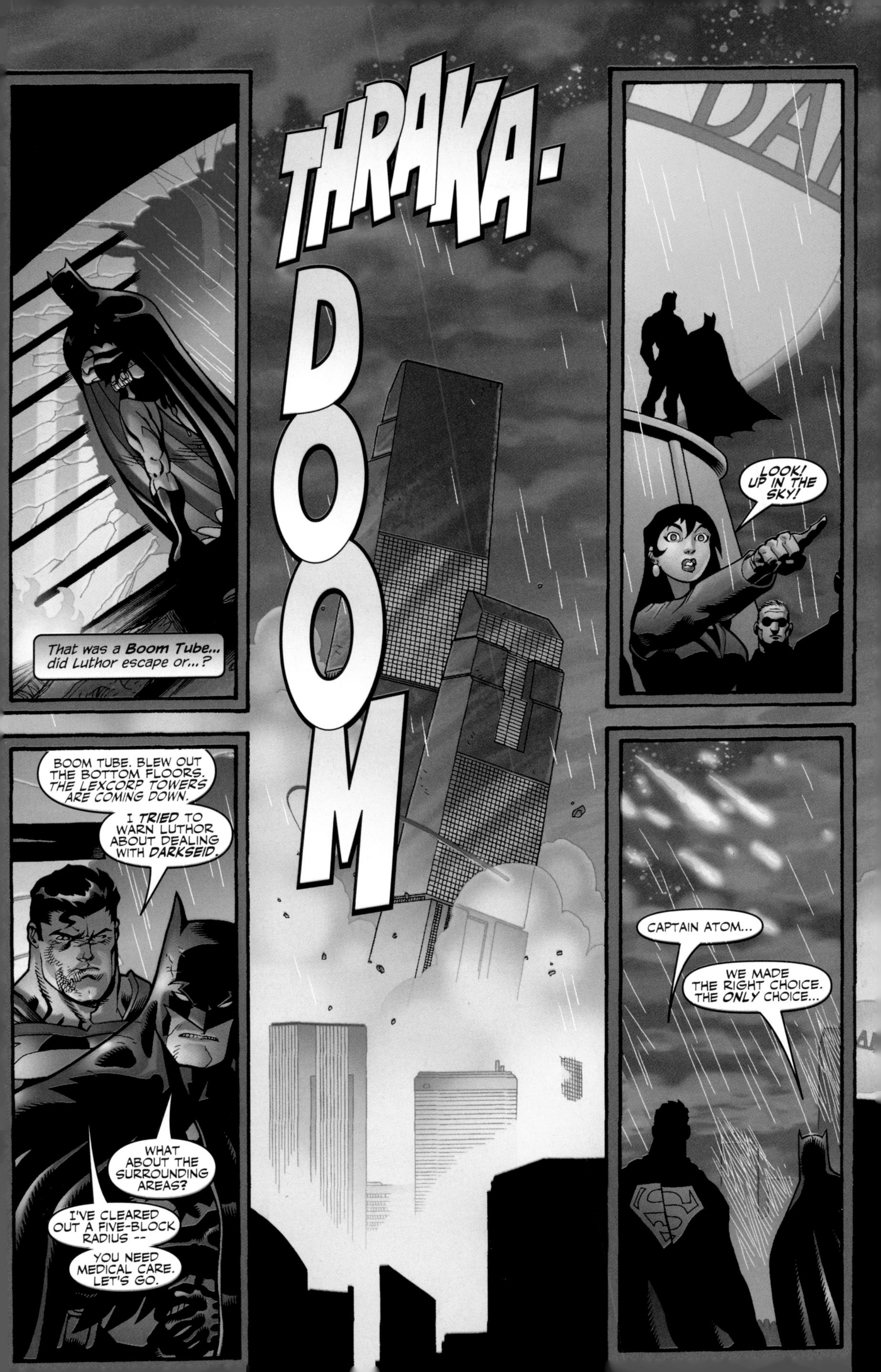
That was a Boom Tube... did Luthor escape or...?
THRAKA-DOOM
LOOK! UP IN THE SKY!
BOOM TUBE. BLEW OUT THE BOTTOM FLOORS. THE LEXCORP TOWERS ARE COMING DOWN.
I TRIED TO WARN LUTHOR ABOUT DEALING WITH DARKSEID.
WHAT ABOUT THE SURROUNDING AREAS?
I'VE CLEARED OUT A FIVE-BLOCK RADIUS --
YOU NEED MEDICAL CARE. LET'S GO.
CAPTAIN ATOM...
WE MADE THE RIGHT CHOICE. THE ONLY CHOICE...

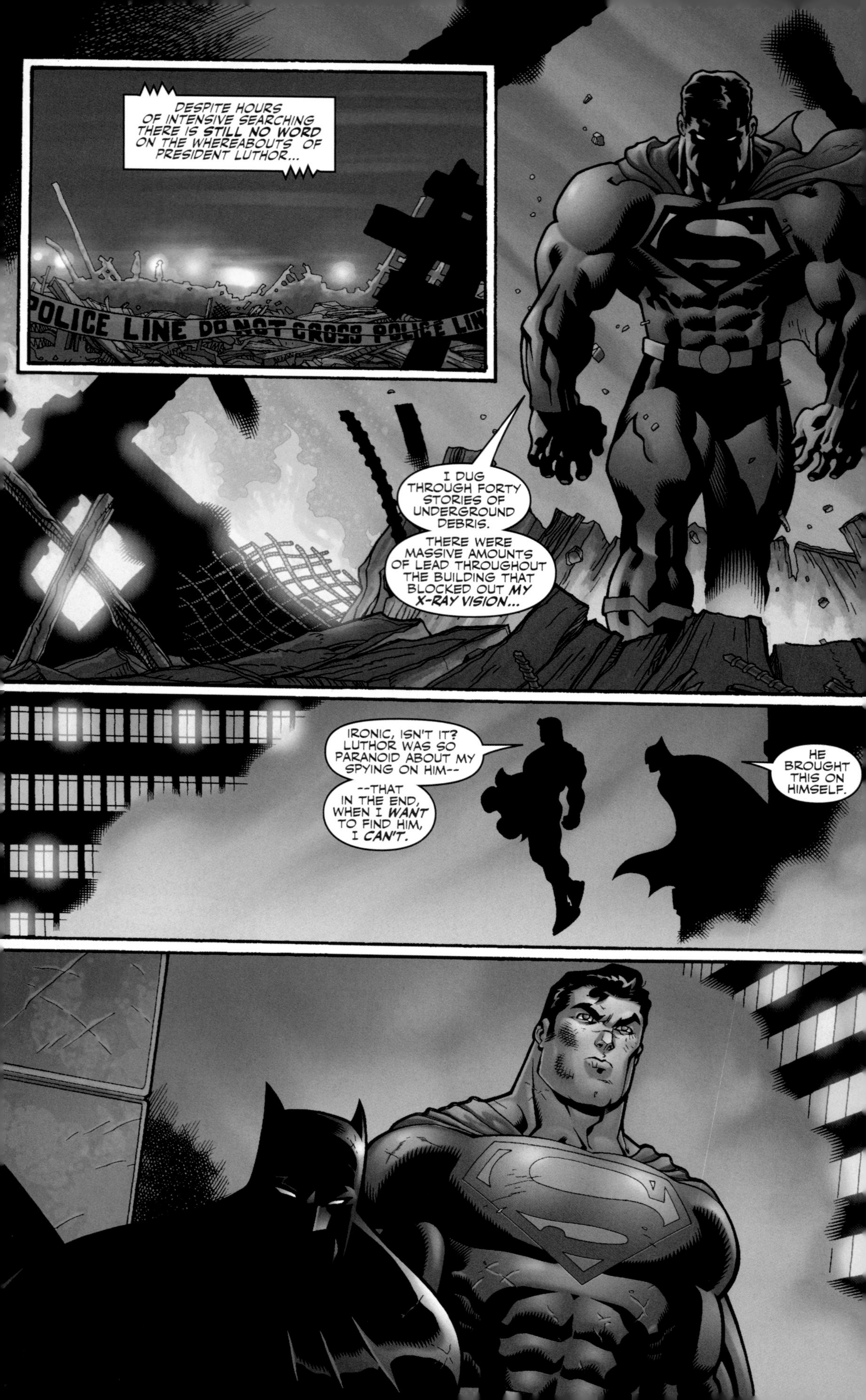
DESPITE HOURS OF INTENSIVE SEARCHING THERE IS STILL NO WORD ON THE WHEREABOUTS OF PRESIDENT LUTHOR...
POLICE LINE DO NOT CROSS POLICE LIN
I DUG THROUGH FORTY STORIES OF UNDERGROUND DEBRIS.
THERE WERE MASSIVE AMOUNTS OF LEAD THROUGHOUT THE BUILDING THAT BLOCKED OUT MY X-RAY VISION...
IRONIC, ISN'T IT? LUTHOR WAS SO PARANOID ABOUT MY SPYING ON HIM--
--THAT IN THE END, WHEN I WANT TO FIND HIM, I CAN'T.
HE BROUGHT THIS ON HIMSELF.

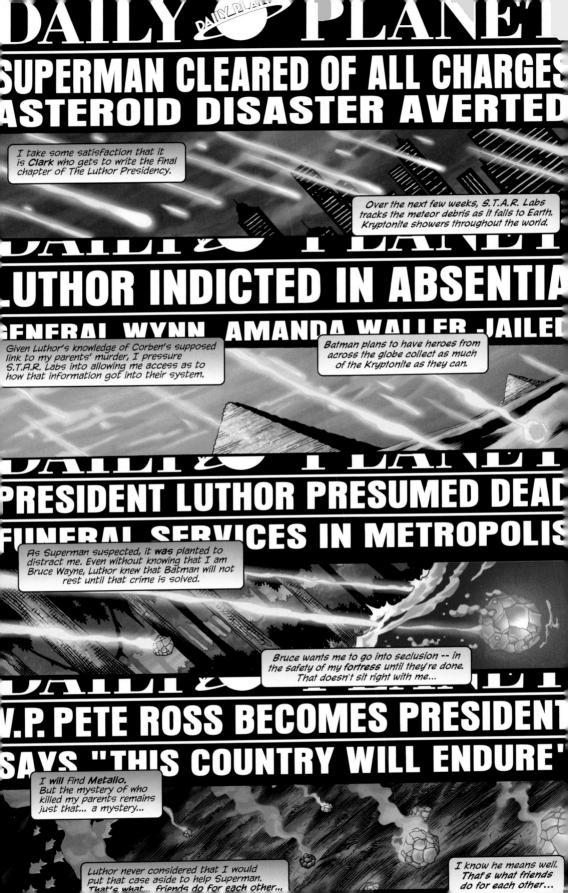

DAILY PLANET

SUPERMAN CLEARED OF ALL CHARGES
ASTEROID DISASTER AVERTED

I take some satisfaction that it is **Clark** who gets to write the final chapter of The Luthor Presidency.

Over the next few weeks, S.T.A.R. Labs tracks the meteor debris as it falls to Earth. Kryptonite showers throughout the world.

LUTHOR INDICTED IN ABSENTIA
GENERAL WYNN   AMANDA WALLER JAILED

Given Luthor's knowledge of Corben's supposed link to my parents' murder, I pressure S.T.A.R. Labs into allowing me access as to how that information got into their system.

Batman plans to have heroes from across the globe collect as much of the Kryptonite as they can.

PRESIDENT LUTHOR PRESUMED DEAD
FUNERAL SERVICES IN METROPOLIS

As Superman suspected, it was planted to distract me. Even without knowing that I am Bruce Wayne, Luthor knew that Batman will not rest until that crime is solved.

Bruce wants me to go into seclusion -- in the safety of my fortress until they're done. That doesn't sit right with me...

V.P. PETE ROSS BECOMES PRESIDENT
SAYS "THIS COUNTRY WILL ENDURE"

I will find **Metallo**. But the mystery of who killed my parents remains just that... a mystery...

Luthor never considered that I would put that case aside to help Superman. That's what... friends do for each other...

I know he means well. That's what friends do for each other.

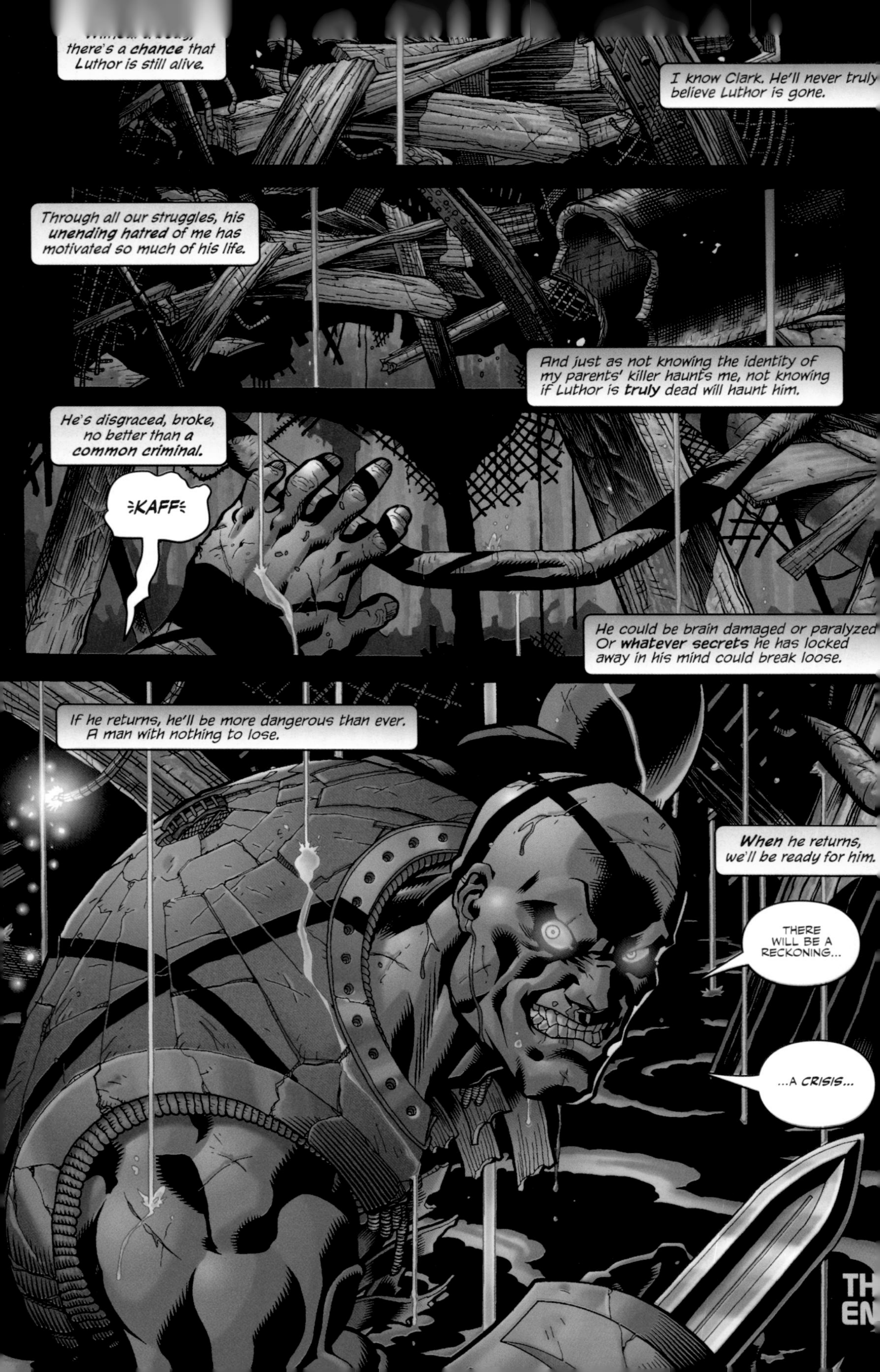

there's a chance that Luthor is still alive.
I know Clark. He'll never truly believe Luthor is gone.
Through all our struggles, his unending hatred of me has motivated so much of his life.
And just as not knowing the identity of my parents' killer haunts me, not knowing if Luthor is truly dead will haunt him.
He's disgraced, broke, no better than a common criminal.
KAFF
He could be brain damaged or paralyzed. Or whatever secrets he has locked away in his mind could break loose.
If he returns, he'll be more dangerous than ever. A man with nothing to lose.
When he returns, we'll be ready for him.
THERE WILL BE A RECKONING...
...A CRISIS...

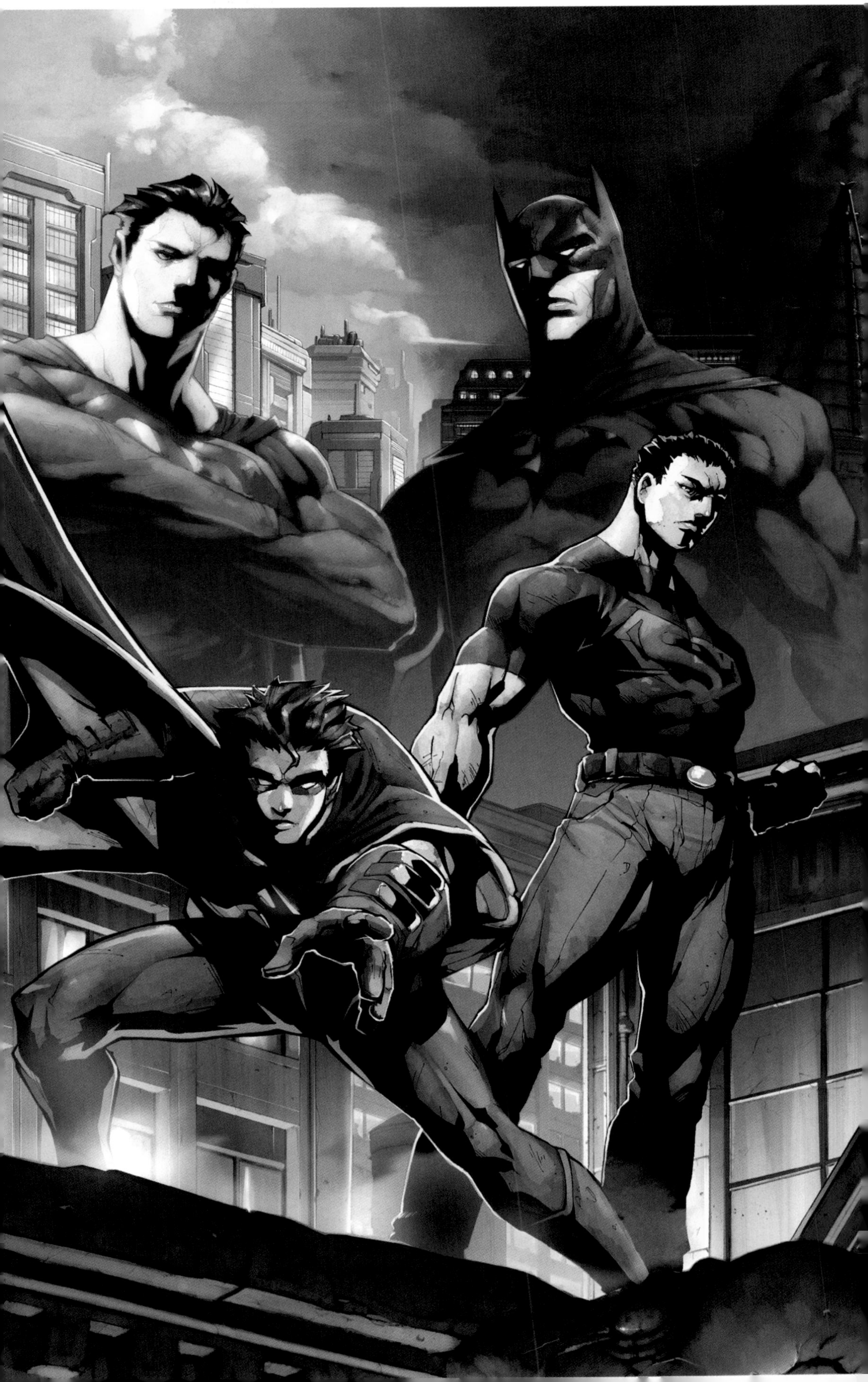

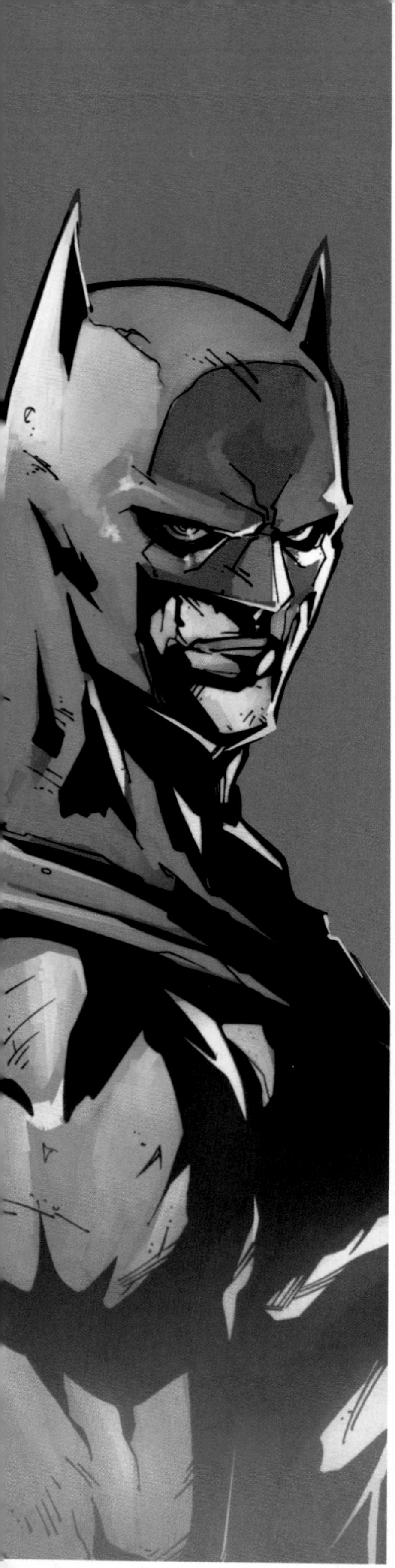

PROTÉGÉ

THE WORLD'S FINEST

JEPH LOEB
WRITER
PAT LEE
PENCILLER
DREAMWAVE PRODUCTIONS
INKER AND COLORIST
RICHARD STARKINGS
LETTERER
PAT LEE
WITH
DREAMWAVE
COVER

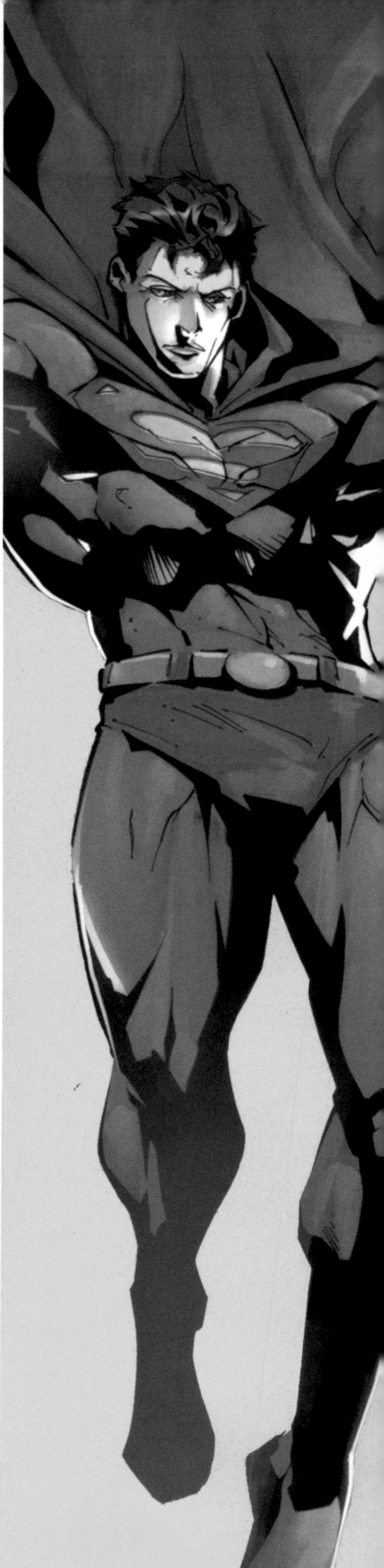

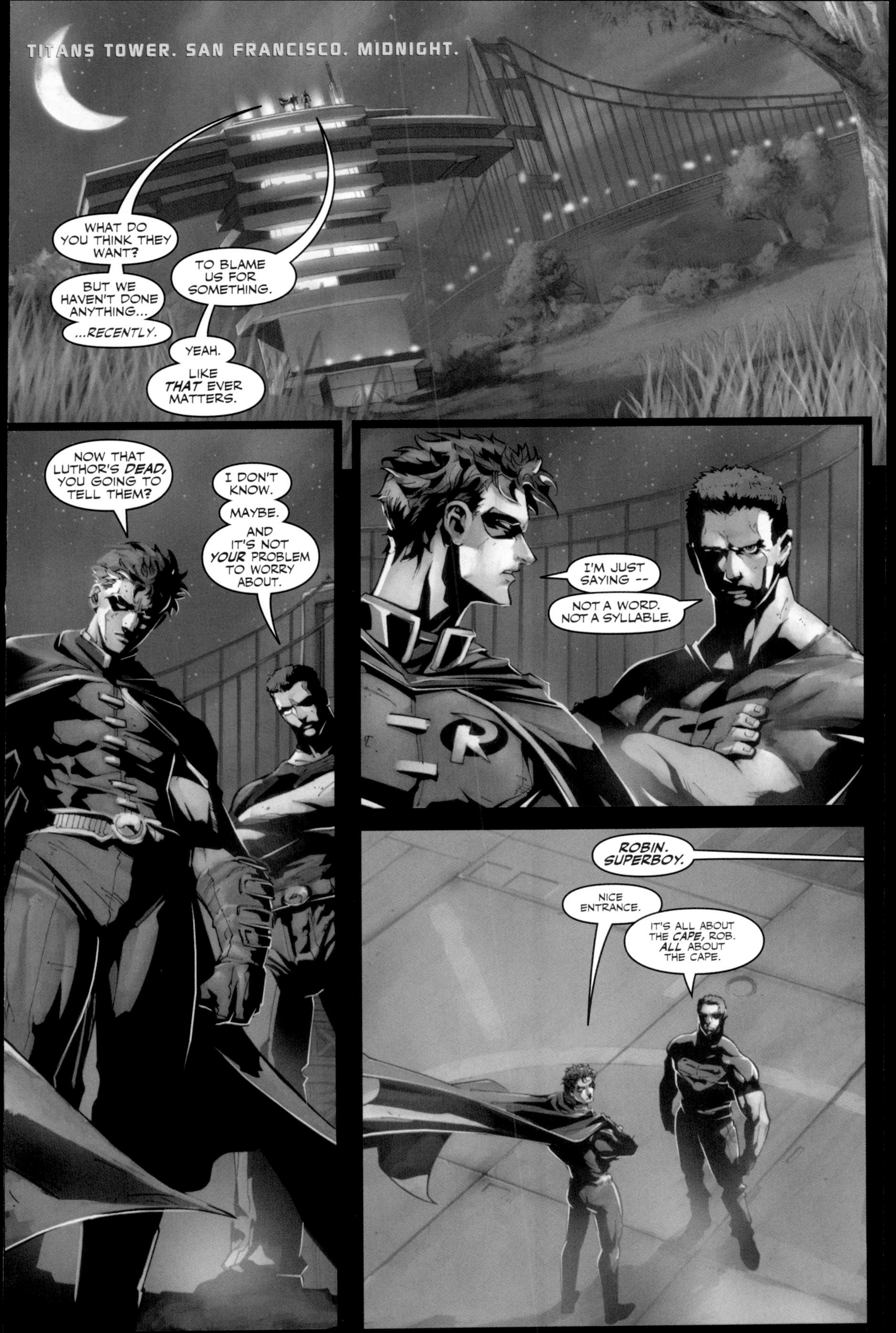

TITANS TOWER. SAN FRANCISCO. MIDNIGHT.
WHAT DO YOU THINK THEY WANT?
TO BLAME US FOR SOMETHING.
BUT WE HAVEN'T DONE ANYTHING...
...RECENTLY.
YEAH.
LIKE *THAT* EVER MATTERS.
NOW THAT LUTHOR'S *DEAD,* YOU GOING TO TELL THEM?
I DON'T KNOW.
MAYBE.
AND IT'S NOT *YOUR* PROBLEM TO WORRY ABOUT.
I'M JUST SAYING --
NOT A WORD. NOT A SYLLABLE.
ROBIN. SUPERBOY.
NICE ENTRANCE.
IT'S ALL ABOUT THE *CAPE,* ROB. *ALL* ABOUT THE CAPE.

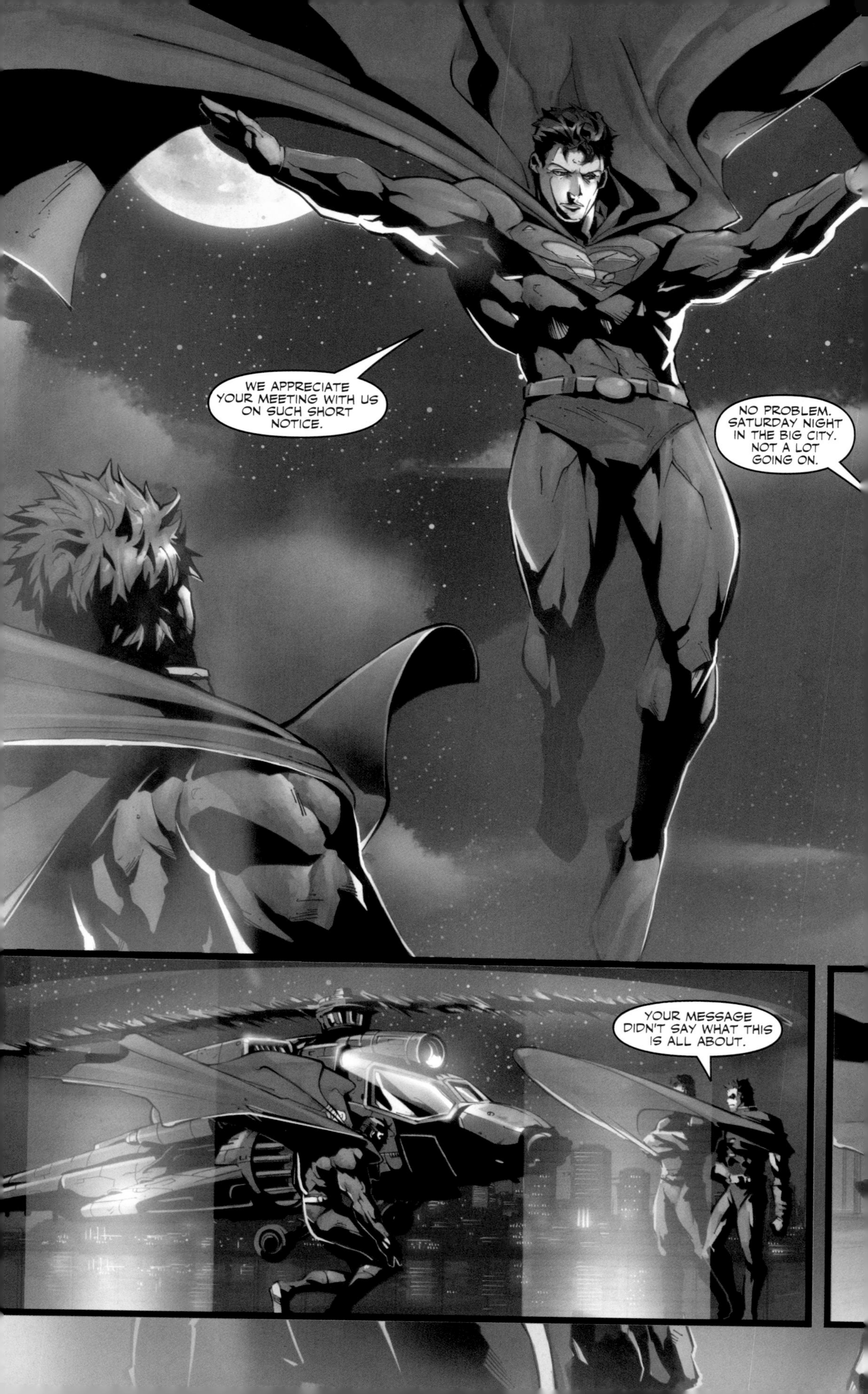
WE APPRECIATE YOUR MEETING WITH US ON SUCH SHORT NOTICE.
NO PROBLEM. SATURDAY NIGHT IN THE BIG CITY. NOT A LOT GOING ON.
YOUR MESSAGE DIDN'T SAY WHAT THIS IS ALL ABOUT.

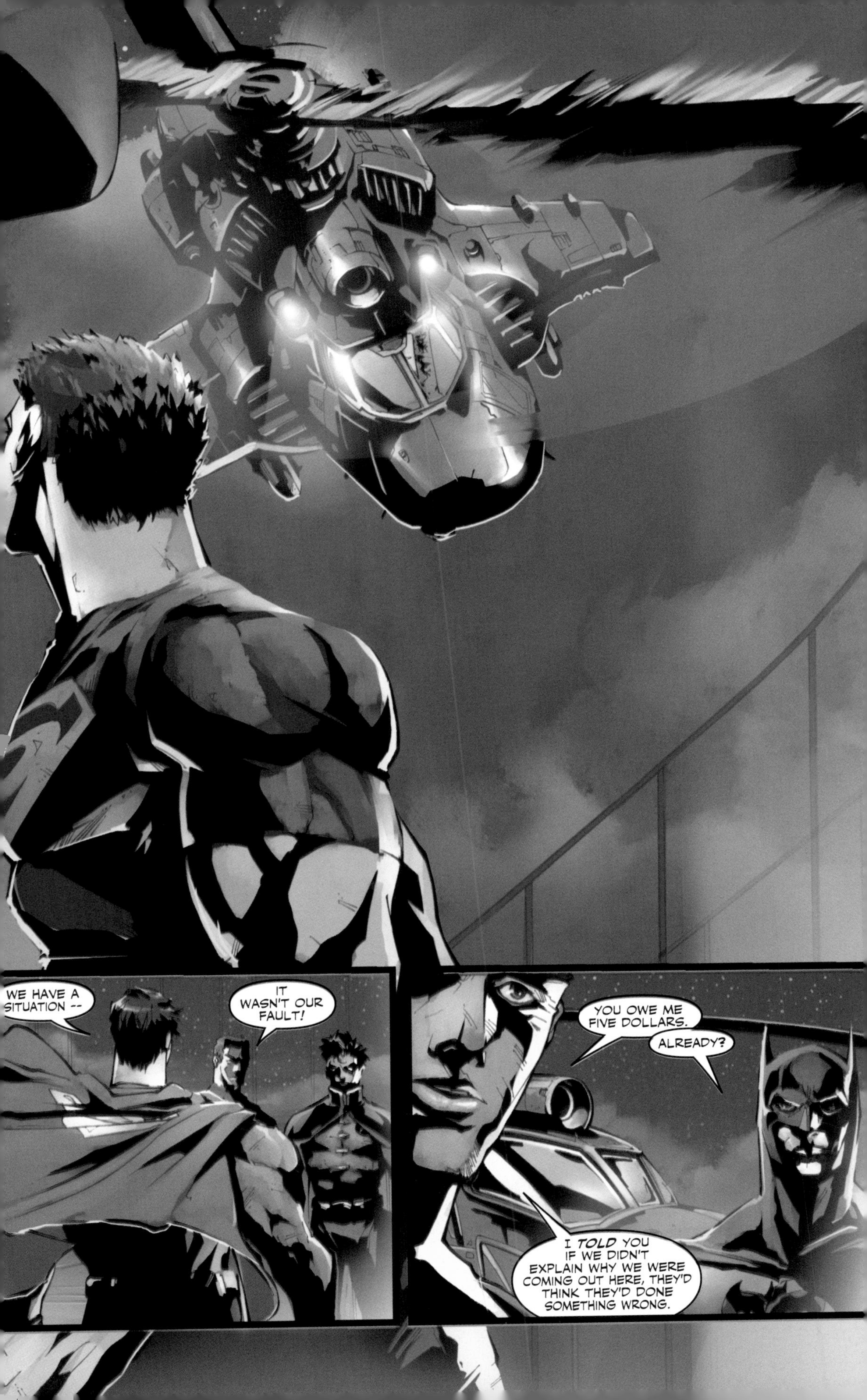
WE HAVE A SITUATION --
IT WASN'T OUR FAULT!
YOU OWE ME FIVE DOLLARS.
ALREADY?
I TOLD YOU IF WE DIDN'T EXPLAIN WHY WE WERE COMING OUT HERE, THEY'D THINK THEY'D DONE SOMETHING WRONG.

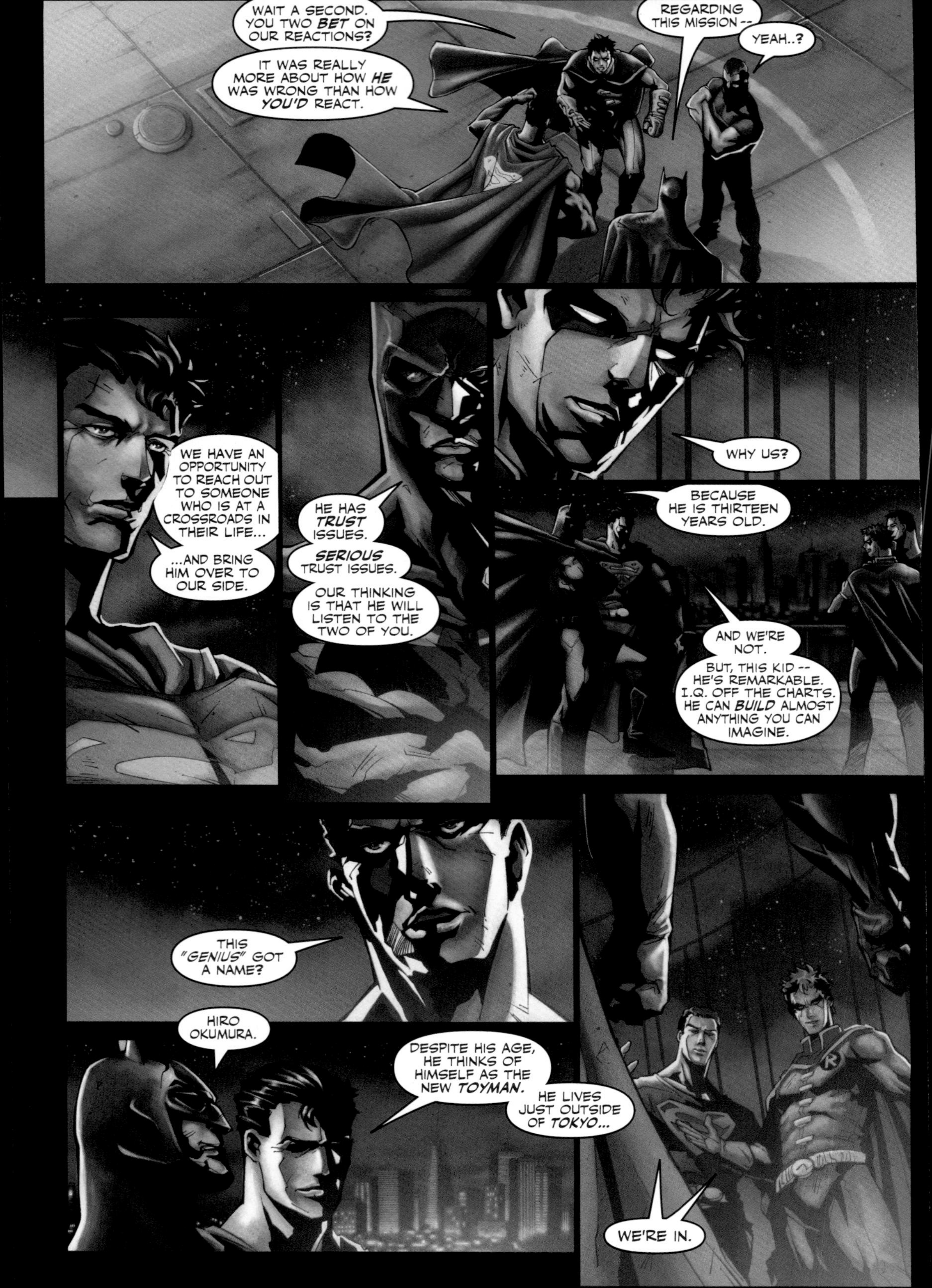
WAIT A SECOND. YOU TWO BET ON OUR REACTIONS?
IT WAS REALLY MORE ABOUT HOW HE WAS WRONG THAN HOW YOU'D REACT.
REGARDING THIS MISSION --
YEAH..?
WE HAVE AN OPPORTUNITY TO REACH OUT TO SOMEONE WHO IS AT A CROSSROADS IN THEIR LIFE...
...AND BRING HIM OVER TO OUR SIDE.
HE HAS TRUST ISSUES.
SERIOUS TRUST ISSUES.
OUR THINKING IS THAT HE WILL LISTEN TO THE TWO OF YOU.
WHY US?
BECAUSE HE IS THIRTEEN YEARS OLD.
AND WE'RE NOT.
BUT, THIS KID -- HE'S REMARKABLE. I.Q. OFF THE CHARTS. HE CAN BUILD ALMOST ANYTHING YOU CAN IMAGINE.
THIS "GENIUS" GOT A NAME?
HIRO OKUMURA.
DESPITE HIS AGE, HE THINKS OF HIMSELF AS THE NEW TOYMAN.
HE LIVES JUST OUTSIDE OF TOKYO...
WE'RE IN.

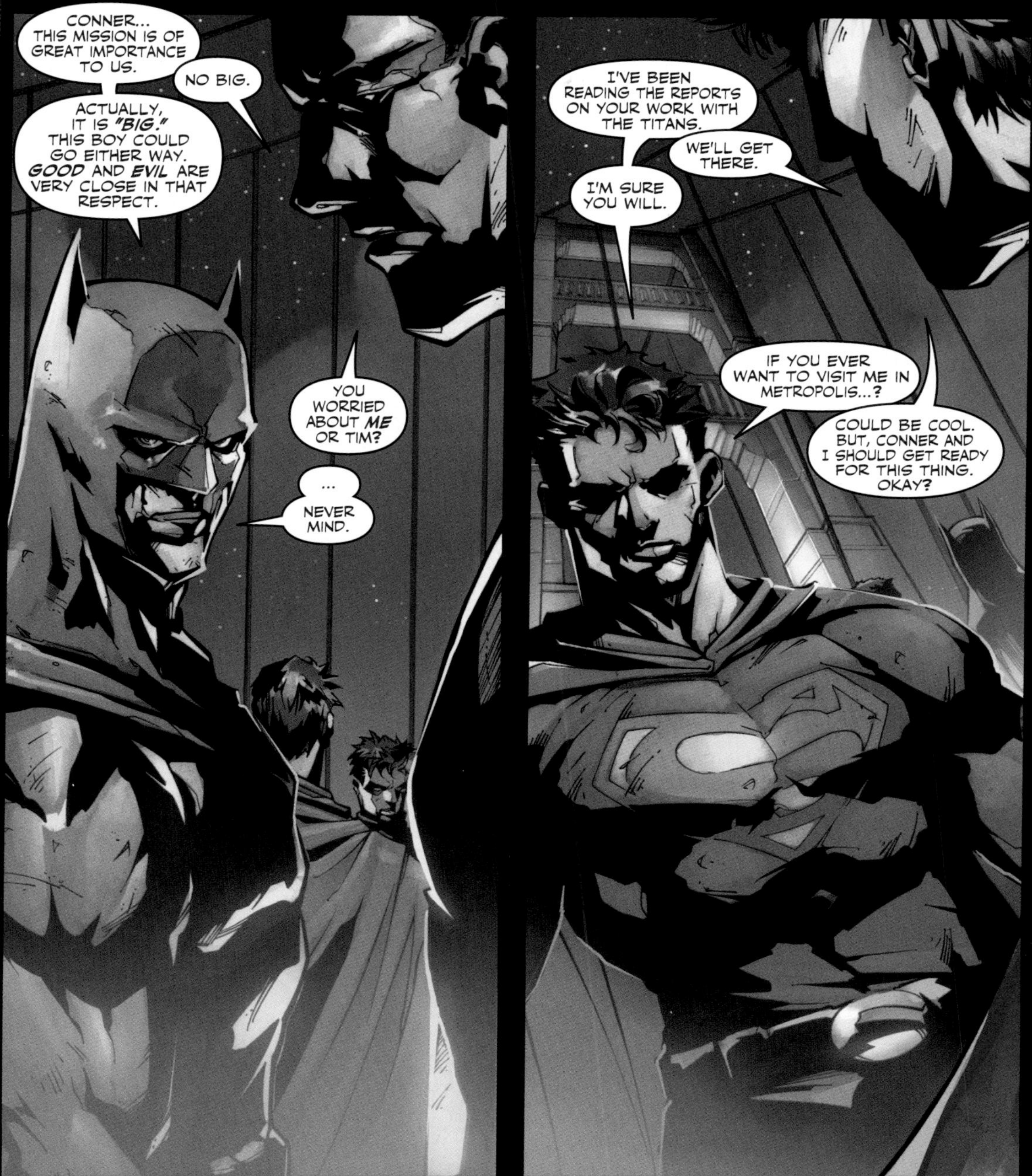
CONNER... THIS MISSION IS OF GREAT IMPORTANCE TO US.
NO BIG.
ACTUALLY, IT IS "BIG." THIS BOY COULD GO EITHER WAY. GOOD AND EVIL ARE VERY CLOSE IN THAT RESPECT.
YOU WORRIED ABOUT ME OR TIM?
...
NEVER MIND.
I'VE BEEN READING THE REPORTS ON YOUR WORK WITH THE TITANS.
WE'LL GET THERE.
I'M SURE YOU WILL.
IF YOU EVER WANT TO VISIT ME IN METROPOLIS...?
COULD BE COOL. BUT, CONNER AND I SHOULD GET READY FOR THIS THING. OKAY?

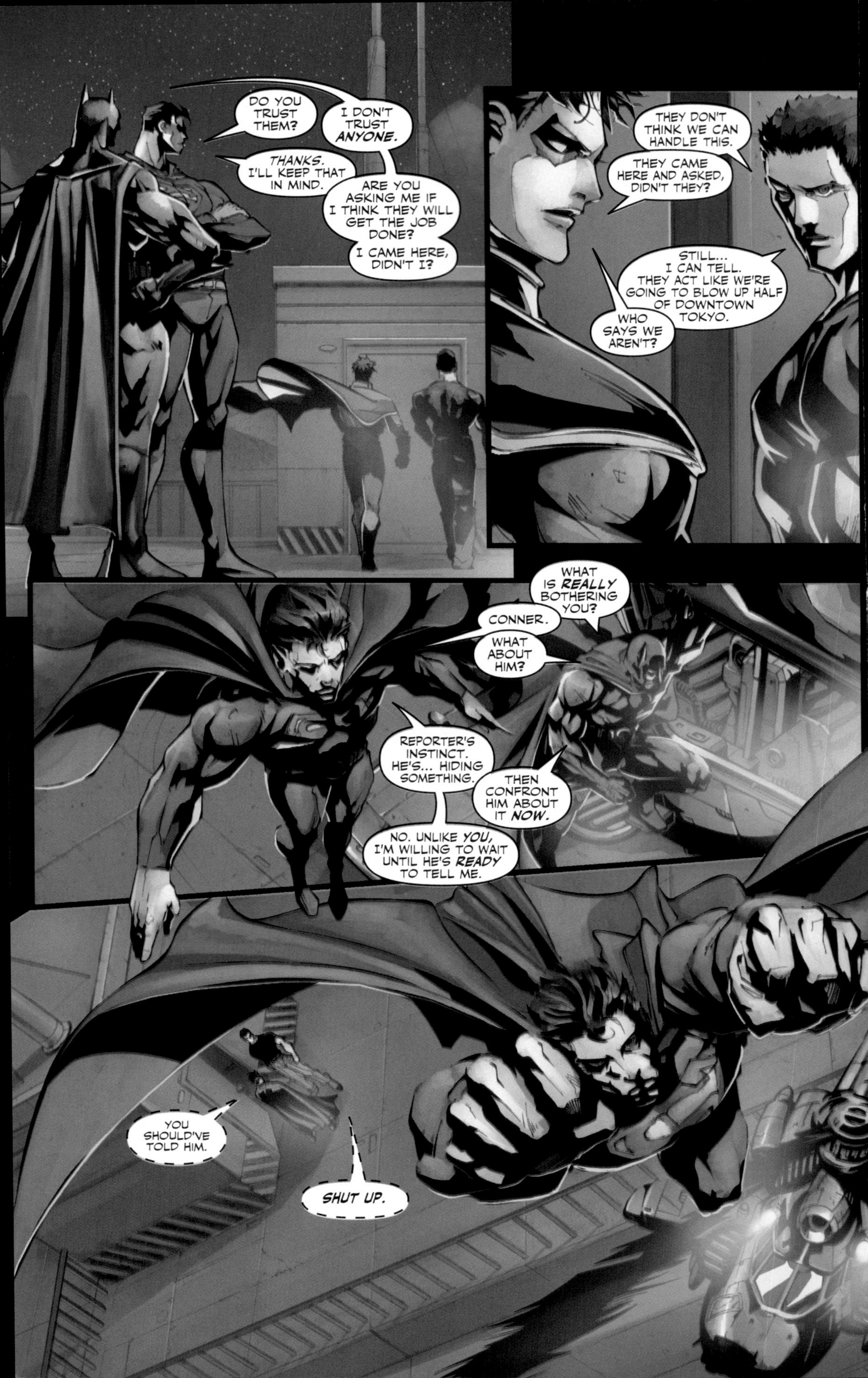

DO YOU TRUST THEM?
I DON'T TRUST *ANYONE.*
THANKS. I'LL KEEP THAT IN MIND.
ARE YOU ASKING ME IF I THINK THEY WILL GET THE JOB DONE?
I CAME HERE, DIDN'T I?
THEY DON'T THINK WE CAN HANDLE THIS.
THEY CAME HERE AND ASKED, DIDN'T THEY?
STILL... I CAN TELL. THEY ACT LIKE WE'RE GOING TO BLOW UP HALF OF DOWNTOWN TOKYO.
WHO SAYS WE AREN'T?
WHAT IS *REALLY* BOTHERING YOU?
CONNER.
WHAT ABOUT HIM?
REPORTER'S INSTINCT. HE'S... HIDING SOMETHING.
THEN CONFRONT HIM ABOUT IT *NOW.*
NO. UNLIKE *YOU,* I'M WILLING TO WAIT UNTIL HE'S *READY* TO TELL ME.
YOU SHOULD'VE TOLD HIM.
SHUT UP.

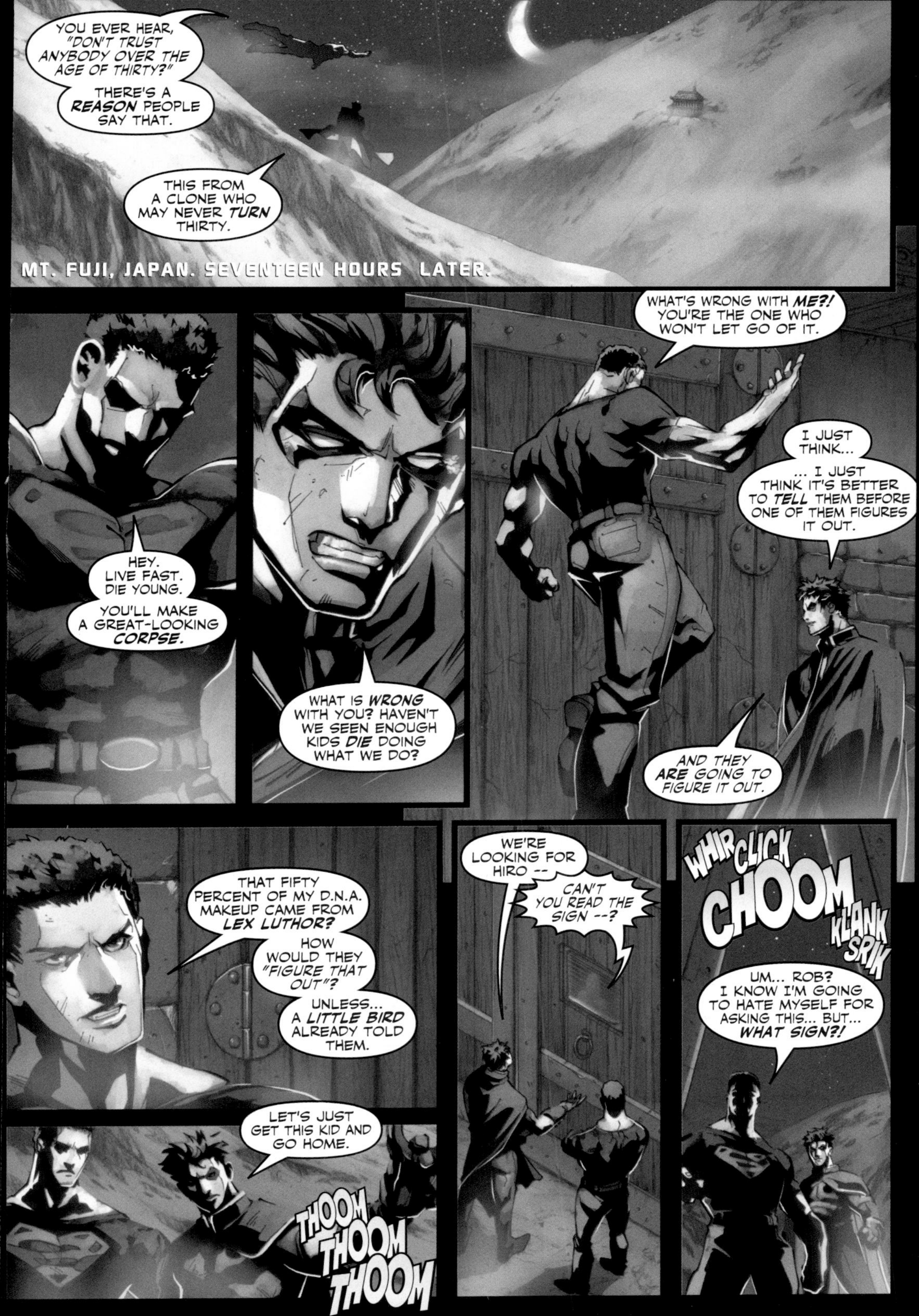
YOU EVER HEAR, "DON'T TRUST ANYBODY OVER THE AGE OF THIRTY?"
THERE'S A REASON PEOPLE SAY THAT.
THIS FROM A CLONE WHO MAY NEVER TURN THIRTY.
MT. FUJI, JAPAN. SEVENTEEN HOURS LATER.
HEY. LIVE FAST. DIE YOUNG.
YOU'LL MAKE A GREAT-LOOKING CORPSE.
WHAT IS WRONG WITH YOU? HAVEN'T WE SEEN ENOUGH KIDS DIE DOING WHAT WE DO?
WHAT'S WRONG WITH ME?! YOU'RE THE ONE WHO WON'T LET GO OF IT.
I JUST THINK...
... I JUST THINK IT'S BETTER TO TELL THEM BEFORE ONE OF THEM FIGURES IT OUT.
AND THEY ARE GOING TO FIGURE IT OUT.
THAT FIFTY PERCENT OF MY D.N.A. MAKEUP CAME FROM LEX LUTHOR?
HOW WOULD THEY "FIGURE THAT OUT"?
UNLESS... A LITTLE BIRD ALREADY TOLD THEM.
LET'S JUST GET THIS KID AND GO HOME.
THOOM THOOM THOOM
WE'RE LOOKING FOR HIRO --
CAN'T YOU READ THE SIGN --?
WHIR CLICK
CHOOM
KLANK
SRIK
UM... ROB? I KNOW I'M GOING TO HATE MYSELF FOR ASKING THIS... BUT... WHAT SIGN?!

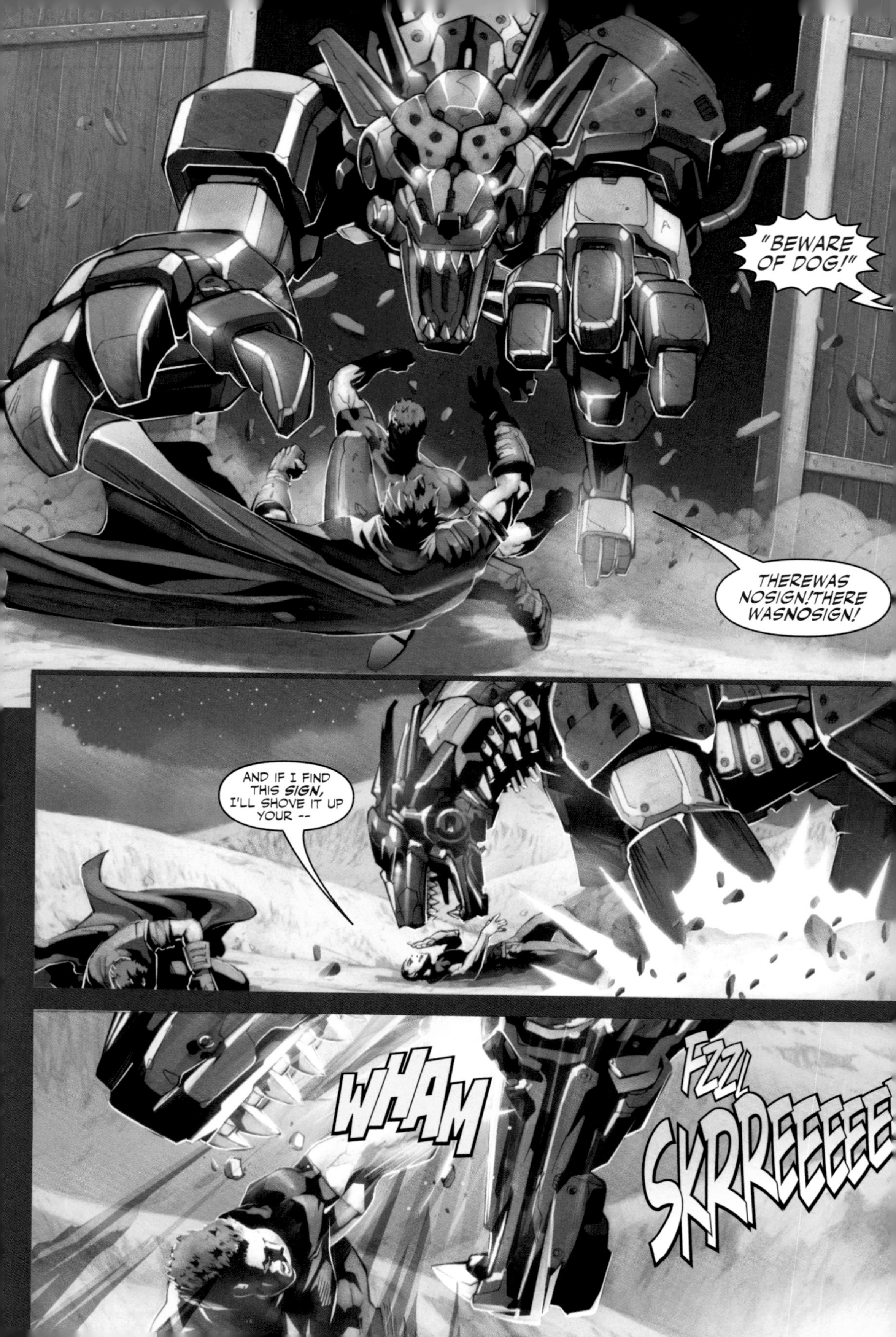
"BEWARE OF DOG!"
THEREWAS NOSIGN!THERE WASNOSIGN!
AND IF I FIND THIS SIGN, I'LL SHOVE IT UP YOUR --
WHAM
FZZL
SKREEEEEE

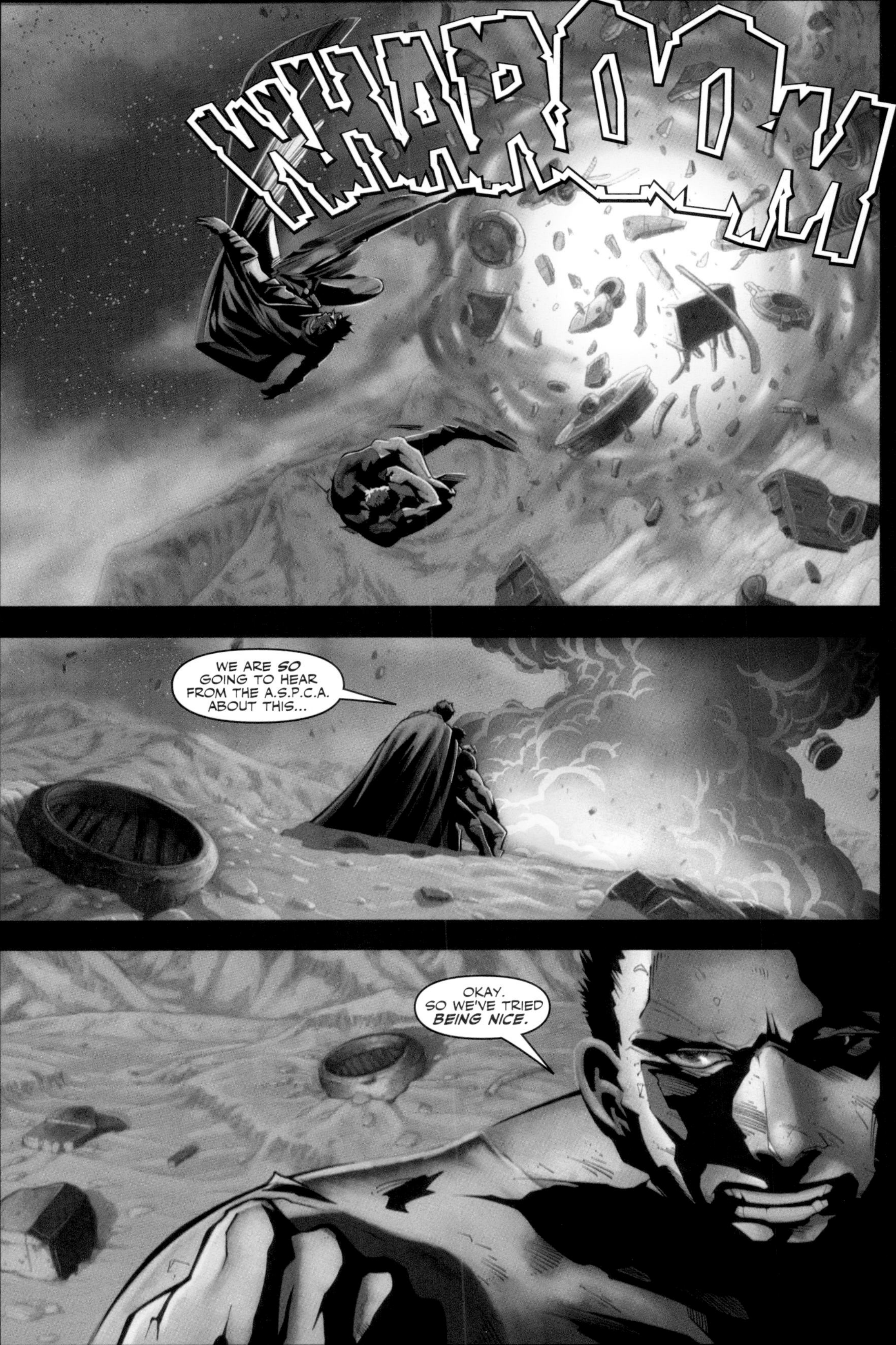
WHAROOOM
WE ARE SO GOING TO HEAR FROM THE A.S.P.C.A. ABOUT THIS...
OKAY. SO WE'VE TRIED BEING NICE.

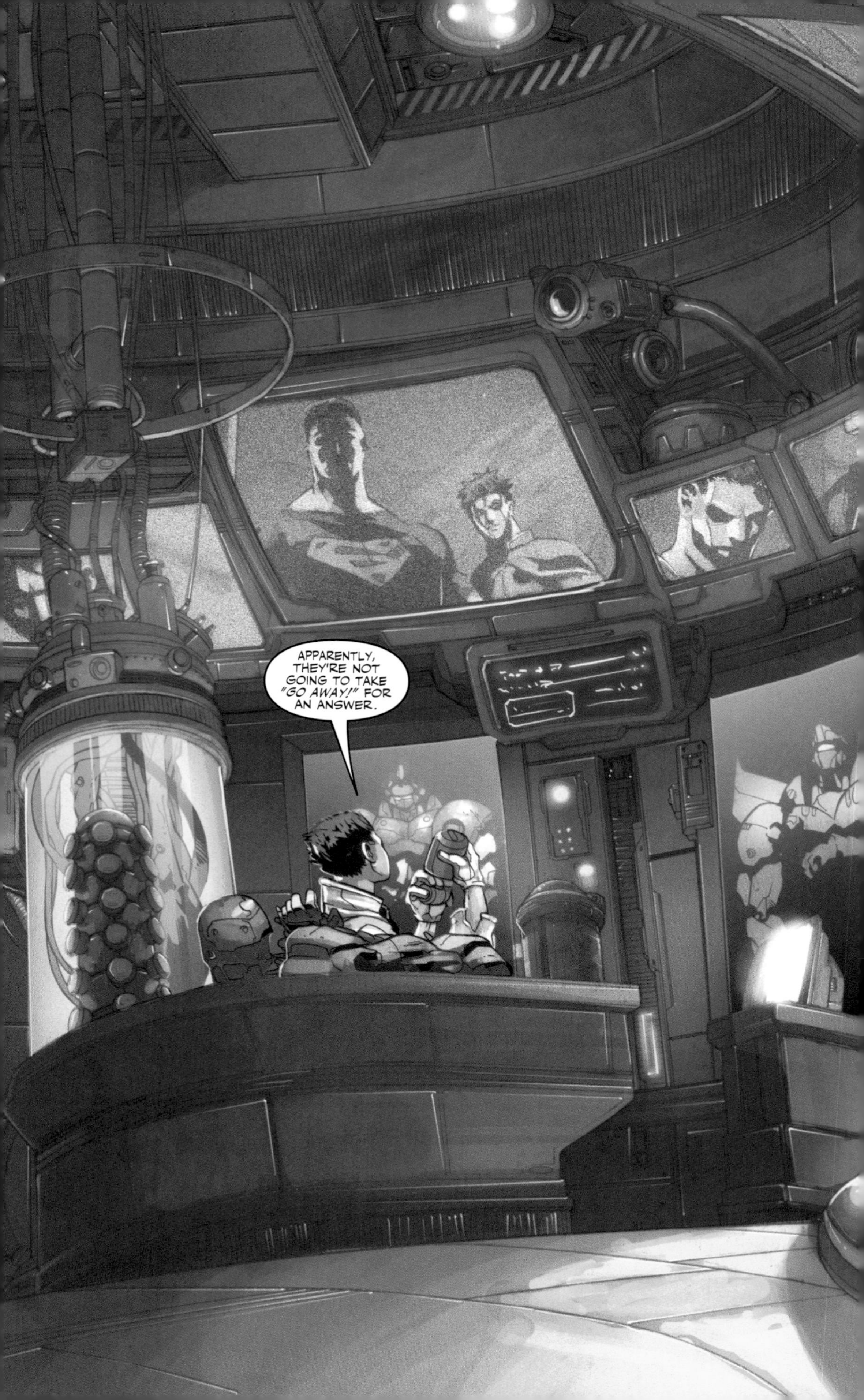
APPARENTLY, THEY'RE NOT GOING TO TAKE "GO AWAY!" FOR AN ANSWER.

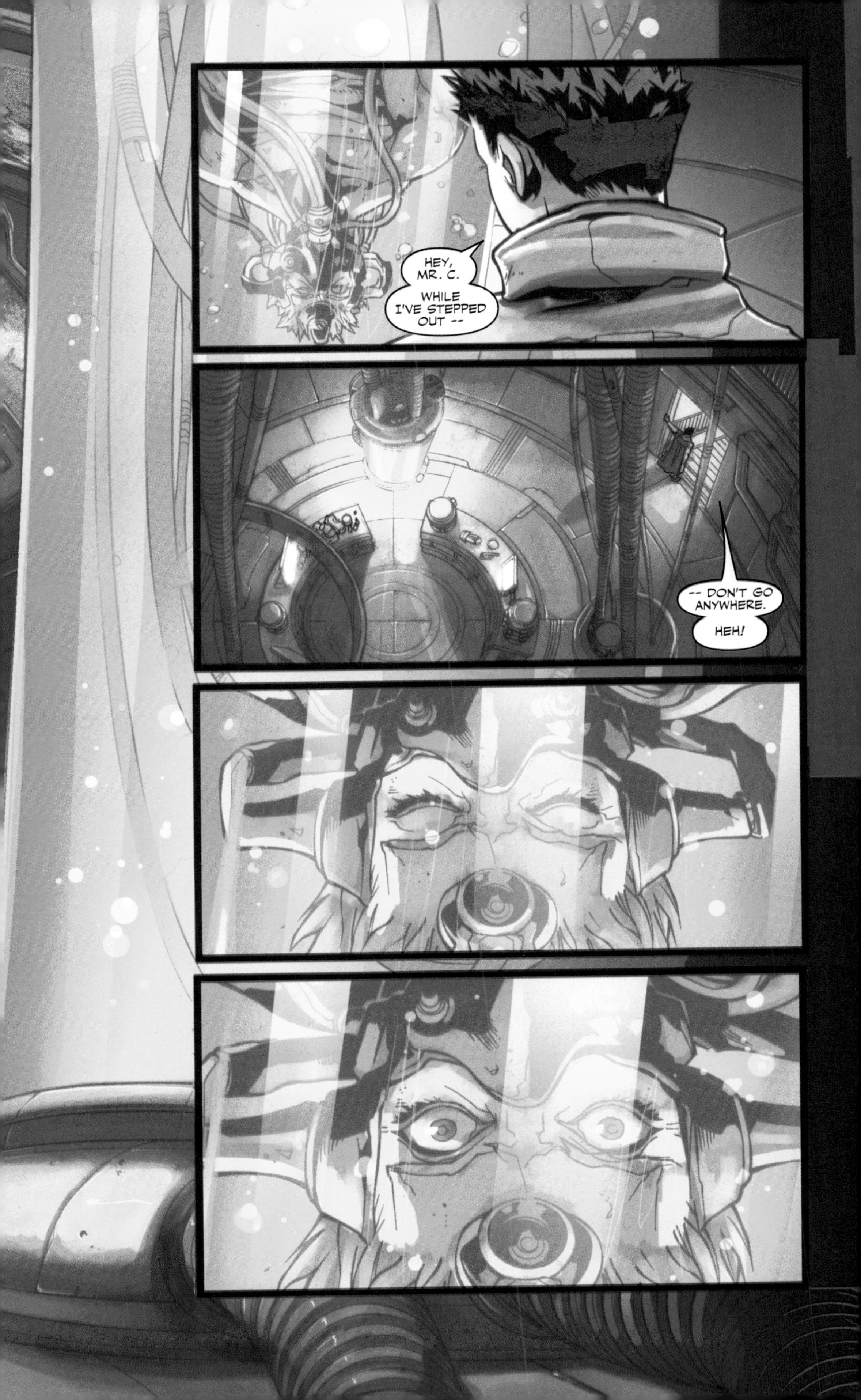
HEY, MR. C.
WHILE I'VE STEPPED OUT --
-- DON'T GO ANYWHERE.
HEH!

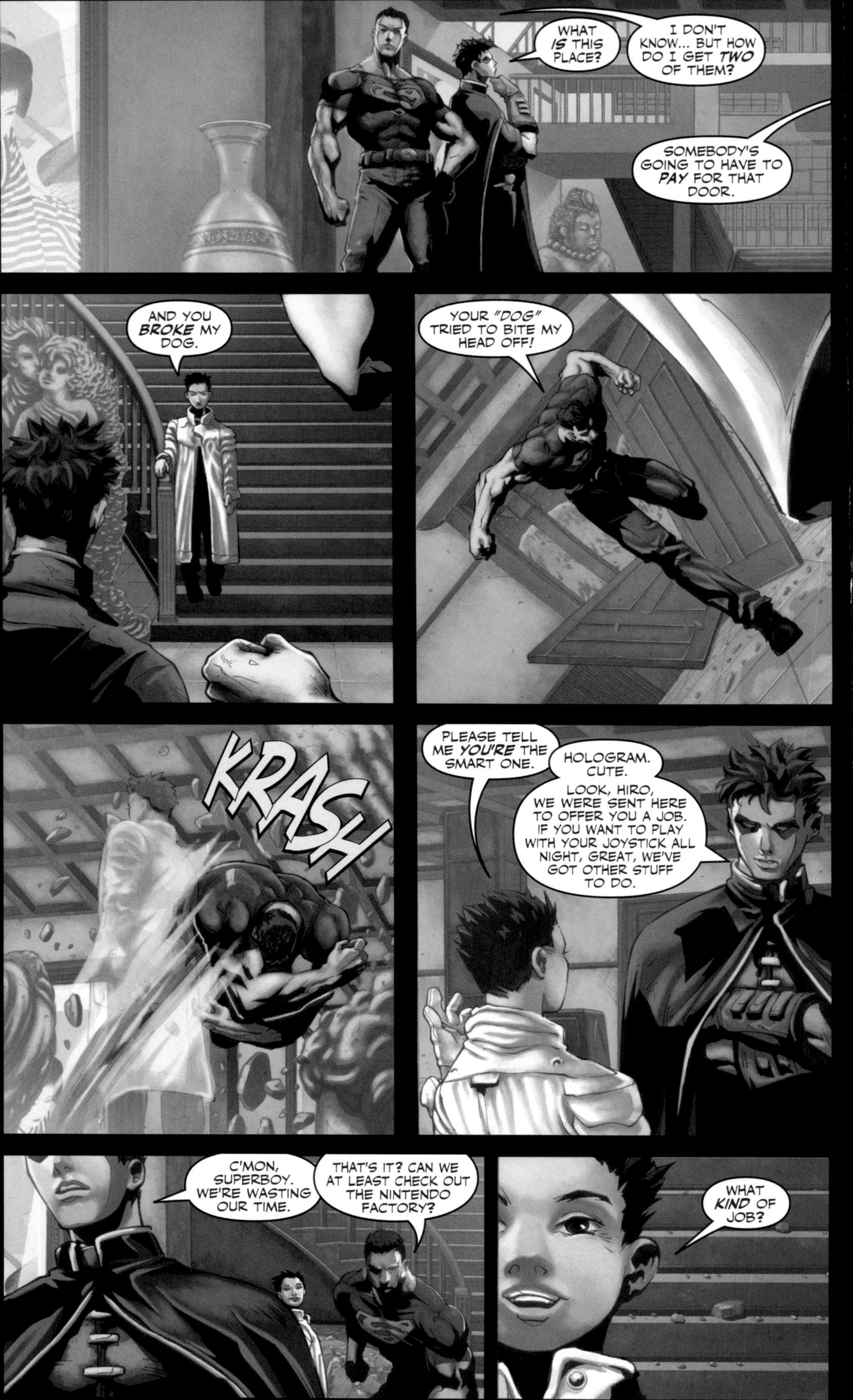

WHAT IS THIS PLACE?
I DON'T KNOW... BUT HOW DO I GET TWO OF THEM?
SOMEBODY'S GOING TO HAVE TO PAY FOR THAT DOOR.
AND YOU BROKE MY DOG.
YOUR "DOG" TRIED TO BITE MY HEAD OFF!
KRASH
PLEASE TELL ME YOU'RE THE SMART ONE.
HOLOGRAM. CUTE.
LOOK, HIRO, WE WERE SENT HERE TO OFFER YOU A JOB. IF YOU WANT TO PLAY WITH YOUR JOYSTICK ALL NIGHT, GREAT, WE'VE GOT OTHER STUFF TO DO.
C'MON, SUPERBOY. WE'RE WASTING OUR TIME.
THAT'S IT? CAN WE AT LEAST CHECK OUT THE NINTENDO FACTORY?
WHAT KIND OF JOB?

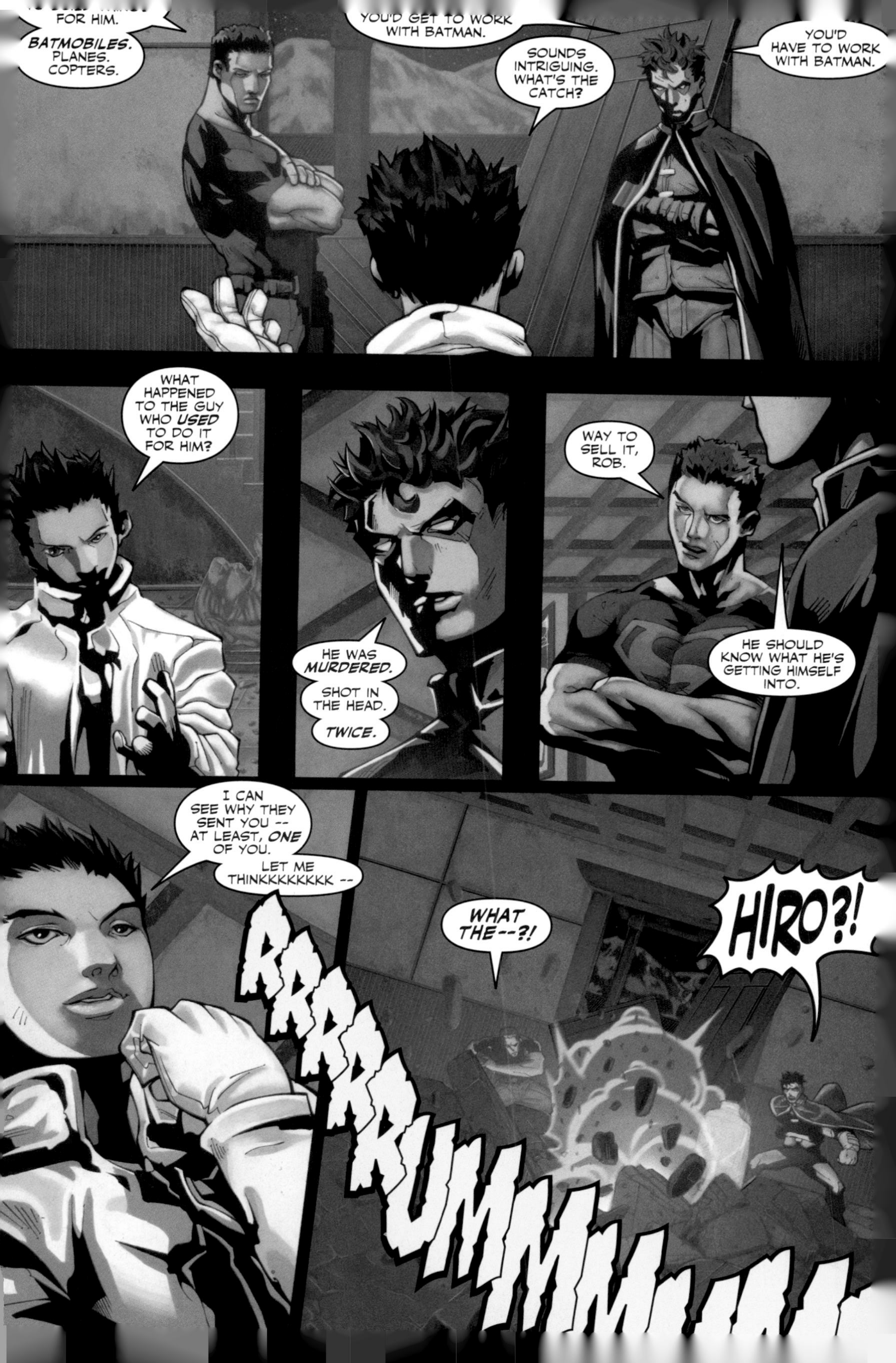
FOR HIM.
BATMOBILES. PLANES. COPTERS.
YOU'D GET TO WORK WITH BATMAN.
SOUNDS INTRIGUING. WHAT'S THE CATCH?
YOU'D HAVE TO WORK WITH BATMAN.
WHAT HAPPENED TO THE GUY WHO USED TO DO IT FOR HIM?
HE WAS MURDERED.
SHOT IN THE HEAD.
TWICE.
WAY TO SELL IT, ROB.
HE SHOULD KNOW WHAT HE'S GETTING HIMSELF INTO.
I CAN SEE WHY THEY SENT YOU -- AT LEAST, ONE OF YOU.
LET ME THINKKKKKKKK --
RRRRRUMMMMMM
WHAT THE--?!
HIRO?!

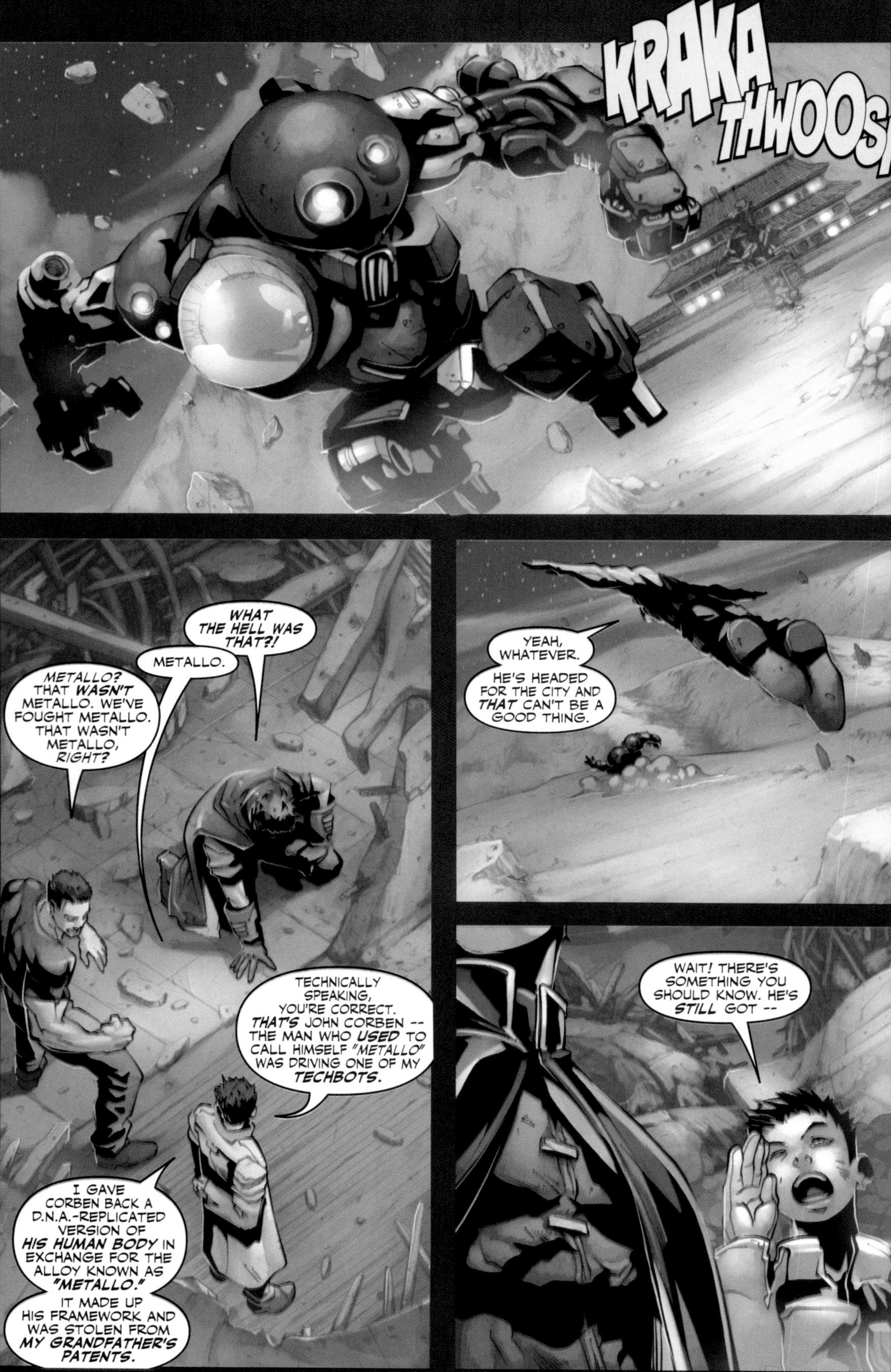
KRAKA THWOOSH
WHAT THE HELL WAS THAT?!
METALLO.
METALLO? THAT WASN'T METALLO. WE'VE FOUGHT METALLO. THAT WASN'T METALLO, RIGHT?
YEAH, WHATEVER.
HE'S HEADED FOR THE CITY AND THAT CAN'T BE A GOOD THING.
TECHNICALLY SPEAKING, YOU'RE CORRECT. THAT'S JOHN CORBEN -- THE MAN WHO USED TO CALL HIMSELF "METALLO" WAS DRIVING ONE OF MY TECHBOTS.
I GAVE CORBEN BACK A D.N.A.-REPLICATED VERSION OF HIS HUMAN BODY IN EXCHANGE FOR THE ALLOY KNOWN AS "METALLO."
IT MADE UP HIS FRAMEWORK AND WAS STOLEN FROM MY GRANDFATHER'S PATENTS.
WAIT! THERE'S SOMETHING YOU SHOULD KNOW. HE'S STILL GOT --

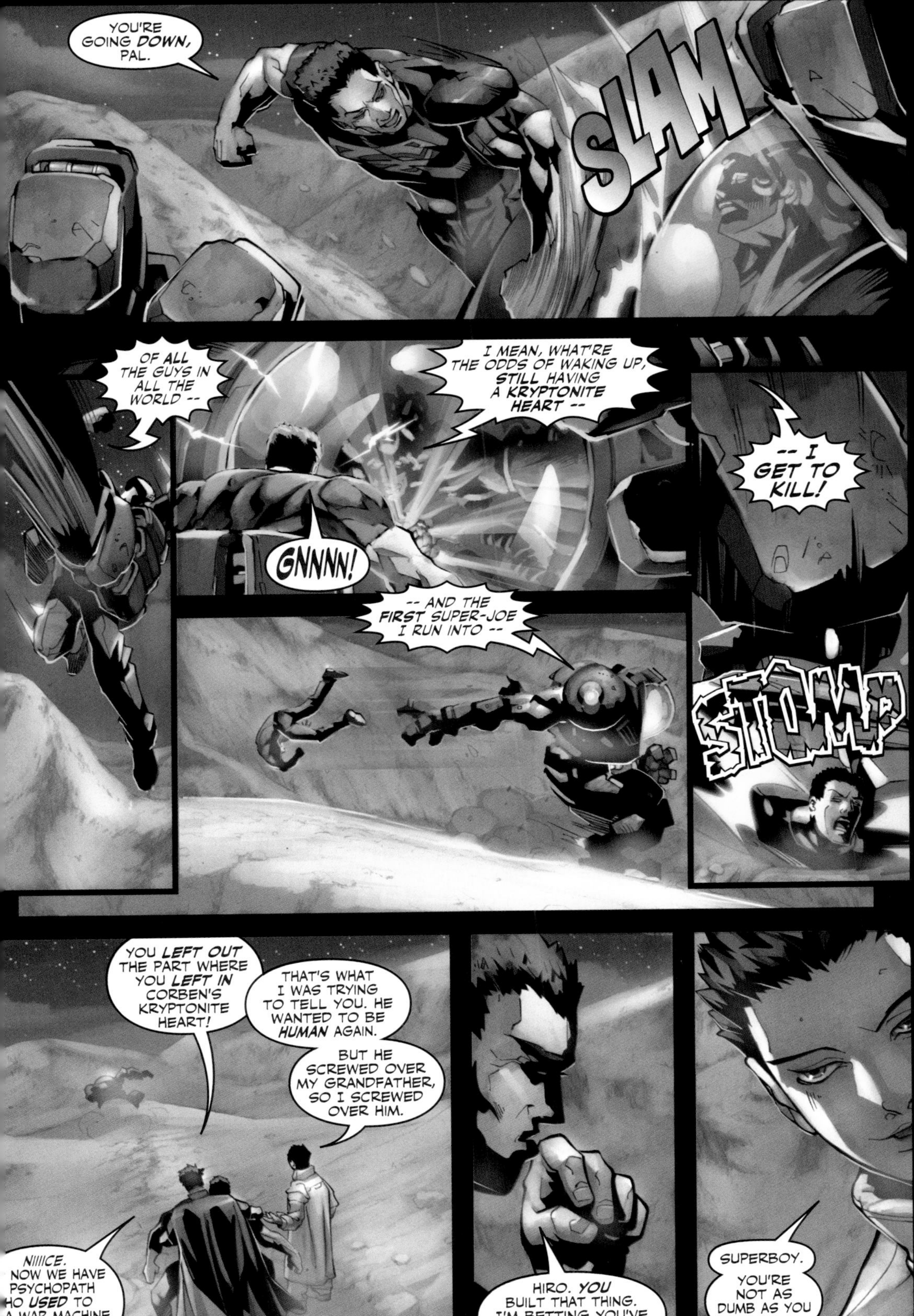

YOU'RE GOING DOWN, PAL.
SLAM
OF ALL THE GUYS IN ALL THE WORLD --
I MEAN, WHAT'RE THE ODDS OF WAKING UP, STILL HAVING A KRYPTONITE HEART --
GNNNN!
-- I GET TO KILL!
-- AND THE FIRST SUPER-JOE I RUN INTO --
STOMP
YOU LEFT OUT THE PART WHERE YOU LEFT IN CORBEN'S KRYPTONITE HEART!
THAT'S WHAT I WAS TRYING TO TELL YOU. HE WANTED TO BE HUMAN AGAIN.
BUT HE SCREWED OVER MY GRANDFATHER, SO I SCREWED OVER HIM.
NIIIICE. NOW WE HAVE PSYCHOPATH HO USED TO A WAR MACHINE RIVING A WAR MACHINE.
HIRO. YOU BUILT THAT THING. I'M BETTING YOU'VE BUILT SOMETHING THAT CAN BEAT IT.
SUPERBOY. YOU'RE NOT AS DUMB AS YOU LOOK...

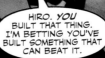

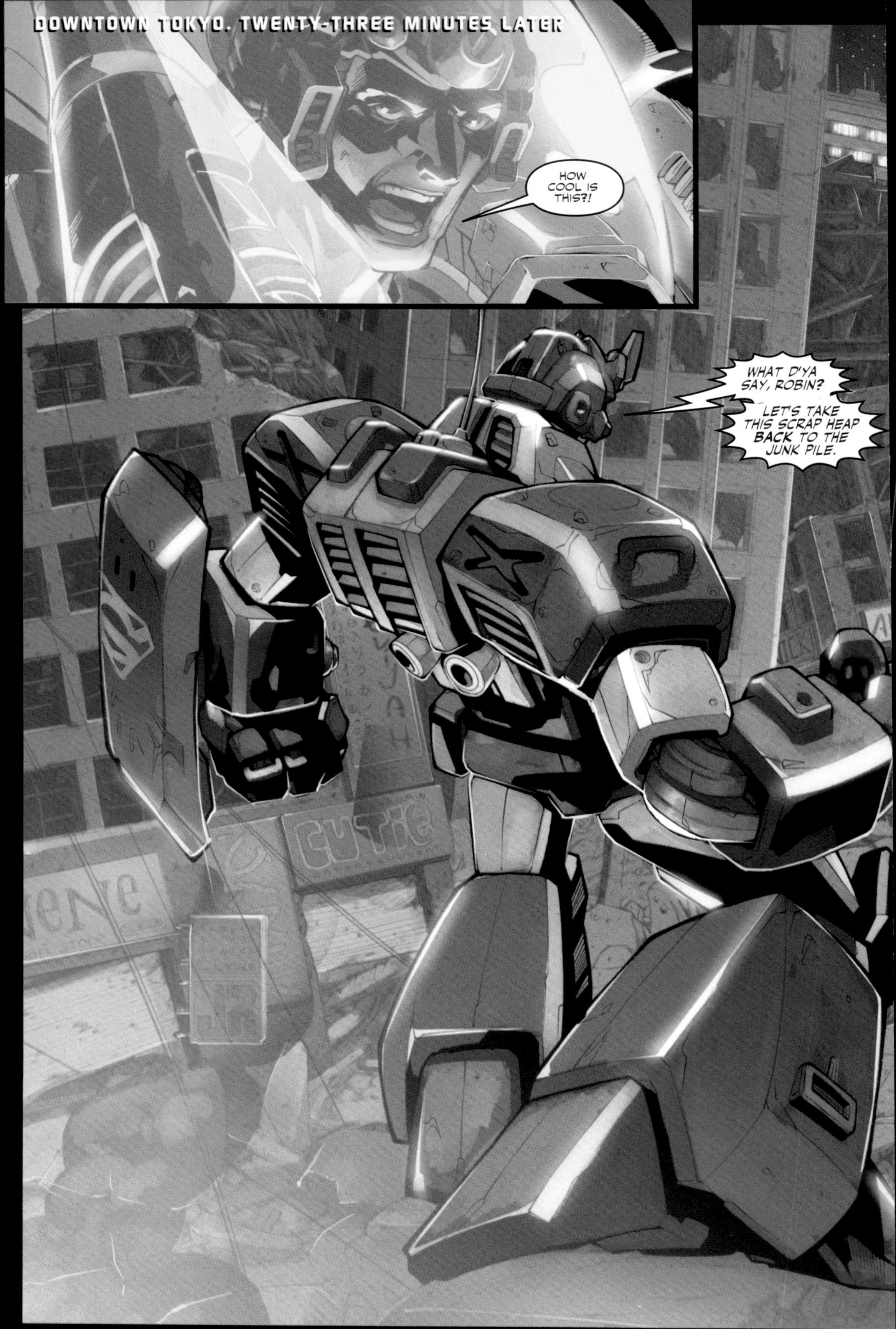
DOWNTOWN TOKYO. TWENTY-THREE MINUTES LATER
HOW COOL IS THIS?!
WHAT D'YA SAY, ROBIN?
LET'S TAKE THIS SCRAP HEAP BACK TO THE JUNK PILE.
CUTIE

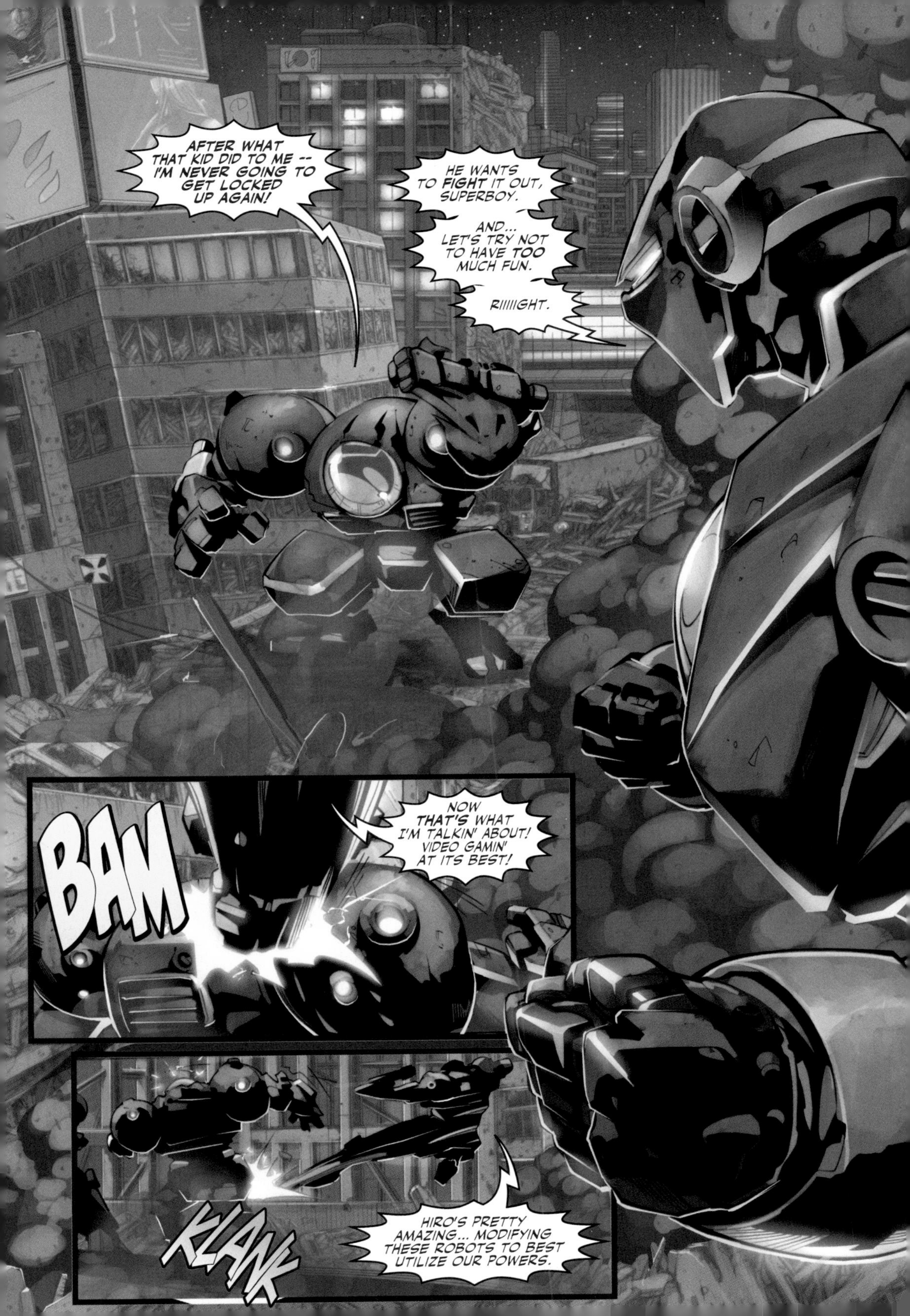
AFTER WHAT THAT KID DID TO ME -- I'M NEVER GOING TO GET LOCKED UP AGAIN!
HE WANTS TO FIGHT IT OUT, SUPERBOY.
AND... LET'S TRY NOT TO HAVE TOO MUCH FUN.
RIIIIIGHT.
BAM
NOW THAT'S WHAT I'M TALKIN' ABOUT! VIDEO GAMIN' AT ITS BEST!
KLANK
HIRO'S PRETTY AMAZING... MODIFYING THESE ROBOTS TO BEST UTILIZE OUR POWERS.

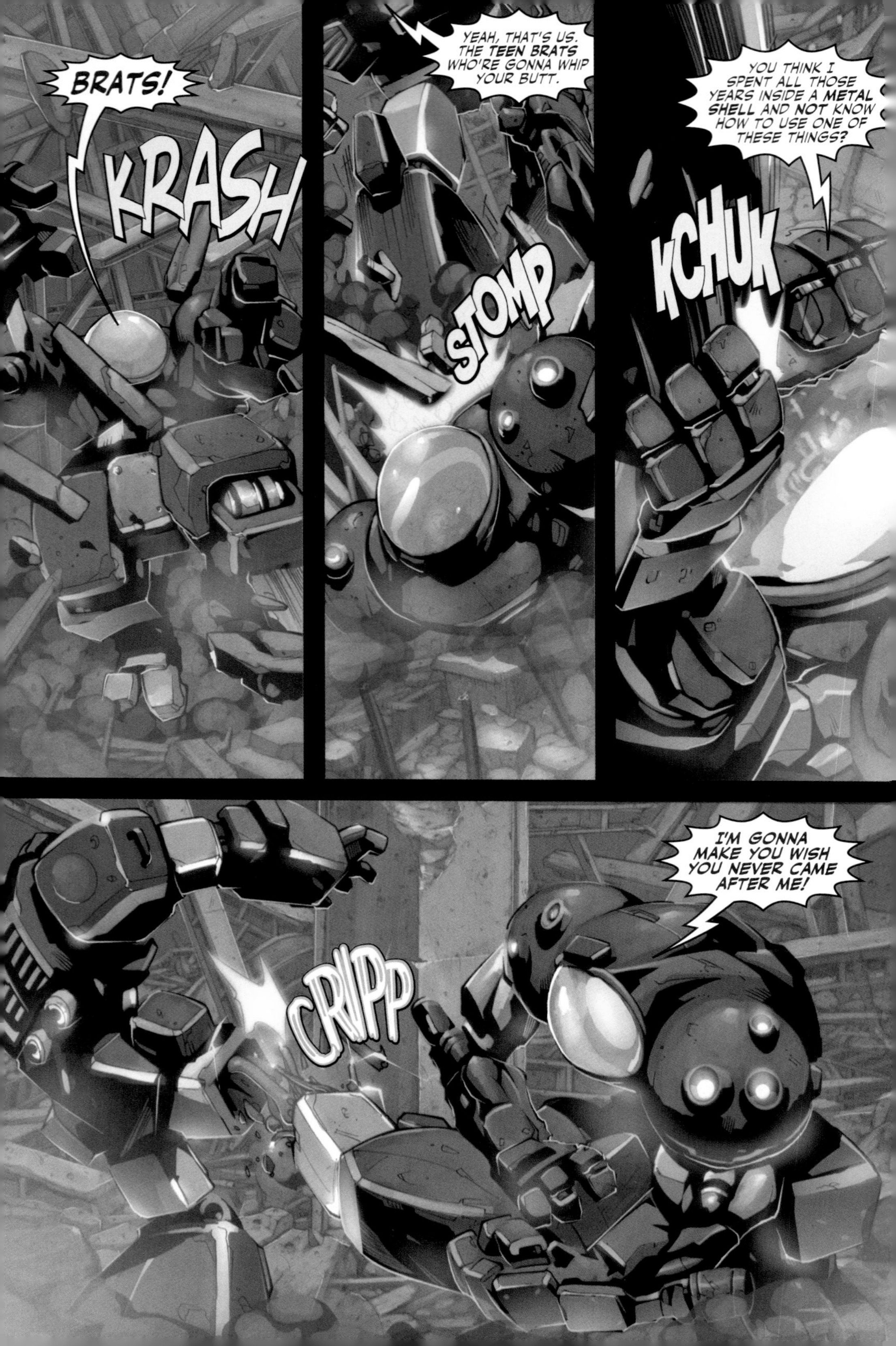
BRATS!
KRASH
YEAH, THAT'S US. THE TEEN BRATS WHO'RE GONNA WHIP YOUR BUTT.
STOMP
YOU THINK I SPENT ALL THOSE YEARS INSIDE A METAL SHELL AND NOT KNOW HOW TO USE ONE OF THESE THINGS?
KCHUK
I'M GONNA MAKE YOU WISH YOU NEVER CAME AFTER ME!
CRIPP

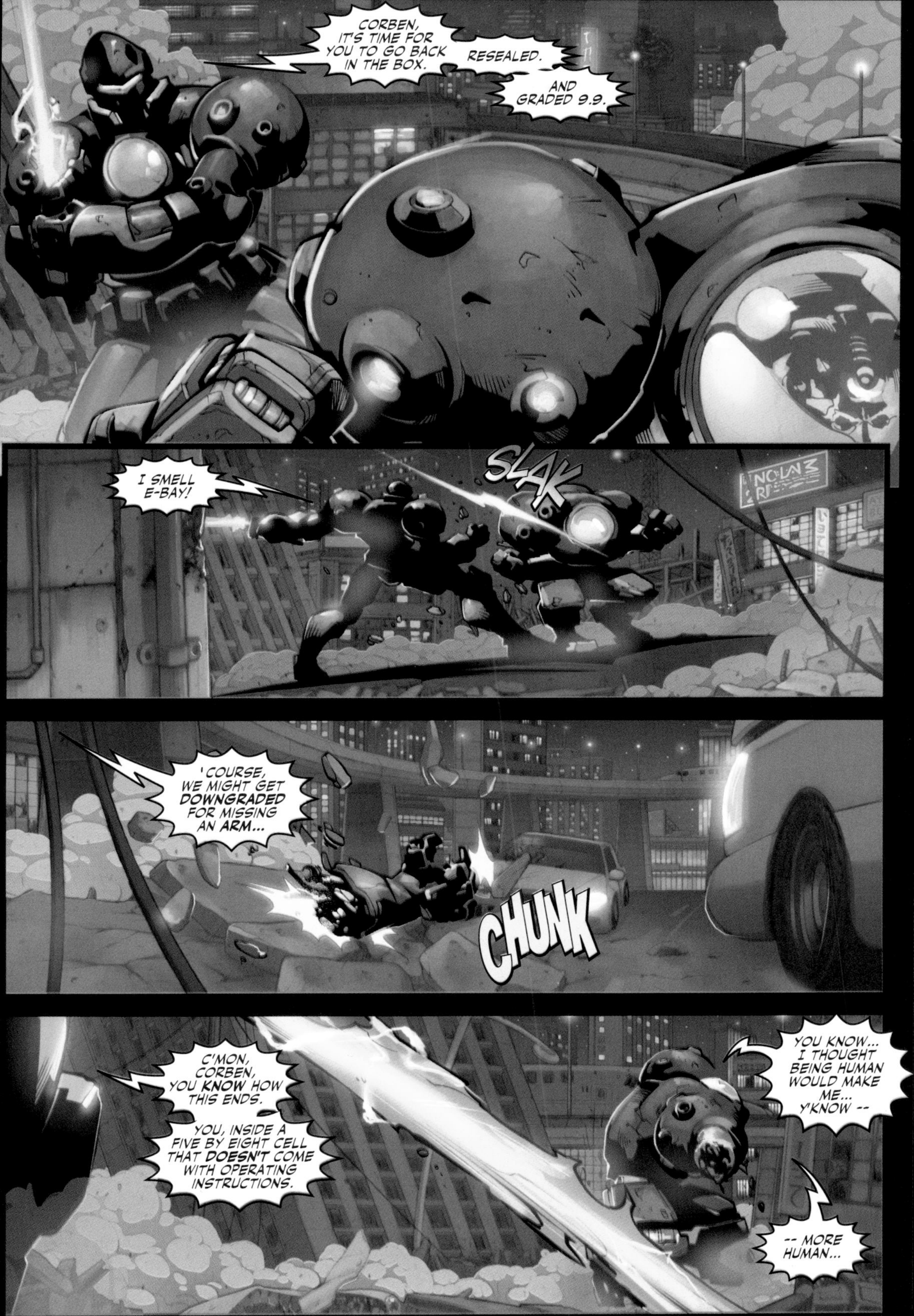
CORBEN, IT'S TIME FOR YOU TO GO BACK IN THE BOX.
RESEALED.
AND GRADED 9.9.
I SMELL E-BAY!
SLAK
'COURSE, WE MIGHT GET DOWNGRADED FOR MISSING AN ARM...
CHUNK
C'MON, CORBEN, YOU KNOW HOW THIS ENDS.
YOU, INSIDE A FIVE BY EIGHT CELL THAT DOESN'T COME WITH OPERATING INSTRUCTIONS.
YOU KNOW... I THOUGHT BEING HUMAN WOULD MAKE ME... Y'KNOW --
-- MORE HUMAN...

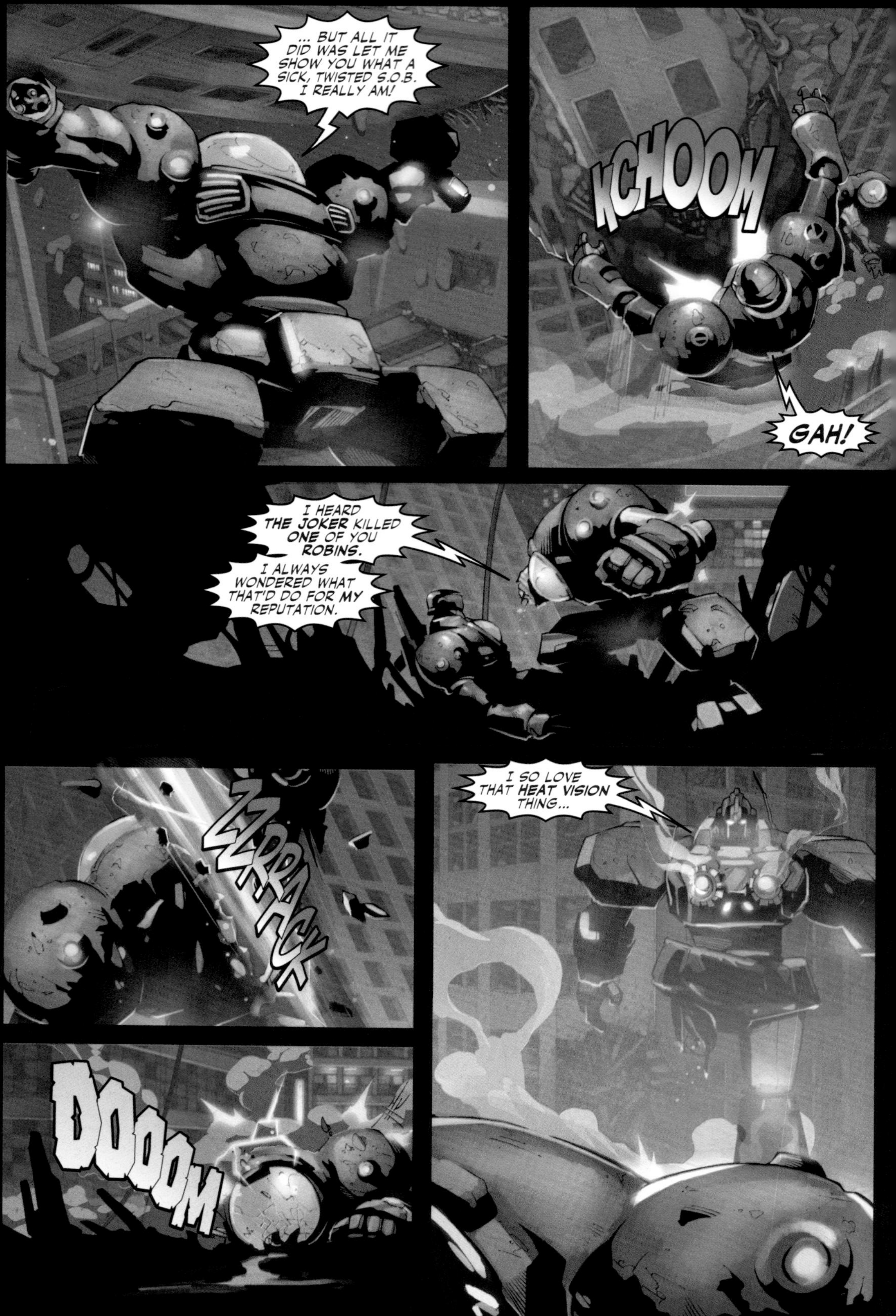
... BUT ALL IT DID WAS LET ME SHOW YOU WHAT A SICK, TWISTED S.O.B. I REALLY AM!
KCHOOM
GAH!
I HEARD THE JOKER KILLED ONE OF YOU ROBINS.
I ALWAYS WONDERED WHAT THAT'D DO FOR MY REPUTATION.
ZZRRACK
DOOOM
I SO LOVE THAT HEAT VISION THING...

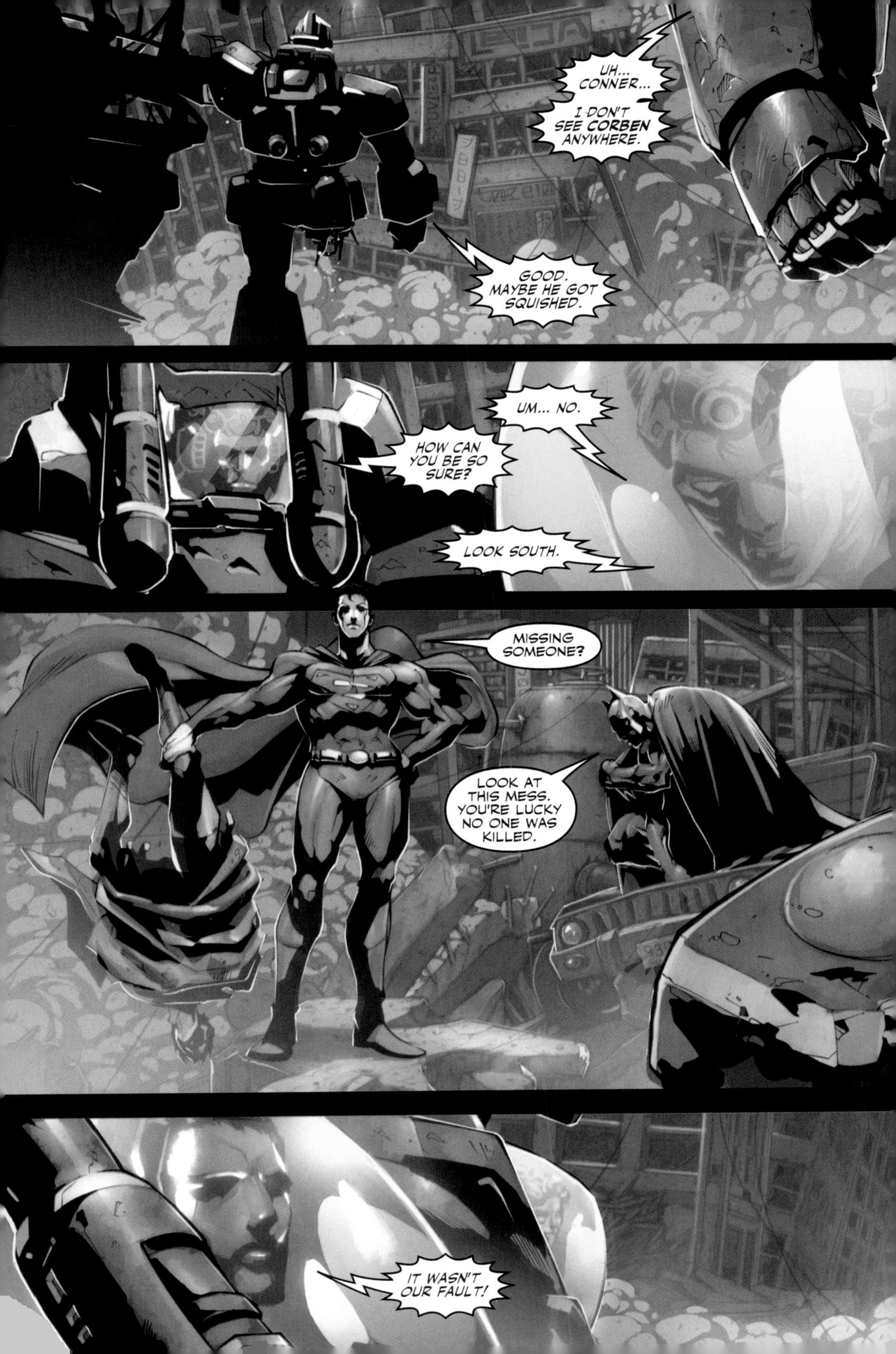

UH... CONNER...
I DON'T SEE CORBEN ANYWHERE.
GOOD. MAYBE HE GOT SQUISHED.
UM... NO.
HOW CAN YOU BE SO SURE?
LOOK SOUTH.
MISSING SOMEONE?
LOOK AT THIS MESS. YOU'RE LUCKY NO ONE WAS KILLED.
IT WASN'T OUR FAULT!

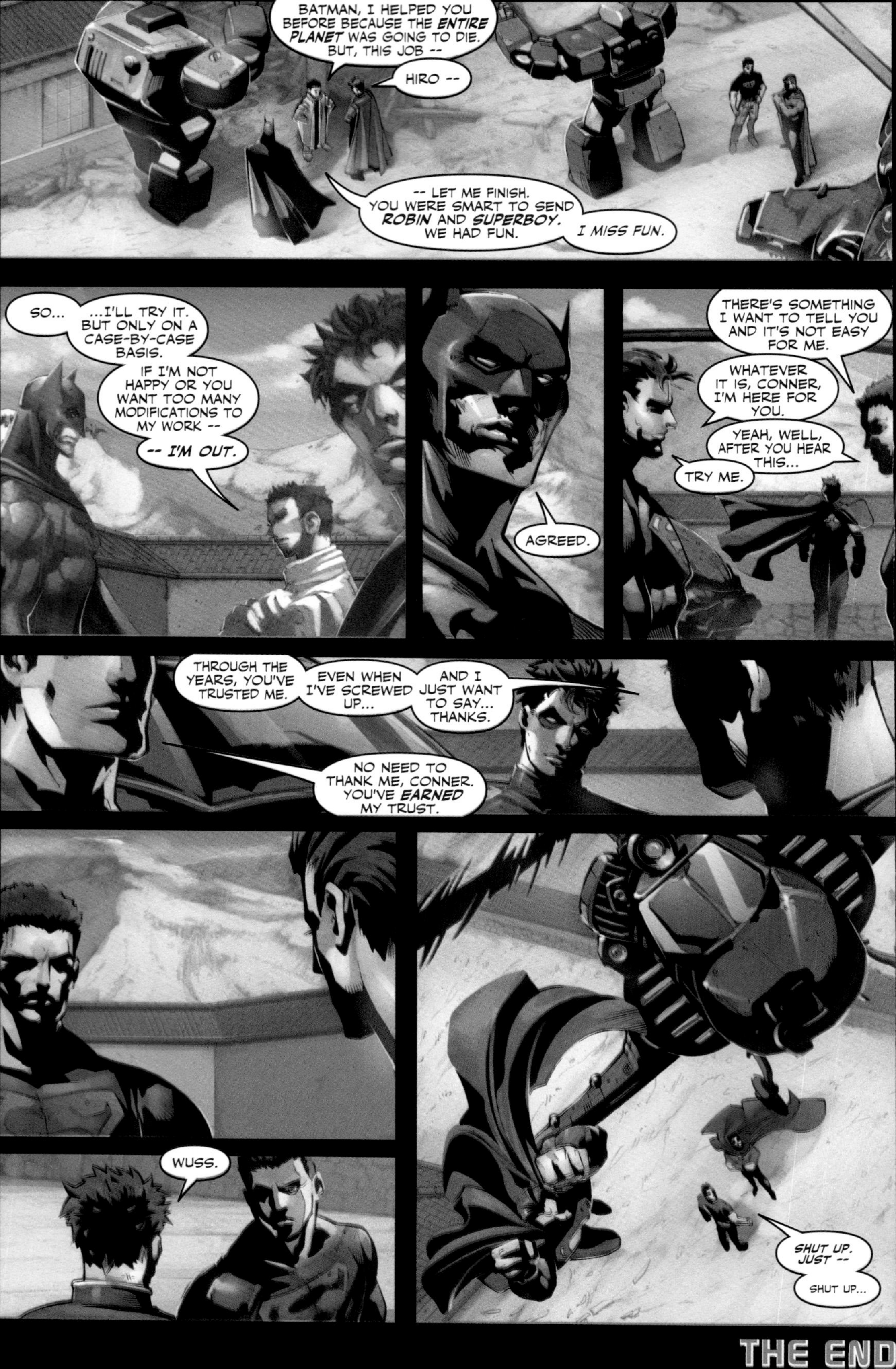
BATMAN, I HELPED YOU BEFORE BECAUSE THE ENTIRE PLANET WAS GOING TO DIE. BUT, THIS JOB --
HIRO --
-- LET ME FINISH. YOU WERE SMART TO SEND ROBIN AND SUPERBOY. WE HAD FUN.
I MISS FUN.
SO...
...I'LL TRY IT. BUT ONLY ON A CASE-BY-CASE BASIS.
IF I'M NOT HAPPY OR YOU WANT TOO MANY MODIFICATIONS TO MY WORK --
-- I'M OUT.
AGREED.
THERE'S SOMETHING I WANT TO TELL YOU AND IT'S NOT EASY FOR ME.
WHATEVER IT IS, CONNER, I'M HERE FOR YOU.
YEAH, WELL, AFTER YOU HEAR THIS...
TRY ME.
THROUGH THE YEARS, YOU'VE TRUSTED ME.
EVEN WHEN I'VE SCREWED UP...
AND I JUST WANT TO SAY... THANKS.
NO NEED TO THANK ME, CONNER. YOU'VE EARNED MY TRUST.
WUSS.
SHUT UP. JUST --
SHUT UP...
THE END

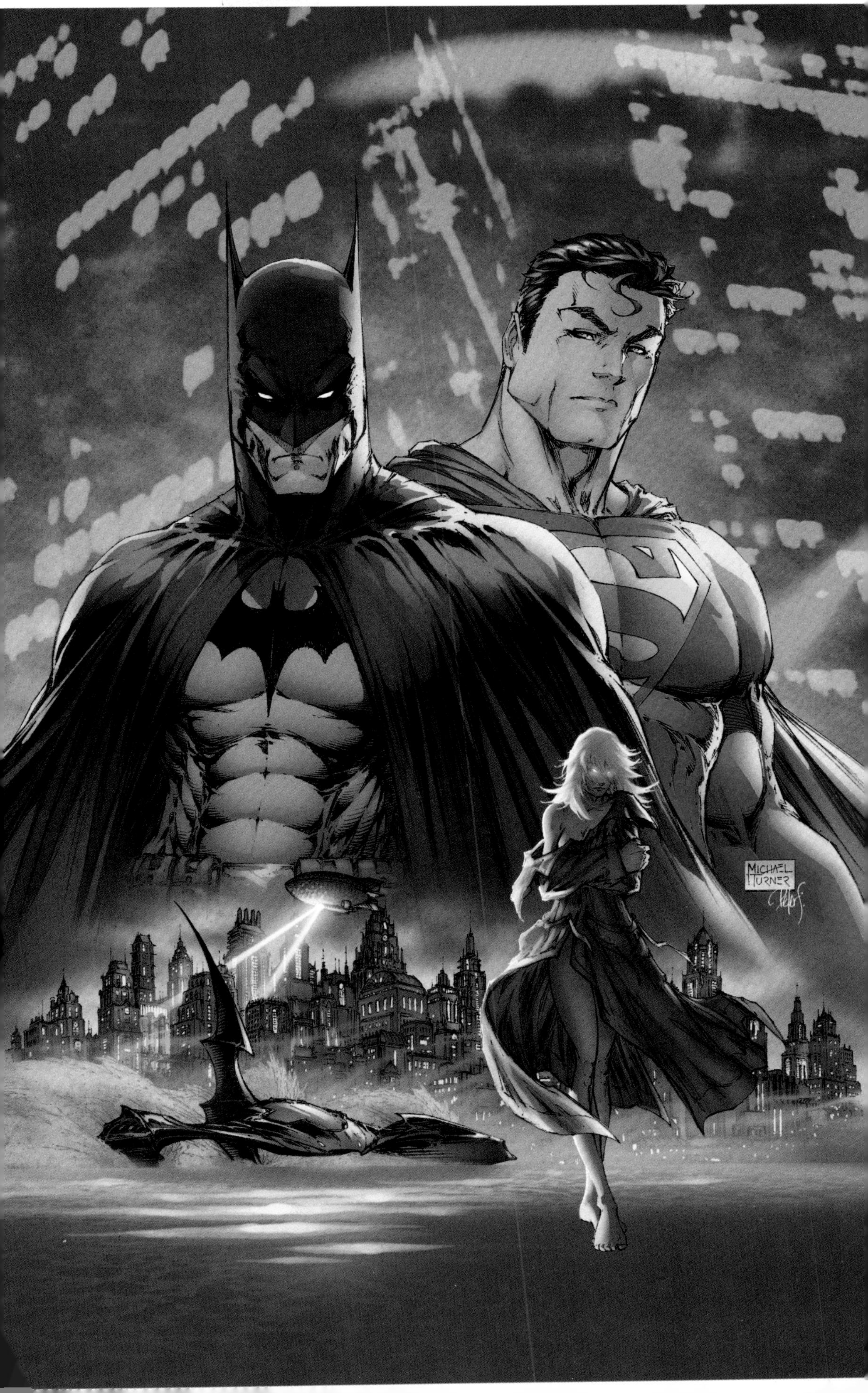
MICHAEL TURNER

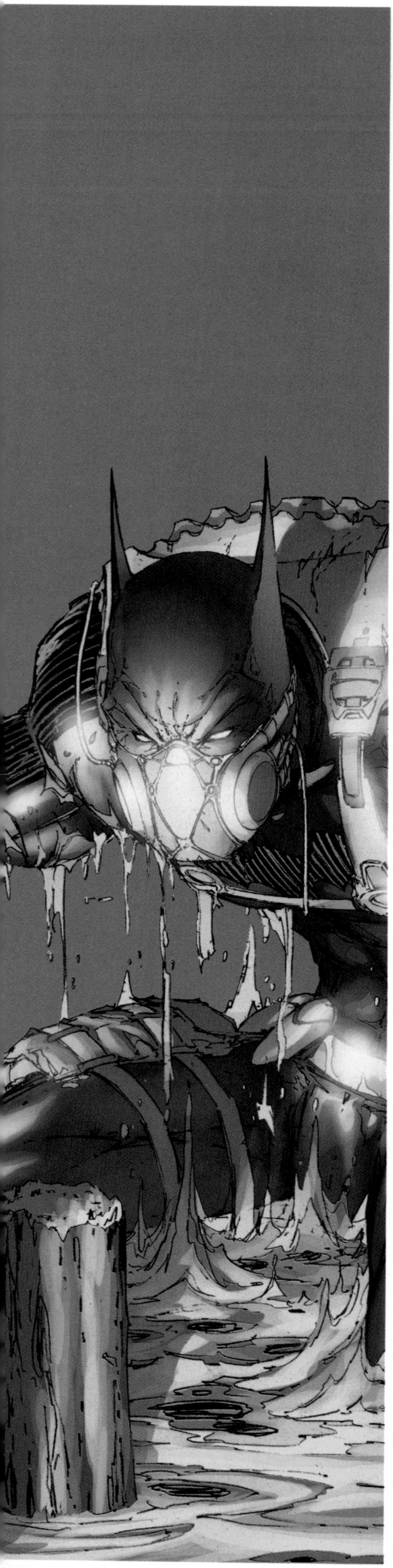

THE SUPERGIRL FROM KRYPTON

PART ONE
ALONE

JEPH LOEB
WRITER
MICHAEL TURNER
ARTIST
PETER STEIGERWALD
COLORIST
RICHARD STARKINGS
LETTERER
MICHAEL TURNER
WITH
PETER STEIGERWALD
COVER

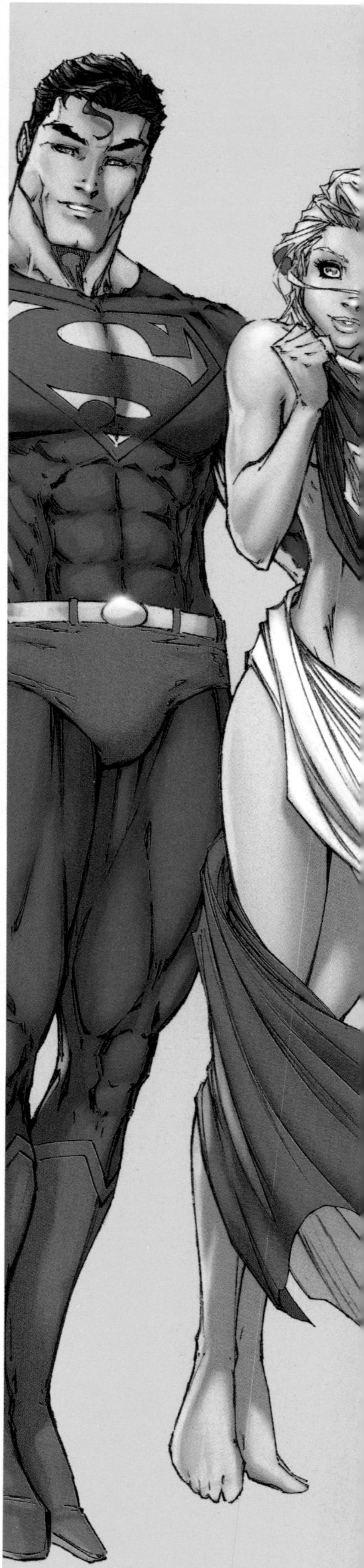

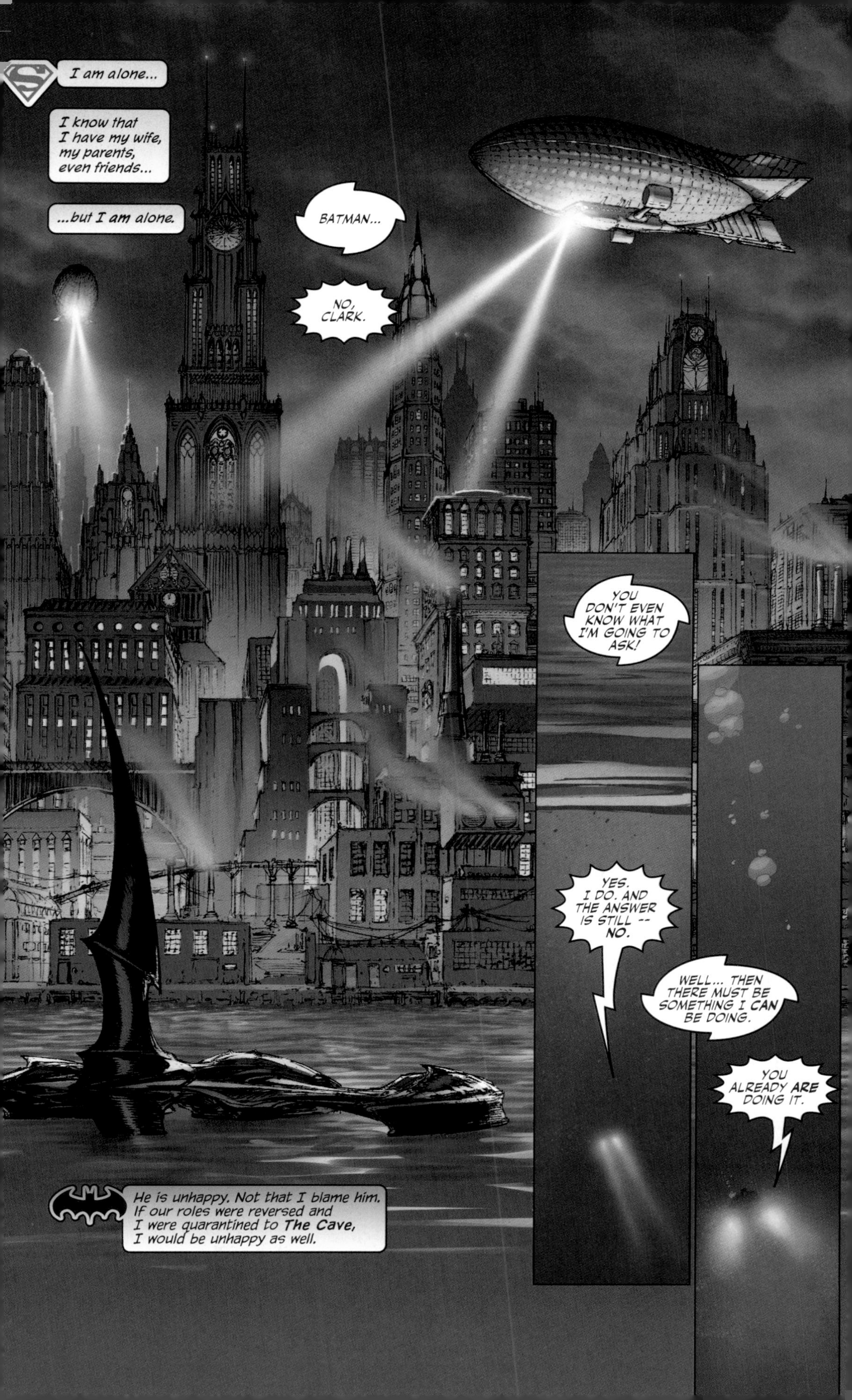

I am alone...
I know that I have my wife, my parents, even friends...
...but I am alone.
BATMAN...
NO, CLARK.
He is unhappy. Not that I blame him. If our roles were reversed and I were quarantined to The Cave, I would be unhappy as well.
YOU DON'T EVEN KNOW WHAT I'M GOING TO ASK!
YES. I DO. AND THE ANSWER IS STILL -- NO.
WELL... THEN THERE MUST BE SOMETHING I CAN BE DOING.
YOU ALREADY ARE DOING IT.

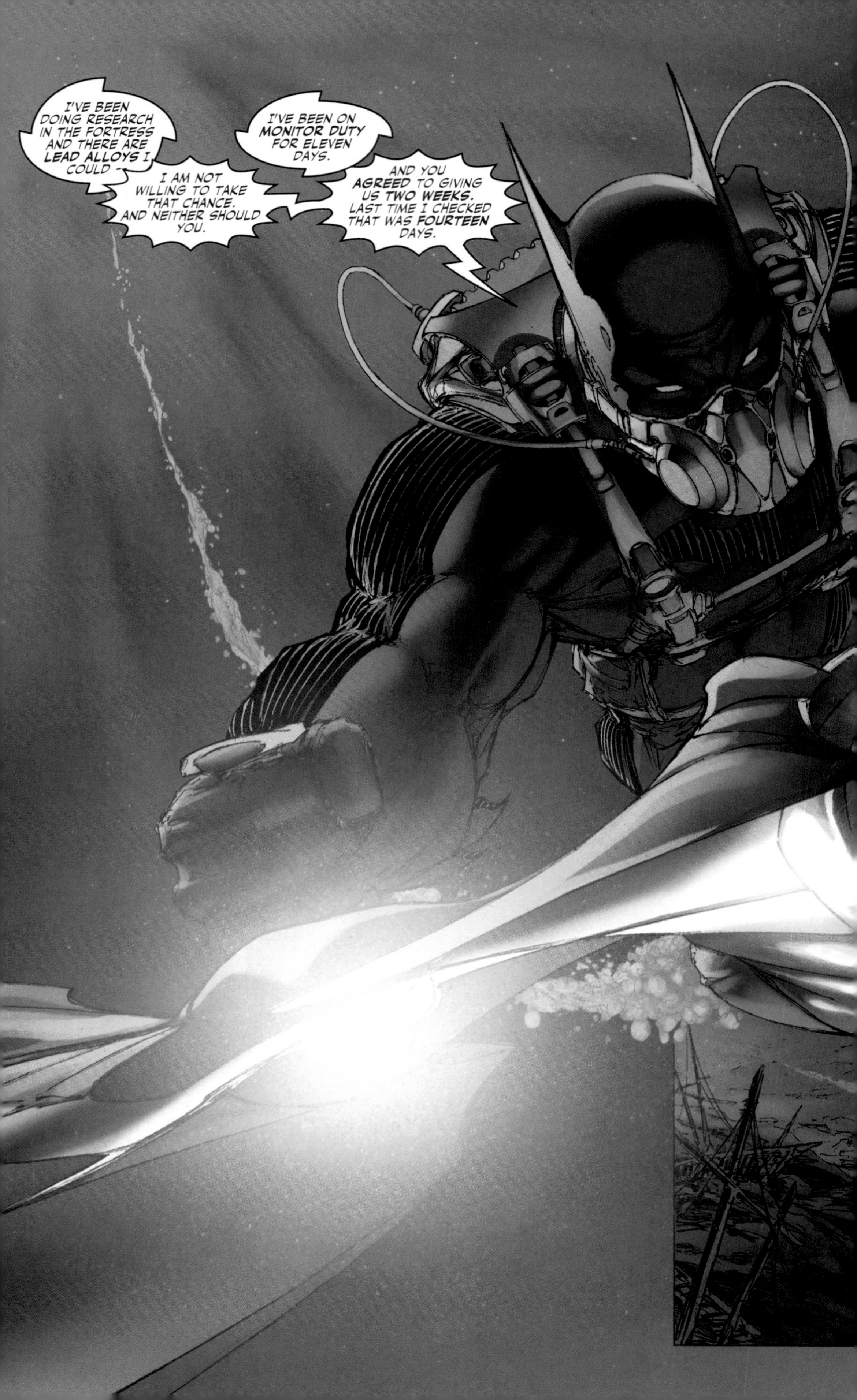
I'VE BEEN DOING RESEARCH IN THE FORTRESS AND THERE ARE LEAD ALLOYS I COULD -
I AM NOT WILLING TO TAKE THAT CHANCE. AND NEITHER SHOULD YOU.
I'VE BEEN ON MONITOR DUTY FOR ELEVEN DAYS.
AND YOU AGREED TO GIVING US TWO WEEKS. LAST TIME I CHECKED THAT WAS FOURTEEN DAYS.

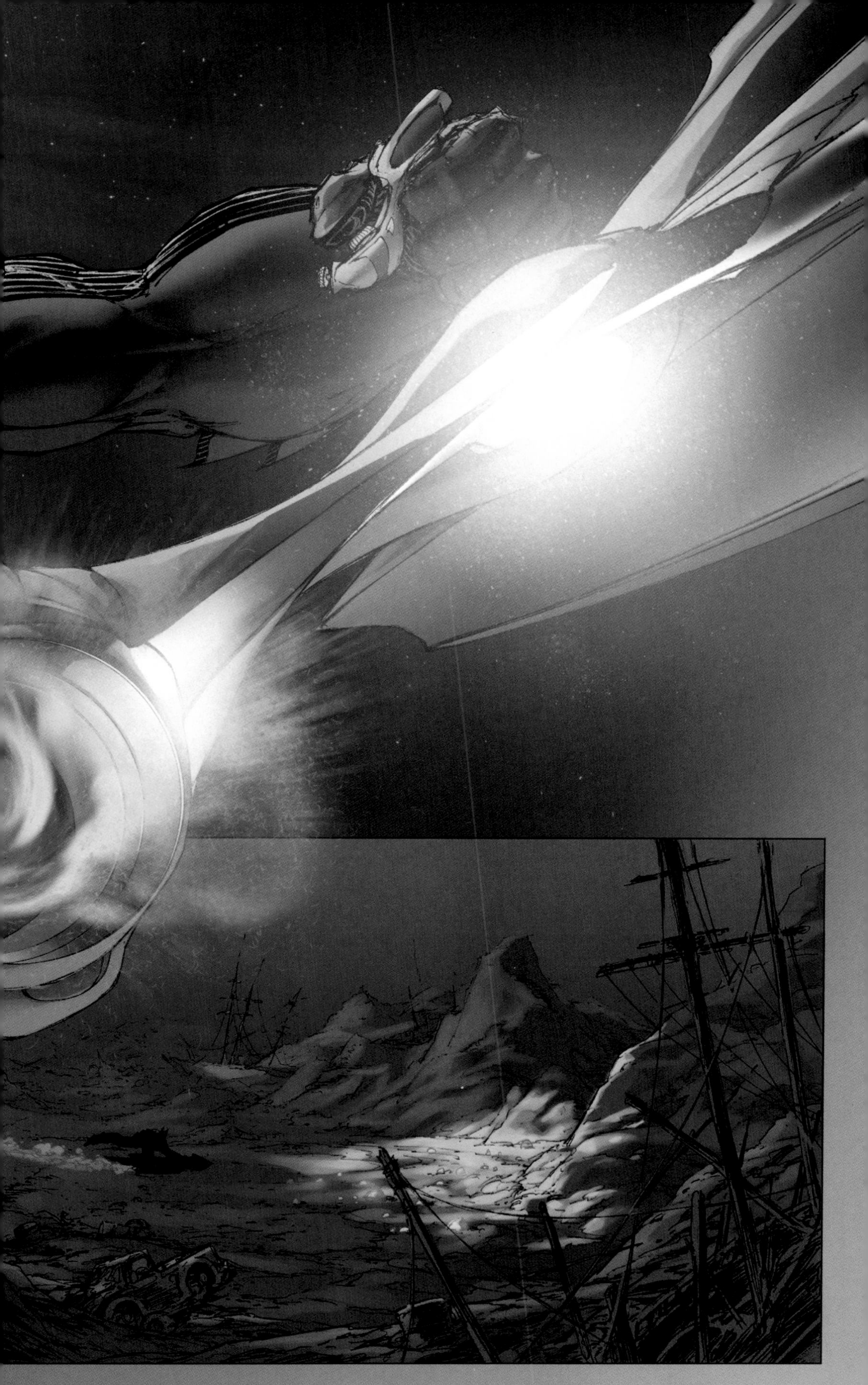

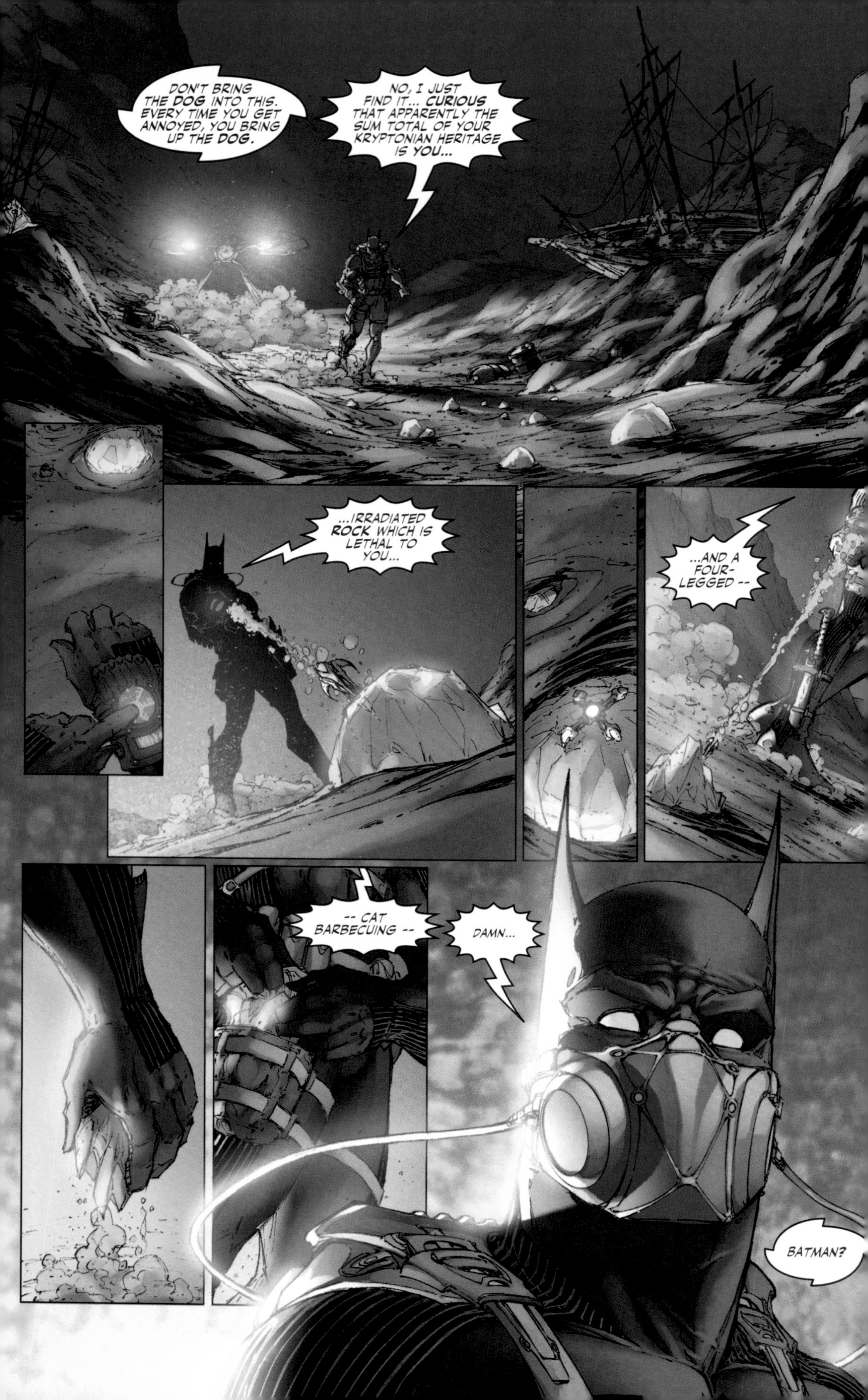
DON'T BRING THE DOG INTO THIS. EVERY TIME YOU GET ANNOYED, YOU BRING UP THE DOG.
NO, I JUST FIND IT... CURIOUS THAT APPARENTLY THE SUM TOTAL OF YOUR KRYPTONIAN HERITAGE IS YOU...
...IRRADIATED ROCK WHICH IS LETHAL TO YOU...
...AND A FOUR-LEGGED --
-- CAT BARBECUING --
DAMN...
BATMAN?

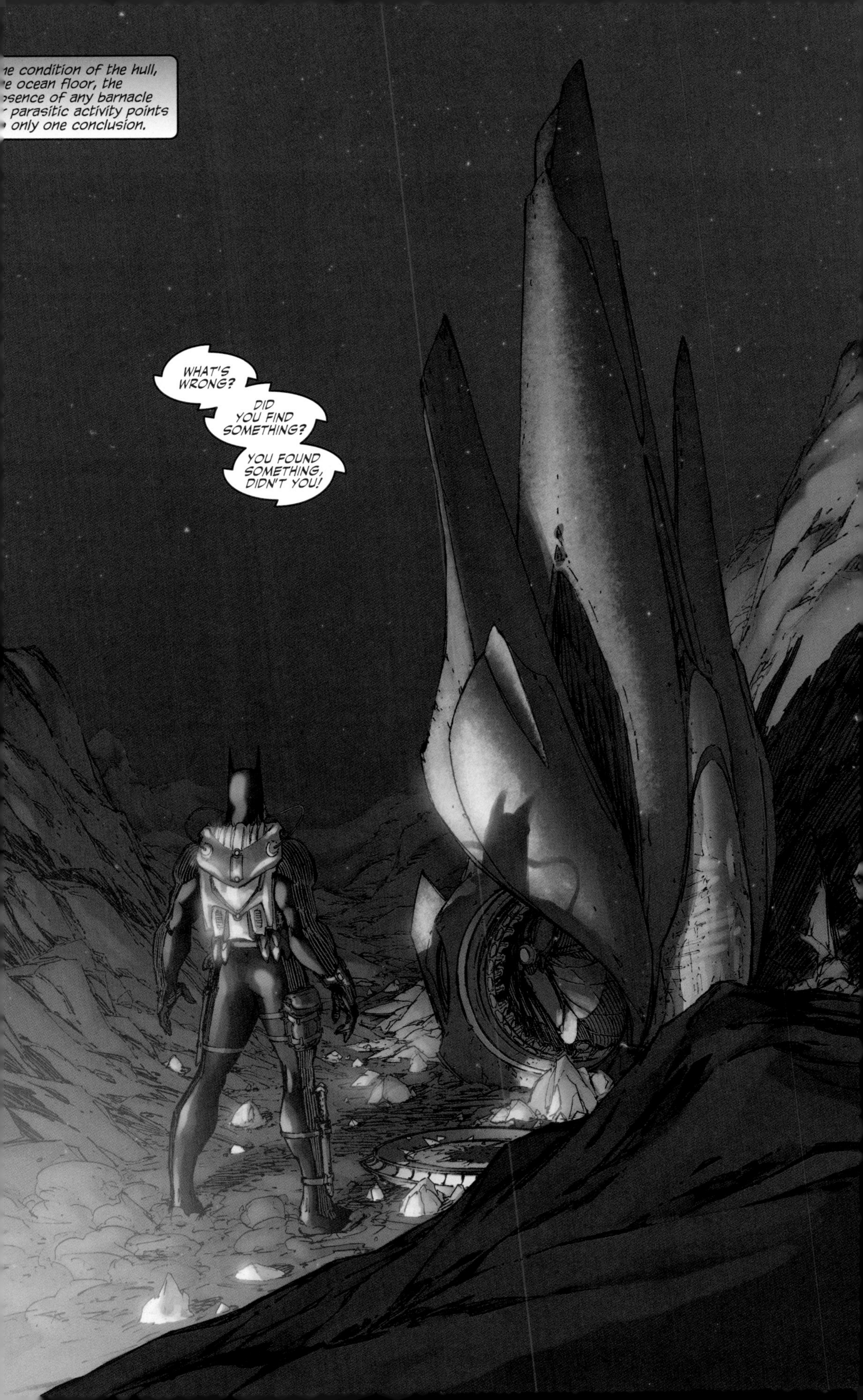

ne condition of the hull, e ocean floor, the bsence of any barnacle r parasitic activity points o only one conclusion.
WHAT'S WRONG?
DID YOU FIND SOMETHING?
YOU FOUND SOMETHING, DIDN'T YOU!

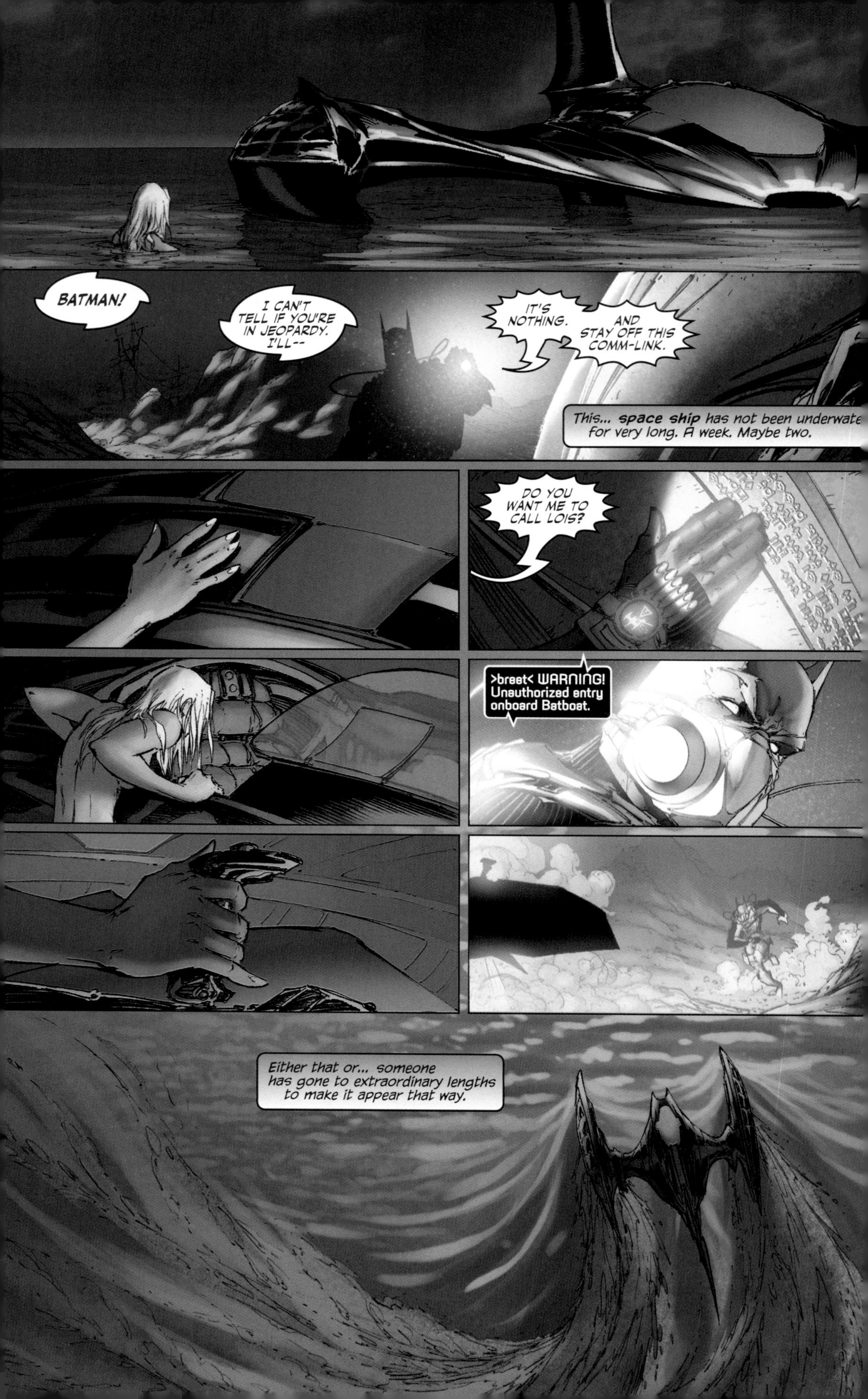
BATMAN!
I CAN'T TELL IF YOU'RE IN JEOPARDY. I'LL--
IT'S NOTHING.
AND STAY OFF THIS COMM-LINK.
This... space ship has not been underwate for very long. A week. Maybe two.
DO YOU WANT ME TO CALL LOIS?
>breet< WARNING! Unauthorized entry onboard Batboat.
Either that or... someone has gone to extraordinary lengths to make it appear that way.

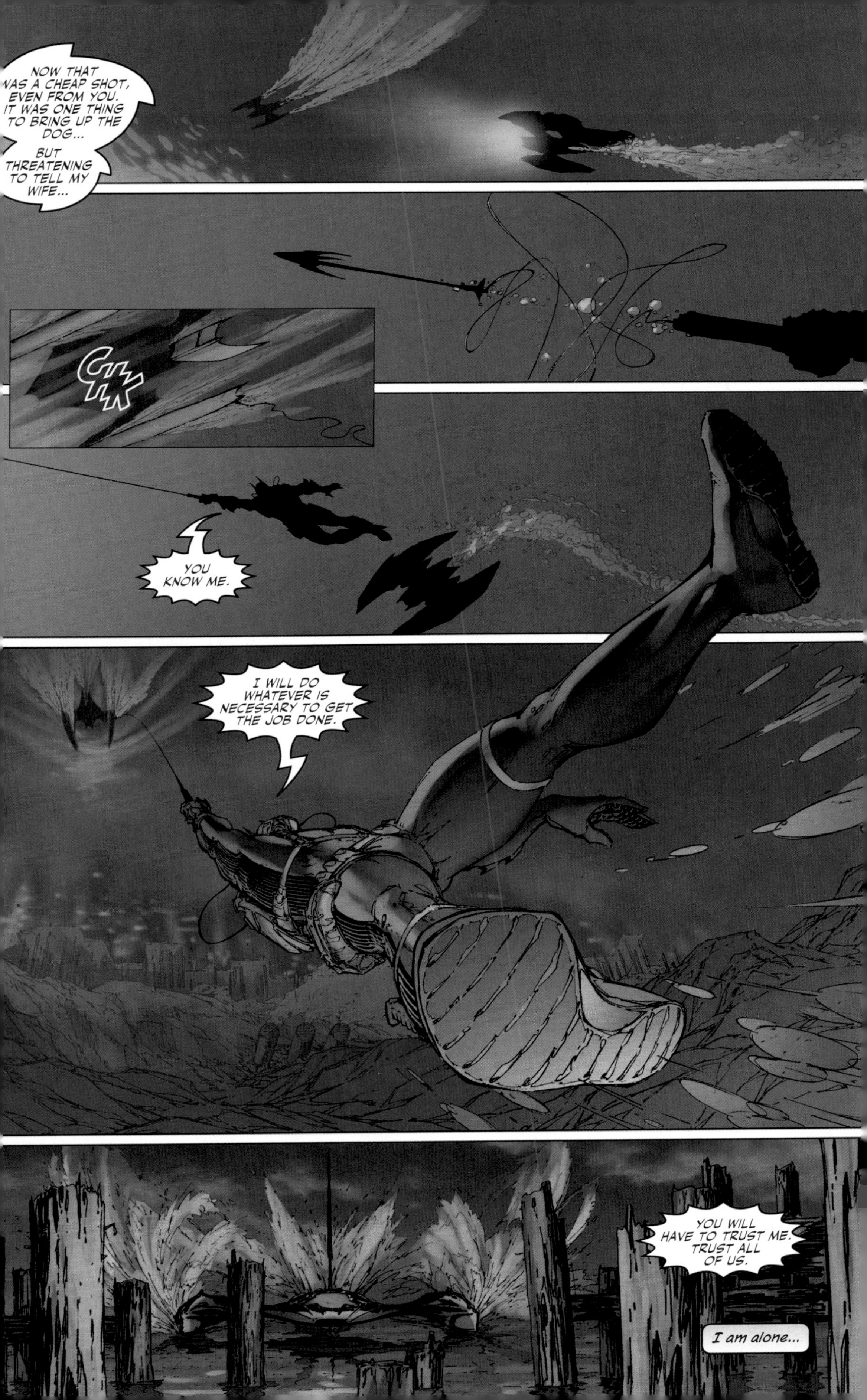
NOW THAT WAS A CHEAP SHOT, EVEN FROM YOU. IT WAS ONE THING TO BRING UP THE DOG...
BUT THREATENING TO TELL MY WIFE...
CHK
YOU KNOW ME.
I WILL DO WHATEVER IS NECESSARY TO GET THE JOB DONE.
YOU WILL HAVE TO TRUST ME. TRUST ALL OF US.
I am alone...

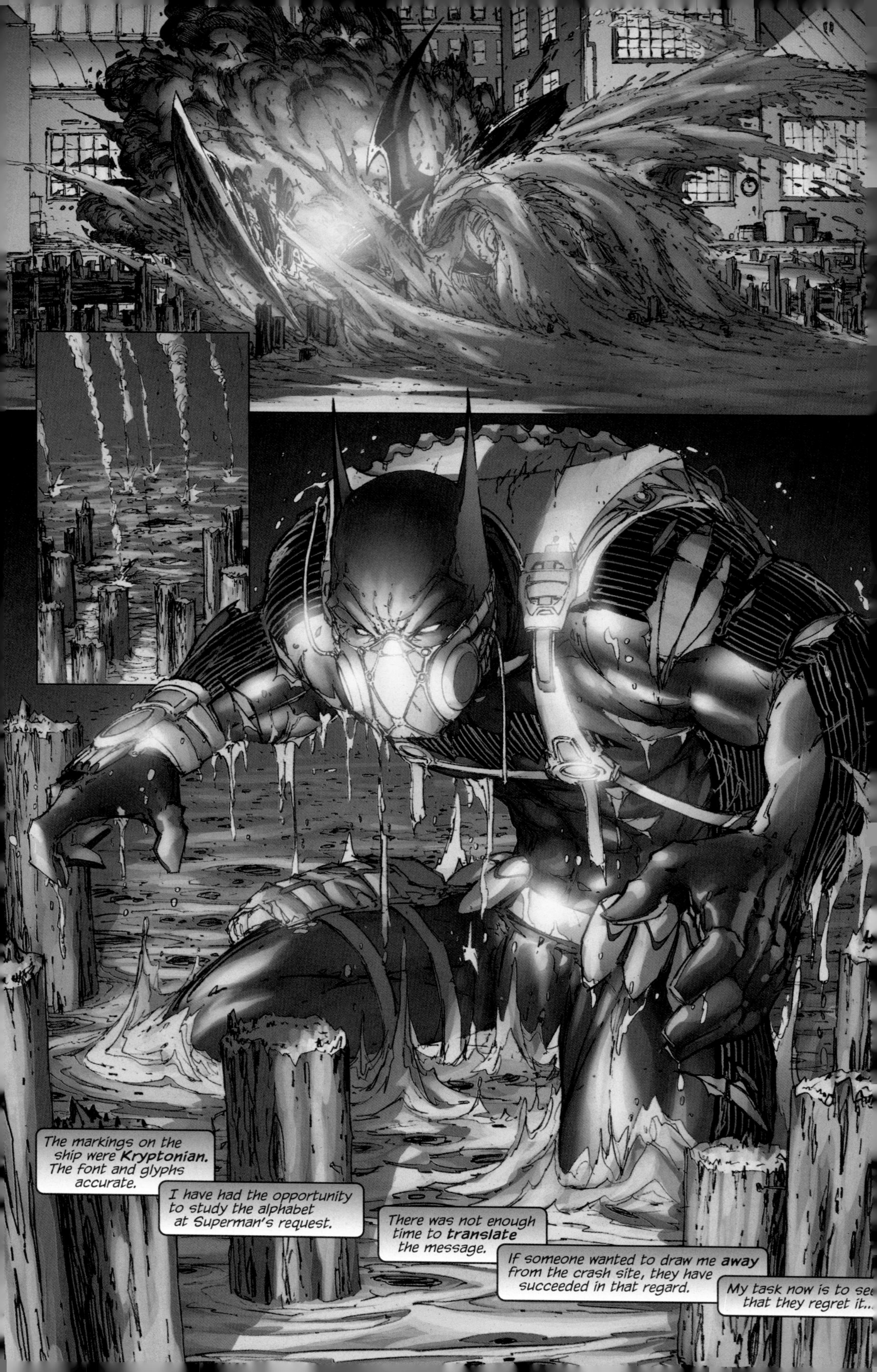

The markings on the ship were **Kryptonian.** The font and glyphs accurate.
I have had the opportunity to study the alphabet at Superman's request.
There was not enough time to **translate** the message.
If someone wanted to draw me **away** from the crash site, they have succeeded in that regard.
My task now is to se that they regret it...

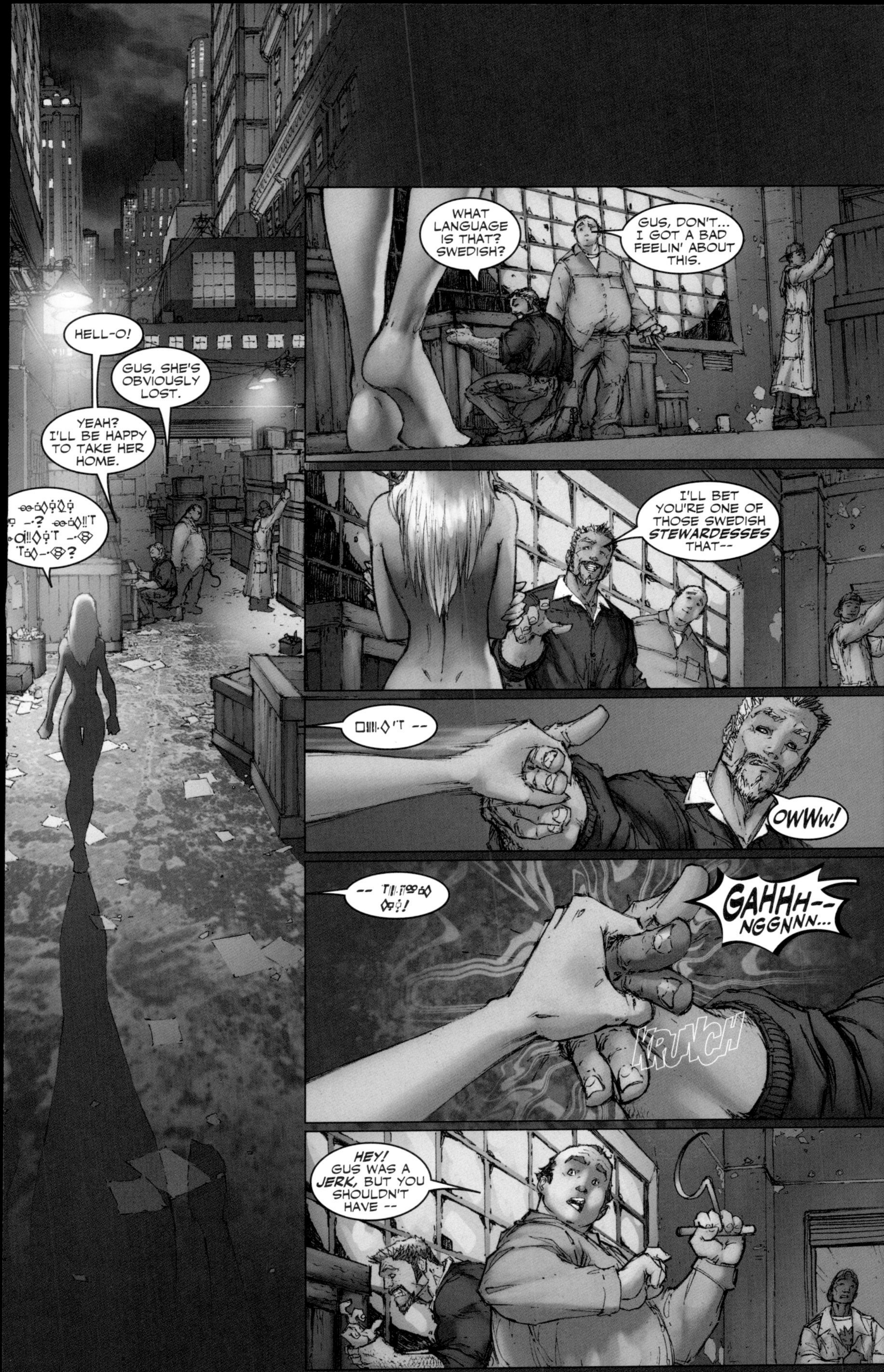
HELL-O!
GUS, SHE'S OBVIOUSLY LOST.
YEAH? I'LL BE HAPPY TO TAKE HER HOME.
WHAT LANGUAGE IS THAT? SWEDISH?
GUS, DON'T... I GOT A BAD FEELIN' ABOUT THIS.
I'LL BET YOU'RE ONE OF THOSE SWEDISH STEWARDESSES THAT--
OWWW!
GAHHH-- NGGNNN...
KRUNCH
HEY! GUS WAS A JERK, BUT YOU SHOULDN'T HAVE --

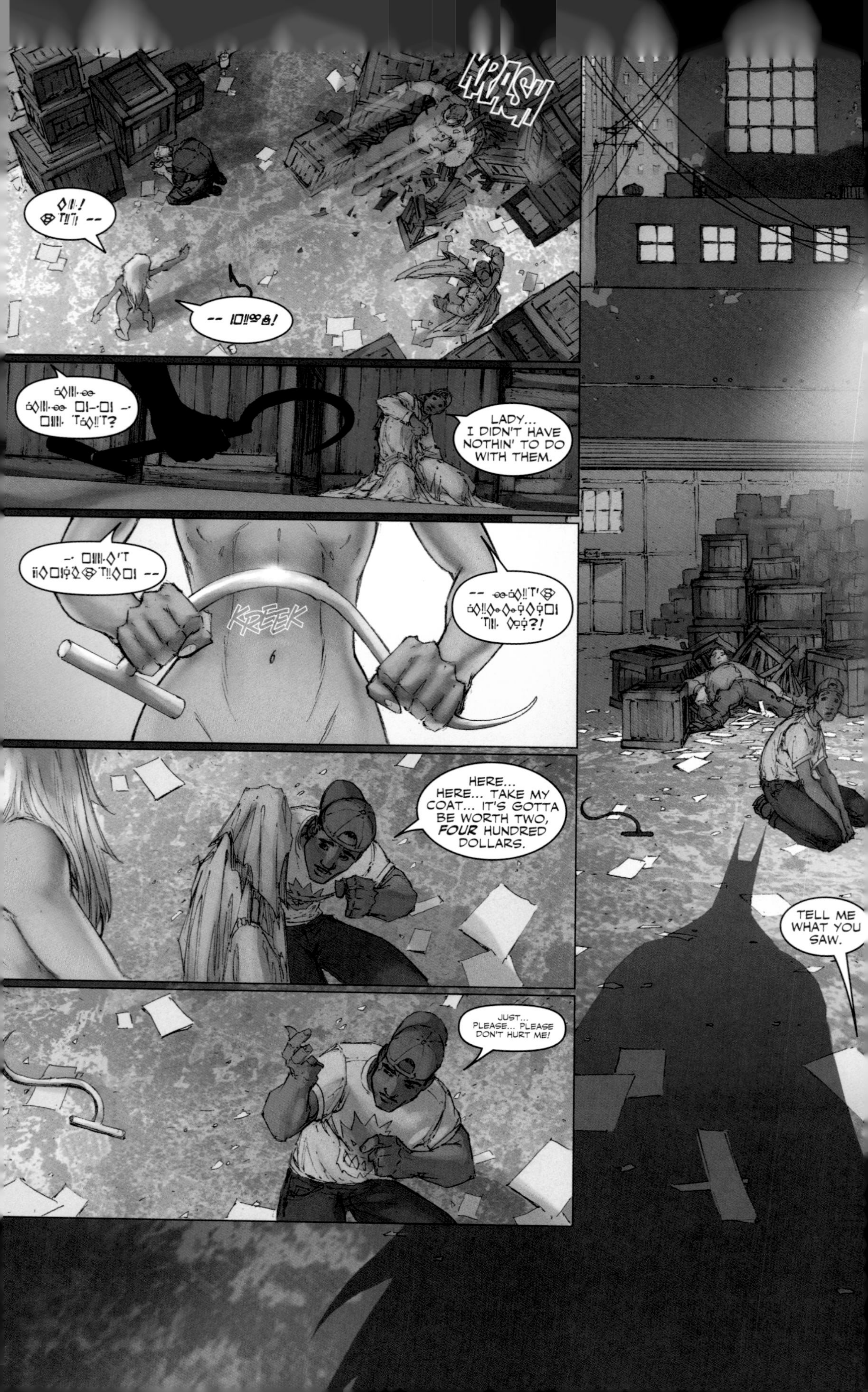
KRASH
LADY... I DIDN'T HAVE NOTHIN' TO DO WITH THEM.
KREEK
HERE... HERE... TAKE MY COAT... IT'S GOTTA BE WORTH TWO, FOUR HUNDRED DOLLARS.
JUST... PLEASE... PLEASE DON'T HURT ME!
TELL ME WHAT YOU SAW.

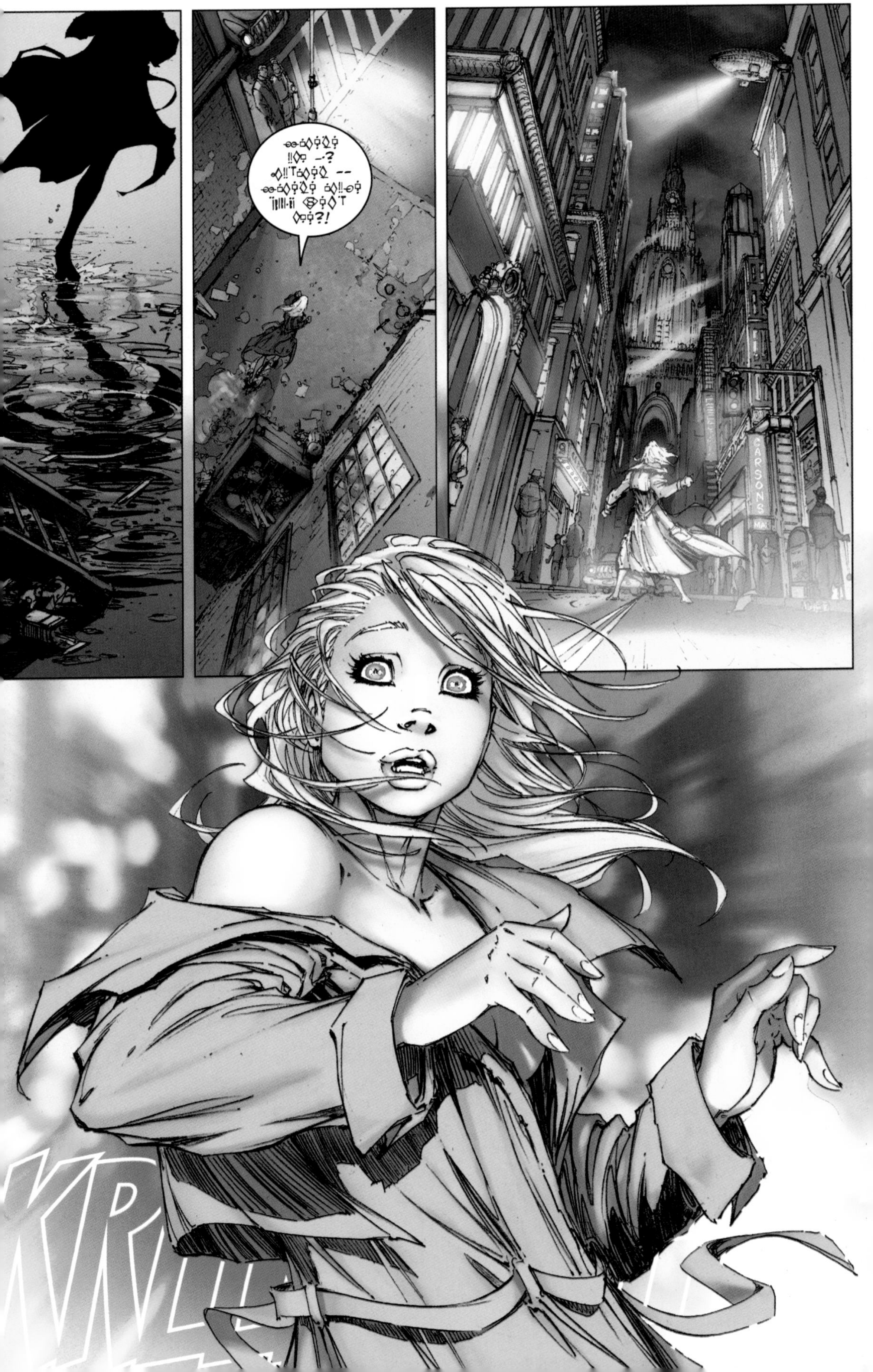
GARSONS

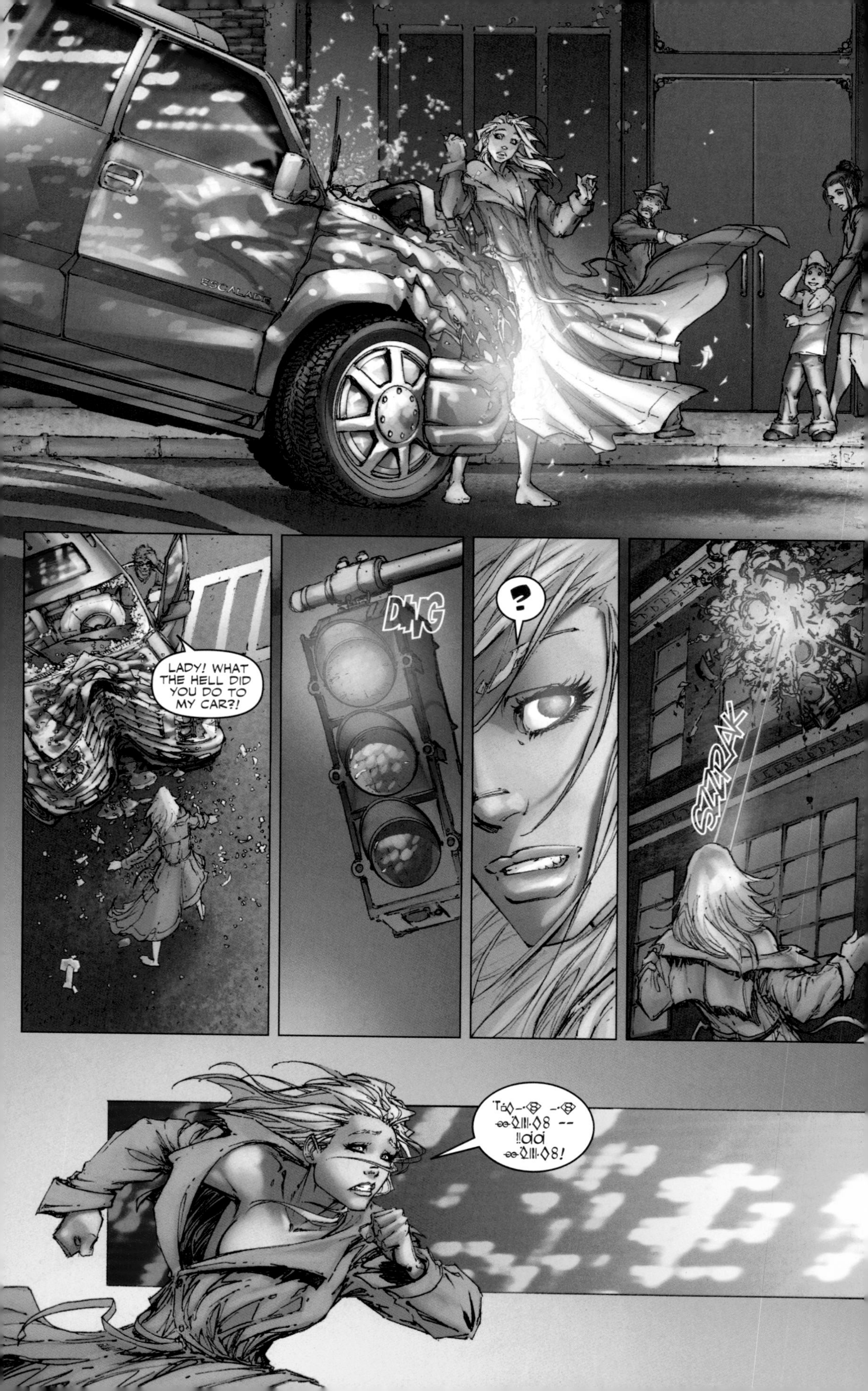
LADY! WHAT THE HELL DID YOU DO TO MY CAR?!
DING
?

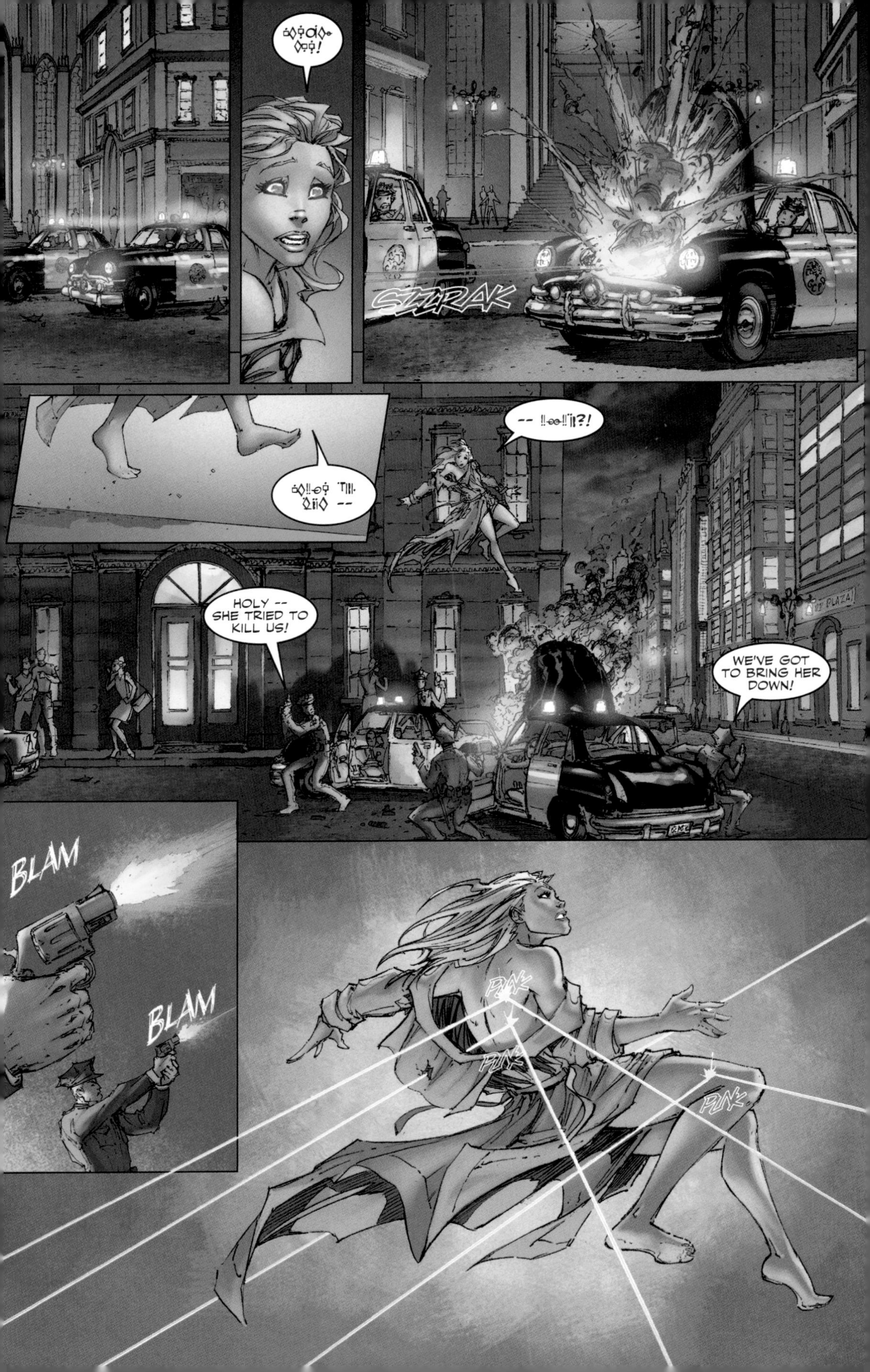

SZZRAK
HOLY -- SHE TRIED TO KILL US!
WE'VE GOT TO BRING HER DOWN!
BLAM
BLAM

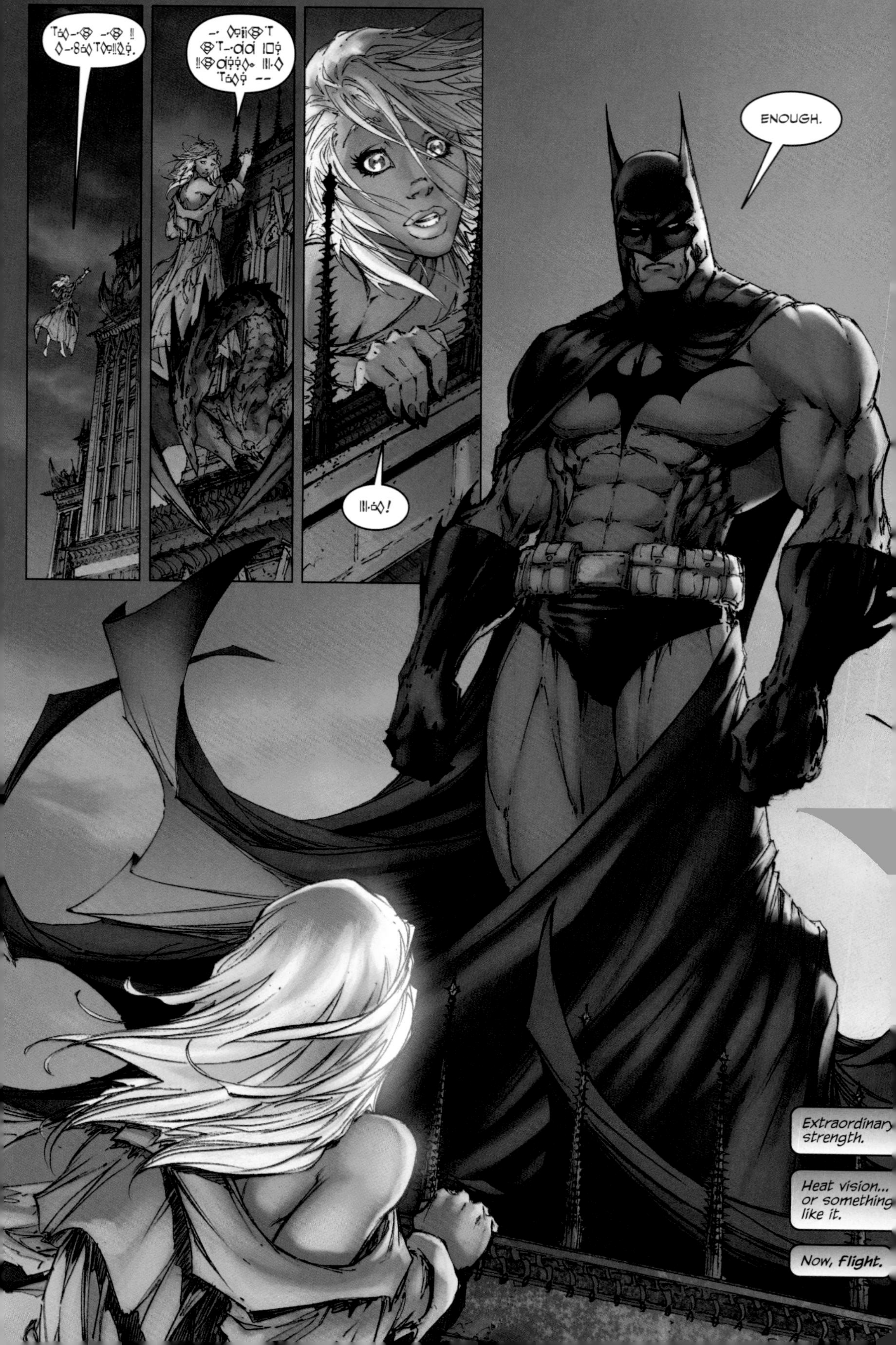
ENOUGH.
Extraordinary strength.
Heat vision... or something like it.
Now, *flight*.

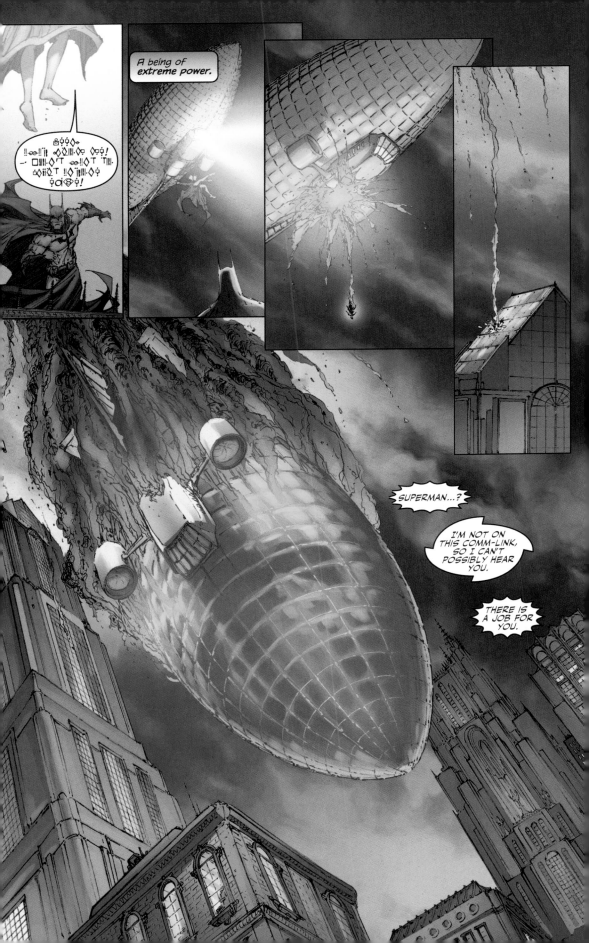

A being of *extreme power.*

!!!\u25c8!!'T\u0131 \u25c8\u25c8\u25c8!!! \u25c8\u25c8\u25cb!
-. \u25a1\u25a0!!-\u25cb'T \u221e!!\u25cbT T!!!-
\u25c8\u25c8\u25cb\u25c8'T !!\u25c8\u25cb!-\u25cb'\u25c8\u25bd
\u0121\u25cb!\u25c8\u25cb\u25c8\u25bd!

SUPERMAN...?

I'M NOT ON THIS COMM-LINK, SO I CAN'T POSSIBLY HEAR YOU.

THERE IS A JOB FOR YOU.

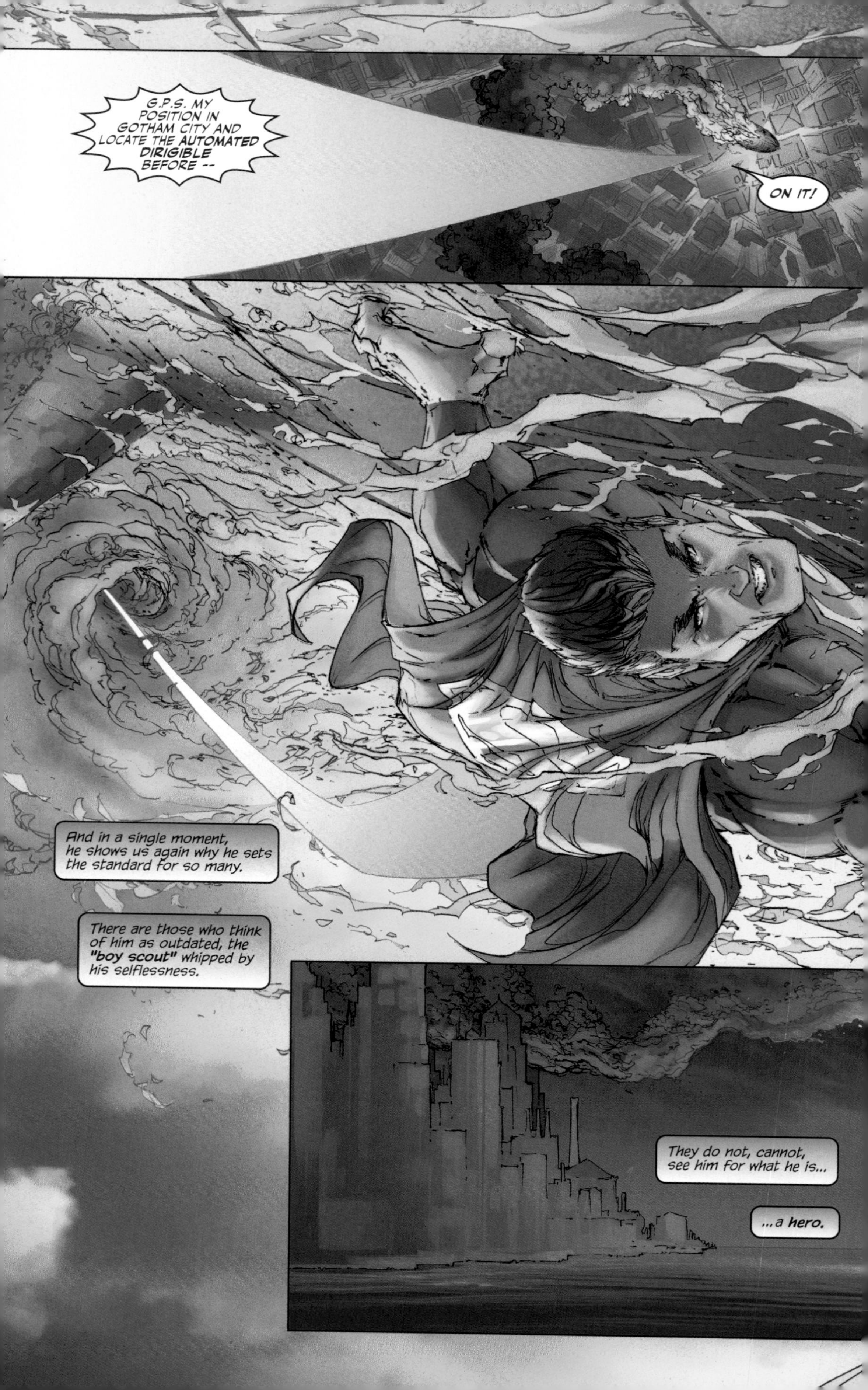
G.P.S. MY POSITION IN GOTHAM CITY AND LOCATE THE AUTOMATED DIRIGIBLE BEFORE --
ON IT!
And in a single moment, he shows us again why he sets the standard for so many.
There are those who think of him as outdated, the "boy scout" whipped by his selflessness.
They do not, cannot, see him for what he is...
...a hero.

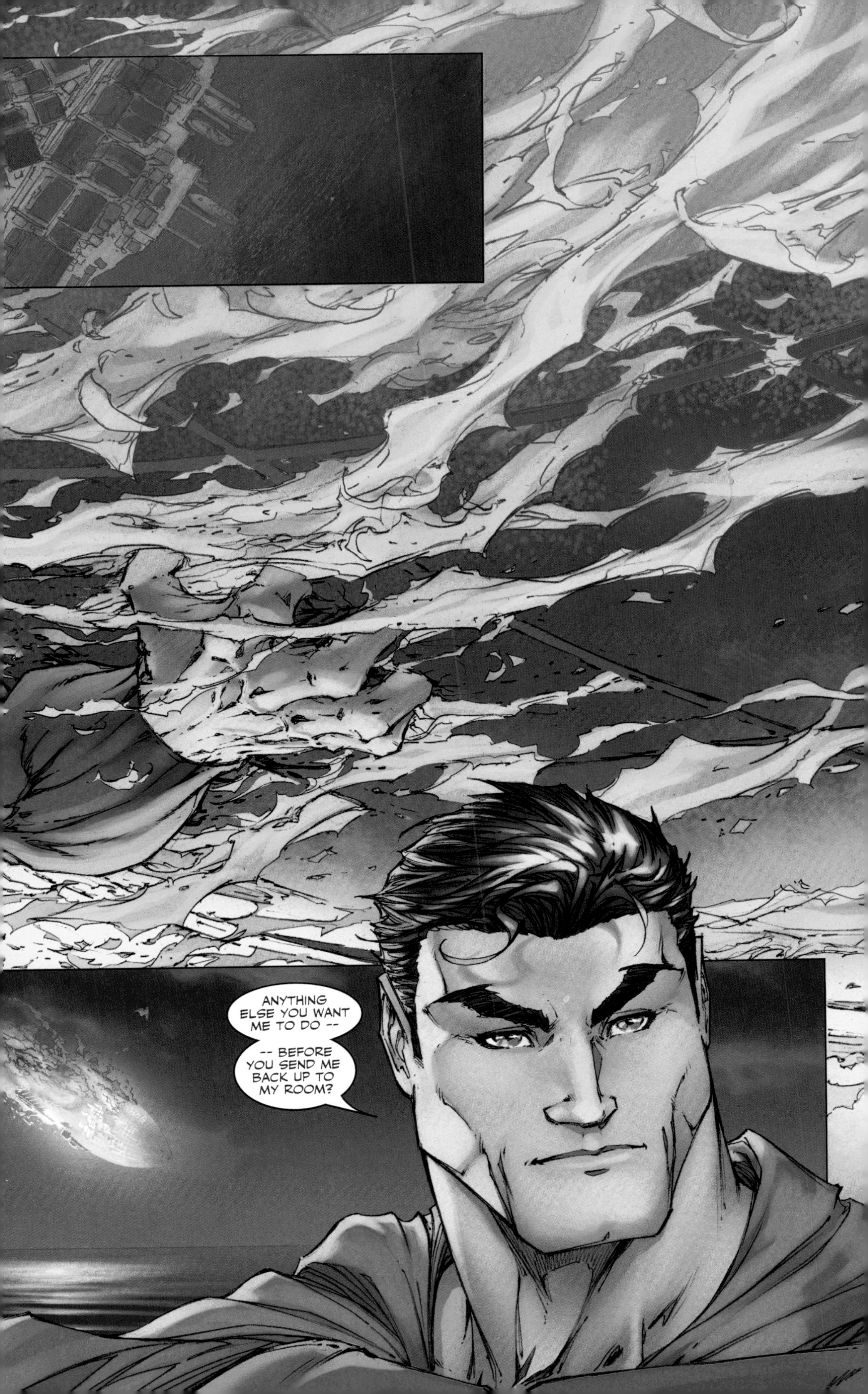
ANYTHING ELSE YOU WANT ME TO DO --
-- BEFORE YOU SEND ME BACK UP TO MY ROOM?

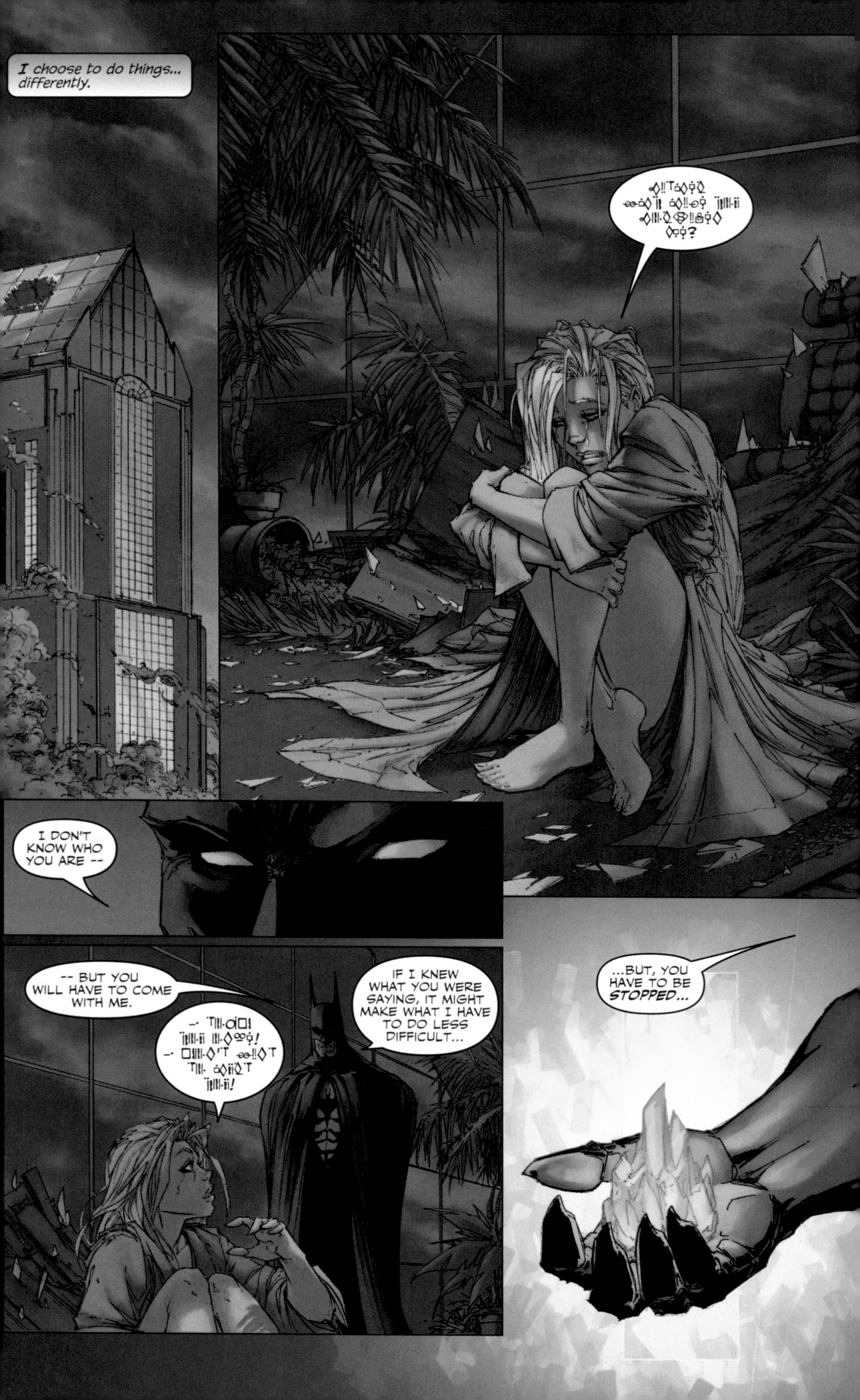
I choose to do things... differently.
I DON'T KNOW WHO YOU ARE --
-- BUT YOU WILL HAVE TO COME WITH ME.
IF I KNEW WHAT YOU WERE SAYING, IT MIGHT MAKE WHAT I HAVE TO DO LESS DIFFICULT...
...BUT, YOU HAVE TO BE STOPPED...

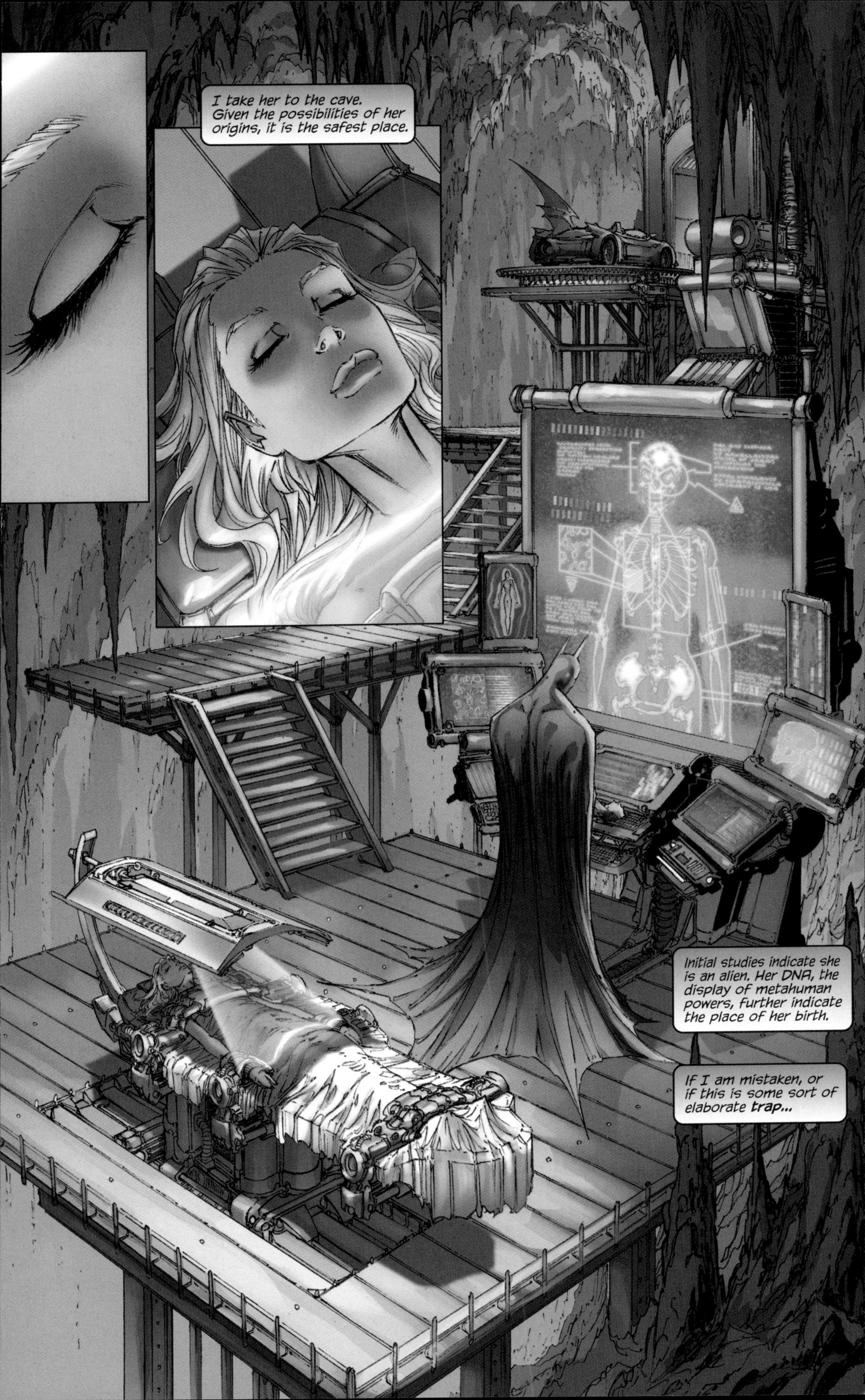
I take her to the cave. Given the possibilities of her origins, it is the safest place.
Initial studies indicate she is an alien. Her DNA, the display of metahuman powers, further indicate the place of her birth.
If I am mistaken, or if this is some sort of elaborate trap...

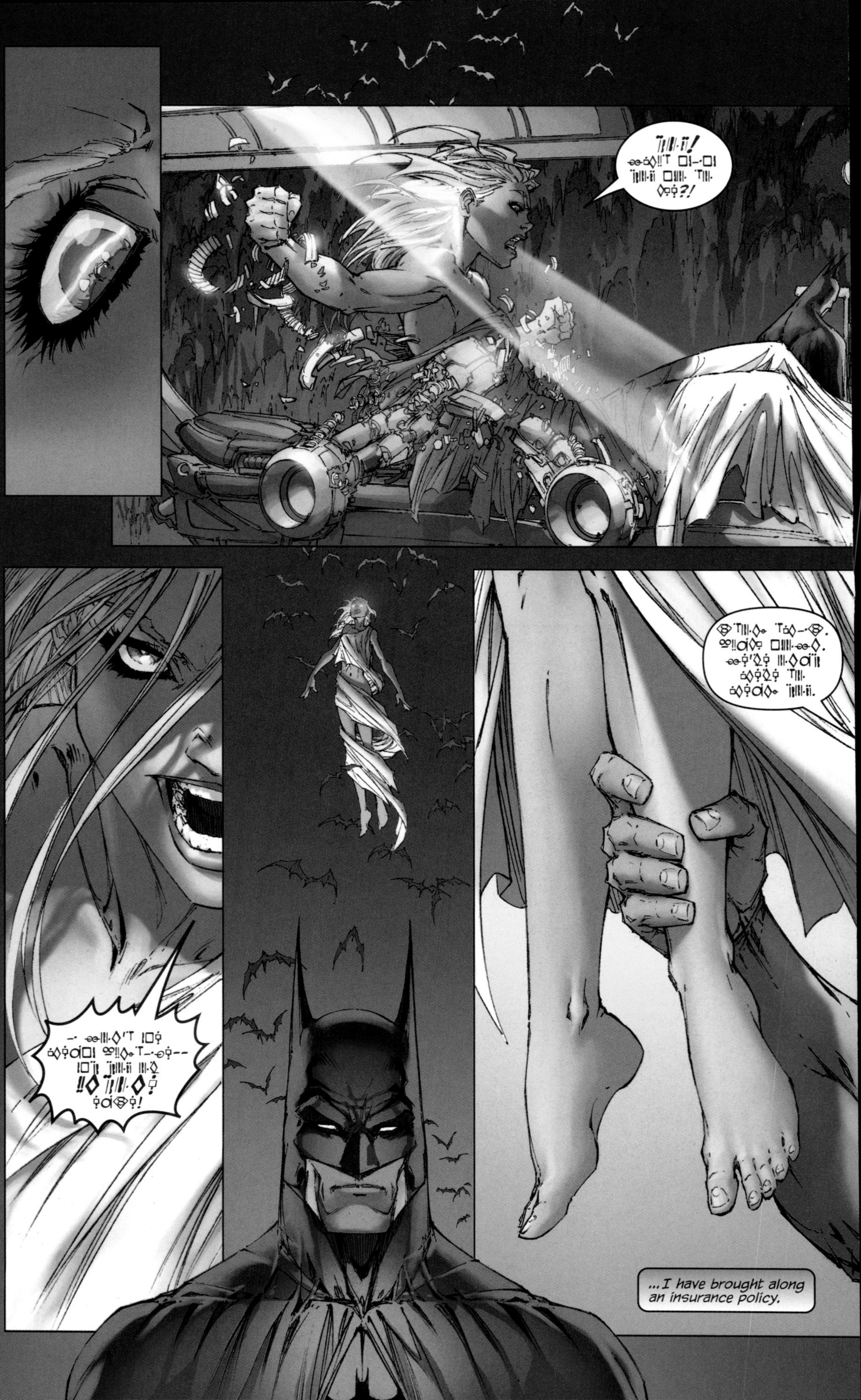
...I have brought along an insurance policy.

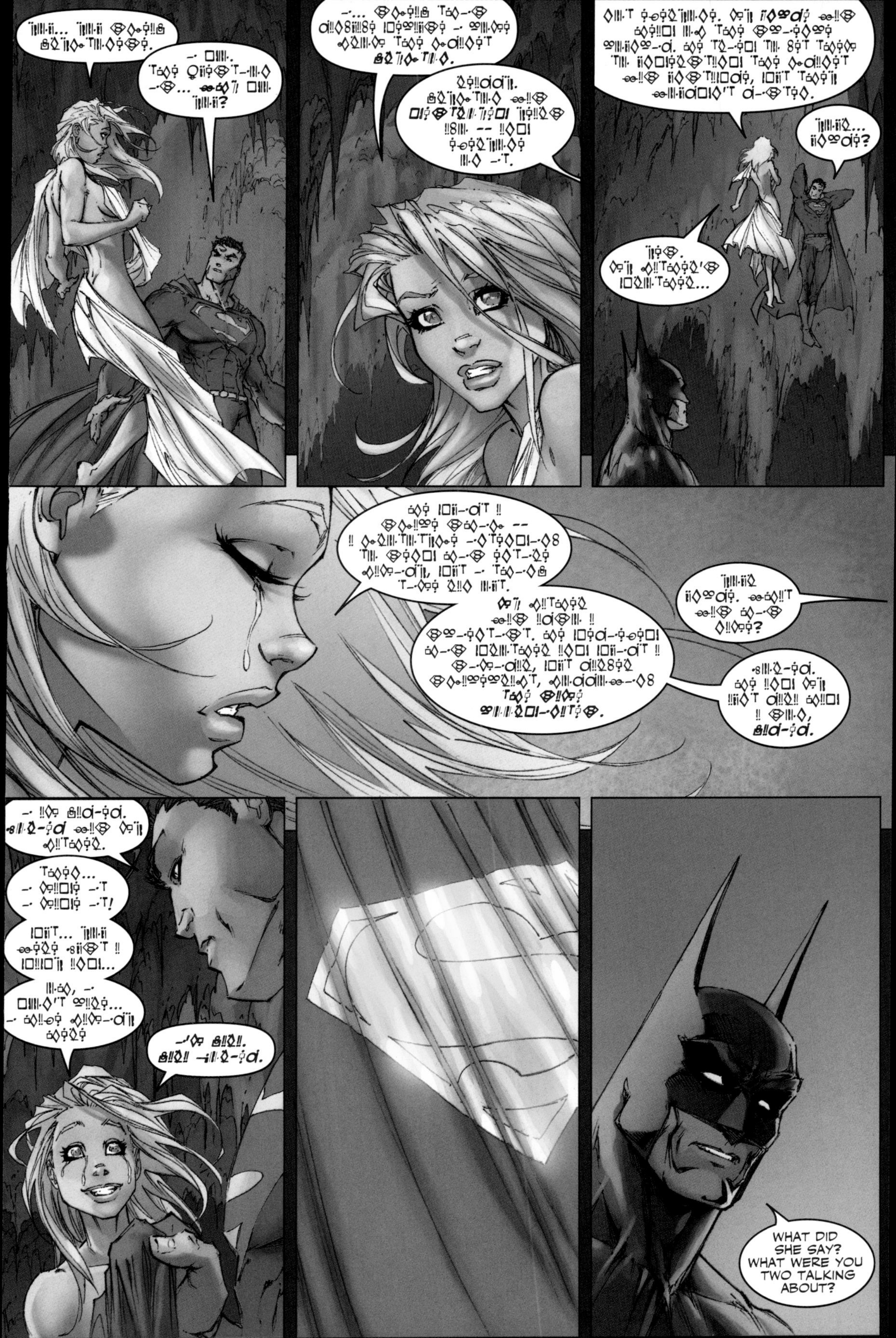
WHAT DID SHE SAY? WHAT WERE YOU TWO TALKING ABOUT?

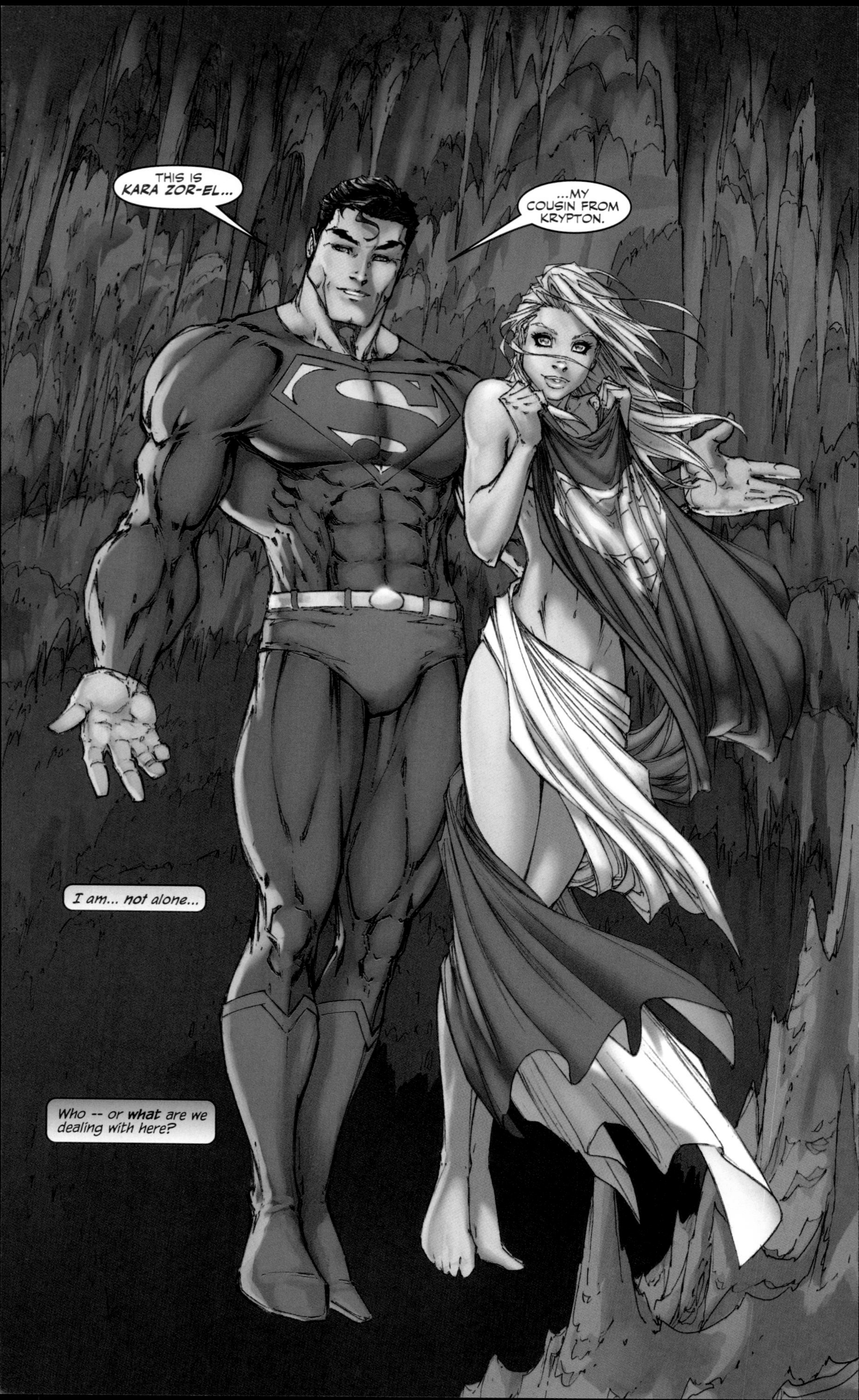
THIS IS KARA ZOR-EL...
...MY COUSIN FROM KRYPTON.
I am... not alone...
Who -- or what are we dealing with here?

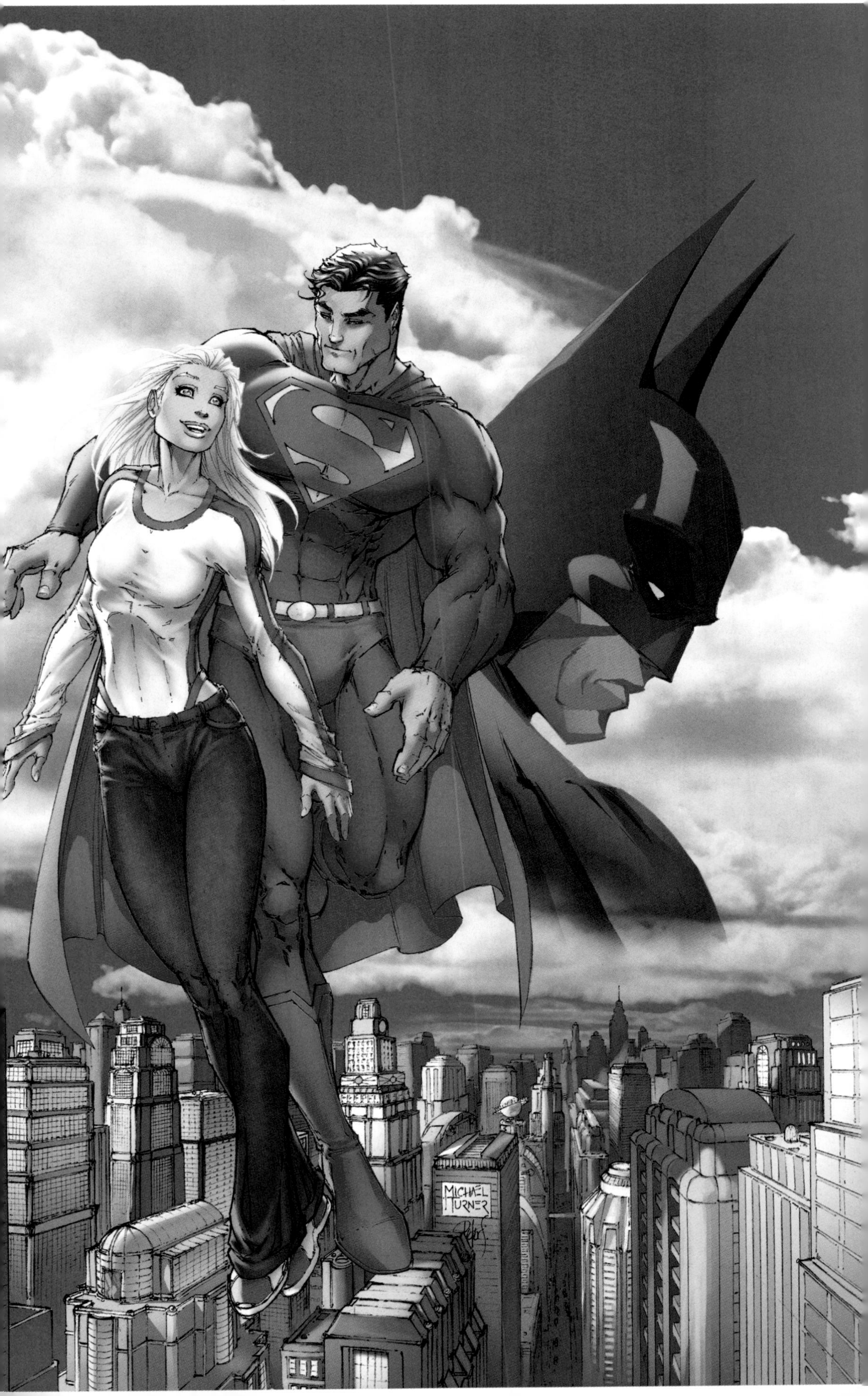
MICHAEL TURNER

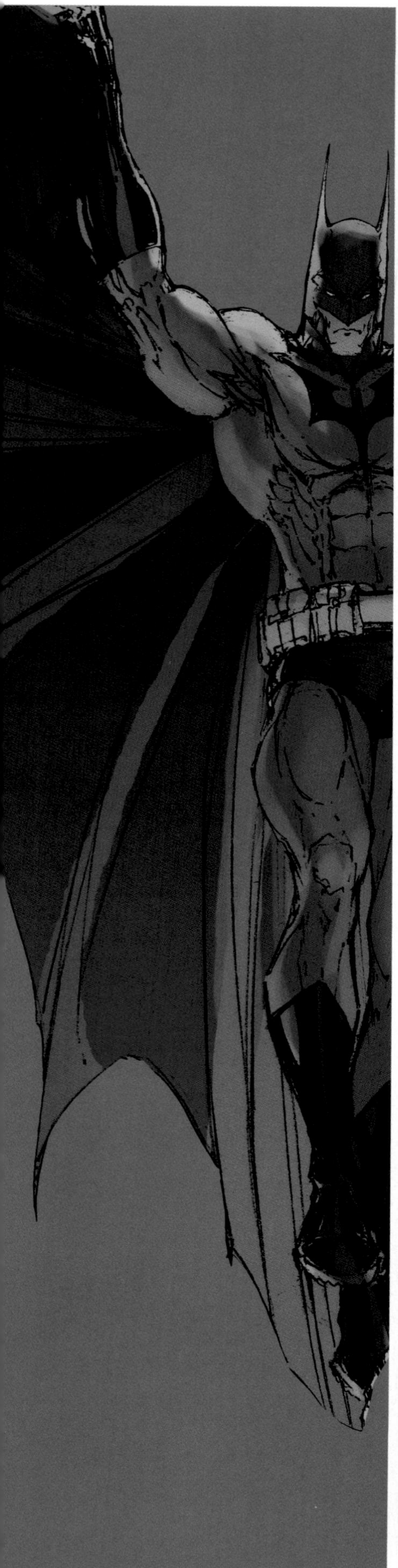

THE SUPERGIRL FROM KRYPTON

PART TWO
VISITOR

JEPH LOEB
WRITER
MICHAEL TURNER
ARTIST
PETER STEIGERWALD
COLORIST
RICHARD STARKINGS
LETTERER
MICHAEL TURNER
WITH
PETER STEIGERWALD
COVER

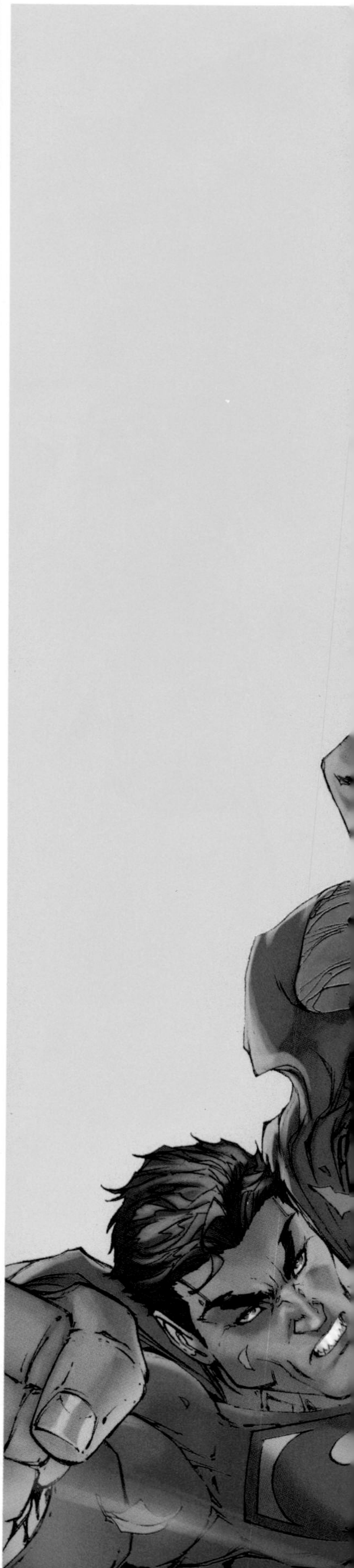

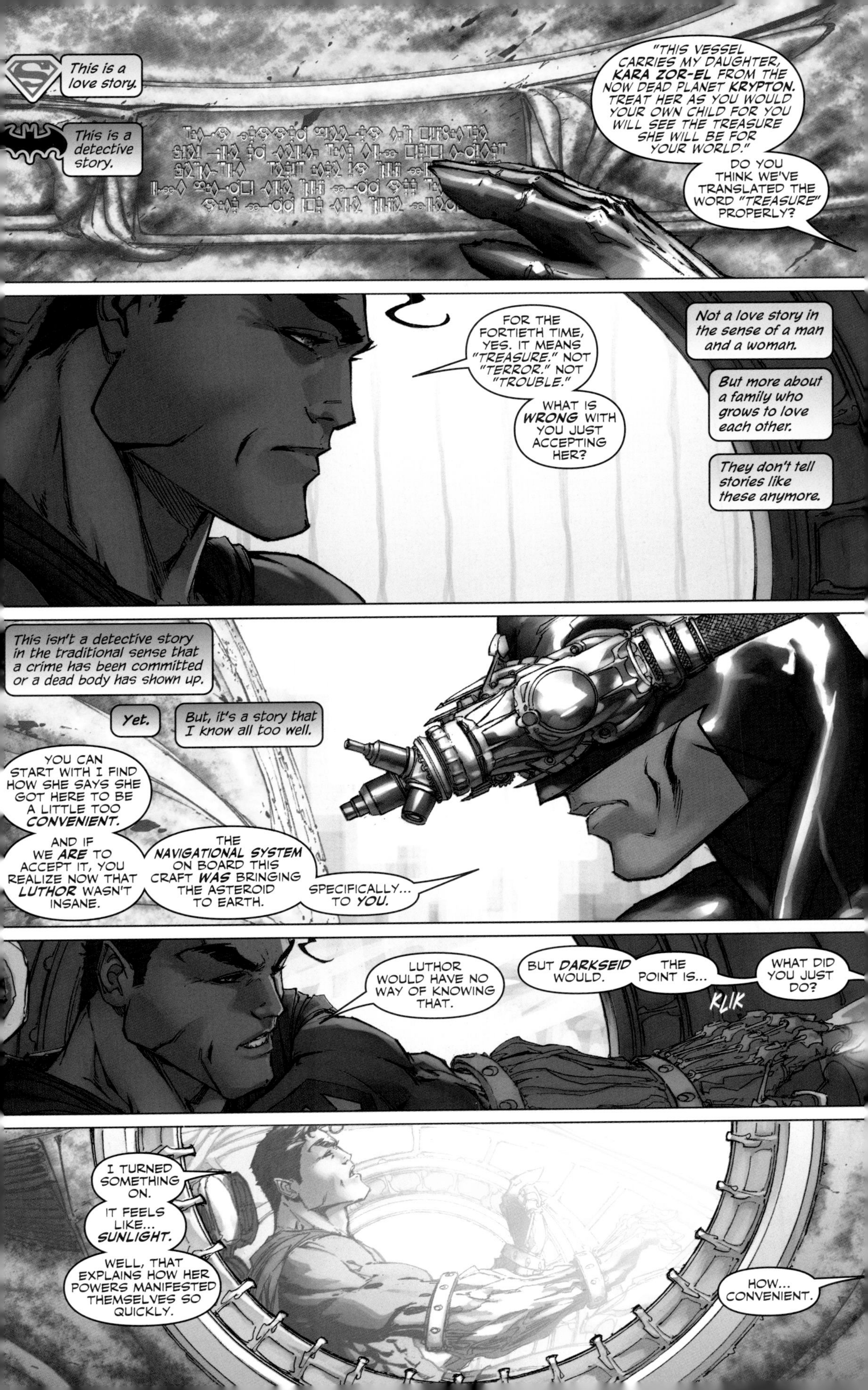
This is a love story.
This is a detective story.
"THIS VESSEL CARRIES MY DAUGHTER, KARA ZOR-EL FROM THE NOW DEAD PLANET KRYPTON. TREAT HER AS YOU WOULD YOUR OWN CHILD FOR YOU WILL SEE THE TREASURE SHE WILL BE FOR YOUR WORLD."
DO YOU THINK WE'VE TRANSLATED THE WORD "TREASURE" PROPERLY?
FOR THE FORTIETH TIME, YES. IT MEANS "TREASURE." NOT "TERROR." NOT "TROUBLE."
WHAT IS WRONG WITH YOU JUST ACCEPTING HER?
Not a love story in the sense of a man and a woman.
But more about a family who grows to love each other.
They don't tell stories like these anymore.
This isn't a detective story in the traditional sense that a crime has been committed or a dead body has shown up.
Yet.
But, it's a story that I know all too well.
YOU CAN START WITH I FIND HOW SHE SAYS SHE GOT HERE TO BE A LITTLE TOO CONVENIENT.
AND IF WE ARE TO ACCEPT IT, YOU REALIZE NOW THAT LUTHOR WASN'T INSANE.
THE NAVIGATIONAL SYSTEM ON BOARD THIS CRAFT WAS BRINGING THE ASTEROID TO EARTH.
SPECIFICALLY... TO YOU.
LUTHOR WOULD HAVE NO WAY OF KNOWING THAT.
BUT DARKSEID WOULD.
THE POINT IS...
KLIK
WHAT DID YOU JUST DO?
I TURNED SOMETHING ON.
IT FEELS LIKE... SUNLIGHT.
WELL, THAT EXPLAINS HOW HER POWERS MANIFESTED THEMSELVES SO QUICKLY.
HOW... CONVENIENT.

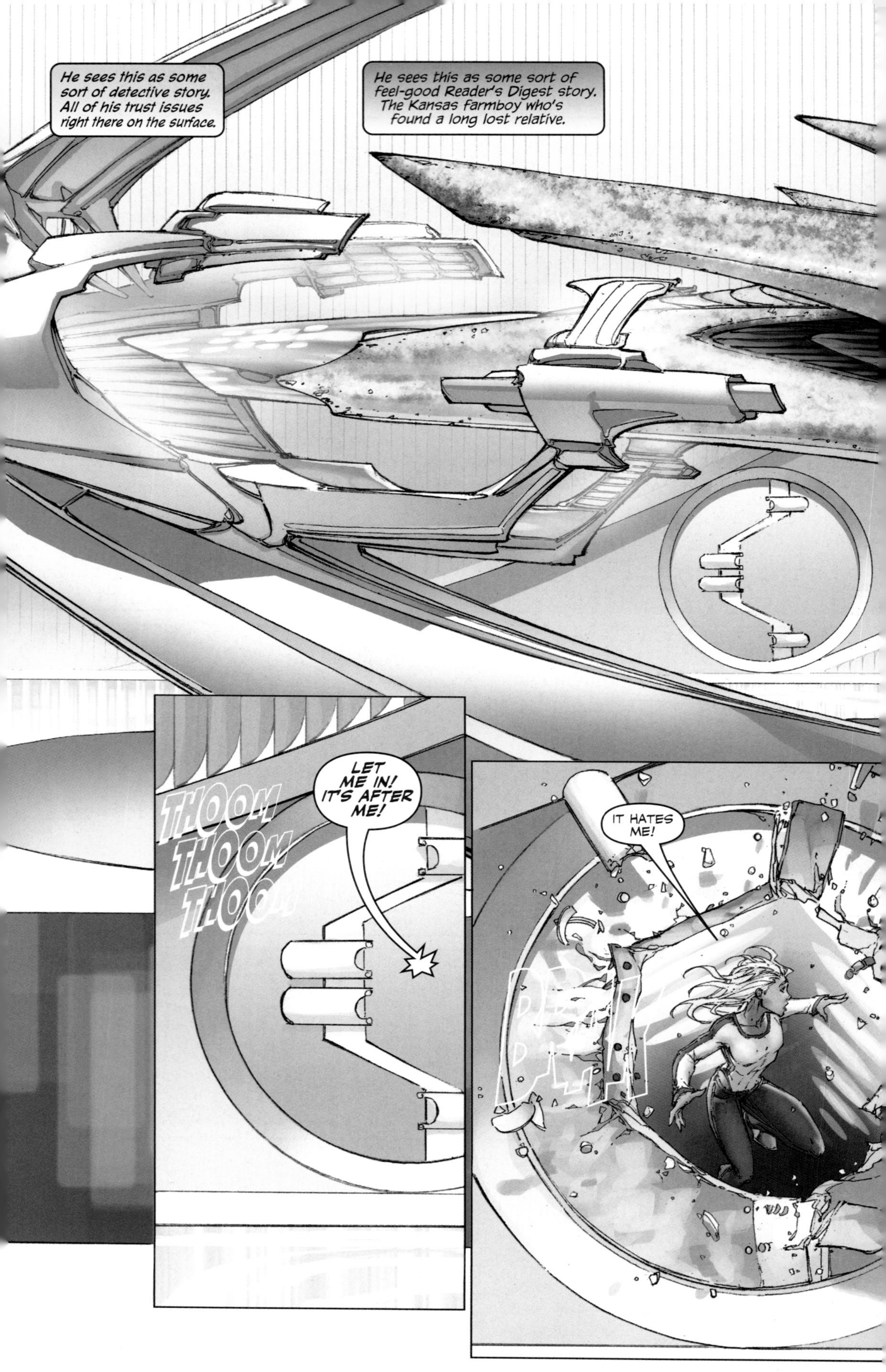
He sees this as some sort of detective story. All of his trust issues right there on the surface.
He sees this as some sort of feel-good Reader's Digest story. The Kansas farmboy who's found a long lost relative.
THOOM THOOM THOOM
LET ME IN! IT'S AFTER ME!
IT HATES ME!

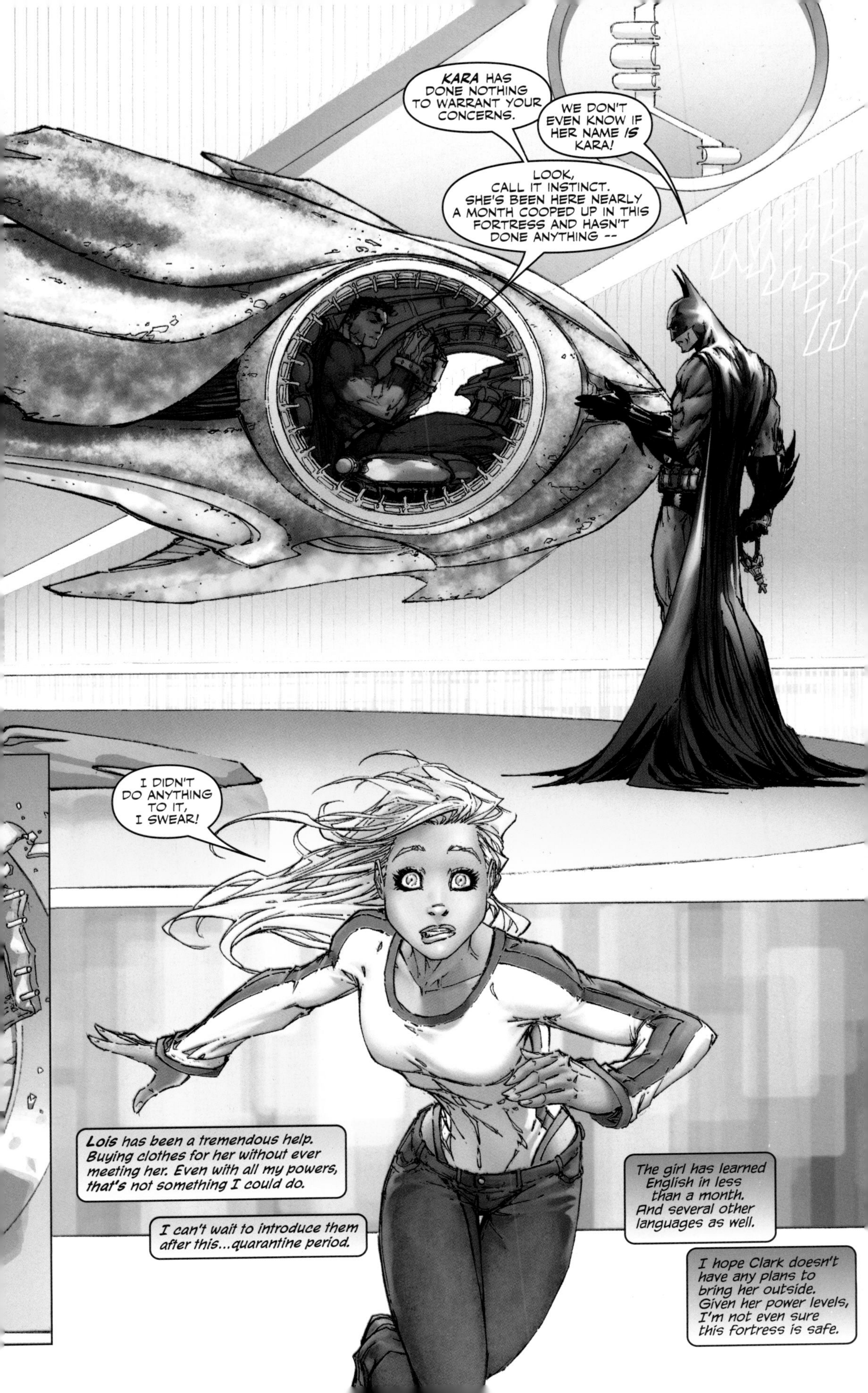
KARA HAS DONE NOTHING TO WARRANT YOUR CONCERNS.
WE DON'T EVEN KNOW IF HER NAME IS KARA!
LOOK, CALL IT INSTINCT. SHE'S BEEN HERE NEARLY A MONTH COOPED UP IN THIS FORTRESS AND HASN'T DONE ANYTHING --
I DIDN'T DO ANYTHING TO IT, I SWEAR!
Lois has been a tremendous help. Buying clothes for her without ever meeting her. Even with all my powers, that's not something I could do.
I can't wait to introduce them after this...quarantine period.
The girl has learned English in less than a month. And several other languages as well.
I hope Clark doesn't have any plans to bring her outside. Given her power levels, I'm not even sure this fortress is safe.

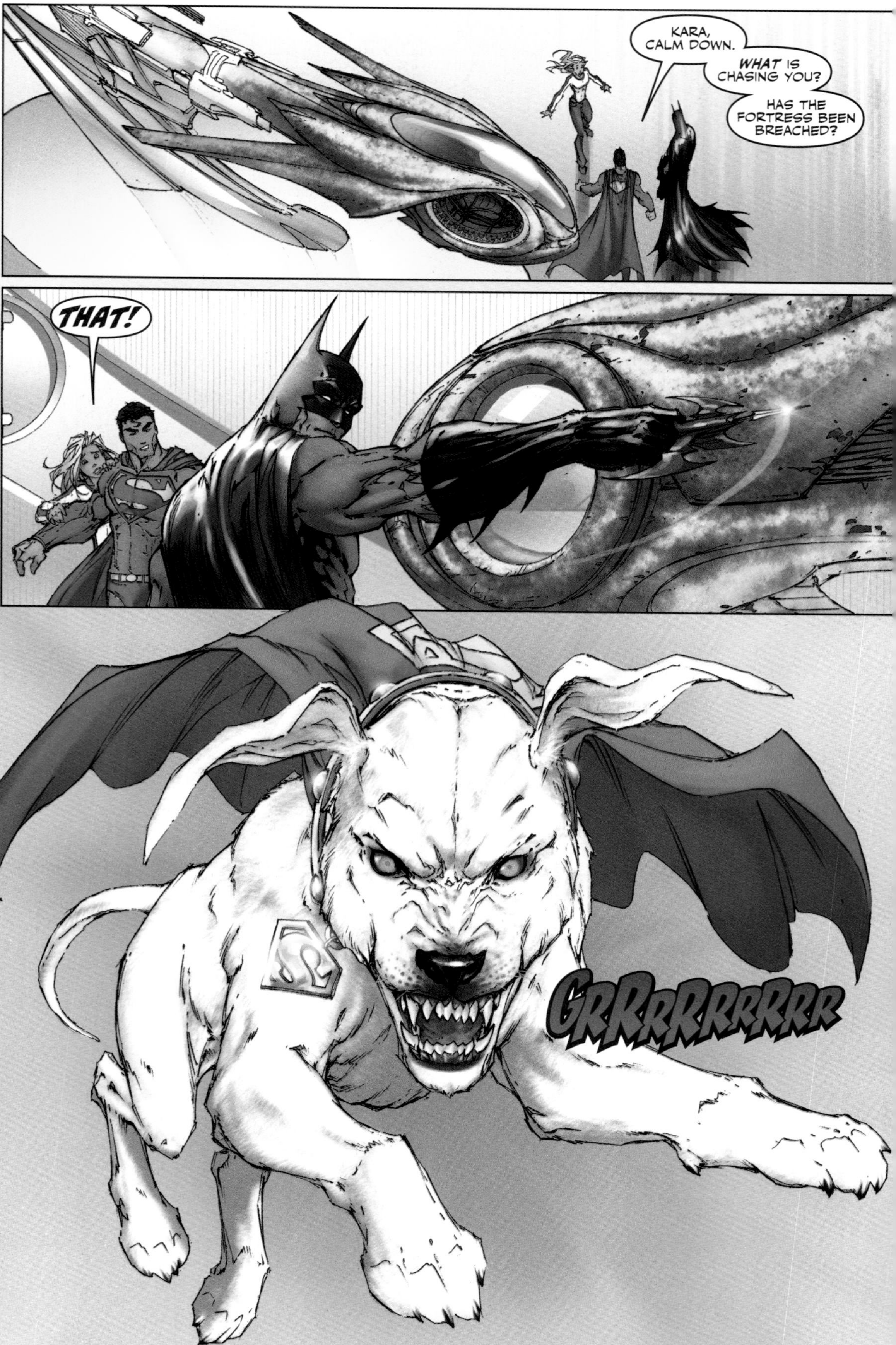
KARA, CALM DOWN. WHAT IS CHASING YOU?
HAS THE FORTRESS BEEN BREACHED?
THAT!
GRRRRRRRRRR

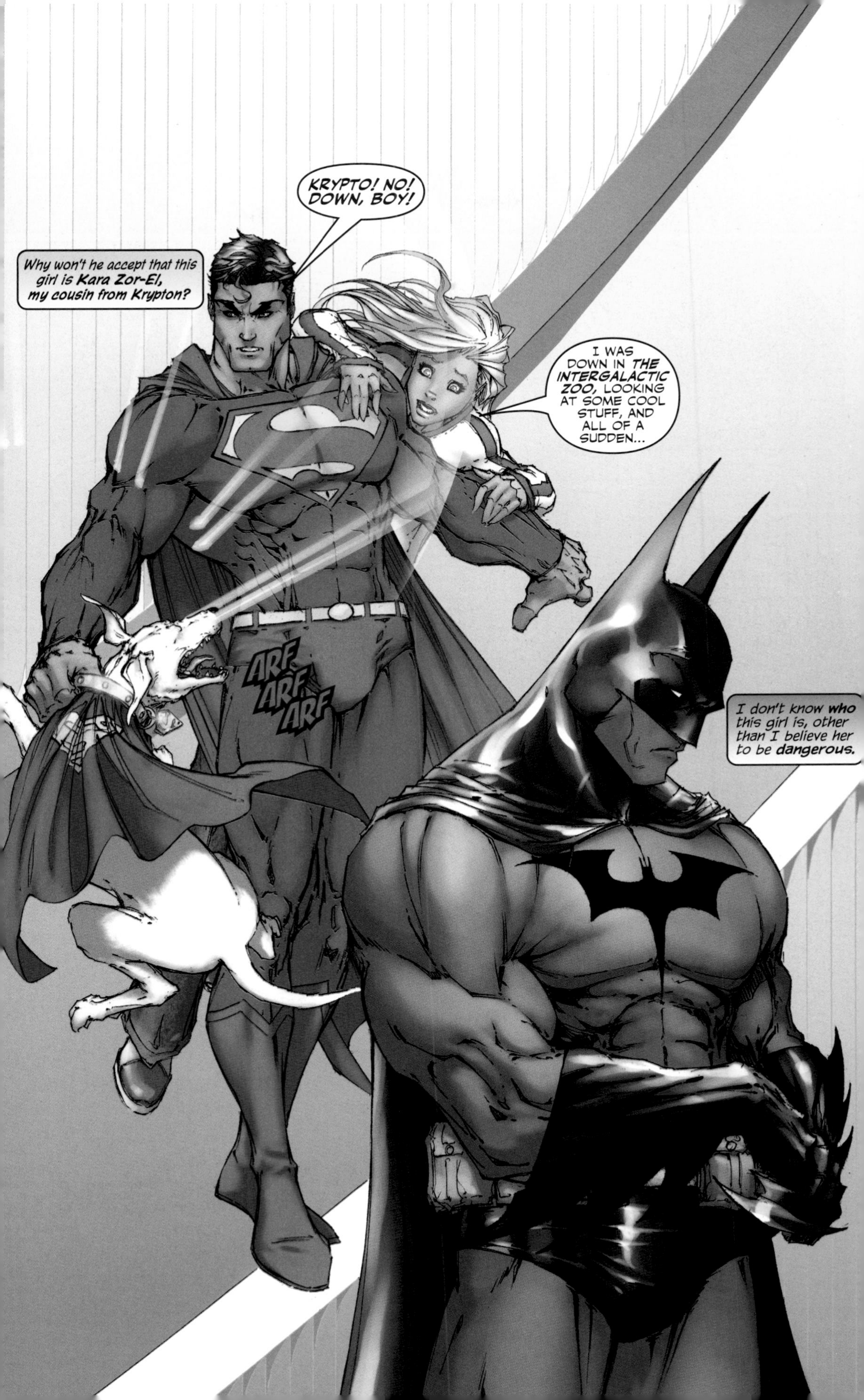

Why won't he accept that this girl is Kara Zor-El, my cousin from Krypton?
KRYPTO! NO! DOWN, BOY!
I WAS DOWN IN THE INTERGALACTIC ZOO, LOOKING AT SOME COOL STUFF, AND ALL OF A SUDDEN...
ARF ARF ARF
I don't know who this girl is, other than I believe her to be dangerous.

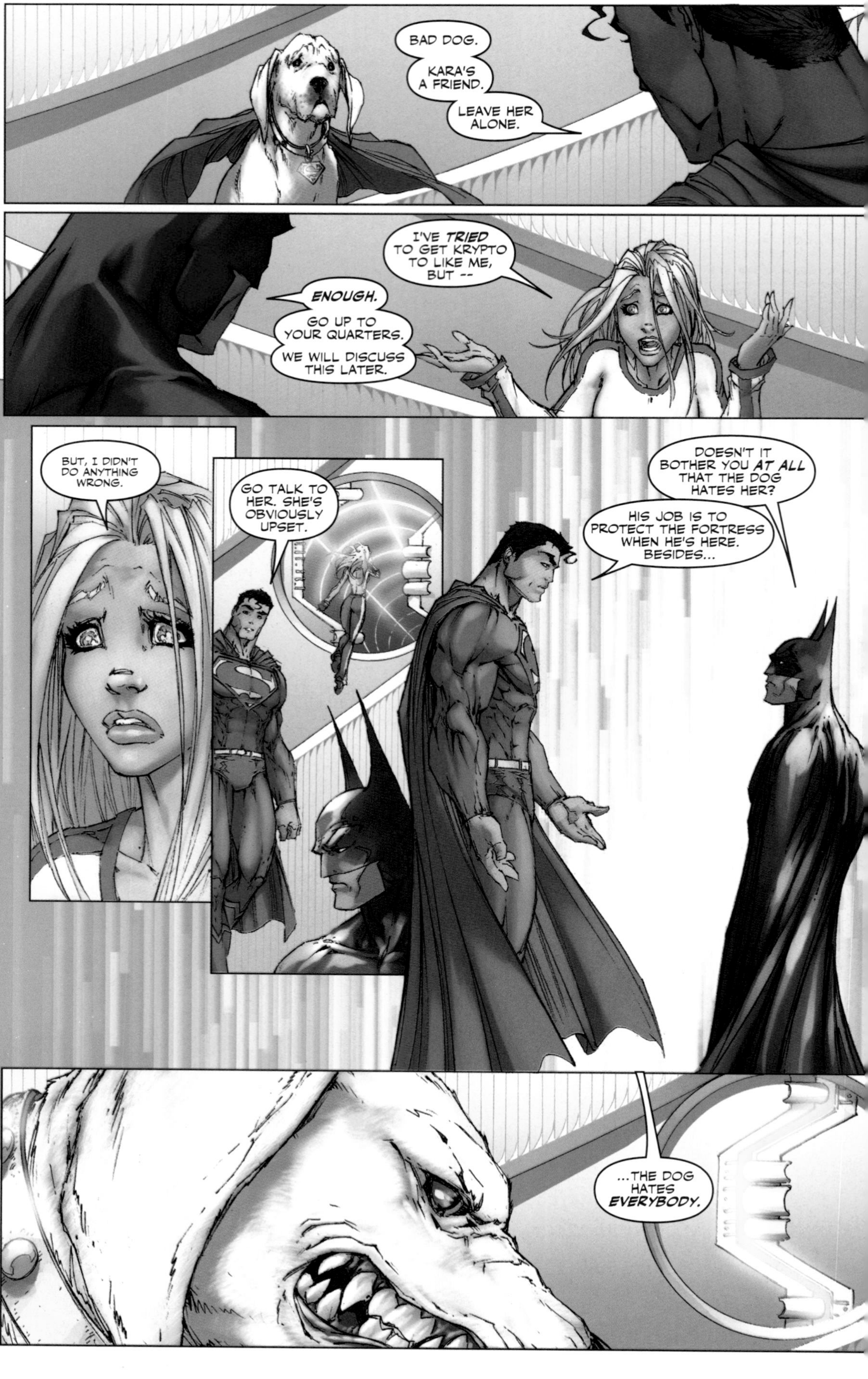
BAD DOG.
KARA'S A FRIEND.
LEAVE HER ALONE.
I'VE *TRIED* TO GET KRYPTO TO LIKE ME, BUT --
ENOUGH.
GO UP TO YOUR QUARTERS.
WE WILL DISCUSS THIS LATER.
BUT, I DIDN'T DO ANYTHING WRONG.
GO TALK TO HER. SHE'S OBVIOUSLY UPSET.
DOESN'T IT BOTHER YOU *AT ALL* THAT THE DOG HATES HER?
HIS JOB IS TO PROTECT THE FORTRESS WHEN HE'S HERE. BESIDES...
...THE DOG HATES *EVERYBODY.*

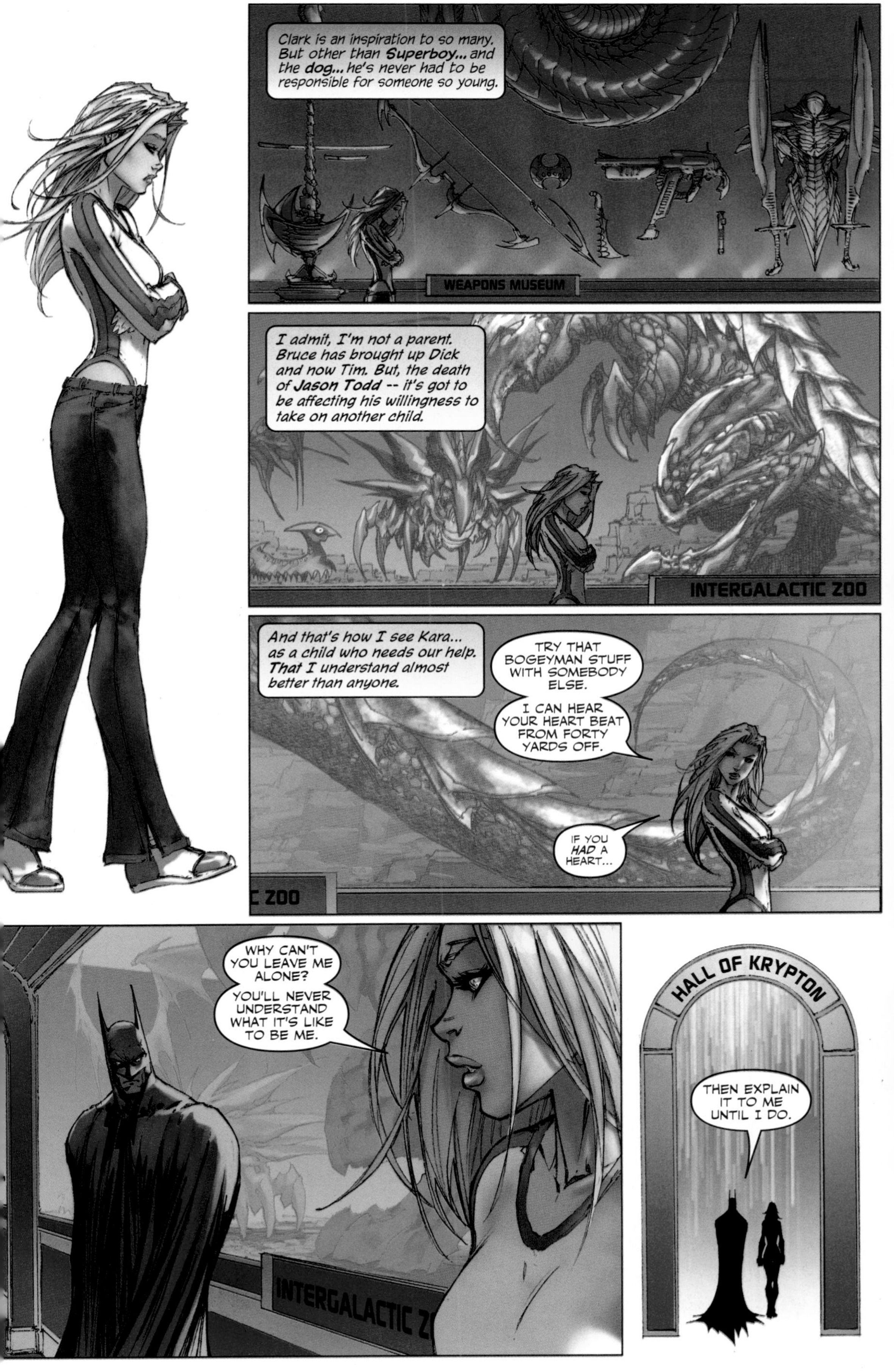

Clark is an inspiration to so many. But other than Superboy... and the dog... he's never had to be responsible for someone so young.
WEAPONS MUSEUM
I admit, I'm not a parent. Bruce has brought up Dick and now Tim. But, the death of Jason Todd -- it's got to be affecting his willingness to take on another child.
INTERGALACTIC ZOO
And that's how I see Kara... as a child who needs our help. That I understand almost better than anyone.
TRY THAT BOGEYMAN STUFF WITH SOMEBODY ELSE.
I CAN HEAR YOUR HEART BEAT FROM FORTY YARDS OFF.
IF YOU HAD A HEART...
C ZOO
WHY CAN'T YOU LEAVE ME ALONE?
YOU'LL NEVER UNDERSTAND WHAT IT'S LIKE TO BE ME.
INTERGALACTIC ZO
HALL OF KRYPTON
THEN EXPLAIN IT TO ME UNTIL I DO.

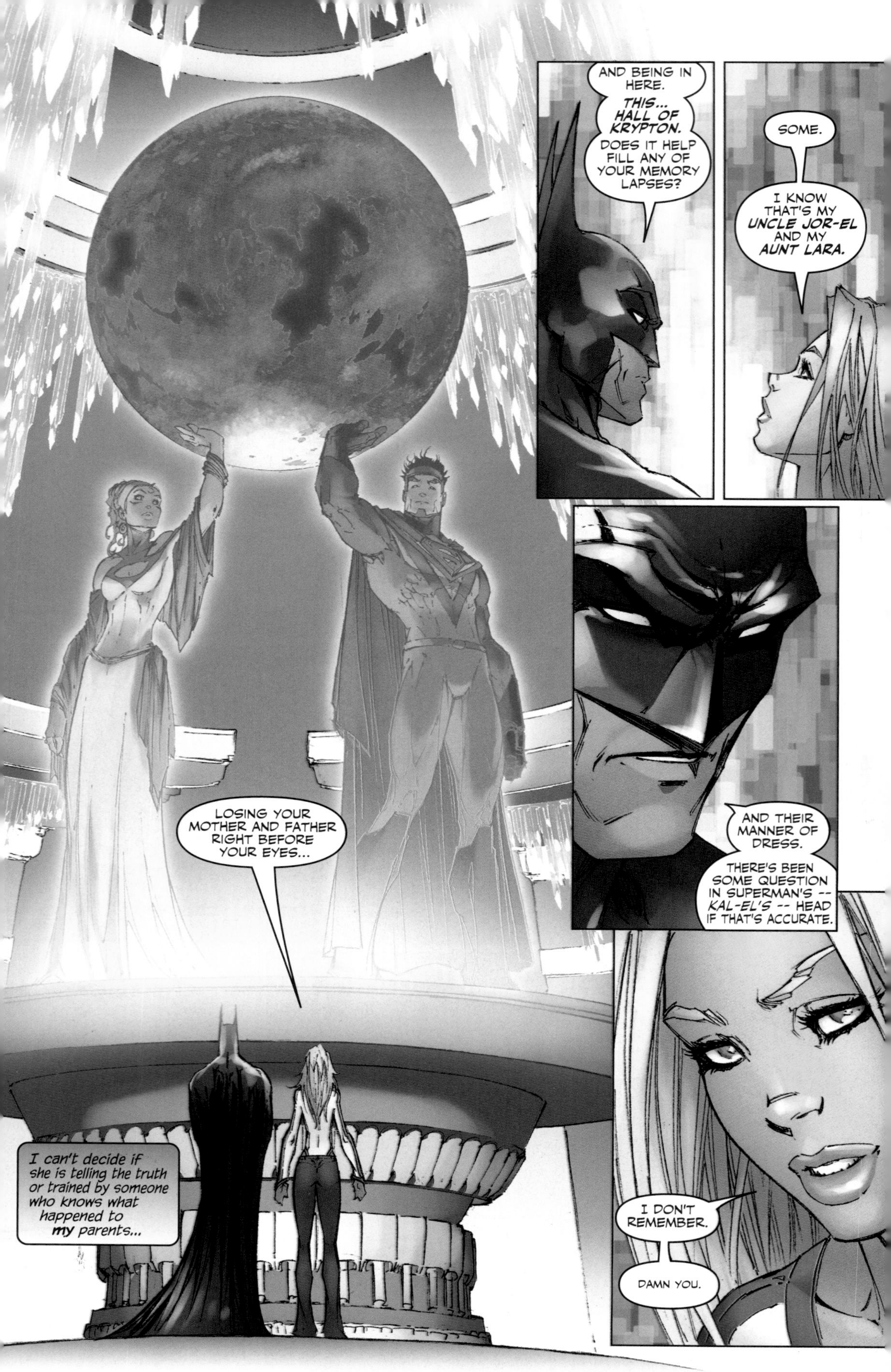
AND BEING IN HERE. THIS... HALL OF KRYPTON. DOES IT HELP FILL ANY OF YOUR MEMORY LAPSES?
SOME.
I KNOW THAT'S MY UNCLE JOR-EL AND MY AUNT LARA.
LOSING YOUR MOTHER AND FATHER RIGHT BEFORE YOUR EYES...
AND THEIR MANNER OF DRESS.
THERE'S BEEN SOME QUESTION IN SUPERMAN'S -- KAL-EL'S -- HEAD IF THAT'S ACCURATE.
I can't decide if she is telling the truth or trained by someone who knows what happened to my parents...
I DON'T REMEMBER.
DAMN YOU.

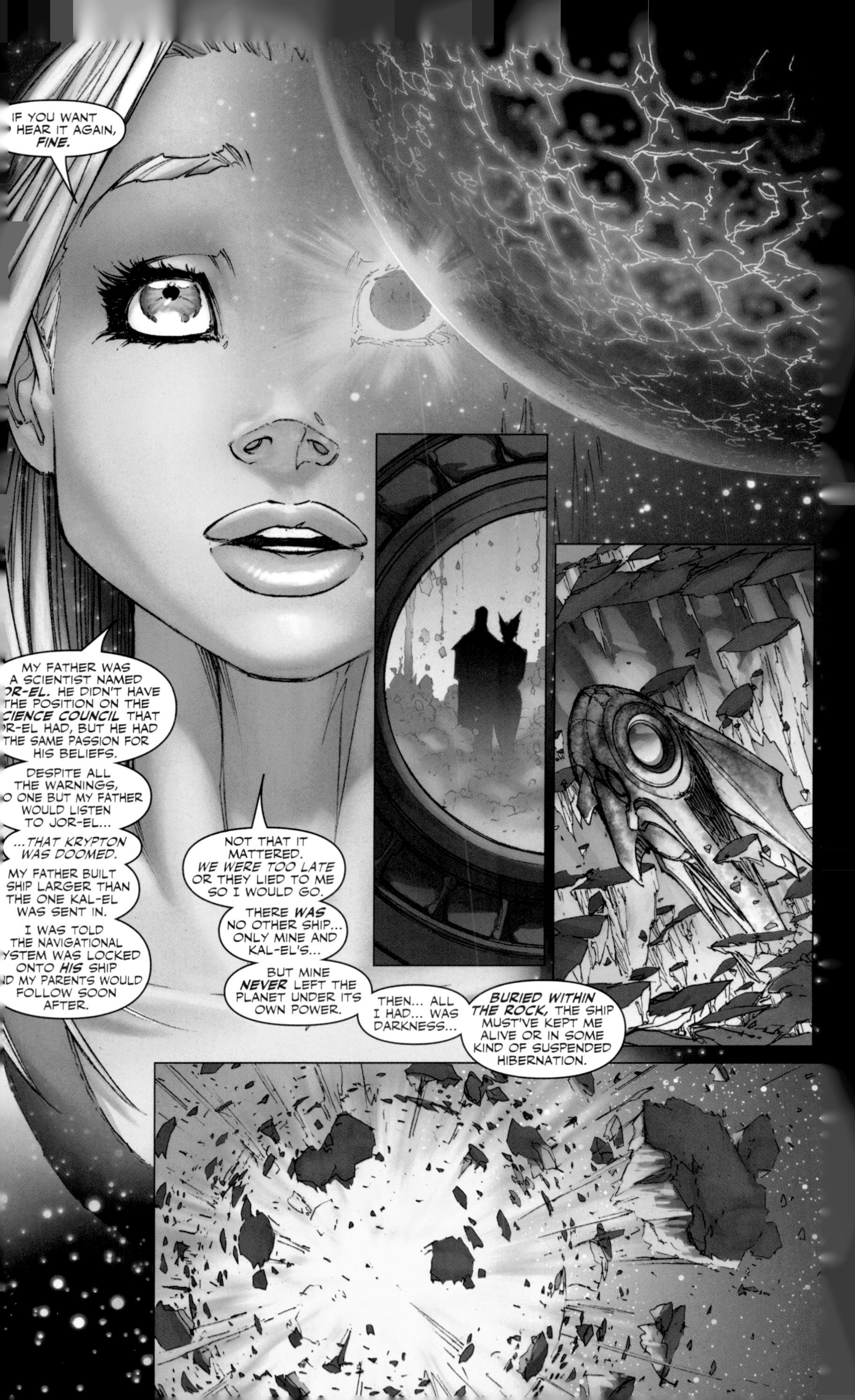
IF YOU WANT HEAR IT AGAIN, FINE.
MY FATHER WAS A SCIENTIST NAMED OR-EL. HE DIDN'T HAVE THE POSITION ON THE IENCE COUNCIL THAT R-EL HAD, BUT HE HAD THE SAME PASSION FOR HIS BELIEFS.
DESPITE ALL THE WARNINGS, O ONE BUT MY FATHER WOULD LISTEN TO JOR-EL...
...THAT KRYPTON WAS DOOMED.
MY FATHER BUILT SHIP LARGER THAN THE ONE KAL-EL WAS SENT IN.
I WAS TOLD THE NAVIGATIONAL YSTEM WAS LOCKED ONTO HIS SHIP D MY PARENTS WOULD FOLLOW SOON AFTER.
NOT THAT IT MATTERED. WE WERE TOO LATE OR THEY LIED TO ME SO I WOULD GO.
THERE WAS NO OTHER SHIP... ONLY MINE AND KAL-EL'S...
BUT MINE NEVER LEFT THE PLANET UNDER ITS OWN POWER.
THEN... ALL I HAD... WAS DARKNESS...
BURIED WITHIN THE ROCK, THE SHIP MUST'VE KEPT ME ALIVE OR IN SOME KIND OF SUSPENDED HIBERNATION.

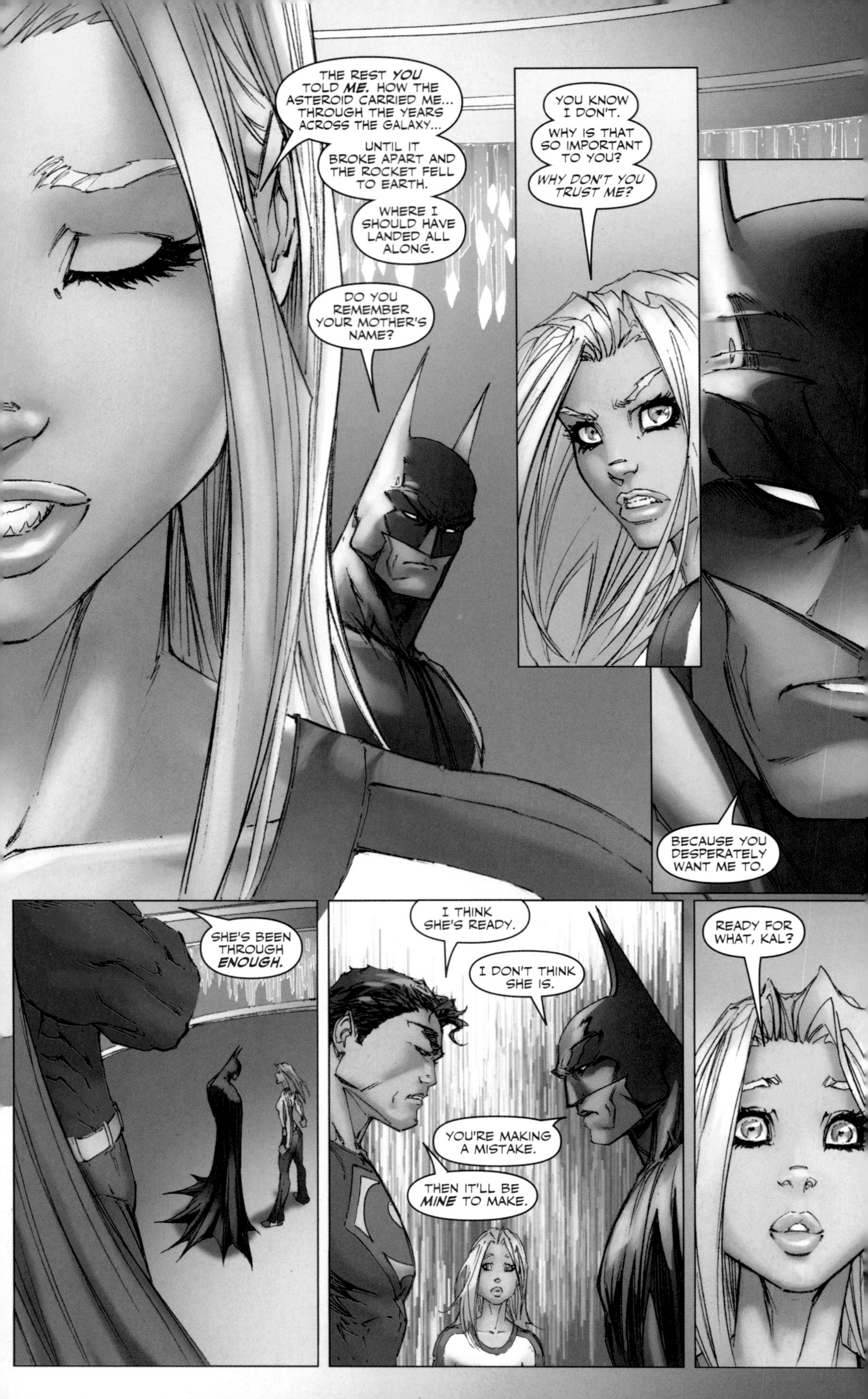
THE REST YOU TOLD ME. HOW THE ASTEROID CARRIED ME... THROUGH THE YEARS ACROSS THE GALAXY...
UNTIL IT BROKE APART AND THE ROCKET FELL TO EARTH.
WHERE I SHOULD HAVE LANDED ALL ALONG.
DO YOU REMEMBER YOUR MOTHER'S NAME?
YOU KNOW I DON'T.
WHY IS THAT SO IMPORTANT TO YOU?
WHY DON'T YOU TRUST ME?
BECAUSE YOU DESPERATELY WANT ME TO.
SHE'S BEEN THROUGH ENOUGH.
I THINK SHE'S READY.
I DON'T THINK SHE IS.
YOU'RE MAKING A MISTAKE.
THEN IT'LL BE MINE TO MAKE.
READY FOR WHAT, KAL?

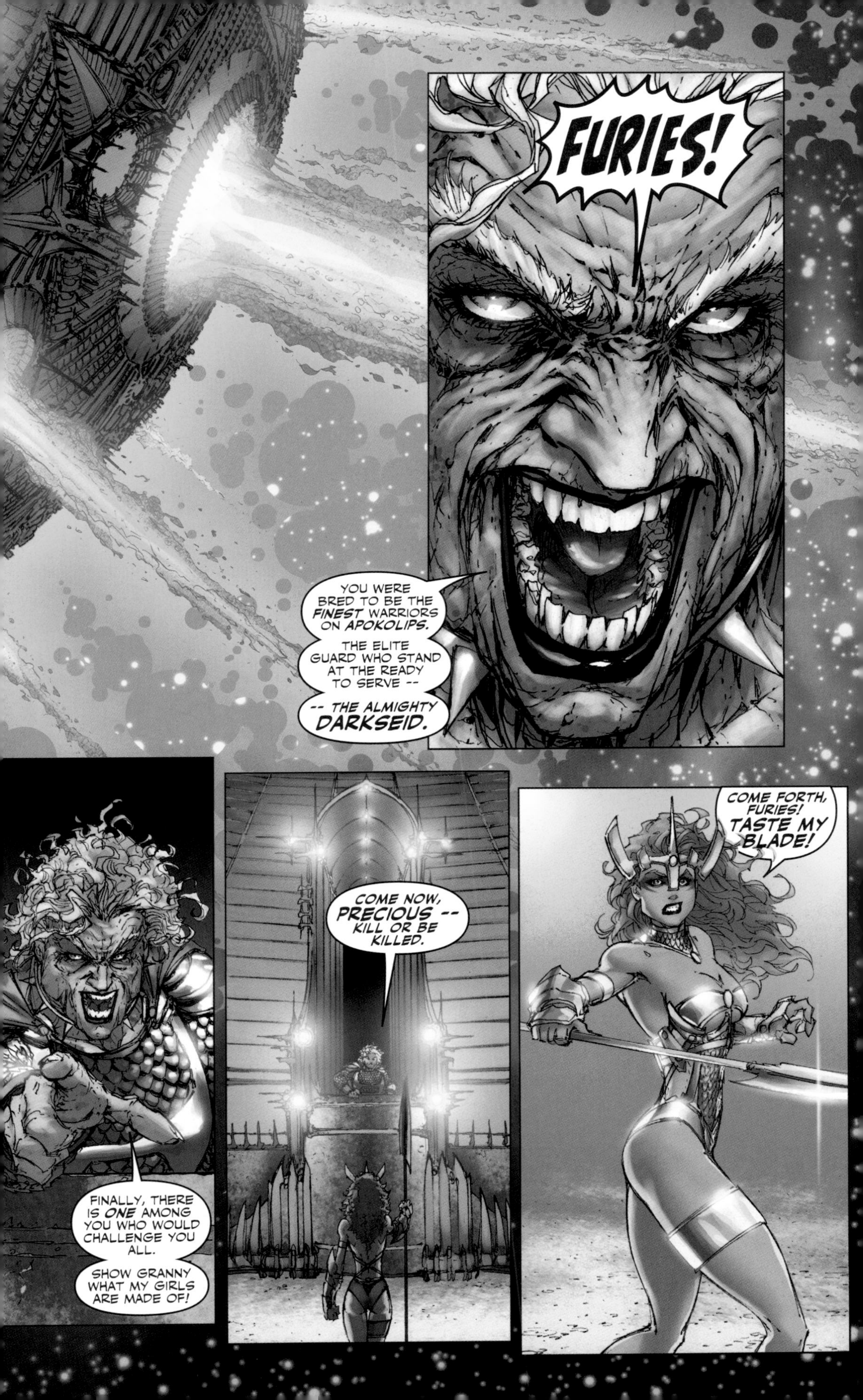
FURIES!
YOU WERE BRED TO BE THE FINEST WARRIORS ON APOKOLIPS.
THE ELITE GUARD WHO STAND AT THE READY TO SERVE --
-- THE ALMIGHTY DARKSEID.
FINALLY, THERE IS ONE AMONG YOU WHO WOULD CHALLENGE YOU ALL.
SHOW GRANNY WHAT MY GIRLS ARE MADE OF!
COME NOW, PRECIOUS -- KILL OR BE KILLED.
COME FORTH, FURIES! TASTE MY BLADE!

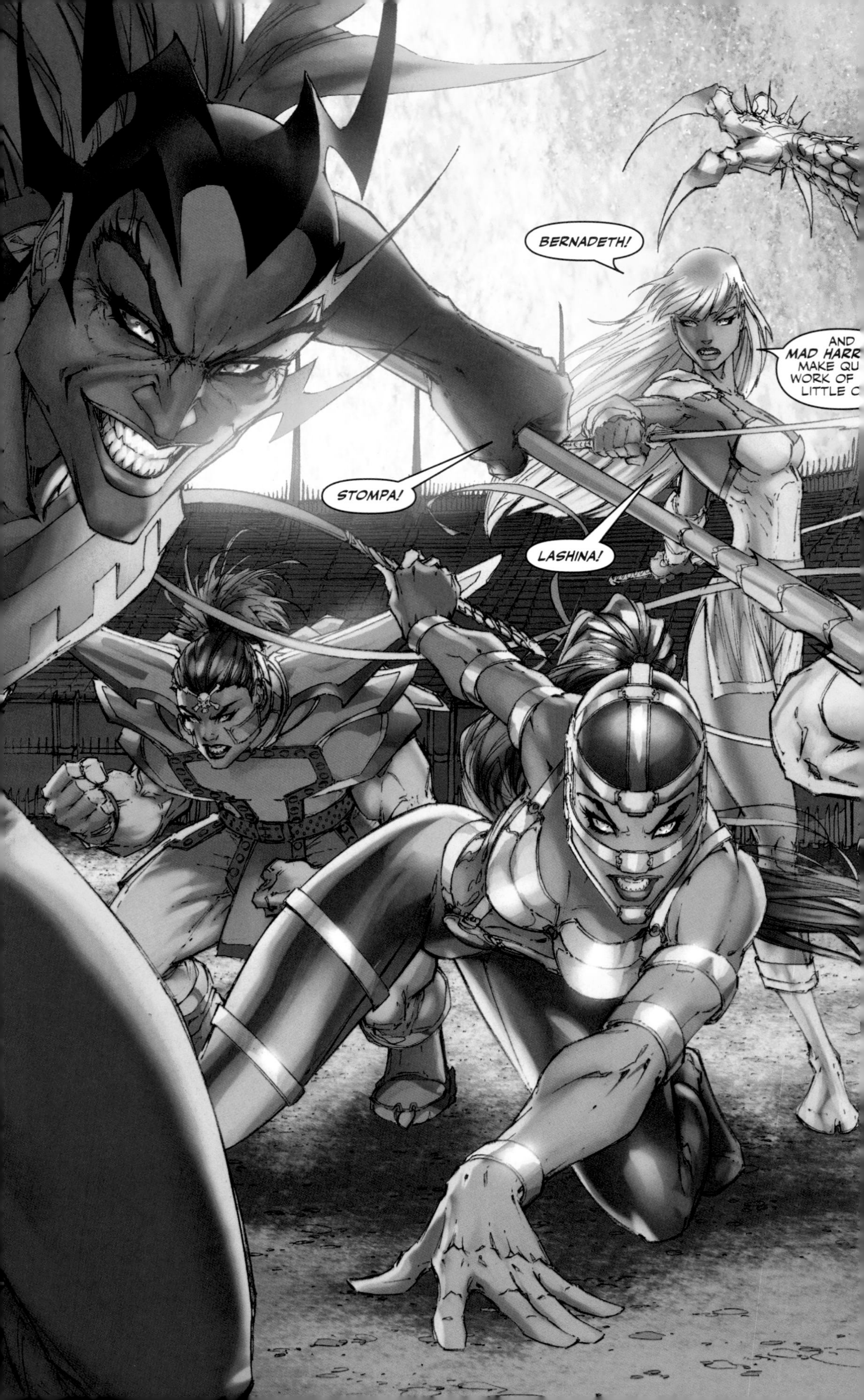
STOMPA!
LASHINA!
BERNADETH!
AND MAD HARR MAKE QU WORK OF LITTLE C

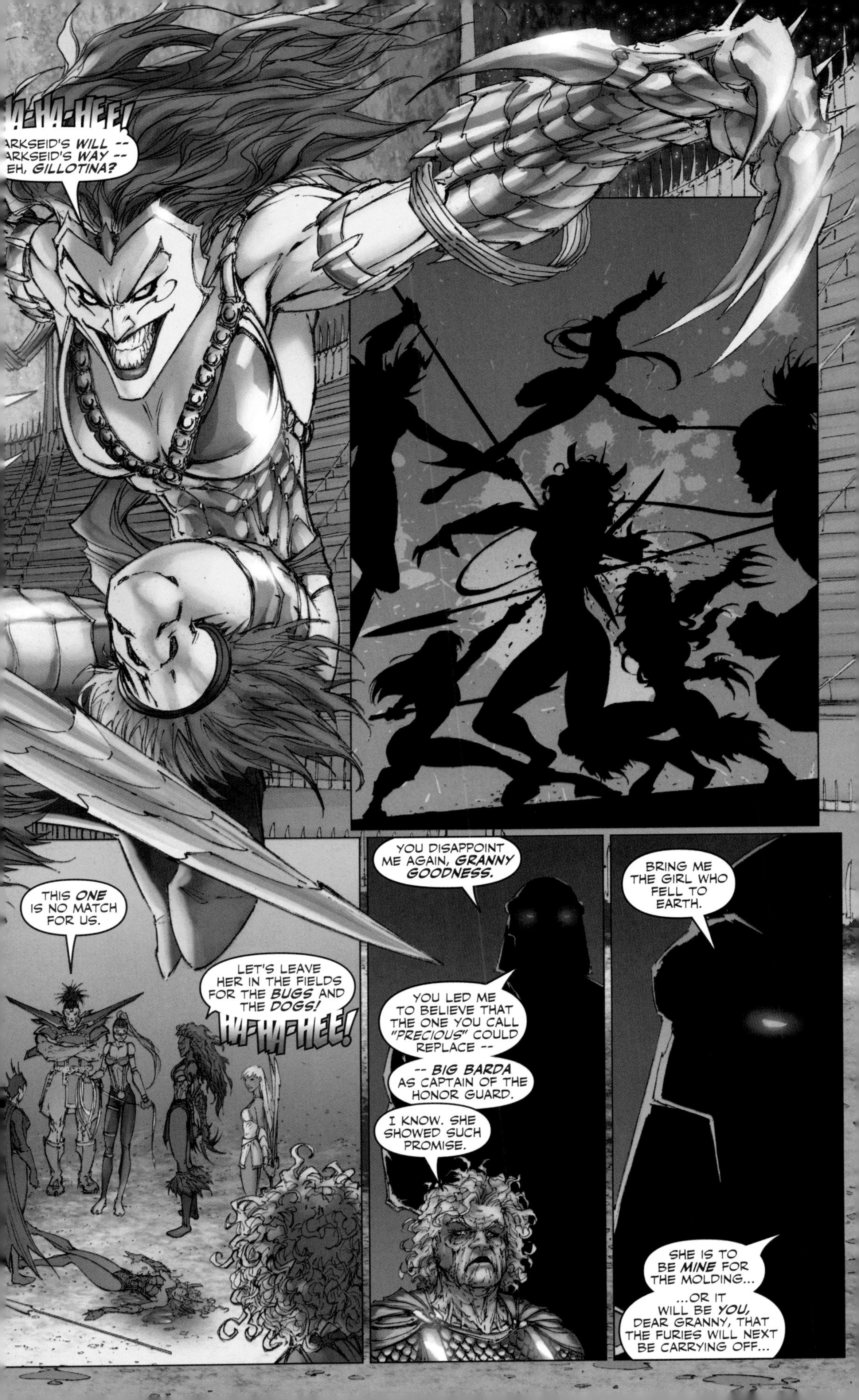
A-HA-HEE!
ARKSEID'S WILL -- ARKSEID'S WAY -- EH, GILLOTINA?
THIS ONE IS NO MATCH FOR US.
LET'S LEAVE HER IN THE FIELDS FOR THE BUGS AND THE DOGS!
HA-HA-HEE!
YOU DISAPPOINT ME AGAIN, GRANNY GOODNESS.
YOU LED ME TO BELIEVE THAT THE ONE YOU CALL "PRECIOUS" COULD REPLACE --
-- BIG BARDA AS CAPTAIN OF THE HONOR GUARD.
I KNOW. SHE SHOWED SUCH PROMISE.
BRING ME THE GIRL WHO FELL TO EARTH.
SHE IS TO BE MINE FOR THE MOLDING...
...OR IT WILL BE YOU, DEAR GRANNY, THAT THE FURIES WILL NEXT BE CARRYING OFF...

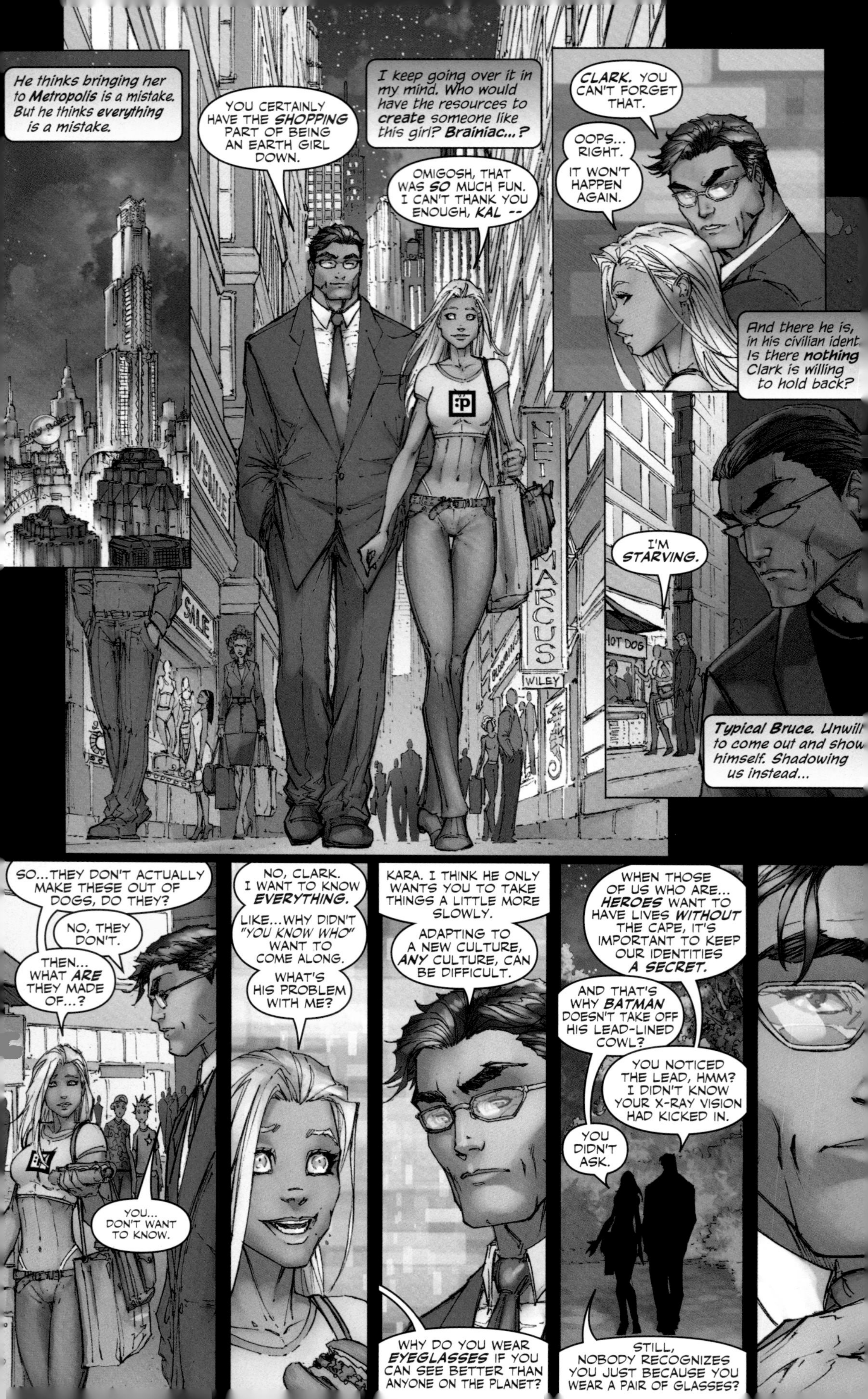

He thinks bringing her to Metropolis is a mistake. But he thinks everything is a mistake.
YOU CERTAINLY HAVE THE SHOPPING PART OF BEING AN EARTH GIRL DOWN.
I keep going over it in my mind. Who would have the resources to create someone like this girl? Brainiac...?
OMIGOSH, THAT WAS SO MUCH FUN. I CAN'T THANK YOU ENOUGH, KAL --
CLARK. YOU CAN'T FORGET THAT.
OOPS... RIGHT.
IT WON'T HAPPEN AGAIN.
And there he is, in his civilian ident
Is there nothing Clark is willing to hold back?
I'M STARVING.
Typical Bruce. Unwill to come out and show himself. Shadowing us instead...
SO...THEY DON'T ACTUALLY MAKE THESE OUT OF DOGS, DO THEY?
NO, THEY DON'T.
THEN... WHAT ARE THEY MADE OF...?
YOU... DON'T WANT TO KNOW.
NO, CLARK. I WANT TO KNOW EVERYTHING.
LIKE...WHY DIDN'T "YOU KNOW WHO" WANT TO COME ALONG.
WHAT'S HIS PROBLEM WITH ME?
KARA. I THINK HE ONLY WANTS YOU TO TAKE THINGS A LITTLE MORE SLOWLY.
ADAPTING TO A NEW CULTURE, ANY CULTURE, CAN BE DIFFICULT.
WHY DO YOU WEAR EYEGLASSES IF YOU CAN SEE BETTER THAN ANYONE ON THE PLANET?
WHEN THOSE OF US WHO ARE... HEROES WANT TO HAVE LIVES WITHOUT THE CAPE, IT'S IMPORTANT TO KEEP OUR IDENTITIES A SECRET.
AND THAT'S WHY BATMAN DOESN'T TAKE OFF HIS LEAD-LINED COWL?
YOU NOTICED THE LEAD, HMM? I DIDN'T KNOW YOUR X-RAY VISION HAD KICKED IN.
YOU DIDN'T ASK.
STILL, NOBODY RECOGNIZES YOU JUST BECAUSE YOU WEAR A PAIR OF GLASSES?

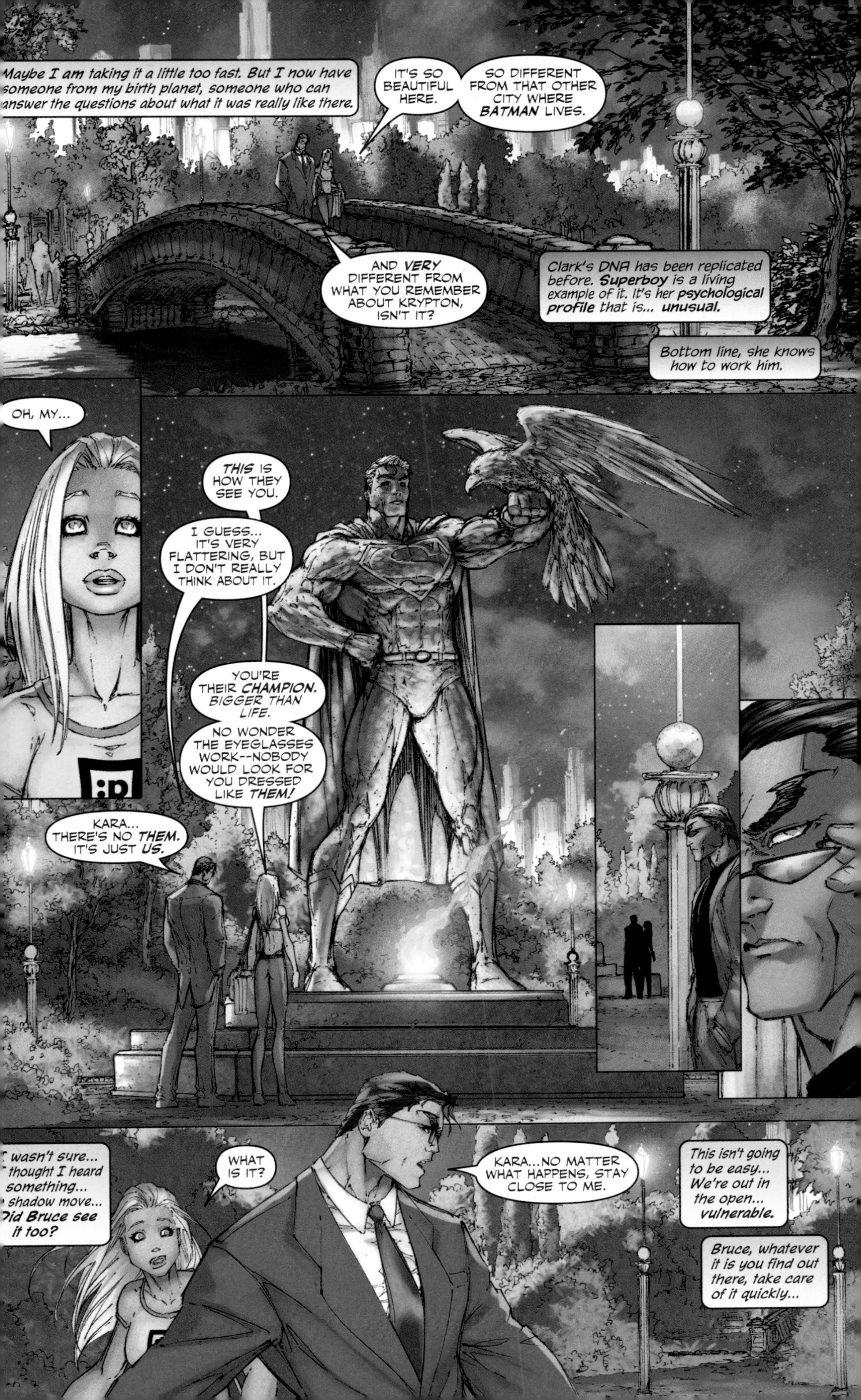

Maybe I am taking it a little too fast. But I now have someone from my birth planet, someone who can answer the questions about what it was really like there.
IT'S SO BEAUTIFUL HERE.
SO DIFFERENT FROM THAT OTHER CITY WHERE BATMAN LIVES.
AND VERY DIFFERENT FROM WHAT YOU REMEMBER ABOUT KRYPTON, ISN'T IT?
Clark's DNA has been replicated before. Superboy is a living example of it. It's her psychological profile that is... unusual.
Bottom line, she knows how to work him.
OH, MY...
THIS IS HOW THEY SEE YOU.
I GUESS... IT'S VERY FLATTERING, BUT I DON'T REALLY THINK ABOUT IT.
YOU'RE THEIR CHAMPION. BIGGER THAN LIFE.
NO WONDER THE EYEGLASSES WORK--NOBODY WOULD LOOK FOR YOU DRESSED LIKE THEM!
KARA... THERE'S NO THEM. IT'S JUST US.
wasn't sure... thought I heard something... shadow move... id Bruce see it too?
WHAT IS IT?
KARA...NO MATTER WHAT HAPPENS, STAY CLOSE TO ME.
This isn't going to be easy... We're out in the open... vulnerable.
Bruce, whatever it is you find out there, take care of it quickly...

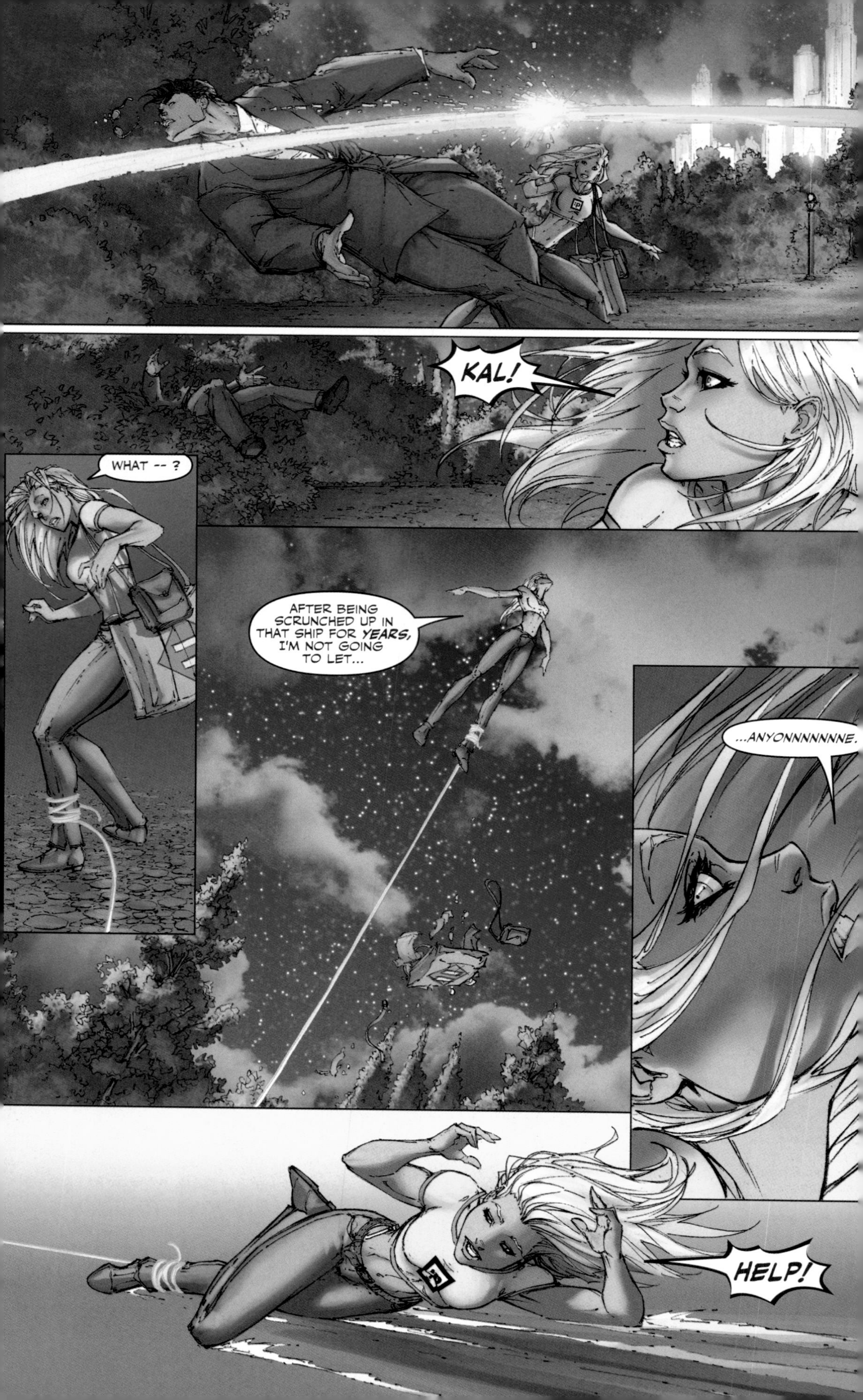
KAL!
WHAT -- ?
AFTER BEING SCRUNCHED UP IN THAT SHIP FOR YEARS, I'M NOT GOING TO LET...
...ANYONNNNNNNE.
HELP!

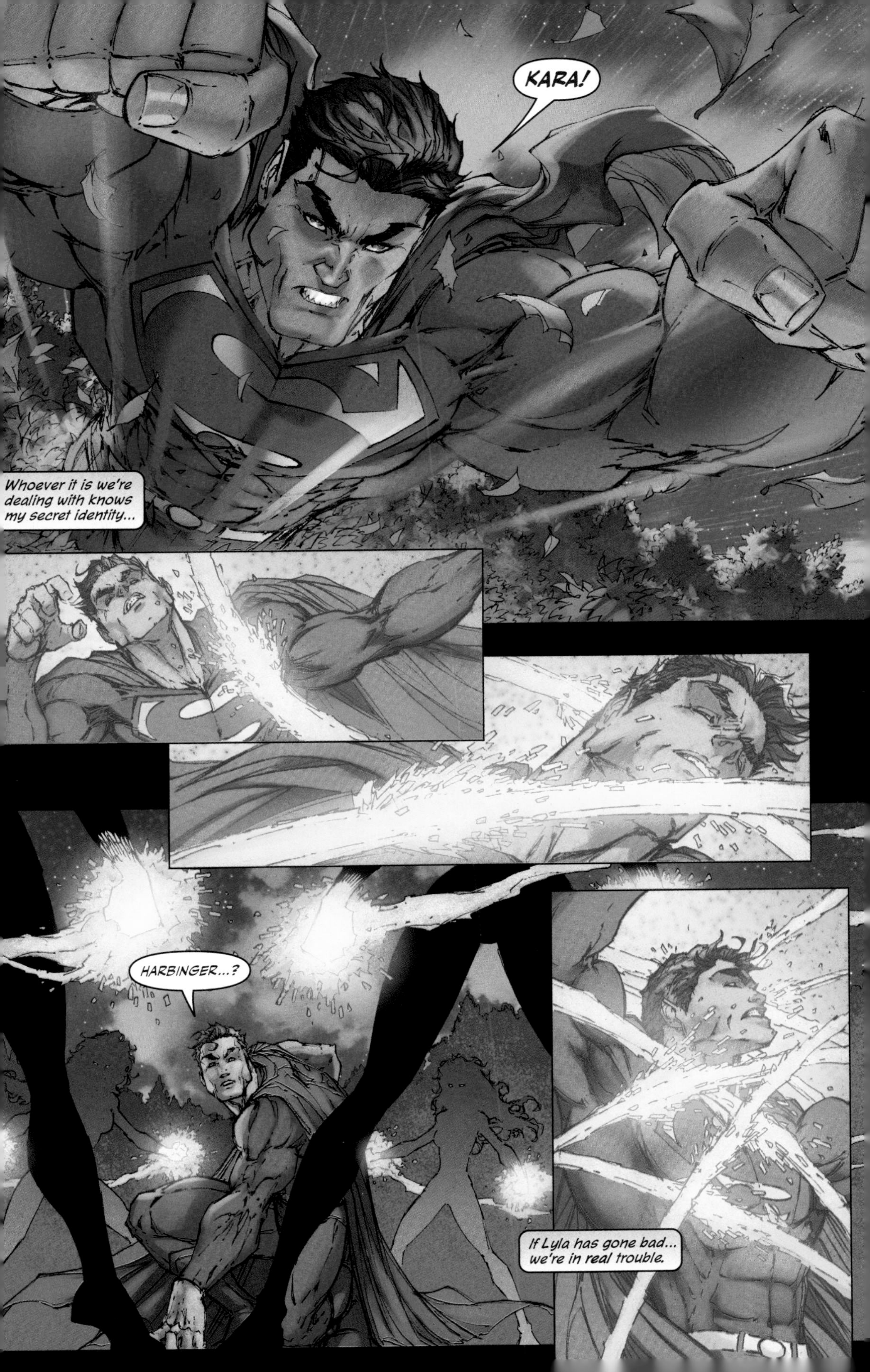
KARA!
Whoever it is we're dealing with knows my secret identity...
HARBINGER...?
If Lyla has gone bad... we're in real trouble.

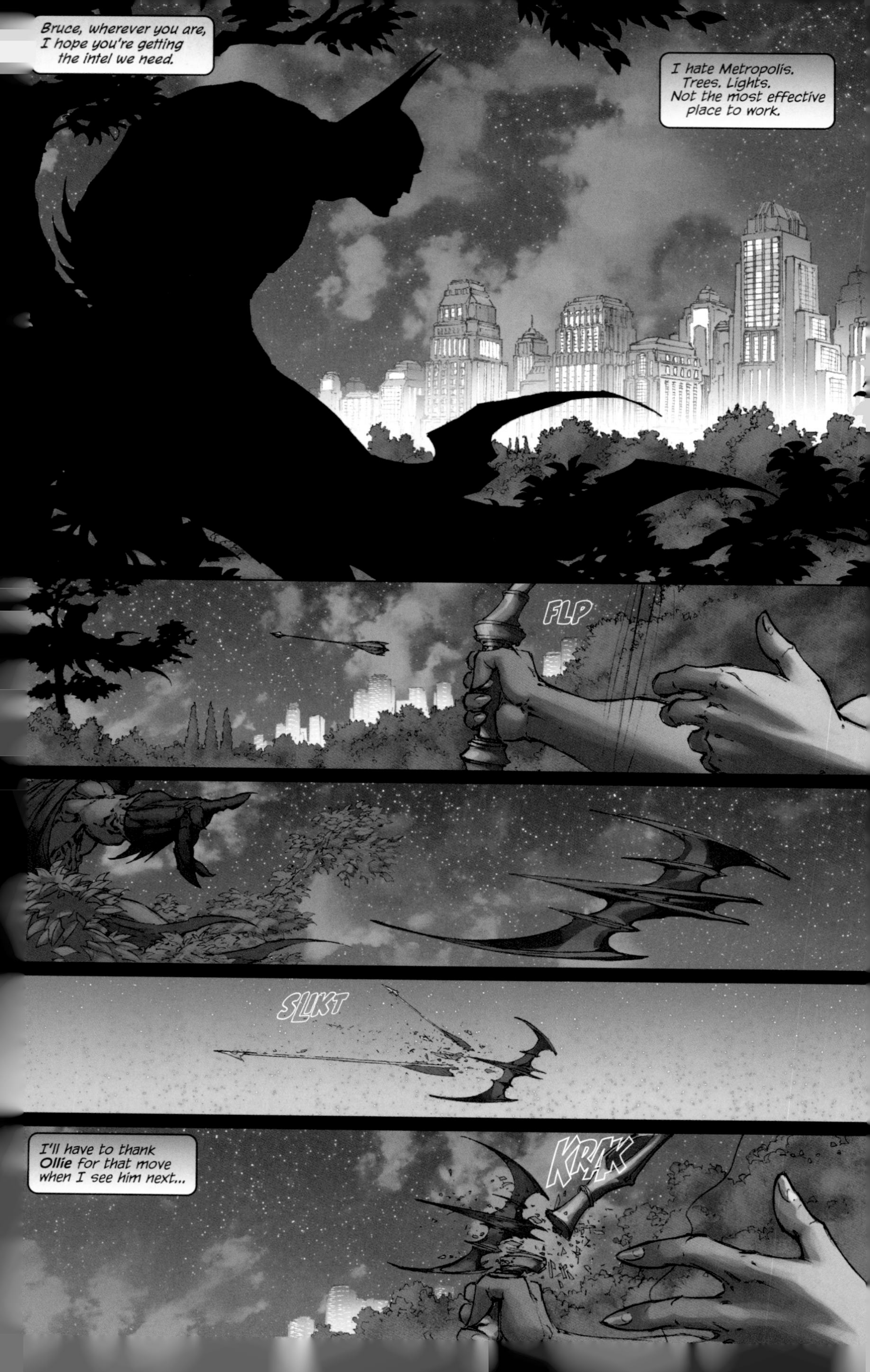

Bruce, wherever you are, I hope you're getting the intel we need.
I hate Metropolis. Trees. Lights. Not the most effective place to work.
FLP
SLIKT
I'll have to thank **Ollie** for that move when I see him next...
KRAK

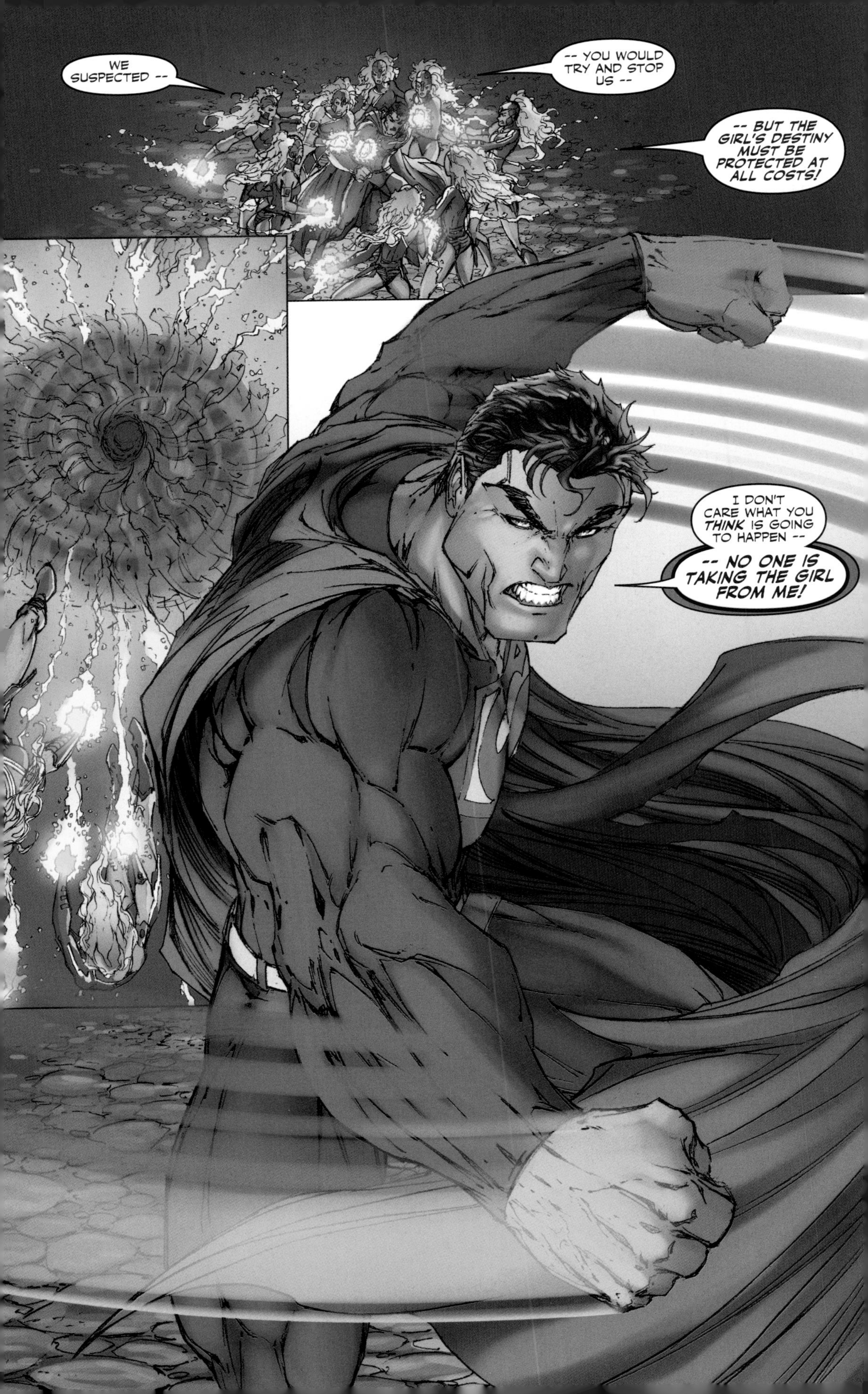
WE SUSPECTED --
-- YOU WOULD TRY AND STOP US --
-- BUT THE GIRL'S DESTINY MUST BE PROTECTED AT ALL COSTS!
I DON'T CARE WHAT YOU *THINK* IS GOING TO HAPPEN --
-- NO ONE IS TAKING THE GIRL FROM ME!

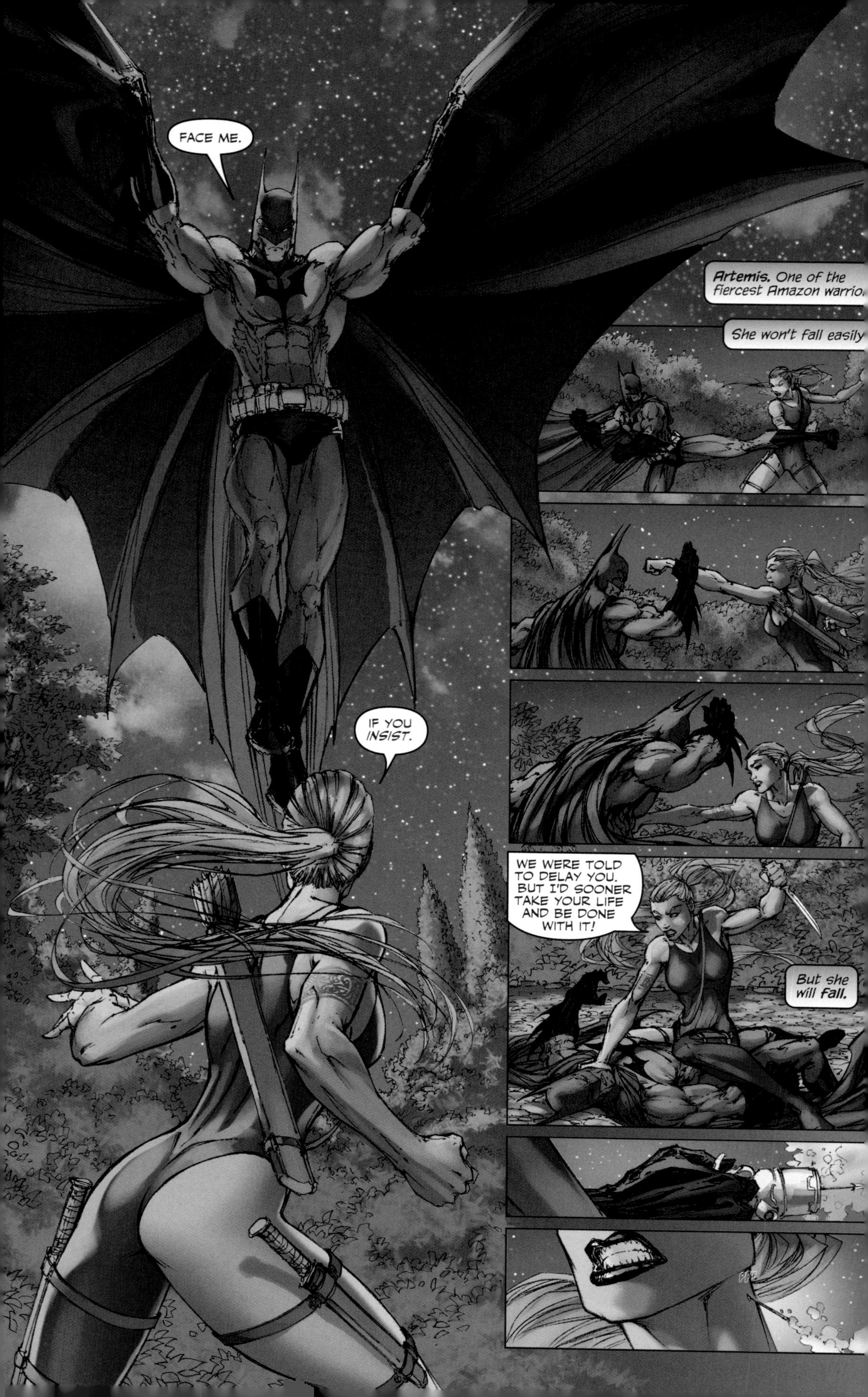

FACE ME.
IF YOU INSIST.
Artemis. One of the fiercest Amazon warrio
She won't fall easily
WE WERE TOLD TO DELAY YOU. BUT I'D SOONER TAKE YOUR LIFE AND BE DONE WITH IT!
But she will fall.

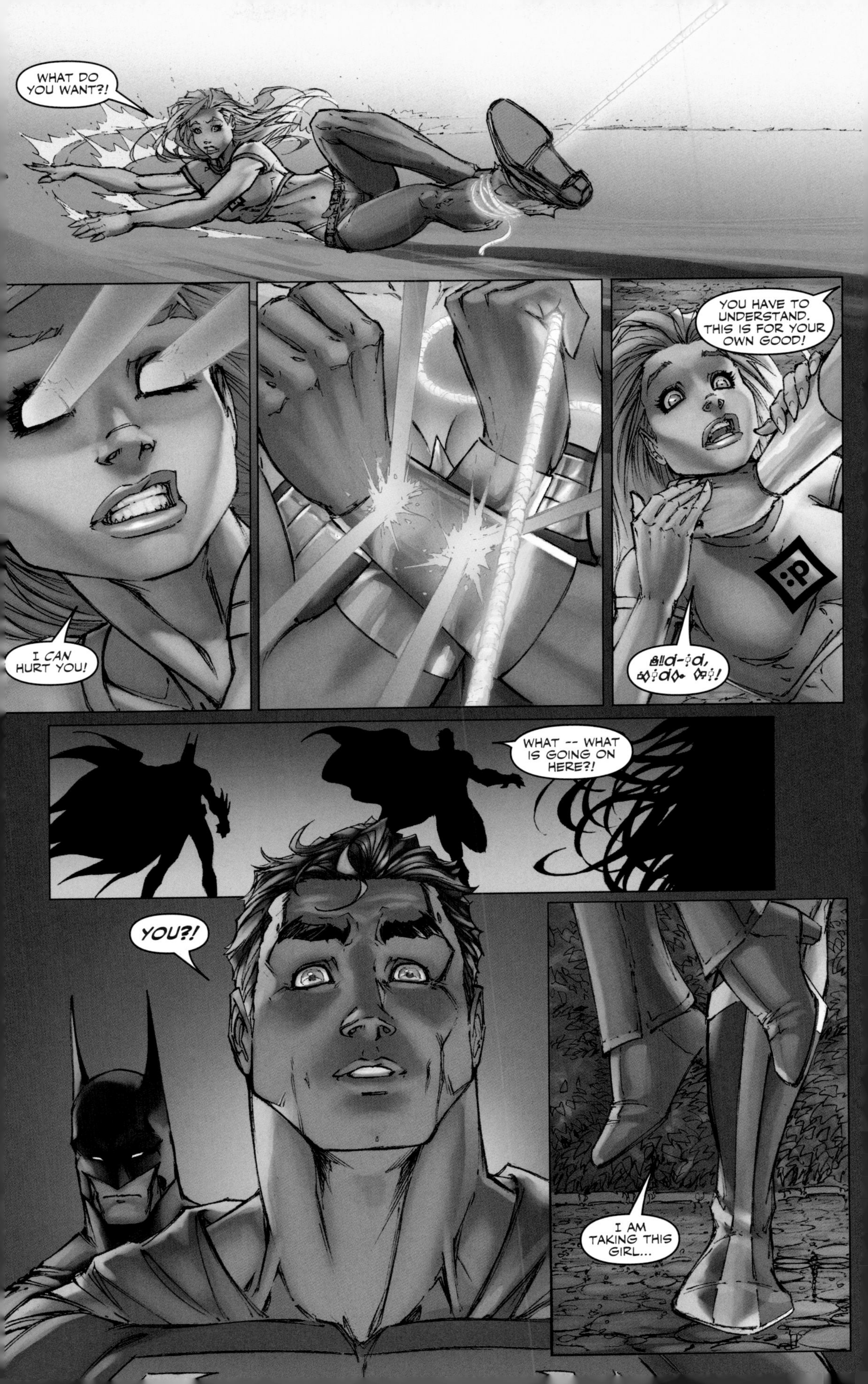
WHAT DO YOU WANT?!
I CAN HURT YOU!
YOU HAVE TO UNDERSTAND. THIS IS FOR YOUR OWN GOOD!
WHAT -- WHAT IS GOING ON HERE?!
YOU?!
I AM TAKING THIS GIRL...

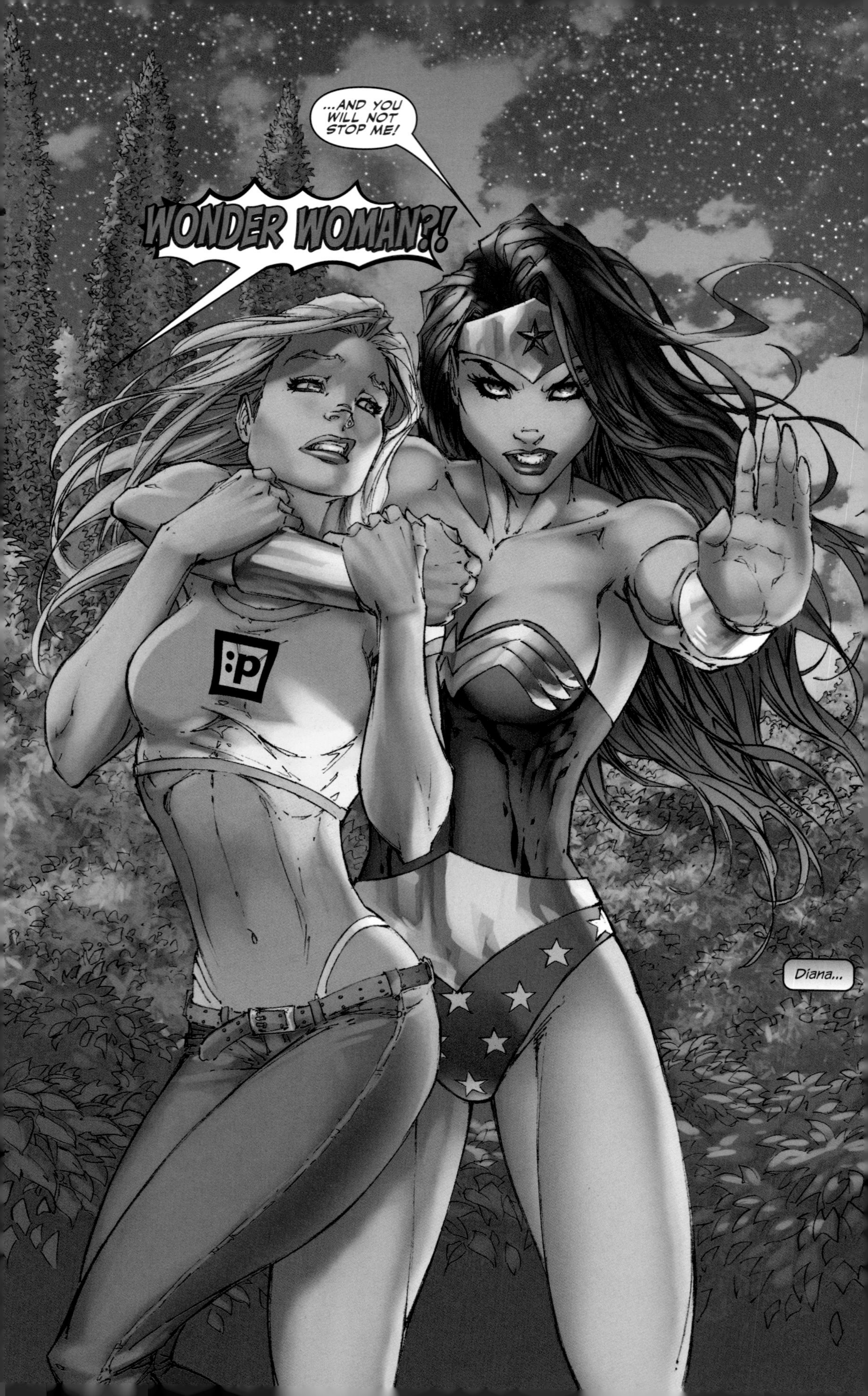
WONDER WOMAN?!
...AND YOU WILL NOT STOP ME!
Diana...

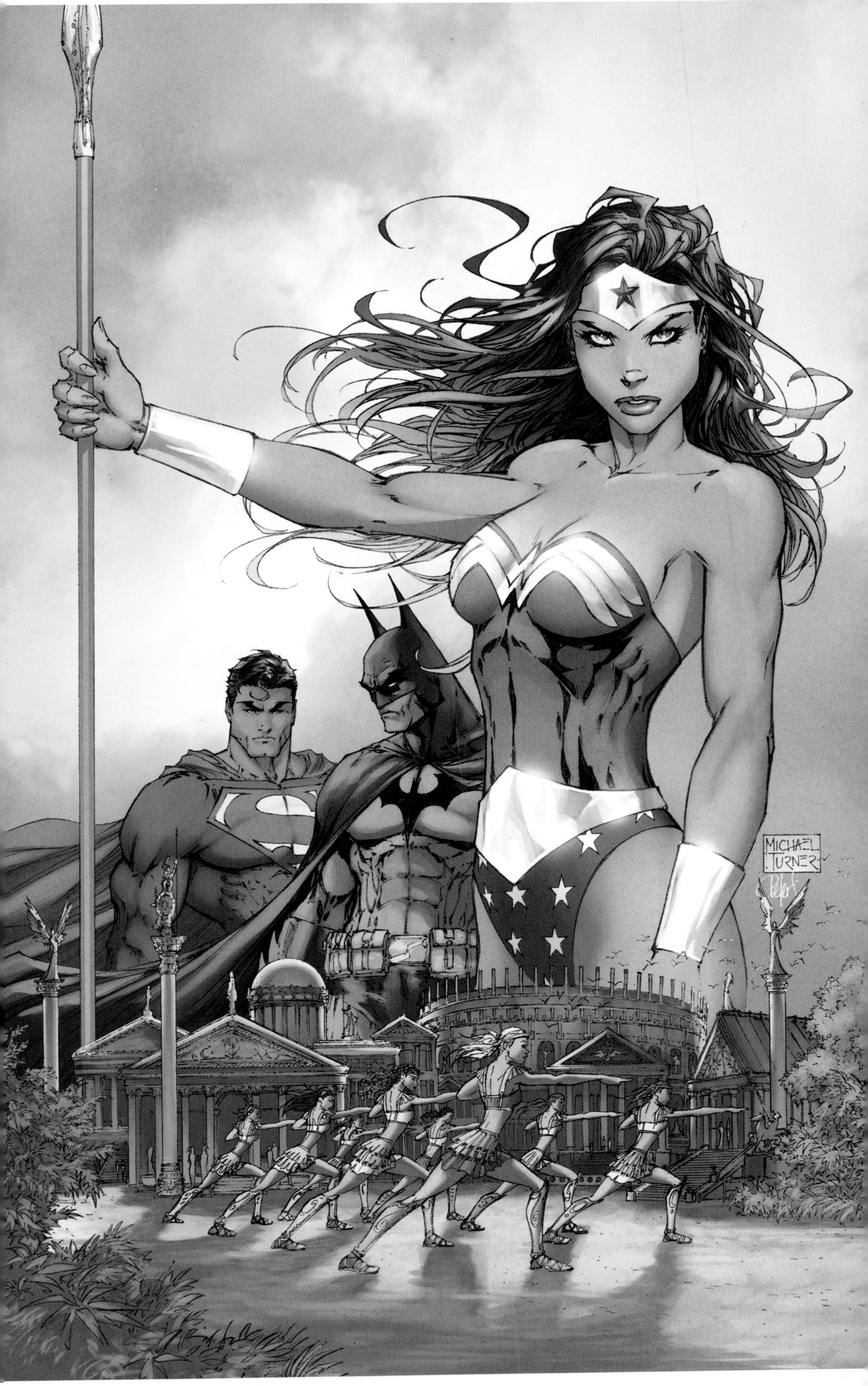
MICHAEL TURNER

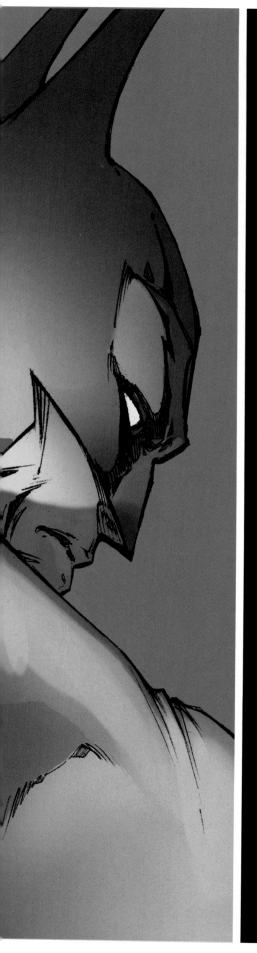
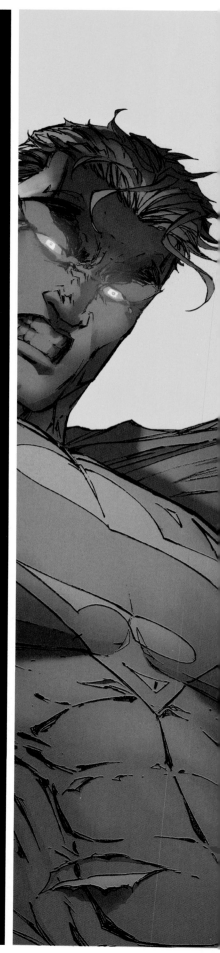

THE SUPERGIRL FROM KRYPTON

PART THREE
WARRIOR

JEPH LOEB
WRITER
MICHAEL TURNER
ARTIST
PETER STEIGERWALD
COLORIST
RICHARD STARKINGS
LETTERER
MICHAEL TURNER
WITH
PETER STEIGERWALD
COVER

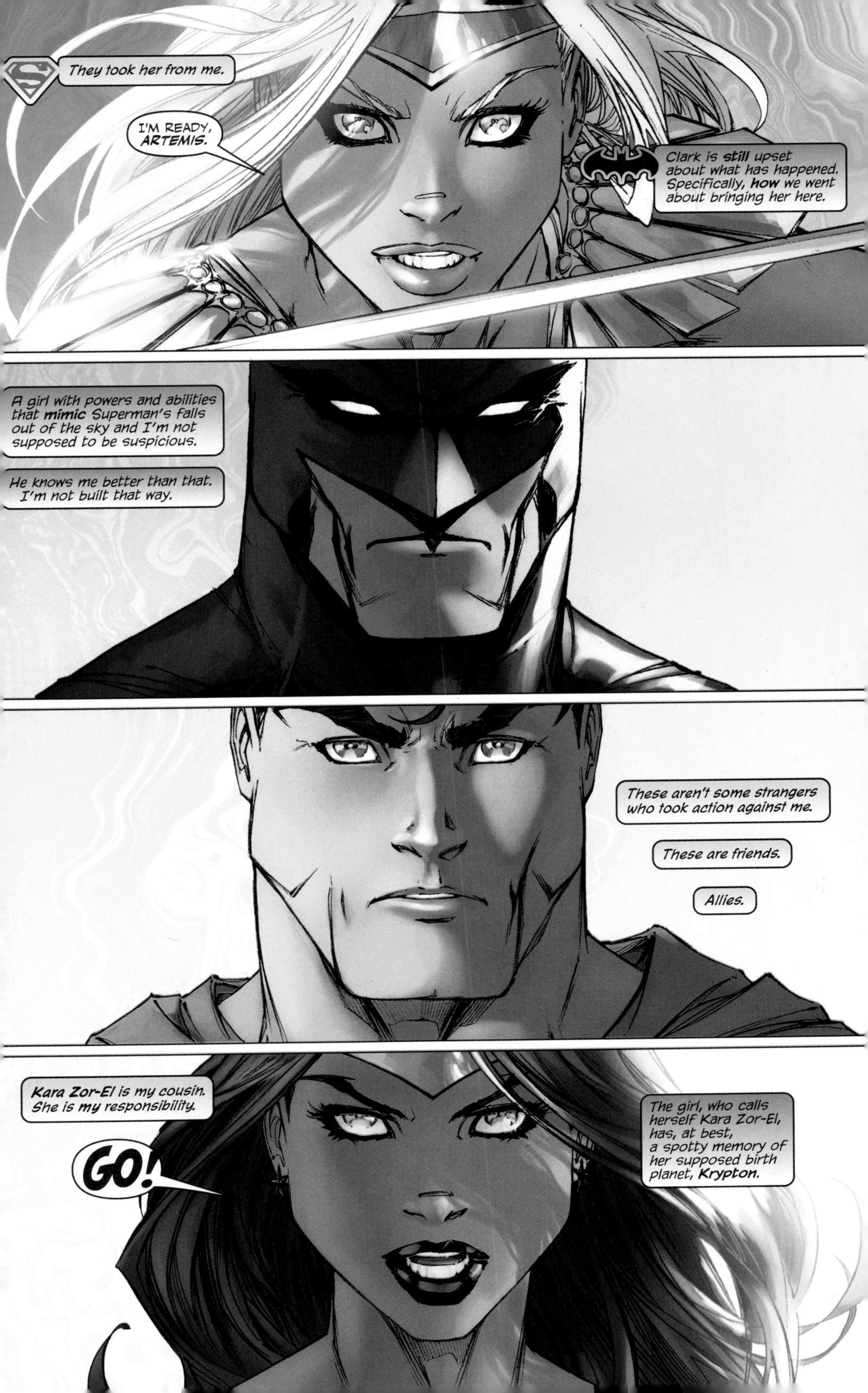
They took her from me.
I'M READY, ARTEMIS.
Clark is still upset about what has happened. Specifically, how we went about bringing her here.
A girl with powers and abilities that mimic Superman's falls out of the sky and I'm not supposed to be suspicious.
He knows me better than that. I'm not built that way.
These aren't some strangers who took action against me.
These are friends.
Allies.
Kara Zor-El is my cousin. She is my responsibility.
GO!
The girl, who calls herself Kara Zor-El, has, at best, a spotty memory of her supposed birth planet, Krypton.

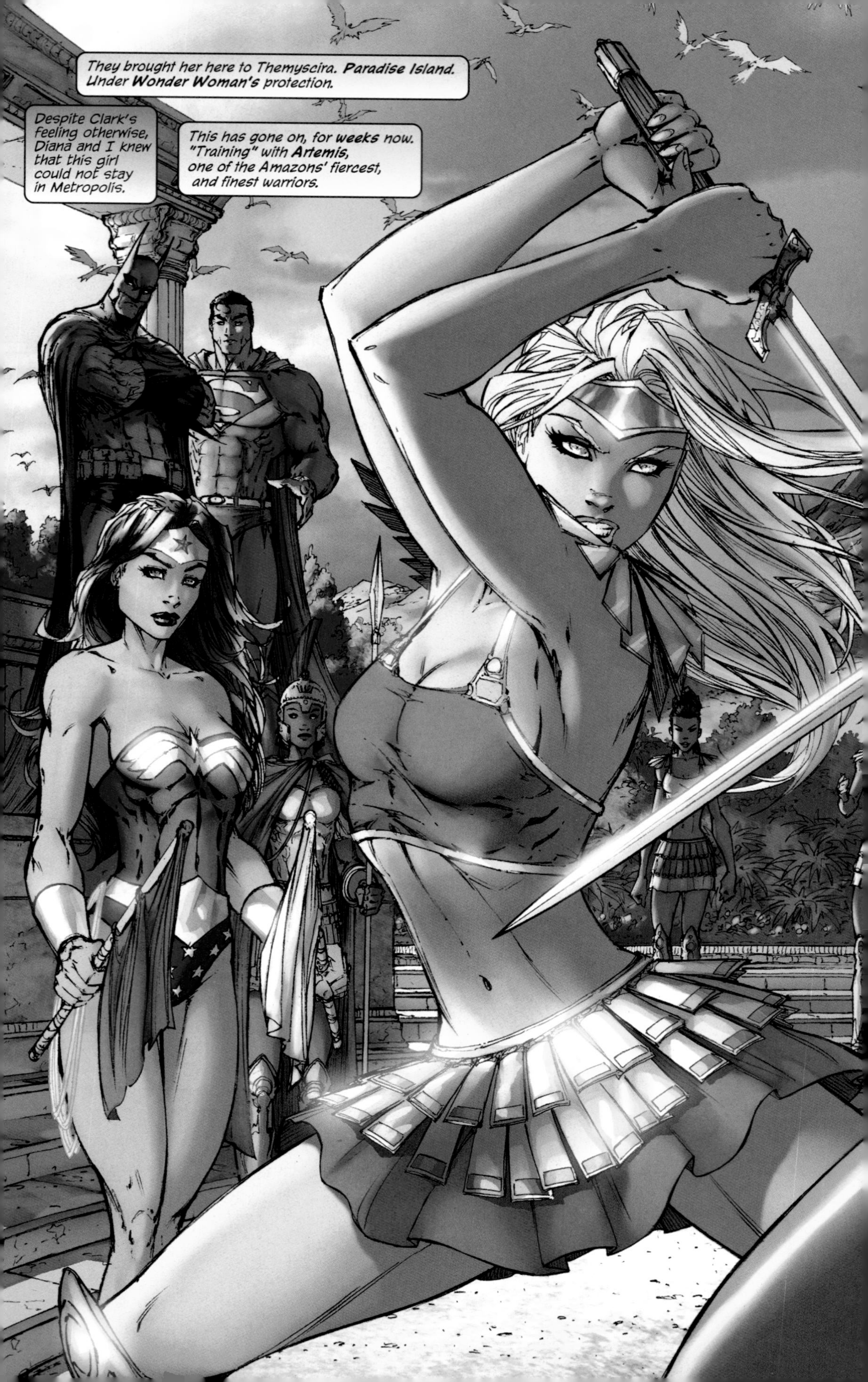
They brought her here to Themyscira. Paradise Island. Under Wonder Woman's protection.
Despite Clark's feeling otherwise, Diana and I knew that this girl could not stay in Metropolis.
This has gone on, for weeks now. "Training" with Artemis, one of the Amazons' fiercest, and finest warriors.

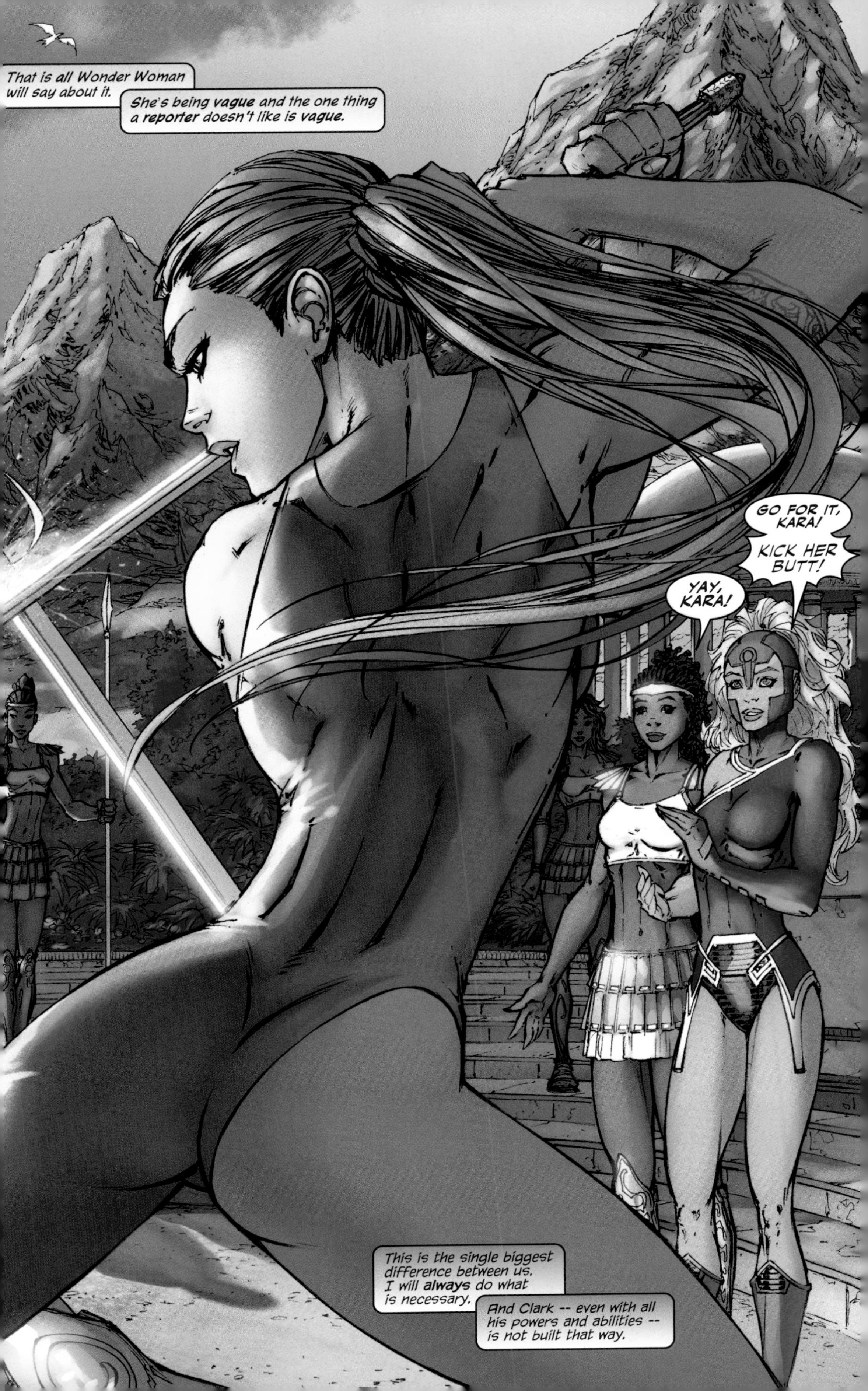
That is all Wonder Woman will say about it.
She's being vague and the one thing a reporter doesn't like is vague.
GO FOR IT, KARA!
KICK HER BUTT!
YAY, KARA!
This is the single biggest difference between us. I will always do what is necessary.
And Clark -- even with all his powers and abilities -- is not built that way.

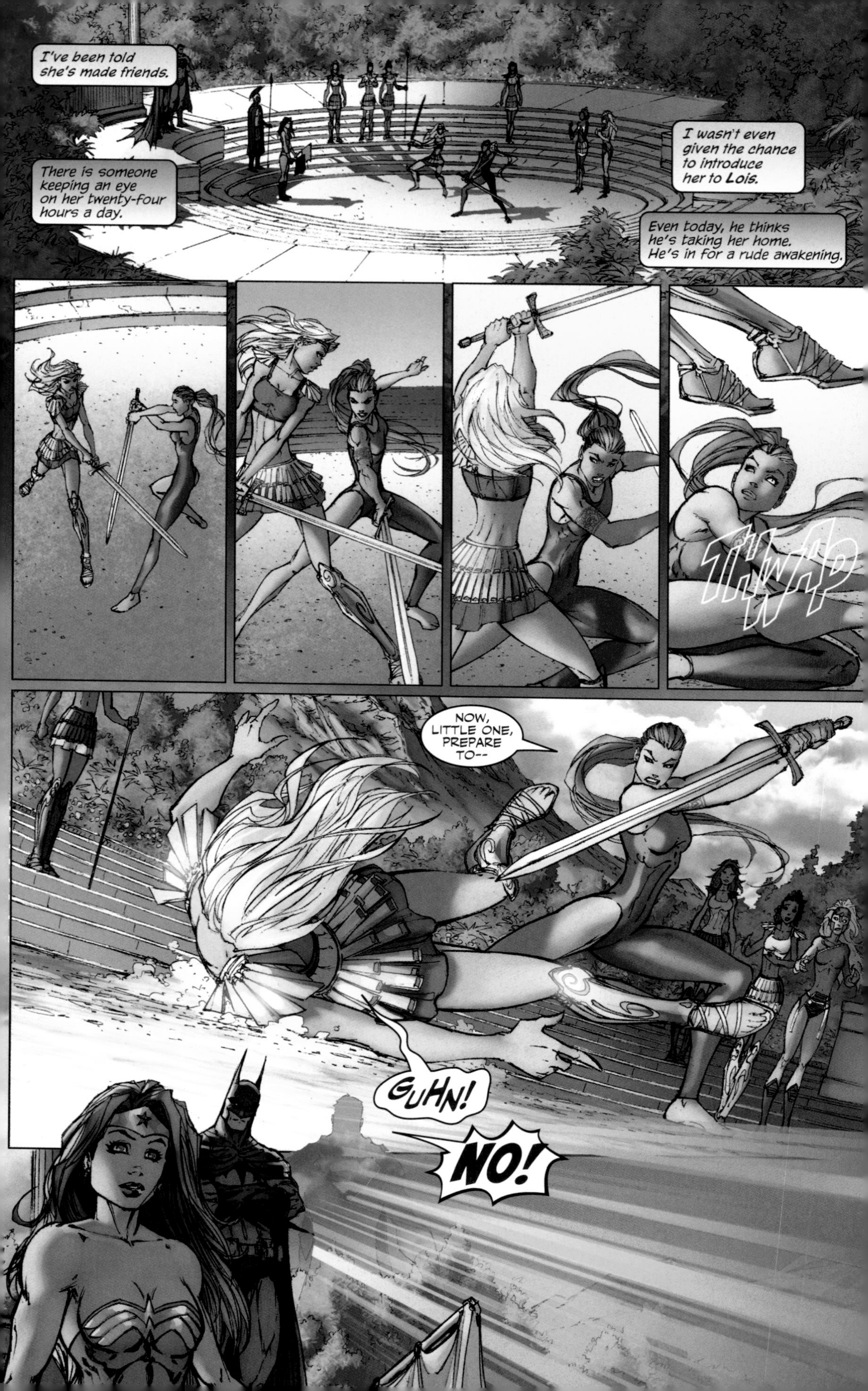

I've been told she's made friends.
There is someone keeping an eye on her twenty-four hours a day.
I wasn't even given the chance to introduce her to Lois.
Even today, he thinks he's taking her home. He's in for a rude awakening.
THWP
NOW, LITTLE ONE, PREPARE TO--
GUHN!
NO!

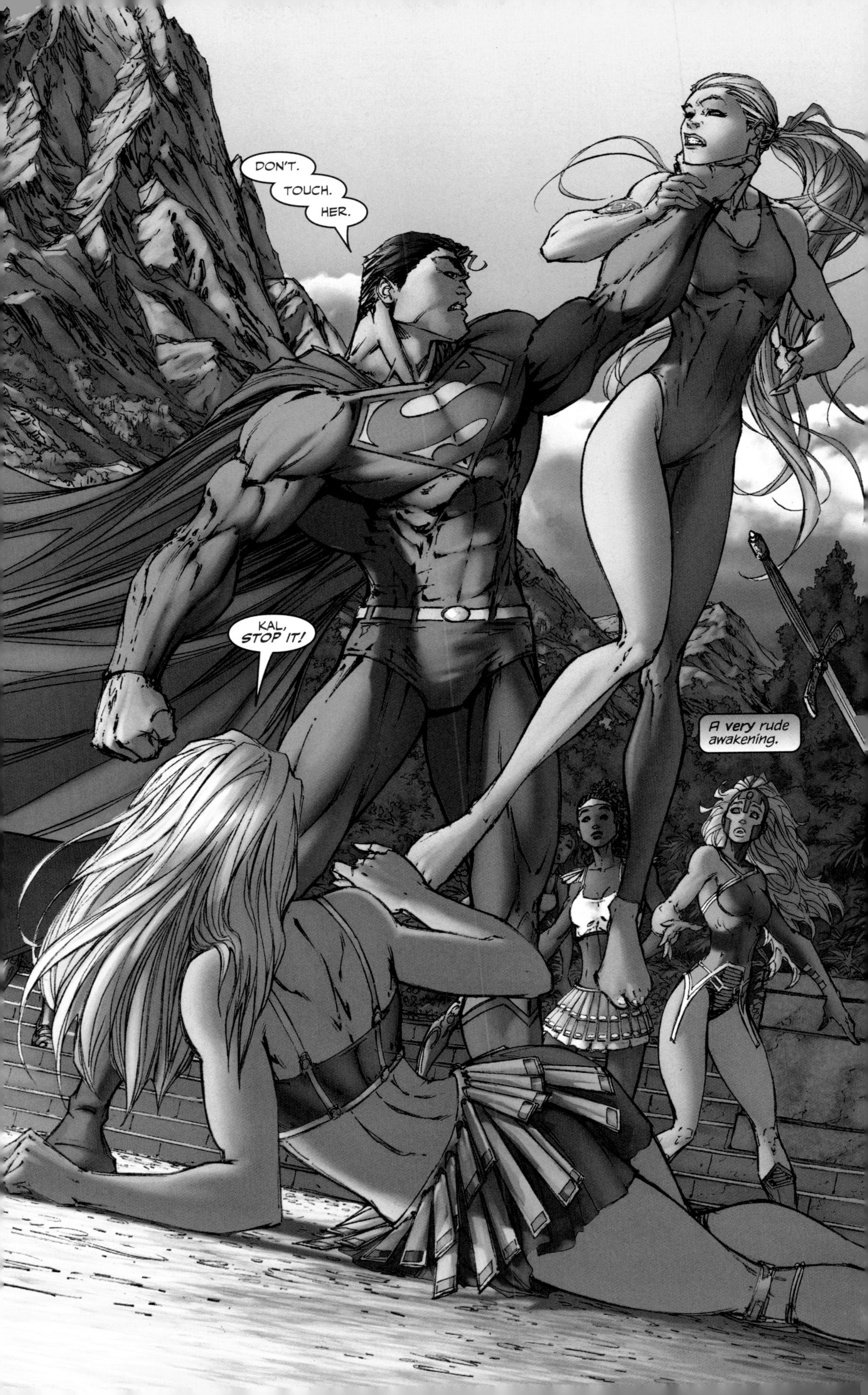
DON'T. TOUCH. HER.
KAL, STOP IT!
A very rude awakening.

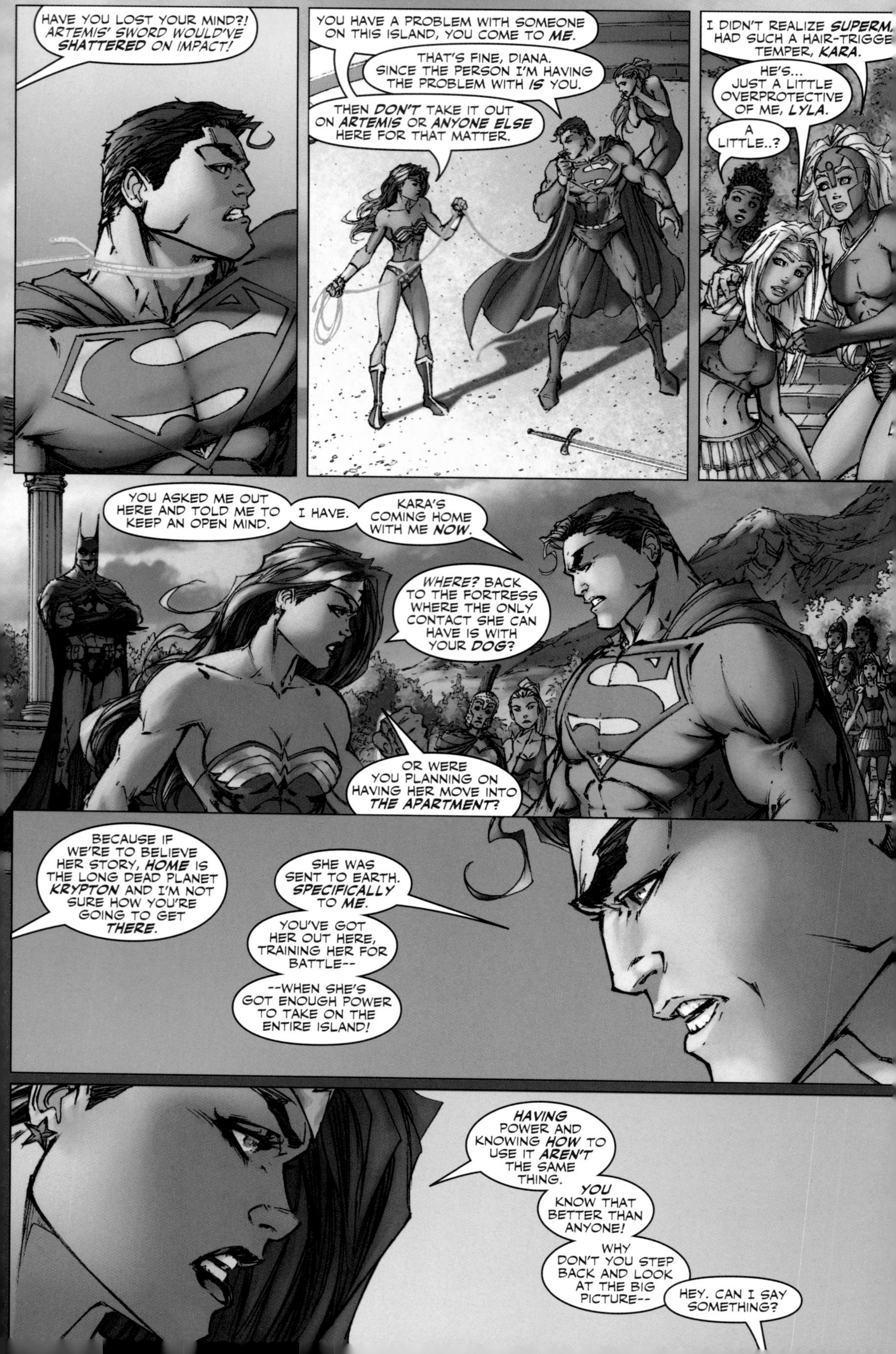
HAVE YOU LOST YOUR MIND?! ARTEMIS' SWORD WOULD'VE SHATTERED ON IMPACT!
YOU HAVE A PROBLEM WITH SOMEONE ON THIS ISLAND, YOU COME TO ME.
THAT'S FINE, DIANA. SINCE THE PERSON I'M HAVING THE PROBLEM WITH IS YOU.
THEN DON'T TAKE IT OUT ON ARTEMIS OR ANYONE ELSE HERE FOR THAT MATTER.
I DIDN'T REALIZE SUPERM HAD SUCH A HAIR-TRIGGE TEMPER, KARA.
HE'S... JUST A LITTLE OVERPROTECTIVE OF ME, LYLA.
A LITTLE..?
YOU ASKED ME OUT HERE AND TOLD ME TO KEEP AN OPEN MIND.
I HAVE.
KARA'S COMING HOME WITH ME NOW.
WHERE? BACK TO THE FORTRESS WHERE THE ONLY CONTACT SHE CAN HAVE IS WITH YOUR DOG?
OR WERE YOU PLANNING ON HAVING HER MOVE INTO THE APARTMENT?
BECAUSE IF WE'RE TO BELIEVE HER STORY, HOME IS THE LONG DEAD PLANET KRYPTON AND I'M NOT SURE HOW YOU'RE GOING TO GET THERE.
SHE WAS SENT TO EARTH. SPECIFICALLY TO ME.
YOU'VE GOT HER OUT HERE, TRAINING HER FOR BATTLE--
--WHEN SHE'S GOT ENOUGH POWER TO TAKE ON THE ENTIRE ISLAND!
HAVING POWER AND KNOWING HOW TO USE IT AREN'T THE SAME THING.
YOU KNOW THAT BETTER THAN ANYONE!
WHY DON'T YOU STEP BACK AND LOOK AT THE BIG PICTURE--
HEY. CAN I SAY SOMETHING?

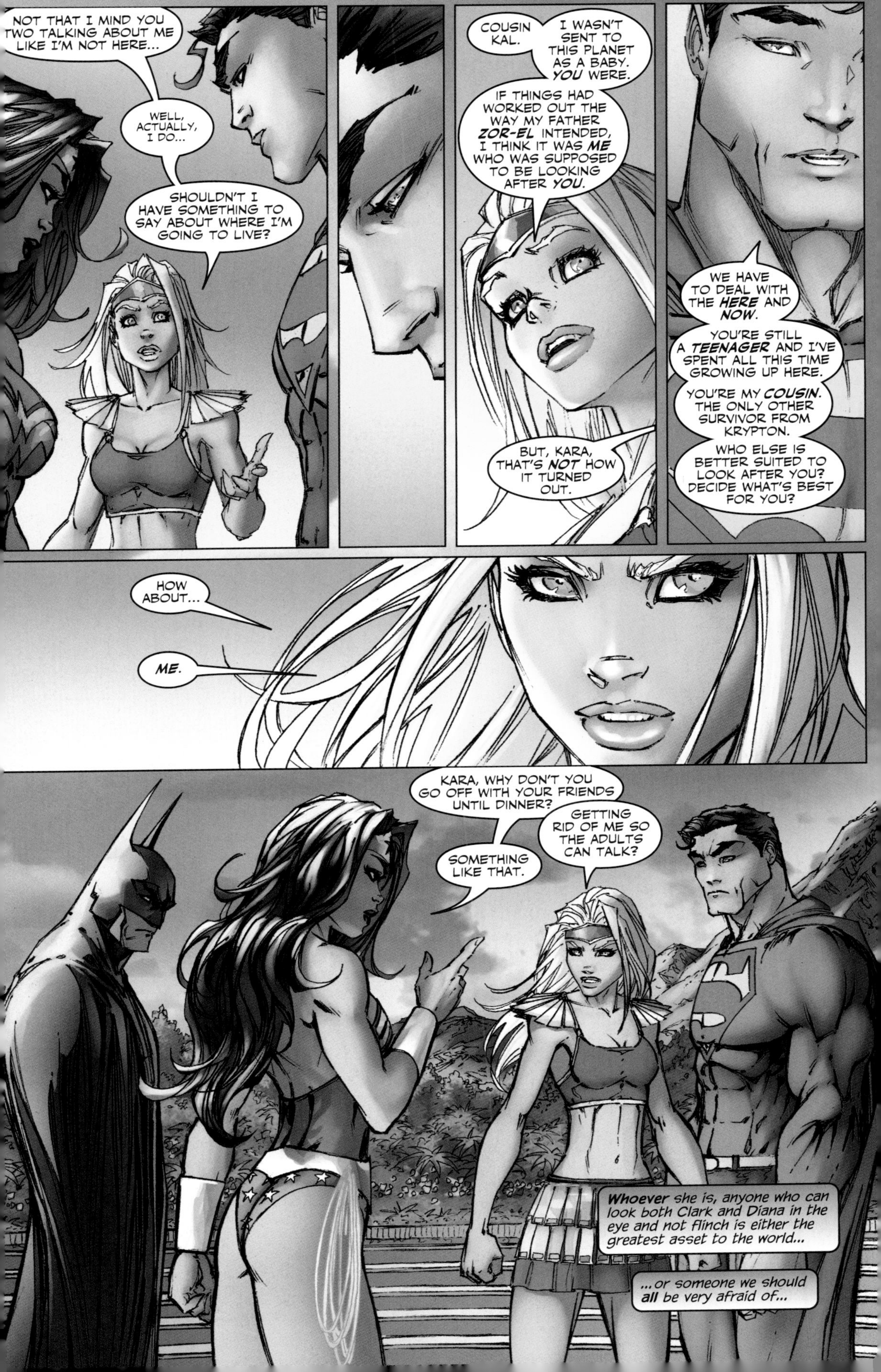
NOT THAT I MIND YOU TWO TALKING ABOUT ME LIKE I'M NOT HERE...
WELL, ACTUALLY, I DO...
SHOULDN'T I HAVE SOMETHING TO SAY ABOUT WHERE I'M GOING TO LIVE?
COUSIN KAL.
I WASN'T SENT TO THIS PLANET AS A BABY. YOU WERE.
IF THINGS HAD WORKED OUT THE WAY MY FATHER ZOR-EL INTENDED, I THINK IT WAS ME WHO WAS SUPPOSED TO BE LOOKING AFTER YOU.
BUT, KARA, THAT'S NOT HOW IT TURNED OUT.
WE HAVE TO DEAL WITH THE HERE AND NOW.
YOU'RE STILL A TEENAGER AND I'VE SPENT ALL THIS TIME GROWING UP HERE.
YOU'RE MY COUSIN. THE ONLY OTHER SURVIVOR FROM KRYPTON.
WHO ELSE IS BETTER SUITED TO LOOK AFTER YOU? DECIDE WHAT'S BEST FOR YOU?
HOW ABOUT...
ME.
KARA, WHY DON'T YOU GO OFF WITH YOUR FRIENDS UNTIL DINNER?
GETTING RID OF ME SO THE ADULTS CAN TALK?
SOMETHING LIKE THAT.
Whoever she is, anyone who can look both Clark and Diana in the eye and not flinch is either the greatest asset to the world...
...or someone we should all be very afraid of...

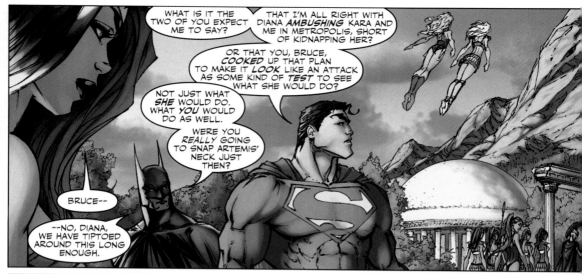

WHAT IS IT THE TWO OF YOU EXPECT ME TO SAY?

THAT I'M ALL RIGHT WITH DIANA *AMBUSHING* KARA AND ME IN METROPOLIS, SHORT OF KIDNAPPING HER?

OR THAT YOU, BRUCE, *COOKED* UP THAT PLAN TO MAKE IT *LOOK* LIKE AN ATTACK AS SOME KIND OF *TEST* TO SEE WHAT SHE WOULD DO?

NOT JUST WHAT *SHE* WOULD DO. WHAT *YOU* WOULD DO AS WELL.

WERE YOU *REALLY* GOING TO SNAP ARTEMIS' NECK JUST THEN?

BRUCE--

--NO, DIANA, WE HAVE TIPTOED AROUND THIS LONG ENOUGH.

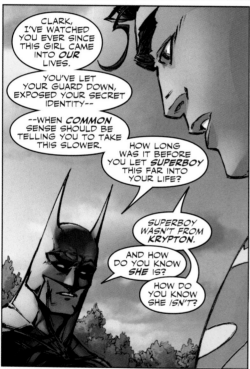

CLARK, I'VE WATCHED YOU EVER SINCE THIS GIRL CAME INTO *OUR* LIVES.

YOU'VE LET YOUR GUARD DOWN, EXPOSED YOUR SECRET IDENTITY--

--WHEN *COMMON* SENSE SHOULD BE TELLING YOU TO TAKE THIS SLOWER.

HOW LONG WAS IT BEFORE YOU LET *SUPERBOY* THIS FAR INTO YOUR LIFE?

SUPERBOY WASN'T FROM *KRYPTON*.

AND HOW DO YOU KNOW *SHE* IS?

HOW DO YOU KNOW SHE *ISN'T*?

UNLIKE YOU, BRUCE, I DON'T LOOK FOR THE *BAD* IN EVERYONE.

MAYBE THAT MAKES ME *NAÏVE* IN YOUR EYES--

-- BUT *EVERY* INSTINCT I HAVE TELLS ME THIS GIRL IS MY COUSIN.

SHE'S DONE *NOTHING* TO SHOW ME OTHERWISE.

IT WASN'T THAT LONG AGO THAT I THOUGHT I HAD A LEAD ON WHO KILLED MY PARENTS.

WASN'T IT *YOU* WHO WARNED ME THAT THE INFORMATION MIGHT NOT BE ACCURATE?

THAT IT COULD'VE BEEN *PLANTED* THERE? THAT IT WAS TOO *DANGEROUS* TO ACCEPT IT AT FACE VALUE?

YOU TWO CAN'T UNDERSTAND...

...IF SHE *IS* FROM KRYPTON...

THEN, LET'S ASSUME SHE IS.

A YOUNG, IMPRESSIONABLE GIRL WITH *AWESOME* POWER.

RAW. UNTESTED. RIPE FOR SOMEONE TO *EXPLOIT*.

DO YOU THINK THAT THE *UNIVERSE* CAN KEEP THAT A SECRET?

WHAT IS IT YOU'RE NOT TELLING ME, DIANA?

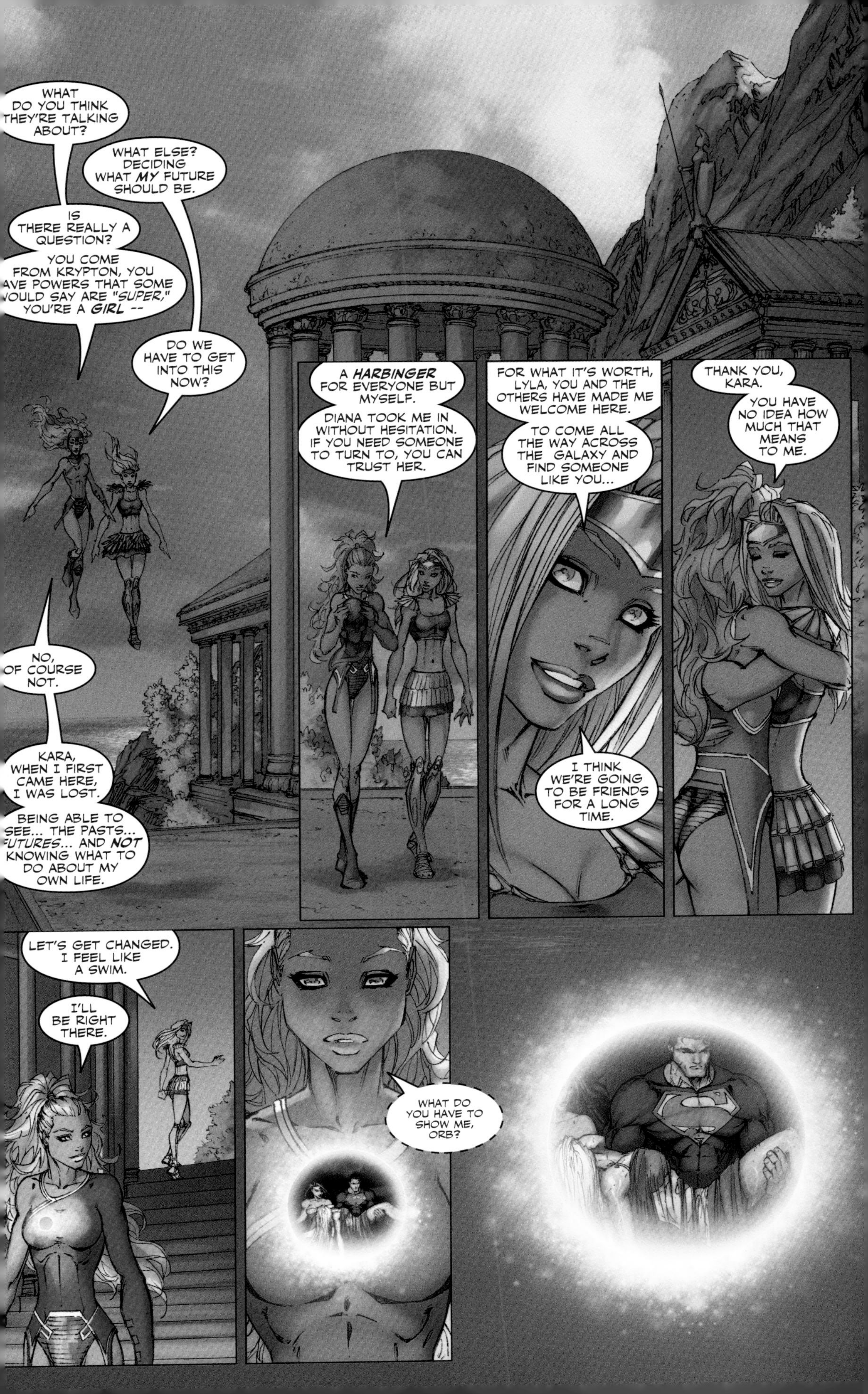

WHAT DO YOU THINK THEY'RE TALKING ABOUT?
WHAT ELSE? DECIDING WHAT MY FUTURE SHOULD BE.
IS THERE REALLY A QUESTION?
YOU COME FROM KRYPTON, YOU HAVE POWERS THAT SOME WOULD SAY ARE "SUPER," YOU'RE A GIRL --
DO WE HAVE TO GET INTO THIS NOW?
NO, OF COURSE NOT.
KARA, WHEN I FIRST CAME HERE, I WAS LOST.
BEING ABLE TO SEE... THE PASTS... FUTURES... AND NOT KNOWING WHAT TO DO ABOUT MY OWN LIFE.
A HARBINGER FOR EVERYONE BUT MYSELF.
DIANA TOOK ME IN WITHOUT HESITATION. IF YOU NEED SOMEONE TO TURN TO, YOU CAN TRUST HER.
FOR WHAT IT'S WORTH, LYLA, YOU AND THE OTHERS HAVE MADE ME WELCOME HERE.
TO COME ALL THE WAY ACROSS THE GALAXY AND FIND SOMEONE LIKE YOU...
I THINK WE'RE GOING TO BE FRIENDS FOR A LONG TIME.
THANK YOU, KARA.
YOU HAVE NO IDEA HOW MUCH THAT MEANS TO ME.
LET'S GET CHANGED. I FEEL LIKE A SWIM.
I'LL BE RIGHT THERE.
WHAT DO YOU HAVE TO SHOW ME, ORB?

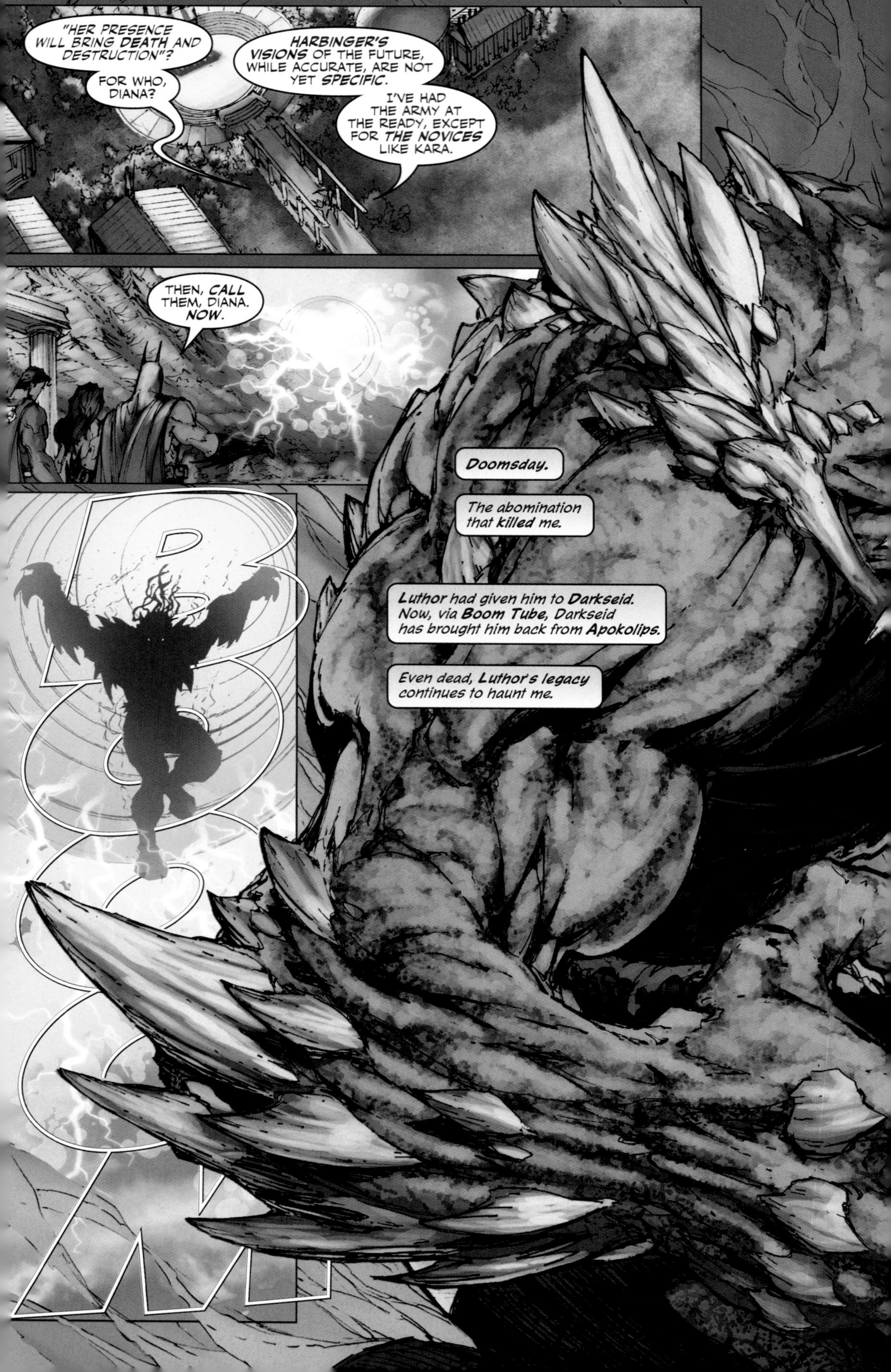
"HER PRESENCE WILL BRING DEATH AND DESTRUCTION"?
FOR WHO, DIANA?
HARBINGER'S VISIONS OF THE FUTURE, WHILE ACCURATE, ARE NOT YET SPECIFIC.
I'VE HAD THE ARMY AT THE READY, EXCEPT FOR THE NOVICES LIKE KARA.
THEN, CALL THEM, DIANA. NOW.
Doomsday.
The abomination that killed me.
Luthor had given him to Darkseid. Now, via Boom Tube, Darkseid has brought him back from Apokolips.
Even dead, Luthor's legacy continues to haunt me.

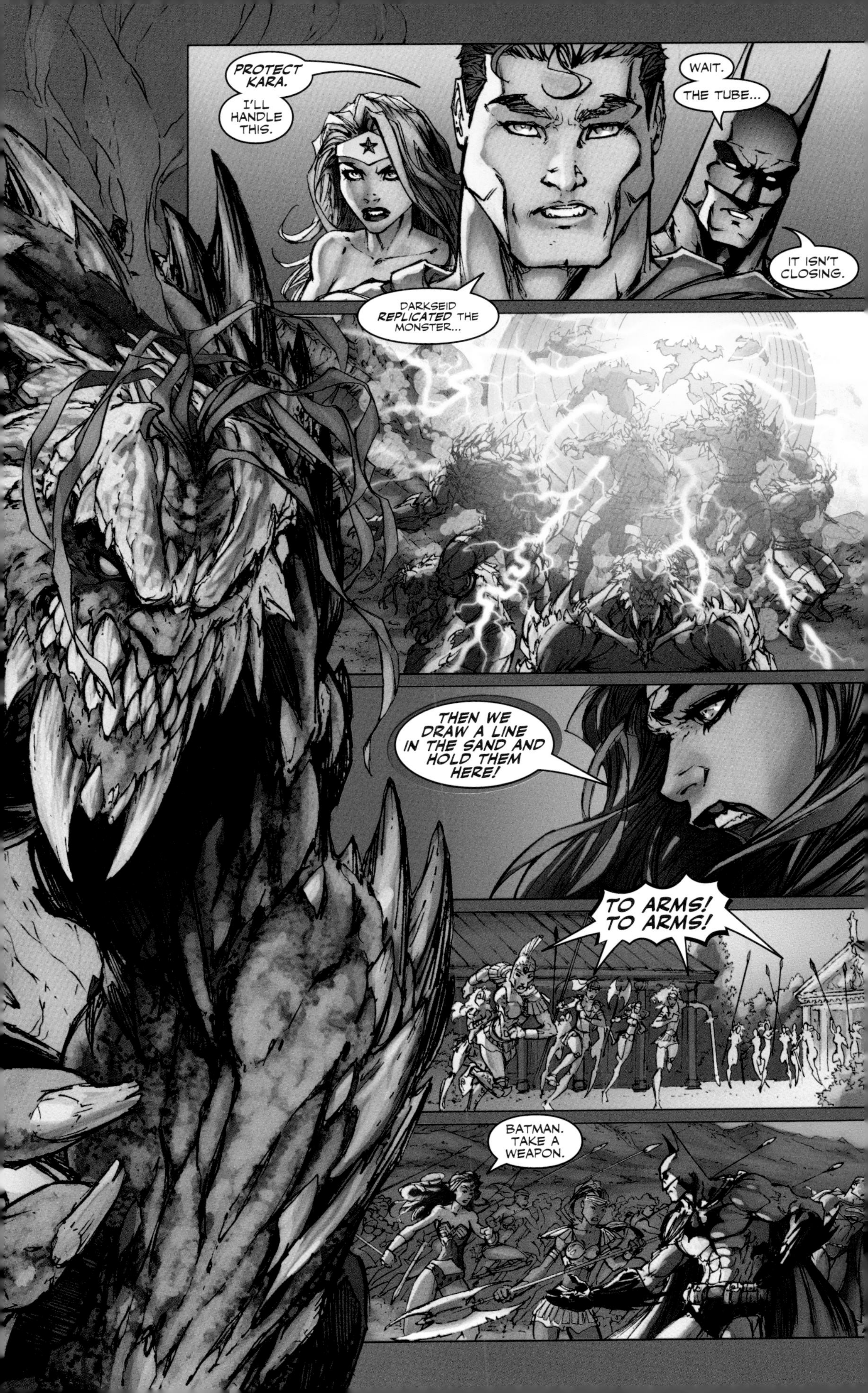
PROTECT KARA.
I'LL HANDLE THIS.
WAIT.
THE TUBE...
IT ISN'T CLOSING.
DARKSEID REPLICATED THE MONSTER...
THEN WE DRAW A LINE IN THE SAND AND HOLD THEM HERE!
TO ARMS! TO ARMS!
BATMAN. TAKE A WEAPON.

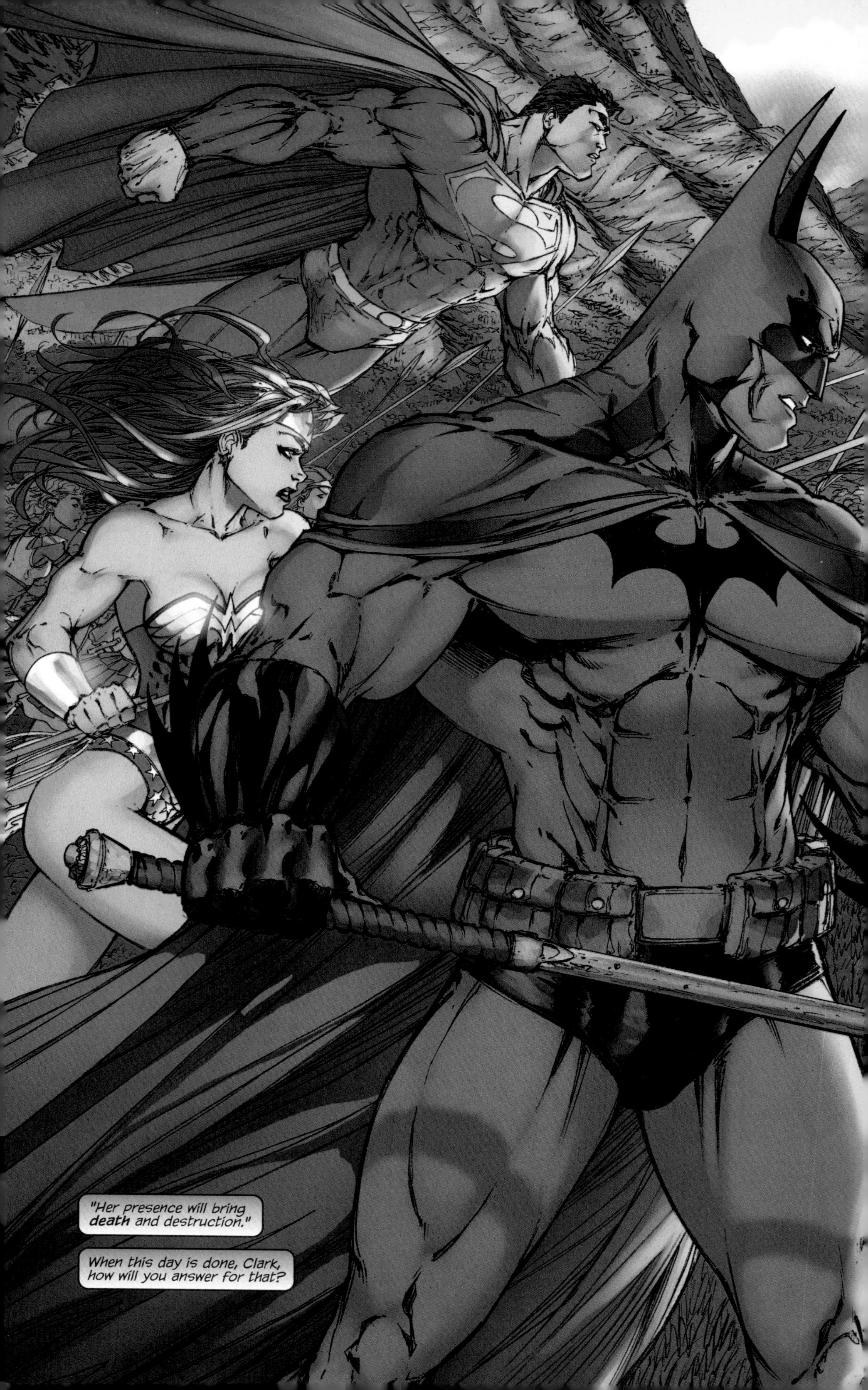
"Her presence will bring **death** and destruction."
When this day is done, Clark, how will you answer for that?

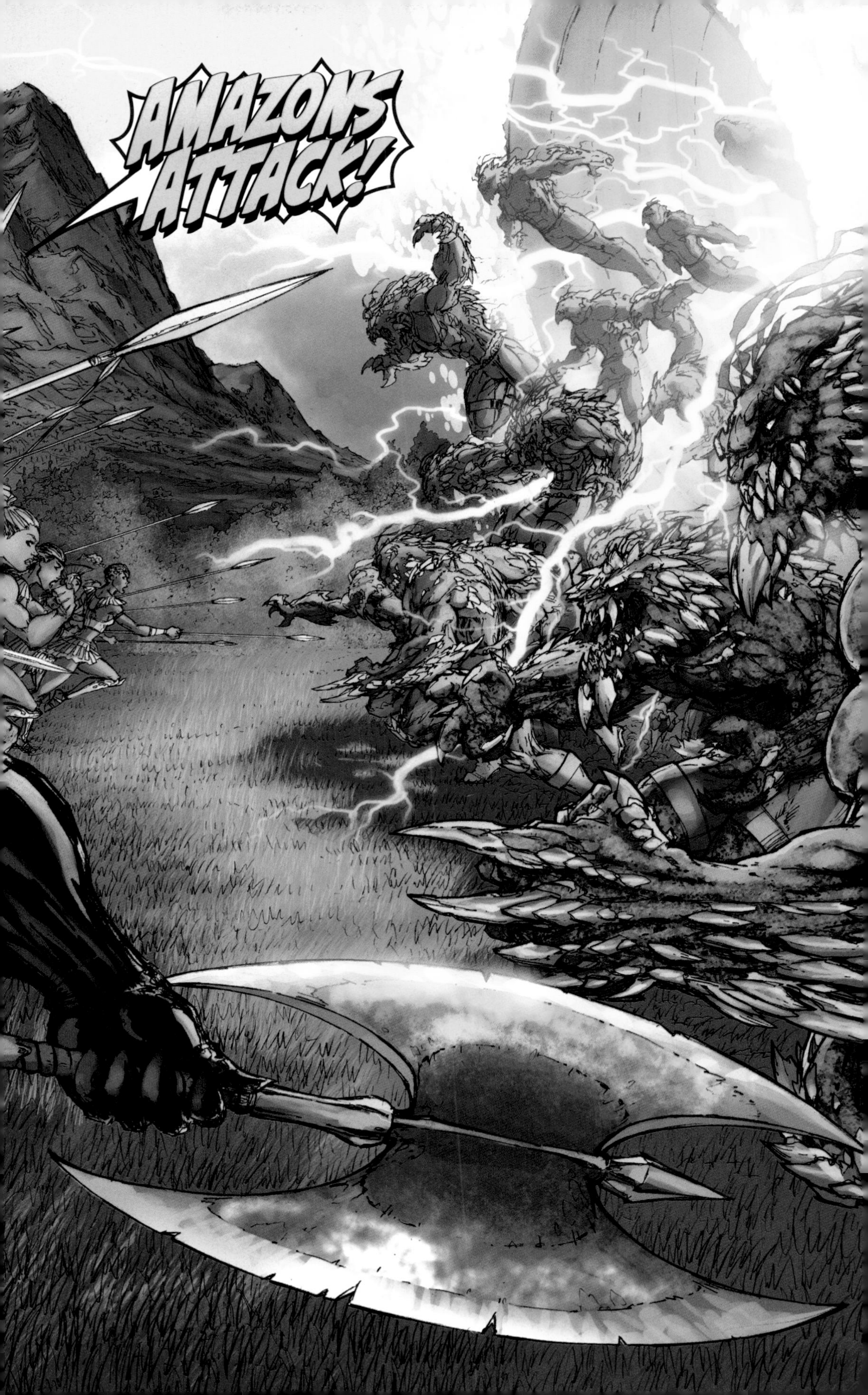
AMAZONS ATTACK!

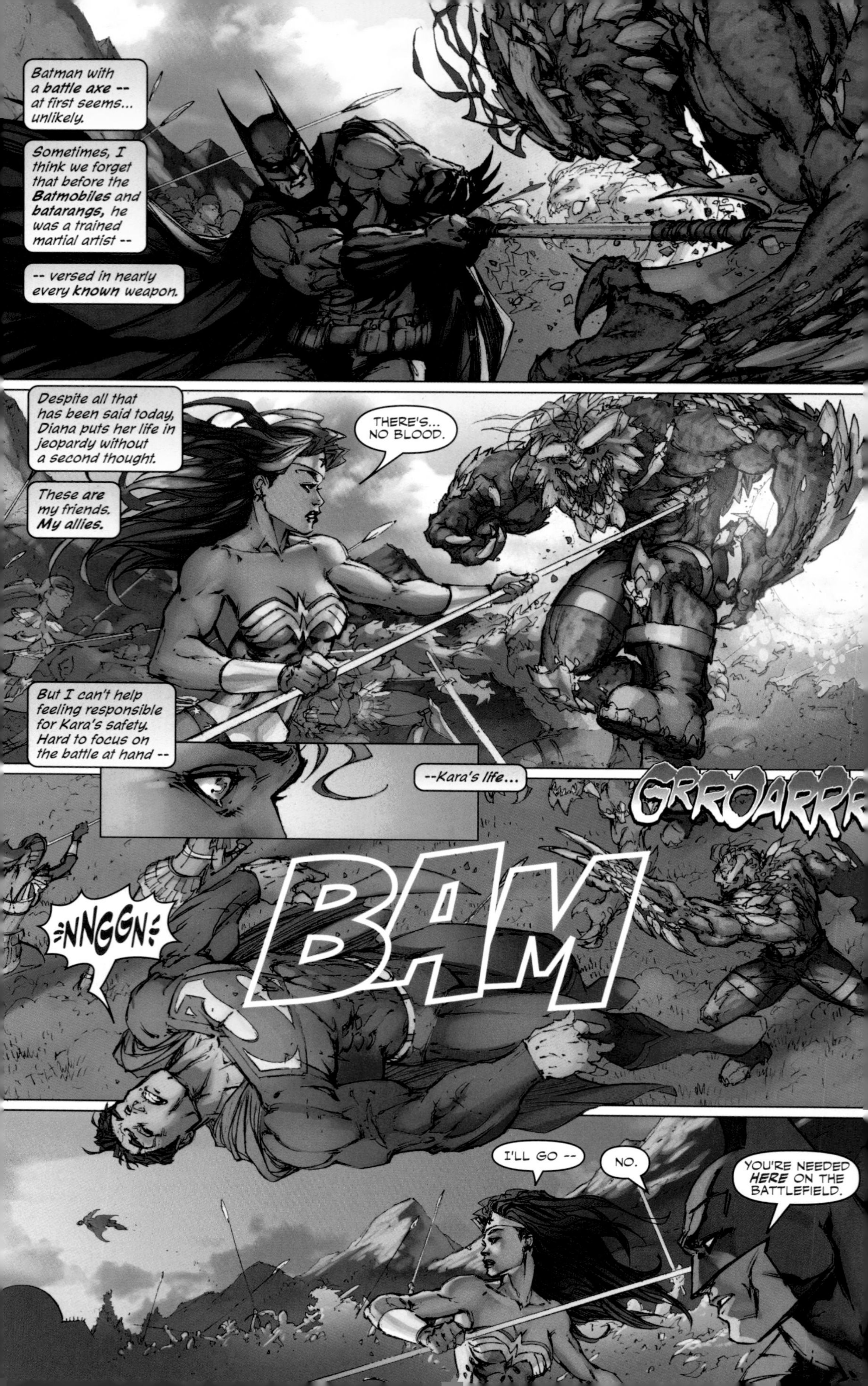
Batman with a **battle axe** -- at first seems... unlikely.
Sometimes, I think we forget that before the **Batmobiles** and **batarangs**, he was a trained martial artist --
-- versed in nearly every **known** weapon.
Despite all that has been said today, Diana puts her life in jeopardy without a second thought.
THERE'S... NO BLOOD.
These are my friends. **My allies.**
But I can't help feeling responsible for Kara's safety. Hard to focus on the battle at hand --
--Kara's life...
GRROARRR
BAM
NNGGN
I'LL GO --
NO.
YOU'RE NEEDED **HERE** ON THE BATTLEFIELD.

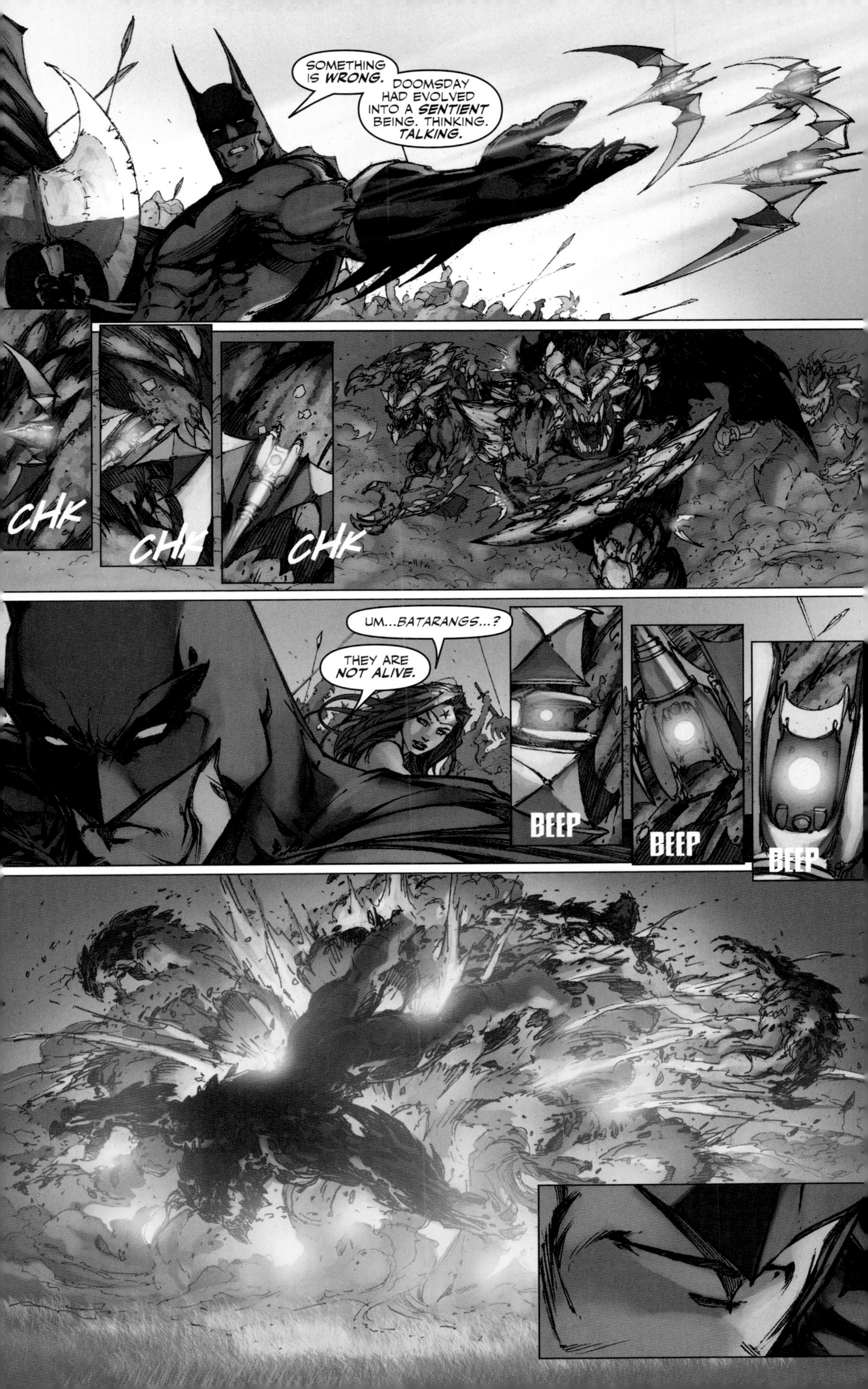
SOMETHING IS WRONG.
DOOMSDAY HAD EVOLVED INTO A SENTIENT BEING. THINKING. TALKING.
CHK
CHK
CHK
UM...BATARANGS...?
THEY ARE NOT ALIVE.
BEEP
BEEP
BEEP

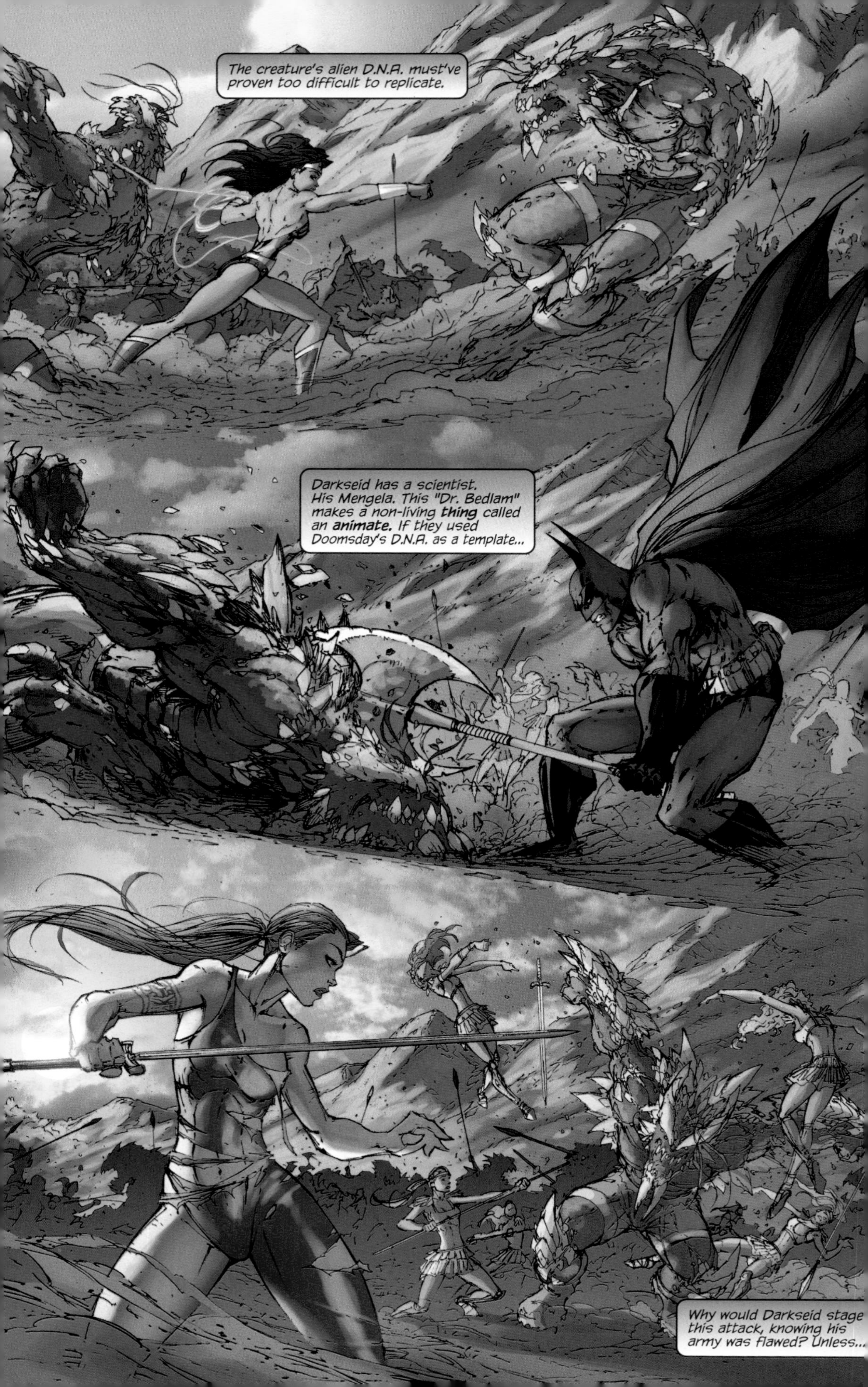
The creature's alien D.N.A. must've proven too difficult to replicate.
Darkseid has a scientist. His Mengela. This "Dr. Bedlam" makes a non-living **thing** called an **animate.** If they used Doomsday's D.N.A. as a template...
Why would Darkseid stage this attack, knowing his army was flawed? Unless...

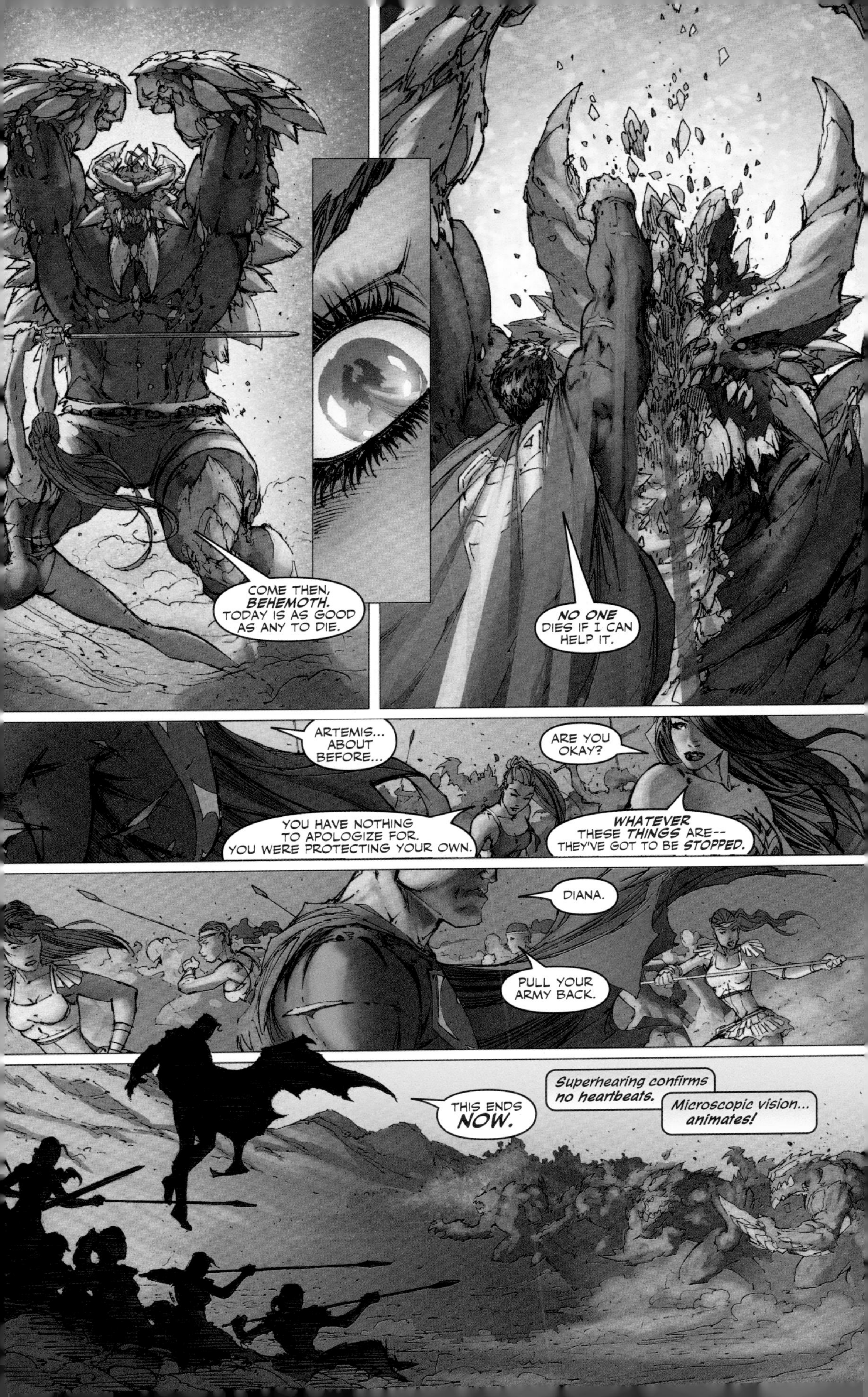
COME THEN, **BEHEMOTH.** TODAY IS AS GOOD AS ANY TO DIE.
NO ONE DIES IF I CAN HELP IT.
ARTEMIS... ABOUT BEFORE...
YOU HAVE NOTHING TO APOLOGIZE FOR. YOU WERE PROTECTING YOUR OWN.
ARE YOU OKAY?
WHATEVER THESE **THINGS** ARE-- THEY'VE GOT TO BE **STOPPED.**
DIANA.
PULL YOUR ARMY BACK.
THIS ENDS **NOW.**
Superhearing confirms **no heartbeats.**
Microscopic vision... **animates!**

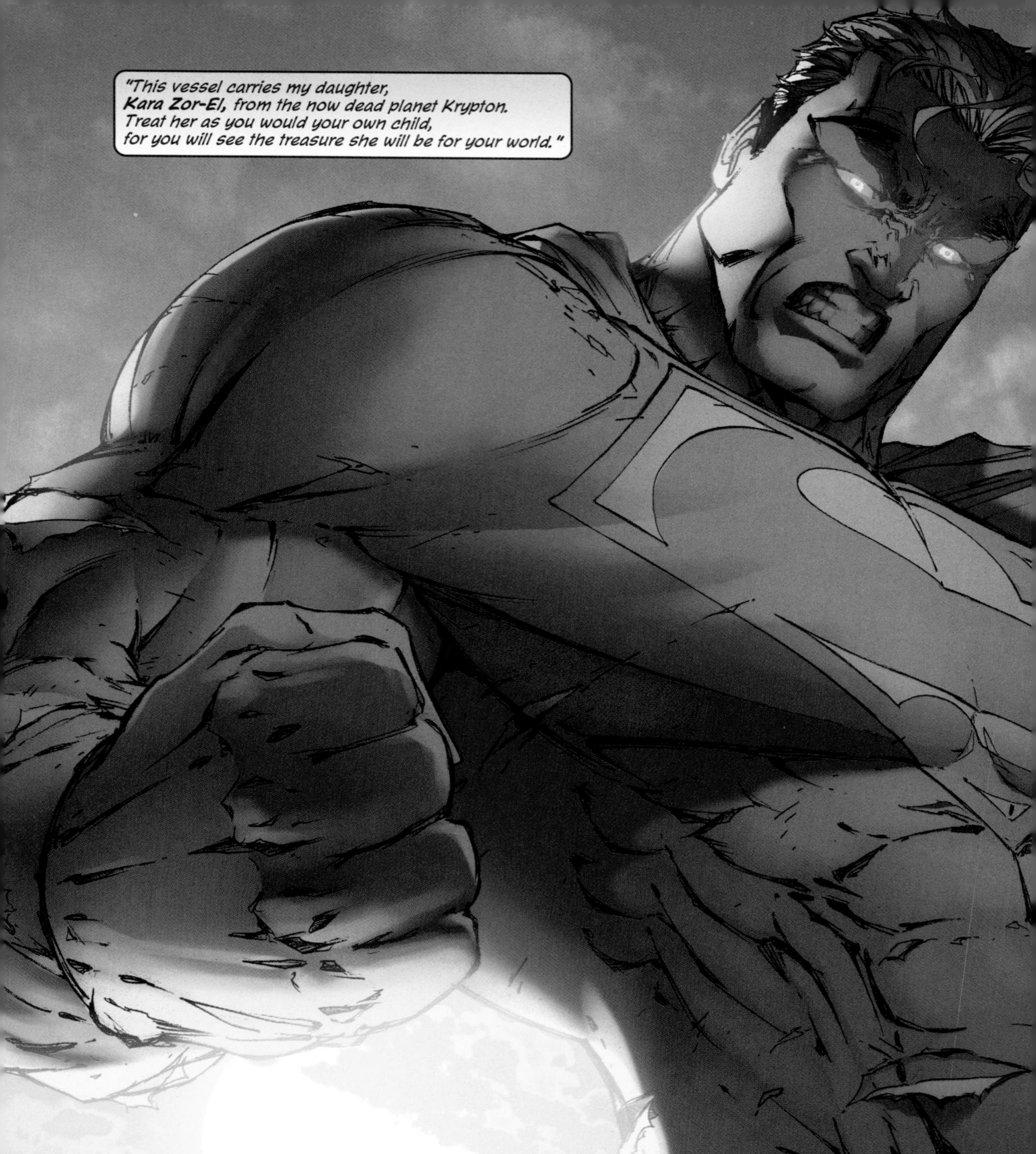
"This vessel carries my daughter, **Kara Zor-El,** from the now dead planet Krypton. Treat her as you would your own child, for you will see the treasure she will be for your world."
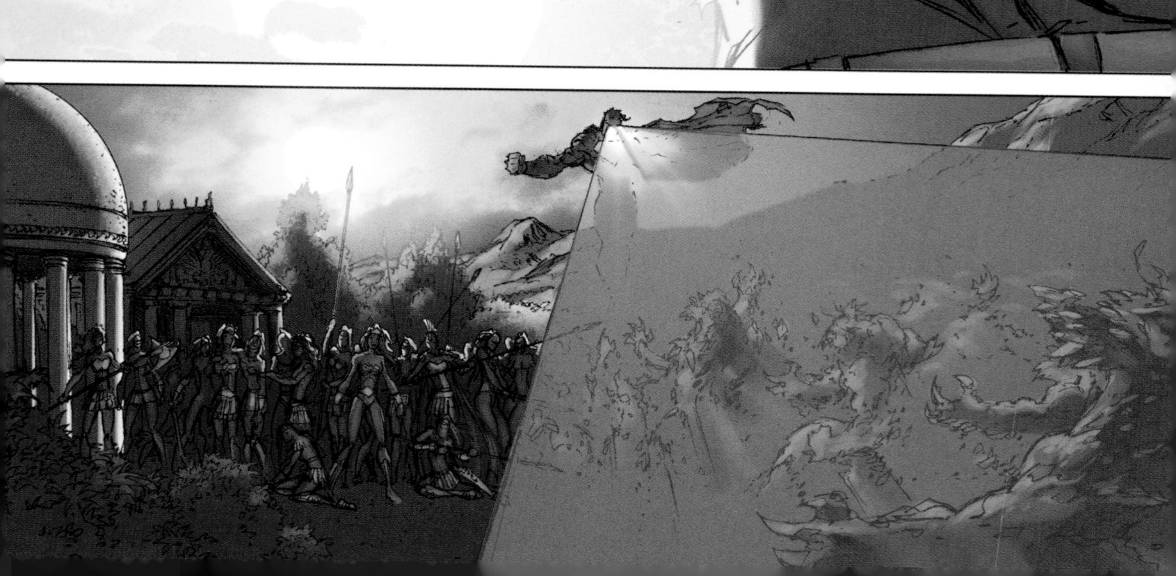

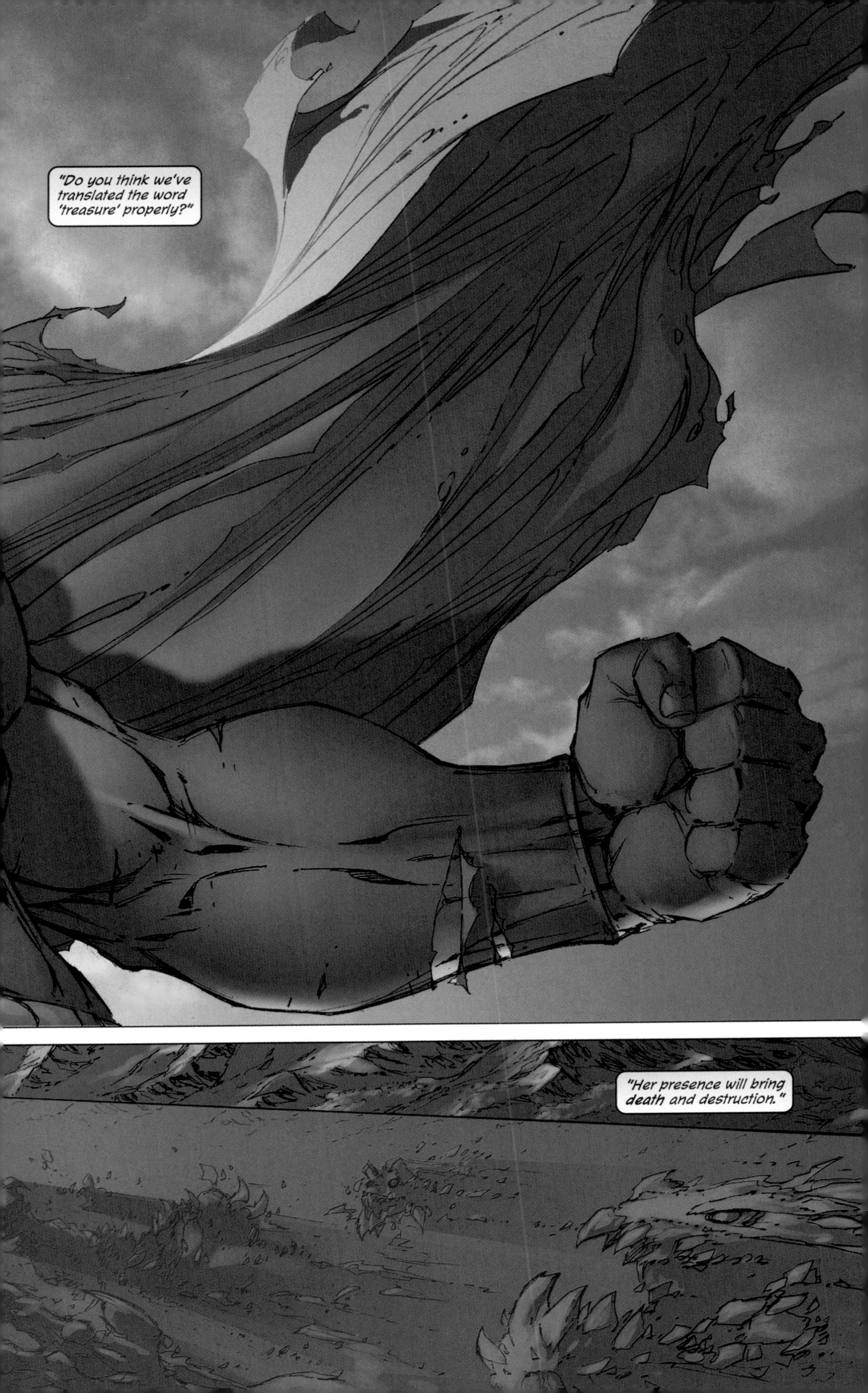
"Do you think we've translated the word 'treasure' properly?"
"Her presence will bring *death* and destruction."

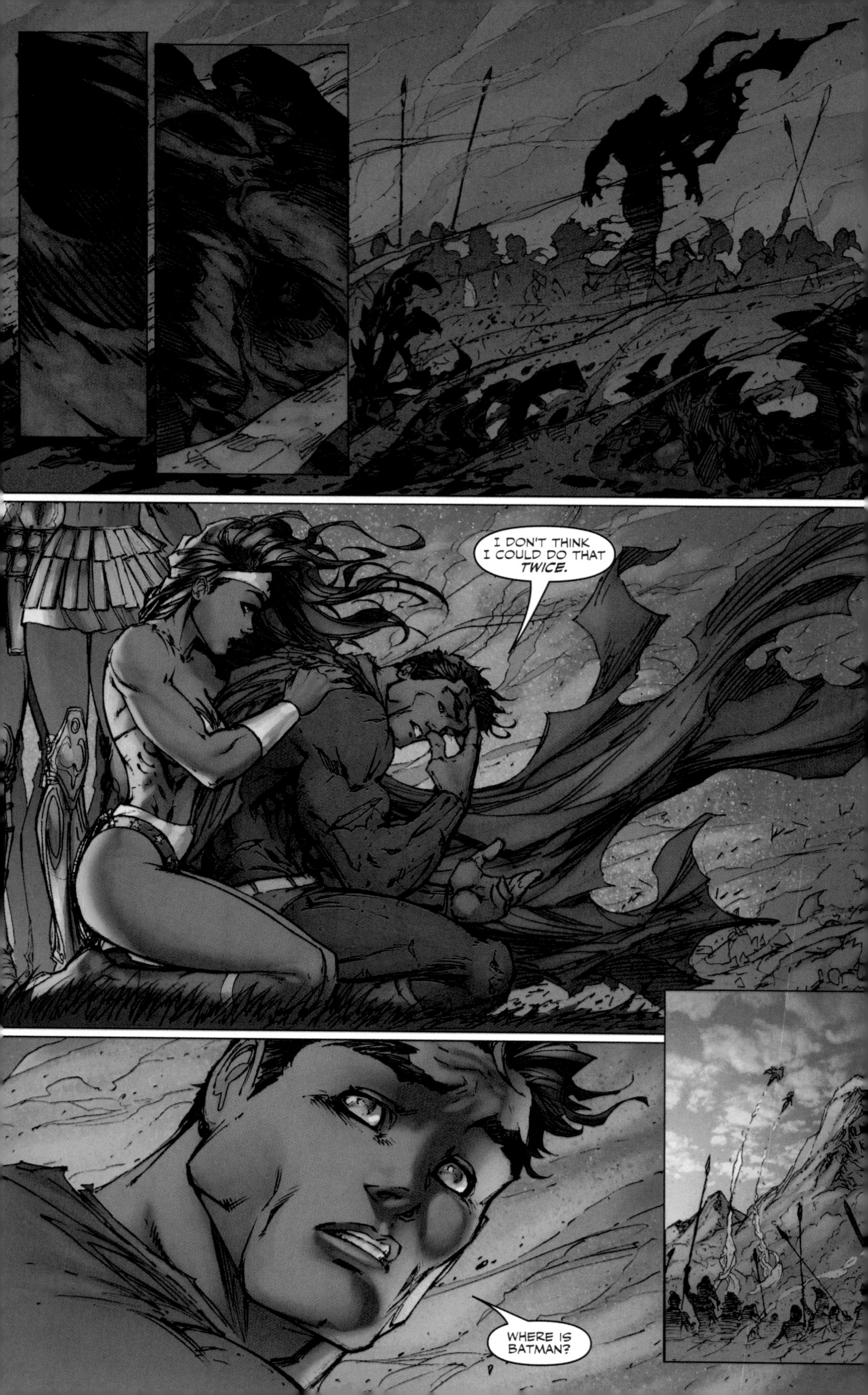
I DON'T THINK I COULD DO THAT *TWICE.*
WHERE IS BATMAN?

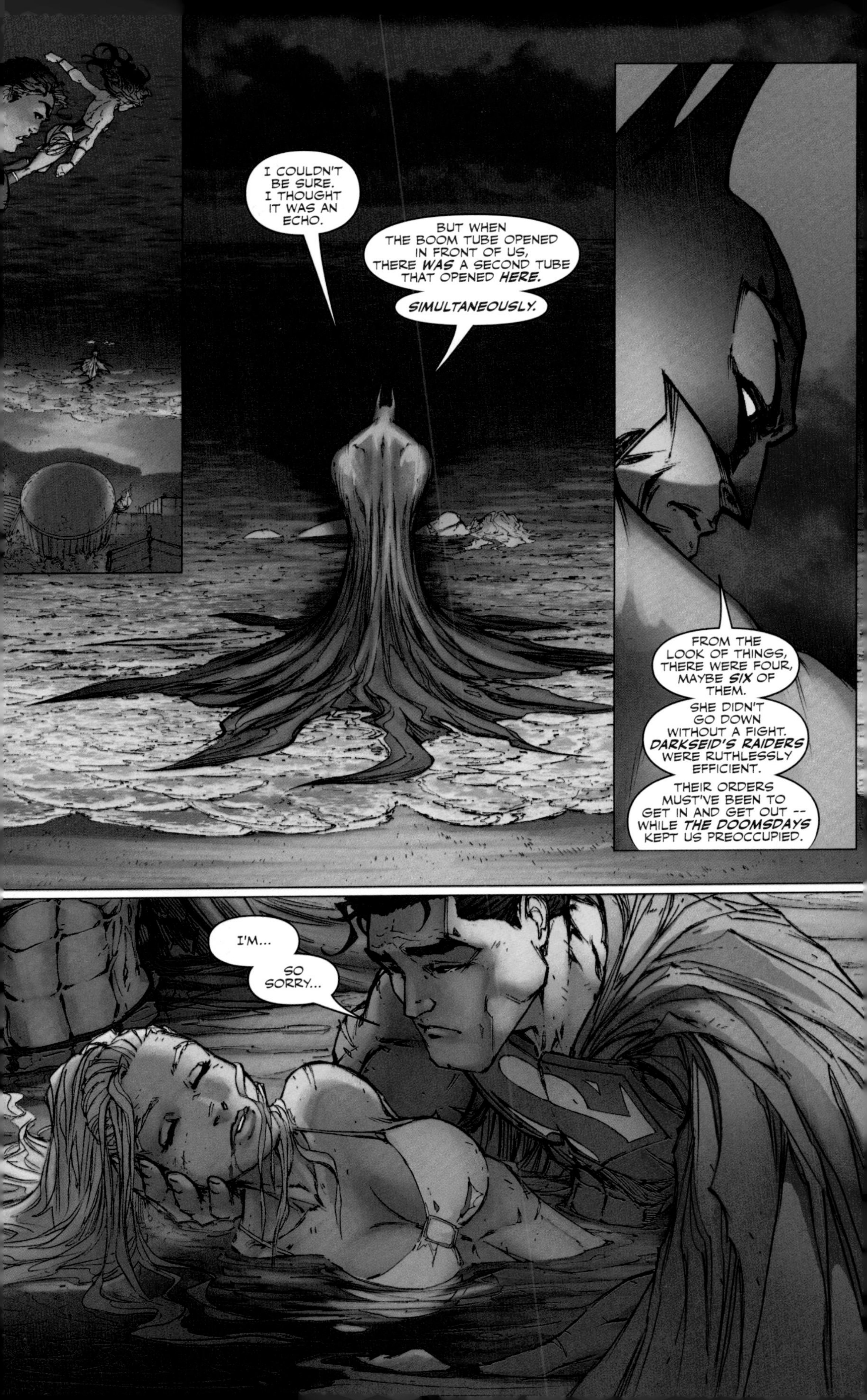
I COULDN'T BE SURE. I THOUGHT IT WAS AN ECHO.
BUT WHEN THE BOOM TUBE OPENED IN FRONT OF US, THERE *WAS* A SECOND TUBE THAT OPENED *HERE.*
SIMULTANEOUSLY.
FROM THE LOOK OF THINGS, THERE WERE FOUR, MAYBE *SIX* OF THEM.
SHE DIDN'T GO DOWN WITHOUT A FIGHT. *DARKSEID'S RAIDERS* WERE RUTHLESSLY EFFICIENT.
THEIR ORDERS MUST'VE BEEN TO GET IN AND GET OUT -- WHILE *THE DOOMSDAYS* KEPT US PREOCCUPIED.
I'M...
SO SORRY...

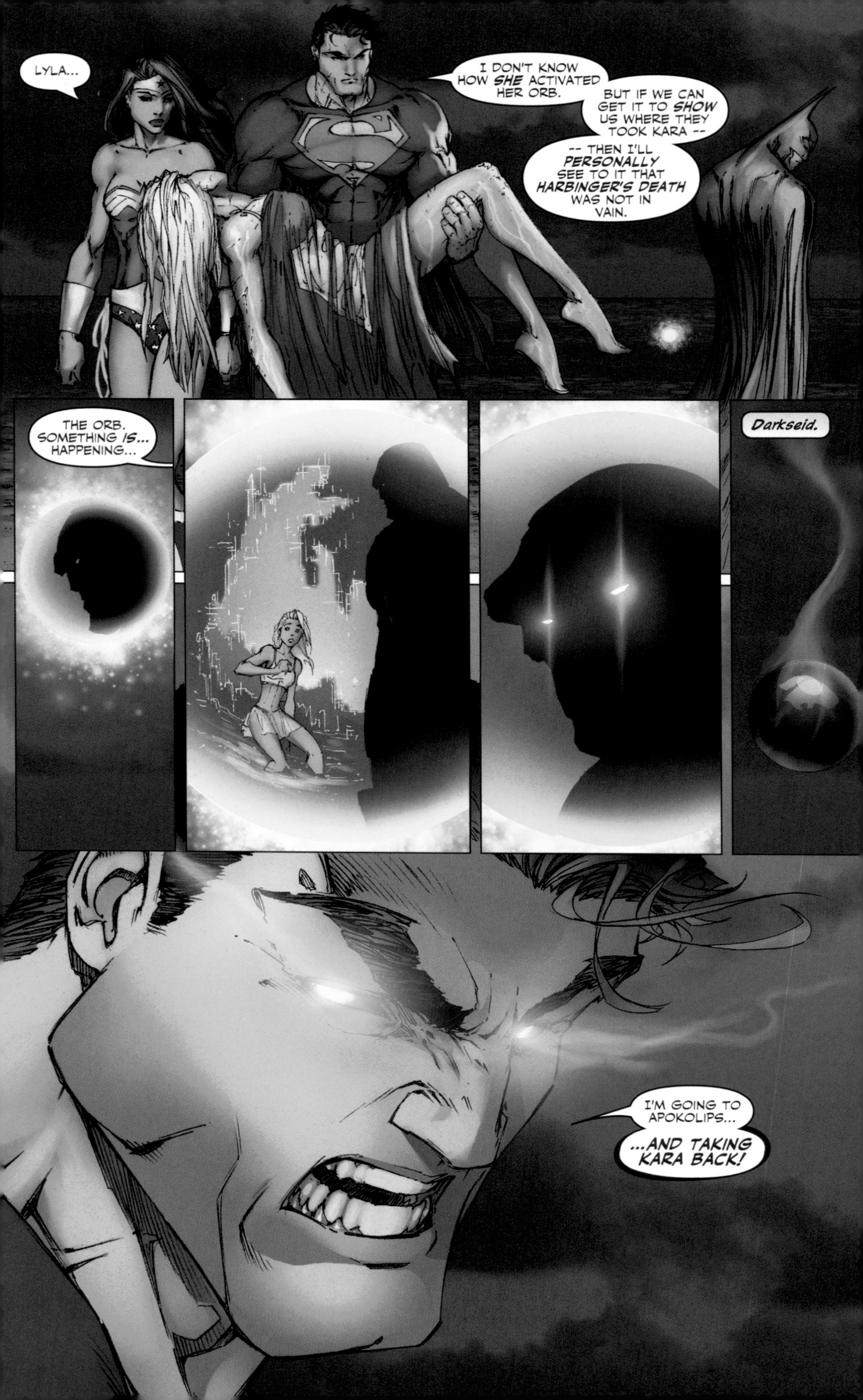
LYLA...
I DON'T KNOW HOW SHE ACTIVATED HER ORB.
BUT IF WE CAN GET IT TO SHOW US WHERE THEY TOOK KARA --
-- THEN I'LL PERSONALLY SEE TO IT THAT HARBINGER'S DEATH WAS NOT IN VAIN.
THE ORB. SOMETHING IS... HAPPENING...
Darkseid.
I'M GOING TO APOKOLIPS...
...AND TAKING KARA BACK!

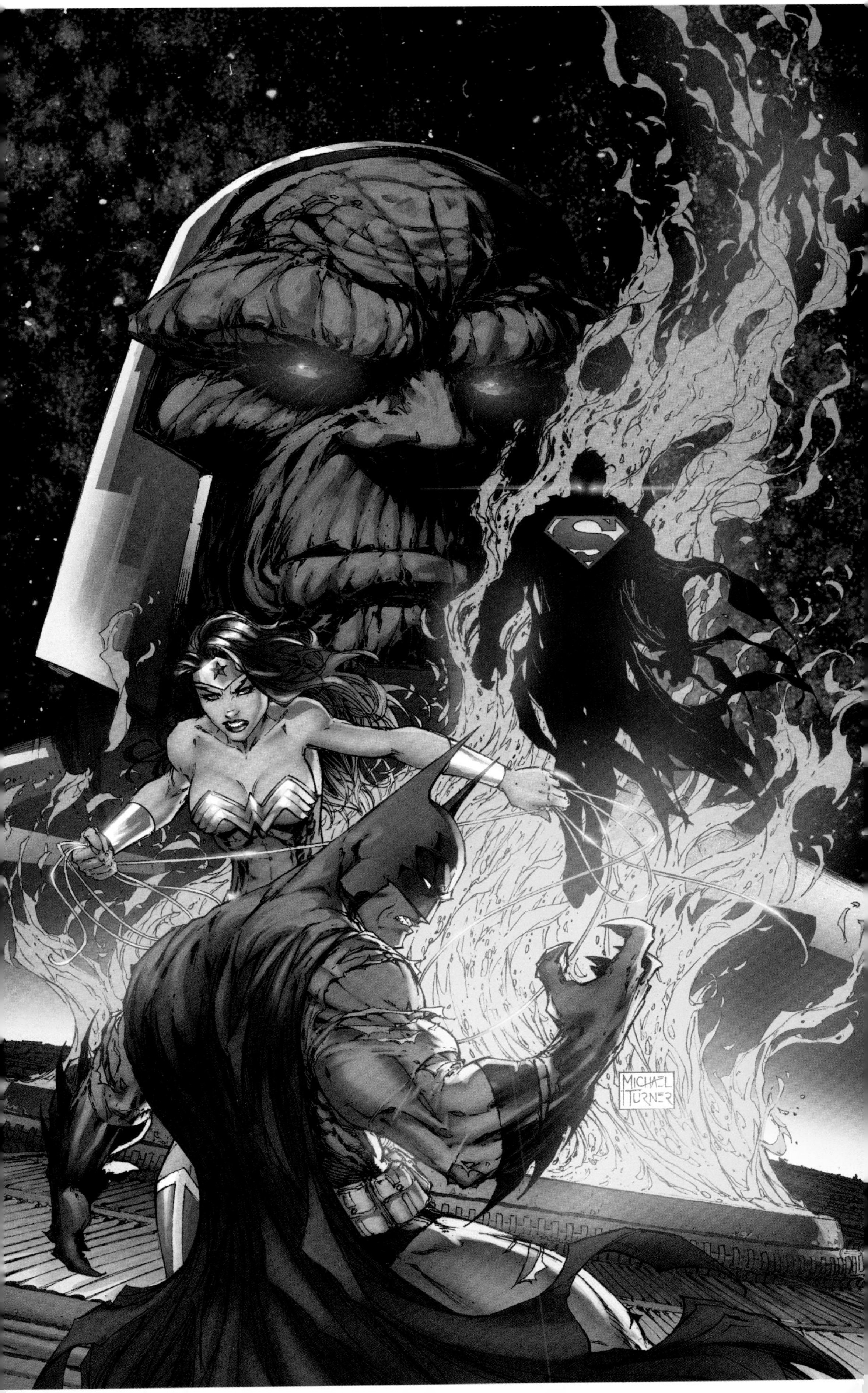
MICHAEL TURNER

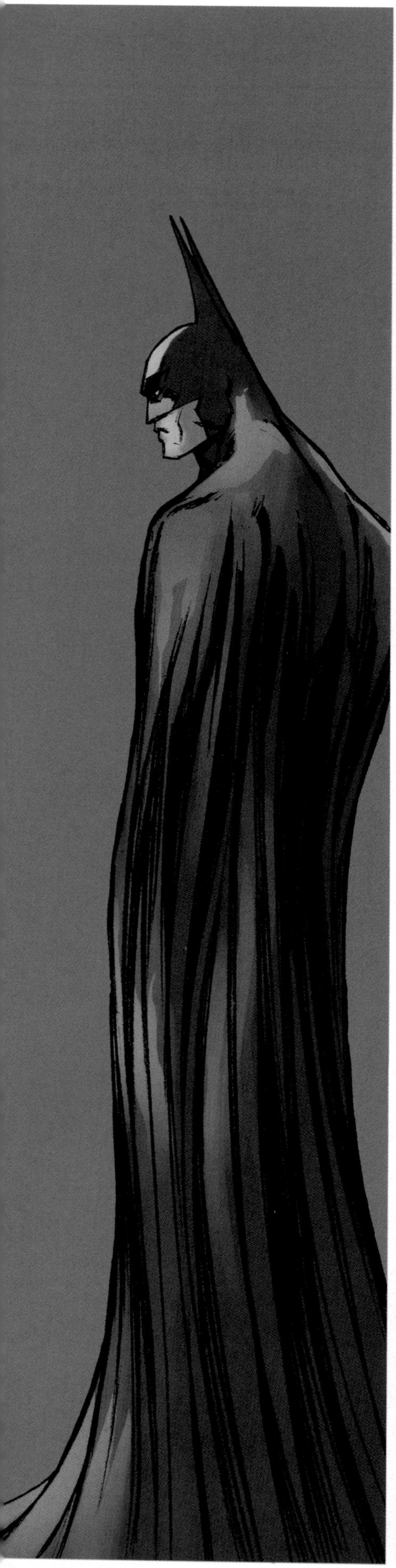

THE SUPERGIRL FROM KRYPTON

PART FOUR
PRISONER

JEPH LOEB
WRITER
MICHAEL TURNER
ARTIST
PETER STEIGERWALD
COLORIST
RICHARD STARKINGS
LETTERER
MICHAEL TURNER
WITH
PETER STEIGERWALD
COVER

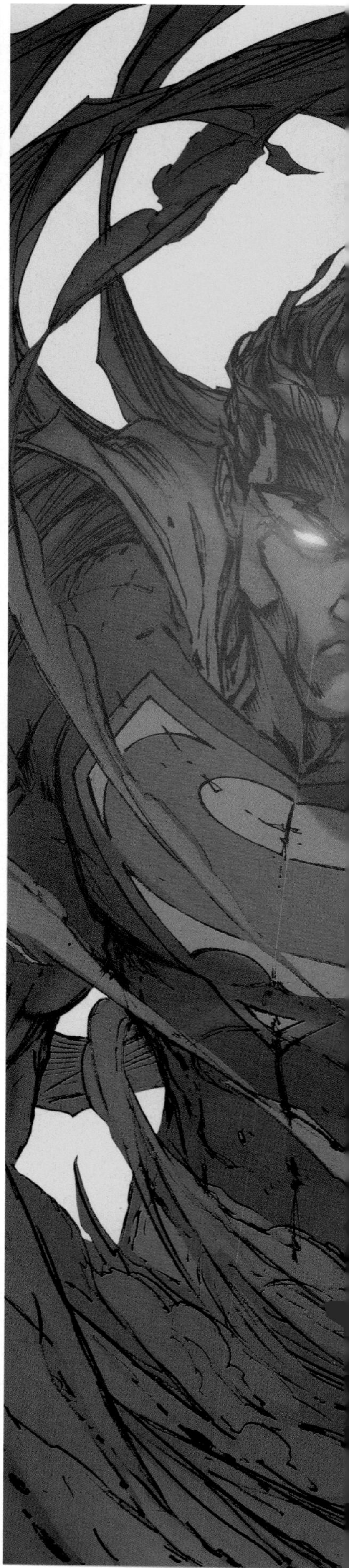

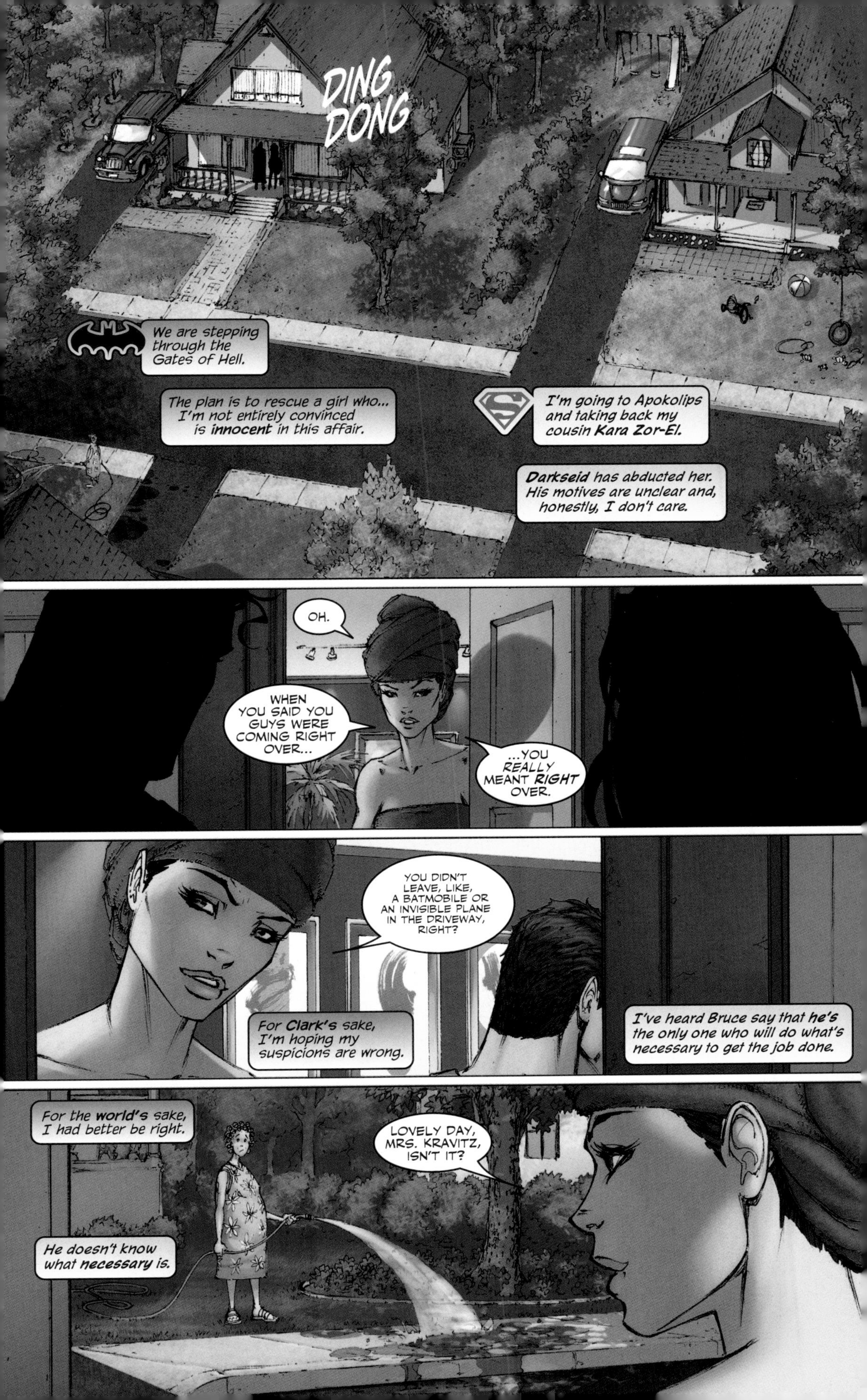

DING DONG
We are stepping through the Gates of Hell.
The plan is to rescue a girl who... I'm not entirely convinced is **innocent** in this affair.
I'm going to Apokolips and taking back my cousin **Kara Zor-El.**
Darkseid has abducted her. His motives are unclear and, honestly, I don't care.
OH.
WHEN YOU SAID YOU GUYS WERE COMING RIGHT OVER...
...YOU *REALLY* MEANT ***RIGHT*** OVER.
YOU DIDN'T LEAVE, LIKE, A BATMOBILE OR AN INVISIBLE PLANE IN THE DRIVEWAY, RIGHT?
For **Clark's** sake, I'm hoping my suspicions are wrong.
I've heard Bruce say that **he's** the only one who will do what's necessary to get the job done.
For the **world's** sake, I had better be right.
LOVELY DAY, MRS. KRAVITZ, ISN'T IT?
He doesn't know what **necessary** is.

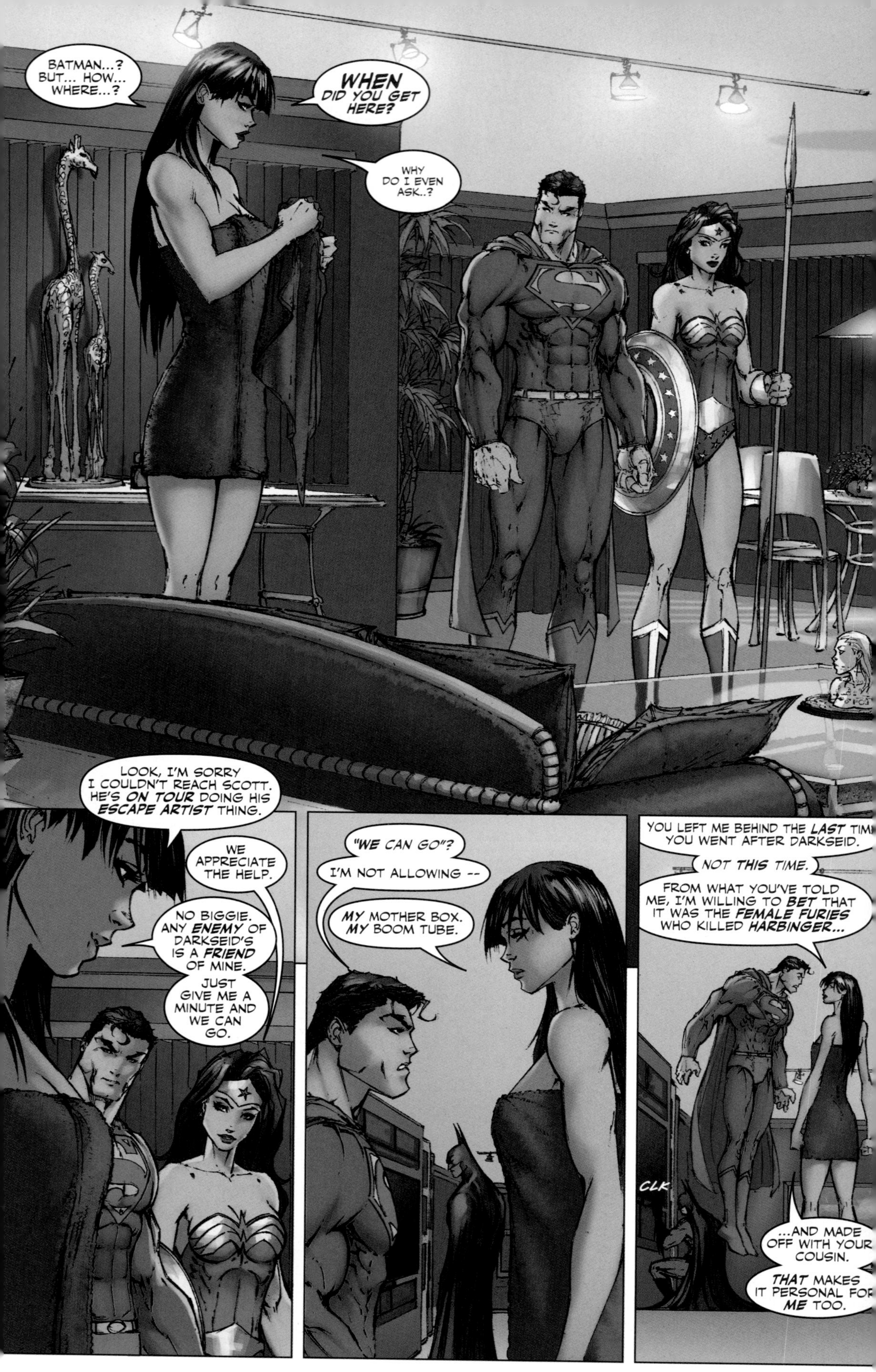

BATMAN...? BUT... HOW... WHERE...?
WHEN DID YOU GET HERE?
WHY DO I EVEN ASK..?
LOOK, I'M SORRY I COULDN'T REACH SCOTT. HE'S ON TOUR DOING HIS ESCAPE ARTIST THING.
WE APPRECIATE THE HELP.
NO BIGGIE. ANY ENEMY OF DARKSEID'S IS A FRIEND OF MINE.
JUST GIVE ME A MINUTE AND WE CAN GO.
"WE CAN GO"?
I'M NOT ALLOWING --
MY MOTHER BOX. MY BOOM TUBE.
YOU LEFT ME BEHIND THE LAST TIM YOU WENT AFTER DARKSEID.
NOT THIS TIME.
FROM WHAT YOU'VE TOLD ME, I'M WILLING TO BET THAT IT WAS THE FEMALE FURIES WHO KILLED HARBINGER...
CLK
...AND MADE OFF WITH YOUR COUSIN.
THAT MAKES IT PERSONAL FOR ME TOO.

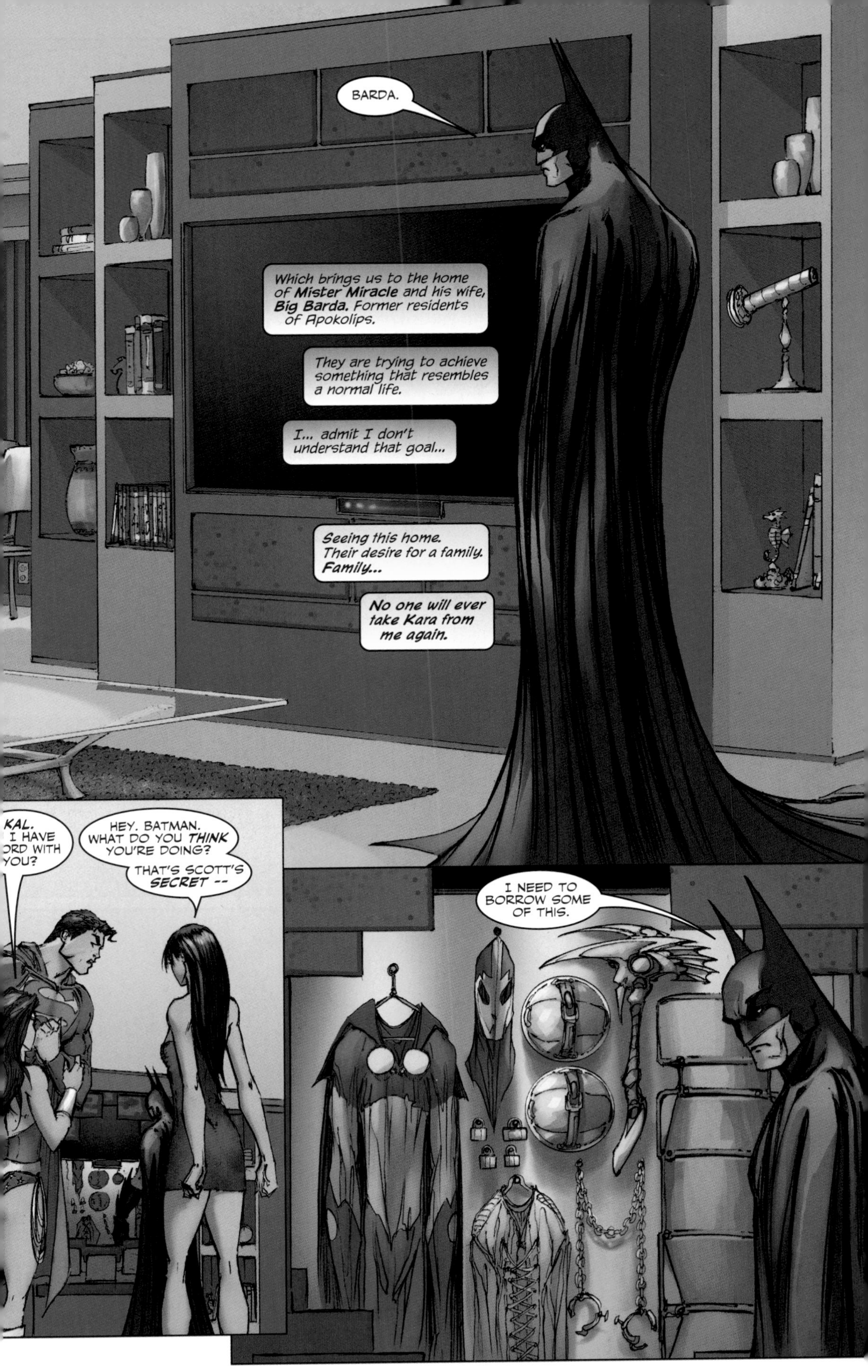
BARDA.
Which brings us to the home of **Mister Miracle** and his wife, **Big Barda.** Former residents of Apokolips.
They are trying to achieve something that resembles a normal life.
I... admit I don't understand that goal...
Seeing this home. Their desire for a family. **Family...**
No one will ever take Kara from me again.
KAL. I HAVE ORD WITH YOU?
HEY. BATMAN. WHAT DO YOU *THINK* YOU'RE DOING?
THAT'S SCOTT'S *SECRET* --
I NEED TO BORROW SOME OF THIS.

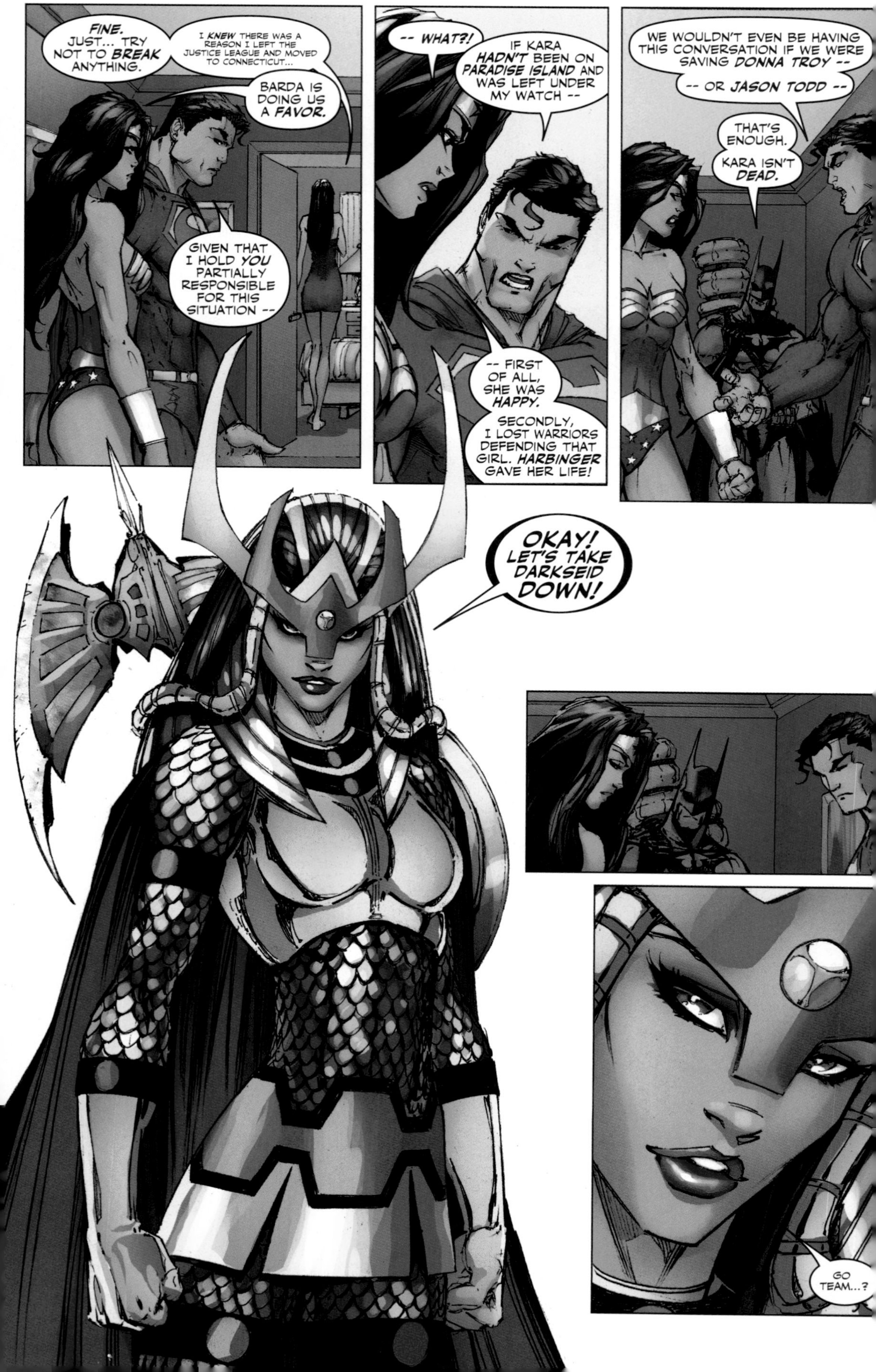
FINE. JUST... TRY NOT TO BREAK ANYTHING.
I KNEW THERE WAS A REASON I LEFT THE JUSTICE LEAGUE AND MOVED TO CONNECTICUT...
BARDA IS DOING US A FAVOR.
GIVEN THAT I HOLD YOU PARTIALLY RESPONSIBLE FOR THIS SITUATION --
-- WHAT?!
IF KARA HADN'T BEEN ON PARADISE ISLAND AND WAS LEFT UNDER MY WATCH --
-- FIRST OF ALL, SHE WAS HAPPY.
SECONDLY, I LOST WARRIORS DEFENDING THAT GIRL. HARBINGER GAVE HER LIFE!
WE WOULDN'T EVEN BE HAVING THIS CONVERSATION IF WE WERE SAVING DONNA TROY --
-- OR JASON TODD --
THAT'S ENOUGH.
KARA ISN'T DEAD.
OKAY! LET'S TAKE DARKSEID DOWN!
GO TEAM...?

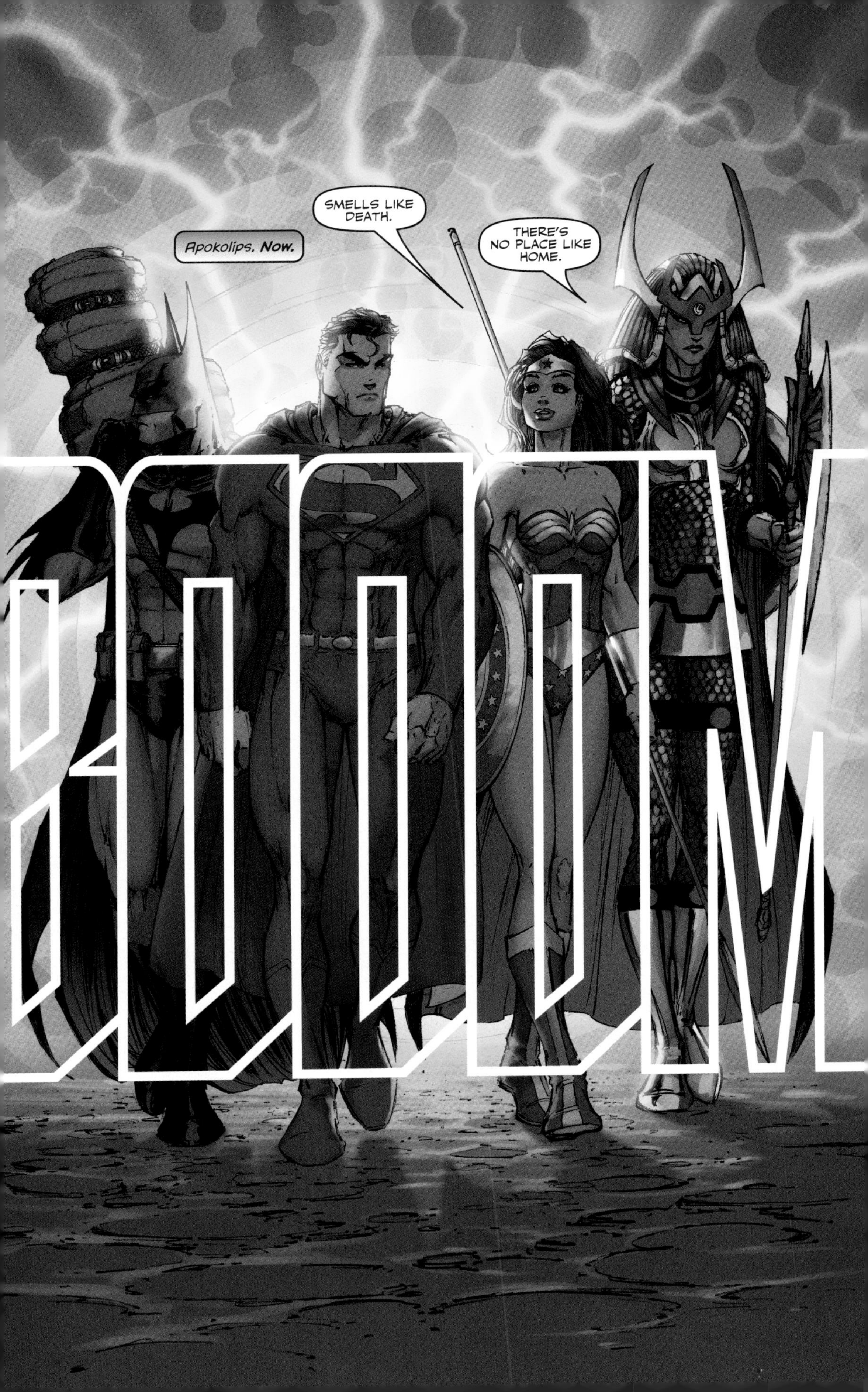
Apokolips. Now.
SMELLS LIKE DEATH.
THERE'S NO PLACE LIKE HOME.
BOOOM

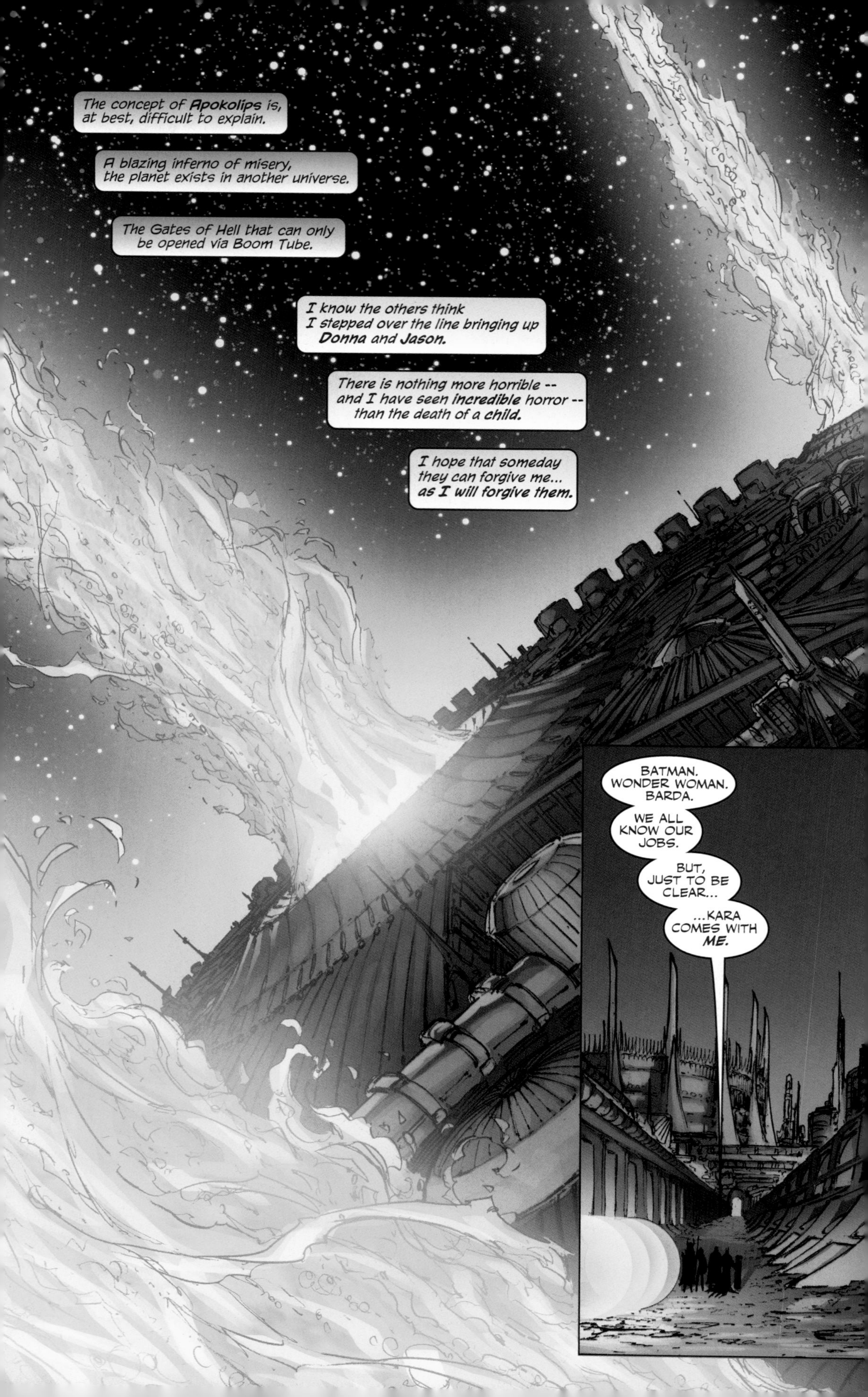
The concept of Apokolips is, at best, difficult to explain.
A blazing inferno of misery, the planet exists in another universe.
The Gates of Hell that can only be opened via Boom Tube.
I know the others think I stepped over the line bringing up Donna and Jason.
There is nothing more horrible -- and I have seen incredible horror -- than the death of a child.
I hope that someday they can forgive me... as I will forgive them.
BATMAN. WONDER WOMAN. BARDA.
WE ALL KNOW OUR JOBS.
BUT, JUST TO BE CLEAR...
...KARA COMES WITH ME.

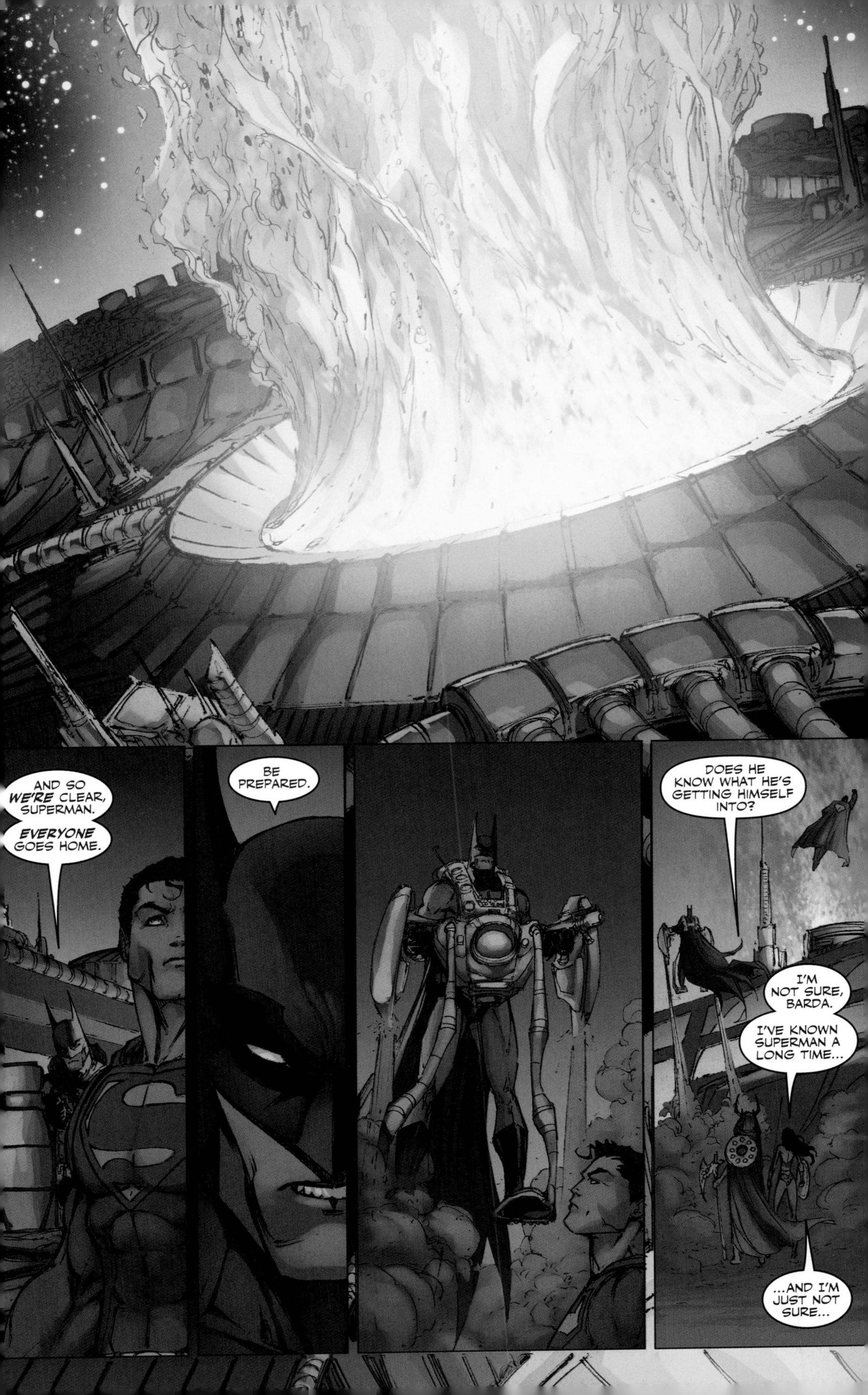
AND SO *WE'RE* CLEAR, SUPERMAN.
EVERYONE GOES HOME.
BE PREPARED.
DOES HE KNOW WHAT HE'S GETTING HIMSELF INTO?
I'M NOT SURE, BARDA.
I'VE KNOWN SUPERMAN A LONG TIME...
...AND I'M JUST NOT SURE...

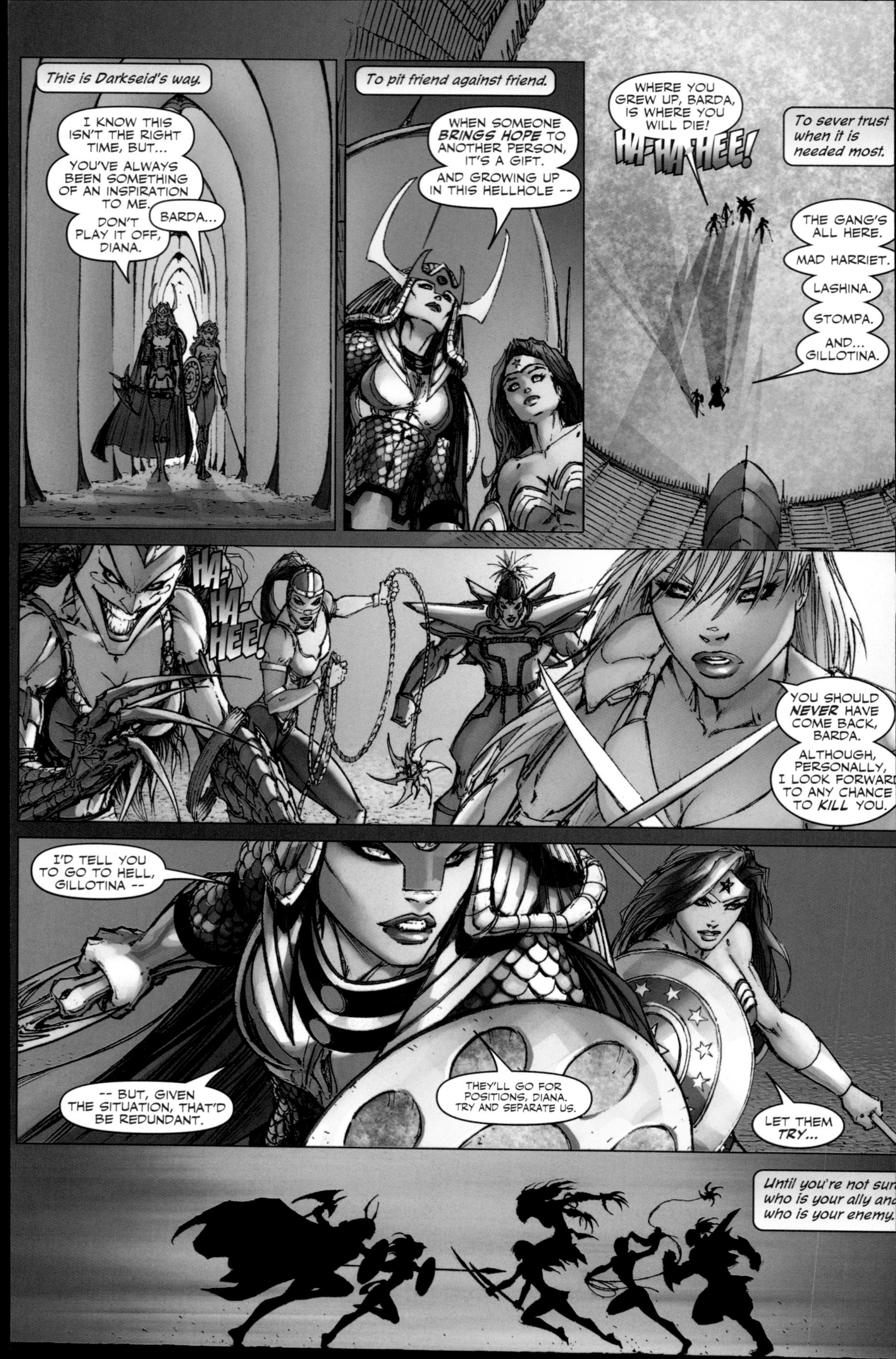
This is Darkseid's way.
I KNOW THIS ISN'T THE RIGHT TIME, BUT...
YOU'VE ALWAYS BEEN SOMETHING OF AN INSPIRATION TO ME.
BARDA...
DON'T PLAY IT OFF, DIANA.
To pit friend against friend.
WHEN SOMEONE BRINGS HOPE TO ANOTHER PERSON, IT'S A GIFT.
AND GROWING UP IN THIS HELLHOLE --
WHERE YOU GREW UP, BARDA, IS WHERE YOU WILL DIE!
HA-HA-HEE!
To sever trust when it is needed most.
THE GANG'S ALL HERE.
MAD HARRIET.
LASHINA.
STOMPA.
AND... GILLOTINA.
HA-HA-HEE!
YOU SHOULD NEVER HAVE COME BACK, BARDA.
ALTHOUGH, PERSONALLY, I LOOK FORWARD TO ANY CHANCE TO KILL YOU.
I'D TELL YOU TO GO TO HELL, GILLOTINA --
-- BUT, GIVEN THE SITUATION, THAT'D BE REDUNDANT.
THEY'LL GO FOR POSITIONS, DIANA. TRY AND SEPARATE US.
LET THEM TRY...
Until you're not sur
who is your ally and
who is your enemy.

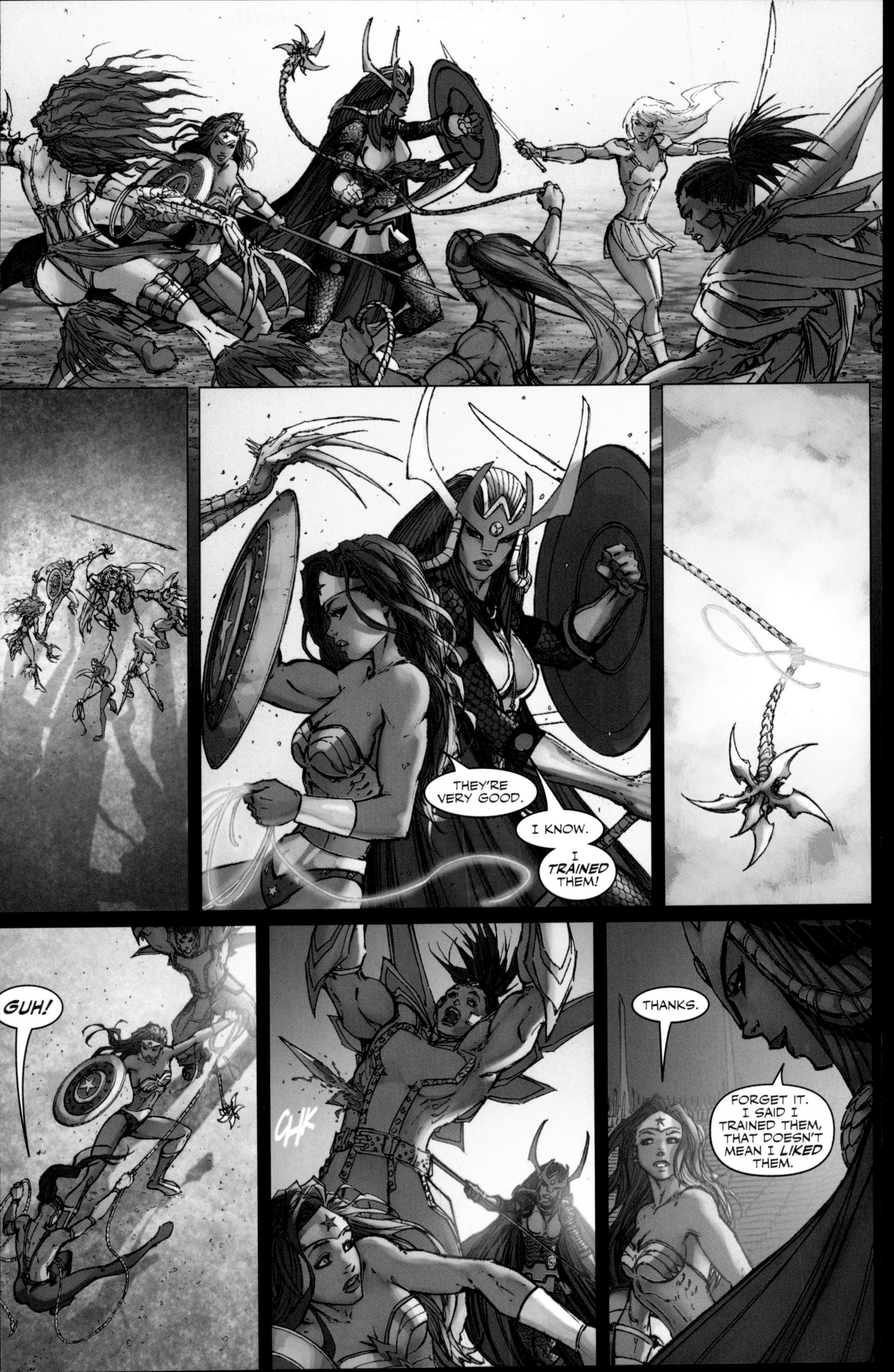
THEY'RE VERY GOOD.
I KNOW.
I *TRAINED* THEM!
GUH!
CHK
THANKS.
FORGET IT. I SAID I TRAINED THEM, THAT DOESN'T MEAN I *LIKED* THEM.

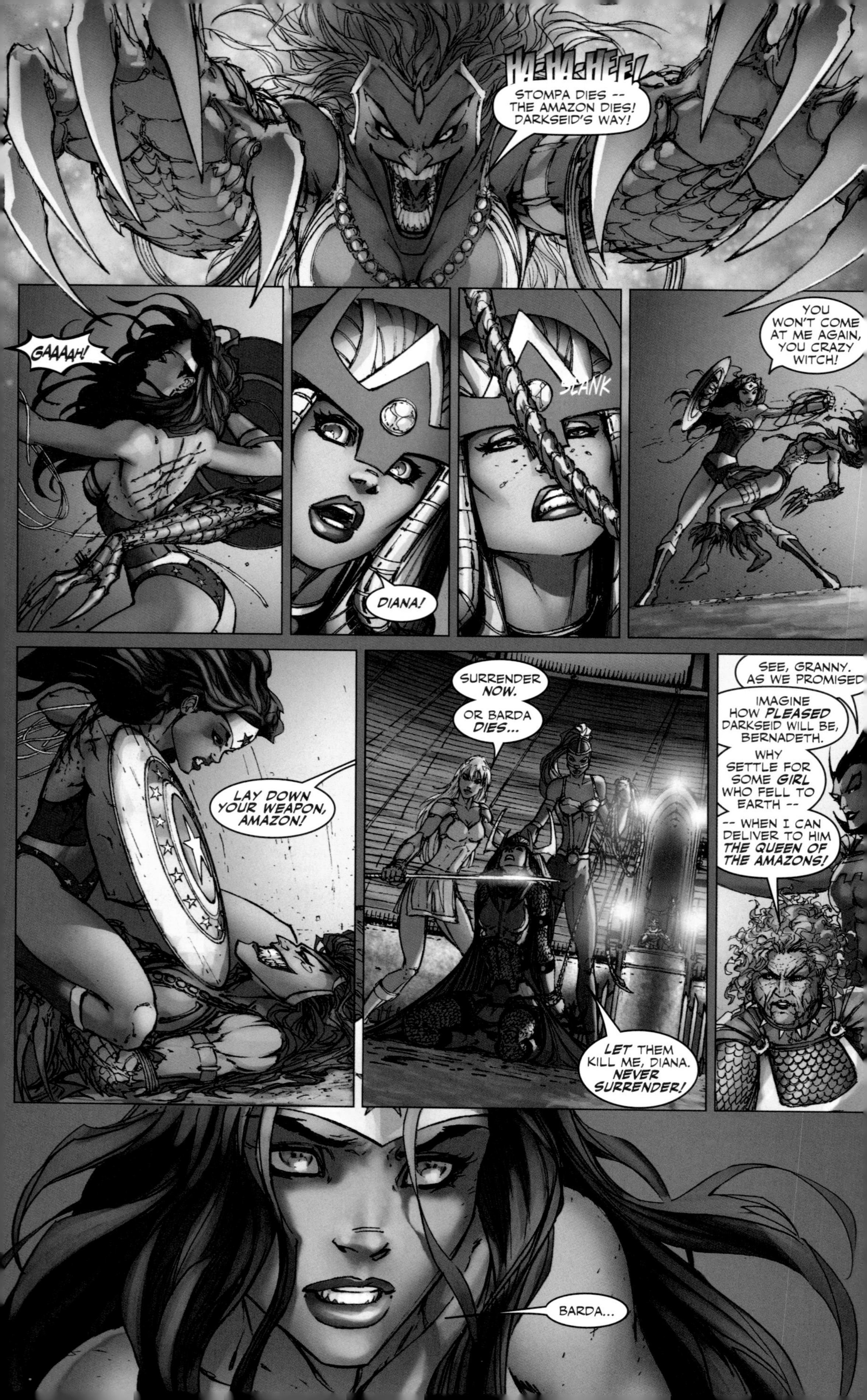
HA-HA-HEE!
STOMPA DIES -- THE AMAZON DIES! DARKSEID'S WAY!
GAAAAH!
DIANA!
SKANK
YOU WON'T COME AT ME AGAIN, YOU CRAZY WITCH!
LAY DOWN YOUR WEAPON, AMAZON!
SURRENDER NOW.
OR BARDA DIES...
LET THEM KILL ME, DIANA. NEVER SURRENDER!
SEE, GRANNY. AS WE PROMISED
IMAGINE HOW PLEASED DARKSEID WILL BE, BERNADETH.
WHY SETTLE FOR SOME GIRL WHO FELL TO EARTH --
-- WHEN I CAN DELIVER TO HIM THE QUEEN OF THE AMAZONS!
BARDA...

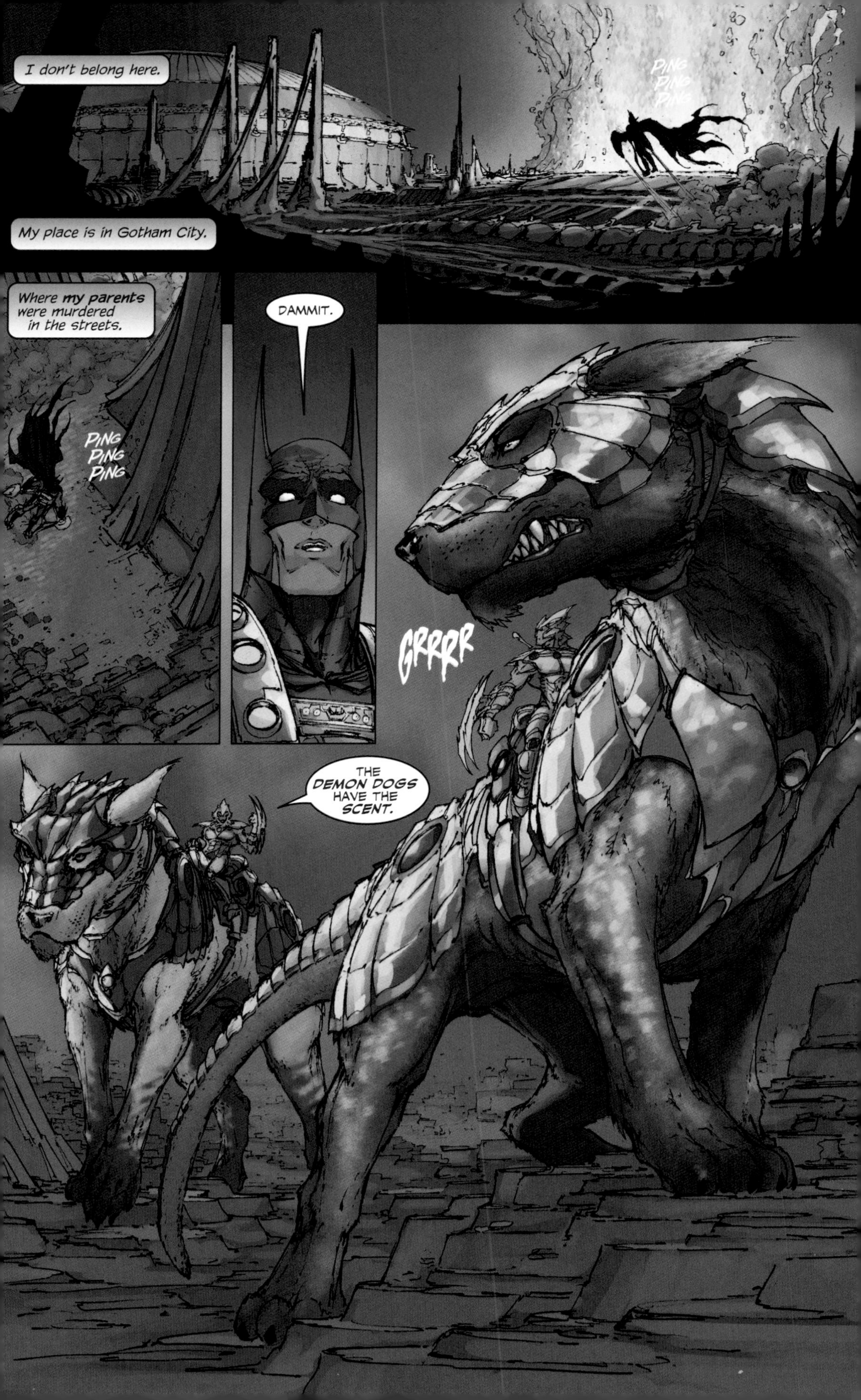
I don't belong here.
PING
PING
PING
My place is in Gotham City.
Where my parents were murdered in the streets.
PING
PING
PING
DAMMIT.
GRRRR
THE DEMON DOGS HAVE THE SCENT.

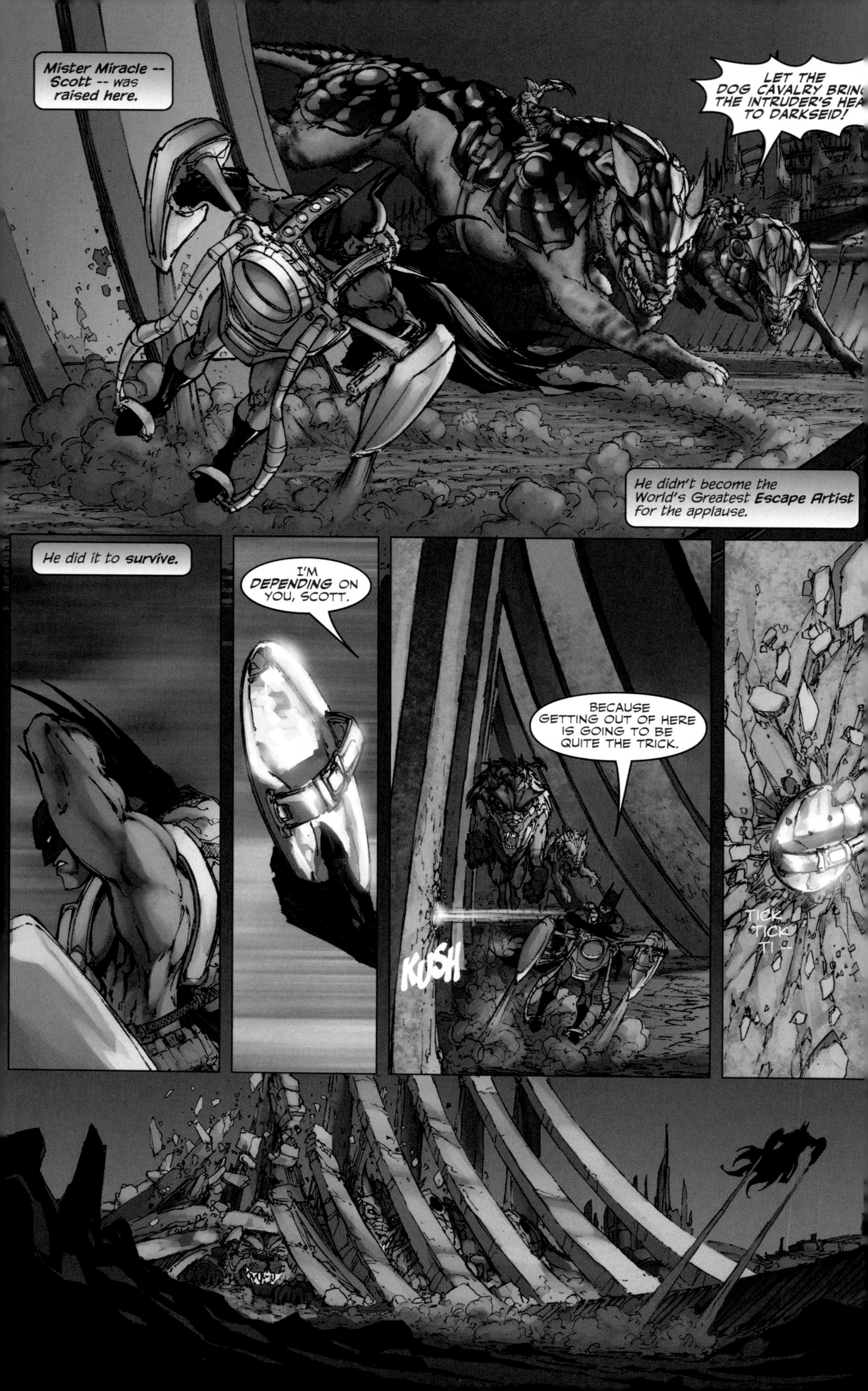
Mister Miracle -- Scott -- was raised here.
LET THE DOG CAVALRY BRIN THE INTRUDER'S HEA TO DARKSEID!
He didn't become the World's Greatest Escape Artist for the applause.
He did it to survive.
I'M DEPENDING ON YOU, SCOTT.
BECAUSE GETTING OUT OF HERE IS GOING TO BE QUITE THE TRICK.
KUSH
TICK TICK TI--

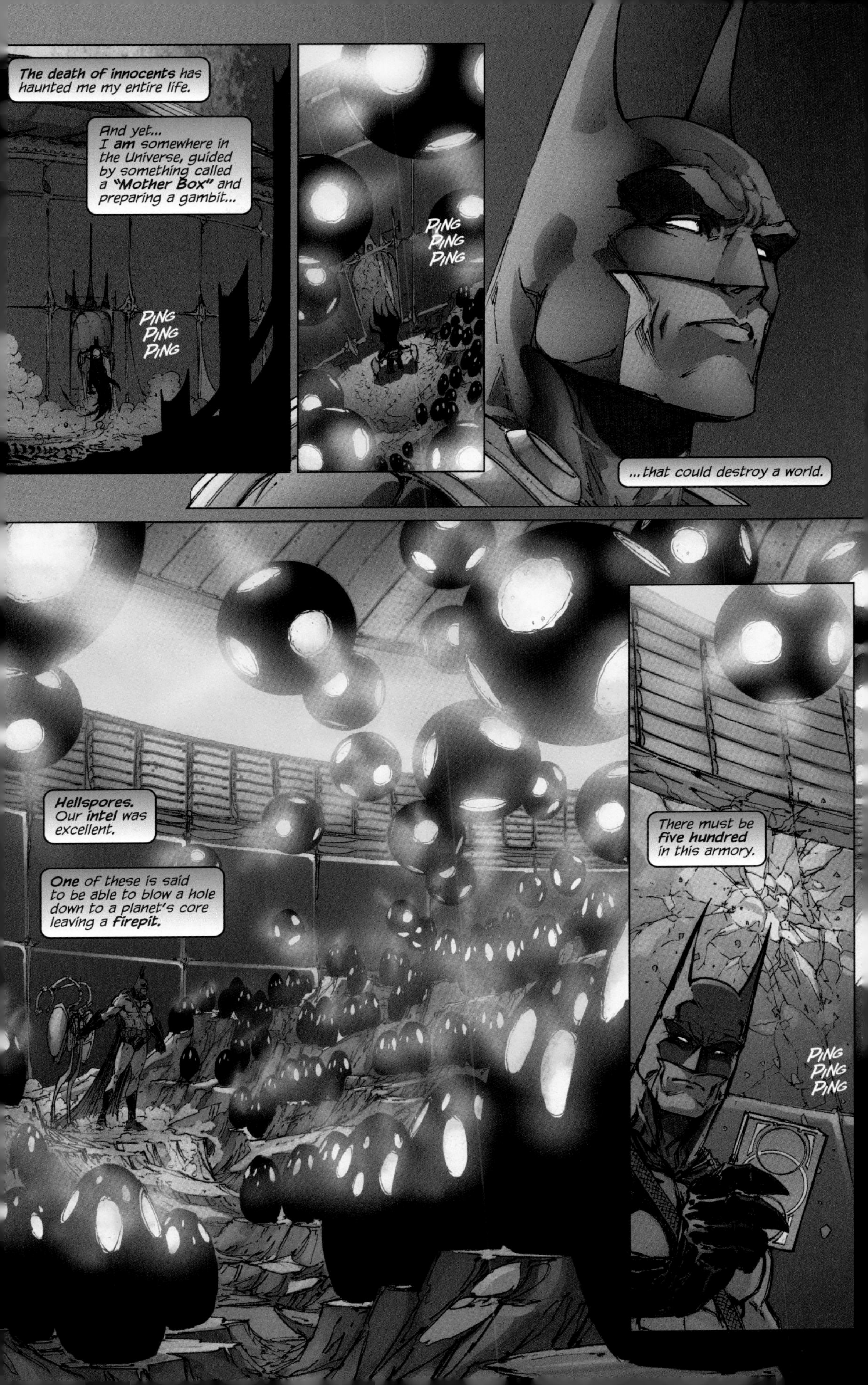
The death of innocents has haunted me my entire life.
And yet... I am somewhere in the Universe, guided by something called a "Mother Box" and preparing a gambit...
PING PING PING
PING PING PING
...that could destroy a world.
Hellspores. Our intel was excellent.
One of these is said to be able to blow a hole down to a planet's core leaving a firepit.
There must be five hundred in this armory.
PING PING PING

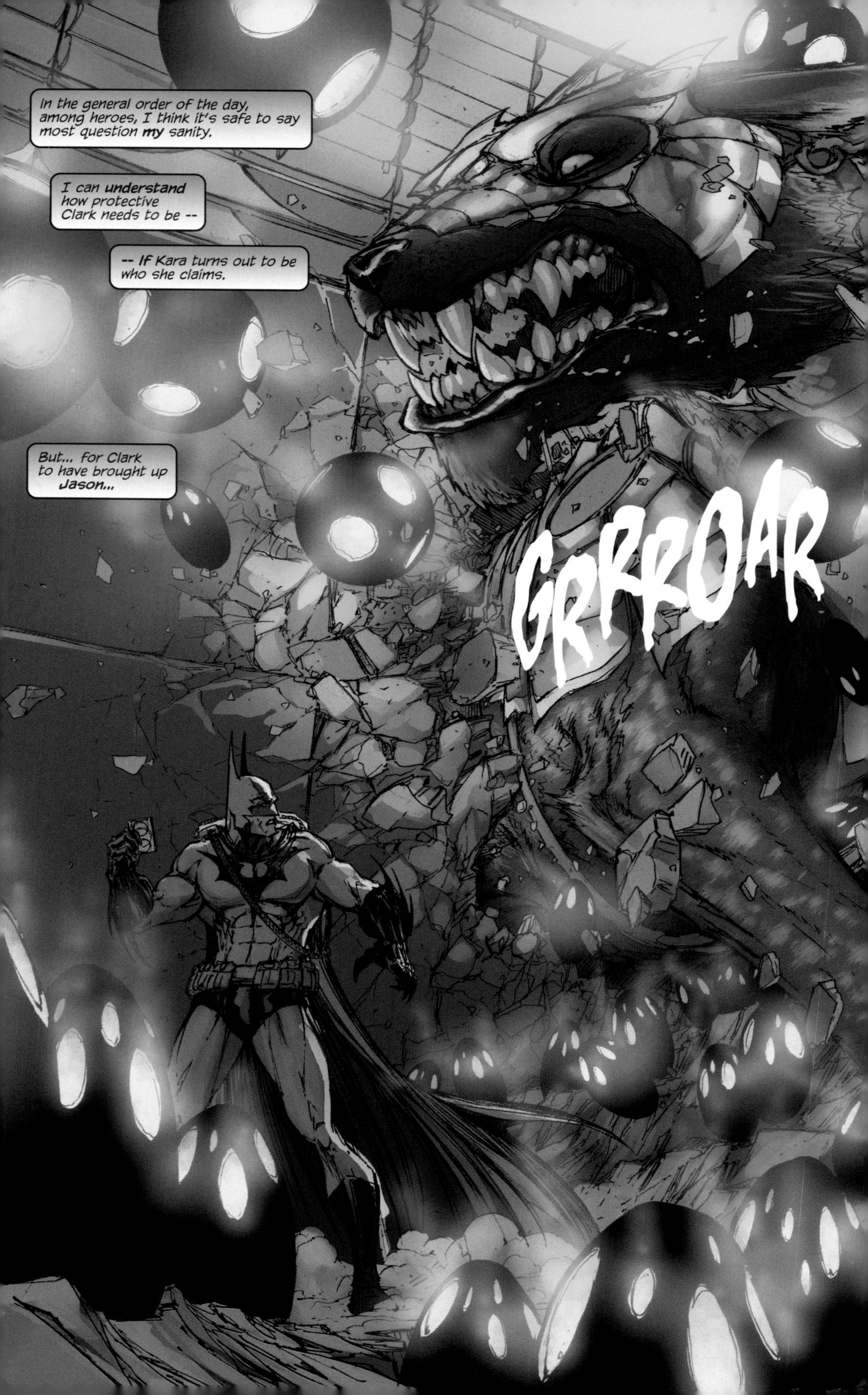

In the general order of the day, among heroes, I think it's safe to say most question **my** sanity.
I can **understand** how protective Clark needs to be --
-- **If** Kara turns out to be who she claims.
But... for Clark to have brought up **Jason**...
GRRROAR

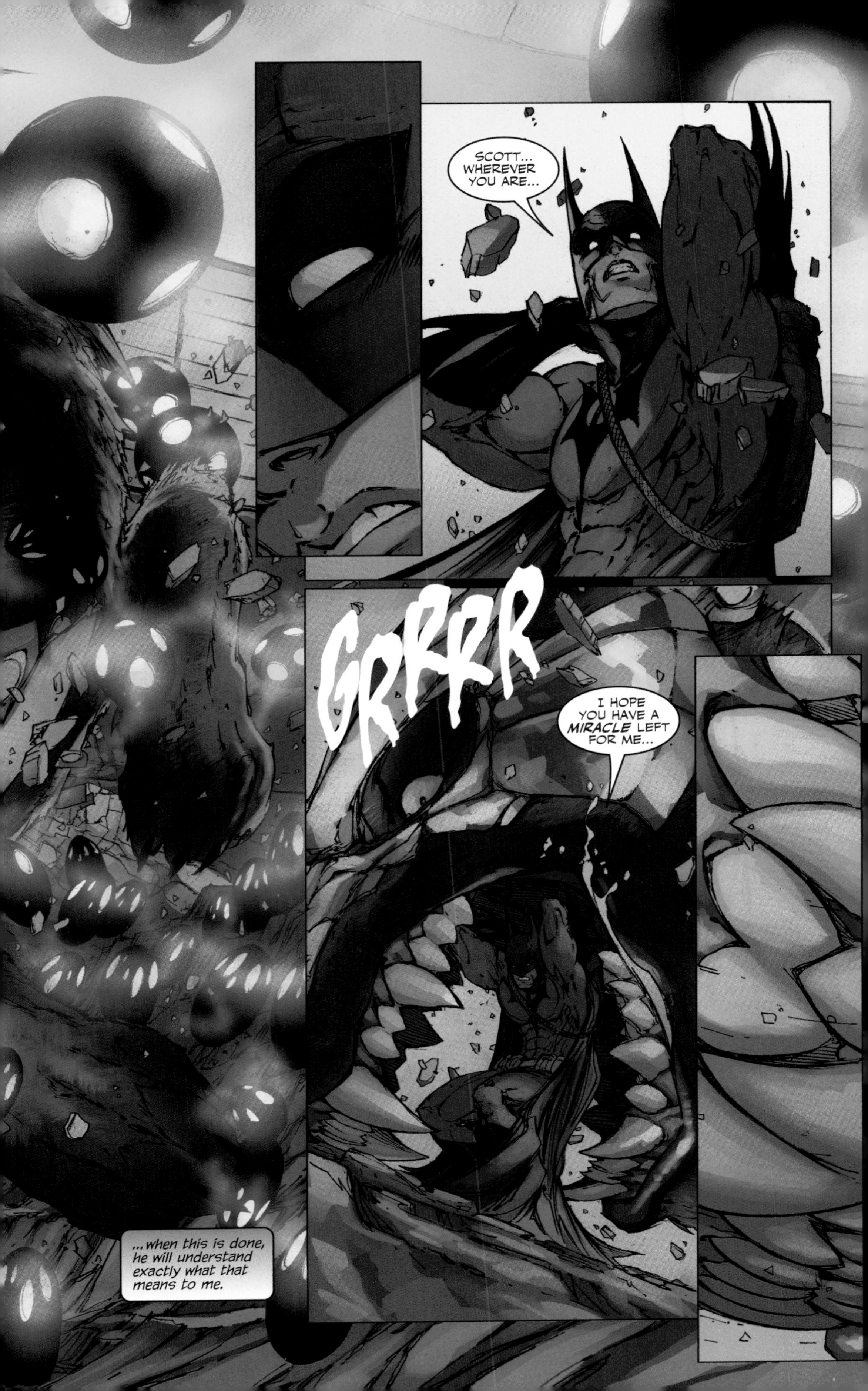
SCOTT... WHEREVER YOU ARE...
GRRRR
I HOPE YOU HAVE A MIRACLE LEFT FOR ME...
...when this is done, he will understand exactly what that means to me.

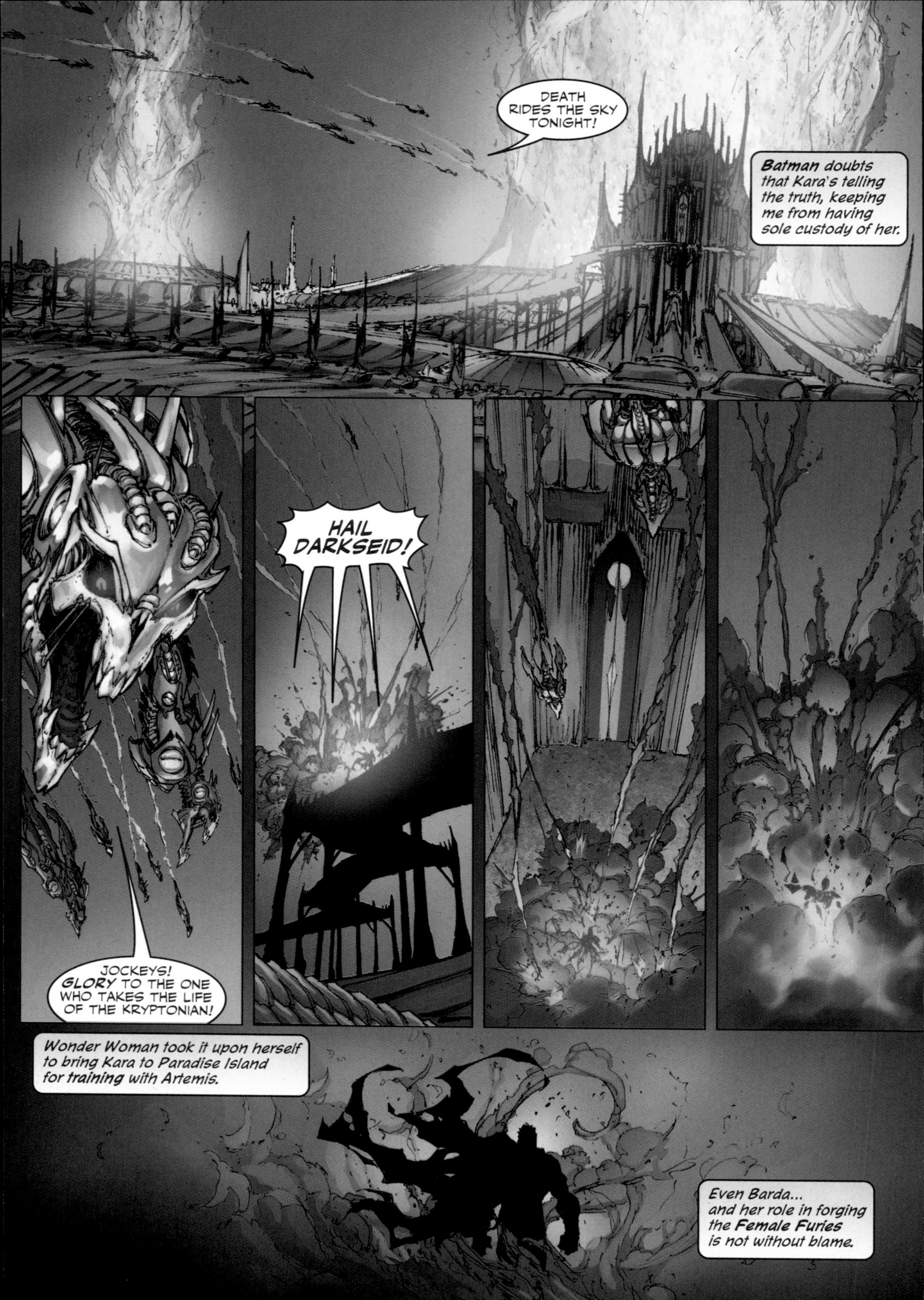
DEATH RIDES THE SKY TONIGHT!
Batman doubts that Kara's telling the truth, keeping me from having sole custody of her.
JOCKEYS! GLORY TO THE ONE WHO TAKES THE LIFE OF THE KRYPTONIAN!
HAIL DARKSEID!
Wonder Woman took it upon herself to bring Kara to Paradise Island for training with Artemis.
Even Barda... and her role in forging the Female Furies is not without blame.

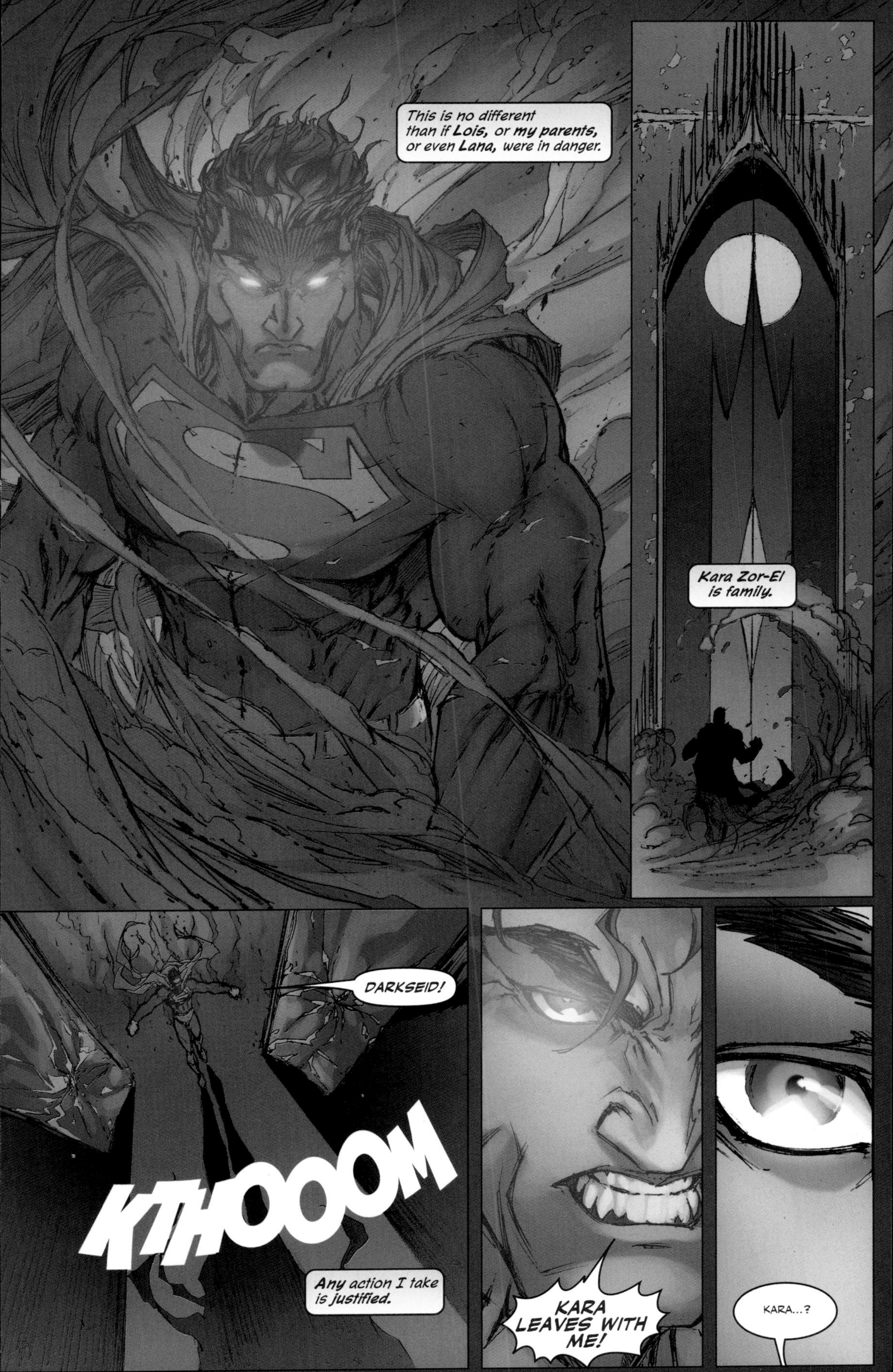
This is no different than if Lois, or my parents, or even Lana, were in danger.
Kara Zor-El is family.
DARKSEID!
KTHOOOM
Any action I take is justified.
KARA LEAVES WITH ME!
KARA...?

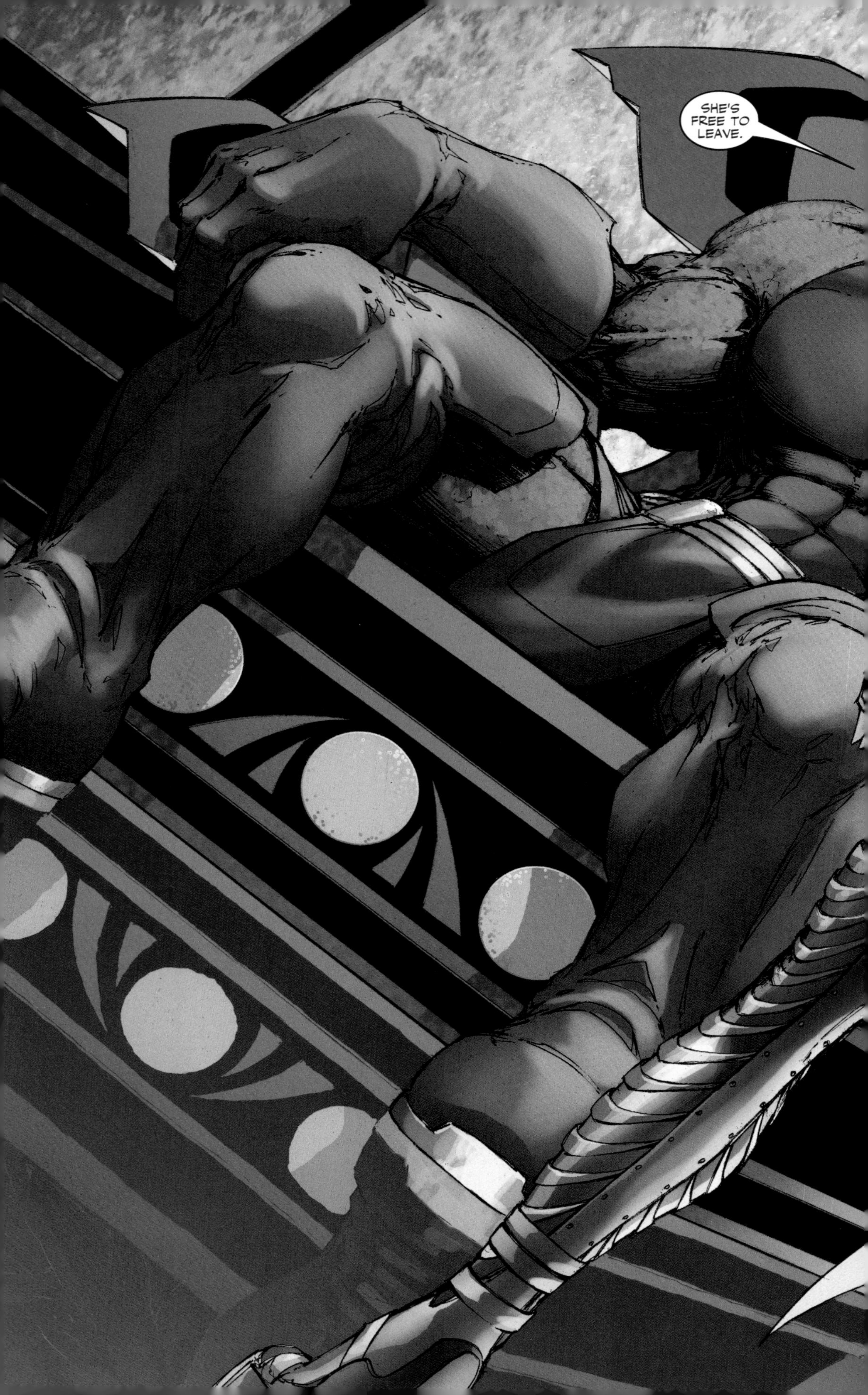
SHE'S FREE TO LEAVE.

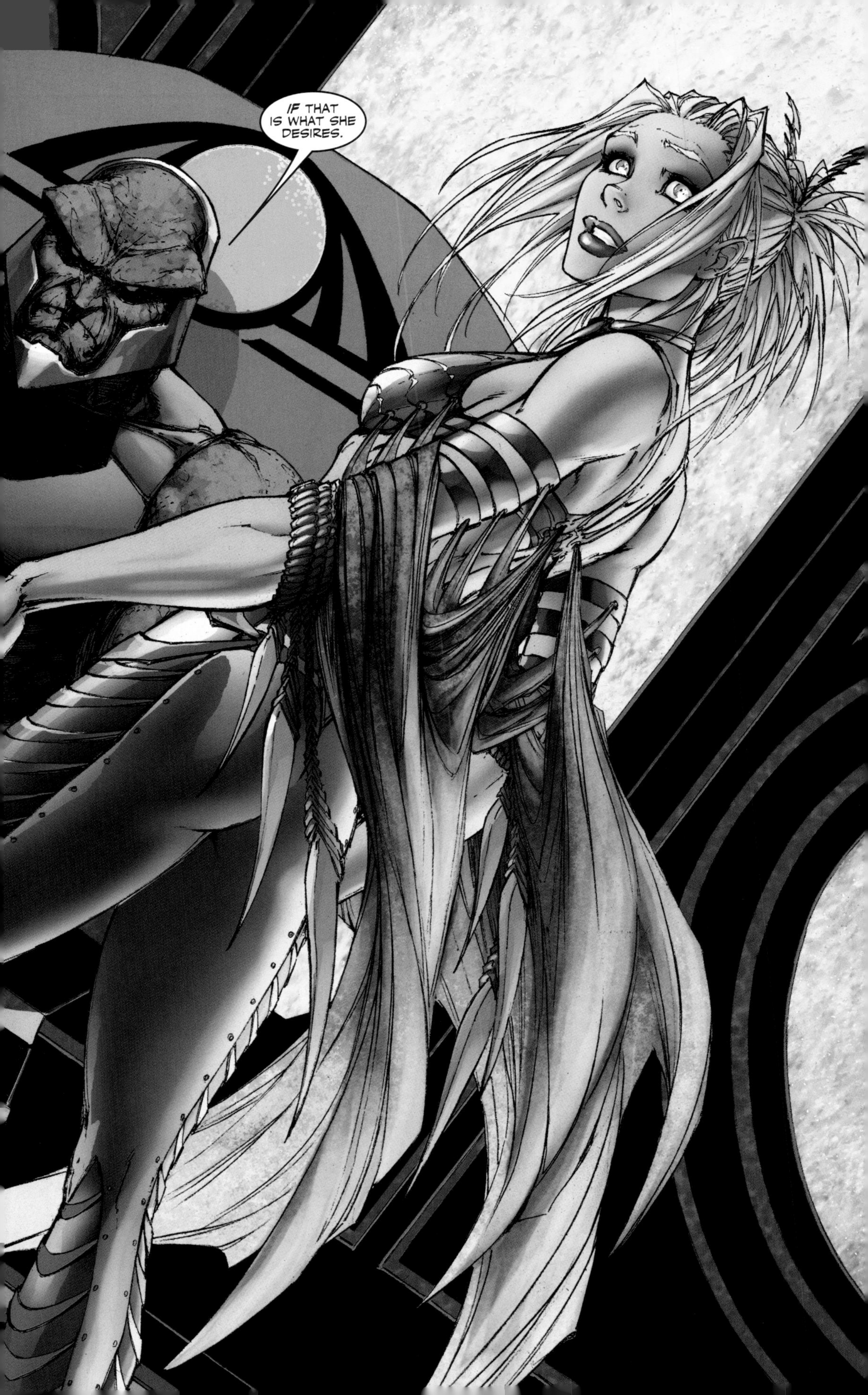
IF THAT IS WHAT SHE DESIRES.

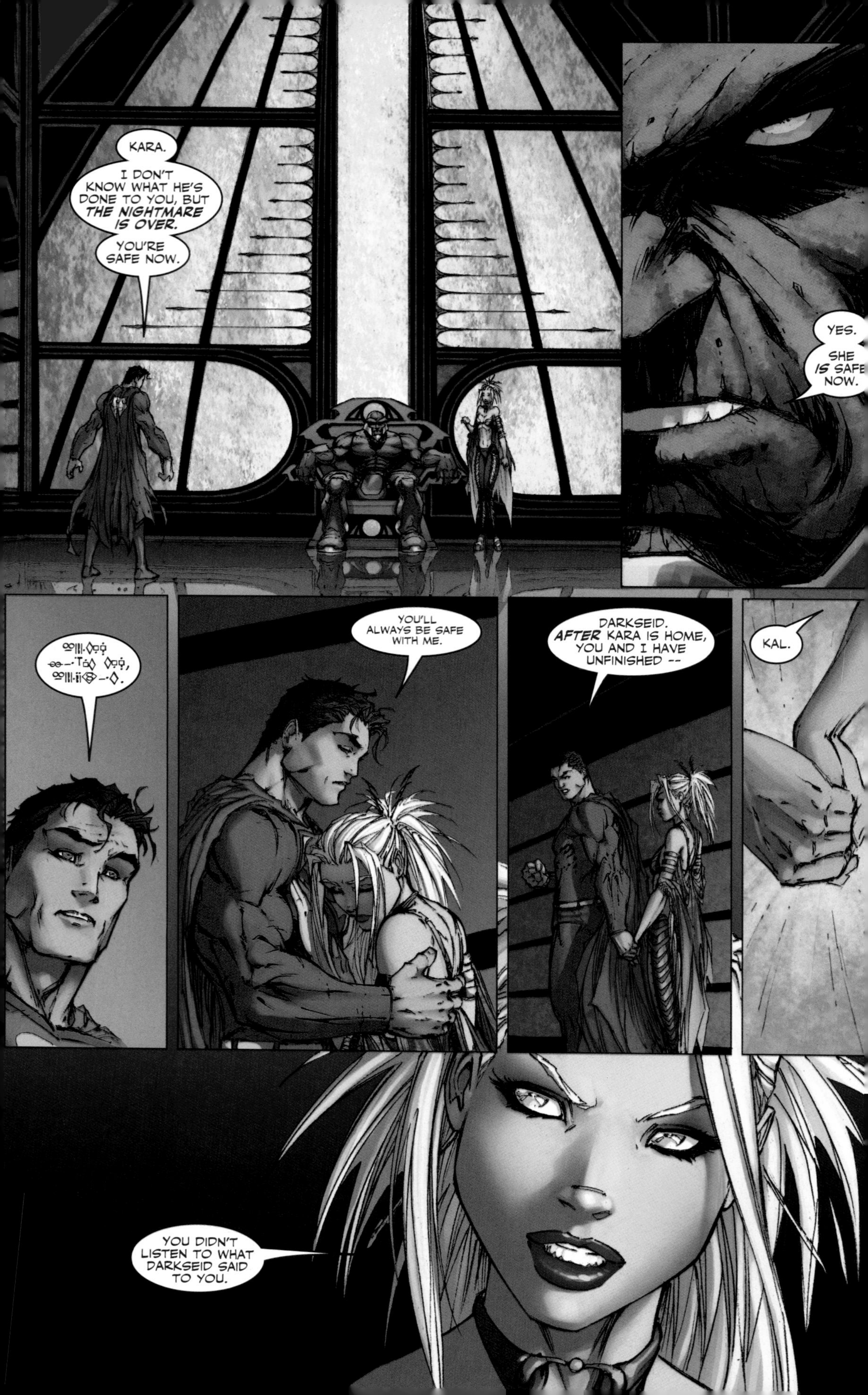
KARA.
I DON'T KNOW WHAT HE'S DONE TO YOU, BUT ***THE NIGHTMARE IS OVER.***
YOU'RE SAFE NOW.
YES.
SHE ***IS*** SAFE NOW.
YOU'LL ALWAYS BE SAFE WITH ME.
DARKSEID. ***AFTER*** KARA IS HOME, YOU AND I HAVE UNFINISHED --
KAL.
YOU DIDN'T LISTEN TO WHAT DARKSEID SAID TO YOU.

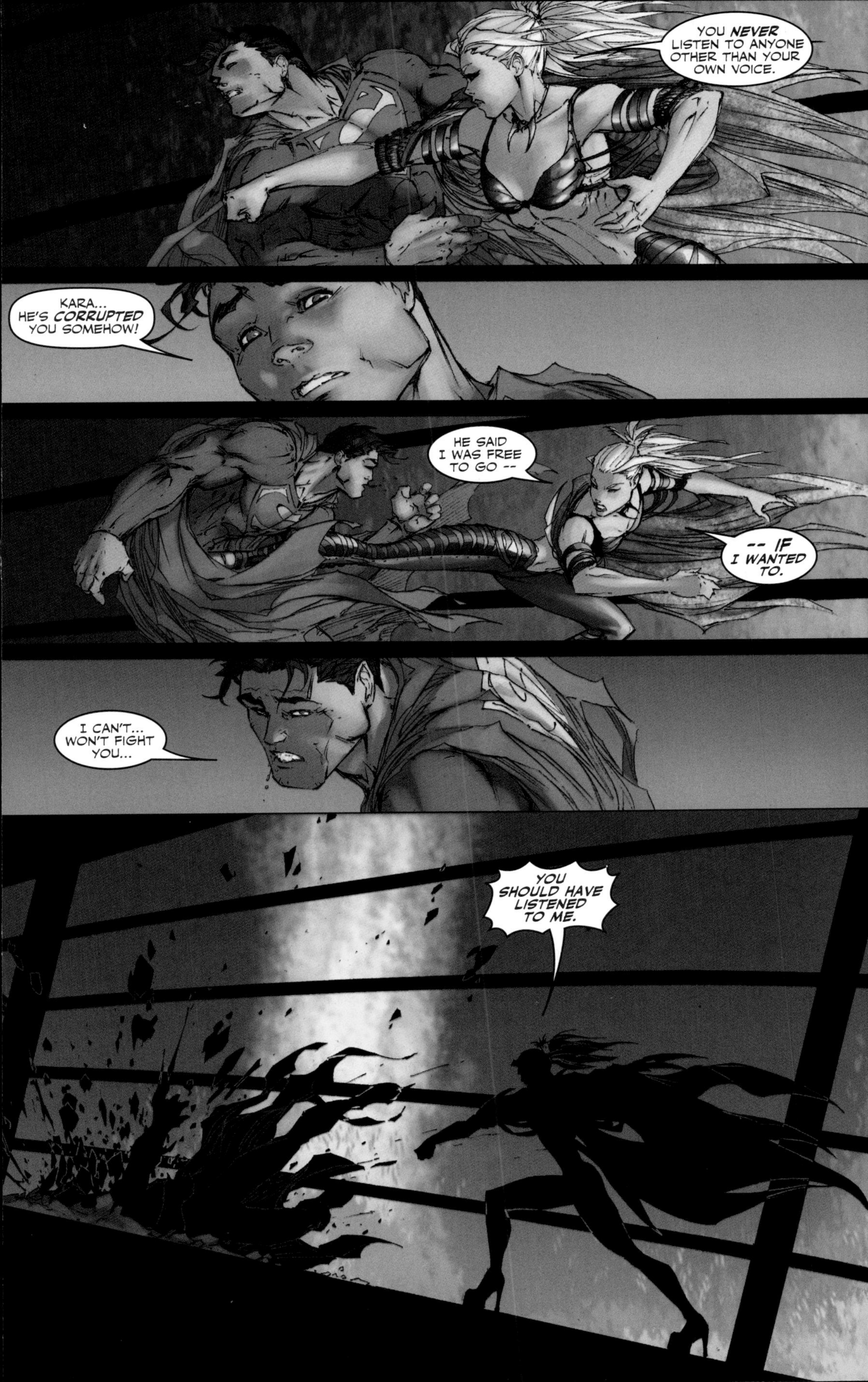
YOU NEVER LISTEN TO ANYONE OTHER THAN YOUR OWN VOICE.
KARA... HE'S CORRUPTED YOU SOMEHOW!
HE SAID I WAS FREE TO GO --
-- IF I WANTED TO.
I CAN'T... WON'T FIGHT YOU...
YOU SHOULD HAVE LISTENED TO ME.

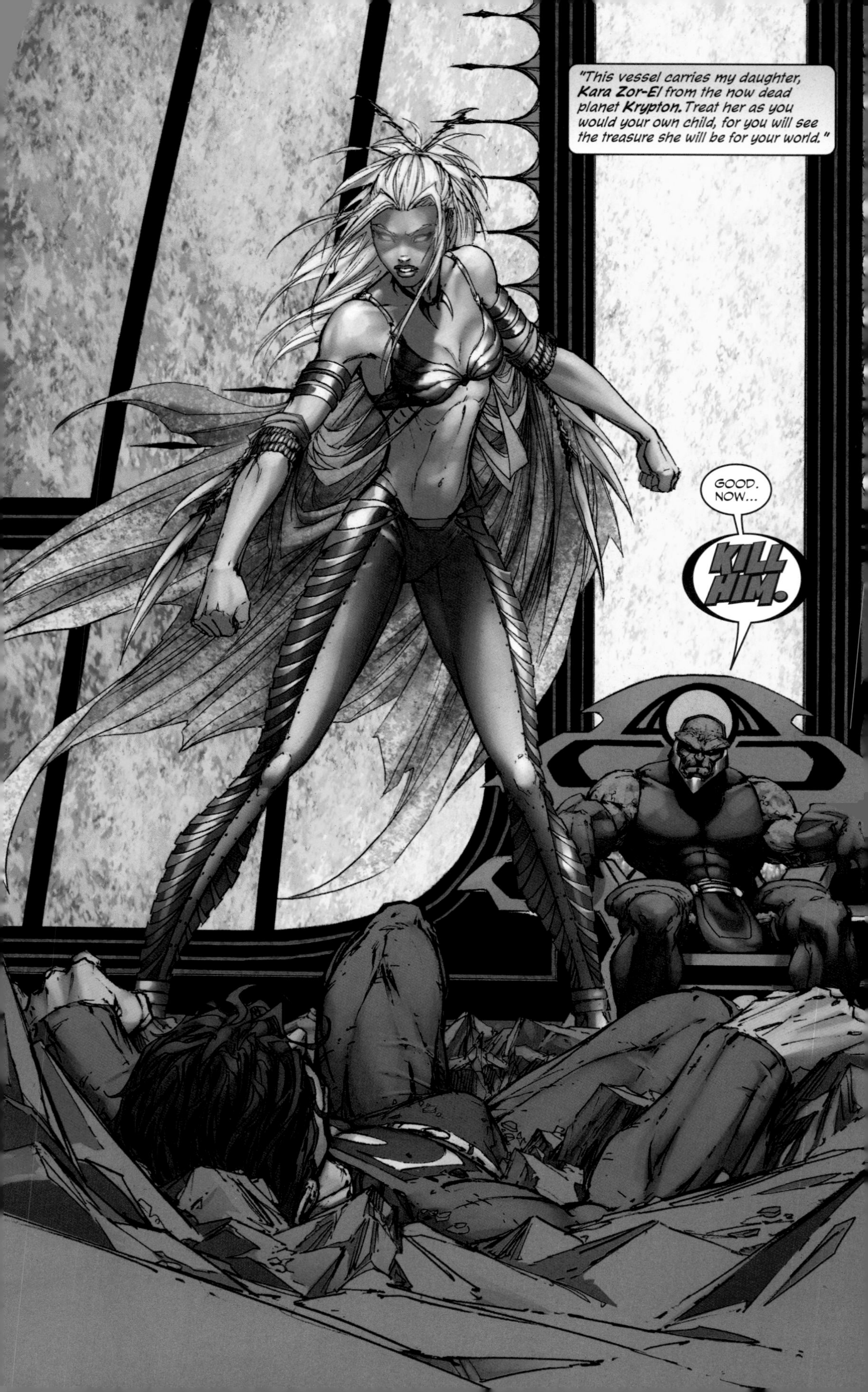

"This vessel carries my daughter, Kara Zor-El from the now dead planet Krypton. Treat her as you would your own child, for you will see the treasure she will be for your world."
GOOD. NOW...
KILL HIM.

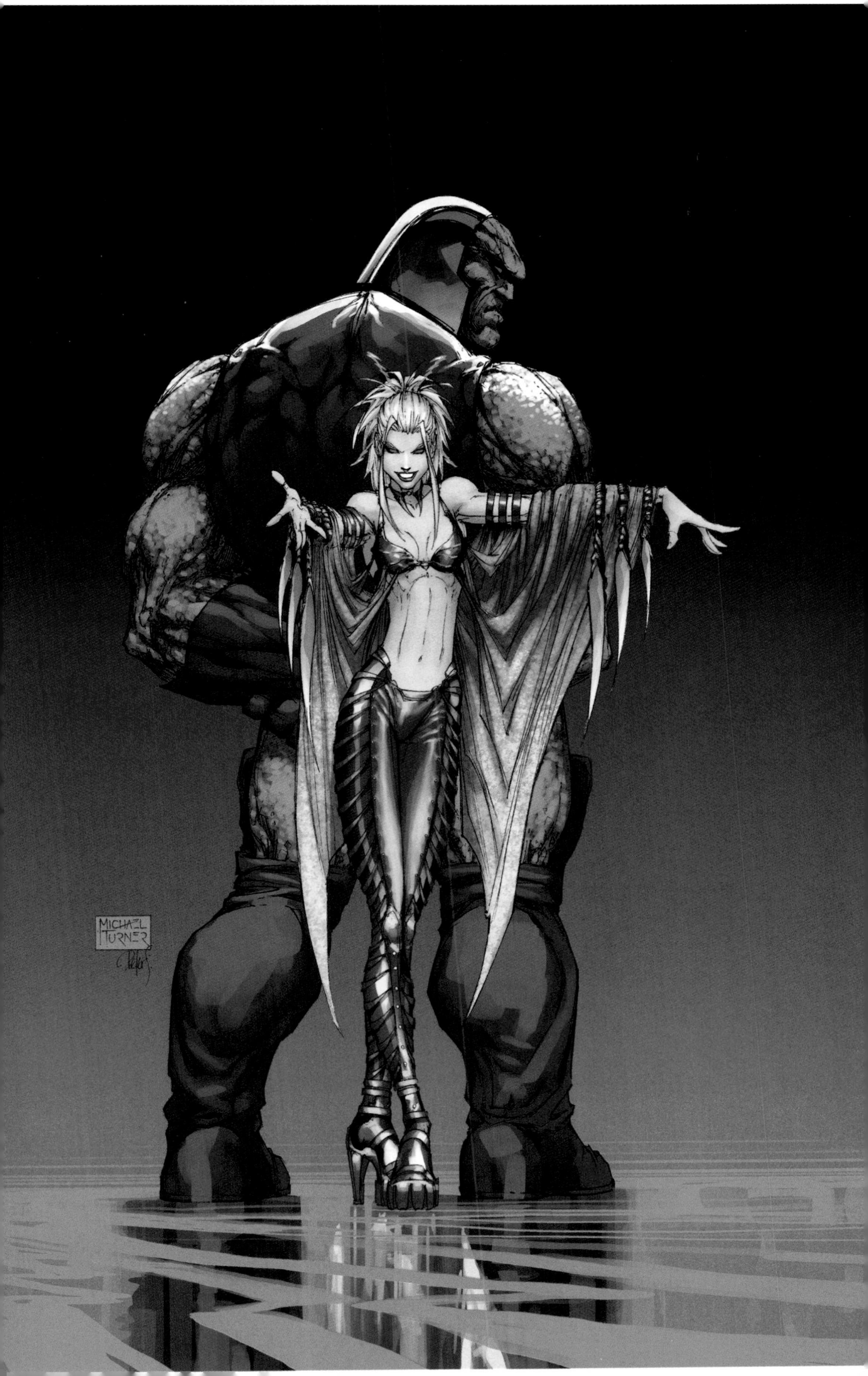
MICHAEL TURNER

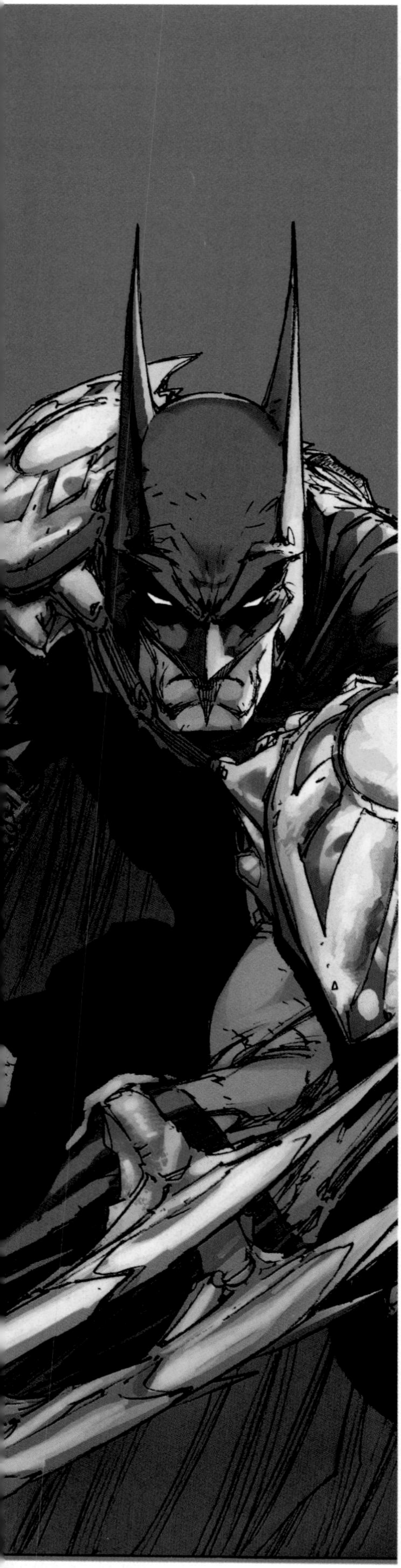

THE SUPERGIRL FROM KRYPTON

PART FIVE
TRAITOR

JEPH LOEB
WRITER
MICHAEL TURNER
ARTIST
PETER STEIGERWALD
COLORIST
RICHARD STARKINGS
LETTERER
MICHAEL TURNER
WITH
PETER STEIGERWALD
COVER

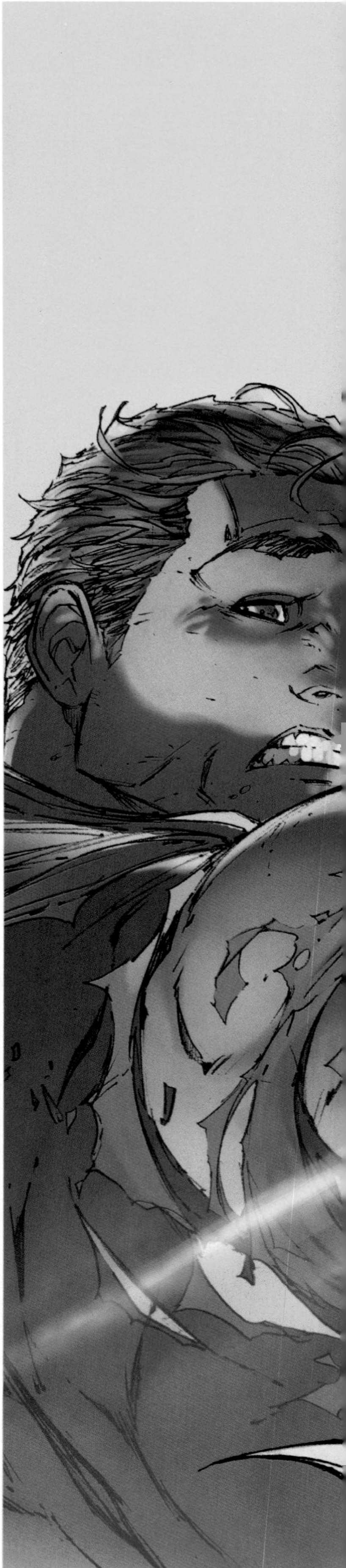

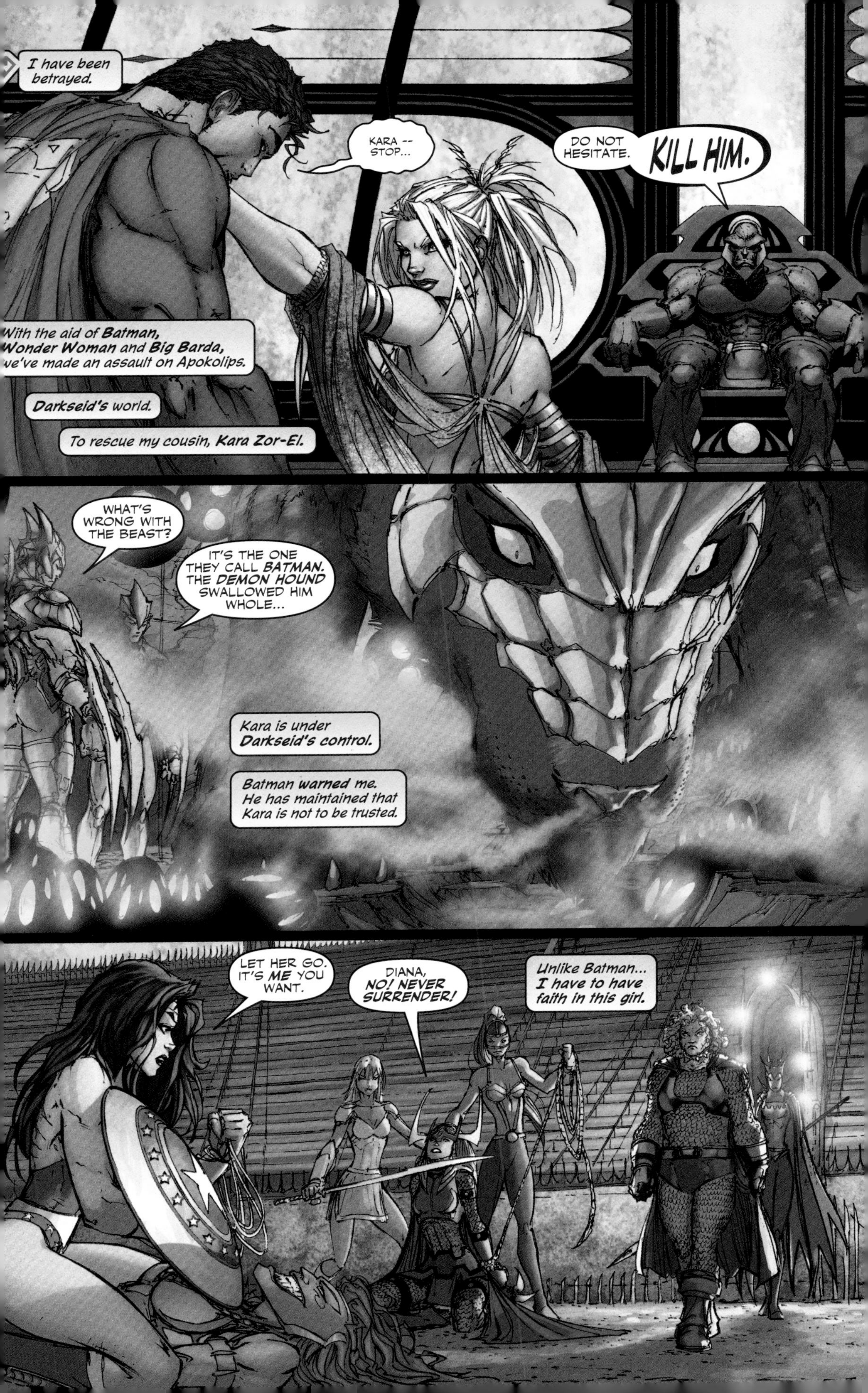
I have been betrayed.
KARA -- STOP...
DO NOT HESITATE.
KILL HIM.
With the aid of Batman, Wonder Woman and Big Barda, we've made an assault on Apokolips.
Darkseid's world.
To rescue my cousin, Kara Zor-El.
WHAT'S WRONG WITH THE BEAST?
IT'S THE ONE THEY CALL BATMAN. THE DEMON HOUND SWALLOWED HIM WHOLE...
Kara is under Darkseid's control.
Batman warned me. He has maintained that Kara is not to be trusted.
LET HER GO. IT'S ME YOU WANT.
DIANA, NO! NEVER SURRENDER!
Unlike Batman... I have to have faith in this girl.

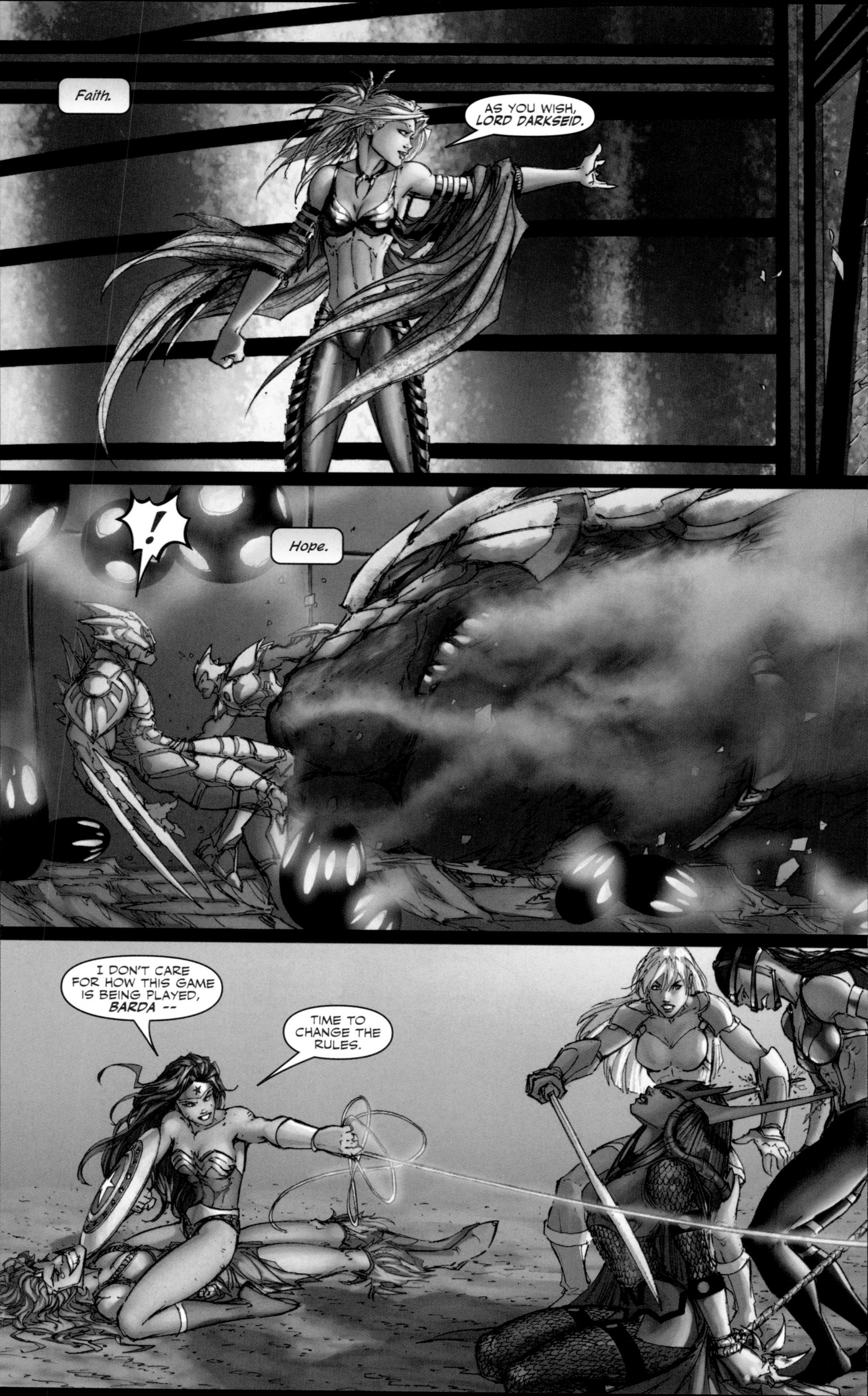
Faith.
AS YOU WISH, LORD DARKSEID.
!
Hope.
I DON'T CARE FOR HOW THIS GAME IS BEING PLAYED, BARDA --
TIME TO CHANGE THE RULES.

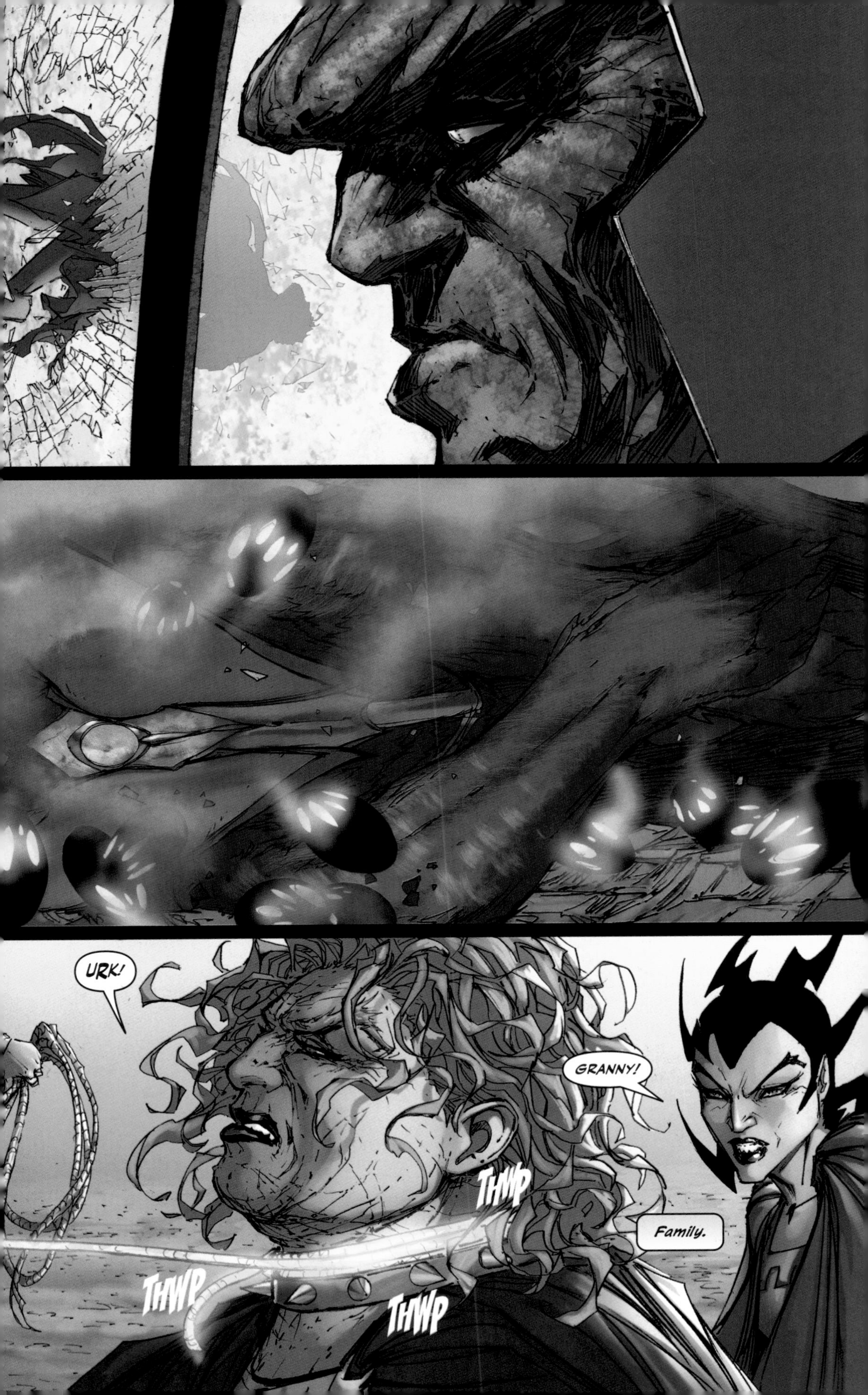
URK!
GRANNY!
THWP
Family.
THWP
THWP

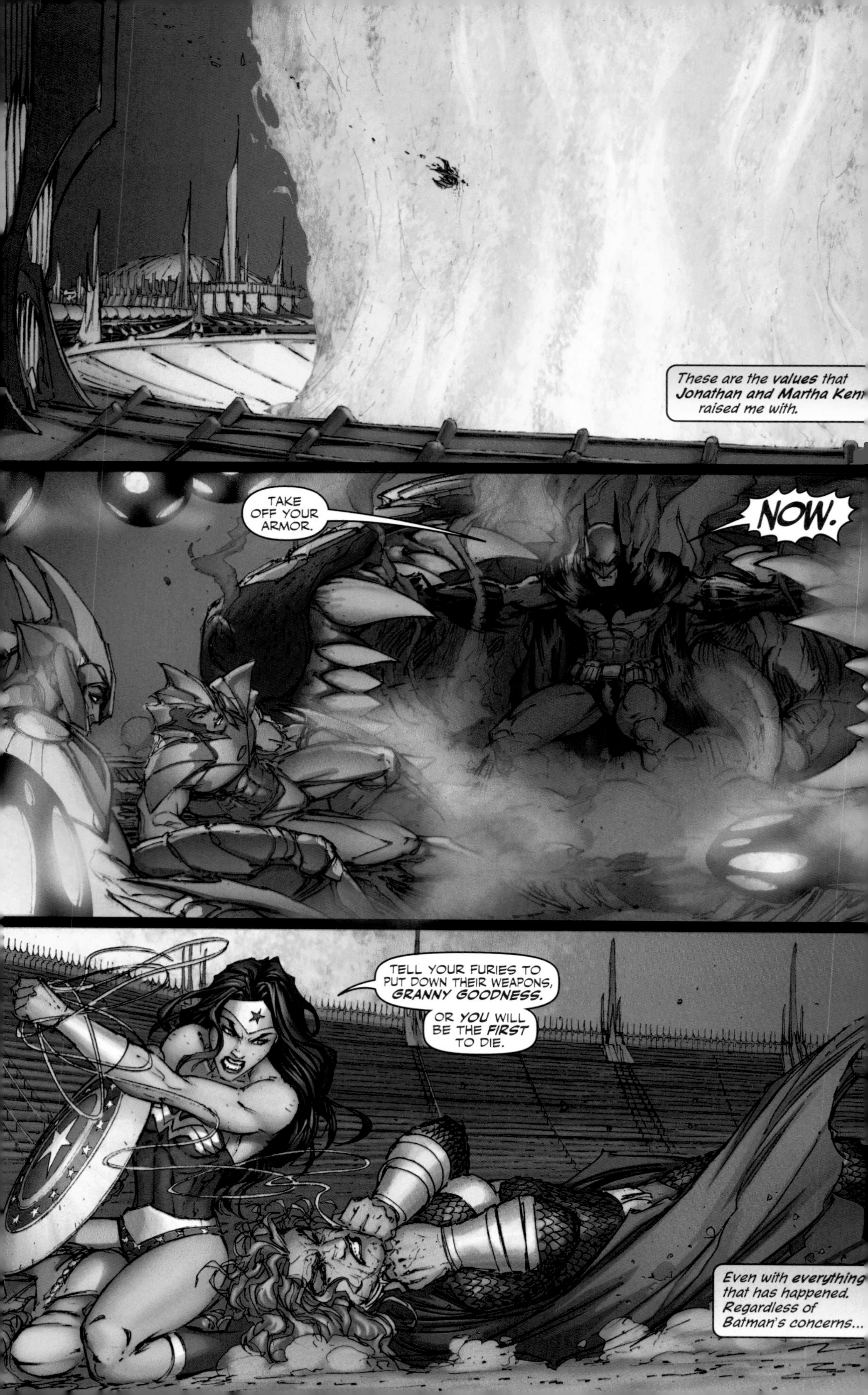
These are the values that Jonathan and Martha Kent raised me with.
TAKE OFF YOUR ARMOR.
NOW.
TELL YOUR FURIES TO PUT DOWN THEIR WEAPONS, GRANNY GOODNESS.
OR YOU WILL BE THE FIRST TO DIE.
Even with everything that has happened. Regardless of Batman's concerns...

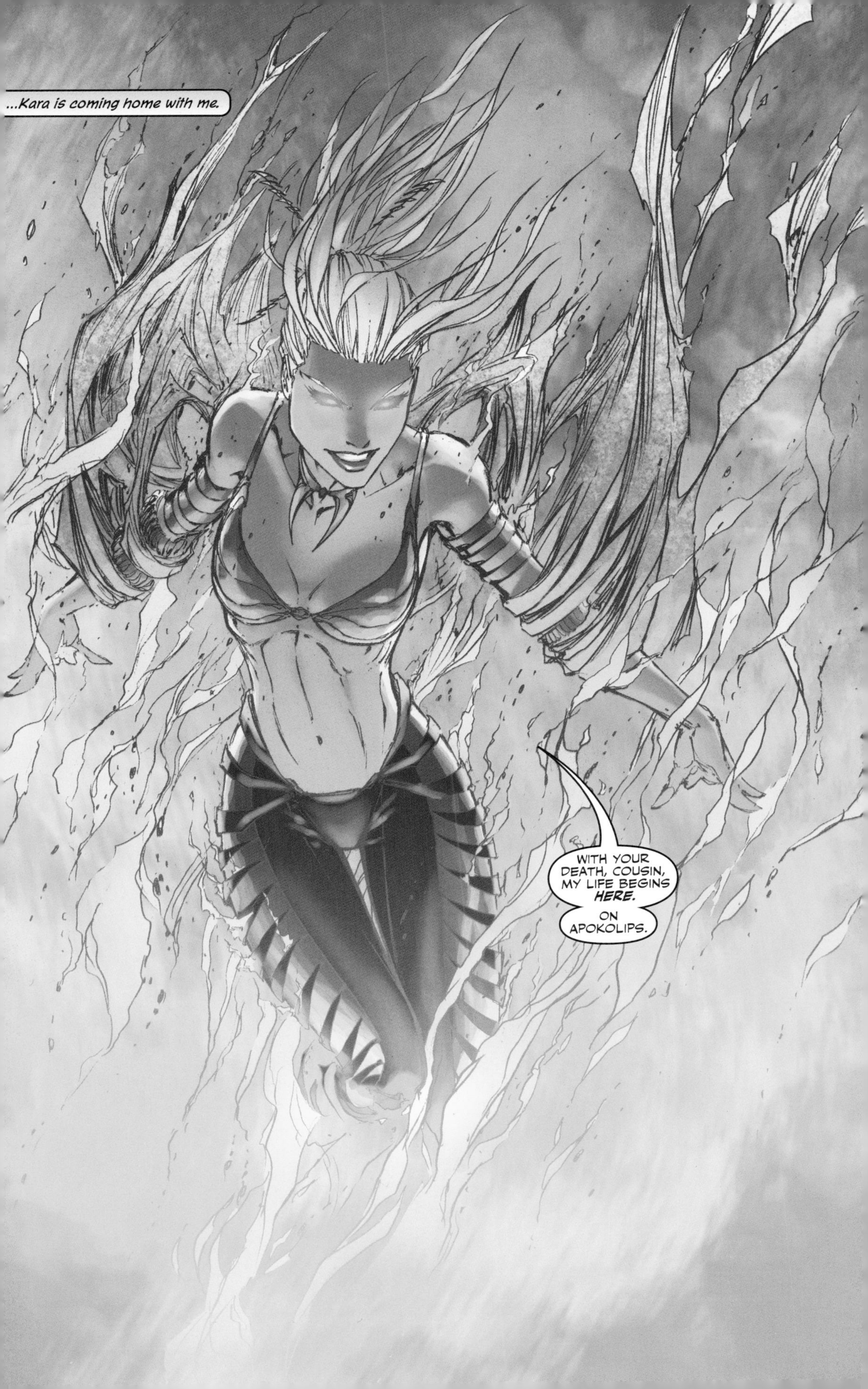
...Kara is coming home with me.
WITH YOUR DEATH, COUSIN, MY LIFE BEGINS **HERE.**
ON APOKOLIPS.

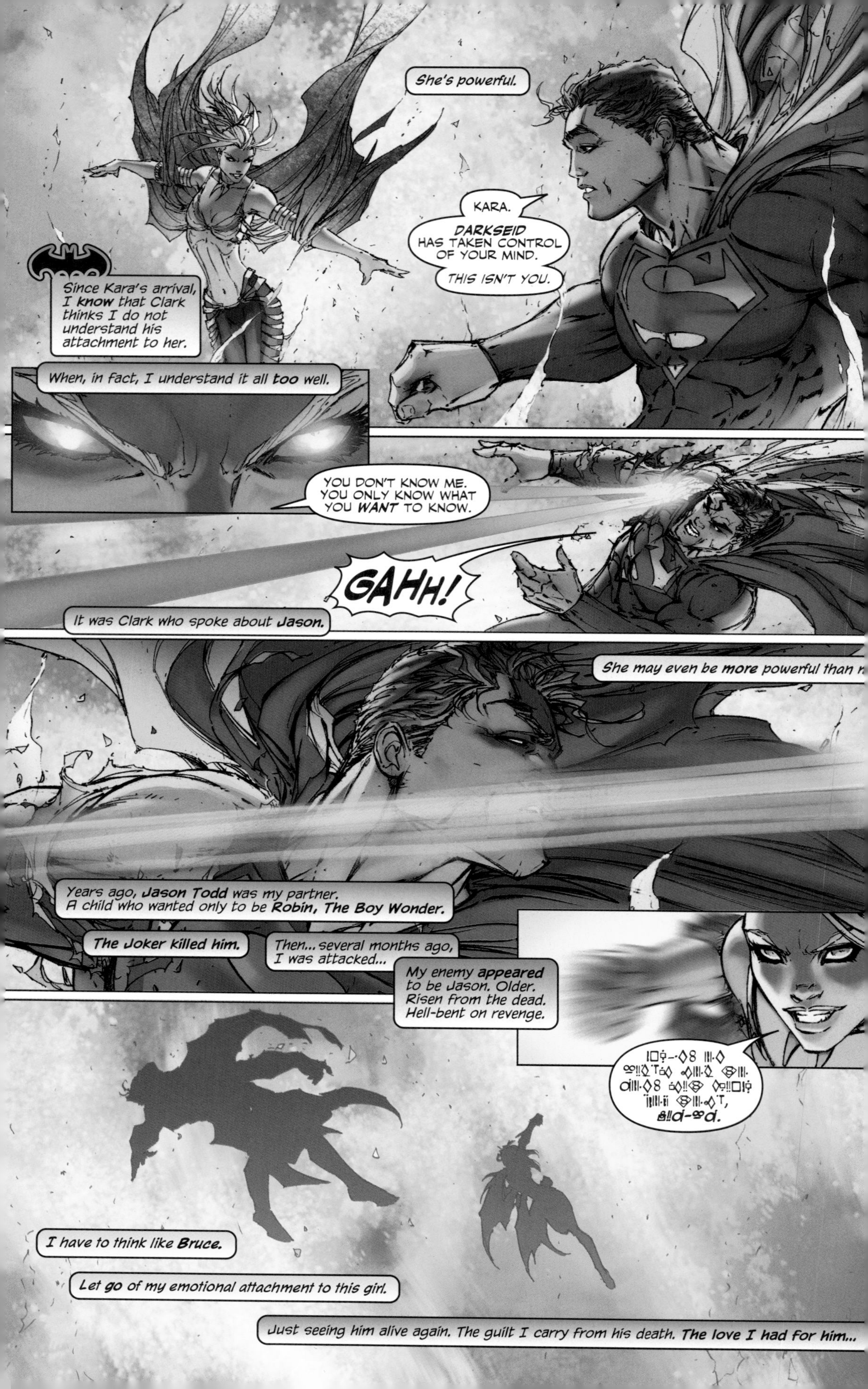
She's powerful.
KARA.
DARKSEID HAS TAKEN CONTROL OF YOUR MIND.
THIS ISN'T YOU.
Since Kara's arrival, I know that Clark thinks I do not understand his attachment to her.
When, in fact, I understand it all too well.
YOU DON'T KNOW ME. YOU ONLY KNOW WHAT YOU WANT TO KNOW.
GAHH!
It was Clark who spoke about Jason.
She may even be more powerful than
Years ago, Jason Todd was my partner. A child who wanted only to be Robin, The Boy Wonder.
The Joker killed him.
Then... several months ago, I was attacked...
My enemy appeared to be Jason. Older. Risen from the dead. Hell-bent on revenge.
I have to think like Bruce.
Let go of my emotional attachment to this girl.
Just seeing him alive again. The guilt I carry from his death. The love I had for him...

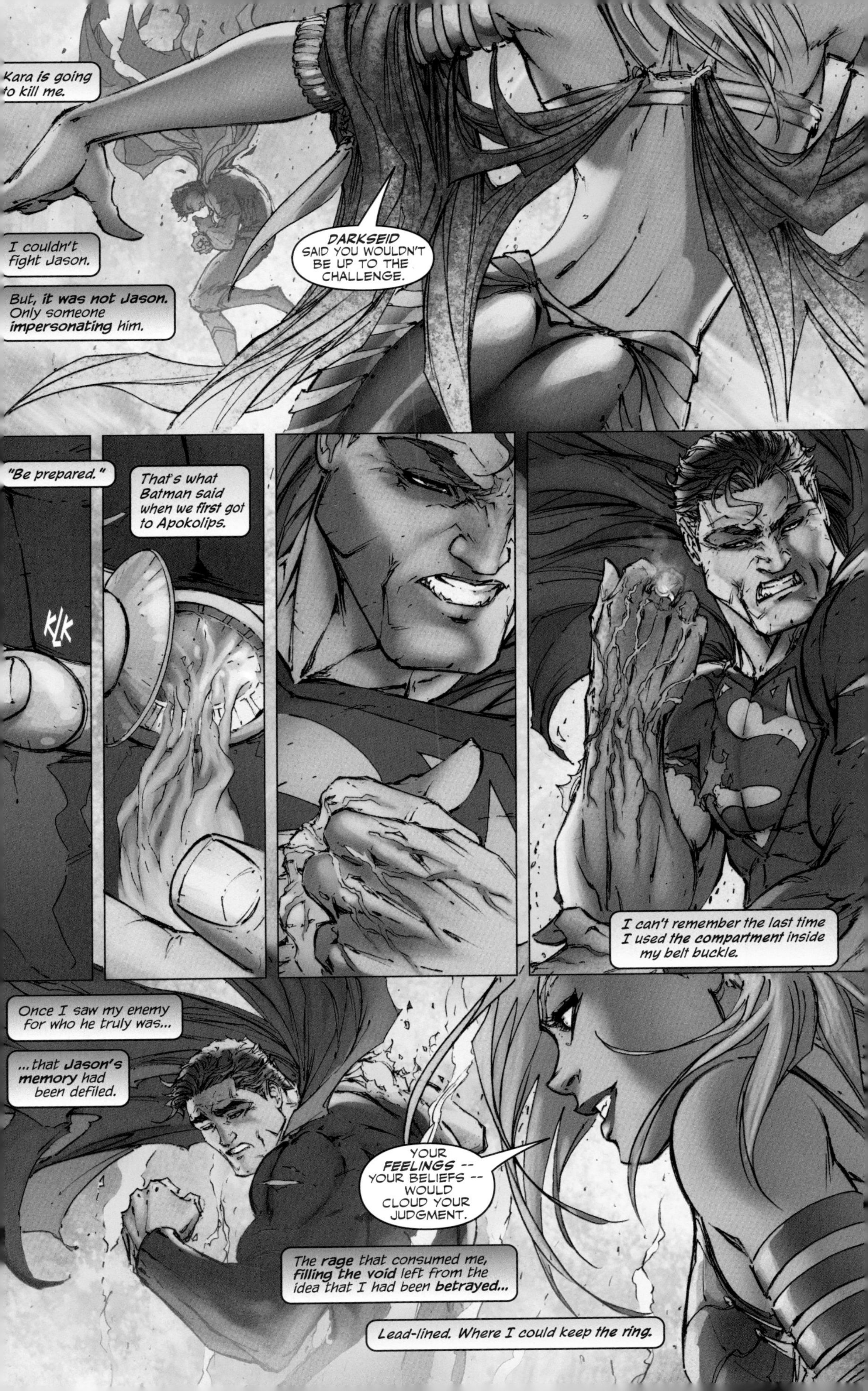
Kara is going to kill me.
I couldn't fight Jason.
But, it was not Jason. Only someone impersonating him.
DARKSEID SAID YOU WOULDN'T BE UP TO THE CHALLENGE.
"Be prepared."
That's what Batman said when we first got to Apokolips.
KLIK
I can't remember the last time I used the compartment inside my belt buckle.
Once I saw my enemy for who he truly was...
...that Jason's memory had been defiled.
YOUR FEELINGS -- YOUR BELIEFS -- WOULD CLOUD YOUR JUDGMENT.
The rage that consumed me, filling the void left from the idea that I had been betrayed...
Lead-lined. Where I could keep the ring.

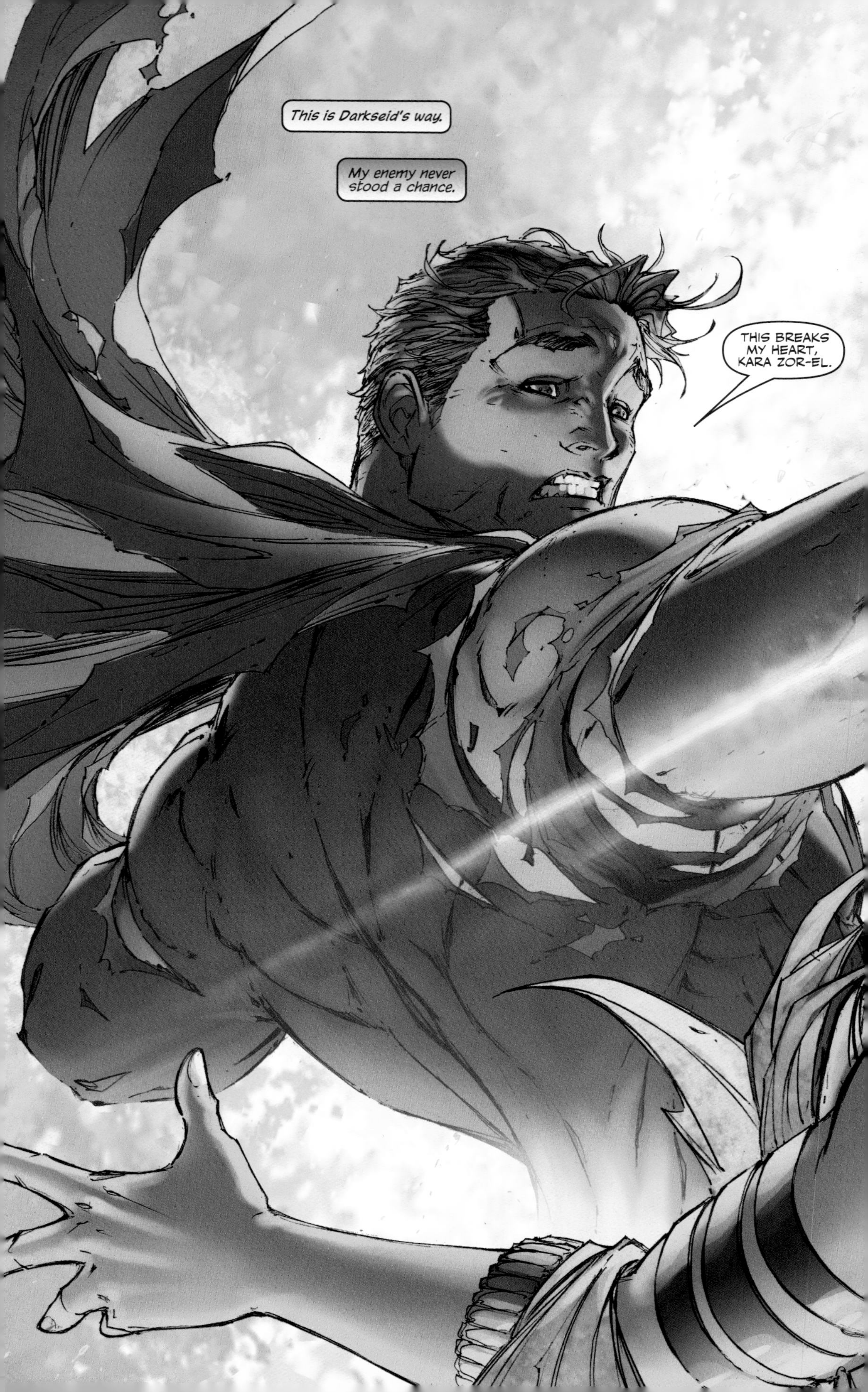
This is Darkseid's way.
My enemy never stood a chance.
THIS BREAKS MY HEART, KARA ZOR-EL.

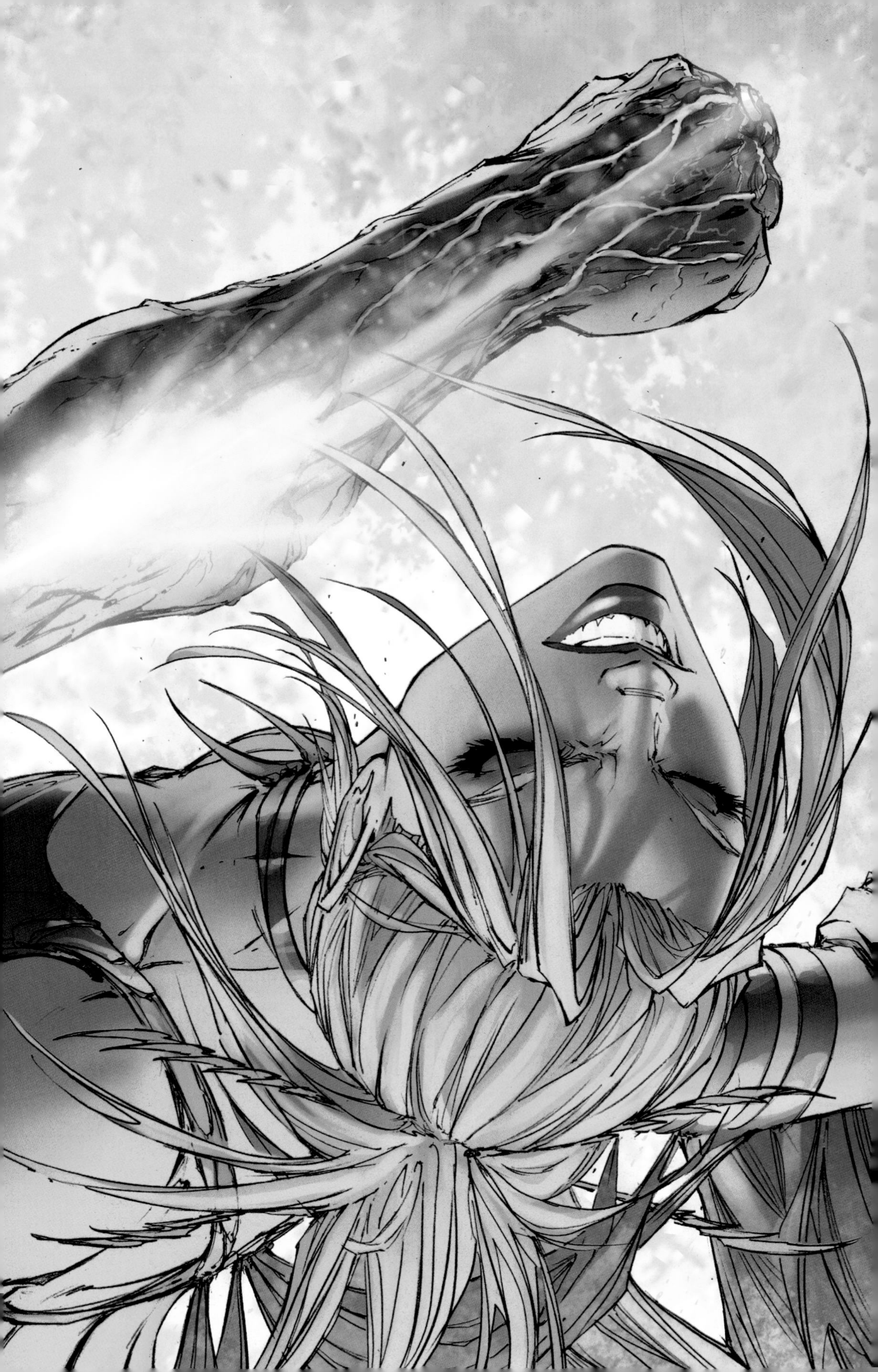

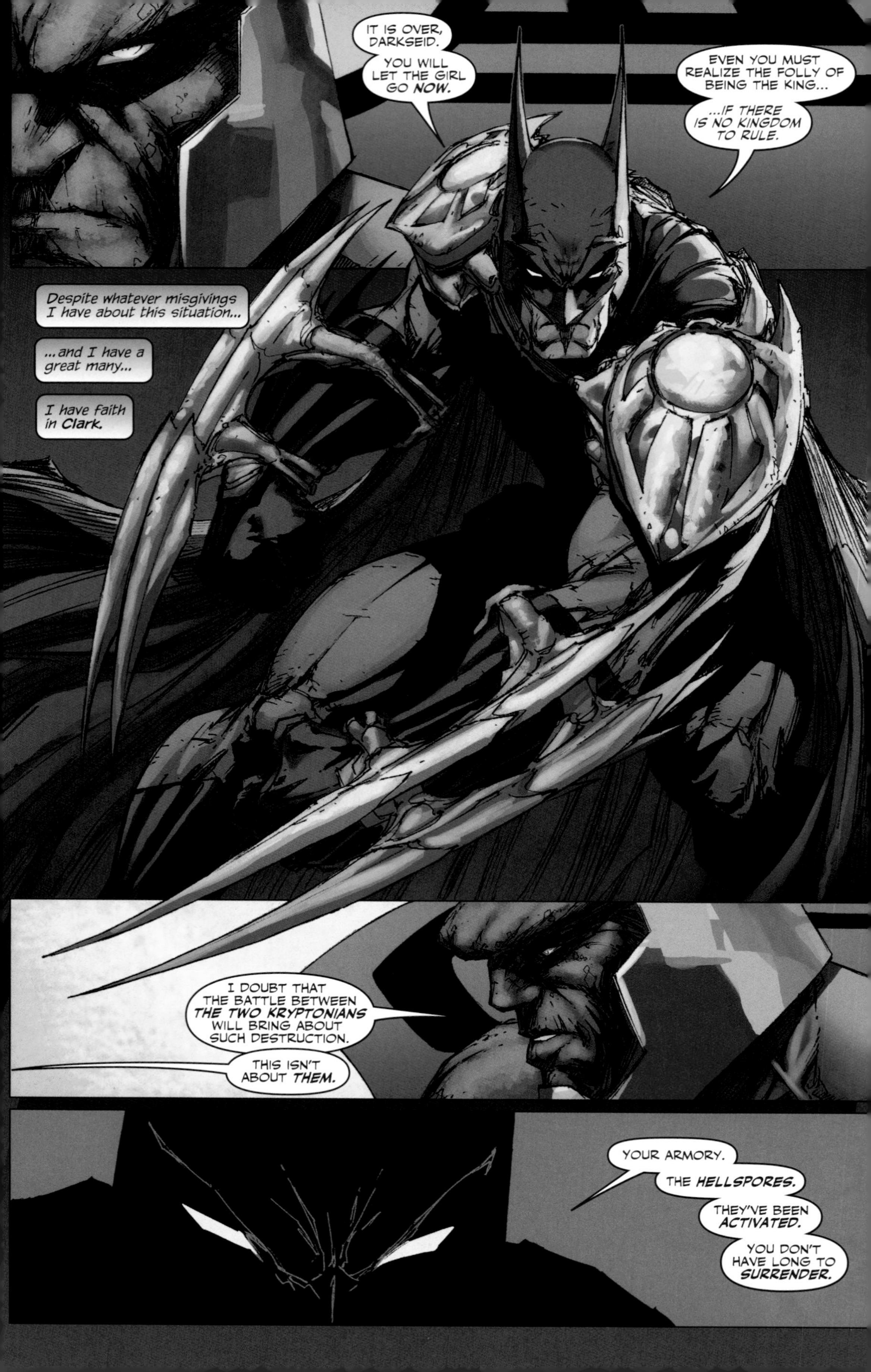
IT IS OVER, DARKSEID.
YOU WILL LET THE GIRL GO NOW.
EVEN YOU MUST REALIZE THE FOLLY OF BEING THE KING...
...IF THERE IS NO KINGDOM TO RULE.
Despite whatever misgivings I have about this situation...
...and I have a great many...
I have faith in Clark.
I DOUBT THAT THE BATTLE BETWEEN THE TWO KRYPTONIANS WILL BRING ABOUT SUCH DESTRUCTION.
THIS ISN'T ABOUT THEM.
YOUR ARMORY.
THE HELLSPORES.
THEY'VE BEEN ACTIVATED.
YOU DON'T HAVE LONG TO SURRENDER.

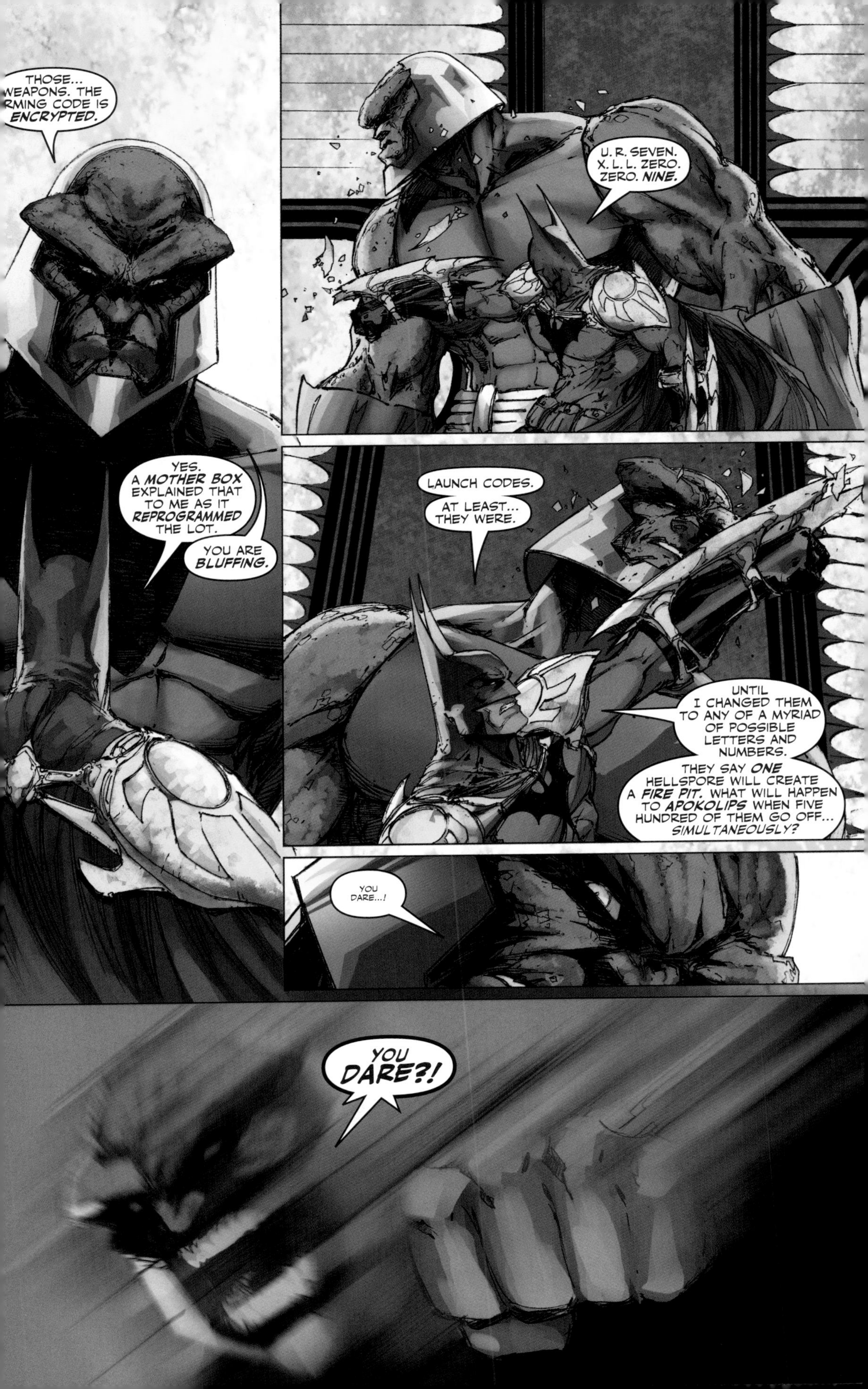

THOSE... WEAPONS. THE ARMING CODE IS ENCRYPTED.
U. R. SEVEN. X. L. L. ZERO. ZERO. NINE.
YES. A MOTHER BOX EXPLAINED THAT TO ME AS IT REPROGRAMMED THE LOT.
YOU ARE BLUFFING.
LAUNCH CODES.
AT LEAST... THEY WERE.
UNTIL I CHANGED THEM TO ANY OF A MYRIAD OF POSSIBLE LETTERS AND NUMBERS.
THEY SAY ONE HELLSPORE WILL CREATE A FIRE PIT. WHAT WILL HAPPEN TO APOKOLIPS WHEN FIVE HUNDRED OF THEM GO OFF... SIMULTANEOUSLY?
YOU DARE...!
YOU DARE?!

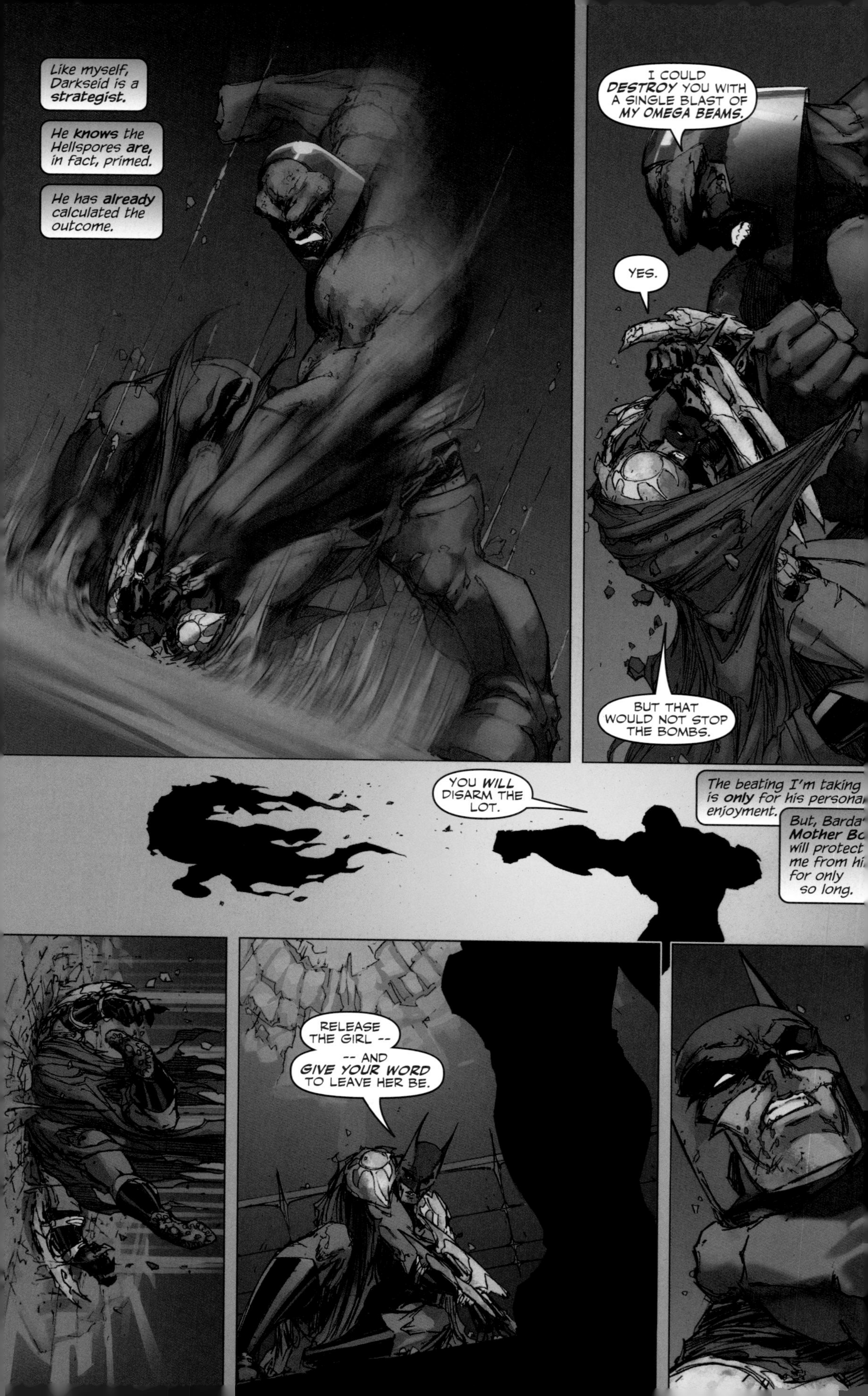
Like myself, Darkseid is a strategist.
He knows the Hellspores are, in fact, primed.
He has already calculated the outcome.
I COULD DESTROY YOU WITH A SINGLE BLAST OF MY OMEGA BEAMS.
YES.
BUT THAT WOULD NOT STOP THE BOMBS.
YOU WILL DISARM THE LOT.
The beating I'm taking is only for his persona enjoyment.
But, Barda Mother Bo will protect me from hi for only so long.
RELEASE THE GIRL --
-- AND GIVE YOUR WORD TO LEAVE HER BE.

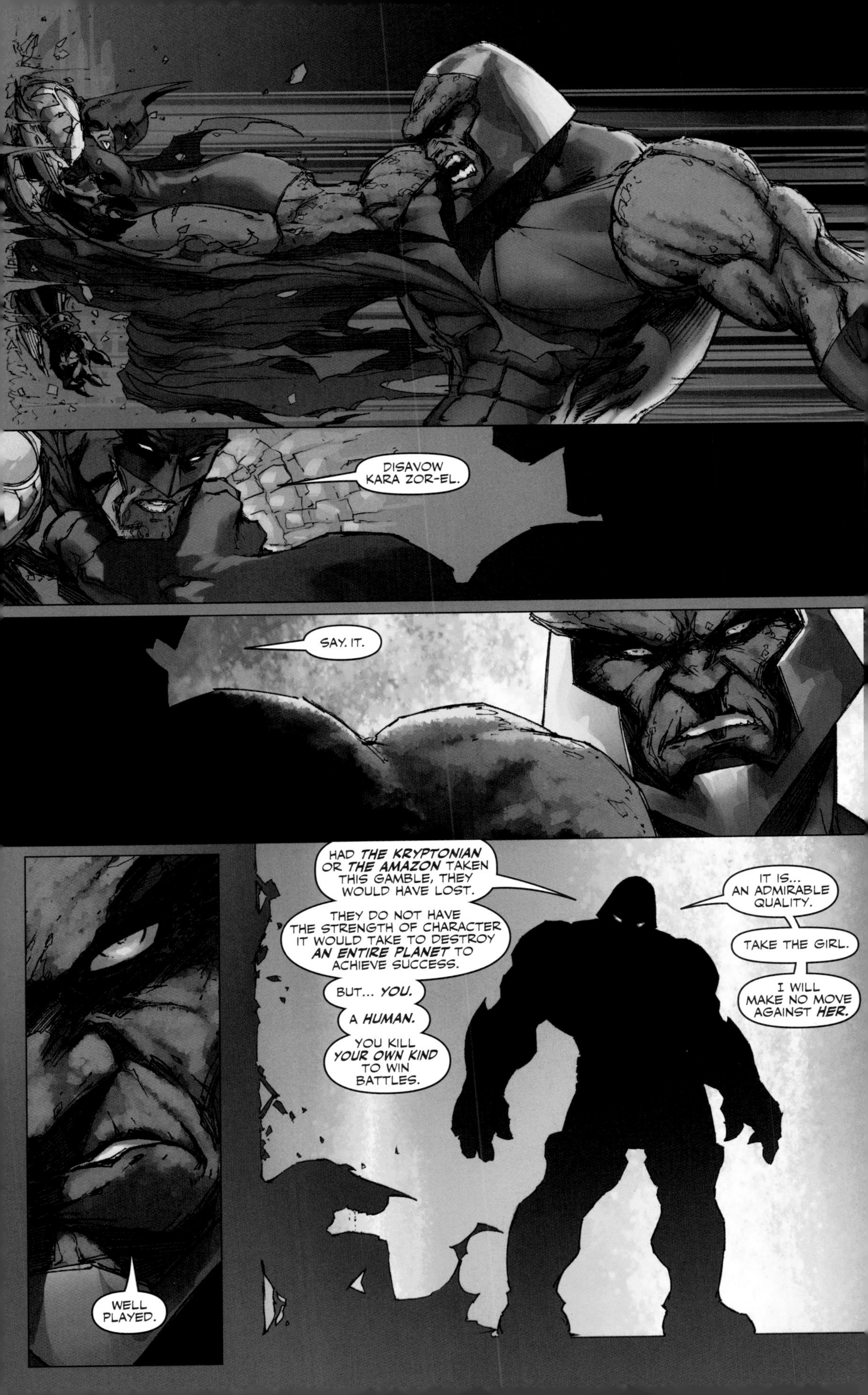
DISAVOW KARA ZOR-EL.
SAY. IT.
WELL PLAYED.
HAD THE KRYPTONIAN OR THE AMAZON TAKEN THIS GAMBLE, THEY WOULD HAVE LOST.
THEY DO NOT HAVE THE STRENGTH OF CHARACTER IT WOULD TAKE TO DESTROY AN ENTIRE PLANET TO ACHIEVE SUCCESS.
BUT... YOU.
A HUMAN.
YOU KILL YOUR OWN KIND TO WIN BATTLES.
IT IS... AN ADMIRABLE QUALITY.
TAKE THE GIRL.
I WILL MAKE NO MOVE AGAINST HER.

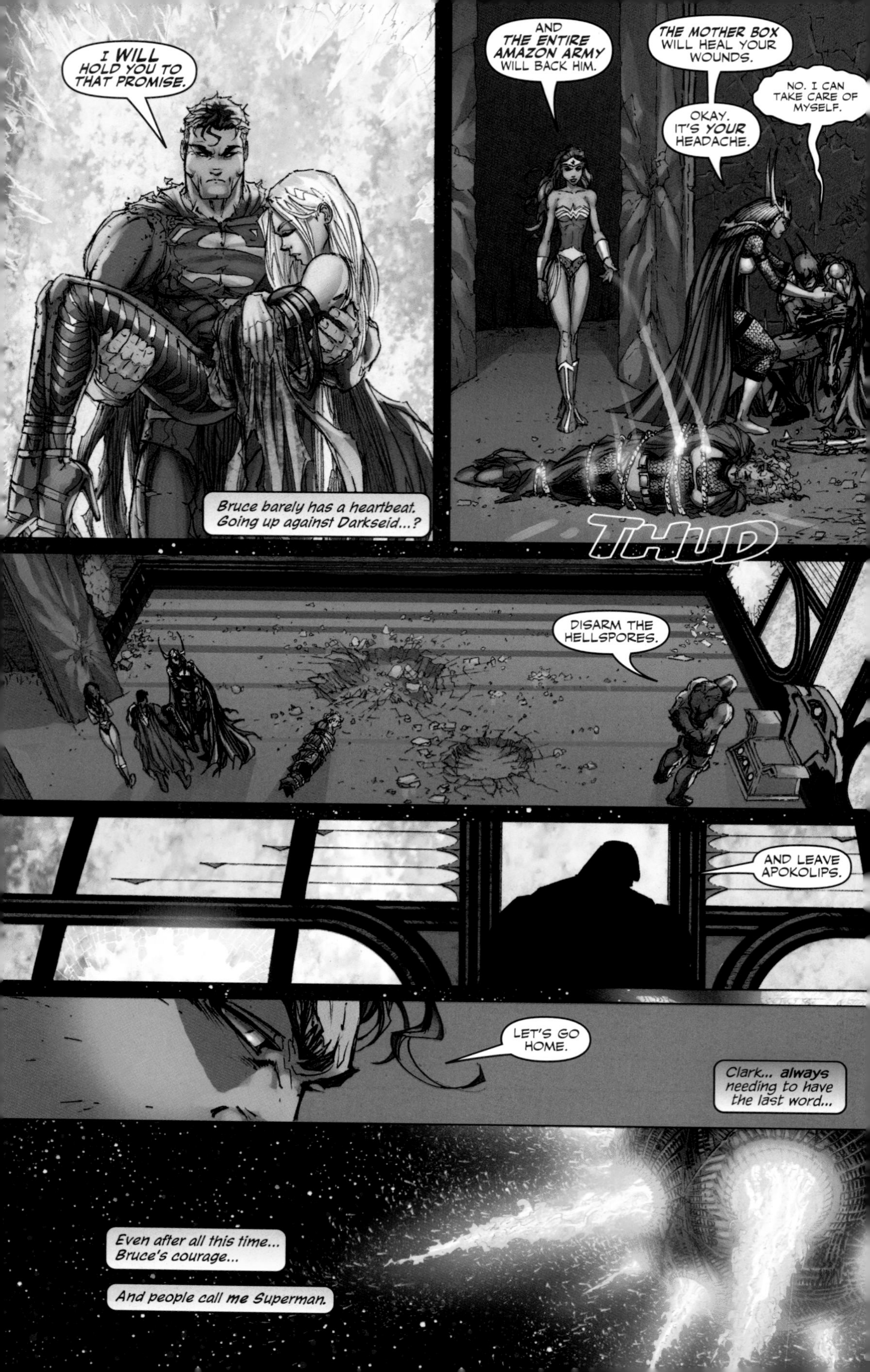
I WILL HOLD YOU TO THAT PROMISE.
Bruce barely has a heartbeat. Going up against Darkseid...?
AND THE ENTIRE AMAZON ARMY WILL BACK HIM.
THE MOTHER BOX WILL HEAL YOUR WOUNDS.
OKAY. IT'S YOUR HEADACHE.
NO. I CAN TAKE CARE OF MYSELF.
THUD
DISARM THE HELLSPORES.
AND LEAVE APOKOLIPS.
LET'S GO HOME.
Clark... always needing to have the last word...
Even after all this time... Bruce's courage...
And people call me Superman.

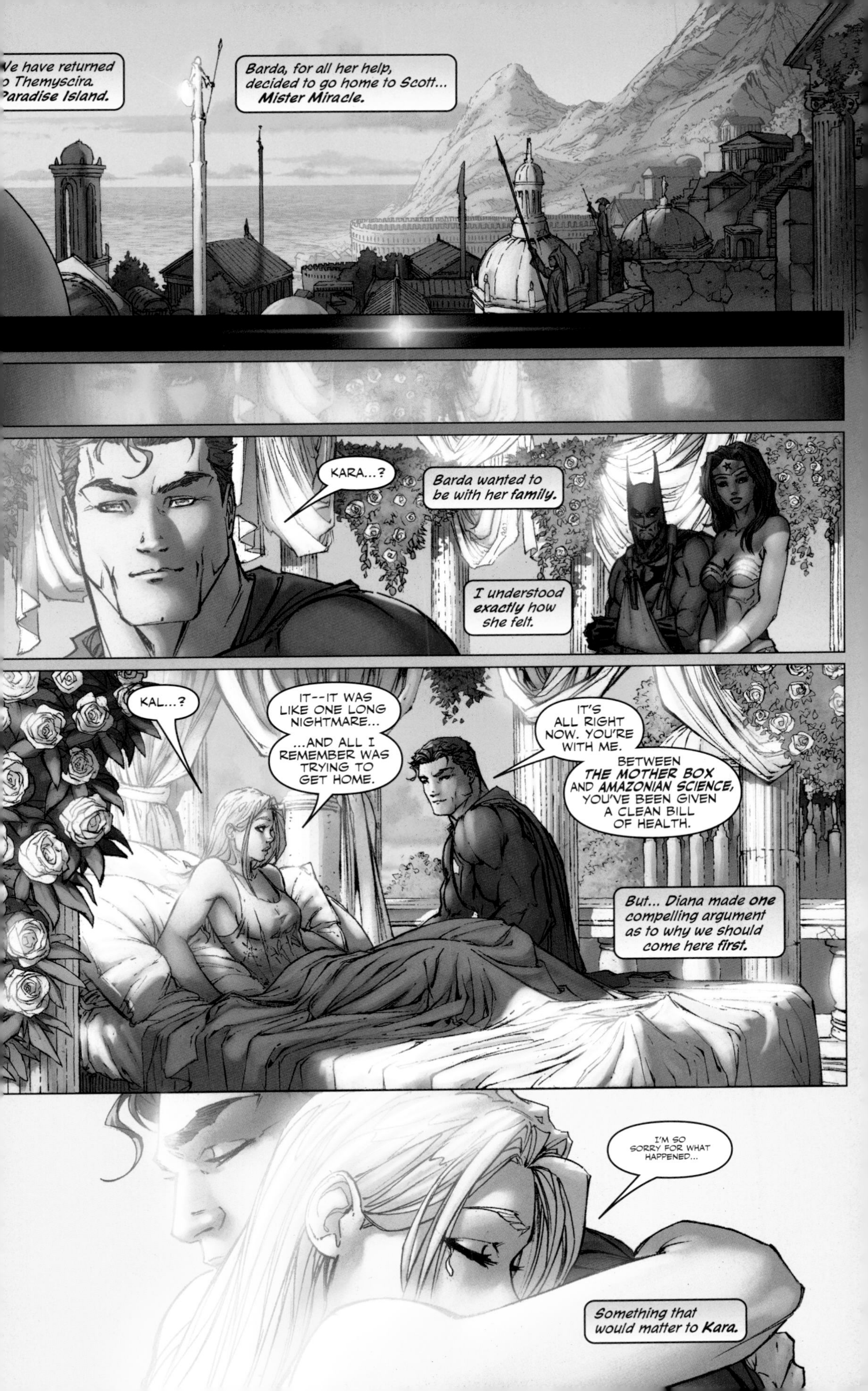

We have returned to Themyscira. Paradise Island.
Barda, for all her help, decided to go home to Scott... Mister Miracle.
KARA...?
Barda wanted to be with her family.
I understood exactly how she felt.
KAL...?
IT--IT WAS LIKE ONE LONG NIGHTMARE...
...AND ALL I REMEMBER WAS TRYING TO GET HOME.
IT'S ALL RIGHT NOW. YOU'RE WITH ME.
BETWEEN THE MOTHER BOX AND AMAZONIAN SCIENCE, YOU'VE BEEN GIVEN A CLEAN BILL OF HEALTH.
But... Diana made one compelling argument as to why we should come here first.
I'M SO SORRY FOR WHAT HAPPENED...
Something that would matter to Kara.

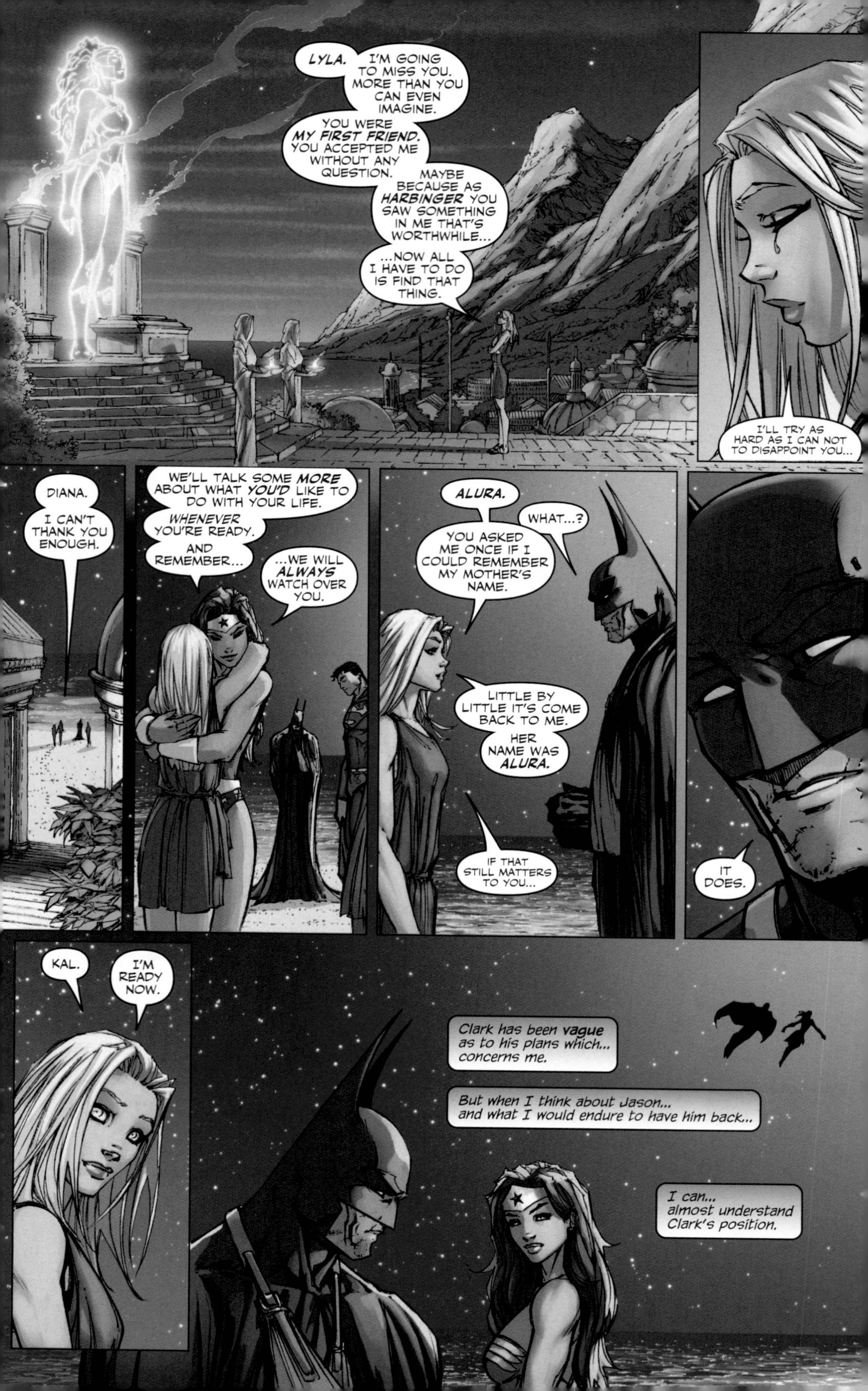
LYLA. I'M GOING TO MISS YOU. MORE THAN YOU CAN EVEN IMAGINE.
YOU WERE MY FIRST FRIEND. YOU ACCEPTED ME WITHOUT ANY QUESTION.
MAYBE BECAUSE AS HARBINGER YOU SAW SOMETHING IN ME THAT'S WORTHWHILE...
...NOW ALL I HAVE TO DO IS FIND THAT THING.
I'LL TRY AS HARD AS I CAN NOT TO DISAPPOINT YOU...
DIANA.
I CAN'T THANK YOU ENOUGH.
WE'LL TALK SOME MORE ABOUT WHAT YOU'D LIKE TO DO WITH YOUR LIFE.
WHENEVER YOU'RE READY.
AND REMEMBER...
...WE WILL ALWAYS WATCH OVER YOU.
ALURA.
WHAT...?
YOU ASKED ME ONCE IF I COULD REMEMBER MY MOTHER'S NAME.
LITTLE BY LITTLE IT'S COME BACK TO ME.
HER NAME WAS ALURA.
IF THAT STILL MATTERS TO YOU...
IT DOES.
KAL.
I'M READY NOW.
Clark has been vague as to his plans which... concerns me.
But when I think about Jason... and what I would endure to have him back...
I can... almost understand Clark's position.

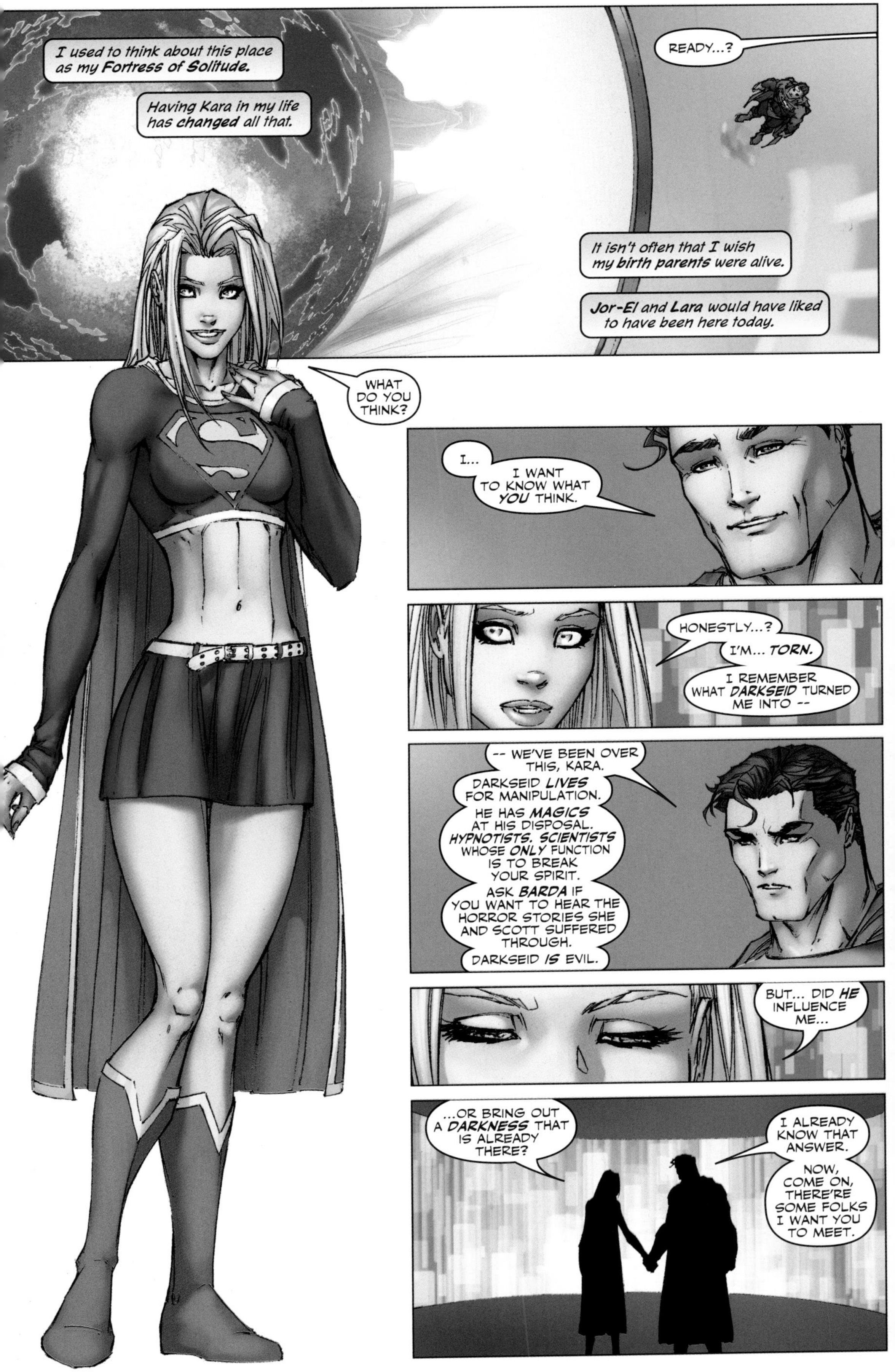

I used to think about this place as my Fortress of Solitude.
Having Kara in my life has changed all that.
READY...?
It isn't often that I wish my birth parents were alive.
Jor-El and Lara would have liked to have been here today.
WHAT DO YOU THINK?
I...
I WANT TO KNOW WHAT YOU THINK.
HONESTLY...?
I'M... TORN.
I REMEMBER WHAT DARKSEID TURNED ME INTO --
-- WE'VE BEEN OVER THIS, KARA.
DARKSEID LIVES FOR MANIPULATION.
HE HAS MAGICS AT HIS DISPOSAL.
HYPNOTISTS. SCIENTISTS WHOSE ONLY FUNCTION IS TO BREAK YOUR SPIRIT.
ASK BARDA IF YOU WANT TO HEAR THE HORROR STORIES SHE AND SCOTT SUFFERED THROUGH.
DARKSEID IS EVIL.
BUT... DID HE INFLUENCE ME...
...OR BRING OUT A DARKNESS THAT IS ALREADY THERE?
I ALREADY KNOW THAT ANSWER.
NOW, COME ON, THERE'RE SOME FOLKS I WANT YOU TO MEET.

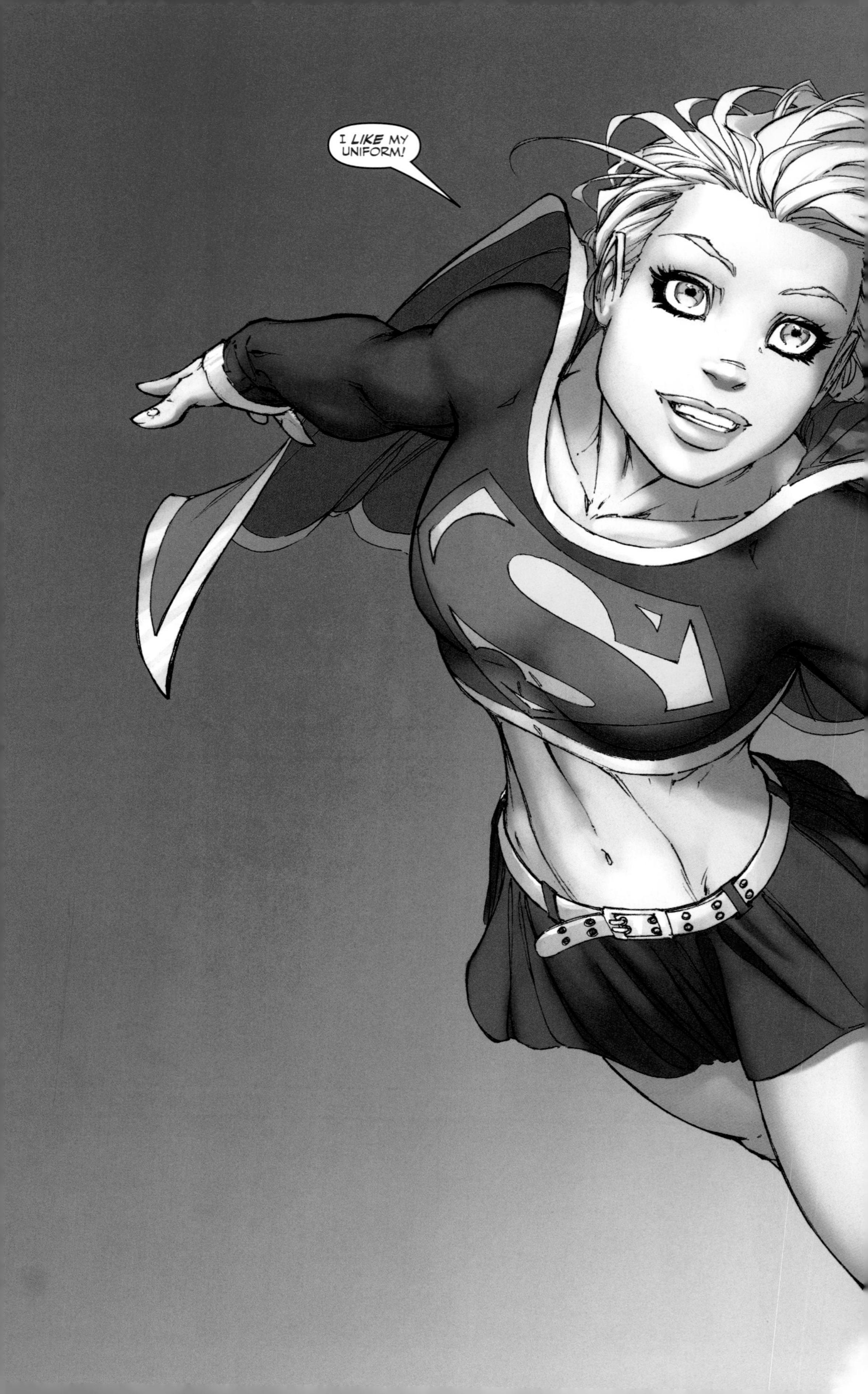
I LIKE MY UNIFORM!

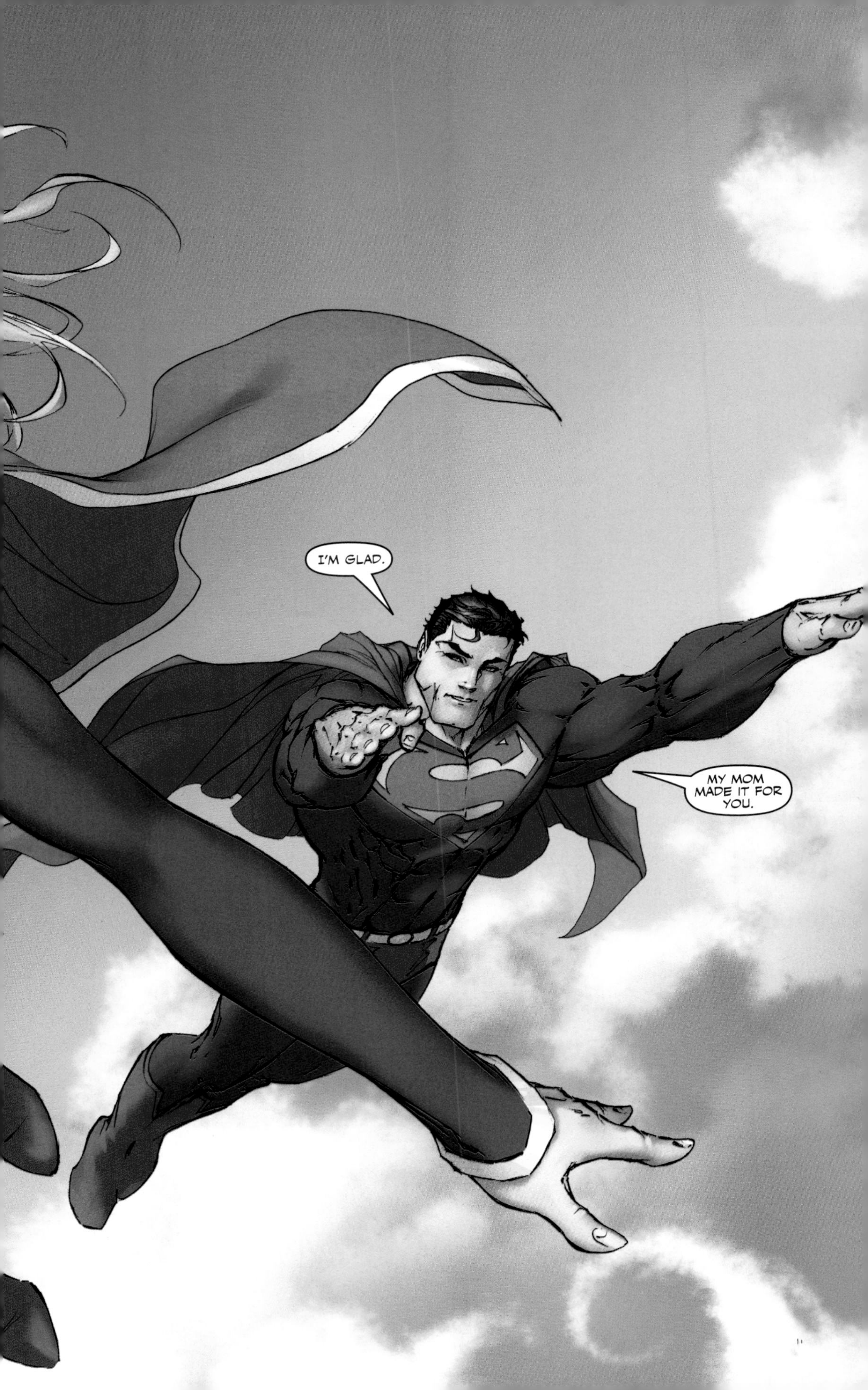
I'M GLAD.
MY MOM MADE IT FOR YOU.

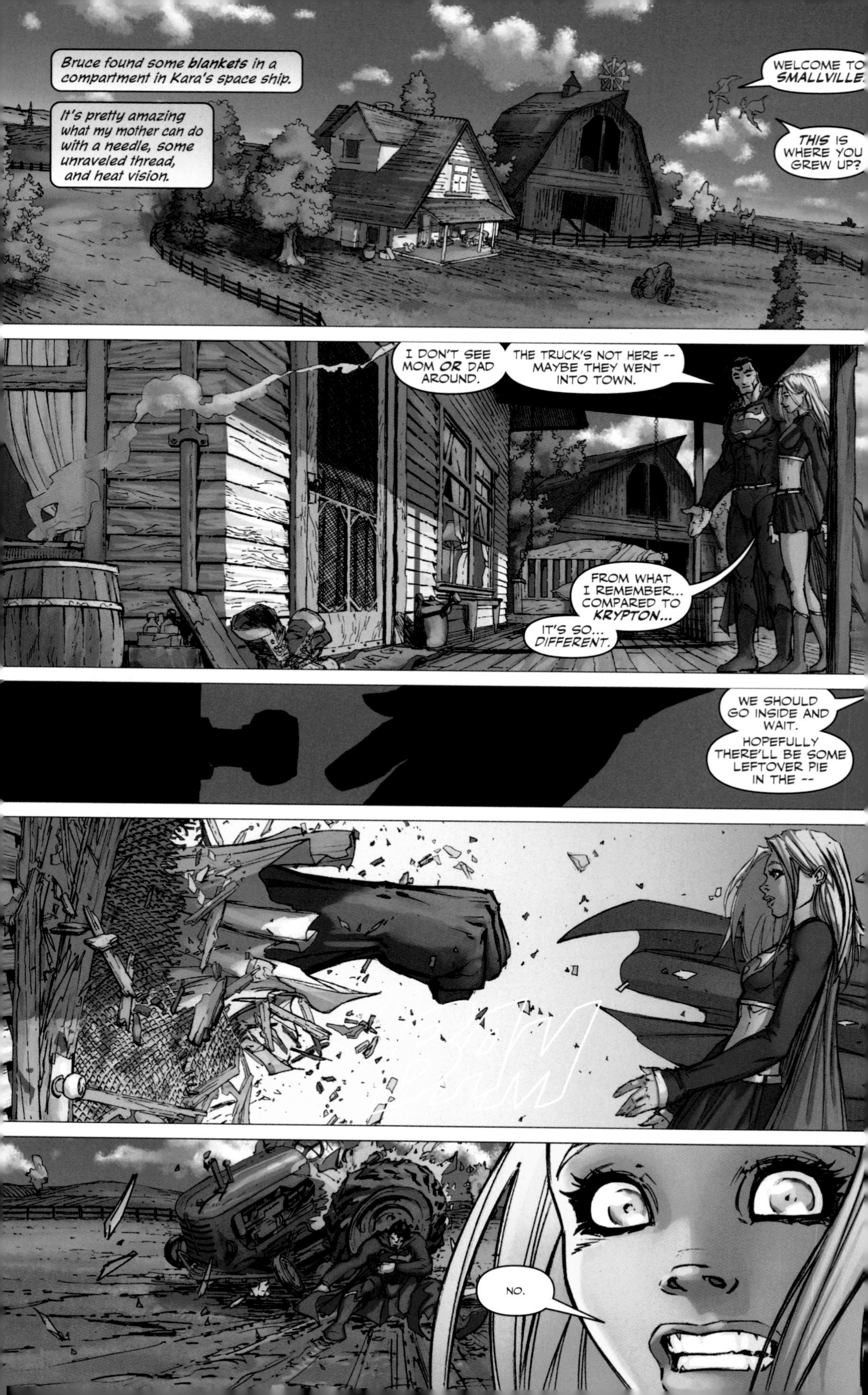

Bruce found some blankets in a compartment in Kara's space ship.
It's pretty amazing what my mother can do with a needle, some unraveled thread, and heat vision.
WELCOME TO SMALLVILLE.
THIS IS WHERE YOU GREW UP?
I DON'T SEE MOM OR DAD AROUND.
THE TRUCK'S NOT HERE -- MAYBE THEY WENT INTO TOWN.
FROM WHAT I REMEMBER... COMPARED TO KRYPTON...
IT'S SO... DIFFERENT.
WE SHOULD GO INSIDE AND WAIT.
HOPEFULLY THERE'LL BE SOME LEFTOVER PIE IN THE --
NO.

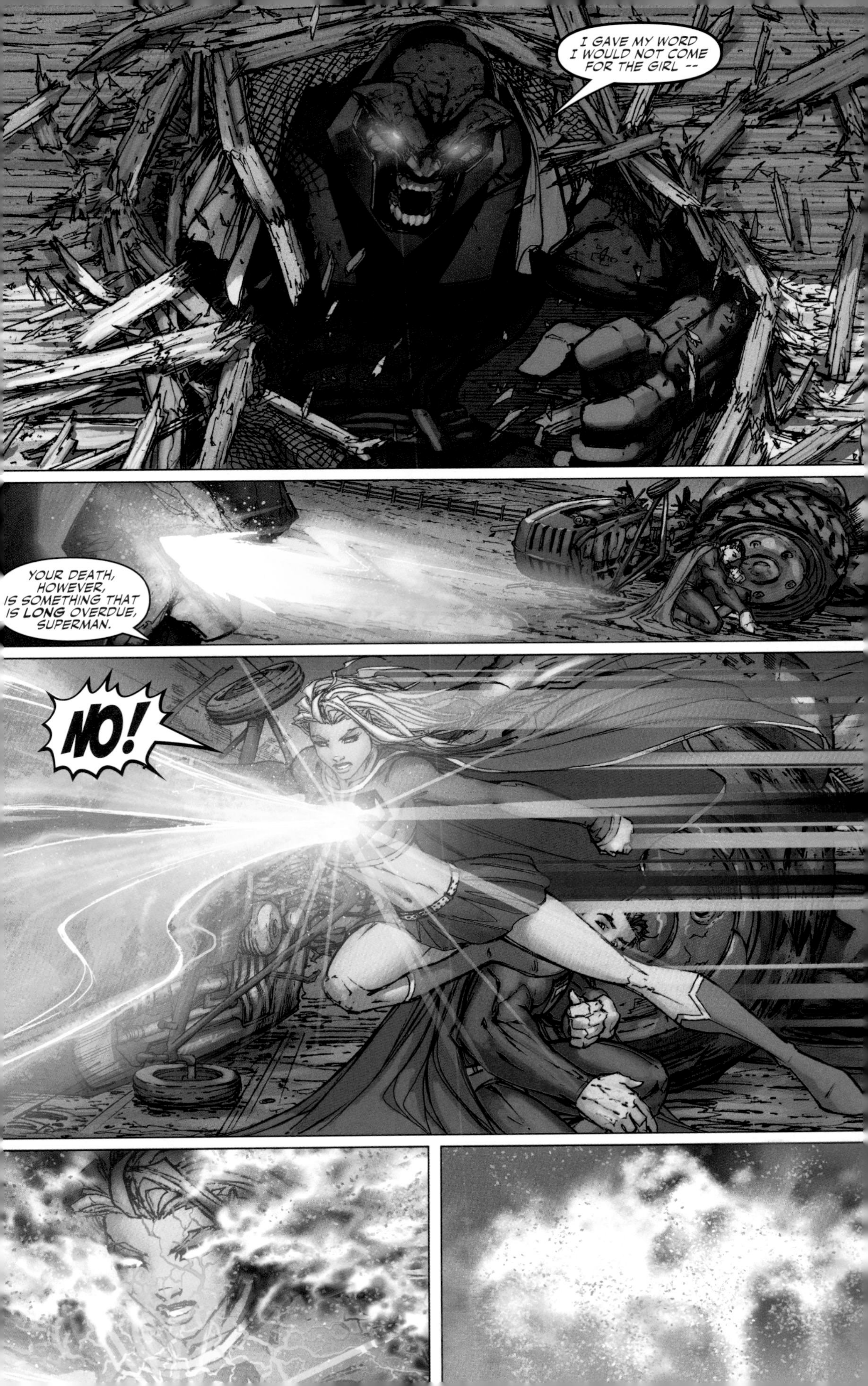
I GAVE MY WORD I WOULD NOT COME FOR THE GIRL --
YOUR DEATH, HOWEVER, IS SOMETHING THAT IS LONG OVERDUE, SUPERMAN.
NO!

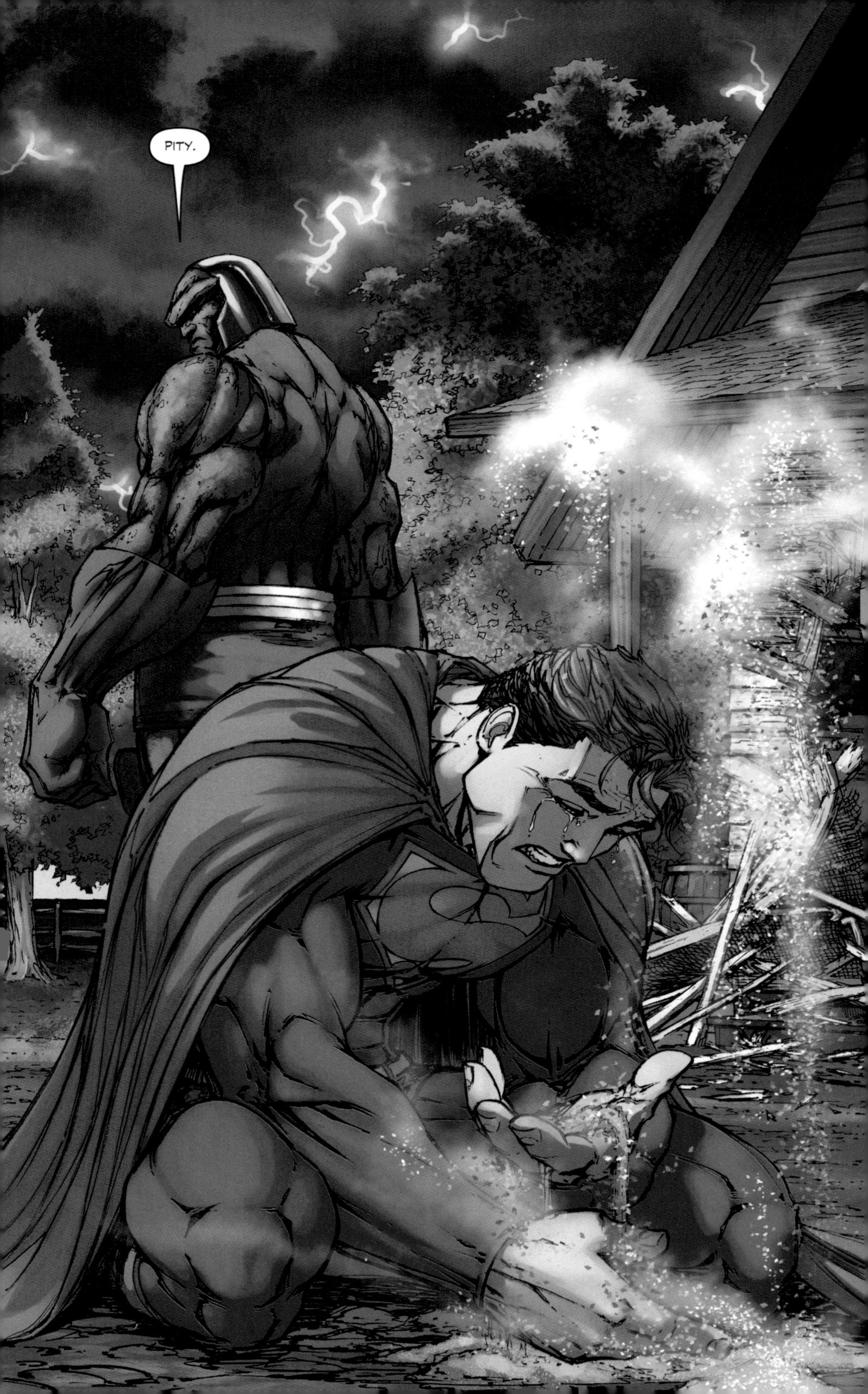
PITY.

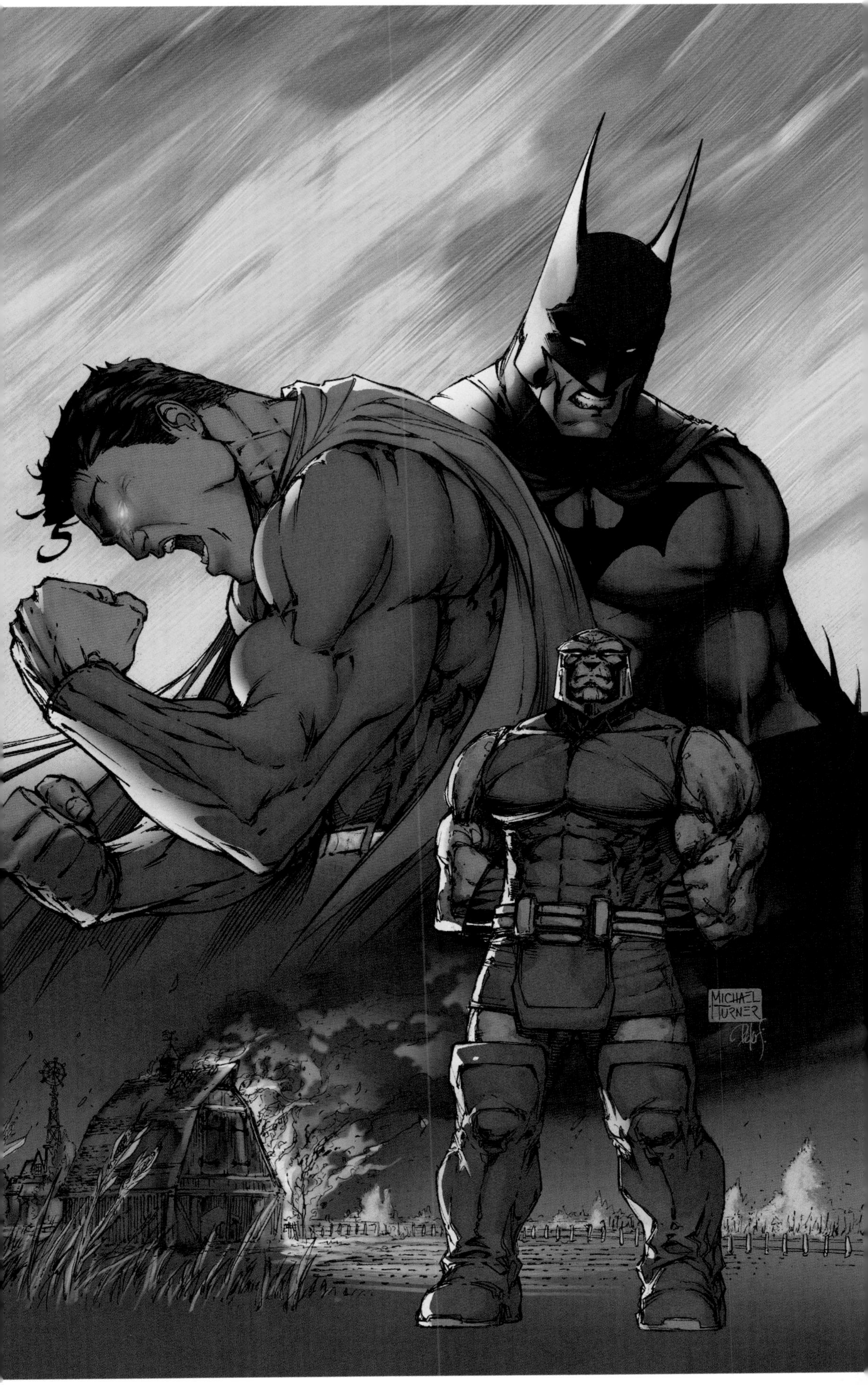
MICHAEL TURNER

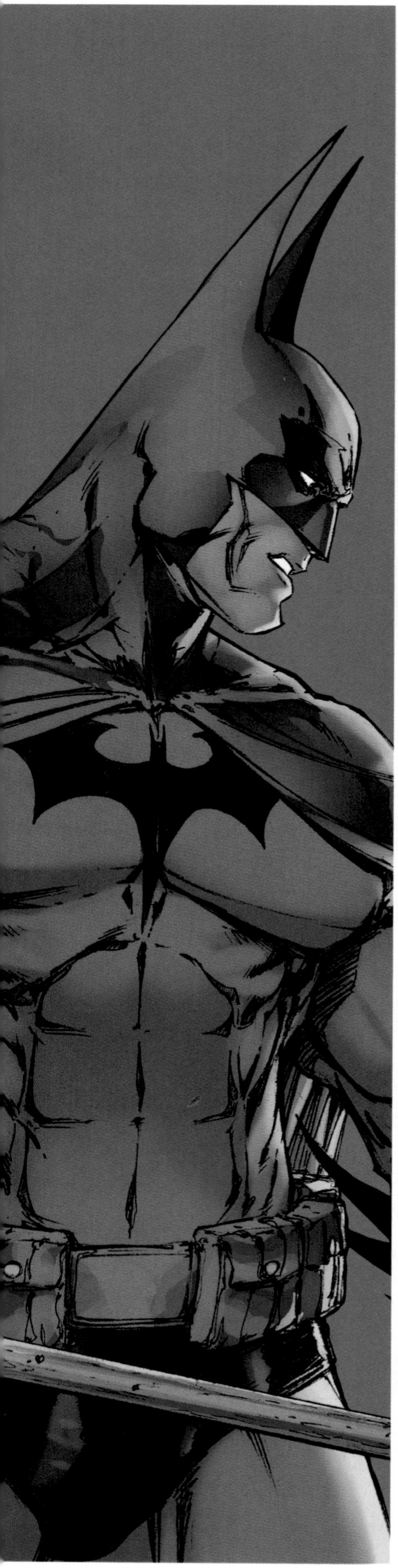

THE SUPERGIRL FROM KRYPTON

PART SIX
HERO

JEPH LOEB
WRITER
MICHAEL TURNER
ARTIST
PETER STEIGERWALD
COLORIST
RICHARD STARKINGS
LETTERER
MICHAEL TURNER
WITH
PETER STEIGERWALD
COVER

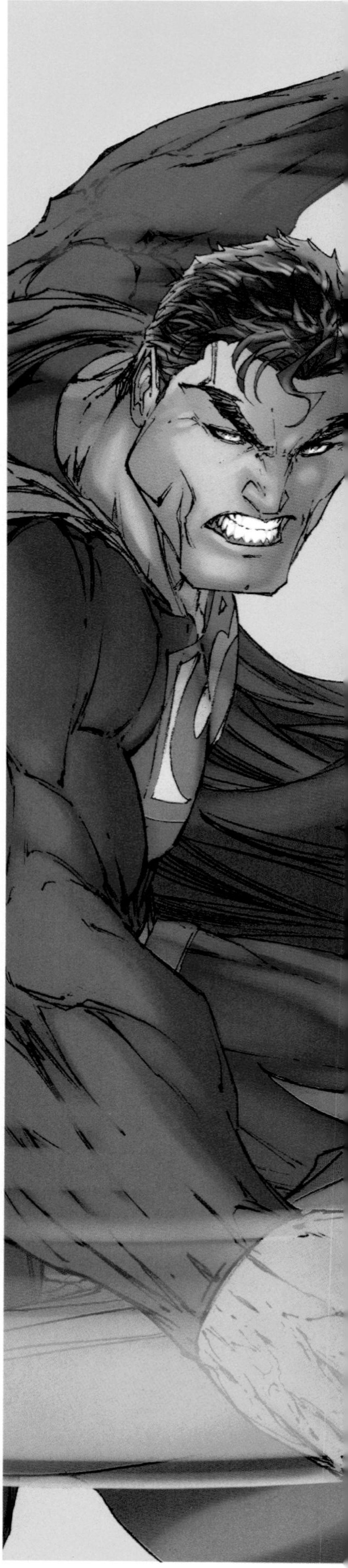

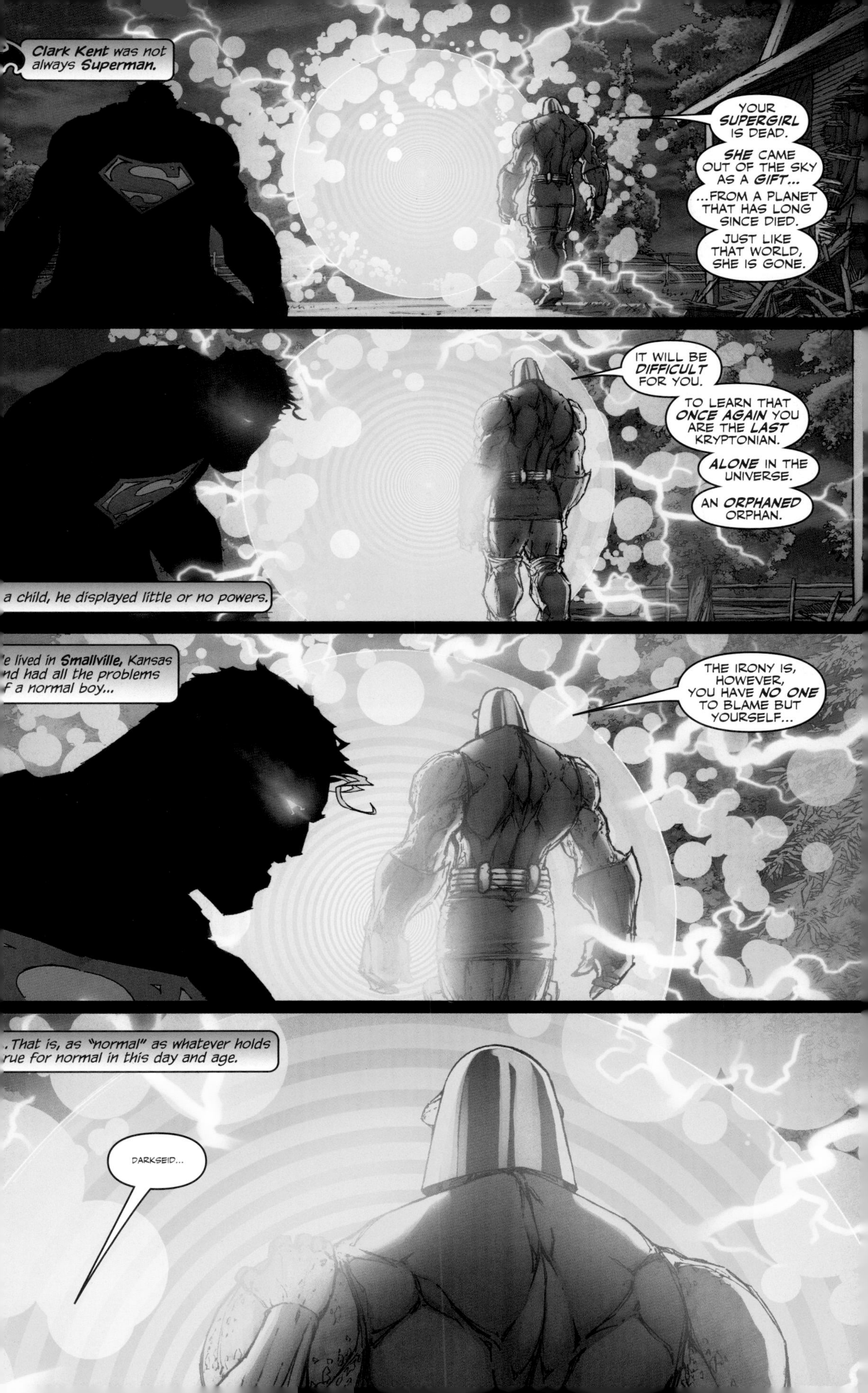
Clark Kent was not always Superman.
YOUR SUPERGIRL IS DEAD.
SHE CAME OUT OF THE SKY AS A GIFT...
...FROM A PLANET THAT HAS LONG SINCE DIED.
JUST LIKE THAT WORLD, SHE IS GONE.
IT WILL BE DIFFICULT FOR YOU.
TO LEARN THAT ONCE AGAIN YOU ARE THE LAST KRYPTONIAN.
ALONE IN THE UNIVERSE.
AN ORPHANED ORPHAN.
a child, he displayed little or no powers.
'e lived in Smallville, Kansas nd had all the problems f a normal boy...
THE IRONY IS, HOWEVER, YOU HAVE NO ONE TO BLAME BUT YOURSELF...
.That is, as "normal" as whatever holds rue for normal in this day and age.
DARKSEID...

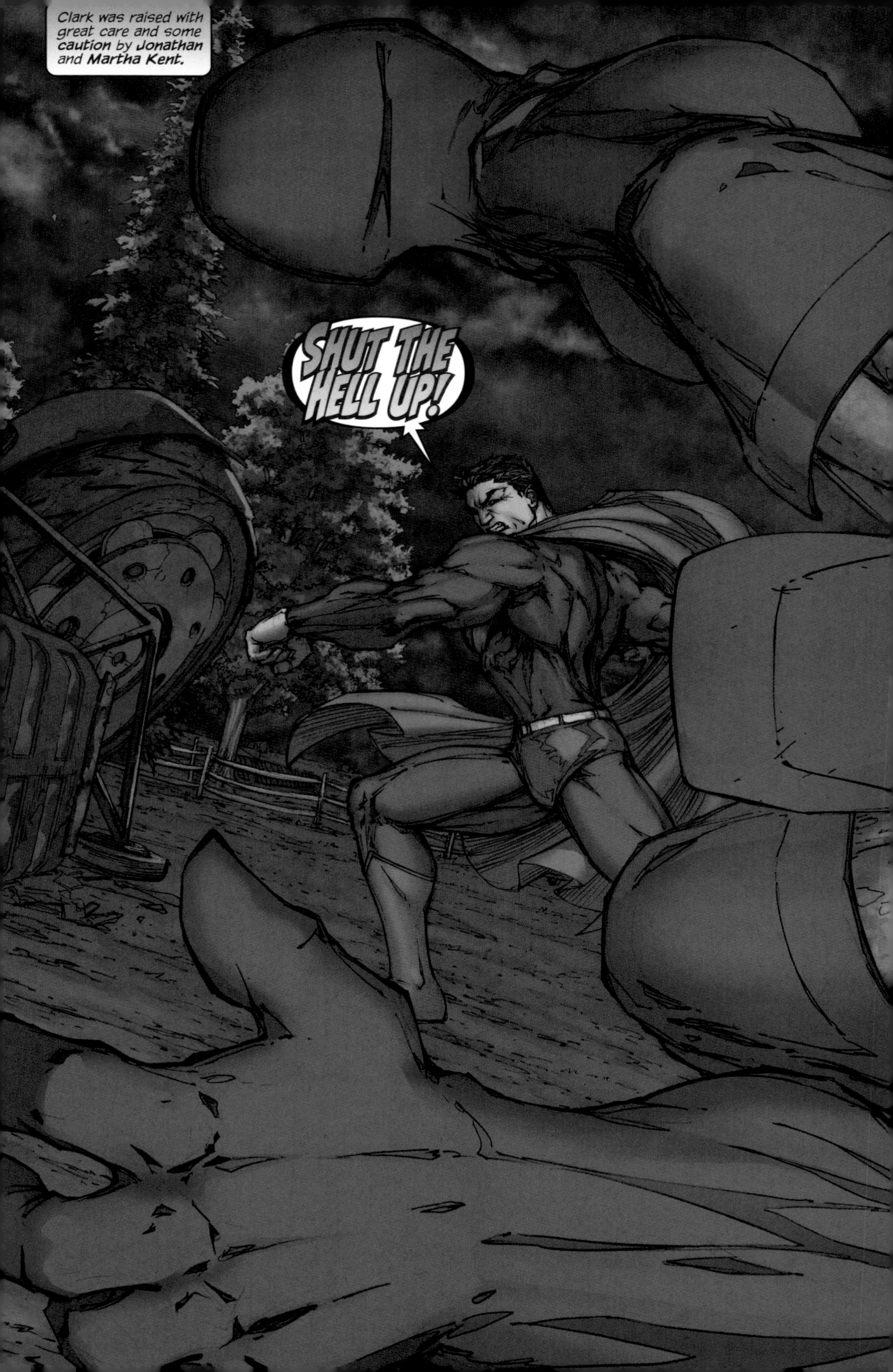
Clark was raised with great care and some **caution** by **Jonathan** and **Martha Kent.**
SHUT THE HELL UP!

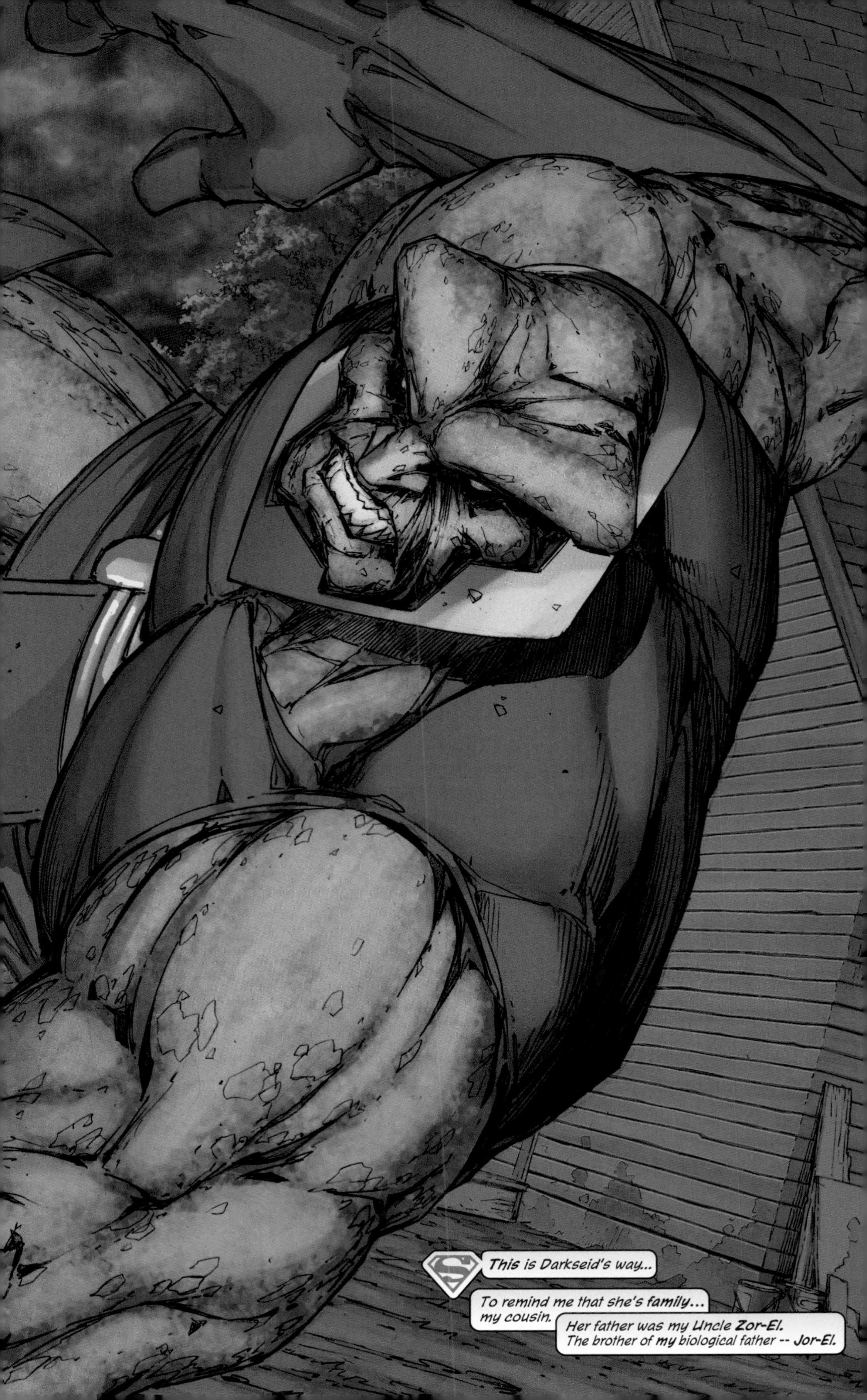
This is Darkseid's way...
To remind me that she's family... my cousin.
Her father was my Uncle Zor-El.
The brother of my biological father -- Jor-El.

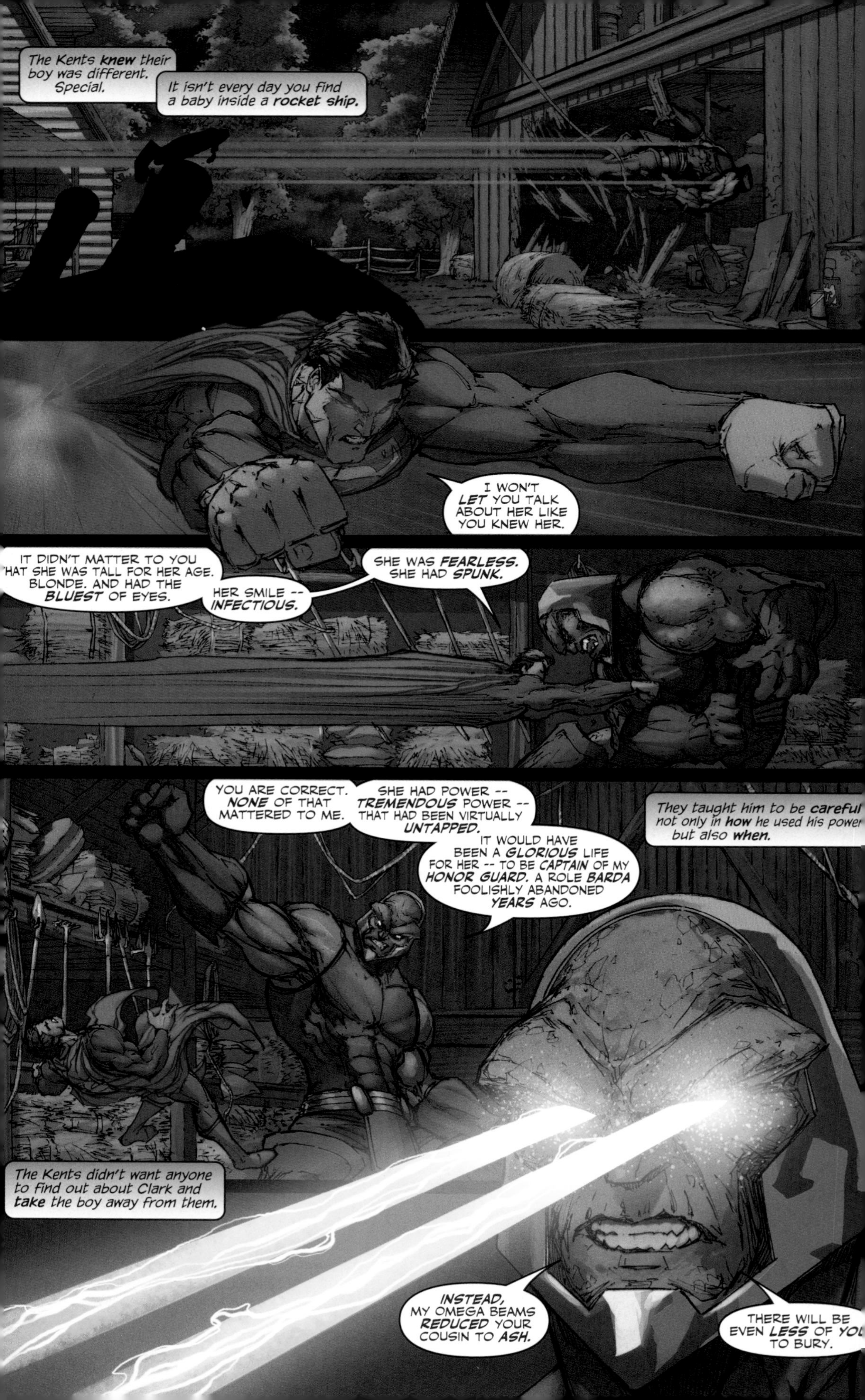

The Kents **knew** their boy was different. Special.
It isn't every day you find a baby inside a **rocket ship.**
I WON'T *LET* YOU TALK ABOUT HER LIKE YOU KNEW HER.
IT DIDN'T MATTER TO YOU THAT SHE WAS TALL FOR HER AGE. BLONDE. AND HAD THE *BLUEST* OF EYES.
HER SMILE -- *INFECTIOUS.*
SHE WAS *FEARLESS.* SHE HAD *SPUNK.*
YOU ARE CORRECT. *NONE* OF THAT MATTERED TO ME.
SHE HAD POWER -- *TREMENDOUS* POWER -- THAT HAD BEEN VIRTUALLY *UNTAPPED.*
IT WOULD HAVE BEEN A *GLORIOUS* LIFE FOR HER -- TO BE *CAPTAIN* OF MY *HONOR GUARD.* A ROLE *BARDA* FOOLISHLY ABANDONED *YEARS* AGO.
They taught him to be **careful** not only in **how** he used his power but also **when.**
The Kents didn't want anyone to find out about Clark and **take** the boy away from them.
INSTEAD, MY OMEGA BEAMS *REDUCED* YOUR COUSIN TO *ASH.*
THERE WILL BE EVEN *LESS* OF YOU TO BURY.

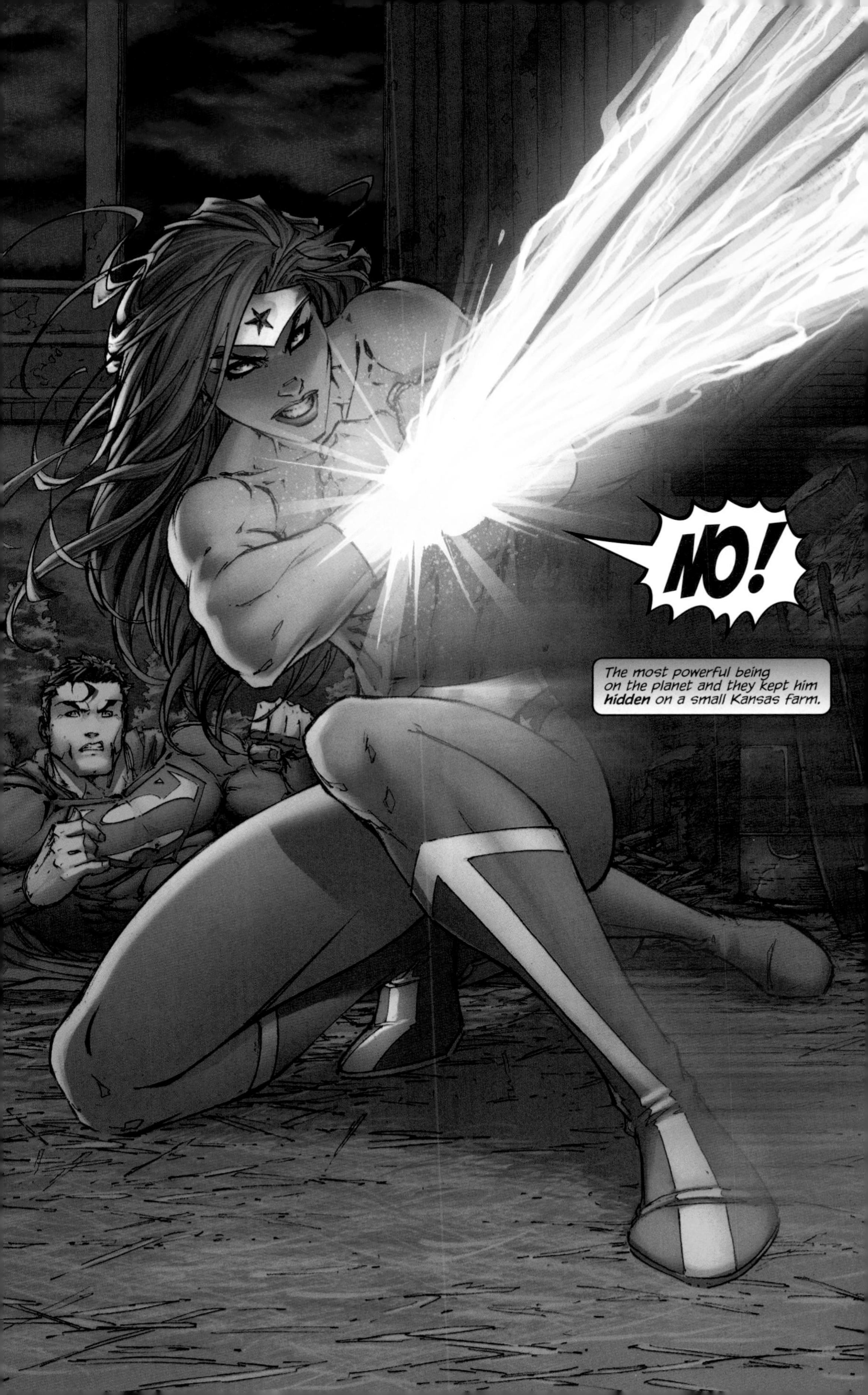
NO!
The most powerful being on the planet and they kept him **hidden** on a small Kansas farm.

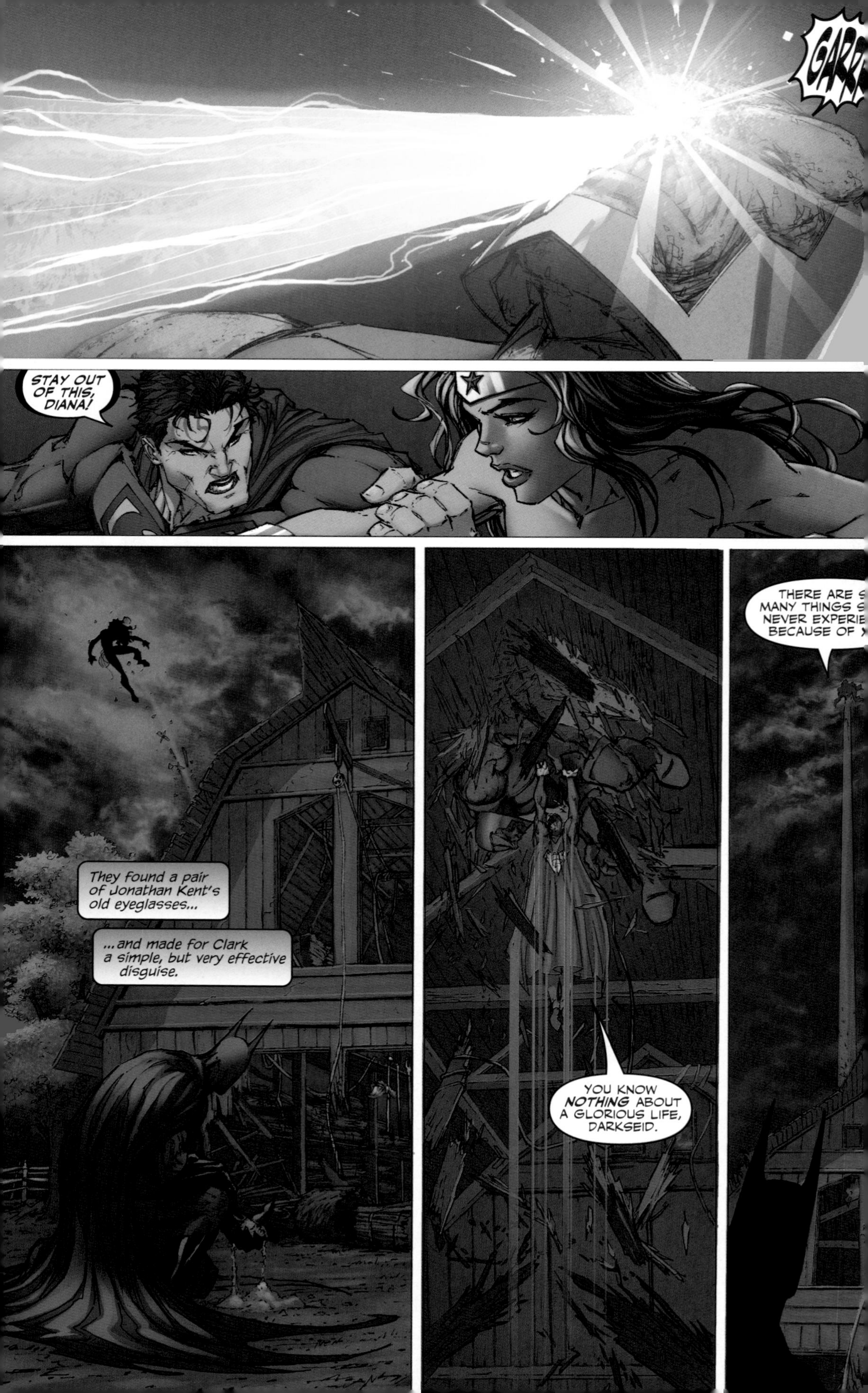

STAY OUT OF THIS, DIANA!
They found a pair of Jonathan Kent's old eyeglasses...
...and made for Clark a simple, but very effective disguise.
YOU KNOW NOTHING ABOUT A GLORIOUS LIFE, DARKSEID.

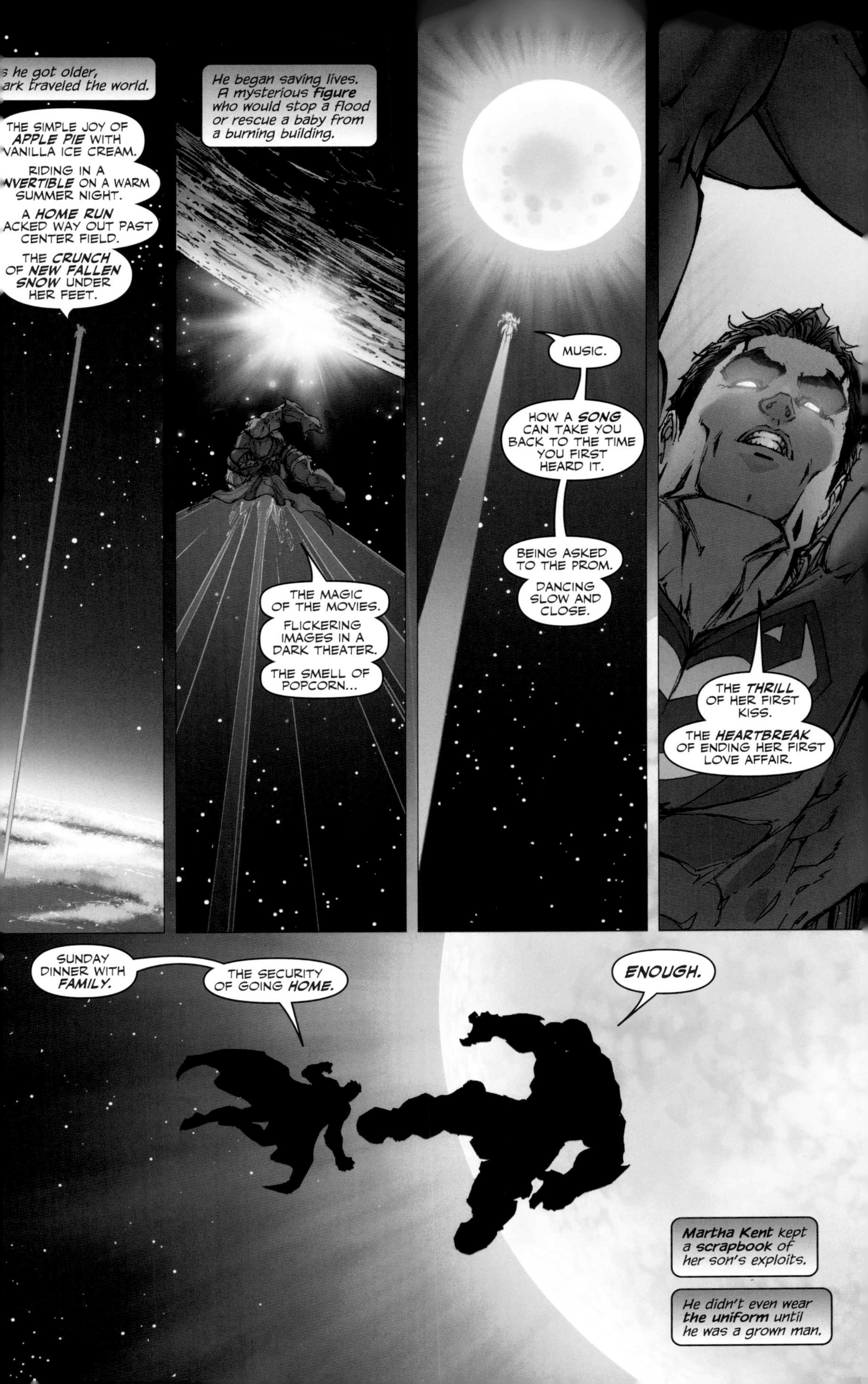
s he got older,
ark traveled the world.
THE SIMPLE JOY OF APPLE PIE WITH VANILLA ICE CREAM.
RIDING IN A NVERTIBLE ON A WARM SUMMER NIGHT.
A HOME RUN ACKED WAY OUT PAST CENTER FIELD.
THE CRUNCH OF NEW FALLEN SNOW UNDER HER FEET.
He began saving lives. A mysterious figure who would stop a flood or rescue a baby from a burning building.
THE MAGIC OF THE MOVIES.
FLICKERING IMAGES IN A DARK THEATER.
THE SMELL OF POPCORN...
MUSIC.
HOW A SONG CAN TAKE YOU BACK TO THE TIME YOU FIRST HEARD IT.
BEING ASKED TO THE PROM.
DANCING SLOW AND CLOSE.
THE THRILL OF HER FIRST KISS.
THE HEARTBREAK OF ENDING HER FIRST LOVE AFFAIR.
SUNDAY DINNER WITH FAMILY.
THE SECURITY OF GOING HOME.
ENOUGH.
Martha Kent kept a scrapbook of her son's exploits.
He didn't even wear the uniform until he was a grown man.

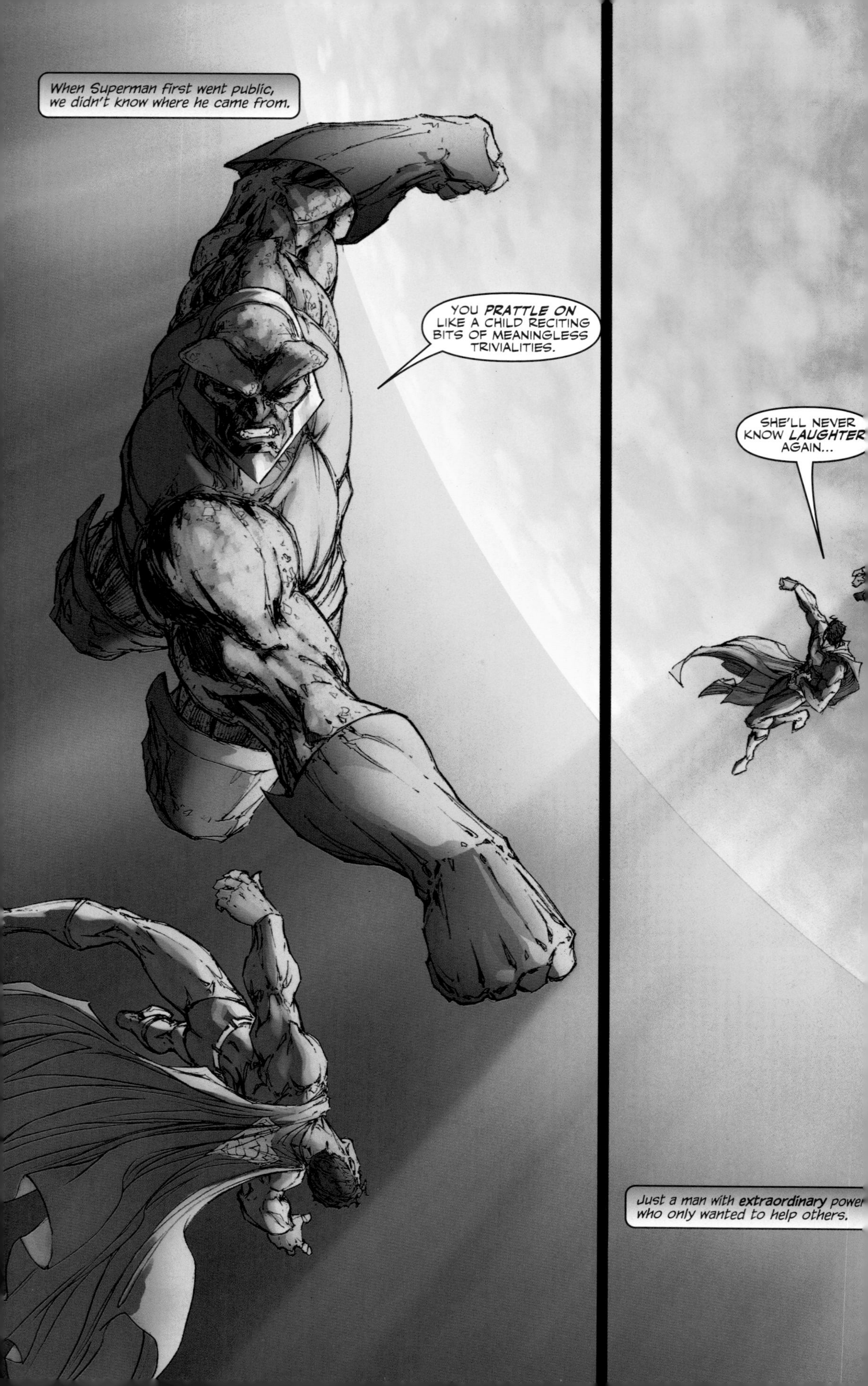
When Superman first went public, we didn't know where he came from.
YOU PRATTLE ON LIKE A CHILD RECITING BITS OF MEANINGLESS TRIVIALITIES.
SHE'LL NEVER KNOW LAUGHTER AGAIN...
Just a man with extraordinary power who only wanted to help others.

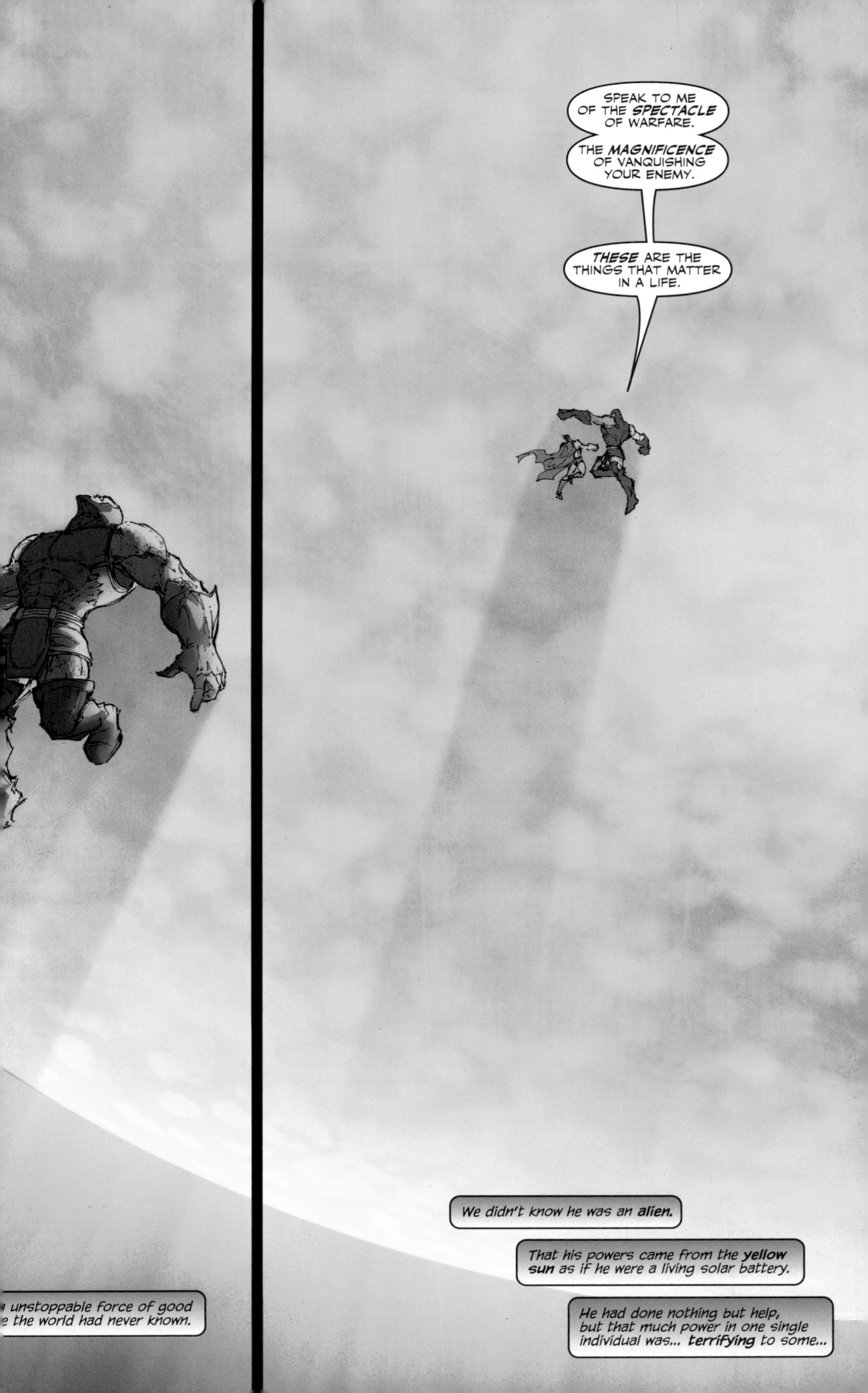

SPEAK TO ME OF THE *SPECTACLE* OF WARFARE.
THE *MAGNIFICENCE* OF VANQUISHING YOUR ENEMY.
THESE ARE THE THINGS THAT MATTER IN A LIFE.
unstoppable force of good the world had never known.
We didn't know he was an **alien.**
That his powers came from the **yellow sun** as if he were a living solar battery.
He had done nothing but help, but that much power in one single individual was... **terrifying** to some...

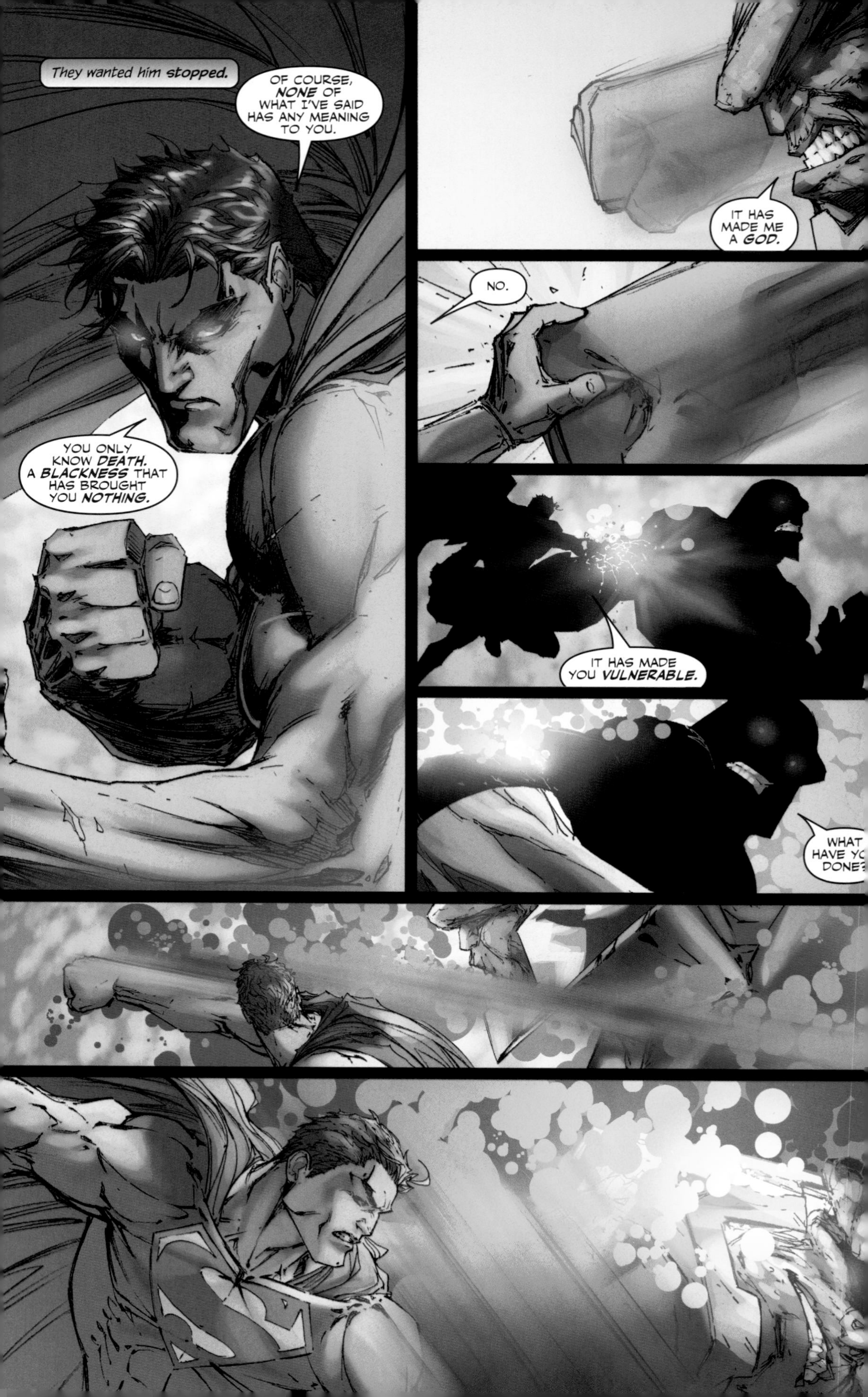
They wanted him stopped.
OF COURSE, NONE OF WHAT I'VE SAID HAS ANY MEANING TO YOU.
YOU ONLY KNOW DEATH. A BLACKNESS THAT HAS BROUGHT YOU NOTHING.
IT HAS MADE ME A GOD.
NO.
IT HAS MADE YOU VULNERABLE.
WHAT HAVE YO DONE?

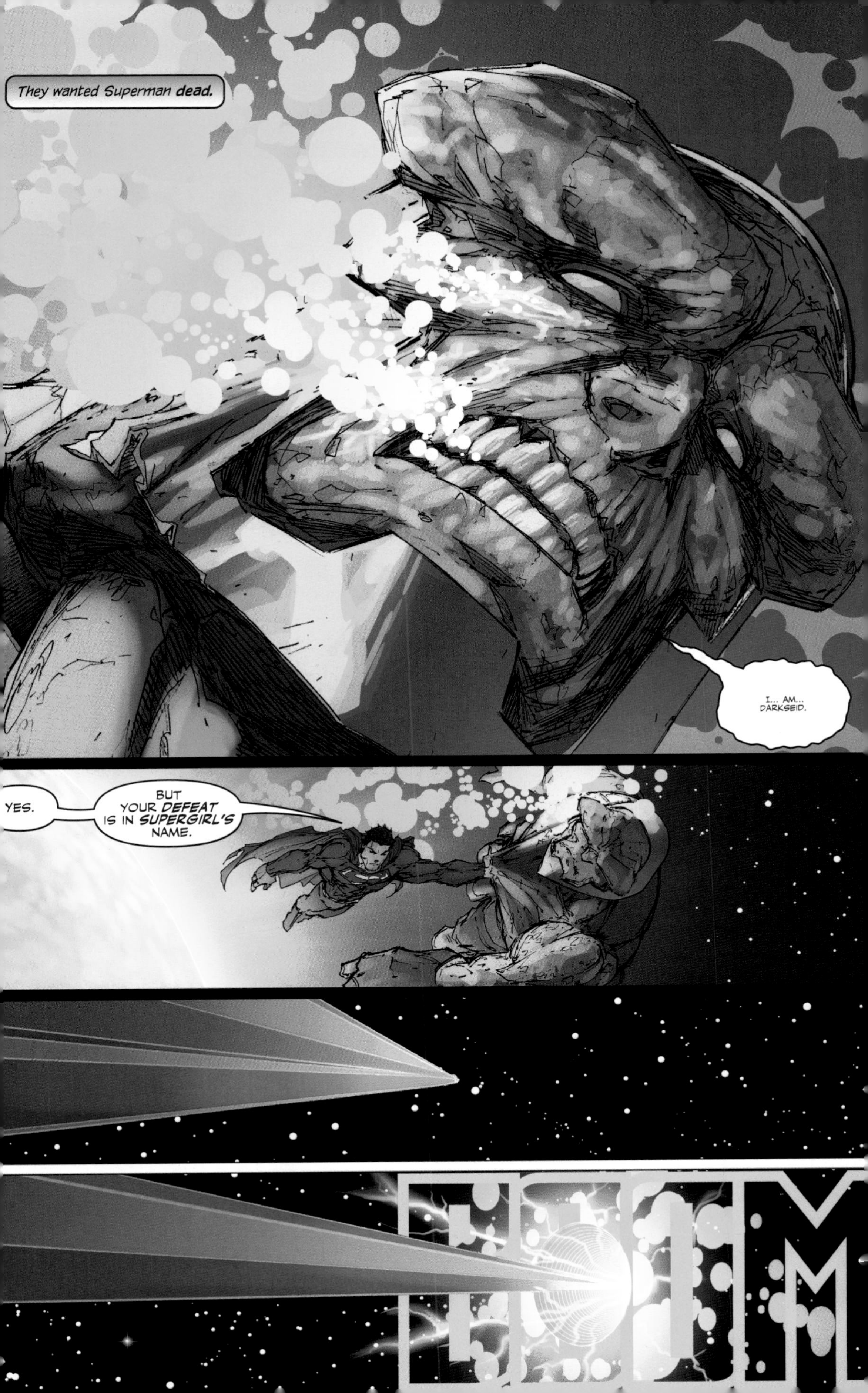
They wanted Superman dead.
I... AM... DARKSEID.
YES.
BUT YOUR DEFEAT IS IN SUPERGIRL'S NAME.

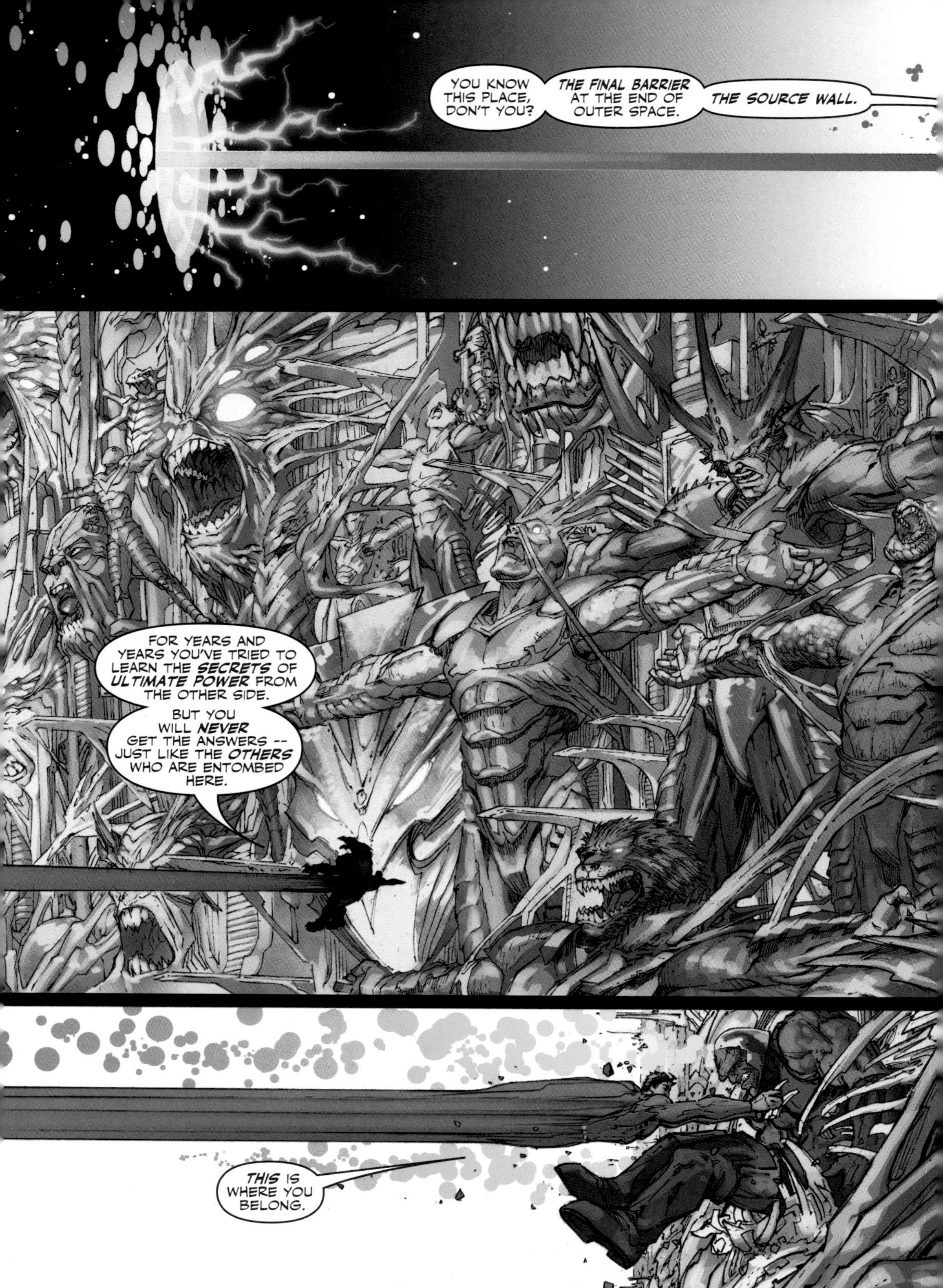

YOU KNOW THIS PLACE, DON'T YOU?
THE FINAL BARRIER AT THE END OF OUTER SPACE.
THE SOURCE WALL.
FOR YEARS AND YEARS YOU'VE TRIED TO LEARN THE SECRETS OF ULTIMATE POWER FROM THE OTHER SIDE.
BUT YOU WILL NEVER GET THE ANSWERS -- JUST LIKE THE OTHERS WHO ARE ENTOMBED HERE.
THIS IS WHERE YOU BELONG.

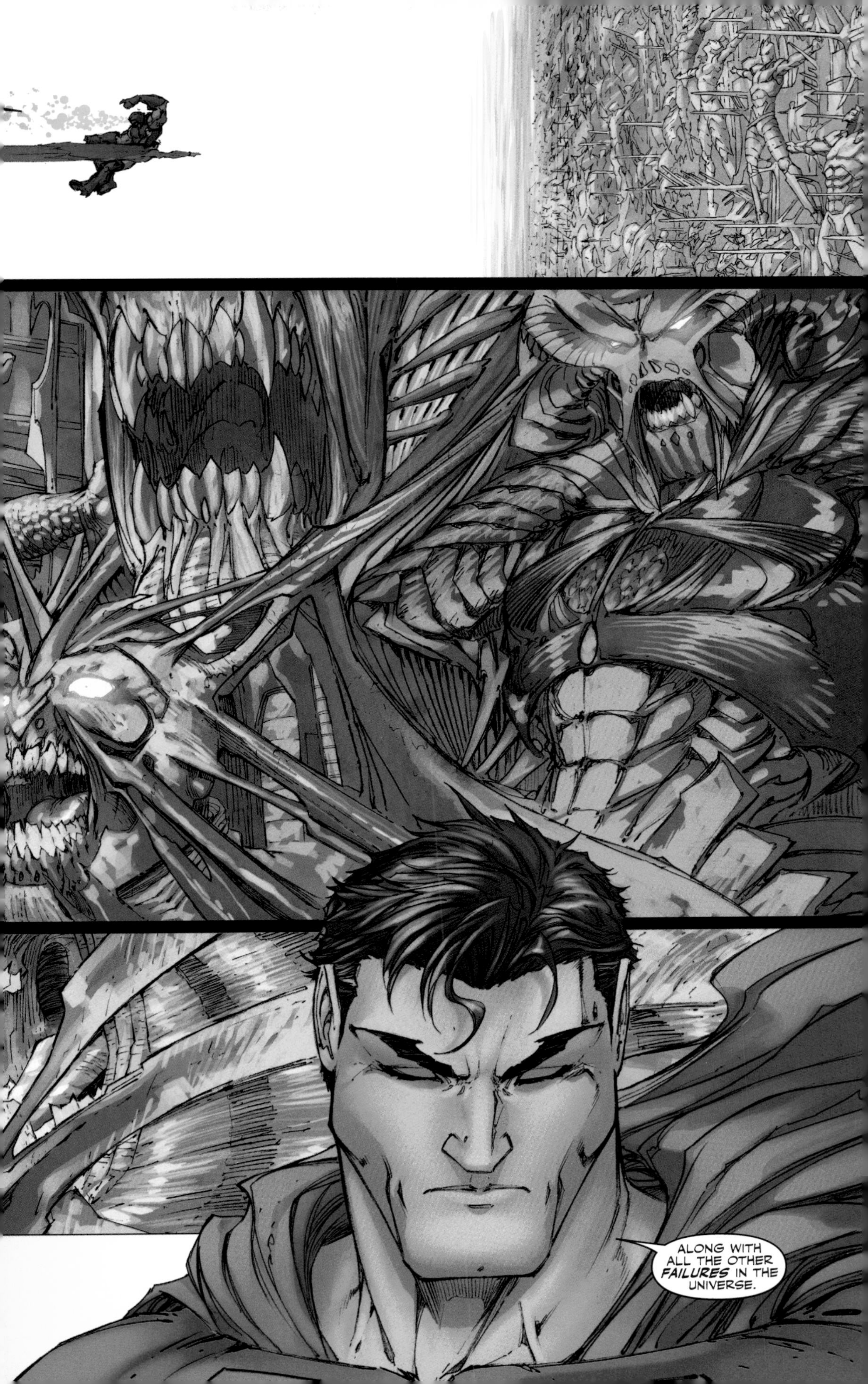
ALONG WITH ALL THE OTHER FAILURES IN THE UNIVERSE.

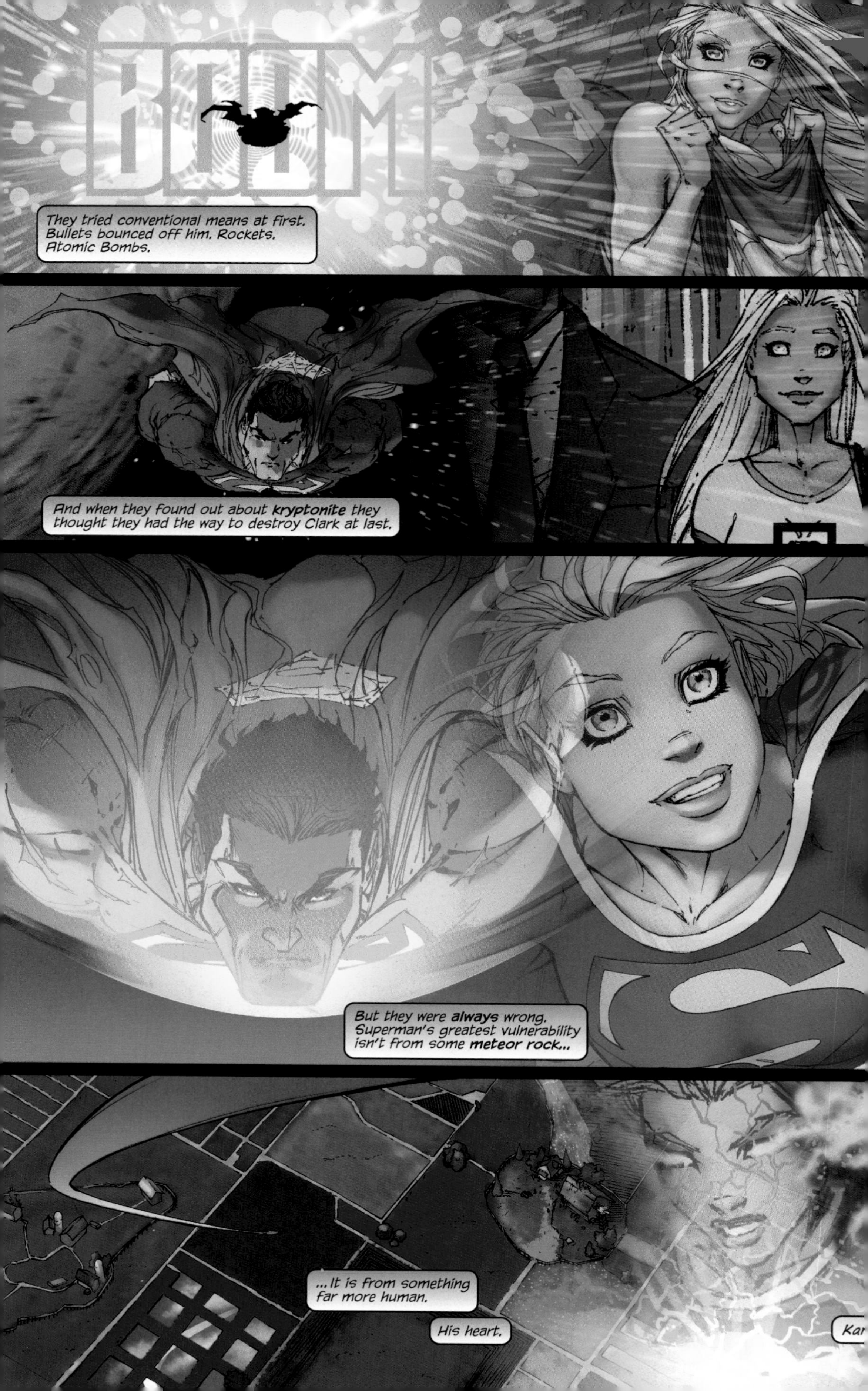
BOOM
They tried conventional means at first. Bullets bounced off him. Rockets. Atomic Bombs.
And when they found out about kryptonite they thought they had the way to destroy Clark at last.
But they were always wrong. Superman's greatest vulnerability isn't from some meteor rock...
...It is from something far more human.
His heart.

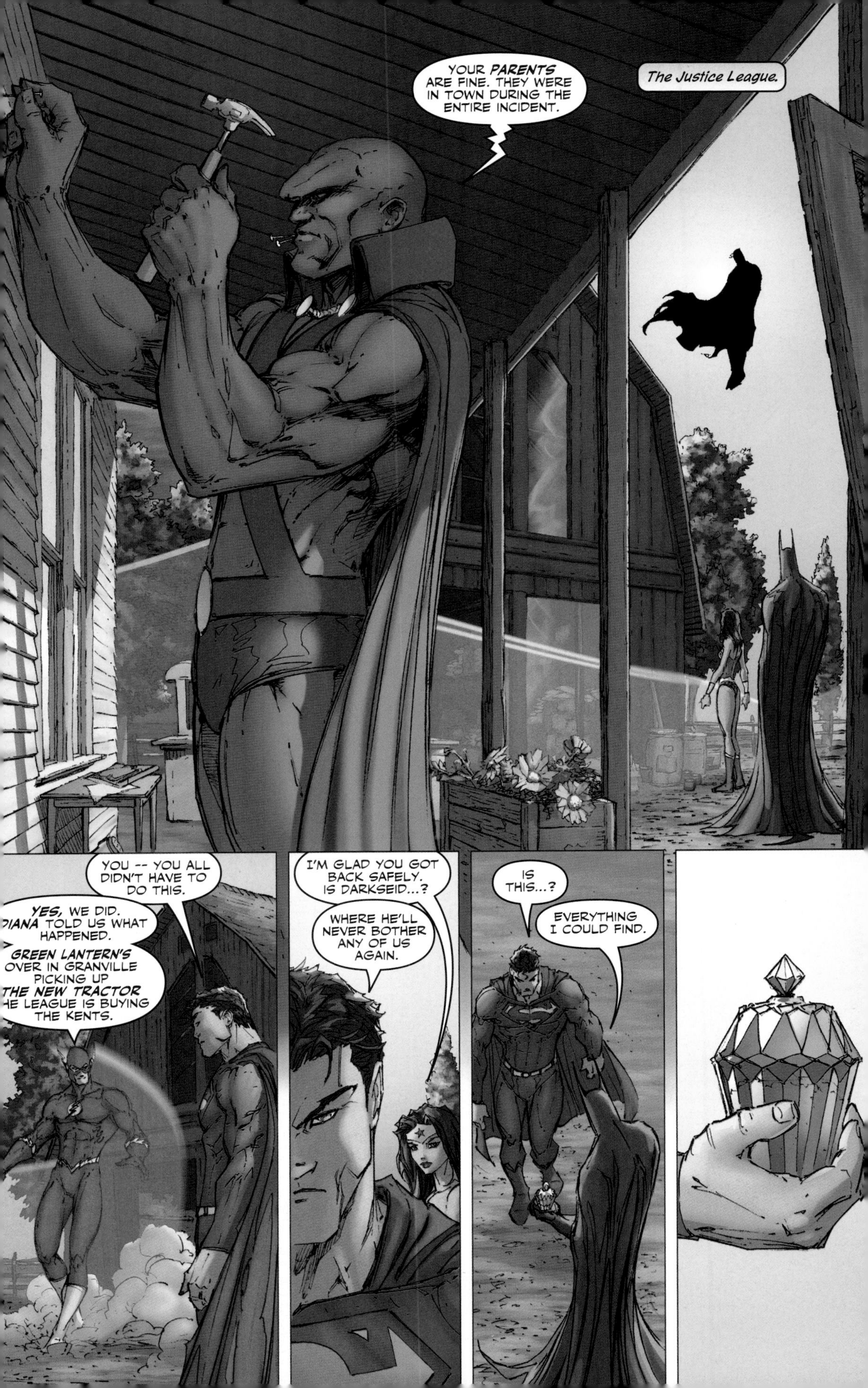
YOUR PARENTS ARE FINE. THEY WERE IN TOWN DURING THE ENTIRE INCIDENT.
The Justice League.
YOU -- YOU ALL DIDN'T HAVE TO DO THIS.
YES, WE DID. DIANA TOLD US WHAT HAPPENED.
GREEN LANTERN'S OVER IN GRANVILLE PICKING UP THE NEW TRACTOR THE LEAGUE IS BUYING THE KENTS.
I'M GLAD YOU GOT BACK SAFELY. IS DARKSEID...?
WHERE HE'LL NEVER BOTHER ANY OF US AGAIN.
IS THIS...?
EVERYTHING I COULD FIND.

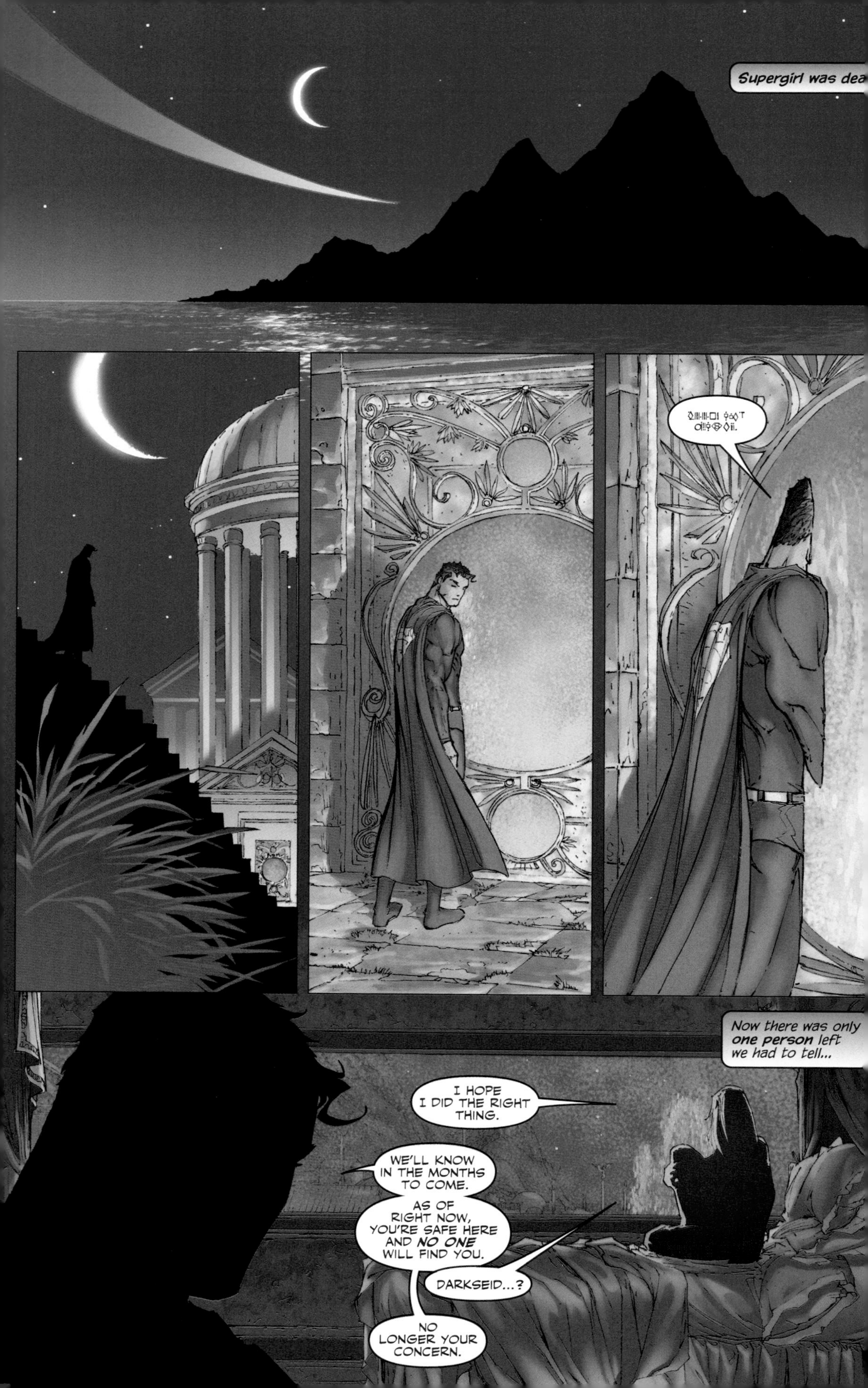

Supergirl was dea
Now there was only **one person** left we had to tell...
I HOPE I DID THE RIGHT THING.
WE'LL KNOW IN THE MONTHS TO COME.
AS OF RIGHT NOW, YOU'RE SAFE HERE AND ***NO ONE*** WILL FIND YOU.
DARKSEID...?
NO LONGER YOUR CONCERN.

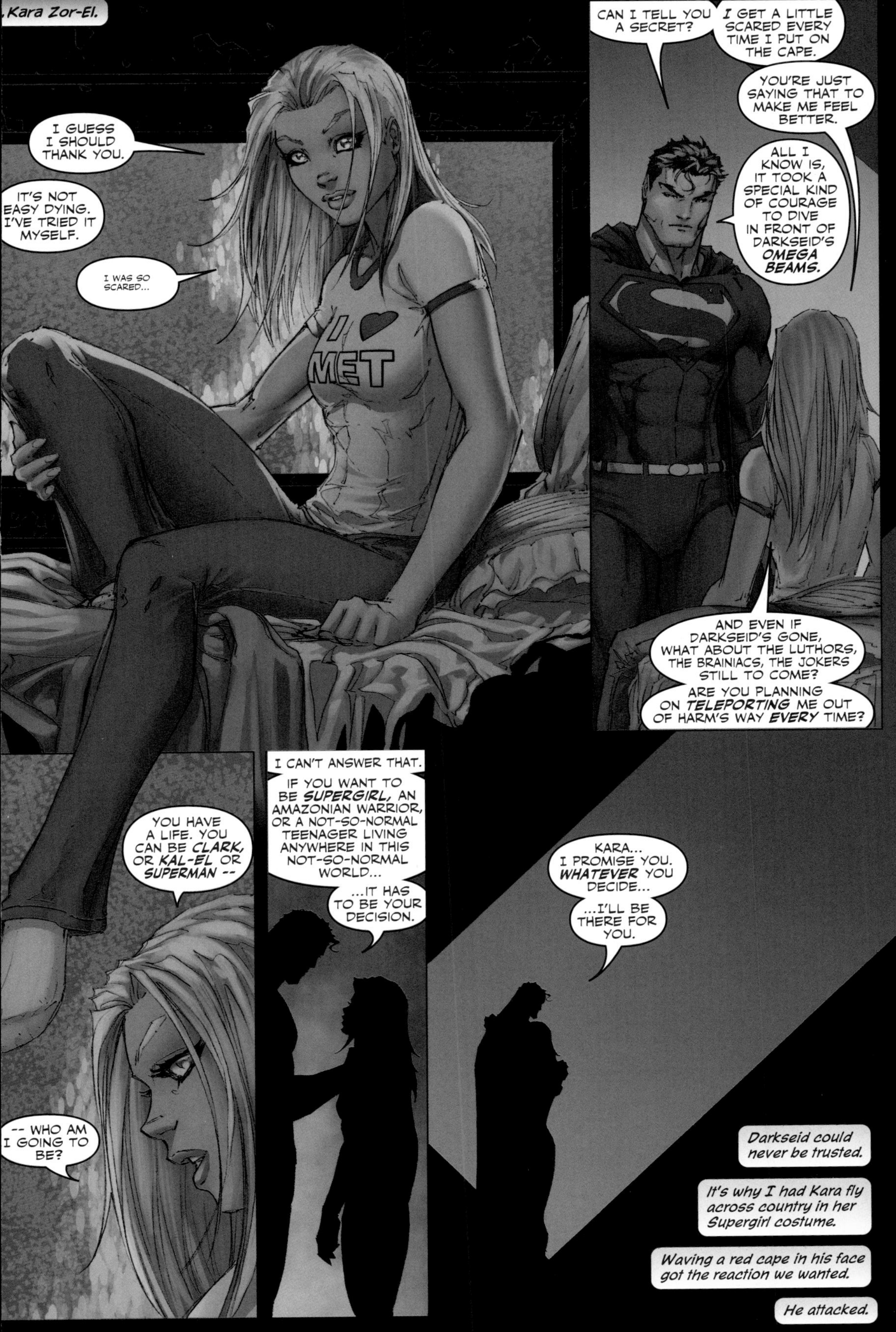

Kara Zor-El.
I GUESS I SHOULD THANK YOU.
IT'S NOT EASY DYING. I'VE TRIED IT MYSELF.
I WAS SO SCARED...
I ♥ MET
CAN I TELL YOU A SECRET?
I GET A LITTLE SCARED EVERY TIME I PUT ON THE CAPE.
YOU'RE JUST SAYING THAT TO MAKE ME FEEL BETTER.
ALL I KNOW IS, IT TOOK A SPECIAL KIND OF COURAGE TO DIVE IN FRONT OF DARKSEID'S OMEGA BEAMS.
AND EVEN IF DARKSEID'S GONE, WHAT ABOUT THE LUTHORS, THE BRAINIACS, THE JOKERS STILL TO COME?
ARE YOU PLANNING ON TELEPORTING ME OUT OF HARM'S WAY EVERY TIME?
YOU HAVE A LIFE. YOU CAN BE CLARK, OR KAL-EL OR SUPERMAN --
-- WHO AM I GOING TO BE?
I CAN'T ANSWER THAT.
IF YOU WANT TO BE SUPERGIRL, AN AMAZONIAN WARRIOR, OR A NOT-SO-NORMAL TEENAGER LIVING ANYWHERE IN THIS NOT-SO-NORMAL WORLD...
...IT HAS TO BE YOUR DECISION.
KARA... I PROMISE YOU. WHATEVER YOU DECIDE...
...I'LL BE THERE FOR YOU.
Darkseid could never be trusted.
It's why I had Kara fly across country in her Supergirl costume.
Waving a red cape in his face got the reaction we wanted.
He attacked.

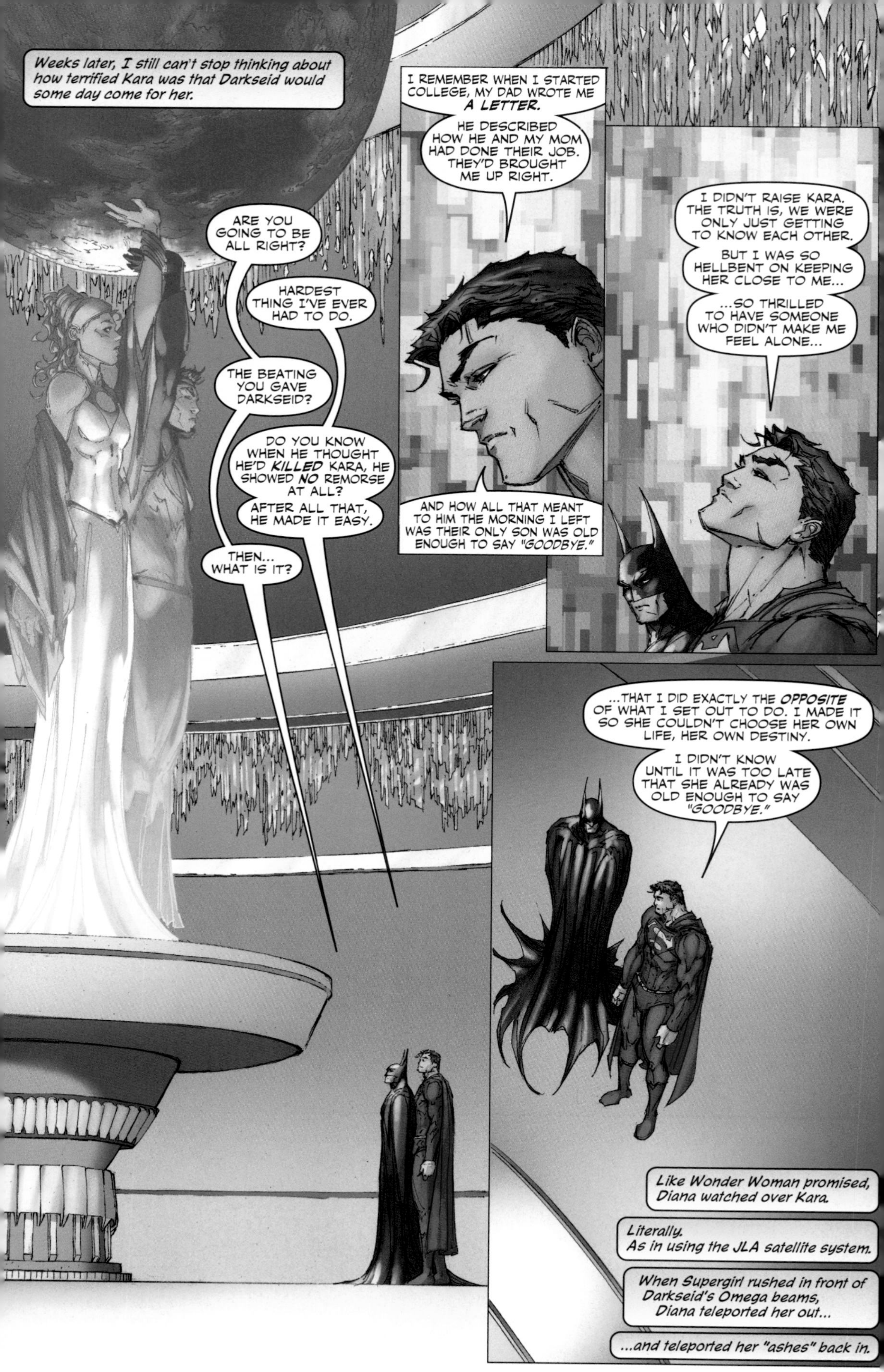
Weeks later, I still can't stop thinking about how terrified Kara was that Darkseid would some day come for her.
ARE YOU GOING TO BE ALL RIGHT?
HARDEST THING I'VE EVER HAD TO DO.
THE BEATING YOU GAVE DARKSEID?
DO YOU KNOW WHEN HE THOUGHT HE'D KILLED KARA, HE SHOWED NO REMORSE AT ALL?
AFTER ALL THAT, HE MADE IT EASY.
THEN... WHAT IS IT?
I REMEMBER WHEN I STARTED COLLEGE, MY DAD WROTE ME A LETTER.
HE DESCRIBED HOW HE AND MY MOM HAD DONE THEIR JOB. THEY'D BROUGHT ME UP RIGHT.
AND HOW ALL THAT MEANT TO HIM THE MORNING I LEFT WAS THEIR ONLY SON WAS OLD ENOUGH TO SAY "GOODBYE."
I DIDN'T RAISE KARA. THE TRUTH IS, WE WERE ONLY JUST GETTING TO KNOW EACH OTHER.
BUT I WAS SO HELLBENT ON KEEPING HER CLOSE TO ME...
...SO THRILLED TO HAVE SOMEONE WHO DIDN'T MAKE ME FEEL ALONE...
...THAT I DID EXACTLY THE OPPOSITE OF WHAT I SET OUT TO DO. I MADE IT SO SHE COULDN'T CHOOSE HER OWN LIFE, HER OWN DESTINY.
I DIDN'T KNOW UNTIL IT WAS TOO LATE THAT SHE ALREADY WAS OLD ENOUGH TO SAY "GOODBYE."
Like Wonder Woman promised, Diana watched over Kara.
Literally. As in using the JLA satellite system.
When Supergirl rushed in front of Darkseid's Omega beams, Diana teleported her out...
...and teleported her "ashes" back in.

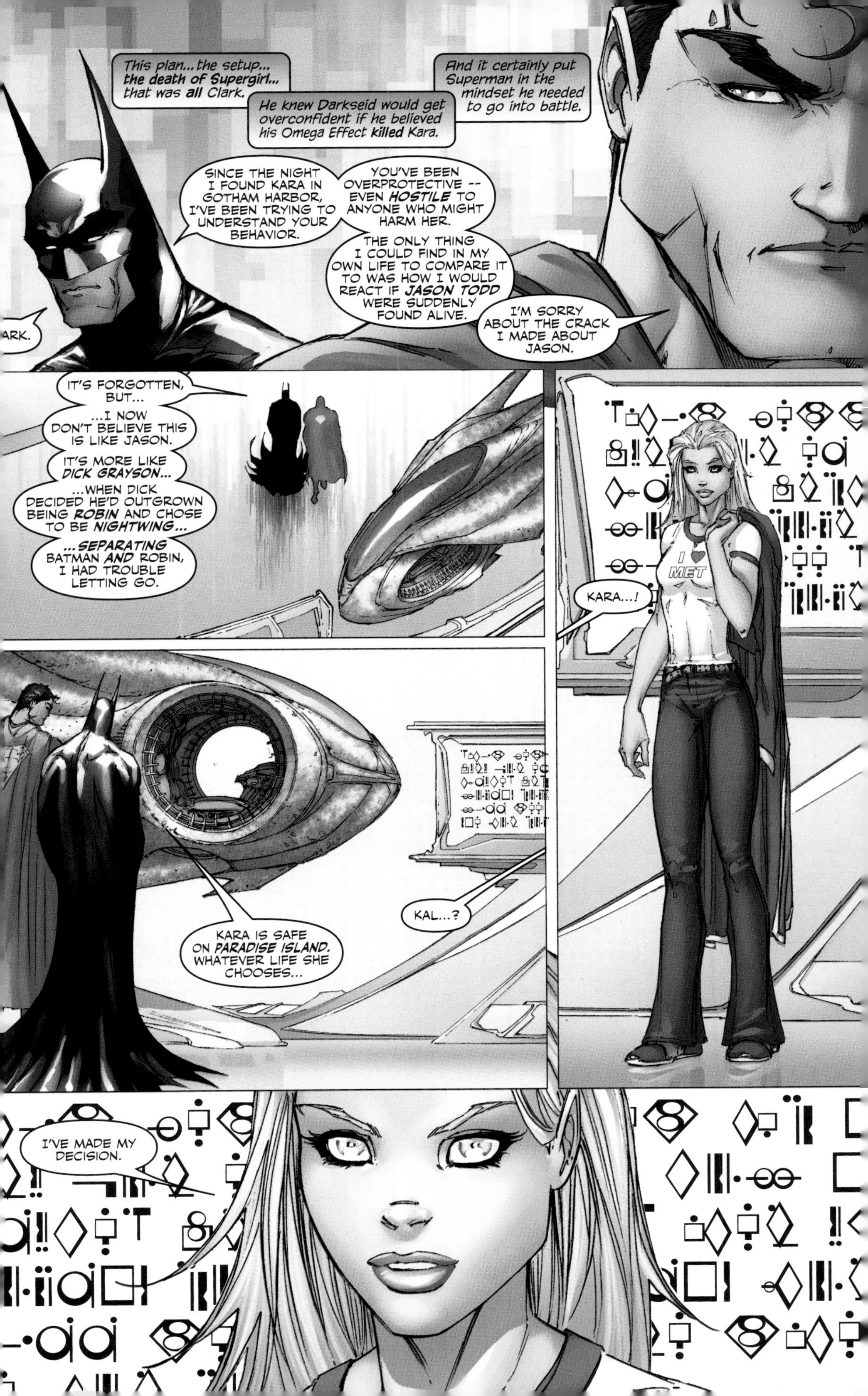
This plan...the setup... the death of Supergirl... that was all Clark.
He knew Darkseid would get overconfident if he believed his Omega Effect killed Kara.
And it certainly put Superman in the mindset he needed to go into battle.
ARK.
SINCE THE NIGHT I FOUND KARA IN GOTHAM HARBOR, I'VE BEEN TRYING TO UNDERSTAND YOUR BEHAVIOR.
YOU'VE BEEN OVERPROTECTIVE -- EVEN HOSTILE TO ANYONE WHO MIGHT HARM HER.
THE ONLY THING I COULD FIND IN MY OWN LIFE TO COMPARE IT TO WAS HOW I WOULD REACT IF JASON TODD WERE SUDDENLY FOUND ALIVE.
I'M SORRY ABOUT THE CRACK I MADE ABOUT JASON.
IT'S FORGOTTEN, BUT...
...I NOW DON'T BELIEVE THIS IS LIKE JASON.
IT'S MORE LIKE DICK GRAYSON...
...WHEN DICK DECIDED HE'D OUTGROWN BEING ROBIN AND CHOSE TO BE NIGHTWING...
...SEPARATING BATMAN AND ROBIN, I HAD TROUBLE LETTING GO.
KARA...!
I ♥ MET
KARA IS SAFE ON PARADISE ISLAND. WHATEVER LIFE SHE CHOOSES...
KAL...?
I'VE MADE MY DECISION.

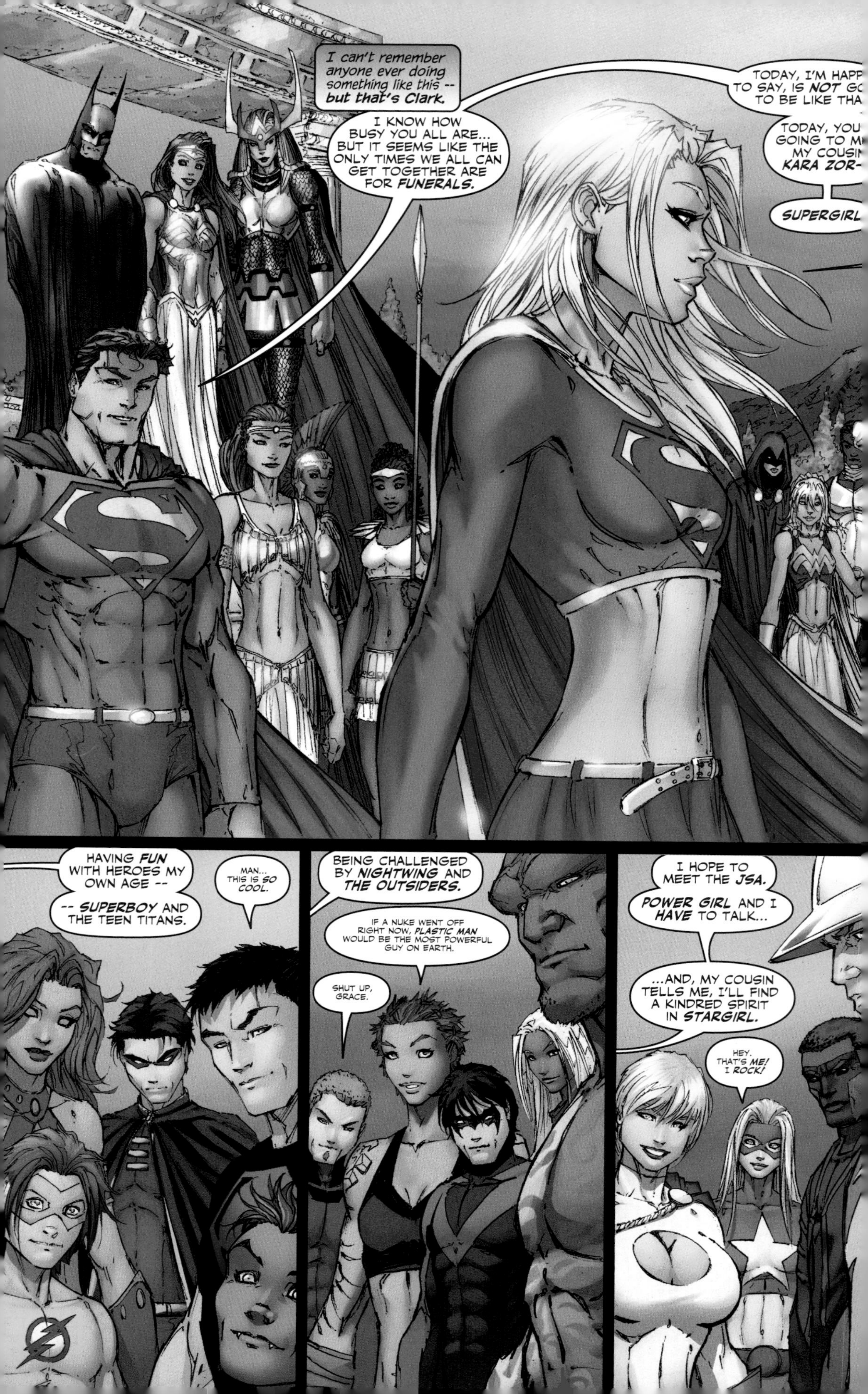

I can't remember anyone ever doing something like this -- but that's Clark.
I KNOW HOW BUSY YOU ALL ARE... BUT IT SEEMS LIKE THE ONLY TIMES WE ALL CAN GET TOGETHER ARE FOR FUNERALS.
TODAY, I'M HAPP TO SAY, IS NOT GO TO BE LIKE THA
TODAY, YOU GOING TO M MY COUSIN KARA ZOR-
SUPERGIRL
HAVING FUN WITH HEROES MY OWN AGE --
-- SUPERBOY AND THE TEEN TITANS.
MAN... THIS IS SO COOL.
BEING CHALLENGED BY NIGHTWING AND THE OUTSIDERS.
IF A NUKE WENT OFF RIGHT NOW, PLASTIC MAN WOULD BE THE MOST POWERFUL GUY ON EARTH.
SHUT UP, GRACE.
I HOPE TO MEET THE JSA.
POWER GIRL AND I HAVE TO TALK...
...AND, MY COUSIN TELLS ME, I'LL FIND A KINDRED SPIRIT IN STARGIRL.
HEY. THAT'S ME! I ROCK!

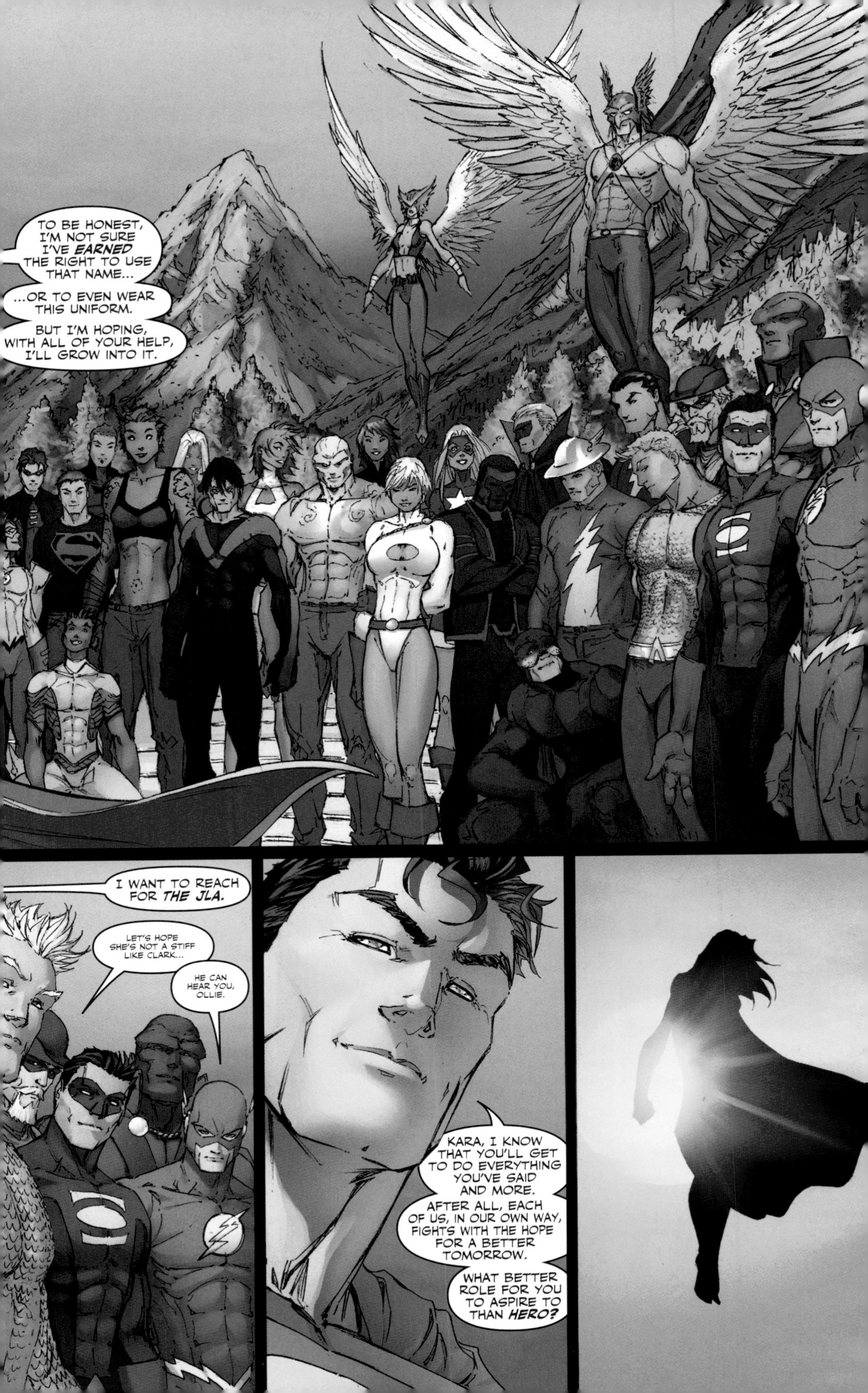
TO BE HONEST, I'M NOT SURE I'VE EARNED THE RIGHT TO USE THAT NAME...
...OR TO EVEN WEAR THIS UNIFORM.
BUT I'M HOPING, WITH ALL OF YOUR HELP, I'LL GROW INTO IT.
I WANT TO REACH FOR THE JLA.
LET'S HOPE SHE'S NOT A STIFF LIKE CLARK...
HE CAN HEAR YOU, OLLIE.
KARA, I KNOW THAT YOU'LL GET TO DO EVERYTHING YOU'VE SAID AND MORE.
AFTER ALL, EACH OF US, IN OUR OWN WAY, FIGHTS WITH THE HOPE FOR A BETTER TOMORROW.
WHAT BETTER ROLE FOR YOU TO ASPIRE TO THAN HERO?

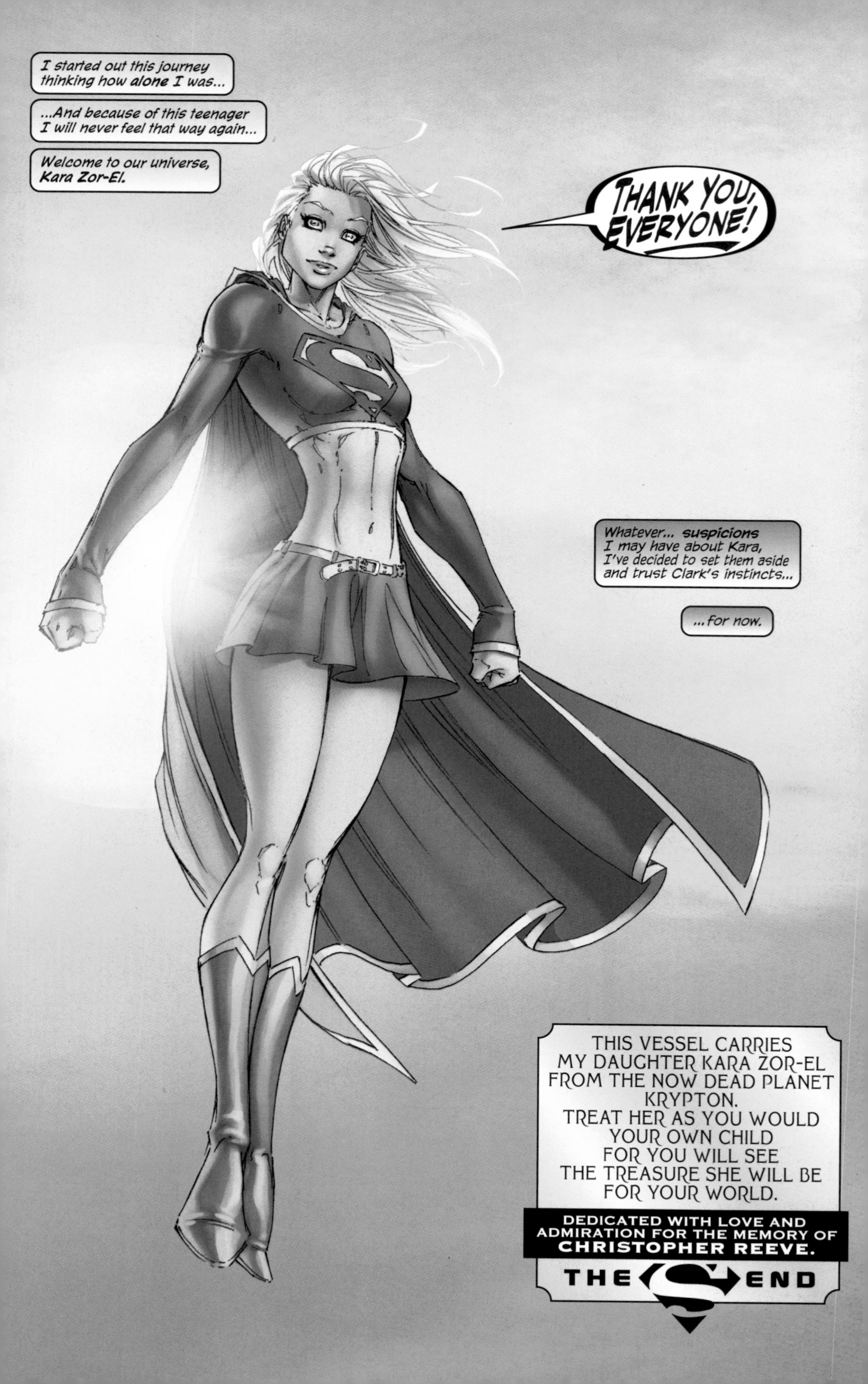
I started out this journey thinking how alone I was...
...And because of this teenager I will never feel that way again...
Welcome to our universe, Kara Zor-El.
THANK YOU, EVERYONE!
Whatever... suspicions I may have about Kara, I've decided to set them aside and trust Clark's instincts...
...for now.
THIS VESSEL CARRIES MY DAUGHTER KARA ZOR-EL FROM THE NOW DEAD PLANET KRYPTON. TREAT HER AS YOU WOULD YOUR OWN CHILD FOR YOU WILL SEE THE TREASURE SHE WILL BE FOR YOUR WORLD.
DEDICATED WITH LOVE AND ADMIRATION FOR THE MEMORY OF CHRISTOPHER REEVE.
THE END

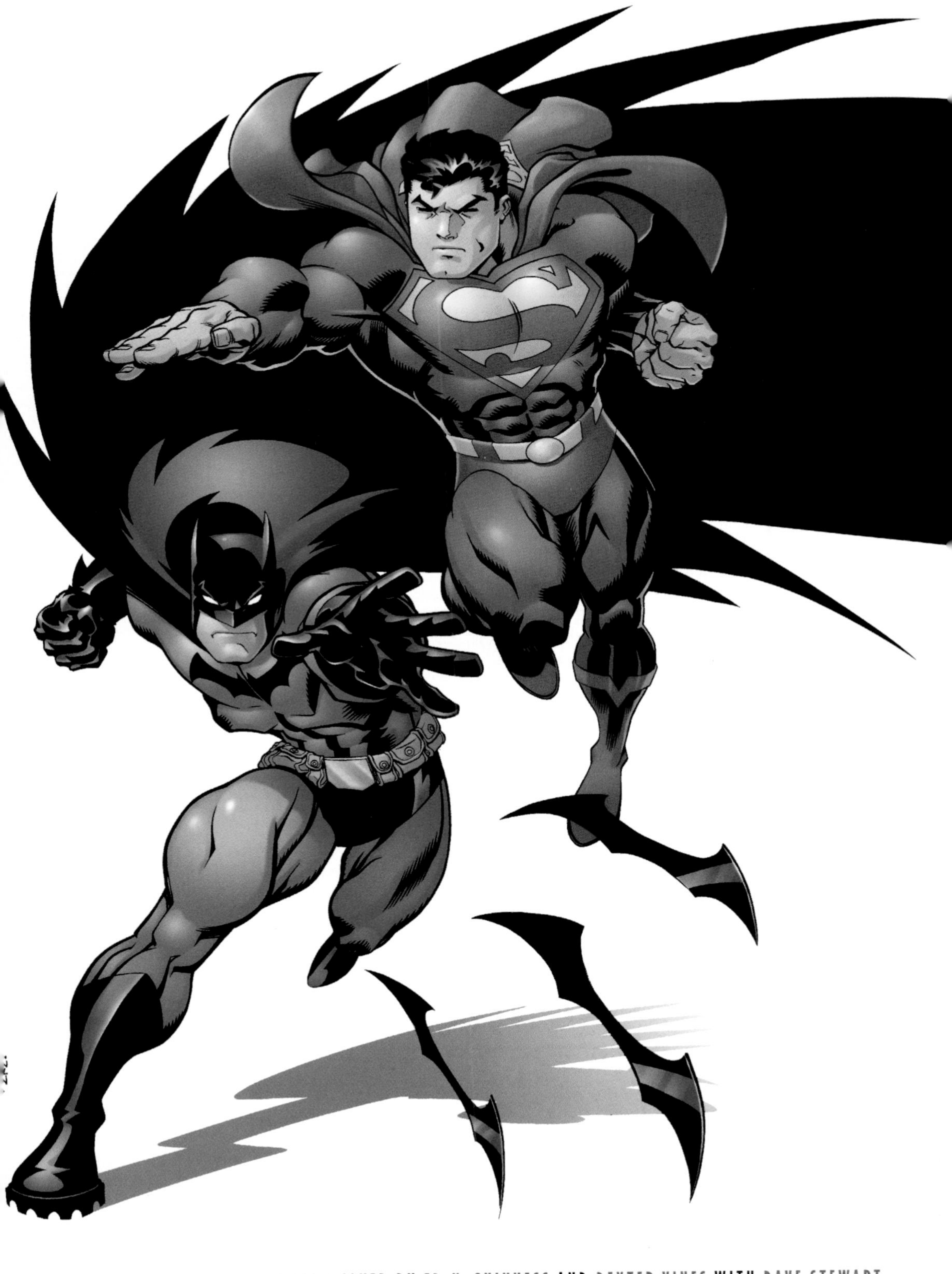

SUPERMAN/BATMAN SECRET FILES 1 COVER BY ED McGUINNESS AND DEXTER VINES WITH DAVE STEWART

When Clark met Bruce

A TALE FROM THE DAYS OF SMALLVILLE

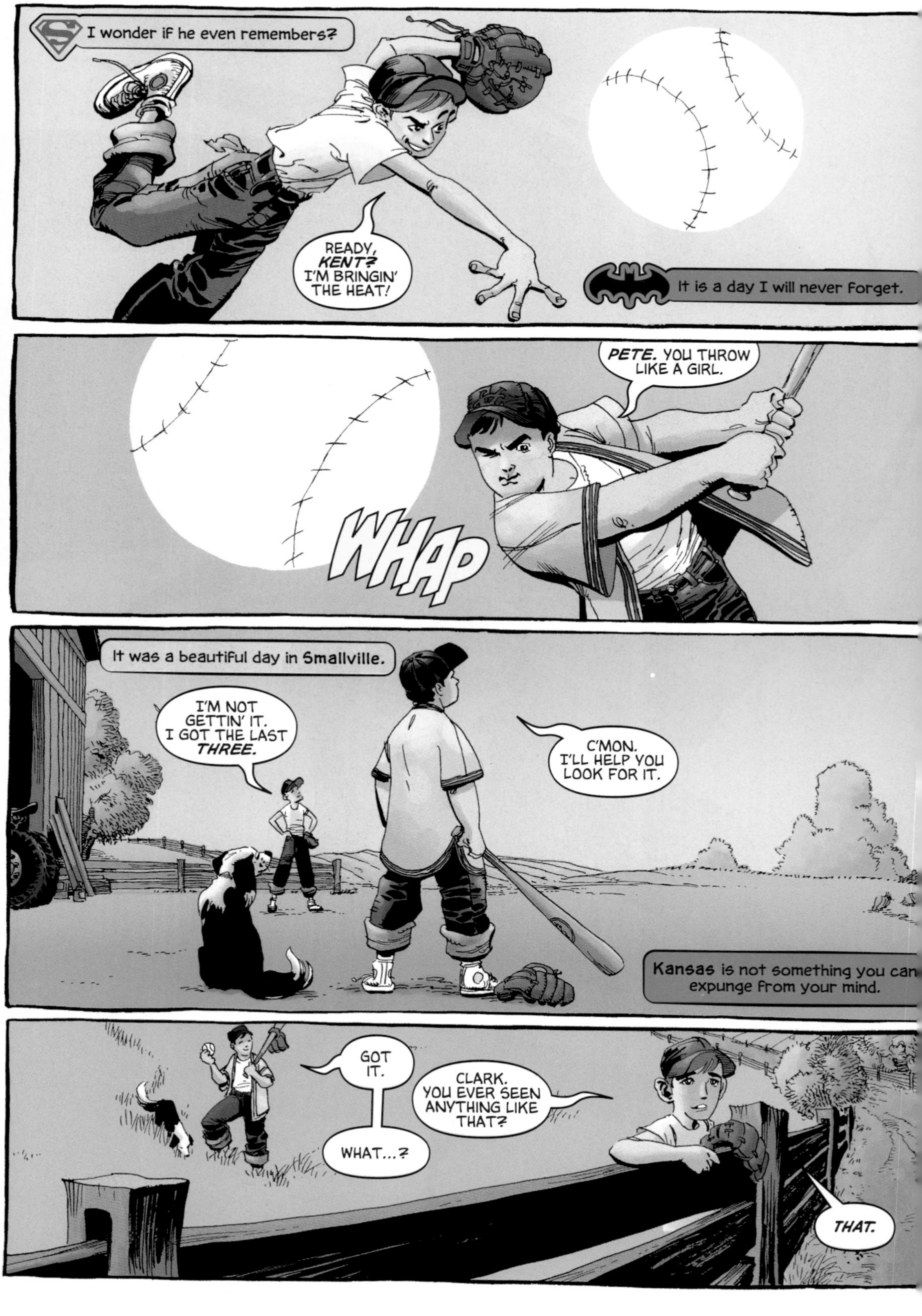

I wonder if he even remembers?
READY, KENT? I'M BRINGIN' THE HEAT!
It is a day I will never forget.
PETE. YOU THROW LIKE A GIRL.
WHAP
It was a beautiful day in Smallville.
I'M NOT GETTIN' IT. I GOT THE LAST THREE.
C'MON. I'LL HELP YOU LOOK FOR IT.
Kansas is not something you can expunge from your mind.
GOT IT.
WHAT...?
CLARK. YOU EVER SEEN ANYTHING LIKE THAT?
THAT.

Pete was right. No one in Smallville had that kind of wealth.

After my parents died, Alfred thought that I needed to get out of Gotham City. We drove to California.

THINK WE SHOULD ASK THAT KID TO PLAY BALL?

CLARK. LOOK AT HIM. THAT KID HAS NEVER PLAYED *ANYTHING.*

By the time we reached the West Coast, I had convinced Alfred we should fly back home.

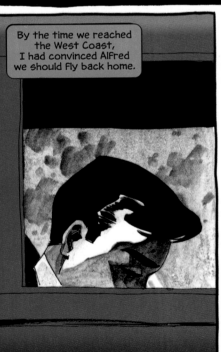

WONDER WHO THAT WAS...?

WHO CARES? RACE YA.

LAST ONE IN HAS TO KISS *LANA!*

I still wonder if we should've asked him to play. If it would've made a difference.

Sometimes, I wish they had asked me to play. But, by then, my life had changed. I had no time for games.

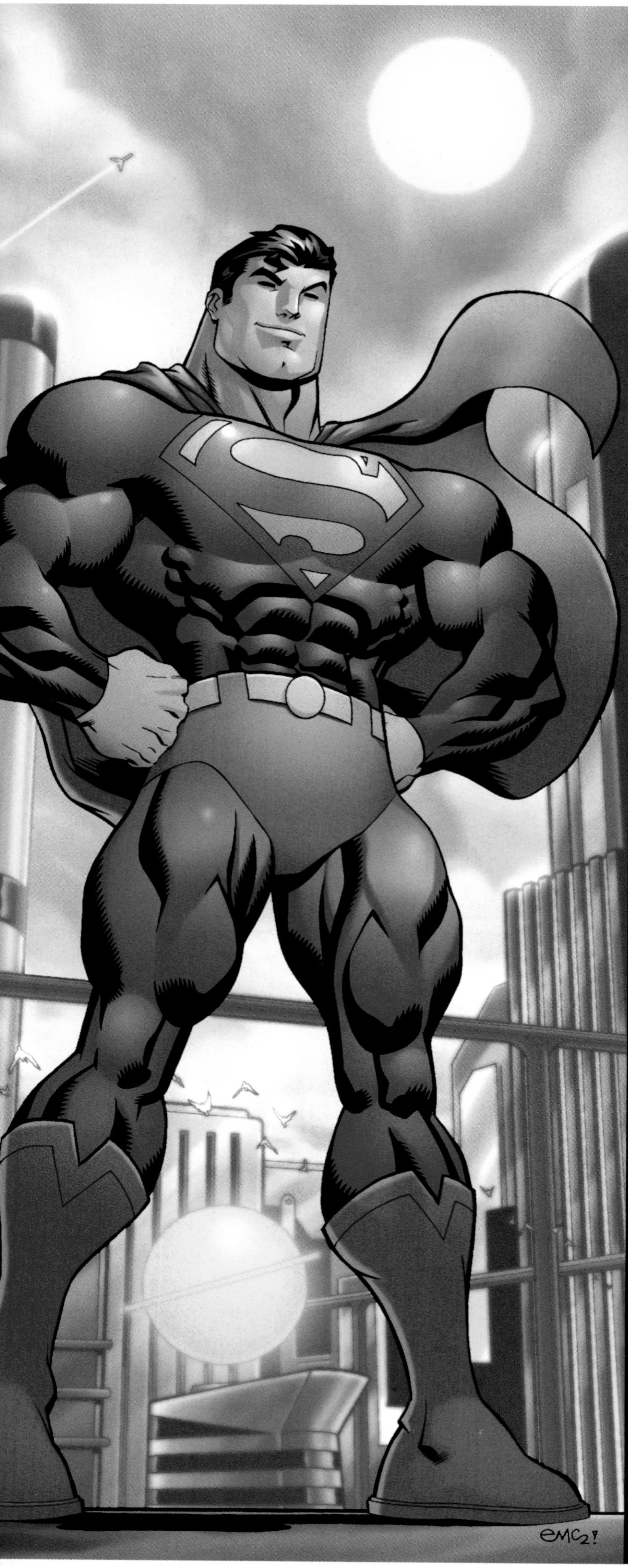

SUPERMAN

REAL NAME: KAL-EL (KRYPTONIAN NAME)/ CLARK JOSEPH KENT (EARTH NAME)
OCCUPATION: REPORTER FOR THE DAILY PLANET
BASE OF OPERATIONS: METROPOLIS
MARITAL STATUS: MARRIED (TO LOIS LANE)
HEIGHT: 6' 3"
WEIGHT: 225 LBS.
EYES: BLUE
HAIR: BLACK
FIRST APPEARANCE: (HISTORICAL) ACTION COMICS 1 (JUNE, 1938); (CURRENT) THE MAN OF STEEL 1 (JUNE, 1986)

Among Superman's extraordinary powers and abilities, the greatest may be his compassion for the world that has adopted him. An orphan of the doomed planet Krypton, Kal-El was rocketed to Earth and discovered in Smallville, Kansas, by farmers Jonathan and Martha Kent. Naming him Clark and raising him as their own, the Kents instilled within the maturing boy a sense of moral responsibility, while Earth's yellow sun imbued his cells with unparalleled strength and energy. By adulthood, the combination would transform Clark into the greatest hero who has ever lived — the Man of Steel, Superman.

Though he lives in Metropolis and is often considered the city's protector, Superman is truly champion of Earth. There are those, however, conspiring to expose him as a menace whose alien origins will destroy the world he has saved countless times.

For all his might, Clark's one constant source of strength is his wife, Lois Lane, with whom he also works as a reporter for the Daily Planet. But if U.S. President Lex Luthor has any say in the matter, Superman's never-ending battle will be fortressed in solitude in the days ahead.

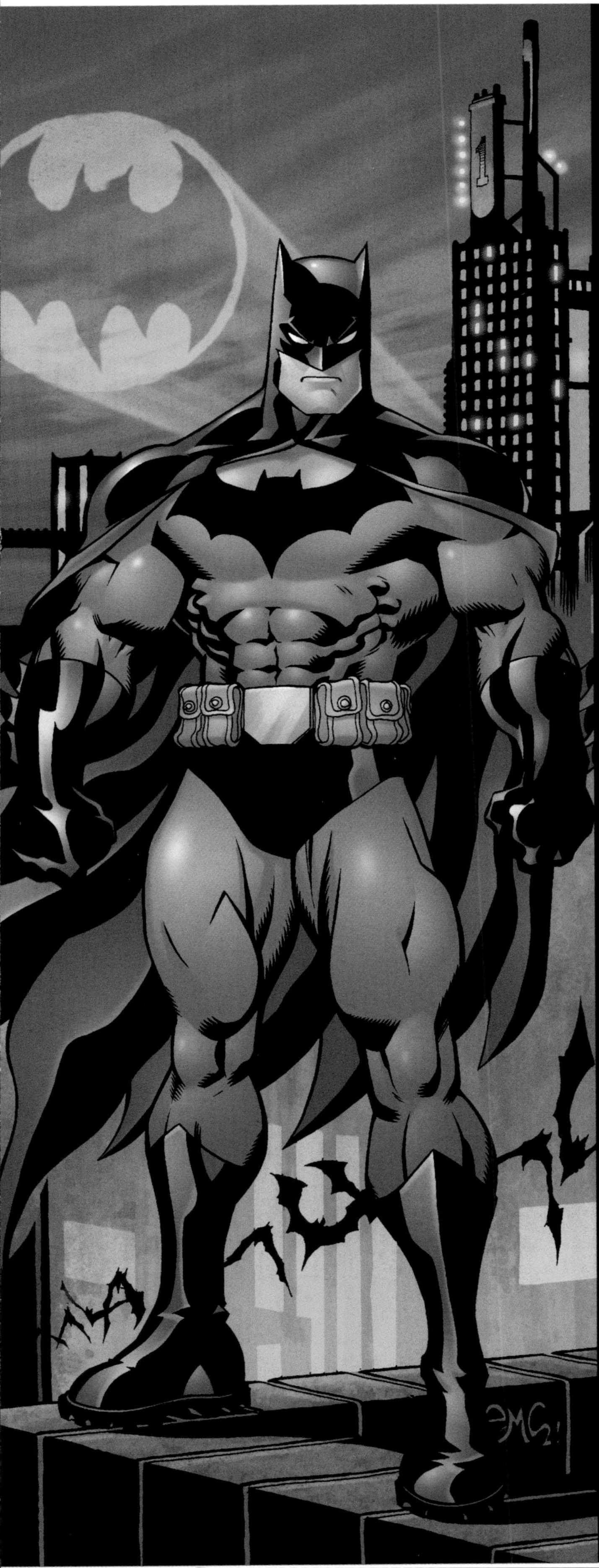

BATMAN

REAL NAME: **BRUCE WAYNE**
OCCUPATION: **INDUSTRIALIST / PHILANTHROPIST**
BASE OF OPERATIONS: **GOTHAM CITY**
HEIGHT: **6' 2"**
WEIGHT: **210 LBS.**
EYES: **BLUE**
HAIR: **BLACK**
FIRST APPEARANCE: **DETECTIVE COMICS 27 (MAY, 1939)**

The defining moment in the life of Bruce Wayne was the instant he witnessed his beloved parents Thomas and Martha Wayne gunned down by a murderous thief in Gotham City's "Park Row" (later nicknamed "Crime Alley"). As the Waynes' bodies lay still on the cold pavement, young Bruce — then just ten years old — vowed to seek justice and apprehend his parents' vicious killer.

Funded by the Wayne fortune and enabled by the family's loyal valet Alfred Pennyworth, Bruce circumvented the restraints of foster care and embarked on a decade-long worldwide trek to learn all he needed to fulfill his promise. Teachers and mentors on both sides of the law taught Bruce the skills — from little-known martial arts to the latest detective processes — that he would use to hone his body and mind into a living weapon in what would eventually become an unrelenting war on crime.

After returning to Gotham, a disastrous first outing as a plainclothes urban vigilante left Bruce broken and bleeding. He realized then that criminals were a superstitious and cowardly lot, and only a fearsome creature of the night could strike fear into their hearts. As if by fate, a wayward bat crashed through a window and provided Bruce the inspiration he so desperately needed: He would become as a bat himself, clad in a daunting costume that would make him a fearsome urban legend amid the crime-ridden streets of Gotham City.

To date, Bruce has never caught the mugger who murdered his parents. Batman's vigil continues, an ongoing onslaught against crime and corruption.

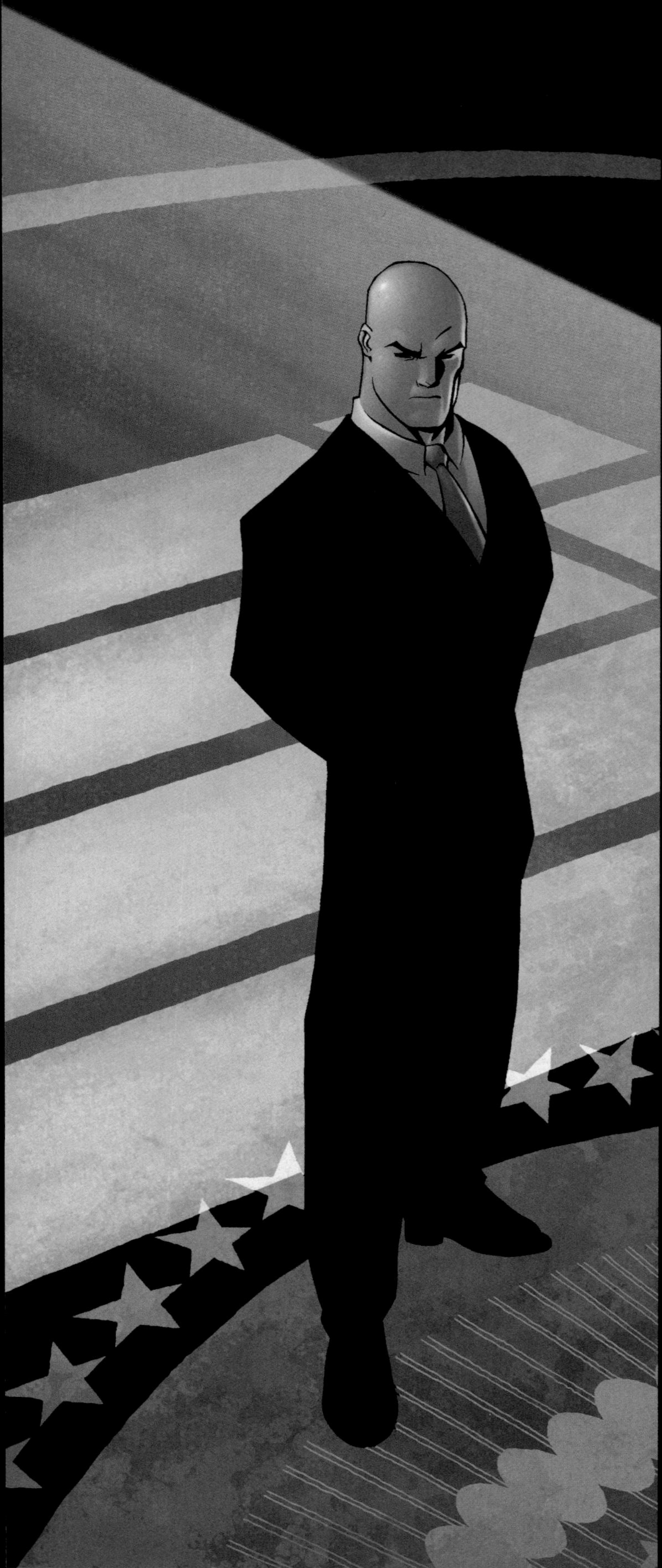

PRESIDENT LEX LUTHOR

REAL NAME: LEX LUTHOR
OCCUPATION: PRESIDENT OF THE UNITED STATES; OWNER OF LEXCORP
BASE OF OPERATIONS: THE WHITE HOUSE, WASHINGTON, D.C.
MARITAL STATUS: WIDOWED
HEIGHT: 6' 2"
WEIGHT: 210 LBS.
EYES: GREEN
HAIR: N/A
FIRST APPEARANCE: (HISTORICAL) ACTION COMICS 23 (APRIL, 1940); (CURRENT) THE MAN OF STEEL 4 (AUGUST, 1986)

There's only one thing the most powerful man on Earth could want: more power. That's all Lex Luthor has ever wanted, and achieved, as an impoverished youth in Metropolis's Suicide Slum, as the founding genius and owner of LexCorp, and as President of the United States. How he has done so is irrelevant; the means have always justified his ends.

Still, being the nation's chief executive isn't enough for this self-professed "man of the people." Luthor wants more, and he'll get it by any means necessary. Not even the one who has always risen above him, literally and figuratively, can stop him this time. Superman can change the course of mighty rivers, but as President, Luthor has altered the course of history. The most powerful armed forces and capability on Earth are at his disposal. He's saved the world from the galactic threat of the planet destroyer Imperiex.

As he carries his political credo of "Truth, Justice and the American Way" into re-election, Luthor will finally convince the people to see Superman through his eyes: not as a champion, but as a self-serving alien whose continued existence threatens every human being's way of life.

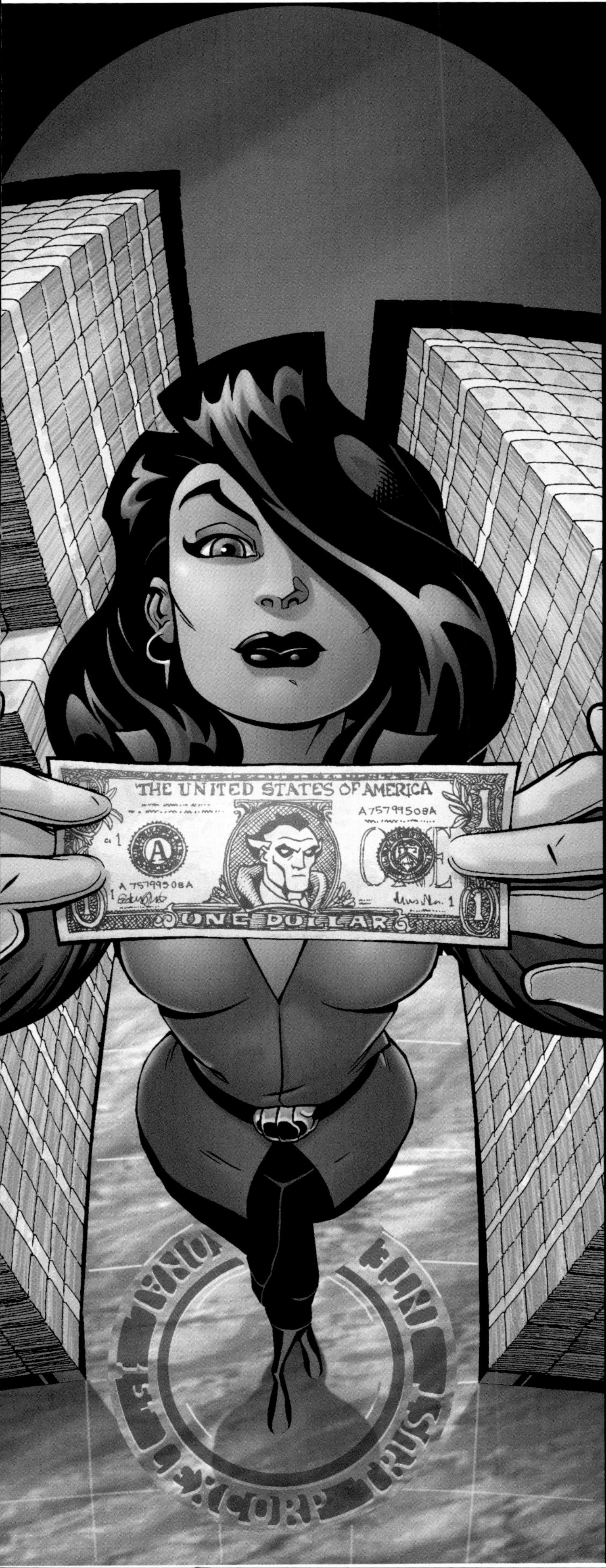
THE UNITED STATES OF AMERICA
A75799508A
ONE DOLLAR
LEXCORP TRUST

TALIA

REAL NAME: TALIA HEAD
OCCUPATION: CHIEF EXECUTIVE OFFICER OF LEXCORP
BASE OF OPERATIONS: METROPOLIS
HEIGHT: 5' 8" **WEIGHT:** 120 LBS.
EYES: ALMOND **HAIR:** BLACK
FIRST APPEARANCE: DETECTIVE COMICS 411 (MAY, 1971)

She is the daughter and sole heir of immortal international eco-terrorist Ra's al Ghul, the so-called "Demon's Head." Talia is also one of the few women Bruce Wayne ever admitted loving.

Batman first met the beautiful-but-deadly Talia when he saved her from one of her father's many enemies. Later, the Dark Knight and the Daughter of the Demon were reunited when Ra's al Ghul abducted Robin in a ruse to coerce Batman into wedding Talia and taking over Ra's al Ghul's agenda of restoring Earth's natural balance through global genocide. Fortunately, Batman balked at saving the Earth via mass murder.

Though attracted to one another, Batman and Talia were divided by her father's extremist ideologies, which would continue to drive a wedge between the star-crossed paramours in the years that followed. Talia has learned to her eternal dismay that loving the Dark Knight and remaining loyal to Ra's al Ghul are — and will forever be — mutually exclusive endeavors.

Acceptance of this great irony fueled Talia's decision to leave her father and strike out on her own. When Lex Luthor was elected President of the United States, the charismatic mogul personally recruited Talia to oversee his vast business empire as acting CEO.

Running the multinational LexCorp's many diverse holdings from its Metropolis-based headquarters seemed like the perfect way to bury her feelings for Batman. But one of LexCorp's closest industrial rivals is WayneCorp, while Bruce Wayne and Lex Luthor are very much less than friends.

Whether Talia's "executive decision" comes from a desire to be closer to Bruce, albeit in the business forum, or is rivalry sparked from her position as spurned lover remains to be seen, as does Ra's al Ghul's reaction to the defection of his beloved daughter.

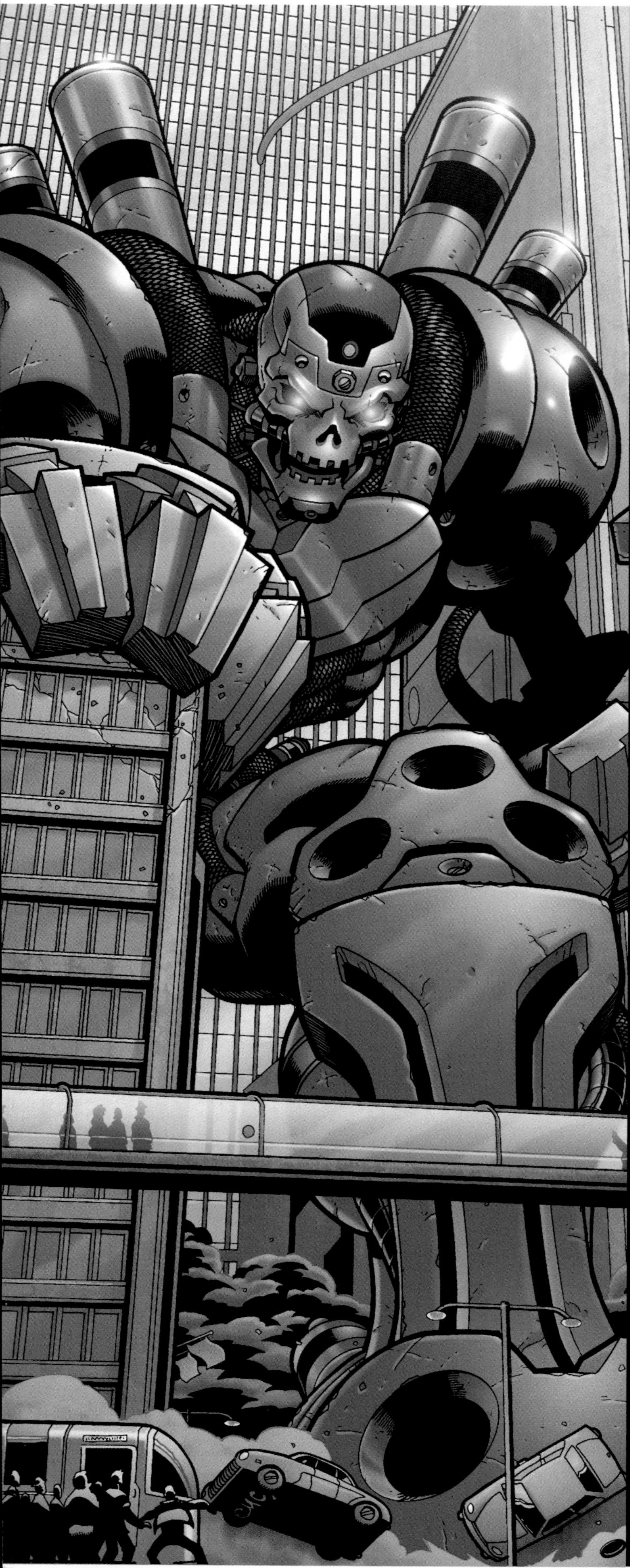

METALLO

REAL NAME: JOHN CORBEN
OCCUPATION: THIEF
BASE OF OPERATIONS: MOBILE
HEIGHT: VARIABLE
WEIGHT: VARIABLE
EYES: VARIABLE (AS CORBEN: GREEN)
HAIR: N/A (AS CORBEN: LIGHT BROWN)
FIRST APPEARANCE: (HISTORICAL) ACTION COMICS 252 (MAY, 1959); (CURRENT) SUPERMAN 1 (SECOND SERIES) (JANUARY, 1987)

To call Metallo a "heartless" monster would be inaccurate. True, only the brain of thief John Corben had survived a horrific car crash. But Professor Emmett Vale, convinced Superman was an alien with hostile intentions for Earth, implanted Corben's brain into a powerful robot body fueled by a "heart" made of Kryptonite: an irradiated fragment of Superman's home world Krypton, and the one substance lethal to the Man of Steel.

Metallo's body has undergone many "upgrades" over the years, the most dramatic coming from the B-13 virus that transformed all technology in Metropolis. While still possessing incredible strength and his Kryptonite heart, he can now "morph" his form as he sees fit, essentially giving himself the right tools for the job every time. Recent mechanical alterations, however, have painfully reminded Metallo that the man he once was no longer exists, making his desire to destroy Superman — the reason he was created — all the greater.

Recent evidence, meanwhile, has given Batman reason to hunt Metallo. His modus operandi and whereabouts in Gotham City years ago suggest that Corben may have murdered Thomas and Martha Wayne, the Dark Knight's parents.

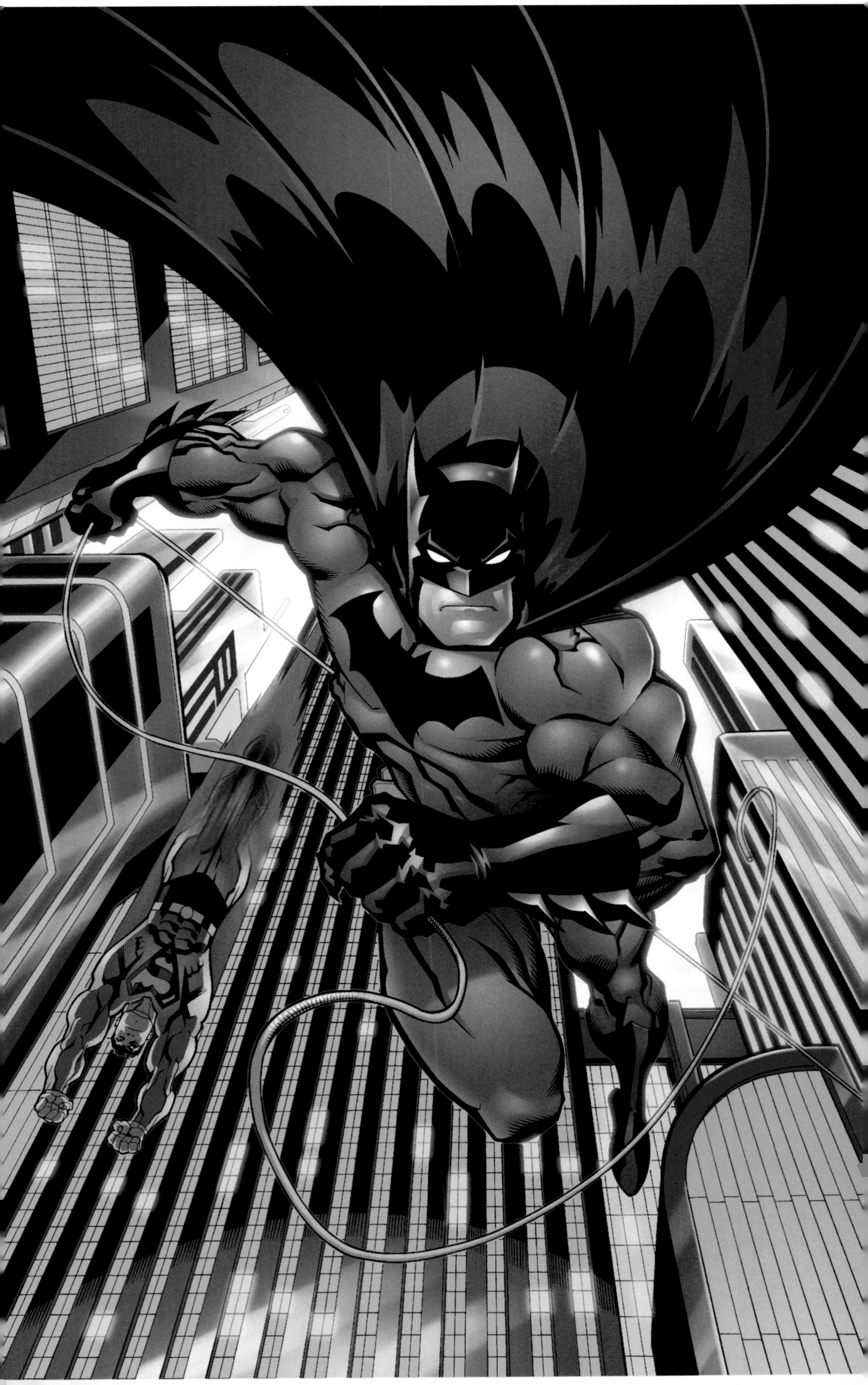

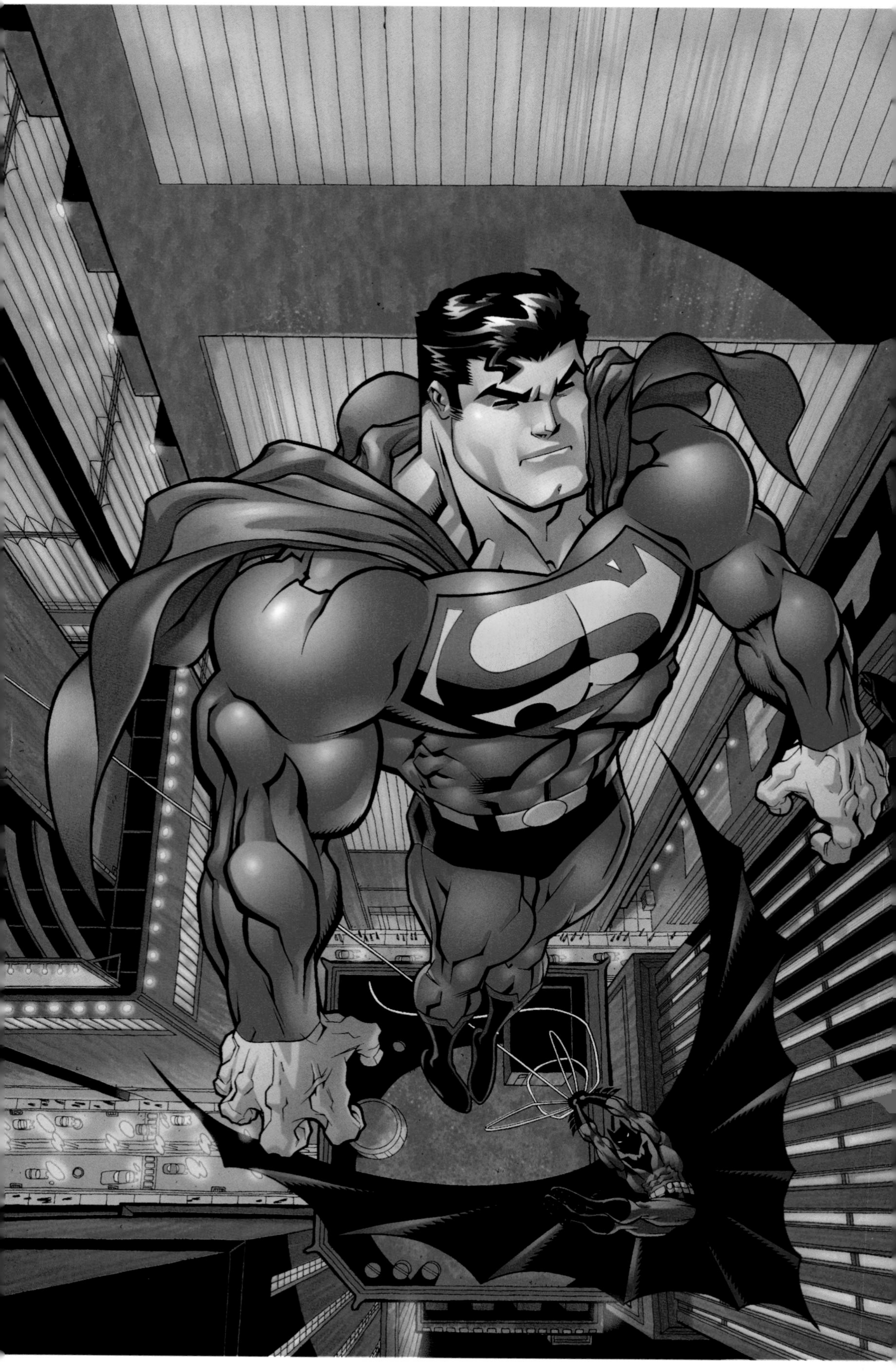

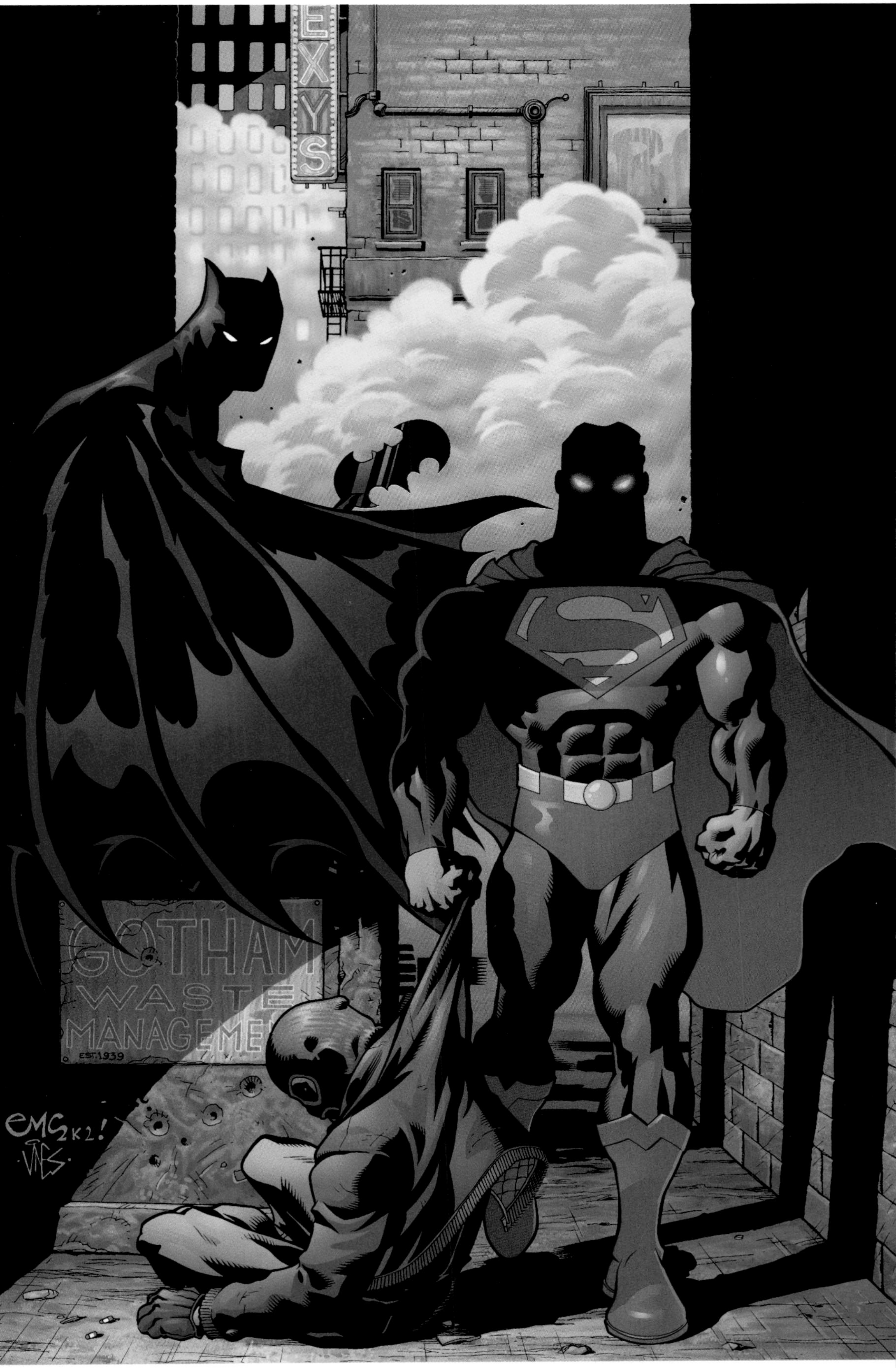
EXYS
GOTHAM
WASTE
MANAGEMEN
EST. 1939
EMC 2K2!
VINES

COVER TO SECOND PRINTING OF SUPERMAN/BATMAN 3 BY ED McGUINNESS AND DEXTER VINES

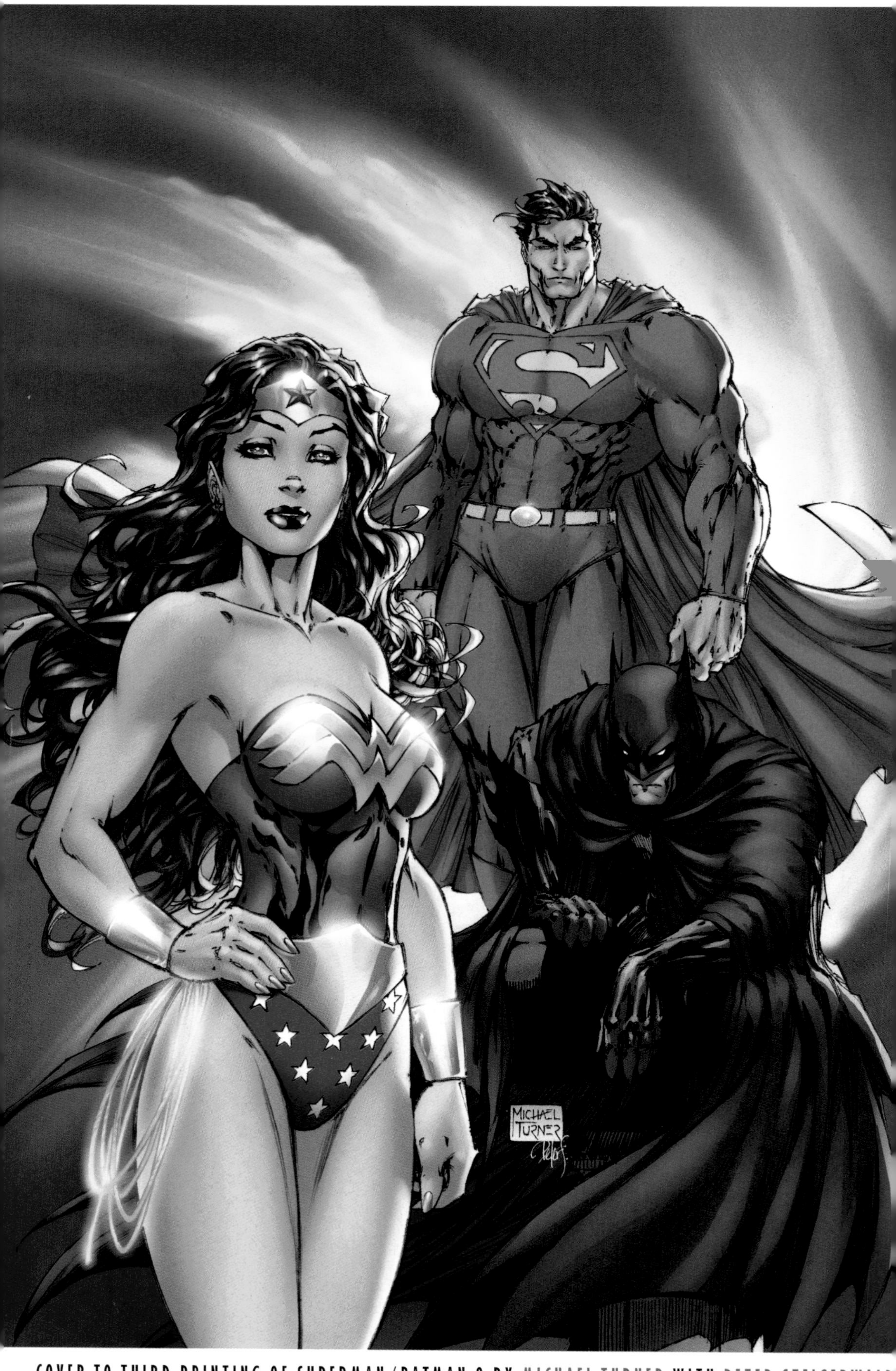
MICHAEL TURNER

COVER TO THIRD PRINTING OF SUPERMAN/BATMAN 8 BY MICHAEL TURNER WITH PETER STEIGERWALD

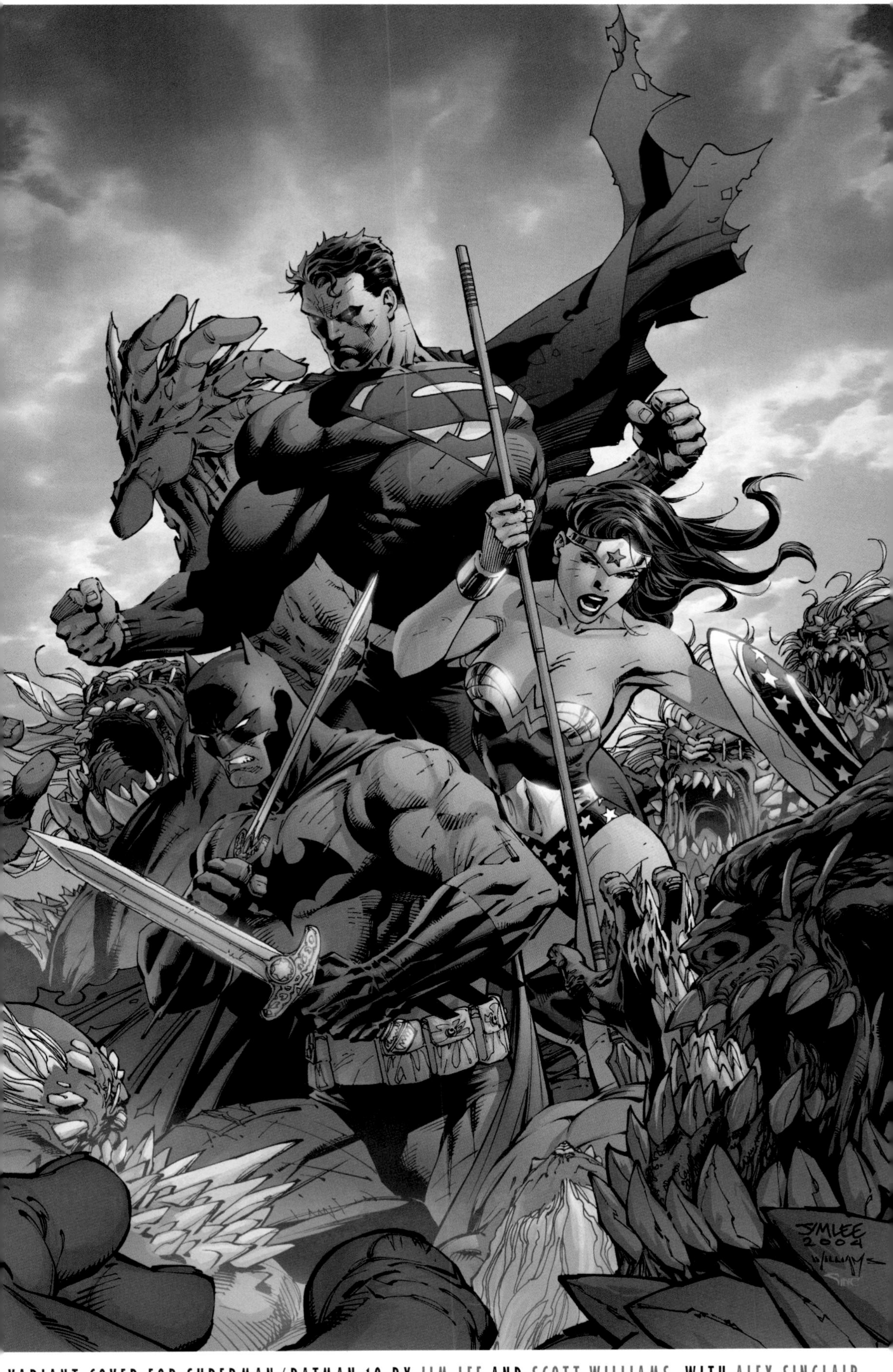
JIMLEE
2004

VARIANT COVER FOR SUPERMAN/BATMAN 10 BY JIM LEE AND SCOTT WILLIAMS, WITH ALEX SINCLAIR

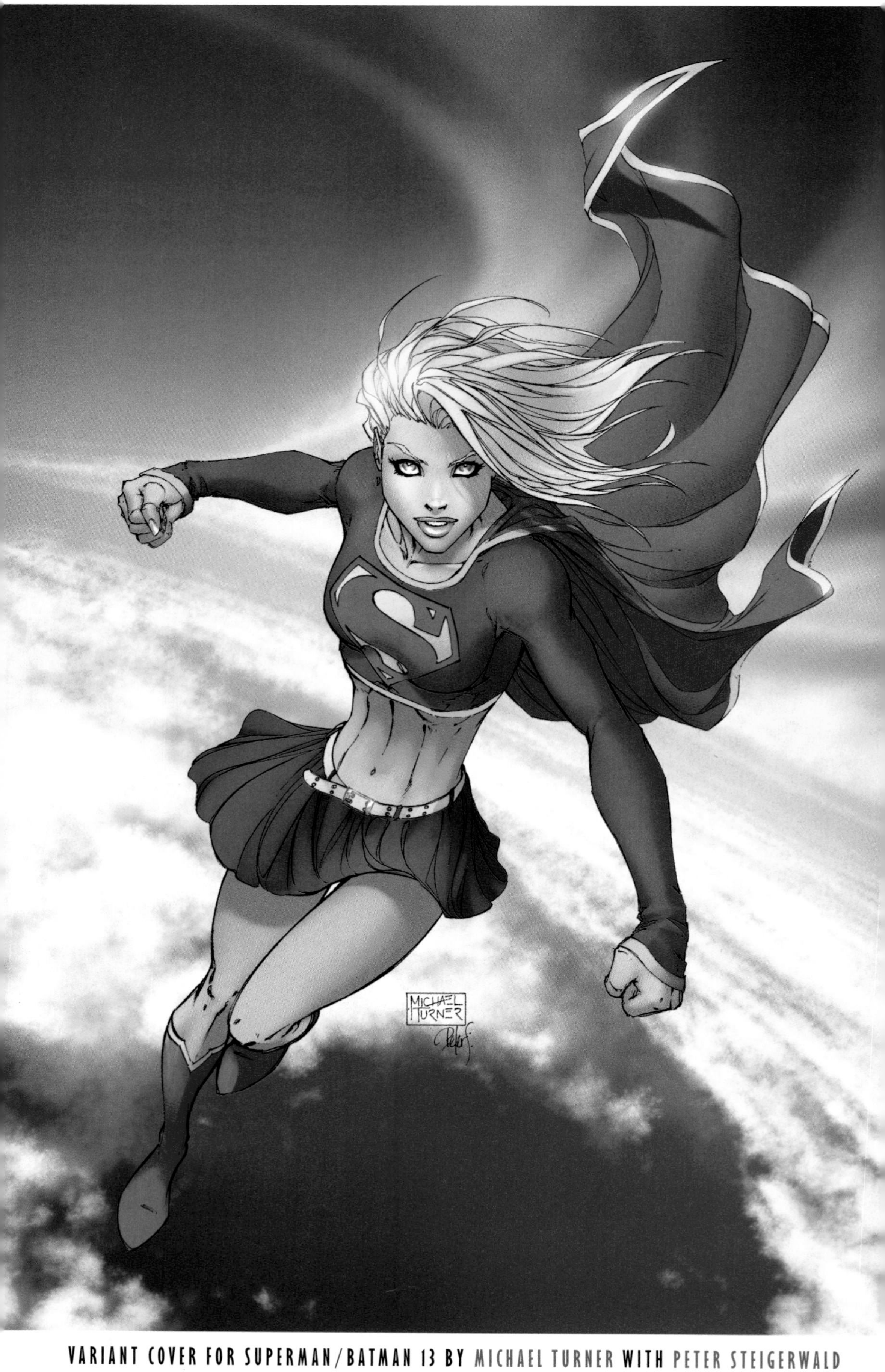
MICHAEL TURNER

VARIANT COVER FOR SUPERMAN/BATMAN 13 BY MICHAEL TURNER WITH PETER STEIGERWALD

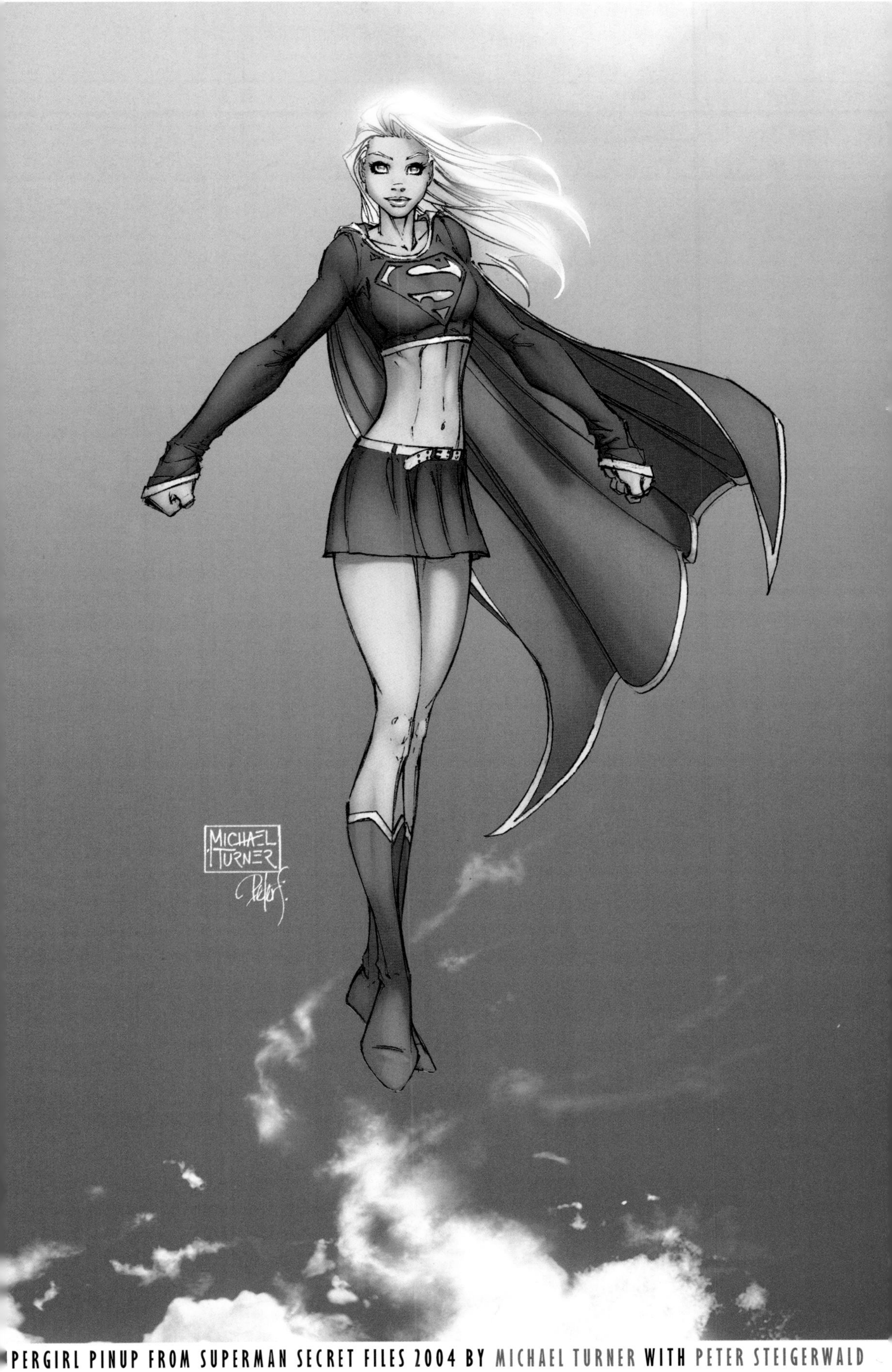
MICHAEL TURNER

PERGIRL PINUP FROM SUPERMAN SECRET FILES 2004 BY MICHAEL TURNER WITH PETER STEIGERWALD

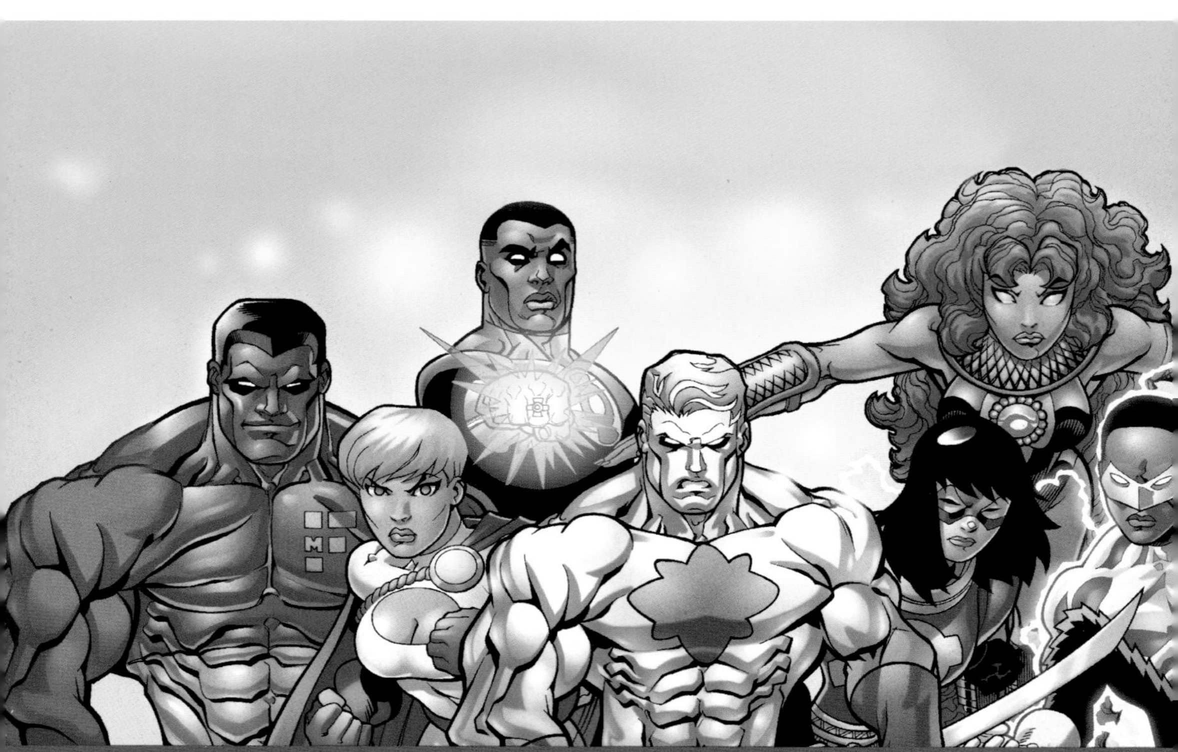

SUPERMAN/BATMAN: PUBLIC ENEMIES BACK COVER ART

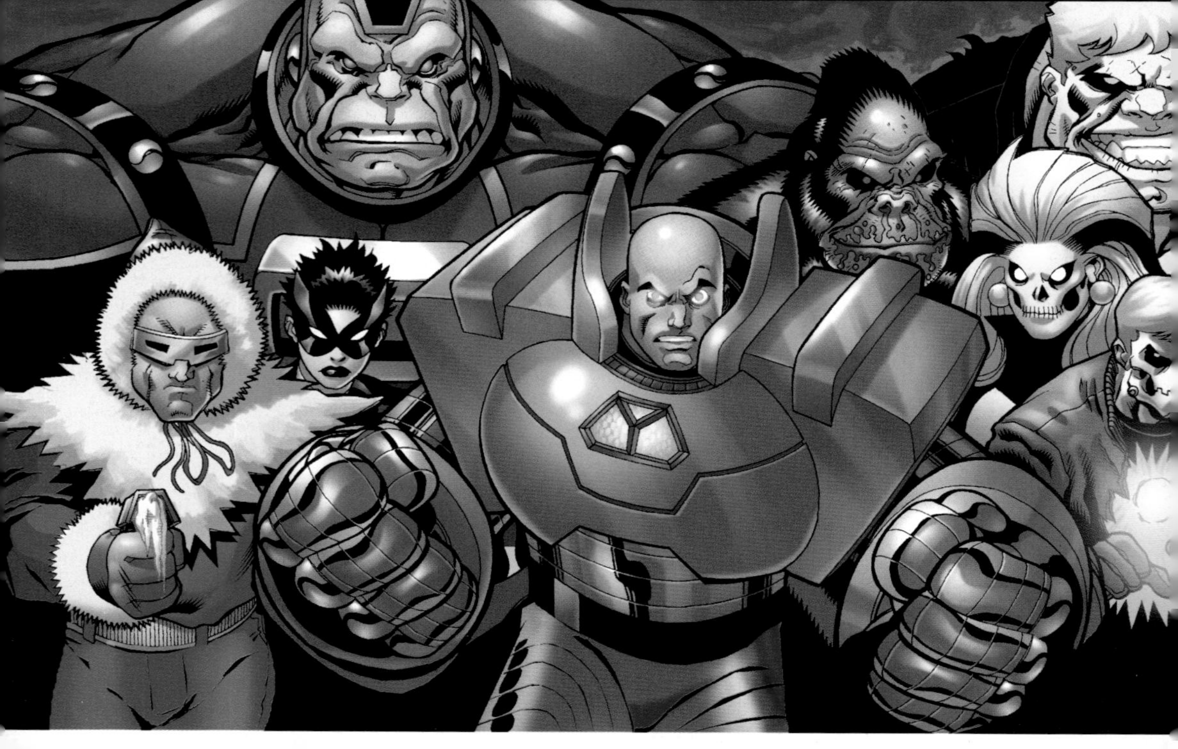

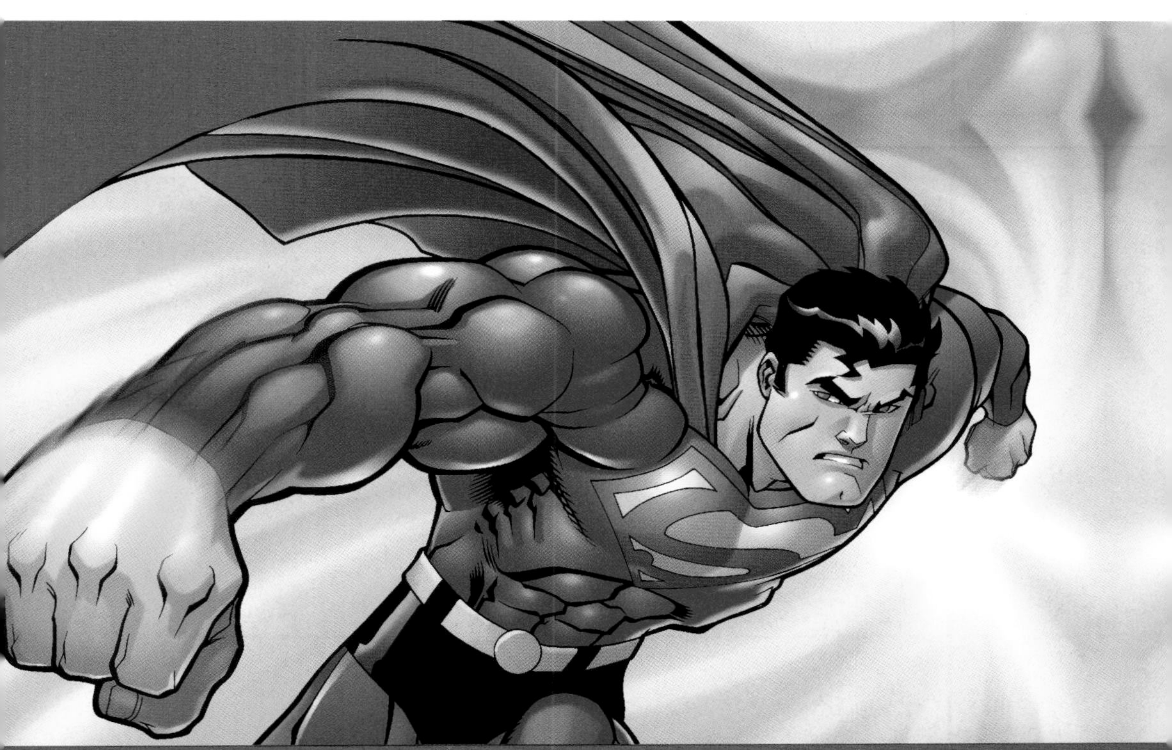

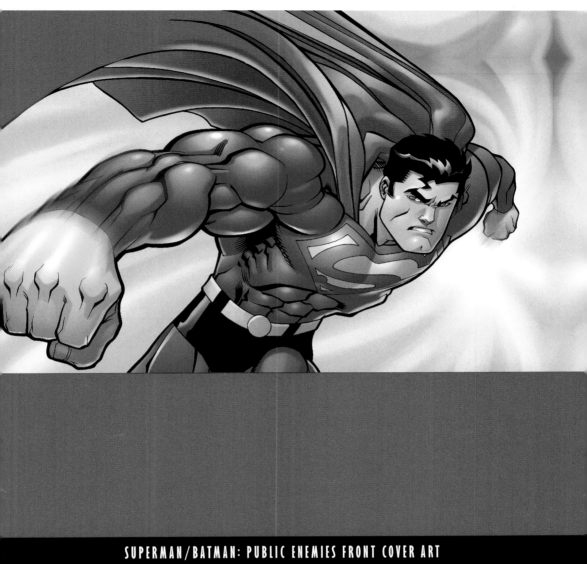

SUPERMAN/BATMAN: PUBLIC ENEMIES FRONT COVER ART

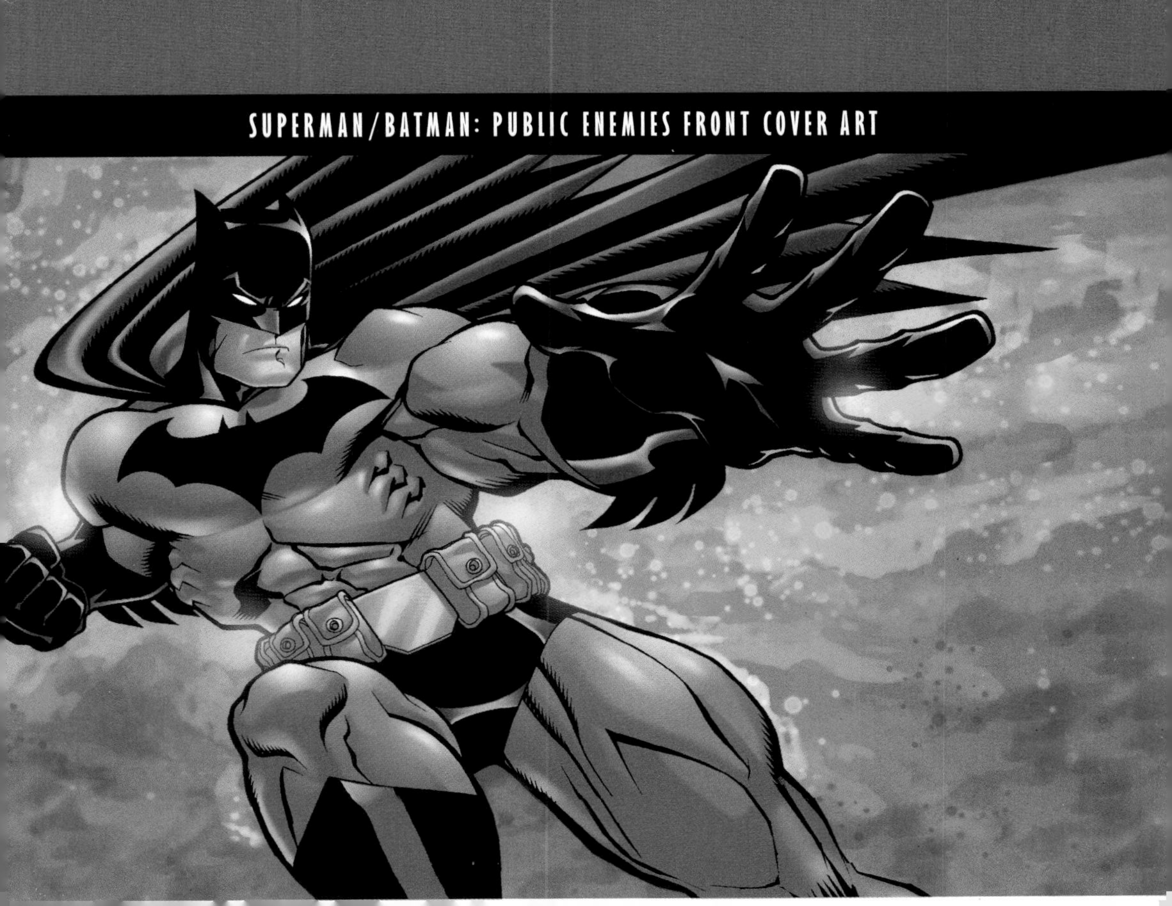

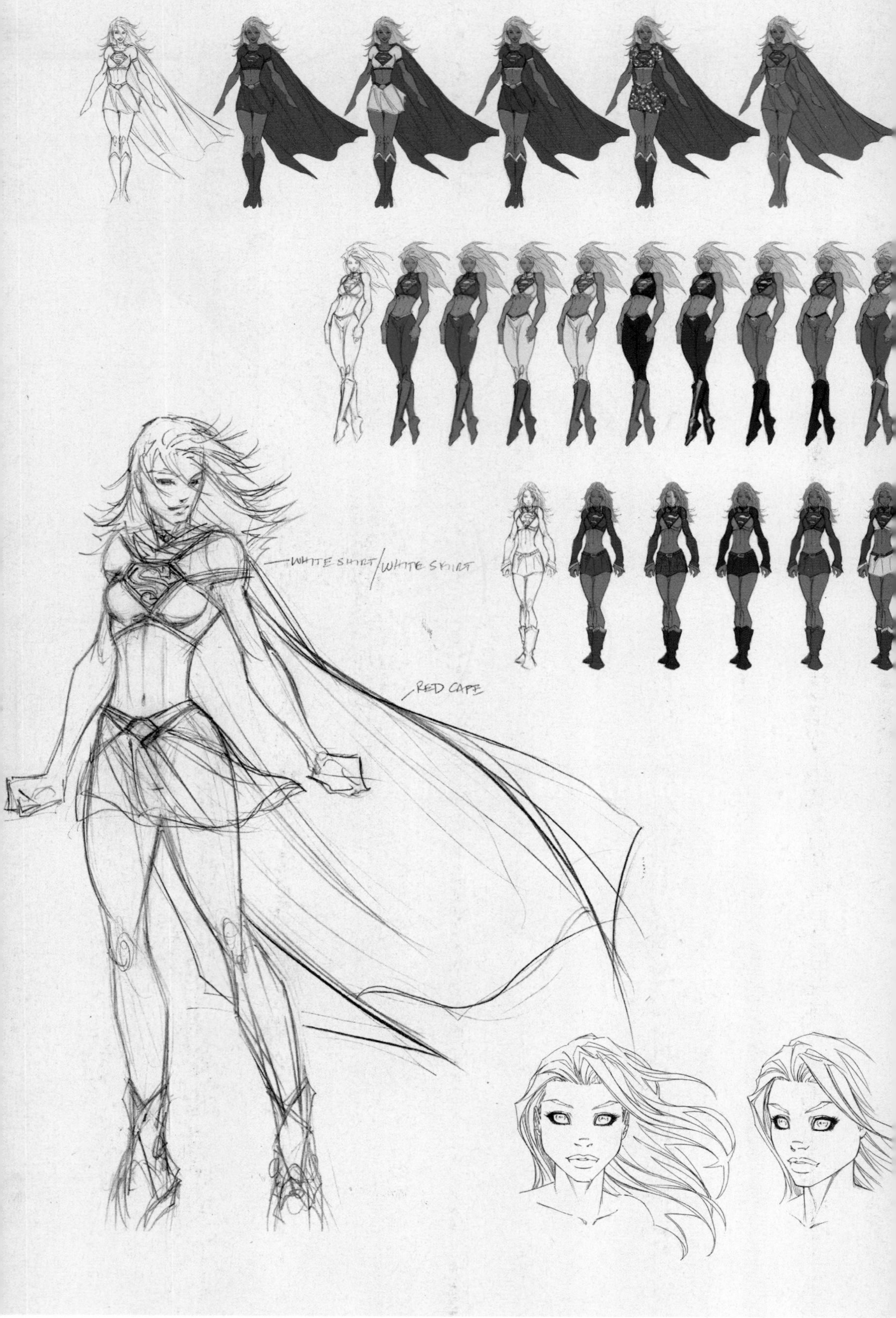
WHITE SHIRT/WHITE SKIRT
RED CAPE

VARIOUS STUDIES OF SUPERGIRL AND HER COSTUME BY MICHAEL TURNER

B
Trains
Dogs
Fish
Busy as a bee.
Idioms

BOOKWORM

Written by Karen Emigh
Illustrated by Steve Dana

FUTURE HORIZONS INC.

Bookworm
All marketing and publishing rights guaranteed to and reserved by

FUTURE HORIZONS INC.

721 W. Abram Street
Arlington, Texas 76013
800-489-0727
817-277-0727
817-277-2270 (fax)
E-mail: info@FHautism.com
www.FHautism.com

ISBN 10:   1-932565-42-6
ISBN 13:   978-1-932565-42-3

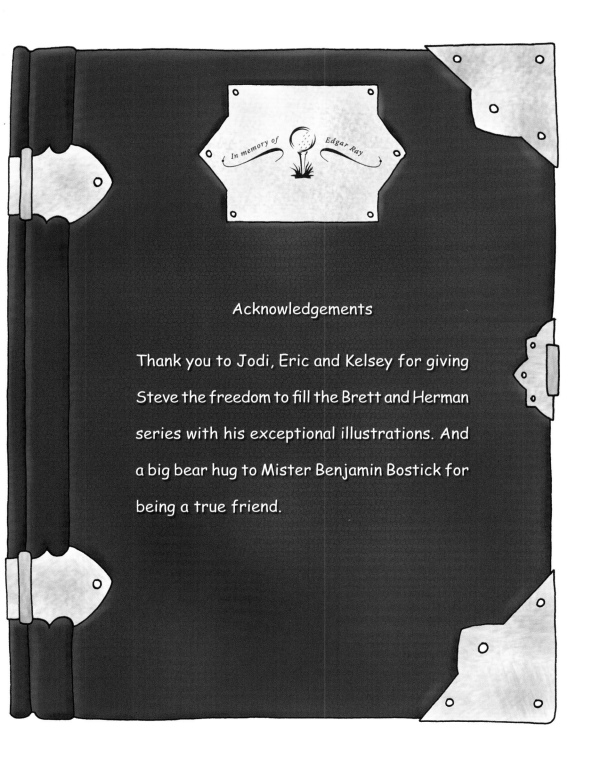

In memory of   Edgar Ray

Acknowledgements

Thank you to Jodi, Eric and Kelsey for giving

Steve the freedom to fill the Brett and Herman

series with his exceptional illustrations. And

a big bear hug to Mister Benjamin Bostick for

being a true friend.

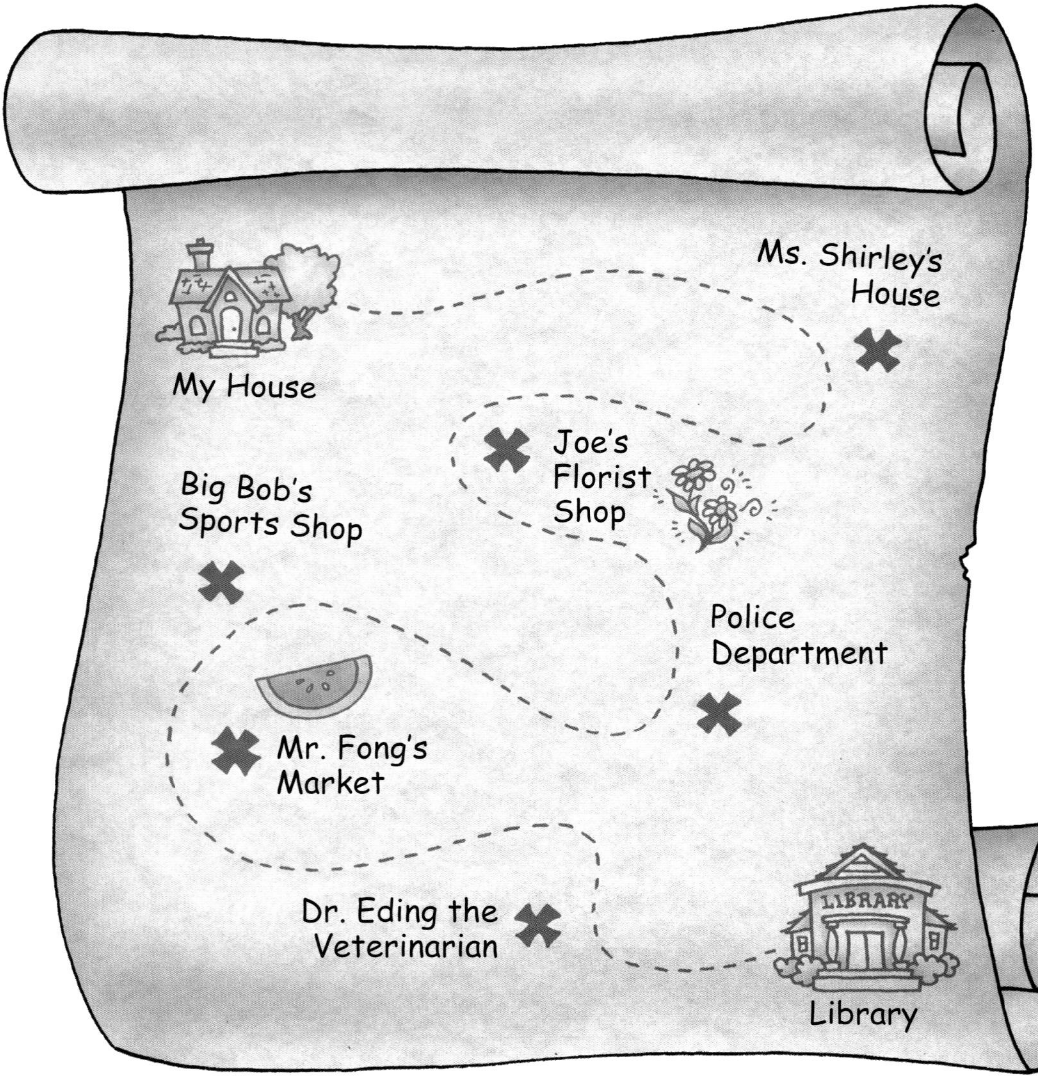
My House
Ms. Shirley's
House
Joe's
Florist
Shop
Big Bob's
Sports Shop
Police
Department
Mr. Fong's
Market
LIBRARY
Dr. Eding the
Veterinarian
Library

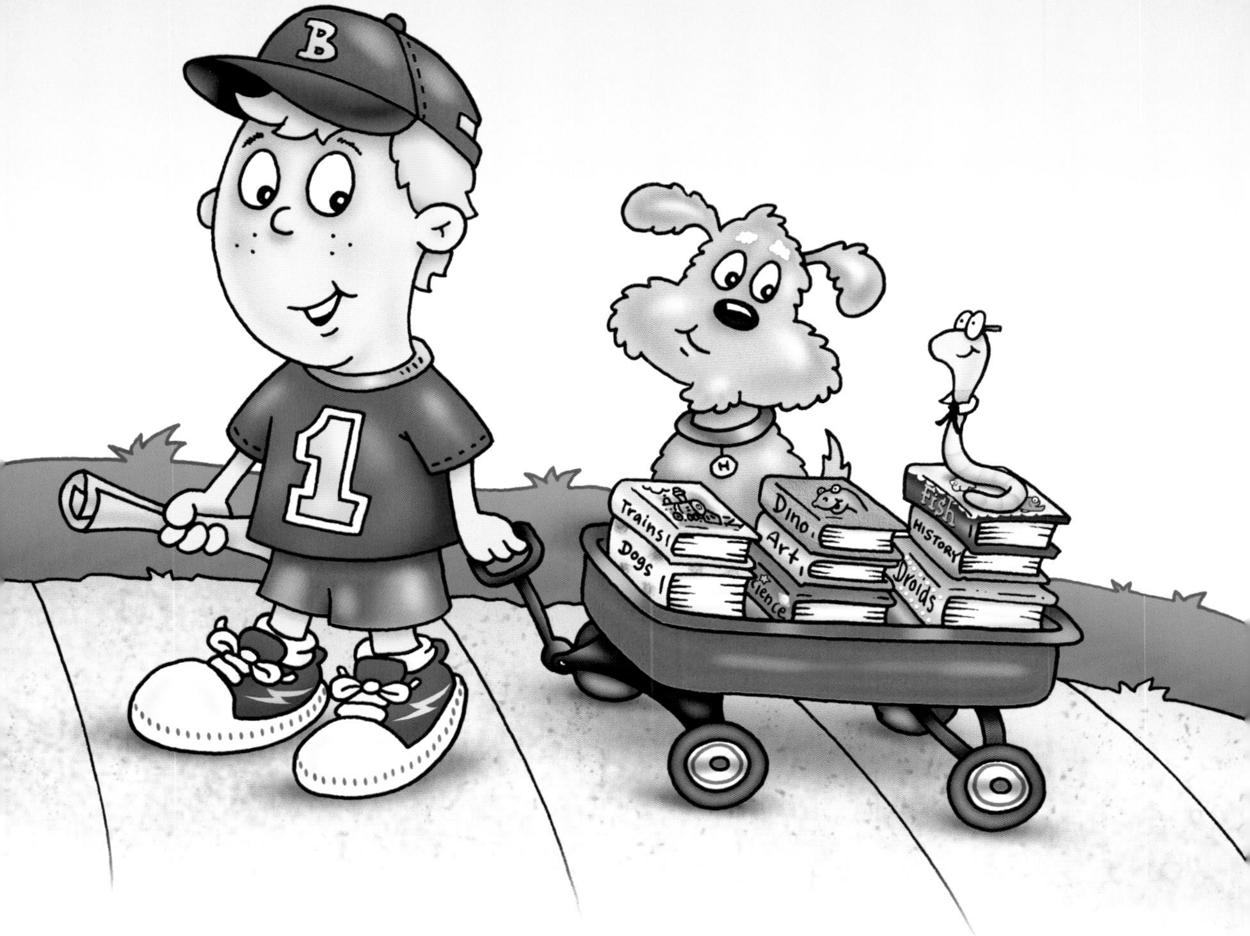
Trains
Dogs
Dino
Art
Fish
HISTORY
Droids

Hi. I'm Brett and this is my dog Herman.

I belong to the library book club and after I read 100 books, I get an award. We're taking these books back to the library and we have a map to show us the way. We might make a few stops to say "Hi" to some friends. You can come, too. Let's go!

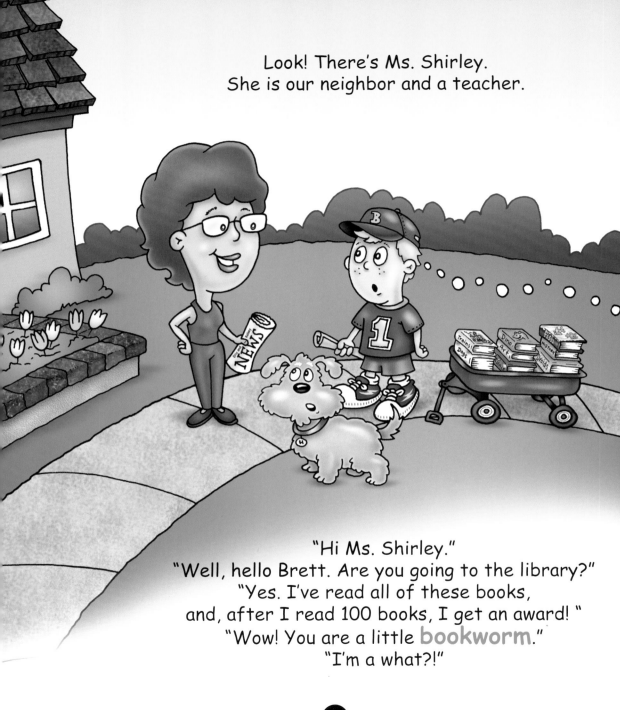

Look! There's Ms. Shirley.
She is our neighbor and a teacher.

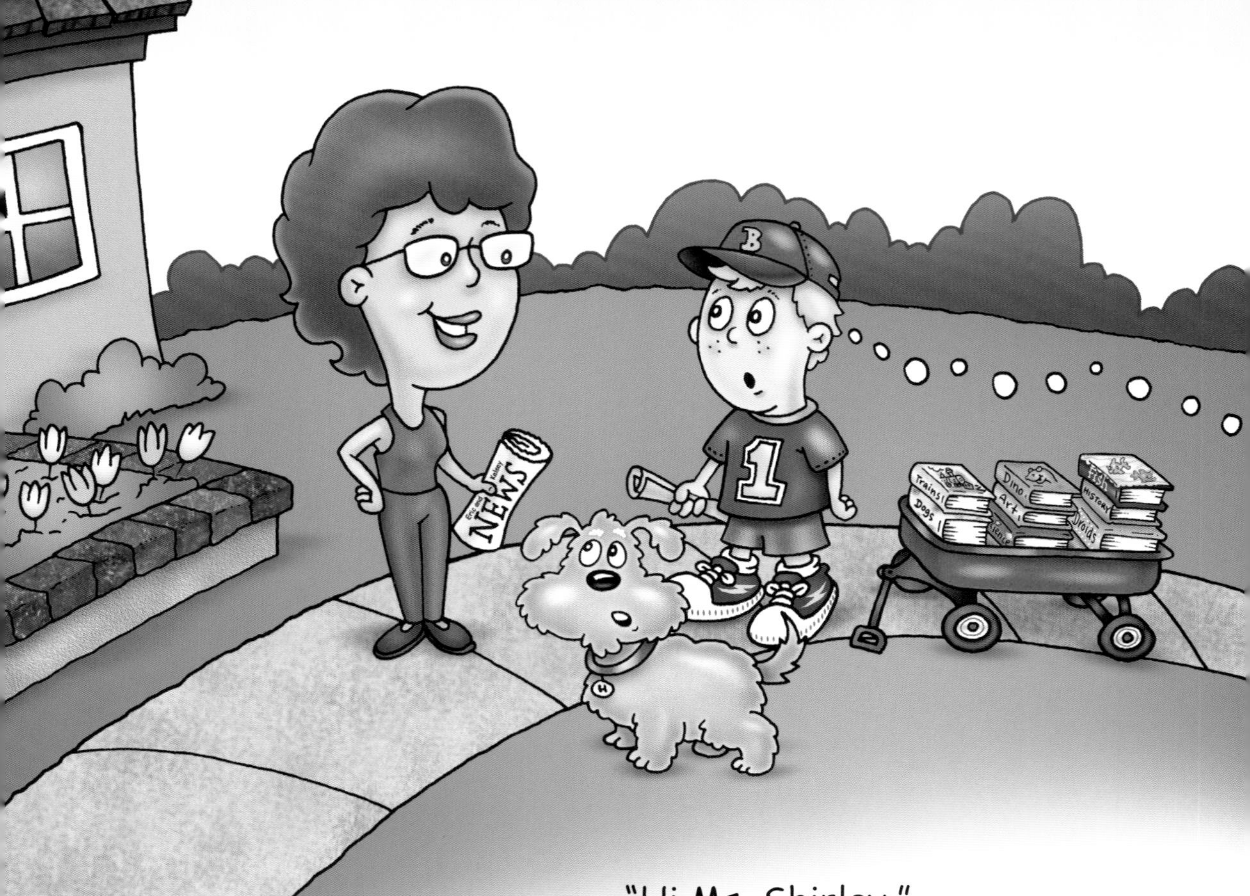
NEWS

"Hi Ms. Shirley."
"Well, hello Brett. Are you going to the library?"
"Yes. I've read all of these books,
and, after I read 100 books, I get an award! "
"Wow! You are a little **bookworm**."
"I'm a what?!"

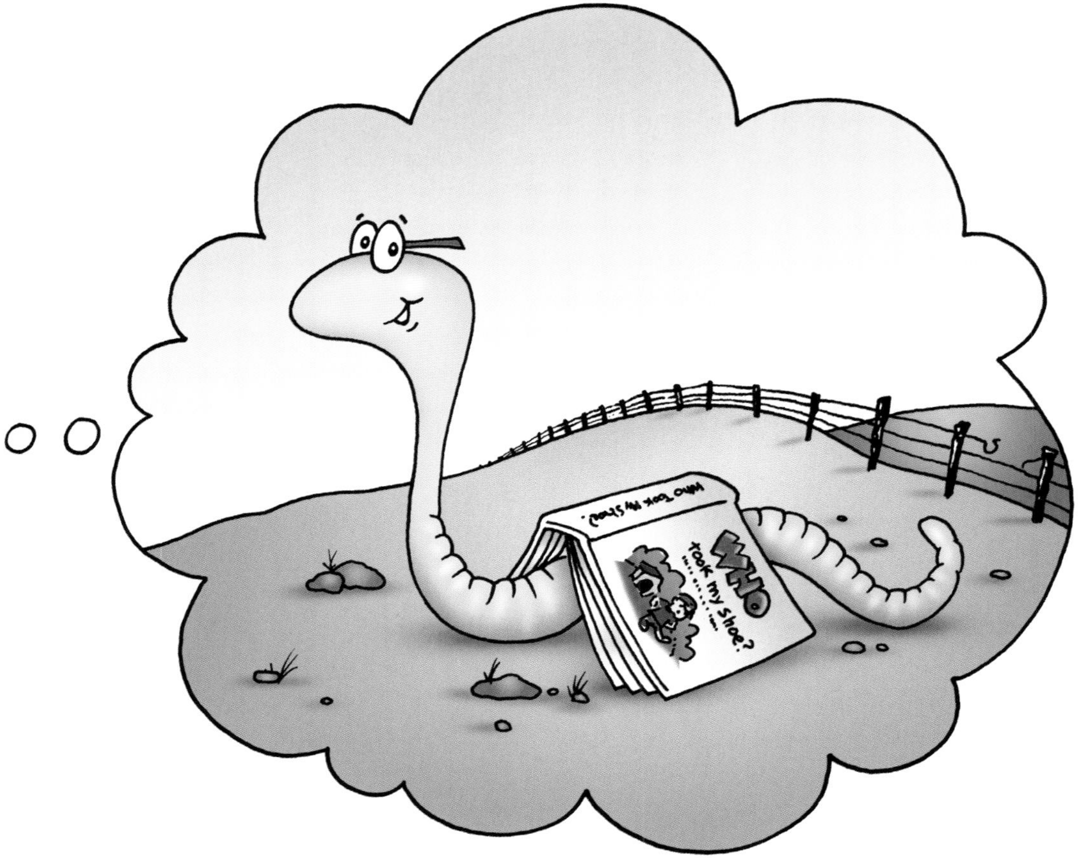
WHO took my shoe?

"A **bookworm**. That just means you enjoy reading a lot. It's called an idiom. People use idioms like that every day and the true or literal meaning doesn't make much sense."

"Because I'm not really a worm, right?"

"That's right, Brett. I think you will hear many idioms today if you listen carefully."

"I'll do that. Bye, Ms. Shirley."

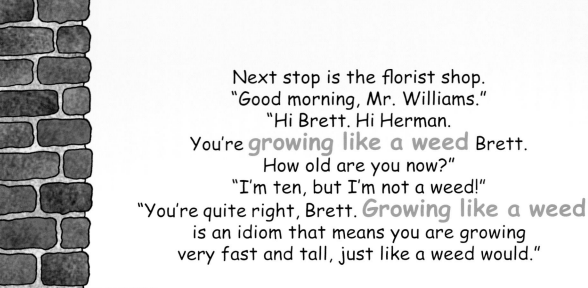

Next stop is the florist shop.
"Good morning, Mr. Williams."
"Hi Brett. Hi Herman.
You're growing like a weed Brett.
How old are you now?"
"I'm ten, but I'm not a weed!"
"You're quite right, Brett. Growing like a weed
is an idiom that means you are growing
very fast and tall, just like a weed would."

FLORIST
& GIFT SHOP

4

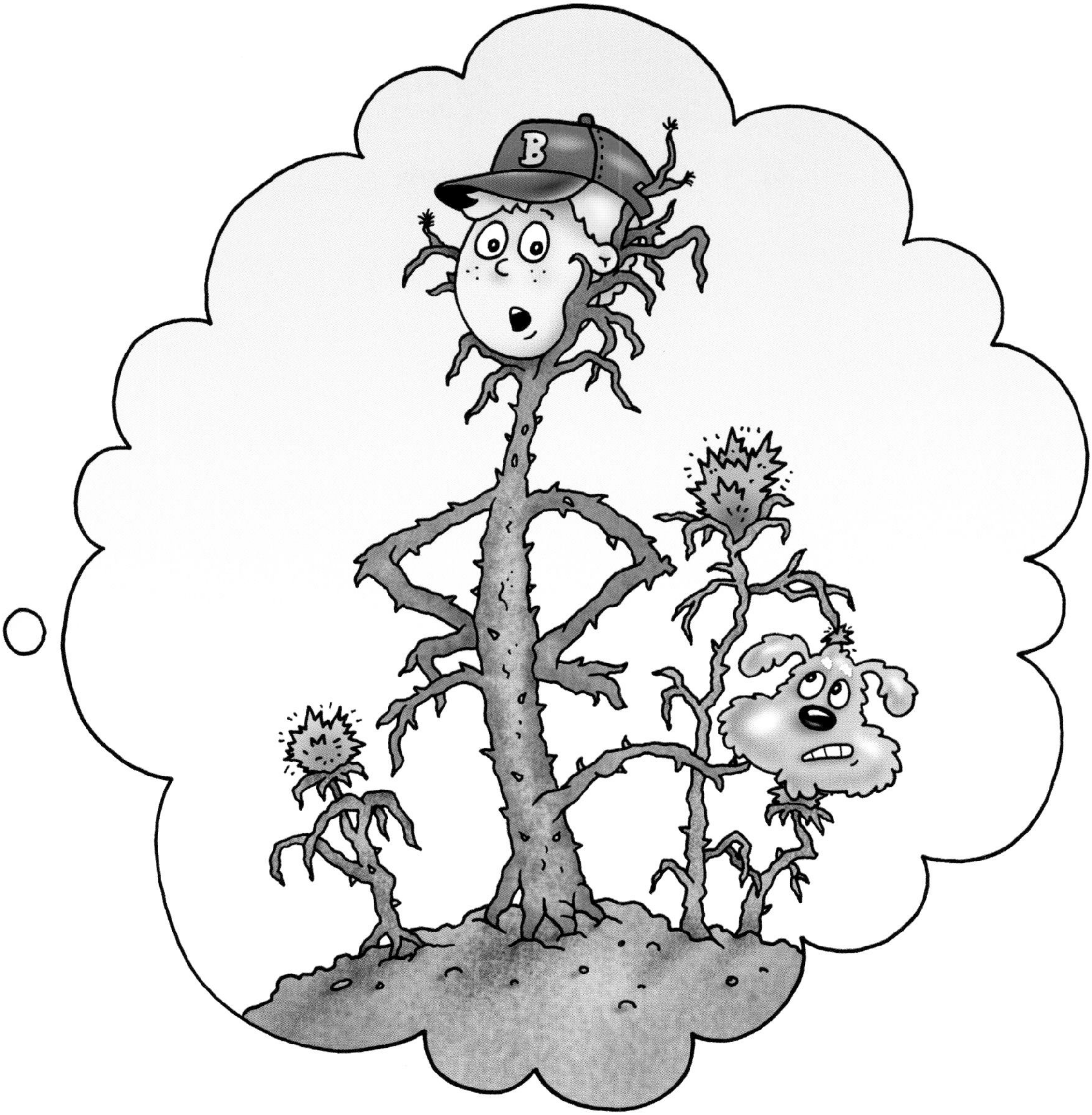

"It sure makes more sense when you say it like that!"
"You're right about that Brett. See you later."
"Bye, Mr. Williams."

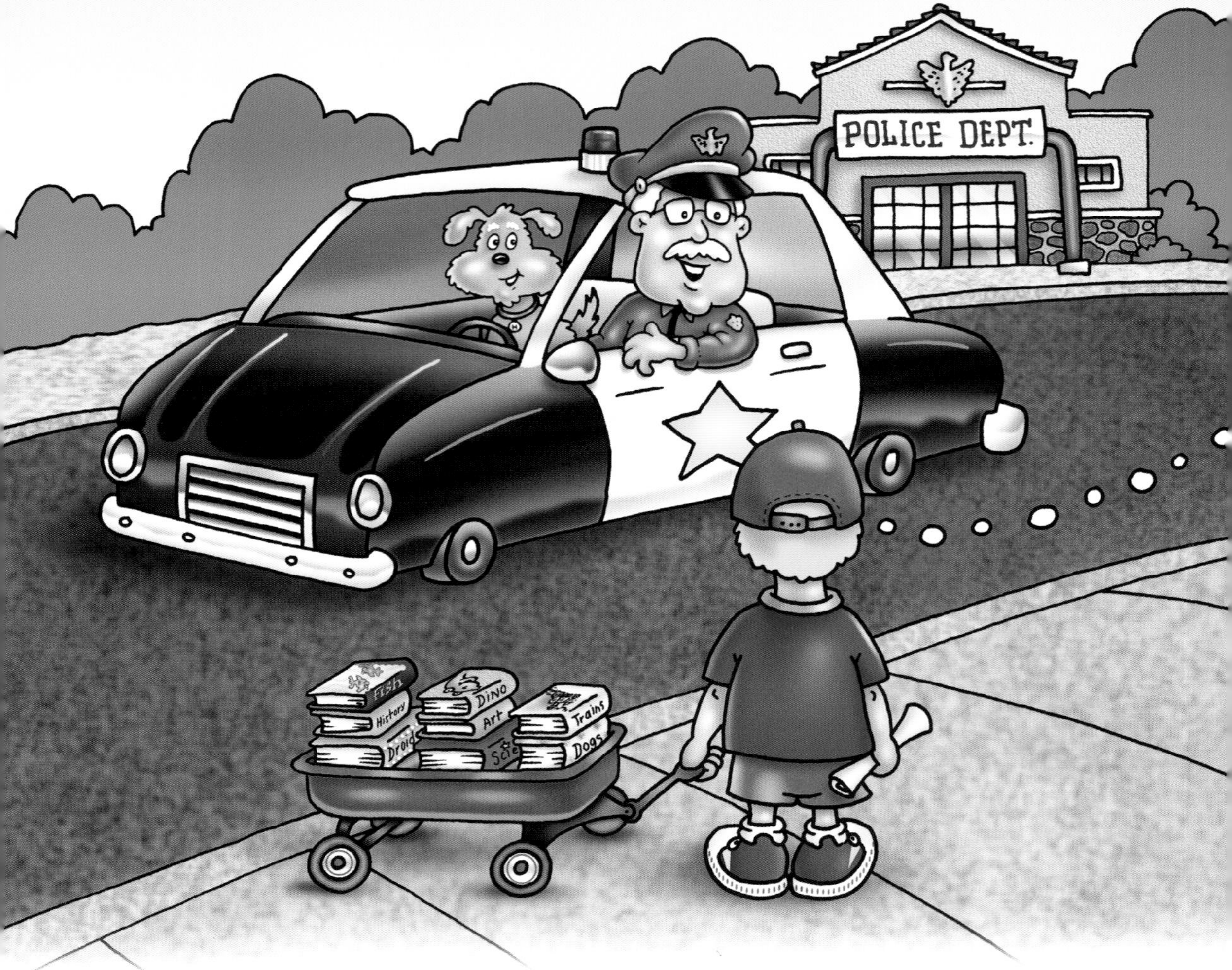
POLICE DEPT.
Fish
History
Droid
Dino
Art
Trains
Dogs

There's the police station and here comes officer Pryor.
"Hi, officer."
"Hi, Brett. I see you're on your way to the library."
"That's right!"
"Okay, but no **monkey business** on the way."
"No sir! I don't have any business with monkeys."
Mr. Pryor laughed, "no Brett. No **monkey business** is just a silly idiom that means don't get into trouble."

"I always try to stay out of trouble,
especially around you."
"That's good. Now be careful going across the street."
"Yes sir. Bye."
"Have fun."

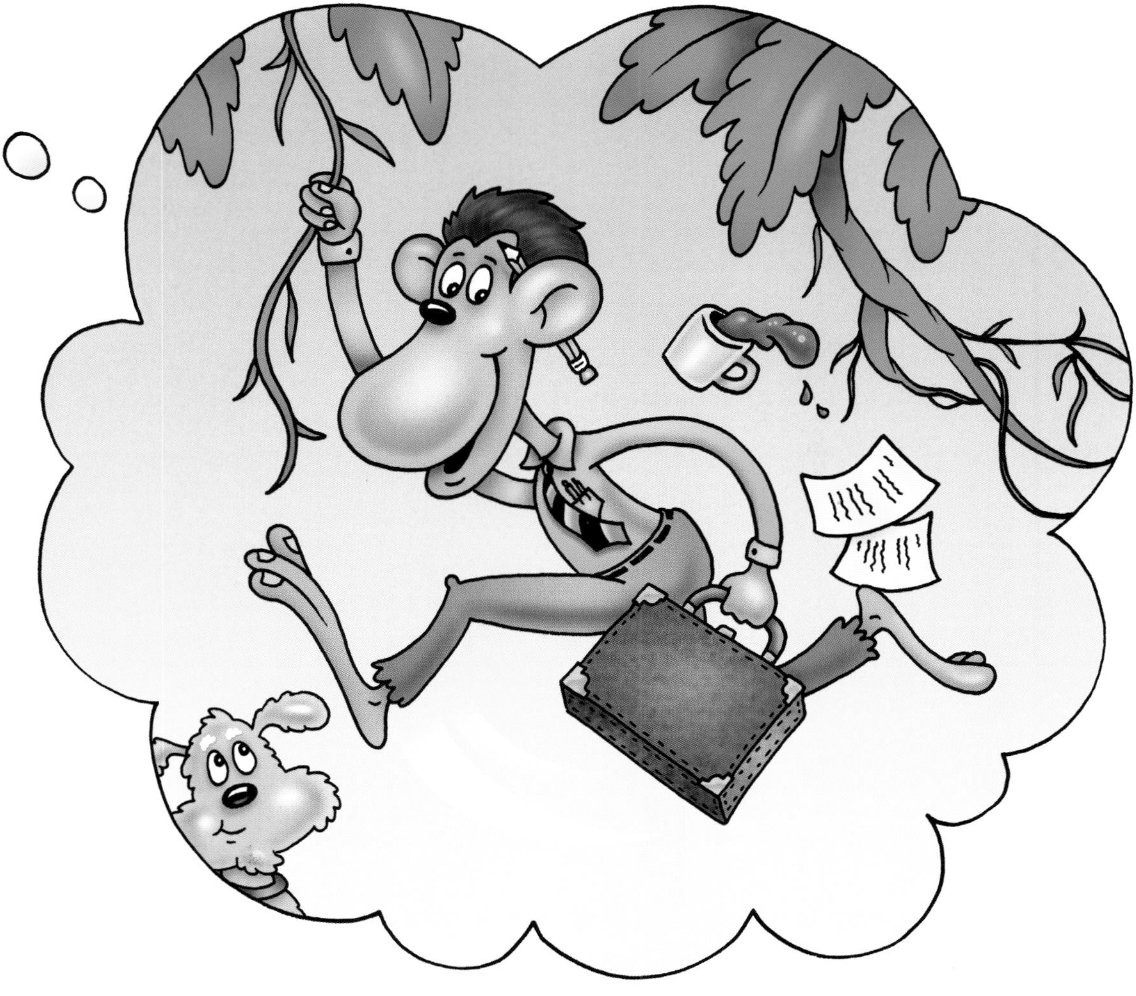

I wonder who we will see next.
Did you check the map?
Who is next on our trip to the library?

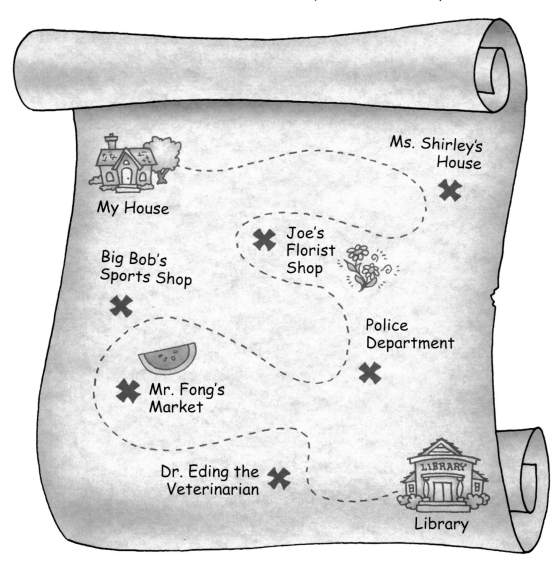

Ms. Shirley's
House

My House

Joe's
Florist
Shop

Big Bob's
Sports Shop

Police
Department

Mr. Fong's
Market

Dr. Eding the
Veterinarian

Library

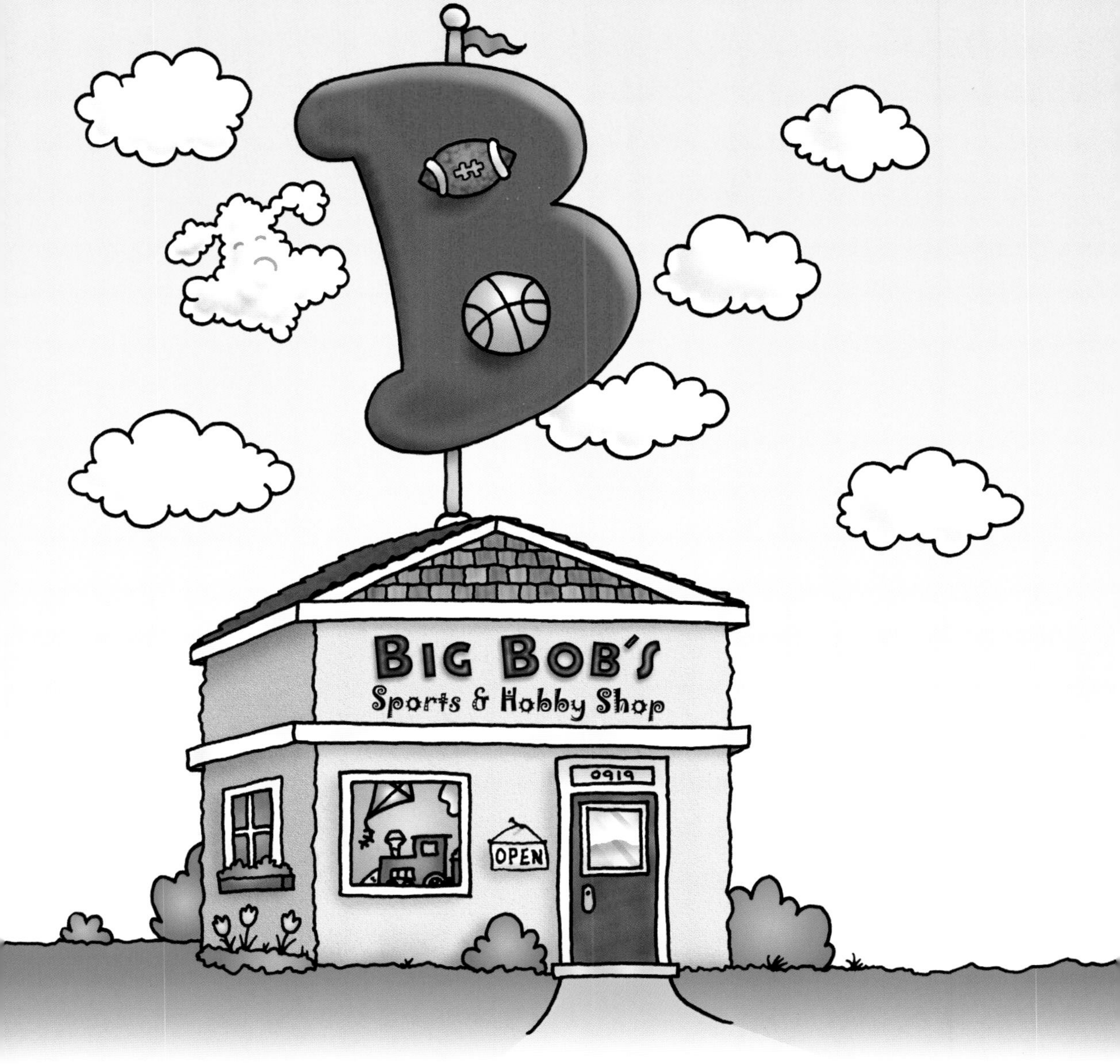
BIG BOB'S
Sports & Hobby Shop
0919
OPEN

The map says that Big Bob's Sports and Hobby Shop is next.
Let's go say "Hello."

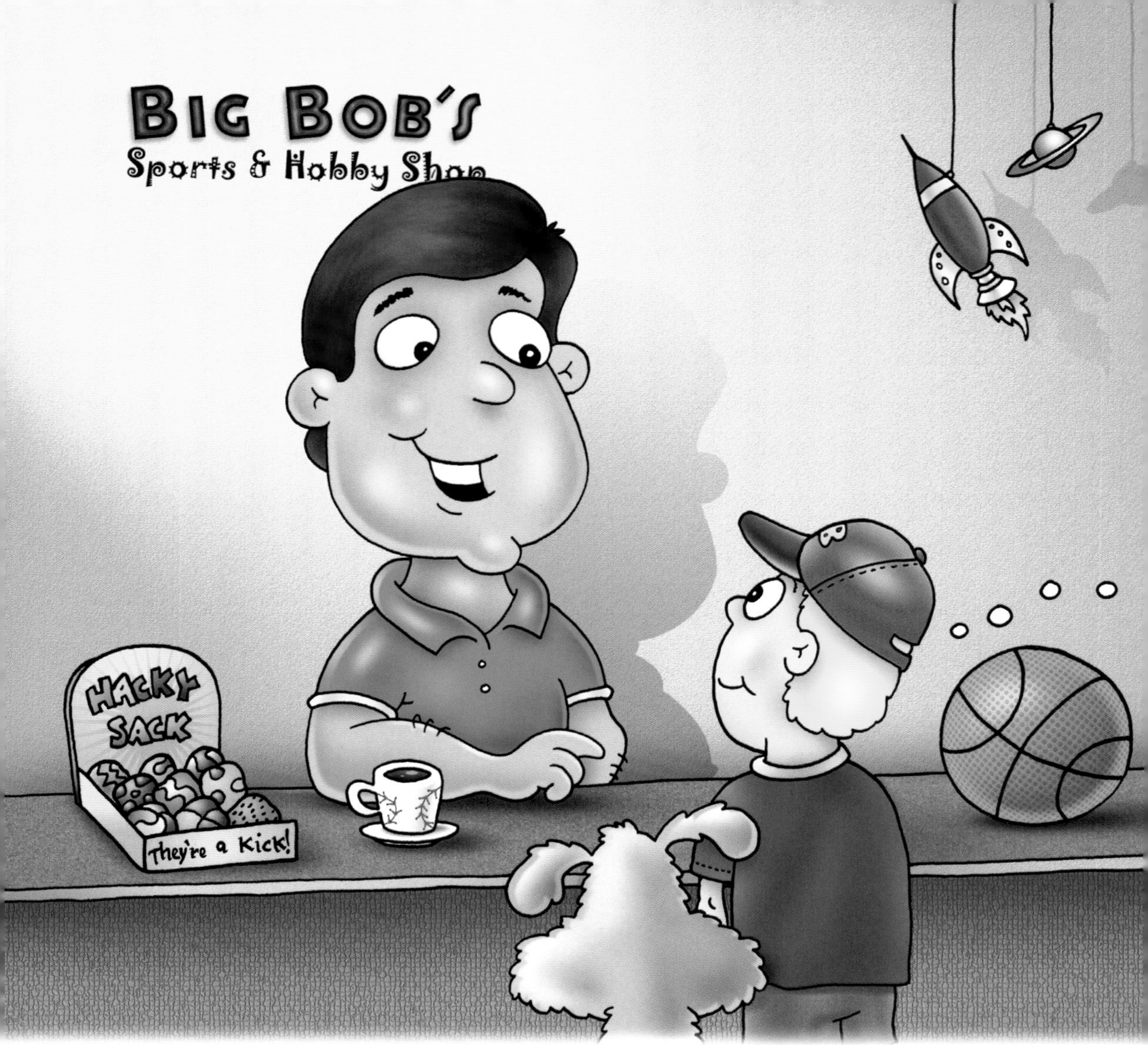
BIG BOB'S
Sports & Hobby Shop
HACKY SACK
They're a Kick!

"Hi, Big Bob."
"Hi, Brett."
"I like the new electric train you have in the window."
"Me, too. Those beauties have been
selling like hotcakes."

"You sell hotcakes, too?"
"No, no. When I say, '**selling like hotcakes**,' I just mean that I've been selling a lot of trains—and very quickly, too."
"I understand now. Well, I'm on my way to the library but I'd like to come back and try out that train someday, if that's okay."
"That would be just fine Brett. See you soon, then."
"See you."

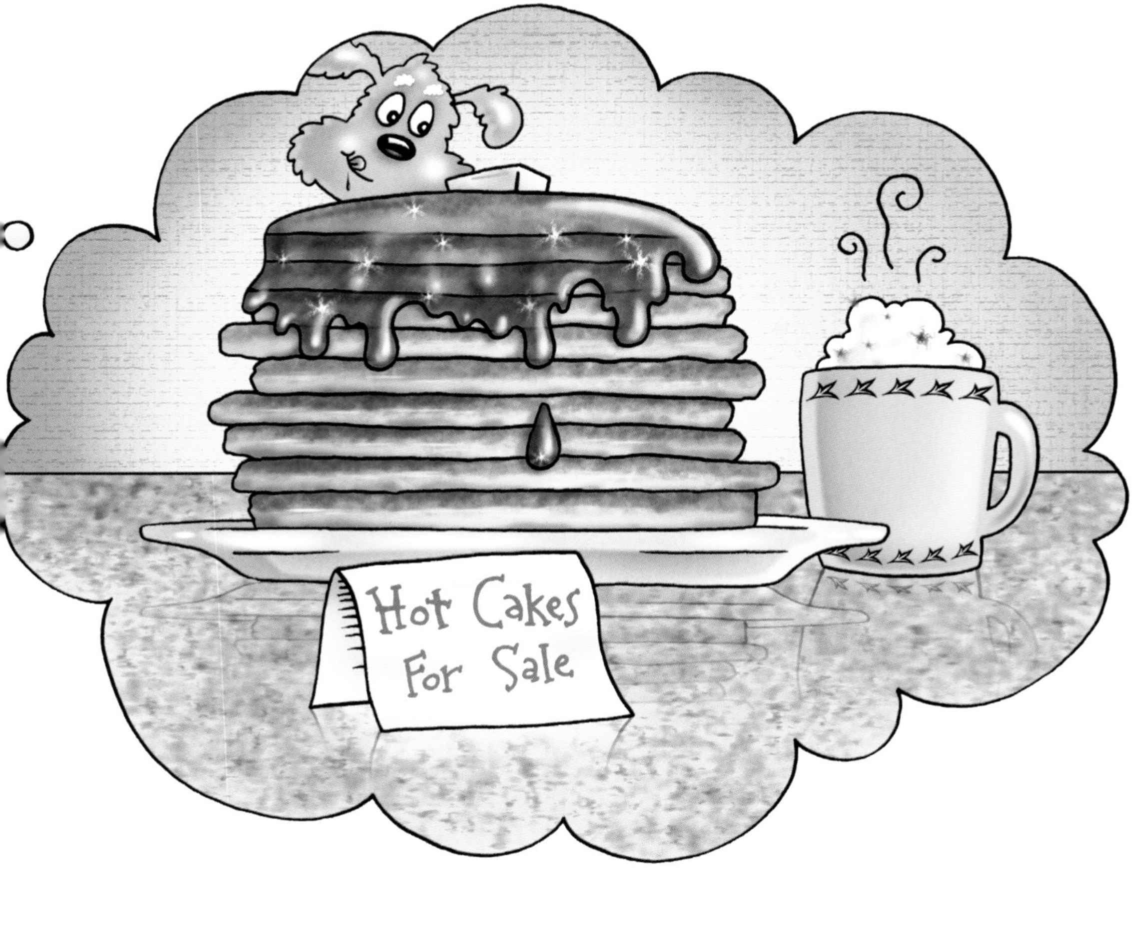
Hot Cakes
For Sale

It looks like Mr. Fong the Grocer is our next stop.
Take a look. He's putting out some fresh fruits and vegetables.

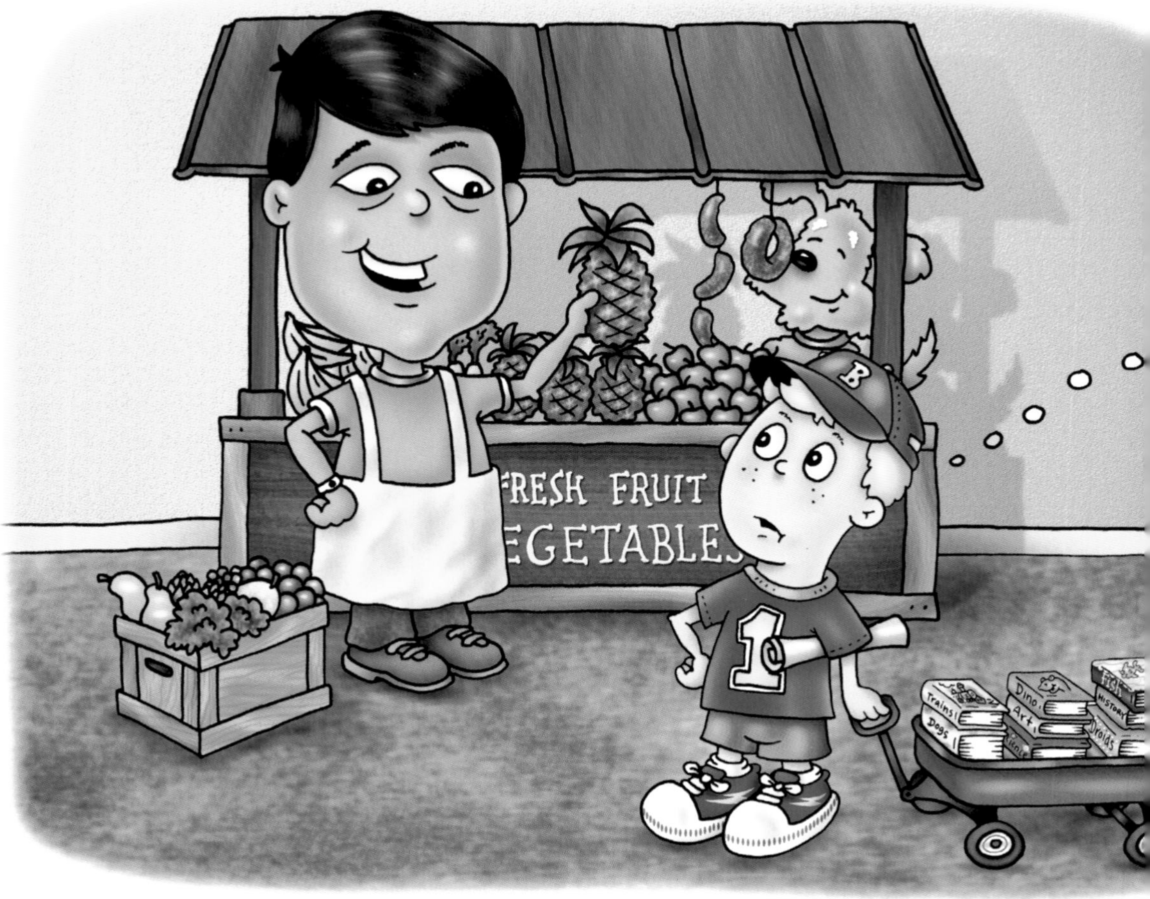
FRESH FRUIT
EGETABLES

"Hi, Mr. Fong."
"Hello, Brett. **I heard through the grapevine** that you are in the book club at the library."
"Yep, we're going there now. But, how could you hear through the grapevine. Don't you needs wires or something for that?"

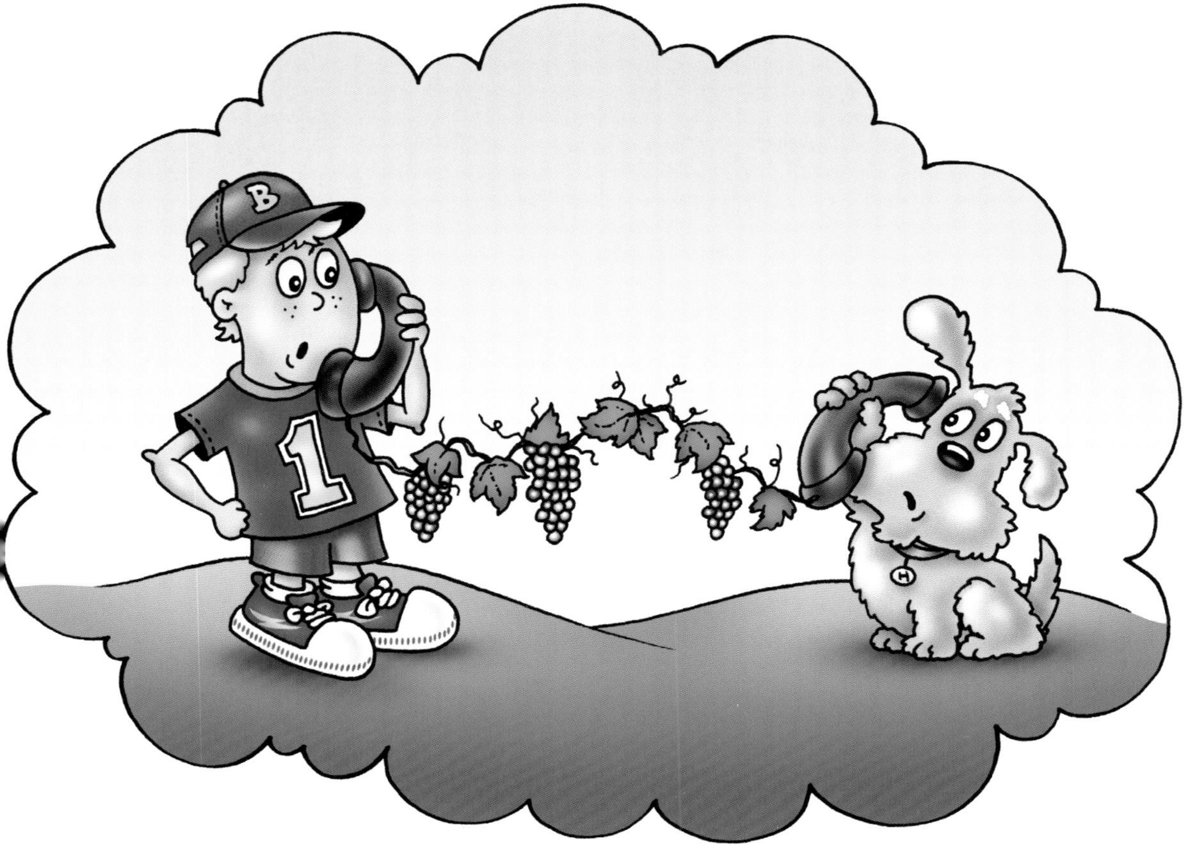
B
1
H

"I suppose you do, Brett. It's just a silly idiom that means I heard it from someone who probably heard it from someone else."

"You're right. That is silly."

"You've got that right. Here's a hotdog for you, and one for Herman."

"Thanks, Mr. Fong. See you later."

"You're welcome, Brett."

Let's stop and see Dr. Eding.
He is Herman's veterinarian
and our next stop.

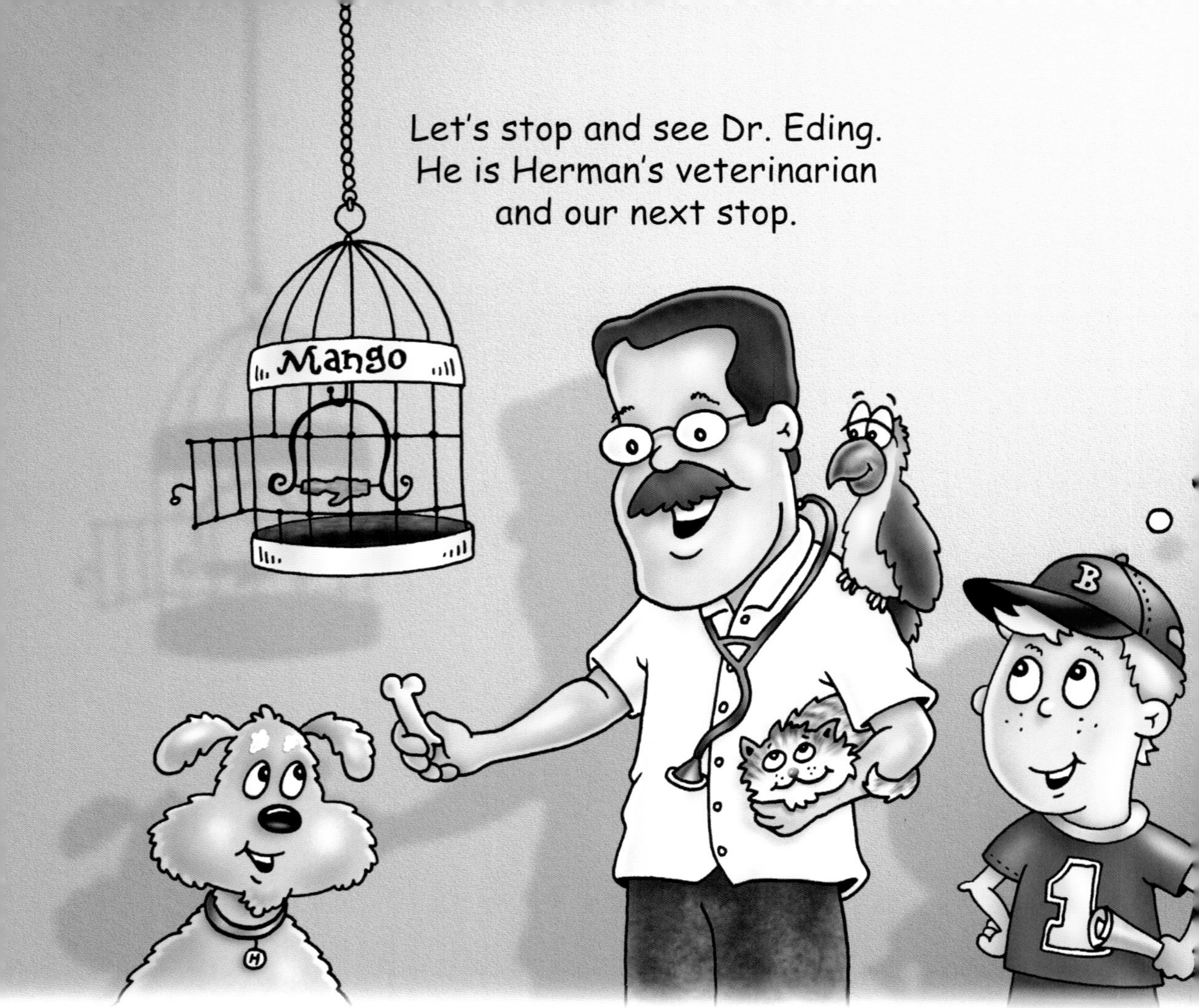
Mango

"Hi, Dr. Eding!"
"Hi, Brett. Going to the library again, I see."
"Yes, and visiting some friends on the way."
"It's a good thing you are going today because tomorrow it's supposed to be **raining cats and dogs**."
"That's not possible is it?"

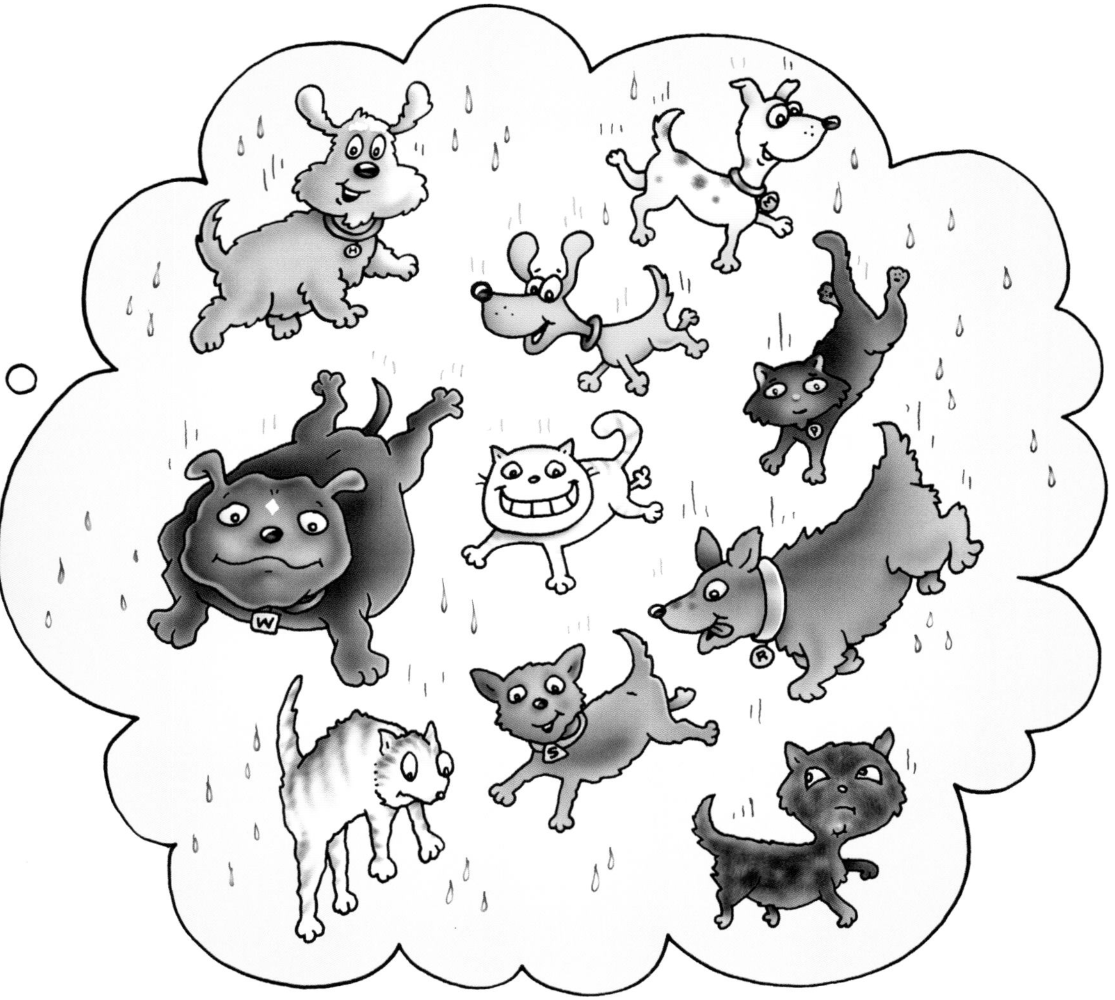

"No, it's not possible. **Raining cats and dogs** is an expression that means it's going to rain very hard."

"It's an idiom! Ms. Shirley told me about those this morning."

"You've got it! Here's a dog biscuit for Herman."

"Have fun."

"We will. Bye."

Okay, time to check the map again.
Look! Next stop, the library.

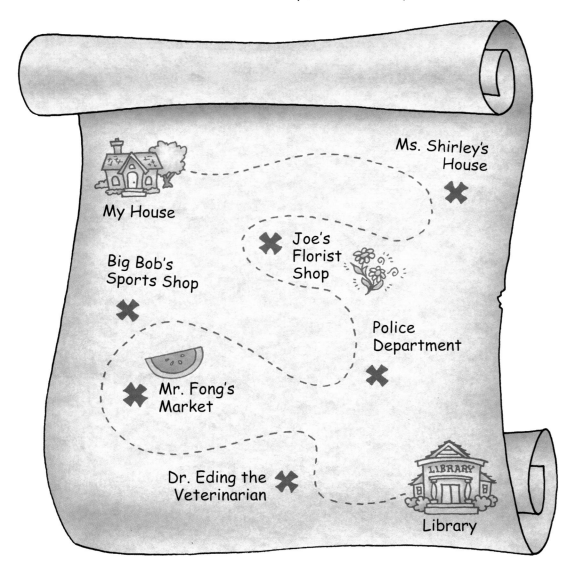

My House

Ms. Shirley's
House

Joe's
Florist
Shop

Big Bob's
Sports Shop

Police
Department

Mr. Fong's
Market

Dr. Eding the
Veterinarian

Library

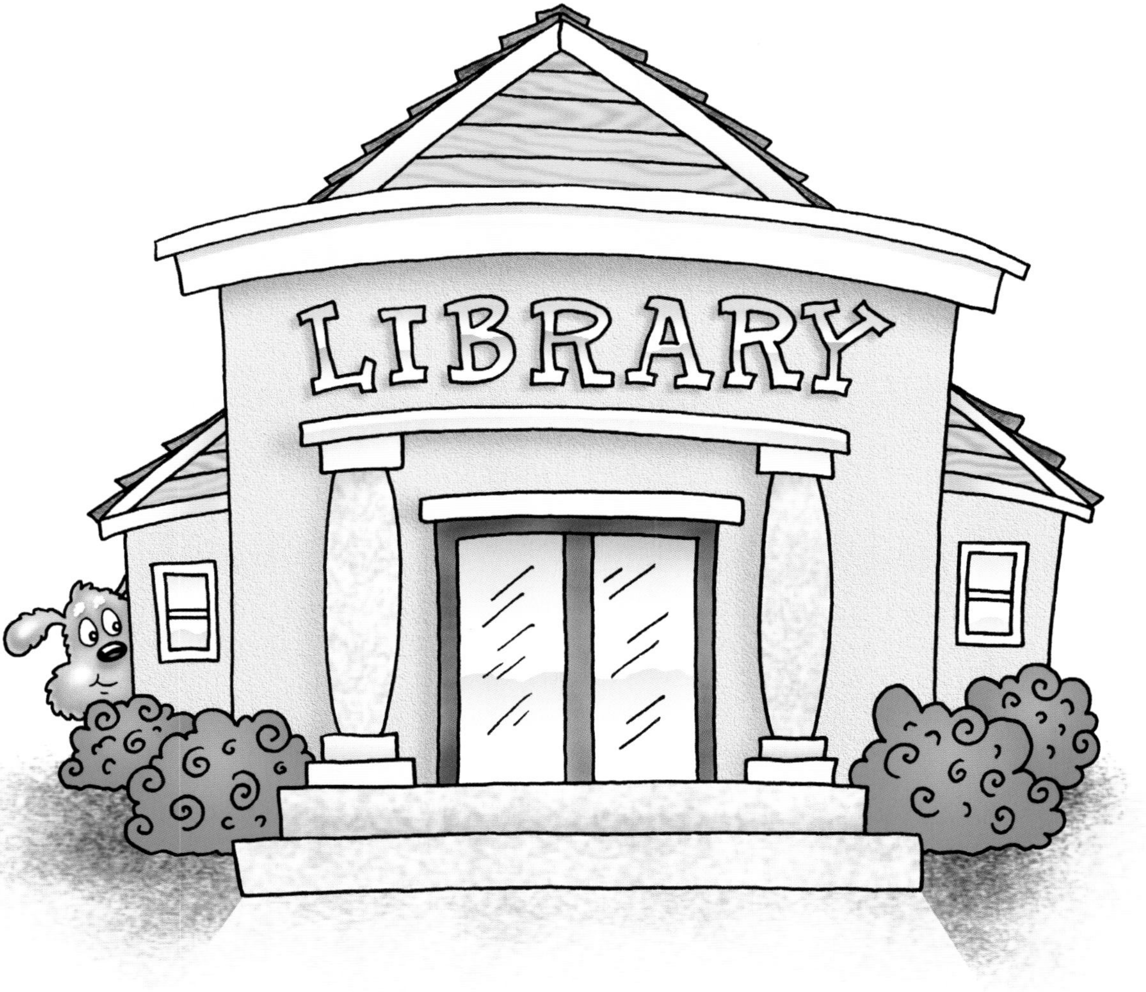
LIBRARY

Here we are.
"Hi, Ms. Ware."
"Good morning, Brett. Did you finish all those books already?"
"Yep. Ms. Shirley says I'm a **bookworm**."
"She just means you read a lot."
"I know. It's an idiom."
"That's right. Idioms are just another way of expressing thoughts and ideas. We have a book here with hundreds of idioms and their meanings if you would like to check it out."

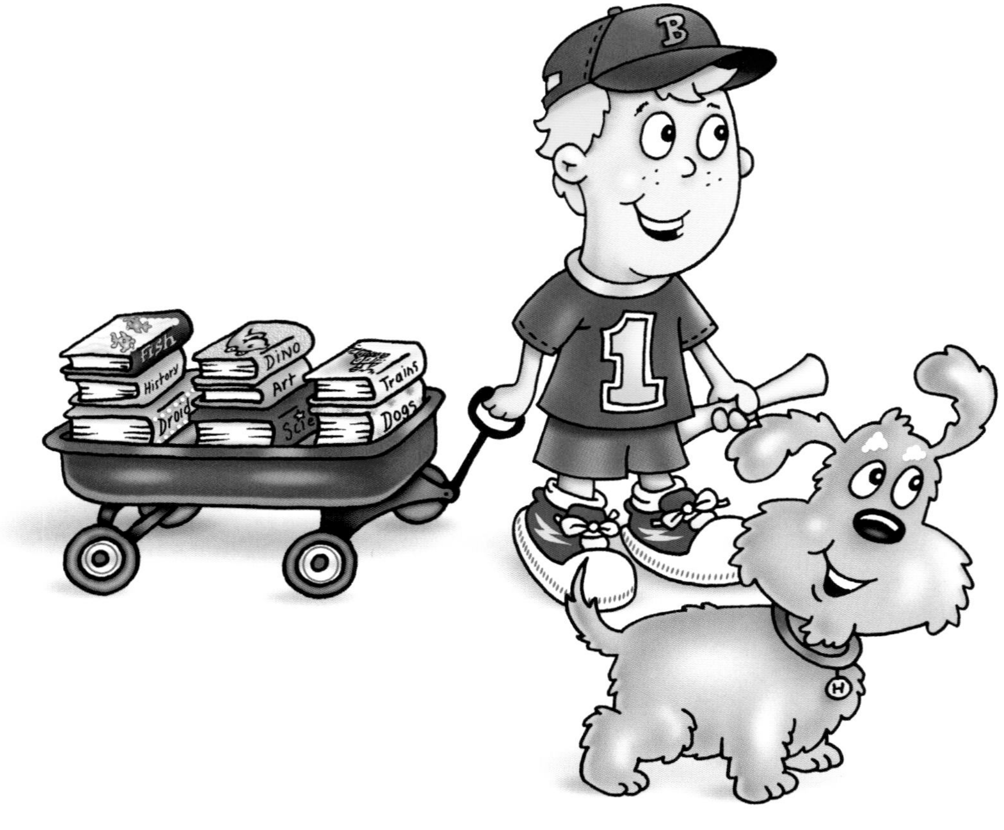
Fish
History
Droid
DINO
Art
Scie
Trains
Dogs

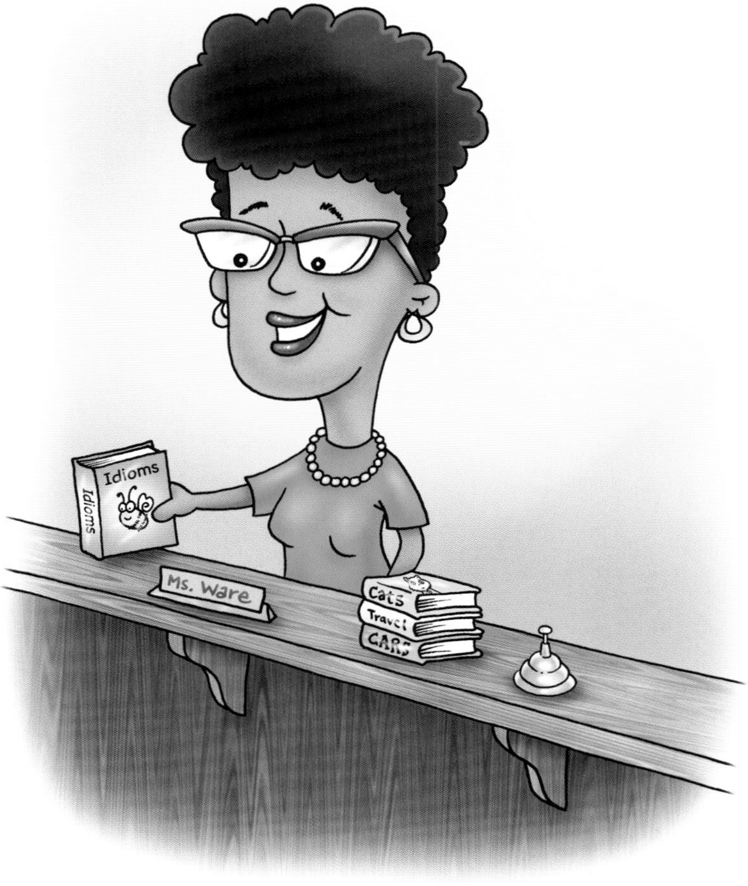
Idioms
Idioms
Ms. Ware
Cats
Travel
CARS

"I'd like that. I've learned a lot of idioms today already."
"Here's the book on idioms and the books on cars,
travel, and cats you asked me to put aside for you.
Plus, now that you have read all those books
in your wagon, you get your award.
Congratulations Brett!"

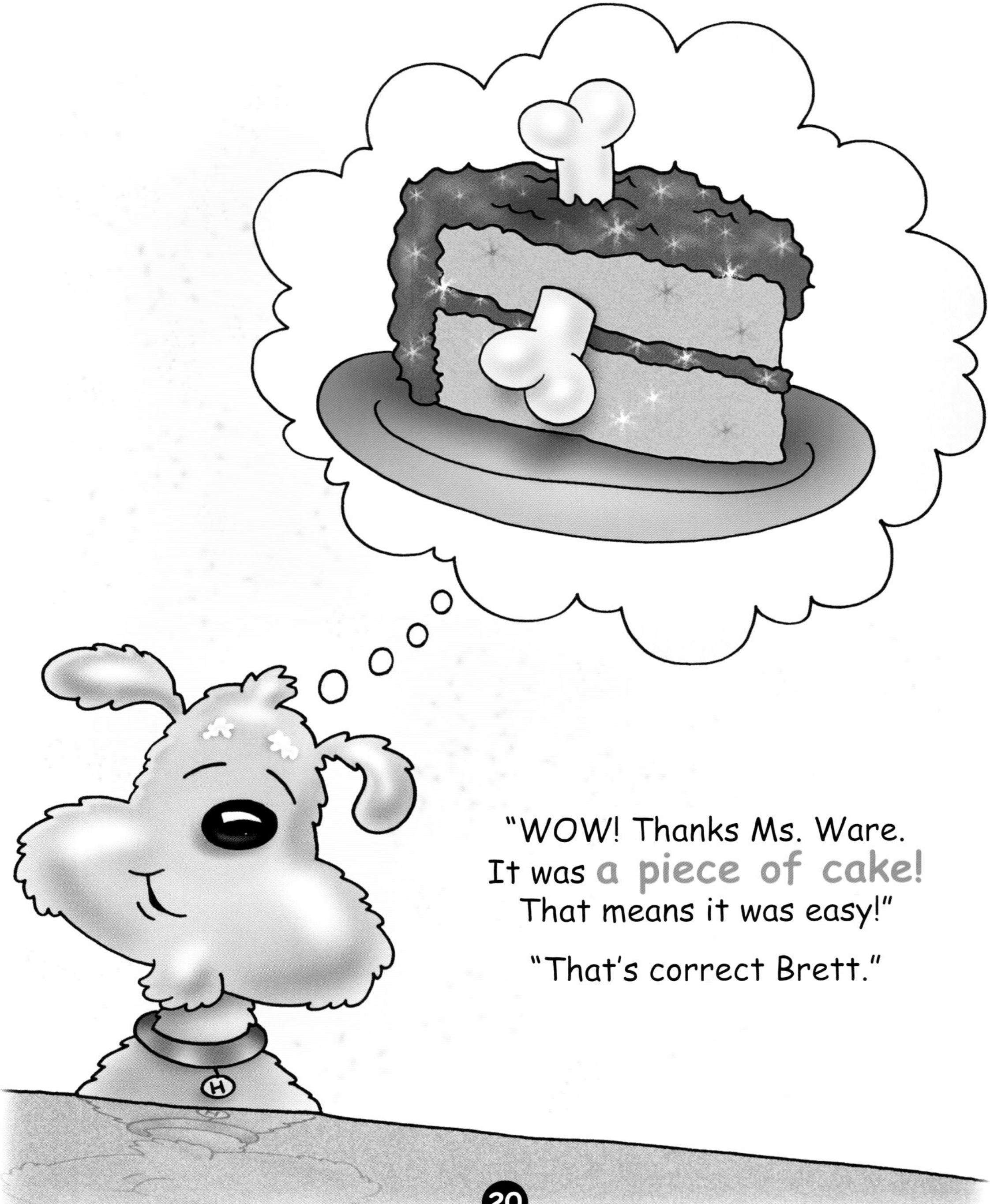

"WOW! Thanks Ms. Ware.
It was **a piece of cake!**
That means it was easy!"

"That's correct Brett."

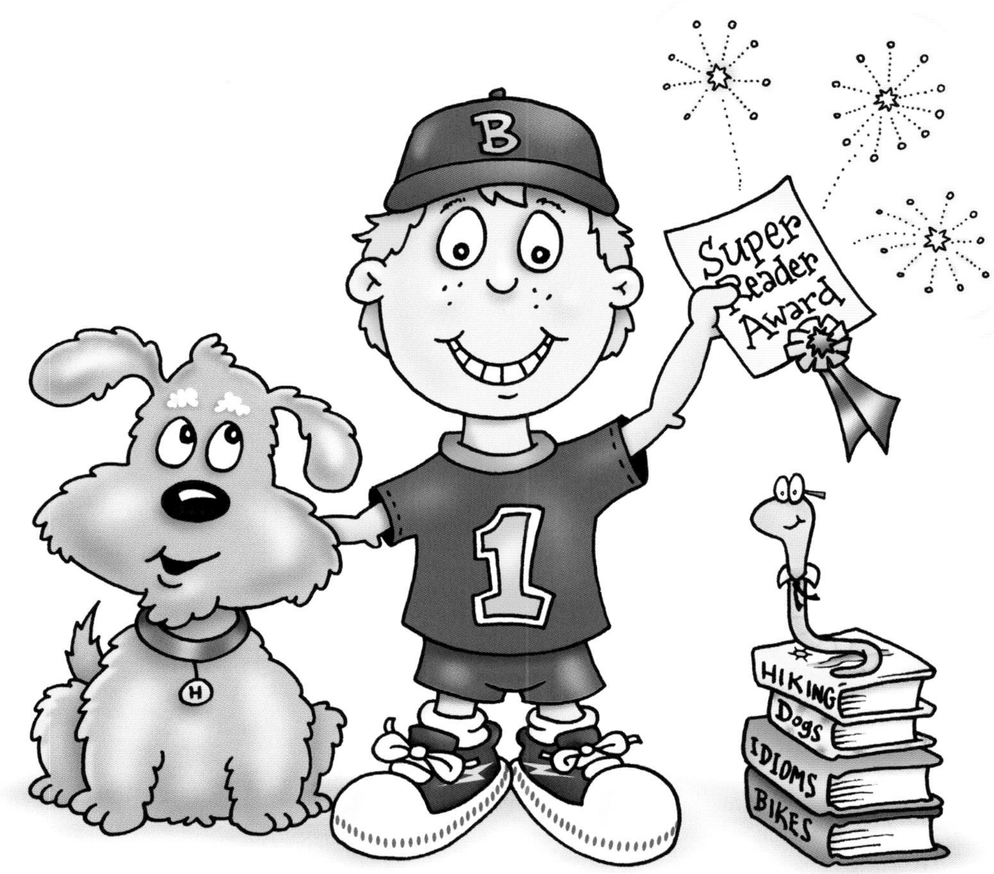
B
Super Reader Award
1
H
HIKING
Dogs
IDIOMS
BIKES

Great Job!

ABOUT THE AUTHOR AND ILLUSTRATOR

Karen Emigh and her husband Ken are the parents of two boys, Brett and Bryce. Karen began writing children's books as a way to help Brett, who is diagnosed with an autistic spectrum disorder, better understand abstract language. They reside in Northern California.

Steve Dana and his wife Jodie are the parents of Eric and Kelsey. They live in the same town as Karen Emigh.

A NOTE TO PARENTS AND EDUCATORS

Idiom: A phrase that, if taken literally, makes little or no sense.

We all use idioms on a daily basis without ever thinking of the literal meaning. Except, that is, when you use one when speaking to someone with an Autistic Spectrum Disorder. A couple of years ago I told my son that I almost "stuck my foot in my mouth." He promptly corrected me by saying that there was no way I would ever be able to get my foot into my mouth. Language for most of our kids is difficult enough without tossing nonsense phrases into the mix. However, idioms are a big part of language, so don't stop using them. Just try to recognize when you're using them and then provide an explanation. Because without an explanation, imagine your child's horror when you tell him or her, "I'm pooped!"

Hang in there!

– Karen

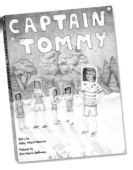